Elizabeth Grant (1797–1885) was born in Edinburgh's fashionable New Town. Most of her childhood was spent in London and on the family estate, Rothiemurchus, on Speyside. She was educated by governesses and in the social graces by various tutors, finally entering Edinburgh society at the end of the Napoleonic wars.

The trauma of a broken engagement was followed by the disastrous failure of her father's career. This involved a huge burden of debt which, in 1820, forced the Grants to retreat to their highland home. As her contribution to improving the family fortunes Elizabeth and both her sisters wrote articles for popular magazines of the day.

In 1827 the family left Scotland for India when her father was appointed to a Judgeship in Bombay. It was here that she met and married Colonel Henry Smith, seventeen years her senior. They left for Ireland the following year to live at Baltiboys, her husband's newly inherited estate situated near Dublin.

She devoted herself to raising a family and took the leading role in managing and improving their impoverished estate. For over half a century Baltiboys was to be her home, her life and her occupation, her resolve never failing even after the death of her husband and her only son. Between 1845 and 1854 she wrote her Memoirs for her family's pleasure; they were later edited by her niece Lady Strachey and published in 1898, thirteen years after her death.

Elizabeth Grant
of Rothiemurchus

The Highland Lady
in Ireland

JOURNALS 1840–50

Edited by Patricia Pelly & Andrew Tod
Introduced by Andrew Tod

CANONGATE

CLASSICS

41

First published as a Canongate Classic in 1991, reprinted in 1997 by Canongate Books Ltd, 14 High Street, Edinburgh EH1 1TE. Copyright to this edition © Andrew Tod and Paricia Pelly 1991. Introduction to this edition © Andrew Tod 1991.

The publishers gratefully acknowledge general subsidy from the Scottish Arts Council Towards the Canongate Classics series and a specific grant towards the publication of this title.

Set in 10pt Plantin by Falcon Typographic Art Ltd, Edinburgh & London. Printed and bound in Great Britain, Caledonian International, Bishopbriggs, Scotland.

Canongate Classics
Series Editor: Roderick Watson
Editorial board: J.B. Pick, Cairns Craig,
Dorothy McMillan

British Library Cataloguing in Publication Data
Grant, Elizabeth, 1797–1885
The Highland lady in Ireland.
I. Title   II. Pelly, Patricia
III. Tod, Andrew
941.5081092

0 86241 361 3

Contents

Introduction

The Highland lady, Elizabeth Grant, was born in Edinburgh on 7 May 1797 in her father's newly-built town mansion at 5 Charlotte Square. She was the eldest of the five children of the 7th Laird of Rothiemurchus, later Sir John Peter Grant, a landed lawyer and Whig Member of Parliament whose political ambitions and financial chicanery were to bring his family close to ruin. The offer of a judgeship in India in 1829 provided a chance to recover his fortunes however, and once his more pressing creditors had been evaded, the family set out for Bombay.

This is the story that was so engagingly told in *Memoirs of a Highland Lady*, the classic which earned Elizabeth Grant the title by which she is so well-known as one of the most fascinating and important Scottish nineteenth-century diarists. She wrote of her childhood in Rothiemurchus with spells in Oxford and London, and of Edinburgh when its reputation was at its height as a city of the Enlightenment. Her early womanhood coincided with the decline in the Grant family situation, so a comfortable existence in the capital had to be exchanged for a penurious life back at the Doune, the family house in the north near Aviemore. Here it was that three talented sisters, Elizabeth, Jane and Mary Grant, wrote the stories and articles that provided their principal source of income until they were rescued by their father's prospects in India. The *Memoirs* ended with Elizabeth's two years in India and her marriage to Colonel Henry Smith of Baltiboys, an Officer in the 5th Bombay Cavalry.

Ten days before the wedding in June 1829, news arrived that Henry's elder brother John, a spendthrift bachelor formerly an officer in the 4th Dragoon Guards, had died in Paris, as a result of which Henry inherited the 1,200 acre

* Edited by her niece, Lady Strachey, they were first published in 1898 and a further revised version was produced by Angus Davidson. The complete text appeared for the first time in 1988, edited by Andrew Tod for the *Canongate Classics*.

estate of Baltiboys some twenty miles south of Dublin in Co. Wicklow. Ill-health (Colonel Smith suffered from frequent bouts of asthma), demanded an early retirement, and so with Janey, their first-born, the Smiths arrived in Ireland in the summer of 1830 for a new chapter in the life of the Highland lady.

The *Memoirs* were specifically written for Elizabeth's children (Annie was born in 1832 and Jack in 1838) over an eight year period, 1846 to 1854. But Mrs Smith had begun a Journal much earlier, on New Year's Day 1840, and with various gaps in later years she kept it going until 1885, the year she died. Her entries to this Journal are particularly complete and informative during the 1840s and these are the years that have been edited to produce the present volume.

It is not the first time a selection has been published. The distinguished writer David Thomson co-operated with the Highland lady's great-grand-daughter Moyra McGusty to produce *The Irish Journals of Elizabeth Smith*, 1840–1850 (O.U.P., 1980), but although her true voice emerged from the dramatic later years of the decade, there was a certain misbalance in the book because only thirty per cent of the text had been taken from the first six years. There seemed, therefore, to be a place for a more representative selection from the Irish Journals to set alongside the *Canongate Classics* edition of the Highland lady's *Memoirs*. The present edition deliberately omits a two year period from 1843 to 1845 when the whole family moved to France, first to Pau and then to Avranches: this seemed to be a self-contained period that might well stand on its own as a separate publication rather than confusing the essential two parts of the Journals – one of which portrays the family's life on a fast-improving estate in a well-described neighbourhood, while the other shows their response to the terrible challenges of the Famine years.

These are, however, only two of many themes that emerge from this fascinating kaleidoscope of a diary. The Highland lady gave several reasons why she kept it so assiduously: it was 'a safety valve . . . for my own great griefs', a 'chronicle of my times' and 'it educated myself in the way of my duties'. But above all (as she wrote on 25 February 1845) this 'indulgence' had the didactic purpose of 'recalling the memory of their mother to my dear children when they will be old enough to understand the moral of my comments upon life.' Later (in July 1856) she did allow herself the observation that

> well weeded, corrected and names with-held, it might bring [Jack] a good penny should the present love of family disclosures remain with the idle publick.

She was nothing if not a practical woman.

There is one problem, however, about treating the *Memoirs* and the *Journal* as a continuous series of autobiographical writings. Elizabeth Smith was well aware that one ended in 1830 and the other started in 1840. This gap is covered in a long and interesting letter to Annie in 1878, helped by a travelling diary kept by her sister Jane Pennington in 1831.

In the first place Baltiboys House, which had been badly damaged in the 1798 rebellion, had to be rebuilt. Jane's diary calls it

> A mere ruin now . . . in a very curious state of abandonment. The house, I believe, was dismantled for the sake of selling the materials when the old proprietor determined to live abroad; but a great proportion of the walls are left standing and cover a very considerable area; and with offices and all, there are more than twice the quantity of stones that it would take to build a convenient mansion.

It was not until 1837 that the family could move into this mansion and when the Journal opens work is still being done. Another great-grand-daughter, who was born at Baltiboys, Ninette de Valois, described it in her autobiography* as 'a long two-storied building with a spacious net-work of basement rooms. It was a typically Irish country house of about 1820–30, late Georgian in part, consisting of one main wing and two smaller ones.' Today, carefully restored, it impresses as an elegant Regency house, tastefully situated by the Blessington Lake created by the confluence of the Liffey and King's rivers.

* Ninette de Valois *Come Dance With Me* (London, 1957).

Annie's 1878 letter described how her mother's sister and brother-in-law, Colonel Pennington, came on their travels to see 'what kind of a place Baltiboys, this neglected property, was like; understandably, it did not make any kind of a favourable impression . . .'

> how could it – ruins – nettles – broken gate – road overgrown with weeds. And when I first saw it, there stood to welcome me a crowd of, as I thought beggars – dirty queer-looking men doffing their remnants of hats with much civility. 'Thim's the tenants' said the only man amongst them with a whole coat. See them now – see the place now – see the farms now! It has taken near fifty years to effect the transformation – fifty years of untiring energy and patience under many disappointments – but the reform is accomplished and is worth all it cost.

The Highland lady saw the 1830s as laying the foundations of all that was to be achieved in the years ahead, as she and the Colonel, with the help of the Agent John Robinson and the Steward Tom Darker, moved towards a more efficient system of managing the estate, based on consolidating farms and direct letting to tenants who lived and worked on their holdings.

> Your father's work and mine lay at home. We had work enough. We determined to get rid of all the little tenants and to encrease the larger farms – and we did it – but not at once – just watched for opportunities and managed this delicate business without annoying any one – or even causing a murmur. The departing were always furnished with the means of setting up in suitable employments, and were fully paid for any value left. We first repaired the thatch of all cabins – then put in windows – then built chimney stacks – not all at once either – little by little as people deserved help. Then your father built his house. The employment thus given completely set his tenants up – the pride they took in the place they had helped to make inspired them with a desire to improve their own dwellings, which was gratified by degrees as we could afford it. A better system of farming followed. The

first field of turnips ever sown in these parts was what is now our front lawn. Then came the draining. The schools were set agoing. I remember that there was a great deal of trouble in the setting up the School – a sign of progress much wanted – none of the men and few of the women could read – none of the women could sew – method equally unknown in the home. Poor creatures they had been neglected for more than a generation.

And all these themes are regularly commented upon in the Journals, as Baltiboys played its part in the steady improvement of the neighbourhood around the market town of Blessington in those pre-Famine years.

This is a neighbourhood, moreover, that comes alive through Elizabeth Smith's descriptions of all classes of society. We meet the stately Marquis of Downshire, one of the greatest landowners in Ireland, whose well-run estates contrast so much with the feckless mismanagement of that broken-down gambler, the Earl of Milltown; the gossiping Dr George Robinson, brother to the Agent, whose life is inter-twined with that of the Smith family right down to Annie's marriage in 1850 with which this volume concludes. (He took her marriage rather badly.) At a humbler level, each and every person living and working at Baltiboys, (whose situation and prospects were analysed in the Catalogue Raisonée the indefatiguable landlord's wife produced at the beginning of that terrible year 1847), can be followed through these pages. There is a wealth of characters to illuminate the detailed recreation of family and estate life at Baltiboys, the range of agricultural change and improvement, and the life led by all groups of society around them. And as David Thomson wrote in his Introduction, all this is achieved by the direct and forceful writing of a character with powerful opinions and an intelligent mind.

My delight is in the vigour of her mind; her wit, the immediacy of her narrative and descriptive style which forwards her life and times to us in a mixture of asperity and warmth of heart, her ventures into practical experiment in education and farming methods.

But, in addition to adding to the Highland lady's reputation as an extremely distinguished diarist, these writings
from the 1840s have an importance over and above the
literary. They are a significant addition to a revised picture
of some parts of Irish landlordism, which shows how some
landed proprietors, while undoubtedly conscious of their
rights, still tried conscientiously to carry out their duties.
This contrasts with the report of the Devon Commission,
for example, which was established in 1843 to inquire into
Irish land tenure, which stressed that the evils of the system
were wellnigh universal.*

It was three months after the Smiths returned from
their retrenching exercise in France that the ravages of
phytophthora infestans, the potato blight, appeared in the
Baltiboys area. The Journals provide a day-to-day account
of how this well-endowed and comparatively prosperous
eastern part of Ireland coped with the challenges of the
disaster, and how it reacted to the despairing and sometimes
belated efforts of the governments of Sir Robert Peel and
Lord John Russell to introduce measures that would relieve
the tragic consequences of failure in the potato crops.

This edition of the Irish diaries kept by the Highland
lady during the 1840s is a little more than 200,000 words
long, perhaps a quarter of all she wrote. Customary editorial
practices, and hopefully common sense, were adhered to
so that Elizabeth Smith's individual voice emerges here as
clearly and as forcefully as Elizabeth Grant's does from the
Memoirs. Sometimes the same story is told in both (after all,
for example, she read Lockhart's biography of his father-
in-law, Sir Walter Scott, in 1840 and commented upon it
in her Journal long before she mentioned it again in the
Memoirs). But the best observations are always good enough
to bear a second reading. She wrote in one continuous flow,
so modern notions of paragraphing have been introduced,
but her spelling has been retained ('philippick', 'atchieved',
'burthen', 'plaister', 'steeple chacing') except in the case of

* For more on the historical background see the magisterial *New History
of Ireland, Volume V, Ireland under the Union I, 1801–1870*, hereafter NH
of I edited by W. E. Vaughan (O.U.P., 1989).

some placenames ('Drumewachta' has a certain charm but it may not be recognised as Drumochter). She consistently wrote 'Blesington' and the 'Milltowns'.

Elizabeth Grant arrived as Elizabeth Smith to her new responsibilities at Baltiboys with a wealth of Scottish experience behind her, and the two extended spells she spent in Scotland in the summers of 1842 (when she wrote her eyewitness account of Queen Victoria's visit) and 1846 (when she returned to her beloved Rothiemurchus) show how she treasured her roots. But she also became fiercely attached to her new loyalties and it is interesting that her sister's 1831 diary should contain this perceptive comment:

> I don't know how it is, but whenever I have been parted from Eliza for more than a month, she has, at our first meeting again, appeared more altered than most people do in the course of years. I believe it is from her extraordinary propensity for falling into the ways, the habits, customs, manners and opinions even, of those she lives with; a faculty of extreme value to the possessor, as it is sure to endear her to everybody by whom she is surrounded, and fits her for every possible change of place or condition.

A little later she makes a final remark: 'They have made an Irishwoman of you now, and may they know the value of the daughter they adopted into their Country' – a fitting summation of the Highland lady and the fascination of her Irish Journals.

Finally, should something of the charm, irritation, intelligence and importance of this marvellous writer have succeeded in being conveyed to her readers, much of the credit must go to my co-editor Patricia Pelly, one of the Highland lady's great-great-grand-daughters, whose family knowledge and committed interest have played an enormous part in preparing this version of her distinguished ancestor's diaries for publication.

Andrew Tod

Dramatis Personae

Colonel Henry Smith of Baltiboys (1780–1862)
Elizabeth Smith, née Elizabeth Grant of Rothiemurchus
(1797–1885) ('the Highland lady'), his wife
their three surviving children, Janie (born 1830), Annie
(born 1832) and Jack (born 1838)
her brothers William and John, (later Sir John) Grant and
their wives Sally and Henrietta
her sisters Mary and Jane and their husbands Charles
Gardiner and, first, Colonel Gervase Pennington then James
Gibson Craig of Riccarton, (later Sir James)
her Aunt, Mary Bourne
her cousin Bartle Frere, (later Sir Bartle)

NEIGHBOURING LANDOWNERS
the third Marquis of Downshire (d. 1845) and his Mar-
chioness
the fourth Marquis of Downshire and his Marchioness
Joseph Leeson, the fourth earl of Milltown (1799–1866), of
Russborough House
Barbara, Countess of Milltown
the Hornidge and Henry families from Tulfarris and
Russelstown
John Finnemore from Ballyward
William Cotton from Humphreystown

IRISH AND SCOTTISH FRIENDS
Francis, Lord Jeffrey
Sir Thomas Dick Lauder
William and Robert Chambers
Mr Caw from Rothiemurchus
Dwarkanoth Tagore
Baron de Robeck
Tom Shehan, editor of the Dublin Evening Mail
the Agents to the Blessington estates of Lord Downshire,

John Murray to 1841, Henry Gore to 1843 and then William Owen
Dr George Robinson
Dr Eckford
Dr Litchfield
John Robinson the Baltiboys Agent
Tom Darker the Baltiboys Steward

CLERGYMEN
Rev William Ogle Moore, Rector of Kilbride
his Curate Mr Foster
Mr Featherstone, Rector of Hollywood
Arthur Germaine, Roman Catholic priest at Blackditches
with his curates James Rickard and Richard Galvin

HOUSEHOLD AND ESTATE
the governesses Jane Cooper, Miss Hart and Miss Clerk
the Housekeeper Margaret Fyfe from Rothiemurchus
the school-teachers Miss Gardiner, Arthur McConnell, Patrick O'Keefe, Fanny MacDonald and John McDarby

TENANTRY
see the index and the *Catalogue Raisonée* of January 1847

ONE

1840

The opening year of the Highland Lady's journal intro-
duces us to the family, the estate and the neighbourhood
of the market town of Blessington. Her varied entries
describe family activities and the life of the tenantry on
the estate; she comments on the wider world of politics
and public affairs, as the Whig government disintegrates
and Daniel O'Connell continues his campaign for the
repeal of the Act of Union; and only in Colonel
Smith's autumn trip to St. Servans to investigate the
possibility of a short term move to 'retrench' is there
a suggestion of any change is the settled pattern of
their lives.

WEDNESDAY, JANUARY 1. A raw dark rainy day yet Hal went
out to look for the harriers and was the better of the ride.
No letters by the post, nor news of any consequence in
the newspapers. In the morning I worked at accounts,
paid all our debts; then gave Janey a musick lesson. In
the evening they danced. After they went to bed I read
aloud the *Life of Wilberforce* till half after eleven.

2. After mending Hal's flannels I finished the year's account
—£6 odd remaining in hands. Luckily at this time of year
there is no outlay. I have myself kept within bounds in
my own private expenses though it was a costly year.
Read Wilberforce aloud from nine to half past eleven
and finished the book to our great regret for it is most
extremely interesting, the first volume dull, rising in
interest every volume after till you quite forgot the
disagreeable plan adopted by the editor.[1] It is a book

1. Edited by his sons Robert, Isaac and Samuel, the 'Life'
(1838) of William Wilberforce the philanthropist (1759–
1833) was, for the DNB, 'no model biography.'

to have, to be often read again, for the times he lived in were full of moment and the people he lived with those of the first note in the moral and political annals of our country—many of them known to me—many of them connected with me—and his truly religious heart, producing an uprightness almost heavenly, is a study for every Christian though to my feelings the *formality* of his religion is to be deprecated and his enthusiasm avoided.

3. The little girls and I went to Widow Redmond's and to Biddy Shannon to send the children to school. How miserable was Shannon's cabin, the two families crowded together to save fuel, the asthmatick old man and his epileptick daughter, poor Biddy with five ragged girls, the three youngest infants—one at the breast, another hardly walking—God help them. Settled the school accounts with Miss Gardiner. I must think over the best plan for increasing the number of pupils.

5. A note from Mrs. Moore, [wife of the Rector of the neighbouring parish of Kilbride] about Caroline Clarke which has greatly annoyed me. A case of real hardship to the poor girl whom I by no means forced on her. Wrote notes to several members of our new Book Club asking for their subscriptions, and then to Mrs. Moore to say that neither Sarah [her first maid] nor I wanted Caroline, that I should have been glad to have had her at the time I offered to take her but now I had engaged another.

6. It will behove me now to throw off a degree of indolence I have I think too much given way to—partly from weak health—partly from having Sarah in whom we had such confidence to trust to. I do not mean to replace her and have thus arranged the household—a cook, a housemaid who will wait on me, a nursery maid, Helen to come to do the washing and to be apart in her laundry as a day labourer—to finish it in four days—her wages 10/- a month, finding her own tea, I feeding her, and every second Saturday to scrub the nurseries for which she will get her dinner. A butler and coachman completes our establishment indoors which a very little exertion

on my part will keep in good order as they are a well disposed set of people.

7. All early astir to prepare for the marriage. The Bridegroom [James the butler,] did all his morning work and then set off with his hamper of provisions to arrange his own breakfast at the Doctor's. Tea, coffee, brown and white sugar, butter, preserved strawberries, bread, hot rolls, ham, corned beef, cake and wine. The Bride dressed all the children and cried too much to dress herself. She was very neat in a blue muslin de laine gown given her by Lady Milltown, a blue plush bonnet given her by me, a white shawl, worked cambric collar, the little girls as bridesmaids in white gloves, their *Dehli scarves* and all their finery, the best man looking as happy as a king and calling for jam. Poor Sarah, she has been nearly ten years with us—within a very few months—the first servant we hired in England, who took Janey from her birth. Never forget, little girls, how much Sarah has done for both of you.

It is for you, dear children, I am keeping this journal. I have often during my life done so before by starts for my mother or my sisters when we were separated, and I have often regretted that I had not continued to do it. Reading Mr. Wilberforce determined me to begin [even] at this eleventh hour. My experience of life, my love for you, all make me anxious to devote myself to your welfare, and if it should be God's will to take your parents from you, the voice of your mother *from the grave* may be a guide and a protection. I am not young—and I am not strong. I shall be 43 next May, your father will be 60 in March and he has been more than 25 years in India. Happiness, comfort, and care may lead us on yet many years—but we may go sooner—before your principles are secured. An uninterrupted course of prosperity you are not to expect nor would I ask it for you. God chastens whom he loves. But I long to see your tempers so controlled, your habits of industry and activity and kindness so fixed, your hearts so truly given to God that you may be enabled to bear the sorrows and disappointments of life with patience, as sent for your good by *Him*—that you may avoid the temptations of prosperity, diligently examining your hearts which will direct you right if you prove them faithfully, remembering for *God's sake* to do your duty in that state of life into which it shall please him to call you.

The post brought a few lines from Mrs. Jameson with a copy made by Harry of his Uncle Woosnam's letter describing the march of the troops into Affganisthan and the taking of the Fort of Guznee at which he assisted, the object being to dethrone one murdering tyrant and place just such another on the vacant throne. A shocking kind of warfare—our disciplined troops against those poor wretches—as may be judged of from the list of mortality on both sides—we the assailants having twenty-three men killed and about eighty wounded, the defenders leaving in the fort above five hundred bodies to be buried, the wounded and the numbers slaughtered by our cavalry in attempting to escape from the walls were unknown. If this be glory it is indeed but tinsel. There seems to me to be nearly as much credit to be gained by an attack like Don Quixote on a flock of sheep—and the King Shah Souja or something for whom we made this slaughter added his own mite to the general sum of corpses by cutting off the heads of all prisoners brought to the camp during his progress.[2]

Mr. Fetherstone called and we had an interesting conversation after dinner. In his parish of Holywood he has a great many protestant parishioners most zealous for their religion—ready to *fight* anyone opposed to it—and perfectly ignorant of its principles—equally superstitious, bigotted, intolerant, and uninstructed with their papist neighbours. I can say the same of most of whom I have had experience here and then we wonder Ireland don't improve. Oh, protestant clergy and landlords of this darkened land what sins of *omission* at least have you to answer for.

2. Shuja-ul-mulk Sadozai, Shah Shuja, deposed 1809 but restored by force of arms during this First Afghan War; the key fort of Ghazni fell in July 1839.

9. The Doctor walked in so much improved by his fortnight's holidays—sad picture of the state of society in
that part of the country near Kilkenny. Gentlemen
all living beyond their means—proud and poor and
ostentatious, badly educated, idle, dissipated, almost
worthless, so drowned in debt as to be crippled in
every feeling. How happy are we to have had our quiet
lot cast here. A letter from John [Robinson, his brother
the Agent] with account current to the end of the year.
All debts paid, fifty pounds in hand and two or three
of the Tenants the back half-year to pay yet—to near
a hundred pounds more, that will do very well and the
pay coming in February.

10. Tom Darker [the Steward] much edified with a very able
article on the Corn Laws I gave him to read—admits the
possibility of the system of agriculture pursued here being
improvable, thinks that lighter fences, corners brought
in, gates to fields, drains and rotation of crops might
greatly increase the value of land; assured me he and
his brother have been improving in these respects. Anne
Henry from Lodgepark came to call. I should be quite
satisfied with such a daughter. I want no daughter of mine
to *shine*. I want no acknowledged *beauty*, no *professor* of
any accomplishment—no learned lady—nothing remarkable, but I wish to see my girls obliging, industrious,
contented, sufficiently accomplished to make their home
agreeable, so intelligent as to be suitable companions to
their father, their brother or their husband.

12. I have been thinking how best to encourage the school,
and not being able to afford more help in money than it
now costs, I have determined on giving fewer prizes—
only one in each Division—and instead I shall send ten
children to school. I have also resolved on resuming
my regular daily business as the only possible way of
keeping things in order. Monday—The washing to be
given out. Clothes mended. Stores for the week given
to the servants. Tuesday—work for the week cut out
and arranged, my own room tidied. Wednesday—accounts, letters, papers all put by. Thursday—house-
keeping, closets, storeroom, etc. arranged, bottles put

by, pastry made—in short every necessary job done for the week. Friday—gardening and poor people's wants. Saturday—put by clean clothes and school. Two hours generally does all, except on Thursday. Thus I am always ready and have plenty of time for other occupations. I also give an hour every evening to the little girls. Janey has a musick lesson every day—Annie every second day—twice a week French—twice a week English—twice a week dancing. Alas, when we see company all this happiness must be forborne, but we owe a duty to society as to other things and in its turn it must be paid and a little intercourse with our acquaintance is good both for ourselves and for our children. With *friends* it is delightful, and we have some even here I should be very sorry to have to part from. In the evening played some of Corelli's solos, read aloud Mrs. Trollope's *Domestic Manners of the Americans*.

14. Janey and Miss Cooper to carry some trifles to poor Biddy Shannon and enquire how many children from Burgage are at school. A poor woman with a sickly baby came for a dispensary ticket: luckily I had some old flannel and socks of Johnny's for the little wretched thing—and mind, dear little girls, never to throw away anything. I consider the servants sufficiently well off with their wages, well fed, well housed, and no hardship, and all old clothes I put carefully away, sure that some day some distressed persons will want them. The merest rag goes into a rag bag which when full a poor woman will sell for a few pennies. Cut out shifts and bibs for some poor—sixty yards of calico for one pound; how much comfort to be given for the price of one smart bonnet.

15. My account day very busy, brought up Tom Darker's books to the end of the year and quite satisfied with the Farm, having sold from it upwards of two hundred pounds worth besides all the hay, corn, straw and potatoes consumed by the family.

16. Too busy moving furniture to get out; reading the paper over the fire saw 'more insults by the French to the British flag' somewhere on the Coast of Africa. Add this to the

West Indies, the Mauritius, etc. and then this nice business in China—the Chartists—the Queen's pecuniary embarrassments with her income of upwards of three hundred thousand a year—the disreputable character of her court composed of the needy, the frivolous, the profligate, and the weakness if not the wickedness of the ministry—what awful times.

A most unladylike letter came from Mrs. Moore to Sarah. I was quite unprepared for the extreme shabbiness, the heartlessness, the total want of gentlewomanly feeling betrayed by this extraordinary production. I was too seriously angry to be able to advise a proper answer till I had waited for near an hour and then it required a little controul to keep the reply sufficiently civil and sufficiently decided. Mrs. Moore after all is but an Irishwoman—uneducated, selfish, peremptory, unfeeling to those beneath her; she is a fair sample of her countrywomen—pleasant and ladylike in the drawing-room and the less that is known of her out of it the better.

17. I write here, my little girls, to let you see the evil consequences of want of propriety in the conduct of a mistress of a family towards her servants. You will be, I hope, too well brought up to find like poor Mrs. Moore any pleasure in the *gossip* of a servant; these undereducated persons are of course apt to quarrel among themselves. And be lenient in judging of them. Do not expect from uncontrolled tempers the same patience strict discipline has I hope produced in yourselves, nor imagine that uninstructed people can perform their duties as conscientiously as you would do. But endeavour by strictness and kindness to induce them to serve you well—teach them to improve themselves by your example and by your advice and by your assistance. Good books, a kind though serious reproof, and above all family prayer properly followed up will effect this in all who are worthy of remaining with you.

I do not know any part of an Irishwoman's character that so ill bears to be scrutinised as her conduct towards her dependants generally—her servants in particular. She is capricious with her tradespeople, and exacting, and bargain-making—almost unknown to her husband's tenants—of very little use to the poor—very fine in her own person—very niggardly in her own house—treating her servants as in other countries people do not treat dogs and her governess as no other lady would treat a servant. All the fault of education, the evils of which of course descend, rendering the lower order of Irish *generally* as unworthy of confidence as the upper are of intimacy. At present with the exception of Tulfarris the Hornidge family home I know of neither ladies nor gentlemen in Ireland—and even there I am not thoroughly satisfied.

18. Queen opened parliament in person with a sad silly speech—things of importance hardly touched on—about the weakest ever uttered of all those unmeaning productions. Great fears of the Chartists doing mischief in London. I can just remember walking on Windsor Terrace when a very little girl, and my brother William at school at Eton to see the old King George III with Queen Charlotte. How much per cent has the value of royalty fallen since those days and like enough to get down to zero before very long if this silly girl has not fixed on a wise husband. We all seem tired of the folly of such a Court, really a disgrace instead of the blessing it might be.

19. Found the Doctor at home in sad distress at Mrs. Moore's discreditable conduct. Made me promise not to whisper it even—seemed delighted I had burned her notes. Indeed I will try to forget them thinking perhaps I have judged her unfairly by a standard with which she is perfectly unacquainted, viz: the feelings of an *English* lady, and then her father one of the profligate though brilliant set that shone when neither religion nor morality was in fashion, her mother not to be mentioned in the line with the word lady, and herself very much spoiled by family flattery before marriage, a husband's folly after, and too clever often to meet with an equal among her own sex; naturally of an arrogant temper, selfish and under-educated—a really fine character that has been irreparably injured.

There is such an evil spirit abroad, in all the manufacturing districts especially that it is impossible not to dread future events, and the links which used to connect the different ranks of society together have been so rudely cut asunder by the haughty bearing of the aristocracy of *birth* that very unkind feelings have been created between classes which might have been mutually agreeable and together most useful to the community at large. A little of the *Highland* manners would have done more for the good of the empire than people are perhaps aware. Who ever there thinks less of the purest blood in Europe because the hand of the highly-born is extended to every fellow creature—his table open to every person of respectability—his assistance at the command of every individual round him? All his dependants known to him by *name*—their well-being as much his object as that of his own family. When did anyone hear of Radicals in the Highlands? Are there any Chartists there? And where can be found such a society of *gentlemen* as among her chiefs and nobles. There was nothing struck me so remarkably when I first came here as the tenants marrying their children—setting them up in different trades, etc. without ever saying one word about it to their landlord. It went through their whole conduct—we were to them only the receivers of a much grudged rent. It has been my endeavour faithfully pursued through many discouragements to establish a more affectionate intercourse between us. I have certainly succeeded in a great degree—time is acting for me—and I hope you, my dear children, will assist in accomplishing the good work which will provide you with humble but *true* friends, and give my little Johnny an improving tenantry.

21. Mr. O'Connell telling unblushing falsehoods as usual and using language in the House such as he uses to his mobs—called to order even by the Speaker. What a disgrace to have him and his *tail* in a British House of Commons—an assemblage *once* of *gentlemen*.

25. Little Post girl came for the little bundle we had made up for her to help her on her way to Australia—the poor thing was going with one shift, one frock, etc. I told her what she would most want. She is a wise girl—a friendless orphan will do better there than here.

28. Janey and I walked through all the mud to school—
twenty-seven children all clean and happy looking; boys
reading—girls at work—three sewing beautifully. Called
at Judy [Ryan's], found it all filthy, house, people,
children and pig! Poor Sarah, if she does take the
vacant room there she surely will not stay long with
such a crew and so nasty.

31. Most beautiful day. What a fine winter. For these windy
storms do incalculable good. They dry the ground—
drive away fever—clear the air of all the miasma our
damp Autumns generate. All the people busy with their
manure preparing for the potato planting. Thus ends the
first month of my Diary. All of us in health. Children
improving—dear Hal happy with plenty of the active
business he likes on his hands, and by good management
money enough to carry on his improvements gradually.
Though far from rich we are perfectly independant.
We live comfortably—can afford to keep all neat about
us—can see our friends in all hospitality—can give a
little way—can assist many—and have the hope of
bringing up our dear children in the station we hold
ourselves—probably the happiest in our mixed society—above want—below parade—leaving us at liberty
to enjoy the quiet domestick life that suits us best.
With a grateful heart do I acknowledge these many
blessings. May God Almighty keep me as I strive to be,
humble. 'Let him that thinketh he standeth take heed
lest he fall.'

SATURDAY, FEBRUARY 1. Hal after the fox-hounds, I busy
preparing for the new laundry maid, much annoyed
at the loss of things mostly by carelessness and the
very improper habits of these lawless Irish replacing
what they have wantonly destroyed by the very first
available article they can lay their hands on. Such as
the ironing blankets disappearing and without a word
to me, a good set of blankets taken off a bed to be
scorched to tinder. A poker broken, a common iron
poker, never mentioned, but a cut steel one from the
best bedroom brought down immediately and burned
so black that there it must now remain. Fifty things of

like nature making it so troublesome to keep house in
Ireland, as unless the mistress sees to every individual
order being *executed* she need not take the trouble to give
one. She must be herself a servant to keep up order. I
am sorry to be obliged to have this fourth maid but I
cannot help it, they are all so slow, so bewildered, so
ignorant that one is forced to have double the necessary
number, of course they can neither be so well fed, so
well paid, nor is the work so well done as where there
are fewer.

2. Read the debate on the Irish side of affairs to Hal,
most extremely interesting, nobody spoke well on the
Ministerial side. Lord Stanley again! the only man
who did not blink the 'no popery' cry, tolerating most
liberally, nay more, willing to employ useful men of any
creed in proper places, but never forgetting that we are
a Protestant country with a Protestant Government and
a Protestant sovereign.

3. Poor Widow Bankes came for some little presents. Do
you remember, Janey and Annie, how frightened you
were of this poor half crazy woman, and how Mama
cured you by making her a sort of pet, giving you clothes
for her, and letting you give her a dinner sometimes, little
foolish girls, were you not?

End of the great Debate. Sir Robert Peel so very
fine, honest, open, manly, straightforward constitutional
English. I cannot see any essential difference between
him, the Duke of Wellington, Lord Stanley, on one
side, and Lord Melbourne, Lord John Russell, on the
other, nothing to prevent their all acting together to
arrest the progress of democracy and impiety, reform
progressively what the changes of time and feelings have
rendered unsuitable to the age, and redeem the honour of
Britain which has been sadly sullied of late. Should this
ever happen we shall be once more a great nation, till it
does, I fear, there don't seem to be enough with talent
on either side alone to fill the offices of Government.

5. Children brought arms full of old stuff frocks and shoes
and two bonnets which we held a council on and assigned
where they would be useful, the best go to a box in

my room, the remainder is distributed in turns to the
deserving poor. I find the *patterns* thus given them have
been of much use in improving their home-made clothes,
they are so clever they can copy anything.

6. Very fine hunting morning, bright but cold. Had cold
luncheon ready in the hall for the hunters, no one called
in but the Doctor who made a good dinner and gave
Janey and me a Latin lesson, and told us Lady Milltown
was not well, complaining of no one ever calling on her,
out of spirits. Her Lord complaining that she never
dresses till near dinner-time, an idle slovenly habit she
learned in France, never stirs out, she that used to be
so active, he don't know on earth what to do with her;
so it must be for she has no pursuit. With that beautiful
house [Russborough] full of the choicest works of art
she has no pleasure in it but to see it now and then
dusted, her fine family of children are no resource to
her. She is incapable of assisting in their education. No
reader, beyond a novel which only wearies the spirits, no
worker.

And here let me remind you, dear little girls, of an old
saying of dear Grandmama's that a woman who had not
pleasure in her needle was never happy, and very seldom
good, it may sound a little forced but it is nevertheless
perfectly true. A woman has so many solitary hours.
Reading through all would be very far from profitable to
her, a scientifick pursuit or a devotion to some particular
art would withdraw her attention too much from these
numberless little duties upon which the happiness of all
around her depends.

Besides this want of occupation poor Lady Milltown
has had the misfortune to yield to a vile, irritable, jealous,
malicious temper which has alienated every friend, and of
what avail to her is all her wit and her talent and her rank
of which she is so vain now that she is getting old? The
spirits that once carried her through are deserting her and
she has nothing to replace them with, no one loves her,
not even her children, I can't excuse her failings though
I make every allowance for her entire want of education,
her early marriage to a profligate man, her later marriage

to an unprincipled one, for she *knows* the right way, and won't pursue it.3

8. Carpenters getting on well upstairs. Dear Hal mightily offended with me because I do not always approve of his taste. Like most men he understands very little about colours, which contrast well, which suit, which shock, neither has he much eye for form or arrangement. Taste like every other talent requiring more cultivation than his active soldier's life has given him opportunity for, but I almost got myself into regular disgrace for hinting this. Men, you are very vain. Not much in the papers, good speech of a frequently troublesome man, the Bishop of Exeter on the Abominations of Socialism.

10. Frightful day, yet the Colonel a good deal out looking after workmen. Disappointed in my laundry maid, but will try her longer, they are all so unneat, so careless, and understand so little what they ought to do, it is really a tiresome business to manage them all, and Hal has worse to complain of outside, real dishonesty, entitled hereabouts cuteness, very sad it is to have so little hope of reforming such errours. Truth is not in the people nor will it ever be in them under the Roman Catholic priesthood.

12. Papers full of the Queen's marriage. The looks of the bridegroom, the dresses, the processions, the banquets, the parties, the cakes, etc. The Queen seems to have shown great calmness combined with great feeling and to be really in love with her young husband. And if he has the talent as well as the beauty of his family this may be a propitious marriage, may rescue her from the gossipping mischief of her bedchamber and raise her thoughts to subjects becoming her important station.4

16. Sunday. Such a beautiful morning, wakened by my three

3. After the death of Eyre Tilson of Coote, Barbara, née Meredyth, married the fourth Earl of Milltown (1799–1866).

4. The 'Bed-Chamber Crisis' of May 1839 ended Peel's brief first ministry. Her marriage to her cousin, Prince Albert of Saxe-Coburg-Gotha (1819–1866) took place on 10. February 1840.

pets all tumbling into bed to me in such glee. Nothing almost raises my spirits so much as a bright Sunday. 'This is the day that the Lord hath made. We will rejoice and be glad in it'. May you ever keep it thus, dear children, not as a day of gloom, as a day of austerity, as a day of privations. Moroseness is no part of the religion of Christ. The Roman Catholic Sunday is in many respects infinitely nearer the proper method of spending the day to my mind than the Calvinistick. The old Church of England nearest of all, not the methodistical section of it, but the real cheerful old English reformed Church.

21. Our book Club begun in earnest, our book—Sir James Mackintosh.[5]

22. Talking over Sir James Mackintosh, I observed how little real value was the greatest genius, the most first-rate talent, compared with the habits of regular industry, how very little the first generally leaves behind it.

It seems to me that there must be something wrong in the Scotch system of education—so many of her cleverest men having in their after life bewailed that desultory reading results as much from idleness as from a desire for knowledge, getting through books unconnected with each other without any purpose, but amusement. To be deprecated at any age, but positively pernicious to youth, encouraging an appetite for novelty merely, unsettling the mind without much informing it, causing over-excitement followed by lassitude without any one good result.

27. Something radically wrong in the character of Sir James Mackintosh I imagine, a want of thoroughly religious principle though he had much religious feeling. He was too much disappointed in his situation at Bombay because he did not seek for it on right grounds. It was all wrong and yet I feel for him, for how desolate did I not myself feel at Bombay, how dull the parties were, how stupid the conversation, and there was great improvement since

5. The 'Life' (written by his son R.J.M) of the celebrated political theorist (1765–1832), who was a friend and contemporary of her father, was published in 1836.

Sir James's day but I took myself to task for my folly
in expecting to find Lord Jeffrey, Mr. Horner, Charles
Grant, the Duke of Gordon, Count Flahault etc. with
their proper accompaniments in a distant Colony, or
rather not expecting, I was not so ill informed as that
implies, but feeling dull because I did not find all of
talent and of polish I had left behind. Here I feel this
too a little, the people are not sufficiently educated to
be to me what my early friends were, but there is much
worth and much talent and much kindness among them.
And I have sobered myself down to be quite happy with
'good home brewed ale' and to think of Highland days
as of a glass of champaign not often attainable.[6]

Walked to Blesinton with the little girls, called at
Mrs. Murray's, found them in, heard a great deal about
Lord Downshire of course, met Mr. Moore in the market
place, talked of our books, he has offered to lend me Sir
James Mackintosh's *Essay on Ethicks* which he says with
the Colonel's help I shall understand. Mr. Murray [Lord
Downshire's Agent] showed us a Temperance Medal
rather handsome. It is really curious what an effect
Father Matthew[7] is producing, the distilleries are in
many places given up, the breweries even injured. Our
brewer told us he does not sell one cask of beer now for
twenty he used to sell; that and the fine of five shillings
really seeme to have produced great effect; that odious
whiskey, it is the bane of Ireland the money spent on this
abominable poison would keep each family in comfort,
besides that with so excitable a people the use of spirits
maddens them and puts them up to the commission of
every crime.

SUNDAY, MARCH 1. Much interested in the journals of Sir J.
M's little Tours, knowing most of the places, his idea
of Indian politicks so correct, projected improvements

6. The H.L. knew India before her marriage and Sir James
   was Recorder of Bombay (1803–1811); both contrasted it
   with what they recalled of Edinburgh in its 'Golden Age'.
7. The Rev. Theobald Matthew was a tireless campaigner in
   the cause of total abstinence from alcohol.

affected. Strange that I should never have seen Sir James himself though we were relations after a Highland fashion, and our families intimate and my father and he great friends. I must write you some Highland tales, dear children, or you will not know your mother well.

10. Children all went to Peeny Kelly's who made much of them Jack in particular, he must be Squire Smith again, no Colonels for her, he must live in his own place among his own people and he will always have plenty for they always had plenty before him. Very likely, when the property was twice as large as it is now.

15. How excessively beautiful is the English of Junius,[8] I never studied it before having only known it read in bits by my father as was his custom with most Authours he liked from whom he used to select passages for our evening's amusement. What pains my father took with us, it did not strike us when we were young, it was done so easily, so much as a part of his own occupations. But every hour since I was separated from him, I have felt the value of early constant intercourse with such a mind as his. We were his companions in all his pursuits—his assistants as far as our powers admitted. What we could comprehend he always so fully explained, yet he led us to enquire for ourselves, seldom either giving us short roads to knowledge, he often let us take a great deal of pains to find out what he could very easily have told us.

John Hornidge called quite in a bustle about the Election for Poor Law Guardian, having nominated Colonel Smith and taken a world of pains to secure his return in opposition to one Riley set up by the Priests. He tried hard to get Hal to promise to accompany him to-morrow to canvass some respectable farmers in Lacken. Sacred musick the first part of the evening, Lord Byron afterwards.

16. I think myself my little hub is acting Coriolanus a little bit, however he says he won't move; if the black-guards

8. This is the pen name of the anonymous author whose savage attacks between 1769 and 1772 on George III's ministers were widely read.

elect him he will do his best for them but he won't solicit one of their most sweet voices. They all know he has consented to the nomination.[9]

19. We met the priest Father Germaine whose Curate has been so busy setting up this Riley, he very much wanted to pass us appearing in the extreme of hurry, but Hal would not let him off. 'How are you, Mr. Germaine'? He was obliged to answer though he quickened his pace. 'Has your Curate been very successful in his canvass?' 'I believe not, Sir', said the poor priest quite taken aback; it was too bad. Coming home my heart filled thinking of all the happiness that awaited us, business going forward everywhere, the ploughman in the field, the labourers splashing [trimming] the hedges, the farm yard full. It is really enjoying life to live as we do.

31. Tumult in the family on account of thefts from the pantry, so many cakes taken away yesterday, the two girls *suspected* but in the absence of proof could accuse none so we called the whole household together. Would allow no one to speak, only listen to a pretty severe rebuke; fancied that we saw guilt on the two faces.

Hal and I walked all about to see what the men were doing, some fencing, some potato planting. Beautiful weather, all prospering round us. Both Hal and I bore the success of the priests and Mr. Riley in the poor law business with equanimity.

WEDNESDAY, APRIL 1. Hal and I walked to Russboro', found Lady Milltown in and so agreeable we staid an hour hearing her talk. In praise of John Robinson as a man of business and talent and as a gentleman. Against the priests and the Irish generally. About the queen and her temper!

6. The Doctor and Tom Darker amusing us with the Priest's

---

9. The English Poor Law, basing relief of poverty on the unpopular workhouses, was extended to Ireland in 1838; an elected Board of Guardians were responsible to the rate payers. See *Coriolanus* Ii:177–9:
   'He that depends/Upon your favours swims with fins of lead/and hews down oaks with rushes.'

denuciations in the chapel against Colonel Smith and anyone who voted for him as a Poor Law guardian in opposition to the Candidate of the true faith. He called on most of our tenants, threatened all, and rated all, yet all but *two* voted for their landlord. Dempsey stoutly insisted that he would, he did not care, he would vote for the man who gave him his land, and he let the priest understand that it would be as well to give over abusing him for he was not the man that would bear it, the Curate struck him when Dempsey turning to the Priest advised him to look after that young man of his for so sure as he ever laid hands upon him again so sure would he knock him down.

They told Farrell the carpenter that if he did not vote for their candidate they would not let him enter their chapel, on which he observed there were other places of worship he could get into without any leave from them. They have refused to christen a child of James Carney's the mason on the same account without he pay them most exorbitant fees. All this is most agreeable to me, the tighter they strain the cord the sooner will it snap. The roused feeling of the people too is really comforting, a ray of light in the darkened land.

The Doctor a good judge says it is surprising the change among the people latterly in their estimation of the priests they are losing much of their fear for them and all their respect. Tom Darker says the same thing, that they talk of their priests now in a way they would never have dreamed of doing a year or two ago. I think nay I feel sure that if we protestants did our duty, if we acted up to our principles, if the landlords visited and assisted and became acquainted with their tenantry and our clergy laboured with zeal in their vocation, there would be few papists in this country in twenty years.

14. Another summer day but windy. Paddy the gardener who had been absent yesterday without leave (whiskey drinking of course) at his work again. Hal went in to the Sessions having heard a bad account of Judy Ryan and her sister big Ellen quarrelling and fighting and drinking, taken up by the police at last.

16. Hal off on a crusade against the impertinent interference
of the Roman Catholic priest with his tenantry, party
work, political scheming beginning here where till now
we never had any of it. Tenants who voted with and
for their landlord denounced from the altar, harrassed
in every way. So on the priest and on the tenants the
Colonel means to call, to request of the first not to trouble
themselves with what should not concern them, to tell the
second to mind what they are about, to inform all that
such as are not thoroughly for him he shall henceforth
consider as against him and treat accordingly, he never
till now interfered with them one way or another, but
war having been proclaimed he will not blink the fight.
If there were more like him we should not have the
country priest-ridden the way it is. The poor people
are well inclined and would be happy and prosperous
if those vile priests would let them alone. Well, he found
Father Ricard the curate at home, Father Germaine was
not at home, and he told him quite plainly all he had
heard and all he thought of what he had heard and all he
certainly should do in consequence and he does not think
they will continue their agitation hereabouts. At first the
little priest tried to shuffle off the accusation but at last he
was obliged to admit its truth though he excused it as an
incidental flourish in an admonitory harangue concerning
dues which I am delighted to find they are beginning to
find some difficulty in collecting.

　　Mrs. John Hornidge called looking most wretched, so
very fine too, just like a corpse dressed up for the grave
in Italy in all the family splendour!

17. These wild people all gone mad, nothing but fighting
in Baltiboys during these odious holidays. Andy Hyland
beat and bruised in a most shocking manner by four
strangers on the Ballymore road who insisted they owed
him a beating though they would not say for what.
Red Paddy Quin and big Pat his cousin a regular
fight unknown for what. Pat Ryan and James Ryan
both on lame James Quin for some mistake about a
cart. Pat Ryan and Paddy the gardener at midnight
on *Monday* quarrelling in Blesinton breaking people's

windows keeping half the town up. Judy Ryan and her
sister Ellen throwing pewter pots at some men's heads
in a publick house and worst of all Dempsey his *four
daughters*, George Cairns, *his wife*, and others setting
on James Ryan with stones and broomsticks and pitch
forks because they were displeased at his having hired
a certain field. Shall we live to tame in any degree such
savages.

18. Lovely day, played with Johnny, saw the little girls off
on the donkeys for the post, then went to put away the
clean clothes and then to start on my tour of lecturing.
Pat Ryan and Judy his wife, James Ryan and his wife,
George Cairns and his wife, Bryan Dempsey three of his
daughters and two sons, Mary Dodson, Judy Ryan etc.
all required it and all got it, all acknowledged they were
wrong but did not seem inclined to do right again, all
thanked me for the *respect* shown them in my taking the
trouble to come to speak to them, none were uncivil,
so I shall continue paying this respect in hopes that by
constantly showing an interest in them and watching over
them and advising them kindly we may in time improve
their tempers. If I could but keep the women quiet, make
them peace-makers instead of wranglers, keepers at home
instead of gadders abroad and induce them to have their
homes comfortable. We shall see, live in hope as they
say, but these people are so untamed, and then their
unfortunate religion and those priests.

27. A great parcel of Club books, came, Sydney Smith's
works[10] in three octave volumes. Life of Sir Walter
Scott in ten small ones.[11] I had read this last before
with such pleasure that I look forward to many delightful
evenings reading it aloud. We began it after tea, read the
fragment by Sir Walter himself with much interest and
Mr. Lockhart's stupid first chapter. It is more pleasant to

10. The Rev. Sydney Smith (1771–1845) was one of the
founders of the *Edinburgh Review*; his collected works
were published in 1839.
11. *Memorials of the Life of Sir Walter Scott* by John Gibson
Lockhart, his son-in-law, was published 1836–8.

me than to many from my knowing so many of the people mentioned. William Clerk so intimate at my father's, so clever, alas! that I should have to add so indolent. I recollect one summer evening that he was drinking tea with us when we lived in George street that he was describing the confession of a felon who was on trial for murder which he related in so impressive a manner that when he drew the paper knife across [my sister] Mary's throat in illustration of the story half of us screamed with horrour so entirely had he rivetted our attention. His memory was so extraordinary his information so extensive that people unable to believe that he really did know everything accused him of reading in the morning to prepare a set of subjects and then artfully turning the conversation at dinner like Sheridan to the point that suited him. If he had talked less one might have fancied this but he never let anything pass as far as I remember and we met him almost daily for years.

He was an oddity like his still cleverer brother Lord Eldin, so were the delightful old sisters, all of them foolishly fond of animals, the house was full of beasts, cats in pelisses, dogs in spencers, eating and drinking all over the rooms, often sitting on the tops of their heads and their shoulders. Lord Eldin had a most valuable collection of pictures, his whole house was one gallery, his port-folios of sketches were still more valuable, he had no greater pleasure in a spare hour than looking over some of these treasures even with us young people, explaining to us the beauties of the art and the defects of the particular painter.[12] Edinburgh was in those days a school for the young mind to be formed in. I did not make the use I might have done of very uncommon opportunities, but it was impossible for the most careless

12. John Clerk, Lord Eldin, built up a large art collection in his house in Picardy Place; after his death it was auctioned and to the disaster of a floor of the building collapsing was added the ignomy that many of the pictures were fakes. His natural daughter was to be governess to the Milltowns and then the Smiths.

not to derive permanent benefit from constant intercourse with society so talented.

28. Lovely and very busy day Hal off to the Sessions, then one of the school children ran down to say the Inspector had arrived there so Jane Cooper [the governess], the little girls and I went up to meet him. He is newly appointed to this district and expressed himself much pleased with the size and cheerfulness of the room, the cleanliness of the children whose appearance he considered superiour to any he had seen. His wife who examined the work praised it highly, she had seen some as neat, none so clean. I mentioned several things to him in which I considered the Board had not used me fairly and he gave me good hopes of redress in time, more particularly as to assistance towards the repairs of the schoolhouse which thus encouraged I shall apply for again.

Hal's Sessions business was a grand affair. Kearns and Dempsey and James Ryan and all their assistants and all their witnesses, furious with one another, Dempsey most impudent to the Colonel who made him make a most ample apology in open Court. How low is morality among these people. Kearns let his grazing to James Ryan and knew that Ryan was to pay the money for it to the Colonel to whom Kearns owed that and much more for rent. Two days after he let the same ground to Dempsey and accompanied him to John Robinson's office in Dublin and saw him there pay the hire of it. Dempsey knowing of the former transaction as many persons say though he has sworn a solemn oath on the Testament that he did not. It is all very shocking.

29. It is singular that with the great intimacy described by Mr. Lockhart to have existed between Lord Jeffrey[13] and Sir Walter Scott that so constantly as we, that is [my sister] Jane and I, were with Lord Jeffrey, almost living at Craig Crook during the summer months, I never saw Sir Walter there nor in all our many delightful conversations

13. The Scottish Judge Francis Jeffrey (1773–1850), well known as the founder and guiding light of the *Edinburgh Review*.

did I ever hear his name mentioned. Not so William
Clerk, his intimacy with Scott certainly was not so close
in after life as it had been in their earlier days, but it
continued and I often heard him talk of Abbottsford
(sic) and of the novels which he never hesitated to
affirm bore internal evidence of their Authour till he
was let into the secret when he never afterwards gave
an opinion upon them. Tommy Thompson[14] too had
cooled in his friendship and many other Whigs, probably
politicks divided these clever men, for party then ran very
high in Scotland. People in Edinburgh were also apt to
get into sets, and to have so many engagements with one
another that they really had no leisure to spend out of
their own circle.

30. Too hot to stir out till quite the evening. Walked till
after eight, then into our book. What a pity that Mr.
Lockhart thought it necessary to publish much of the
early love of Sir Walter and the very silly letters of the
Countess Purgstall[15] and the most childish nonsense of
poor Lady Scott whom he only married out of pique,
though probably he was not aware of it. She was ever
from the time I ever knew anything about her a most
ridiculous little person, frivolous and stupid as far as
a stranger could judge, without conversation, generally
dressed an object, rouge and garlands of roses on a crop
head when an old wrinkled woman and I should suppose
incapable of bringing up her daughters for they always
flew about just as they liked, came to church in old
bonnets and dirty frocks and without gloves, while she
herself never came there at all. Miss Macdonald Buchanan
however who was extremely intimate in the family and a
good judge told Uncle Ralph that she was not so deficient
as she appeared, that she possessed good sense and a most
amiable temper kept an hospitable clean tidy house and
that although she could not comprehend her husband she
looked upon him as a very great man. I fancy when quite

14. Deputy Clerk Register of Scotland (1806–39).
15. Jane Cranstoun (who married Godfrey Wenceslas Count
    of Purgstall) was an early confidante of Sir Walter.

young she had been pretty. Latterly poor woman from bad health accompanied by pain and asthma she was said to have taken to drinking. I saw her one night at a party at the Miss Pringles', certainly very odd, her daughter Anne in great distress, and William Clerk and Sir Adam Ferguson came and coaxed her away.

And here ends another happy month during which sorrow in no shape has visited us. And except that we have imprudently run ourselves too close in money matters we have not had a care. On the 1st of May, to-morrow, another quarter's pay becomes due and we will be wise enough in future to endeavour to have a little in hand rather than just barely to pay our way.

TUESDAY, MAY 5. Another drive to the new Shop in Blesinton. How that little village has improved since we first settled in this country eight years ago. And all since the market was established there, though John Hornidge, John Murray and other croakers declared it never would succeed and refused to encourage it. Colonel Smith, Ogle Moore, and Doctor Robinson advanced the funds to set it agoing. Nothing more was required. Each week increased its business, by the end of the second year we were all repaid our advances. All the people round, better dressed, all busier, upwards of twenty new houses in Blesinton, most of them shops, each year the description of Shopkeeper and the style of goods improves. Those idle old men would keep a country back a generation.

It is a great pity Mr. Lockhart repeats so much and gives so many long letters. We are becoming introduced to a great many new characters, the English literary Tories, amongst whom I have seen William Rose often at my Uncle George Frere's and had to listen every Sunday of the spring of 23, in a bower! to his Ariosto, or Tasso, I forget which[16] And Coleridge whom I though quite mad, it was the fashion of the house to be amazed at his flow of eloquence, the flow of *words* amazed me, but as they came a great deal too quick to be comprehended I

16. He was a friend of Scott who encouraged him to publish his translation of *Orlando Furioso* between 1823 and 1831.

was not able to judge of the mind that prompted them, it was a torrent of language that never stopped and as the wildest eyes that ever glanced from a head accompanied this deluge with the most piercing flashes and a quantity of long grey hair stood bolt upright upon his large head as if it had been electrified he really looked as if he had escaped from Bedlam.[17]

7. It is a pity that Walter Scott did not travel into the *North* Highlands when he was about it, he would have found the manners much more primitive, the whole style of the *Clans* from the Chiefs downwards very much superior to any thing he had had an opportunity of seeing.

8. Sir Walter improving as a letter writer except on State occasions when he is very formal, far fetched, long-winded and much too *respectful* in his style to those he considers great people. Not having been brought up among them at all I suppose he felt awed by their titles.

10. Sir Walter's tour to the Hebrides tiresome yet in parts interesting. Many years afterwards when Jane was at Abbotsford he gave her a seal the stone of which he had picked up at Iona on this occasion. It has two characters on it of some old kind of letters, a relique indeed now.

12. Book very interesting, how singular the fulfilment of some of those old Highland prophecies, that which Scott alludes to about Seaforth uttered hundreds of years ago, that whenever there should be at the same time 'A deaf Seaforth, a childless Chisholm, a mad Lovat, and an Applecross with a buck tooth there should be an end of the male heirs of that branch of the Mackenzies.' Such an odd combination of circumstances, and all to happen in my day, and I knowing every one of the people. I could multiply these superstitions, *what* a pity that Scott never came into our highlands.

13. In our drive this evening met Lord Milltown looking miserable—he said nothing of winnings, and as his horses certainly lost I fear he has made a bad business of it. What

---

17. When Coleridge's brief sojourn in the army to escape his debts ended, the authorities explained his sudden discharge on the grounds of 'insanity'.

a life, feverish excitement or despair leading to everything that is bad, by slow but sure degrees eradicating all that is good. I never see him without a mixed feeling of sorrow and pity and shame that is really painful, for nature though she inflicted one very dreadful personal infirmity on him [see p. 489] gifted him with many admirable qualities, fine talents, good understanding, amiable temper, very handsome countenance, and rank and wealth and zealous friends. A bad education and disreputable society and an ill assorted marriage have altogether made him to be shunned instead of courted, and he is himself most unhappy.

14. We took our drive in the evening the children and I, then Hal and I walked. After tea read as usual. How all these well remembered names of people, times, and places recall the feelings of my early days. Days altogether of much enjoyment but embittered by the recollection of much sorrow, for my youth had a very stormy dawn, how could it be otherwise. Taken out of the schoolroom in which I had been kept as a child and thrown without preparation upon the world without a guide, without a direction, without ever having been taught to think and possessing many dangerous qualities, great beauty, the wildest spirits, the deepest feelings, and an ardent imagination, how could such a girl of seventeen avoid errour,[18] errour which led to suffering, for I was of a timid temper and dared not to act altogether for myself, you have been accustomed dear children to see your mother so calm, always cheerful, never elated, never sad. May you never understand all she went through before attaining this enviable state of sober happiness. I think you never will, for you will have a *watchful friend* in me.

19. Took no drive for the sake of the brown mare but had abundant occupation in a Court of Enquiry held on the conduct of Catherine the housemaid who had propagated

18. This is a reference to her broken engagement (described in her *Memoirs*); there are further tantalising references in her *Journals* (e.g. 26.5.40, 9.6.40 and especially 19.8.46).

so scandalous a story of little Caroline Clark that Sarah and James were obliged to inform us of it in order to have the matter examined into. Convicted of false witness and many falsehoods she showed no contrition, no shame neither, her manner was doggedly disagreeable. Poor thing, this disposition is the worst feature in the case.

20. Called Catherine to my room and discharged her. Her behaviour was improper, stubborn, sulky, had I not been very gentle though very firm and very cold she would have been impudent. She first insisted on being paid to the end of the quarter, then expected to have her expenses paid home, next brought forward a claim to some balance of last quarter's wages, and then tried to persuade me she had hired for higher wages than I give. But I brought down her evil spirit. Bitterly did I make her cry, I made her too acknowledge that all this was not only nonsense but wrong, *and that she had seen nothing* about Caroline, only she knew them that had. In short she is an unprincipled young woman and glad am I to get quit of her. And she quite deceived me for though I never liked her she was so plausible upstairs we all believed her to be thoroughly correct. The last person in the house I should have suspected of stealing out to Sunday dances though I used to think her too late in shutting her windows. I made her sign a receipt for her wages after all this, not trusting her at all.

22. Every evening we go on with Sir Walter. The King's visit to Scotland amused us much. That very August 1822 Hal sailed a second time for India hearing of Lord Castlereagh's suicide in the Channel. I was in my room at the Doune where I had been confined for many months, my sisters and my father and William went up to Edinburgh to all the splendour, but without any *tail*. Indeed very very few of the Highland nobles gave into poor Sir Walter's folly about the Clans with their pipes and tartans and gatherings. His making the great big fat King appear at his Levée in the kilt, (a dress only worn by a small portion of his Scotch subjects of the lower order, for the Highland Chiefs in ordinary always wore *trews* and on occasions of ceremony the full dress

of every other gentleman of their day) was considered as a mistake more serious than a folly for it very highly offended the Lowlanders who indeed during the whole pageant, in despight of their wealth and their numbers, acted only as very secondary to their wild neighbours. I believe the King and half his Court really believed all the *Scotch* were *Highlanders*. I think it was old Lady Saltoun who thus wittily answered the complaint of a Lowland Lady on this subject, 'why since his stay will be so short the more we see of him the better'.[19]

24. At six o'clock I had the three servant girls in to prayers and to read the Bible which I explained to them as they went along, Kitty listening though a Roman Catholic, I only made her read in the National School Extracts as totally ignorant of religion as the Papists are, it is better to begin with her as with a child. I hope this may be of use to these poor untaught girls, at any rate it keeps them at home and occupies them for an hour on a Sunday evening.

27. Wrote to the Secretaries of the National Board to know what is become of Miss Gardiner's salary, that certainly does seem to be a strangely mismanaged concern. What they do with the immense sum of money voted yearly to them by parliament it really is difficult to make out, they shamefully underpay the teachers and even the pittance they give them is generally due for months, there is no getting any assistance towards improvements or repairs, nor is there any training school as yet for instructing female teachers, and the Institution being going on these six years, and such a farce as the Inspector is. One merit they have and it is a great one, they are most liberal in their supply of school requisites. All their books are admirable and very cheap and they give every four years a complete set *to be used in the School*, gratis.

Mr. Featherstone called and walked into Blesinton with us which we found quite gay with a detachment of the

19. The natural daughter of Lord Chancellor Thurlow, she married the Waterloo hero who had had four horses shot underneath him on the battlefield.

22nd on their march southward. We did all our business
then called on the Doctor and brought him back with us
to dinner which was delayed till five o'clock by Mrs. John
Hornidge and Mrs Finnemor coming to call, the two
poor old women were dressed up like two characters
in a Comedy,[20] ringlets and flowers and feathers and
Mrs. Hornidge with nearly a dozen flashy colours about
her. And the ghastly looking false teeth and cadaverous
countenances making them truly melancholy spectacles.

28. A holiday, nobody working, Paddy asked leave to go
to Naas to purchase clothing, I will try him this once.
Mr. Darker went to buy wedders for fattening and a
bit of beef. We have reached a melancholy part in the
life of Scott, his ruin, from two causes. Commercial
engagements both with printers and booksellers which
he had no business ever to have entered into, and utter
carelessness in the management of everything he was
concerned in. The Printer's books were never balanced,
the Bookseller's affairs he never enquired into, he bought
land, built a castle, lived like a Prince, without an idea of
his means. Immense sums were made by his works the
sound of which seemed to satisfy him. He sometimes got
money, sometimes Bills.

Oh those Bills, the bane of Scotchmen, the ruin of
many a fine estate, the whole miserable business is doubly
melancholy to me from reminding me of the ruin of my
own father, who with a larger certain income than Sir
Walter, ready money at the beginning, quite as much
for his annual falls of timber as ever Sir Walter made
by his brains, much less expensive house-keeping, very
little building, very moderate improving, lost in contested
elections as much as Sir Walter by speculations by the
help of those dreadful Bills and a set of Agents and
flatterers who most successfully enacted towards him
the part of the Bannatynes. The children of both have
suffered. We are none of us where we should have been
as the heirs of such parents. In *our* case however we have

20. Lady Brute and Lady Fanciful, from Vanbrugh's *The
    Provoked Wife*, perhaps?

gained by adversity for we all required her rugged lessons, and though our paths in life have lain much below the proud promise of our birth I question whether they have not led to much more certain happiness which depends neither on rank nor success nor on wealth but on a properly regulated temper.

William can never be of the consequence his father was, but he will be independant and from his own exertions, and he will have a moral influence from the rectitude of his conduct in very difficult circumstances worth infinitely more in the estimation of good men than any that station alone could give him. John might have run a more brilliant career at home, because more in the eye of the world, than the creditable and lucrative official life he is passing in India but he don't regret the difference, and he will return young enough to enjoy many cheerful years in his native country. On the girls the blight fell heaviest, the younger girls, for my early indiscretions deserved no light doom,[21] and I can only attribute the favour of God in blessing me after many years of distress with such a home as with grateful affection I feel to be mine, to the unfeigned humility with which I repented the unhappy consequences of a faulty education on an unreflecting mind.

29. No Paddy, nor sign of him. It really is a sad failing this detestable punch drinking, well he shall pay half a crown for his headache and never will I give him leave to a fair again. Tom Darker bought ten wedders for £9 1 0 the beef was 7½d per pound, the dearest I ever paid in Ireland.

30. Paddy and I a very serious conference, he is in a fright. John Robinson arrived. Tenants all ready to meet him. And in general paid well, Pat Quin in the Bottoms, a defaulter as usual. Kearns of course and Widow Doyle and Widow Farrell, some of the rest did not pay up, but these paid nothing.

SATURDAY JUNE 6. Finished Sir W. Scott—a work it would have been better in half the number of volumes, and if

21. Scottish judicial sentence associated with the death penalty.

some judicious friend had sobered down the panagerical style of his son in law's enthusiastick veneration and admiration it would have been another improvement. But faults and all it is an admirable book and will correct many prejudices entertained both against the conduct and the disposition of 'good Sir Walter' whose worth really has been equal to his genius.

9. Your father says, dear children, that I shall quite frighten you into fancying your mother had been in her youth a monster of wickedness from the severity with which in mature age I have censured the follies and the flippancies of girlhood, for my indiscretions amounted to no more serious crime, bad enough. What can be more odious than a pert flirting girl, often betrayed by her giddiness into little better than a jilt. First of all inconsiderately entangled herself, then without reflecting on her duty to him whose whole object she had become or on her own feelings towards him, or on his character, or on the reasons urged against him; was easily frightened into giving him up, and weakly led to act a heartless part in affecting levity very ill timed and God knows very unlike the reality. The whole tale was melancholy, none acted rightly and each I believe suffered for it. Let it rest with the *Dead*.

18. Drove after dinner. Met quantities of Teetotallers who had all walked in procession from Ballymore to the Water fall [at Polaphuca] all looking so decent, well dressed and happy. I do hope there is no latent mischief under this temperance pledge, its present effects are so excellent apparently.

19. Paddy the gardener absent again, yesterday was a holiday, what must we do with the unfortunate man.

20. Paddy very penitent, I very serious with him, his fine of 2/6 seems to have but little effect, if he does not reform we really must look about for another gardener as valuable things might be destroyed by a day and night's neglect.

THURSDAY JULY 2. We had taken such a long drive last night that we proposed to give ourselves only a short one this evening and were just setting out when Doctor Eckford [their old Indian friend] drove up to the door. Very little changed in the ten years that have passed since we parted in the 'Isle of France', [Mauritius].

7. Doctor Eckford went by the caravan after much too short a stay for he is very agreeable in a house from his constant cheerfulness. He has overturned all I have been doing these ten years in less than so many days having infected my restless husband with such a desire to economise in France instead of at home that, his own inclination for such a scheme being very great, I feel it is more than probable he will yield to the temptations of a fine climate and the society of an old friend. If it will make him happier why should he not do it, he certainly would save in two years or at most three as much as would entirely relieve him from every embarrassment, and give us a little ready money besides, while here it is almost impossible to contract our expenses sufficiently as the occupations which make his life agreeable to him are all of a very expensive kind. Whether an idle life in a foreign country would suit him as well I have my fears. We must both take a little time seriously to reflect on all the circumstances of our position and when our minds are made up act with decision.

17. Never was such horrid weather. Heard of poor Major Hornidge's death. Alas, thus do our old friends leave us. Tom Darker spoke of it with tears.

19. Mr. Foster preached a sort of funeral sermon of which I could make very little. It was certainly his own for it was full of flourishes, splendid descriptions in flowery metaphorical language leading to nothing. Hal grieves in earnest for the poor Major, his last remaining old friend in this country, whom he served under in the Yeomanry during the rebellion [of 1798], who was consistently kind to him under every circumstance, he was as the sermon said a model for a country gentleman. A good Landlord, a kind master, an accommodating neighbour, as a husband, a father, a friend most exemplary. Many will long feel his loss, he was my boy's Godfather and should we be so far favoured by God as to rear our dear child to manhood we may propose this good kind man to him as an example,

for his life exhibited most Christian virtues, his end was
that of the righteous.

20. Wrote to Mr. Fetherstone to ask him to tea. He came
and the Doctor and two old Mr. Murray's with two wives
and six young people making a party of twenty-one. We
had a long tea table, plenty of dancing, then wine and
water and all seemed very happy. The Doctor was most
good-natured doing all he could to keep up the fun,
but the two curates declined dancing as too frivolous
an act for the clerical profession and the two Carrolls
on account of being in deep mourning, a mistake on
the one part and folly on the other. What can be the
sin of a clergyman standing up to dance with children in
a small and perfectly private party, and when did young
men ever introduce their feelings into society. Annoying
a whole set of people for a piece of *self ceremony*, for they
are quite able to laugh and eat most heartily black crepe
and all!

28. I am not quite sure that I like the St. Servans plan but
I see very plainly that Hal prefers it to circumscribing
his *expenses here* and honest Tom Darker will manage
for him so faithfully that the utmost will be made of
the ground and we shall take the opportunity of getting
quit of several insolvent tenants whom it would not be so
agreeable to turn out while we were living among them,
as they are all ill living reckless people quite inclined to
be mischievous as well as drunken and idle. I therefore
mean to consider the plan as set.

30. Another lovely day. Paddy the gardener absent all yesterday, having had some money given him to buy meal,
he has sent in the keys this morning, knowing he has
dismissed himself. Unfortunate creature, after so many
warnings, but go he must, he is unfit to be trusted with
any plants of value, and it would be wrong to others to
forgive him.

SATURDAY AUGUST 1. A very beautiful day, delightful for
hay-making, excellent for ripening the crops which are
very heavy. I in the garden with John Kearns who must do
for the present at least, till we are more settled whether to
go abroad or to stay. Hal and I looking over accounts and

calculating what saving we could effect by breaking up our establishment, what expenses we must leave behind us, how we should arrange our plans. Paid Paddy the gardener in full, sending him off between ready money and savings book with £13. He who came here ragged and starving, there will be little remaining this day week.

8. The heat so oppressive there is no stirring out till after seven in the evening, yet the Colonel will go out to look at his hay and in consequence is feeling his side. It is very odd, but I never yet knew any man who had the least sense in his conduct with regard to himself, their knowledge that certain things are hurtful to them does not seem to make the least difference—they appear to have no power of control over themselves. I am sure I hope dear Hal you will read this and think of it and without getting angry just consider whether it is likely we should have you long well in a French climate with French fruits without a horse.

10. Johnny was out in the morning and in such extravagant spirits in the afternoon he appeared as crazy as Prince Louis Napoleon[22] who tried to get up a little revolution in Boulogne with five men and ten horses out of a steam boat and an edict ready drawn up proclaiming M. Thiers his prime minister, it was all over in a couple of hours, and they were all half drowned trying to escape.

18. Poor Law Commission sat again, Hal sent John Darker not being able to move himself. On the whole it all seems to be fairly done, a very just value laid on lands and houses too, generally speaking and a very fair attention paid to such corrections as persons of superiour local knowledge propose. And *Riley* the Colonel's opponent! An admirable guardian, one of the best of them. Wide awake, shrewd, intelligent, and quite acquainted with the value of property. We got our house lowered and some of the bad land planted on the top of the hill. The tax will by no means fall heavy, it is not known, but the Commissioner supposes about three per cent.

22. Bonaparte's nephew, later Emperor Napoleon III: for Alfred Cobban this incident was 'a day excursion to Boulogne.'

The landlord besides his own rate for his own house and grounds etc. will pay for each tenant the half of what his farm and tenements are rated at. We expect to have to pay about £20 yearly, not so much as we spend now by many a good pound, doing but little either towards lessening the evils of poverty, which to say the truth are principally brought on the people by their own vices, for a more improvident, idle set of human beings never were collected in a plentiful land. And then being taught by their priests to believe that the more they suffer here the less they will have to endure in purgatory, they are deprived of any stimulus to exertion.

Lord Milltown and John Hornidge unfortunately came to very high words yesterday at the meeting which is a pity, Lord Milltown was quite wrong in an observation he made regarding some valuation he was inconsiderate enough to call *unfair* and John Hornidge retorted in a passion instead of gravely. How invaluable in every relation of life, private and public, is a perfect command of temper; remember this, my own dear boy, in case I do not live to help you. A country gentleman, which we look forward to your making yourself, ought more particularly to be very guarded on this count, so many little irritating accidents are apt to happen to him both in the management of his own affairs and in his intercourse with his neighbours, they are a class very apt to fall out without care about their roads and their assessments and their different jobs, and to do good a man must have influence, *and to have influence he must have temper*, it would be all in good order always with all of us if our hearts were rightly with God.

29. Hal drew up the minutes for his will which he wishes to make before leaving home. Neither he nor I having any foolish superstitions about these things but both of us liking to have all our affairs so arranged that in case of accident all may be found in good order, properly settled that there may be neither trouble nor perplexity left behind us. He read the rough draft over to me and it appears to me to be extremely just, very proper in every respect, and very, very kind to me, proving that he really

has confidence both in my affection and in my prudence. Still woman is but woman and in matters of business even where the good of her own children is concerned she requires the counsel of a sterner mind, so we agreed that he should ask Richard Hornidge to undertake a joint charge.

If it be my lot to survive you, my dear, kind Hal, I will endeavour to the utmost to fulfil every wish of yours, to do as I think you would like to have done, and you may depend upon my paying to the few relations you value the same respect and the same attention as I believe you have always seen me show to them. And I sometimes wish that it may be my lot for you would be very wretched without me, encumbered with business and frightened about the children and lonely, and if you were ill how wretched you would be without her who for so many years has been your anxious attendant.

WEDNESDAY SEPTEMBER 2. Hal wrote his Will over fair on one of the printed papers and signed it in presence of the Doctor, and Tom Darker, who subscribed it as Witnesses. He leaves all his property to Johnny, and with a portion of £2,500 each to the dear little girls.

5. We consider that the sale of our horses and our carriages will take us over to France and give us a good sum besides to have by us for accidents and that the pay—£320—will keep us there well. The gross rent of the property here is about £380—head rents, cess[23], pensions, wages, &c., all the necessary expenses that must be left upon it, allowing for bad rents, etc., £350—leaving John £630 to lay up annually, besides the profits of the farm, which must at least be another £100. And then, if we are so lucky as to let the house, we might allow ourselves the rent of it, as John would certainly have £600 a year, maybe more, to pay our little debt of a £1,000 with. So that if we tire of the Continent in two years we can come home rather more than free, and if we can stay a third year, we shall have near £1,000 in our pockets. So Hal is right, and the scheme is a good one when looked fairly in the face, and

23. Local tax based on the value of land.

all set down in black and white figures arithmetically. Yet all my heart is in Baltiboys, rain and all I wish to live and die here.

7. Took a long walk: went to school and was much pleased. Called in by Tom Kelly to see his new haggard. His whole range of offices is very complete, well laid out, well built and most creditable to him. He is in despair at the Colonel going away. So are they all, poor people. Old Mrs. Tyrrell came to give up her land looking wretchedly ill. She has made some arrangement with Mick Tyrrell, which the Colonel seems to approve of, and which I hope may be agreed on, as the poor old woman would have her cabin and garden for life and a little turf, and be rid of her ill-tilled field, which keeps her in poverty and pays us no rent, and thus another patch would be got quit of, which fits in very well to little Tyrrell's good farm.

9. Miserable night of asthma—in consequence of taking a tumbler of negus at night, eating meat at dinner and taking no exercise. Medicine won't do alone—he must abstain from wine and meat till the stomach come round again; he was still suffering so much at six o'clock that he sent to tell the Doctor he should not go this day; but he got better, and the day was fine with the wind in his favour, and the Doctor came and revived his spirits; so they started at one o'clock. He never looked up once after turning from the hall door, and we—how desolate we were—for of later years I have been spoiled, he has never left us, and this month that we are to be alone seems to me as if it would be endless. Frank came back by nine o'clock, his master was off in good spirits.

10. Began the round of visits I intend to make before leaving the Country, and took the Burgage side first. The Redmonds seem pretty comfortable; the eldest married daughter in a good place, paying the Mother for caring her fine child, and though receiving neither money nor kindness from her husband, able to maintain herself perfectly without him. The second daughter married too rather in a hurry we think, and so well—to a woollen draper's shopman, quite a lift in the world—but when it happened and how she and *her baby* came so unexpectedly

upon the scene so immediately after the announcement
of the husband seems queer, however married she is and
well, and has a comfortable lodging, and has taken her
little sister Margaret to live with her. Biddy, too, is with
a laundress, so only the two least girls are at home. Mick
always in work, and always dutiful to his Mother, so is
her eldest son; her third son little help to her, but able
to support himself, and she has a little boy as good as
Mick. The house is in good repair, clean and decent,
and she is so industrious there is no fear but that the
worst days of that family are over. The poor Delanys
looked miserable, their house a ruin and the two sick old
people seated each side their chimney in patient misery.
They have a little crop, straw enough to thatch the house,
hay enough for the cow, the two little wee boys beginning
to be some help to them, three daughters in good places,
two at home—one must stay to mind those old cripples,
but the other must get a place. Hal has left some warm
clothing for the old man, and I must do something to
enable them to get over the winter; it is heart-breaking
to think of what will become of the creatures when we
are away—it is the good dinner that has kept old Delany
alive and free from pain so long. Then to the dear old
cottage now almost a ruin, so dirty, so damp, windows
overgrown with the creepers we trained so neatly, papers
peeling off the walls, damp breaking through the ceilings,
garden a wilderness. Mary Fitzpatrick wants what I can't
give her—a contented temper—always fretting for evils
she can't cure, and forgetting her many comforts. She
would marry a Widower with three children, but only
two of them are thrown upon her, and he is kind to her
and a good workman. She has two nice babies of her own,
wants nothing from me but a small supply of medicine,
for her health is certainly very bad and most likely the
principal cause of her fretfulness.

14. We walked up Burgage Lane to pay all remaining visits
there, and found a great improvement in its inhabitants since we first remember them. All thriving except
old Shannon, suffering from asthma, and Henry Wall's
family, who don't look so well off as they used to do.

The wife is too fond of tea; she has another baby, so I sent her physick. Mary Doolen I will leave a little money for with Tom Darker to be given to her occasionally.

15. The Doctor tells me Lord Milltown could not come home just now, that he can live at Leamington while the £200 he has just won will last, and what he will do after that nobody can tell; he is unable to raise money to pay the renewal fines of some farms on his wife's property, the leases of which have fallen in, so that her income will be lessened for the future; and he knows the authour of *Harry Lorrequer*[24] a class fellow of his own, a wild, very clever, hare-brained creature, who himself played off many of the tricks he describes, now living at Brussels, I fear not very creditably, since his present employment is fleecing Hugh Henry at Ecartez.

17. Great commotion in the yard, Mary Highland having been seen at the peach trees. I gave it them well at all sides, being very angry and for sundry reasons of my own being very glad of an opportunity *publickly* to find fault with her. Tom Darker has distrained the three bad Tenants, Kearns, Doyle and Quin.[25]

25. No letter from Hal by the early post, the second brought me his first from St. Servans. Says if I like he will return to sweet Baltiboys, where perhaps we might economise just as well as anywhere else after all. I will say the word, he may depend upon it, too happy to get him back at this small cost to the place where he is best and happiest, and where he ought to be. And may God grant that this new trial, backed by so many more equally unsuccessful, may cure his restless temper, which I sincerely believe was at the bottom of this whim, though he fancied it resulted from prudence. The dreadful society is worse in my eyes

24. This was Charles Lever who lived in Brussels from 1840 to 1842. *Harry Lorrequer* for Thomas Flanagan (NH of I p. 493) is a 'picaresque romance of rakehell heroes moving through a dowdy, amiable and inefficient society of fox hunts, garrison town and ruined big house').

25. The legal process whereby goods and chattels were claimed for rent arrears.

than the ugly, wretched seaport. What could he expect from a set of people among whom Dr. Eckford figured chief. Henry Robertson is so captivated by the scenery and the air here, that he seriously thinks of coming to live in Dublin or near it. His £800 a year, which is a bare maintenance for them in Edinburgh, would enable them to keep a carriage here; he says that if we could gather a little knot of Indians about us, we might laugh at the world.

27. The Doctor came and carried me to Henry Wall's wife to see whether she would do for Mrs. Cotton, Mary Nowlan having become so intolerable they cannot keep her. The old Irish story: for the first six weeks no one could behave better, but as soon as the good feeding had given her spirits and she had got some clothes and a little money, her senses seem to have deserted her. First she wanted five meals a day, she having never had but two in her cabin, and they only potatoes, with very seldom milk to them; then *beer* at command, which in her life before she never could have tasted; then angry at getting no presents; then sulky at the English nurse insisting that the baby should be kept cleaner, etc., etc. How can one help these creatures? And Mary Wall, whom we found to-day actually without sufficient clothes to cover her, will be perhaps just as absurd in her turn. Patience, time and care may improve at least the young.

29. John had no difficulty with the poor creatures whose crops he seized. He left them all that they would require for the support of their families, merely took what they would have improperly otherwise disposed of, and before May comes, when they will be dispossessed, we must see to get something done for them. Farm they never will—Quin from vice and Kearns from folly, and Doyle from something between the two. Doctor called to hear about the Colonel, as indeed he has done most days, and to ask me if I wanted money. Took a long walk, gave Mary Wall good advice and something better.

30. Not quite so comfortable a month as many, Hal having given his health another shake, not a very safe thing at his age, and spent money instead of saving it; but if it

teach him wisdom we won't grudge it; his own warm, luxurious, happy home is the place for him at his age with his health, and, when he sees the good train his affairs are now in, I think he will not again be tempted to wander.

THURSDAY OCTOBER 15. A melancholy end to the St. Servans expedition, [the Colonel being bed-ridden with asthma for a fortnight after his return] but one to be expected, for change of air very seldom suits his asthmatick disposition. He has had a great shake, and he is not recovering from it so well as he used to do. A warning to him to take better care of his valuable life, and stay in the home filled with comforts suited to his age.

17. I must get to the garden, now looking as it used to do under *Paddy* reformed—his temperance medal and the entreaties of himself and friends having softened my hard heart after some weeks of obduracy, for I was very angry with him. We had the Duke of Wellington's *Life* here by Maxwell from our club—very badly done, I though—and now Beckford's *Travels*, which the Colonel tells me are equally stupid. We ought to have a new round of books ordered, these being out; but our indolent secretary [Ogle Moore] is too busy rocking his babies and fondling his wife to attend to any thing besides—how can we expect him to mind a book society when he neglects his parish?

19. Old Mrs. Grant sent us some periodicals to amuse the Colonel, among them a number of *Chambers' Magazine*, with which I am delighted. How is it that the Scotch always get to the top of every thing—do all best—early education of temper and habits, as well as school learning.

24. The Doctor was quite agitated yesterday in telling us of a most shocking piece of negligence—worse—neglect of positive duty in our Vicar and Curate. A girl thirteen years of age, for whom they are receiving an annuity from the County, allowed to live among papists, unacquainted with the nature of an oath, remembered two years ago to have said some prayers, etc. This shocks him and others because it came before them in a Court of Justice, where

her testimony could not be received by the magistrates on account of her ignorance; but I could rake up fifty such cases or such like, where the total inattention of our clergy is every day increasing evils that a generation of better care will not eradicate. And people wonder that the reformed religion does not spread here. I wonder it is *tolerated*—it seems to fail to produce even in gentlemen an idea of their duty. What effect can it have on the poor. Mr. Moore is greatly more culpable than Mr. Foster—*he knows his duty*, which the other poor creature really does not—poor Ireland!

30. Poor Sarah spent her night in tears. She is fretting herself to death, and I feel for her leaving us after eleven years happy service, and I feel for myself losing such an affectionate and useful creature; and though I do not value James equally, thinking he has some of the *cuteness* and plenty of the selfishness of an Irishman, I full well feel that as a servant we can never hope to replace him. The whole house is weeping.

31. The last day of October—upon the whole a very harassing month to me. We were too prosperous, all was going on too brightly with us, we needed some little check to keep us in mind that we are but pilgrims and sojourners here below and can't expect always to travel in pleasant places or in sunny weather. I hope, and I firmly believe, that the worst is over.

MONDAY NOVEMBER 2. I am no worldly mother, dear children, I wish for no splendour for any of you. If my two dear girls marry men of worth with a profession which their talents and industry will enable them to live comfortably by and to leave their children in the same station they hold themselves, it is all that I desire. A small establishment, some years of strict economy, would be no objections with me, but I think we owe it to our parents and to our children not to sink them below their birth, which we most certainly do when we cannot educate them for and in that rank in society they have a right to join.

3. Old Lord Seafield dead[26] my Chief—puffed off in the

26. The fifth Earl died unmarried at Cullen House, 26.10.1840

papers as a noble Earl, which indeed he was, but it was a dignity he and his family and his race and his people think very secondary indeed to his being the head of the Clan Grant. In my young days, at least, and in our part of the Highlands the clannish feeling was as ardent as ever it could have been, though they tell me it is wearing out like other good old things that don't seem to me to be replaced by better.

7. Hal rode and I walked, and then came the butcher with a quarter of beef and a poor man with a quarter of veal, which he had overbled and had to kill. I remember thinking it very disagreeable in your grandpapa, children, my dear father, that he made me, when I had grown up, attend the cutting up of the meat. The sight of so much raw flesh and the smell made me nearly sick at first, and I thought I should never learn the names of the pieces, nor understand where to look for them all. 'If you don't marry a rich man,' said Grandpapa, 'you will thank me for this.' 'Even if she do,' said Grandmama. 'she will not be the worse for her servants knowing she understands her business.' I was a foolish little girl in some things. I used to faint when I saw blood, so Grandpapa made me attend the Doctor whenever he had to bleed any one, and very soon I could hold the cups and even assist him in many surgical operations. It is mere selfishness prevents women being thus useful. Nature intends them for nurses, and if they thought more of the sufferings they could relieve than of the unpleasantness to themselves, they would soon lose their nervousness.

8. Jane Cooper quite shocked at my family troubles. Caroline requiring more rubbing in consequence of disobeying the Doctor's injunction—little naughty girl, one would have thought her seven weeks' penance would have frightened her. And Mary Byrne needing several more ablutions before she will be free from a swarm of very unpleasant companions. Decent and clean as she looks with a neat bonnet and shawl and two tidy gowns, she has but *one* shift—*one* petticoat—so she must wash, and I must lay out her money for her in Linen if she is to stay here.

Absentees, you ought to be at home instructing these poor savages.

Father Matthew to preach at Black Ditches to-day. Such crowds already on the road, the hill and the bridge swarming. All the country will be there; and no one before him ever did so much good to it, already rags are disappearing, the people are looking fat, clear, clean and more cheerful. In Blesinton, where I *know* every second house once sold whiskey, there are not above *three* in the whole town now where it is to be had. Coffee, tea and bread to be had in the teetotal shops instead, and on a market day quantities of meat bought. Drinking was the curse of the country, it is by no means so poverty stricken as it looked. The means of the people for the most part were fully adequate to their comfort, but they wasted in riot what would have supported their families well. I have known a farmer take his oats to market and spend every shilling of the price of them in whiskey before he left it. Punch and a pipe—that was the Irish comfort, and to enjoy it he sat in a ruined cabin in a ragged dress by a cold hearth, with a starving set of children round him.

9. Little girls and Miss Cooper went to church, so did Marianne—and didn't some home again, leaving us to get our dinner as we could. So I sent for her and scolded her well. My former gentle fault-finding making no impression on any of them, they never believed me in earnest. Mary, too, remained at chapel till five o'clock to take the pledge. The Doctor called in on his way to dine at Tulfarris. He had been talking to Father Matthew, and says he is a gentlemanly, nice-looking man about forty. None of the people hereabouts much disposed to follow him, but their priests make them. I wonder what becomees of all the money collected—the poorest person pays 1/- for the medal, the better sort 2/6 or more, and near a million have bought them.

16. My new maid Mary Byrne, who seemed so good a servant and had endeavoured to do all her work to my satisfaction, has got her head turned already. On Saturday she could not eat her dinner—a stew of beef and cabbage. To-day she declined washing the clothes without

assistance, so I desired her to return to her cabin—such
sort of tempers not suiting me. All spring and the early
part of summer they had only one meal a day, and she was
working out in the fields on 6d a day without food when
I was struck with her tidy appearance. How can one help
such creatures?

17. Dull morning. About half after seven Mary Byrne sent
me word that she would stay with me still if I would give
her help. I was very angry, ordered her off without delay
and sent for Nancy Fox to come and wash for me. They
are most extraordinary people.

28. Getting ready for John Robinson, who came by the
mail at 11 and had all his business over by dinner
time. The tenants paid well with the exception of Pat
Quin in the Bottoms, who never will be made anything of, and Kearns. Little Doyle paid up all arrears,
his fright having made him industrious—that and the
Temperance pledge. Old Mrs. Tyrrell has given up her
little holding to Mick Tyrrell, one of the most thriving
farmers in the place. Commons, as usual, had a mere
nothing to give—three or four pounds and his tickets
for butter.

30. John off to Commons early to distrain his goods and
began in form to make an inventory of stock and
crop amounting in value to several hundred pounds,
when the old wretch told him he might take whatever would make up the rent at Mr. John Darker's
valuation. So John helped us to two good milch cows,
a yearling and some oats—altogether equal to the nine
months rent owing. Why the old creature did not sell
his things himself at the different fairs and markets
and bring the money decently it would be hard to
say.

John says that in the King's County when he is
receiving Lady Milltown's rents the tenants will pay
a small proportion, fall on their knees, declare they
cannot pay another penny, a thousand excuses from
different pieces of ill-fortune, when he calls in the
Driver, orders him to proceed immediately to distrain
their goods, and then from out of some secret pocket

comes the whole rent to a fraction. They are the strangest people! What has made them so it would be hard to tell: maybe misgovernment and certainly want of education and most indubitably the priesthood; but here they are, neither honest nor truthful nor industrious and full of wild fearful passions that won't be rooted out for many generations.

The poor *Delanys*, who owe a dozen years' rent, gave up their bit of ground at once and were forgiven their £15 or £16, which they were quite incapable of making in their best day, and now the old man's ill-health and the old woman's want of energy, for she is not so old or so weakly but what she could very well earn her bread, were it not for an indolent habit and the frightful doctrine that the more she suffers here, the less will she suffer hereafter. John got altogether upwards of £220. Rutherfurd and Williams have still to pay—another hundred nearly—and all the Bills we have in Dublin won't be quite a hundred, so that leaving me £60 for present expenses he will have a very nice little sum in hand, £150 I think, which we will not touch if we can help, that we may have a little ready money by us. We felt it so very uncomfortable to be run so close. Before the end of February pay will come again, and before any more bills are due in May, both rent and pay will come, and another good balance I hope after clearing all debts may be added to the sum in Bank, so we shall get on capitally, and if we could but get more land into our own hands we should really make a fortune. By taking advantage of every windfall, I hope in time we may manage this.

TUESDAY DECEMBER 8. Dempsey has been most extremely disagreeable about the same piece of ground of Kearns' that he was so unruly about in spring,[27] threatening James Ryan and his whole family, getting Counsel's opinion, going to the Sessions, and using such language himself and his daughters to everyone whom

27. See 28.4.40

he thinks fit to consider of the opposite faction. Altogether he is a regular savage, and threatens to be very troublesome.

Miss Gardiner called upon me in great distress to know how to conduct herself in the following circumstances: since the measles broke out, she has never got her school gathered again. On going to enquire for her different scholars, she was told they should not return, for that I had burned all their Roman Catholic catechisms, that their priest was informed of it, that he was exceedingly angry and determined to make a great noise about it. She wanted to know whether she should call upon him to refute their folly, but, after considering a minute, I told her not. I bid her take no notice of the story whatever, and if the priest called on her to make enquiries, to take him extremely coolly, merely to say the tale was not true, and that there were no catechisms in the school, none being allowed to be taught there by the rules. I think it not unlikely that the tale may have originated with the priests themselves. They do not like my school, they do not like the knowledge the children gain there, nor the attachment they feel for me. They are beginning to find their power shaking, and they are trying desperate plans to retain it. How difficult it is to do good here. Much can't be done in this generation.

19. Finished six shifts and six nightcaps and sent them to Mr. Foster for the six old women on the Church list and have determined on endeavouring to alter the arrangement concerning the charity money. At present it is given in single shillings to any of them who beg hard or on the first Sunday in the month they each get three or four. They are all in rags, all starving, lodge where they can, and spend this money on the people who let them in and in tea, snuff, etc. I will myself give no money to be so misapplied, and as our Vicar takes no sort of trouble with his parish nor any one else, as I have the Curate's ear, I'll try and do what good I can, and for a beginning give them all linen instead

of putting a sum of money in the Box on Christmas
day. Went to Peggy Nary, who is much in want of
Christmas comforts. She is Hal's pensioner, but I look
after her for him, and before many days she will be very
comfortable.

25. Christmas day. What a pity—I forgot teetotalism when
I mixed the puddings, and not one of the outside men
would taste them. Now when those unruly people have
such self-command where they think it a sin to yield to
temptation, is it not plain that properly educated they
would be a fine and a moral race, almost equally plain
that those thousand crimes they do commit they have
not been taught to consider sins.

26. A regular réveillée—The Wren—under our windows.
What can have been the origin of this strange custom?
It is St. Stephen's day—the first martyr, who was
stoned to death—and what has a little harmless bird
to do with that? They hunt the poor little thing to
death, then set it on a pole, fix a kind of bower
round it, and then carry it all over the country with
musick and dancing and all of them dressed up with
all the rags and ribbons and bits of coloured paper
they can collect. This morning there were no young
women of the party as there used to be. Maybe they
don't find it merry enough now that whiskey a'n't in
fashion.

A visit from Mr. Moore and chatting on from one
subject to another, he and I got quite confidential; he
lamented his dereliction of duty, said he was firmly
resolved to 'turn over a new leaf'. 'But you have said
so so often.' 'Never to you,' etc. He then went into
some very painful family details, which did in some
degree excuse his neglect of his parish duties, and
appeared altogether so touched with the *omissions* of
his proper business that I am in hopes he will seriously
set to work to repair them. And few could do it better,
for his heart is kind, his temper gentle, his judgement
good, his piety sincere and his manner delightful, yet
I fear to trust him, he is indolent and facile, and
unless his wife be impressed with the feeling of duty

belonging to their station, I doubt his keeping his resolution.

31. Thus ends 1840. A year of quiet happiness spent entirely in our pleasant home, and in which by prudence we have managed to get before the world again. And all well. God be thanked for every mercy.

TWO

1841

Everything comes into a sharper focus with this second year—the ways she brought up her children and looked after her husband; the methods used to cajole a sometimes reluctant tenantry into improvements; their relationships with the Agent and Steward; their views on friends and neighbours, priest and teacher; and (in an election year) how she regarded the politicians of the day from Peel (whom she revered) to O'Connell (whom she loathed).

FRIDAY JANUARY I. A little note from Jane complaining of the excessive severity of the weather—Never felt any cold like it since the days of our Highland winters when we girls occupied the barrack room in the roof of the Doune, without a fire, without warm water, when we groped for our clothes a little after six o'clock, washed in ice and descended to the comforts of Cramer's exercises on the piano-forte, or worse Bochsa's on the *harp* till daylight allowed of our using our eyes; really children were cruelly used in those days, and for what purpose. Could we do any good with numb fingers, starving with cold and hunger and cross from actual suffering. Should we not have been better in our warm beds. Mary and I are wiser with our children. We never wish them to get up till they can see to dress and we have a warm room and good fire for them to go to afterwards and they never touch the pianoforte till they have had their breakfast and as I at least wish for no professors in my family, Janey has never yet any day practised an hour.

8. Miss Gardiner down with an order from the Inspector to attend at Naas to-morrow to furnish accounts and receive directions for the future management of our School. I took the reply on myself and made it like my father

of old in the 'brimstone and butter' style sending them every account they could want but not sending the poor young woman, thinking their Inspector may come here himself if he has anything particular to say to us.

12. How taste changes. I remember as a girl being so delighted with Horace Walpole's *Letters*, now they almost disgust me, so frivolous, such an absence of principle, such mere trifling through life, without an aim or an end, and vice so familiar to the society of the day, yet the charm of the style carries one on from one gossippy letter to another, all unsatisfactory though they be, and he had mind enough for better things had he lived in a better age, though naturally cold and ill-natured.

13. A letter from Mary—still delighted with Pau. She has got an admirer too, of course. She can't live without one, but 'tis only the landlord of the maison Puyoo—rather a descent in the scale of lovers, but even beautiful women approach forty.

27. Very much interested in my book,[1] which I finished with regret. Both Hal and I think that insanity was constitutional in him and would have broke out before had his life been unfortunate.

    I cannot, when reading of these times and of these men avoid recurring in my thoughts to my father who lived with them and was of them and yet does not hold his proper station among them. In talents he was inferiour to few, in accomplishments superiour to most, but he had two great weaknesses, a wish to do too much and a desire that what he did do should be known and fully appreciated, he had the misfortune to be born heir to a very large fortune, to step into its possession when a boy, to find himself in his own country from his position a man of consequence and in his own family the one flattered idol of a large and needy connexion. He married, too, so very young, a beautiful and a clever woman, but he

    1. The *Memoirs* of Sir Samuel Romilly (1757–1818), the radical reformer; the H.L. writes a little later that he 'just mentions my father as among the clever men at the Scotch Bar whose politicks were in the way of their advancement.'

had to educate her and then he thought his own pupil too perfect and she was as young as himself, utterly ignorant of the world and her temper often prevented her using her judgement. There is nothing like the school of adversity, how can we make up to *our* children for their never knowing it.

How will O'Connell talk of his recent failure? He drove to Belfast under a borrowed name and left it in fear of his life under the escort of the police. The ministry are weak and ridiculous and contemptible but they have not been wrong in not putting down O'Connell, it was wiser to let him annihilate himself.

No children at my school but three and the hedge school full to overflowing, the priests, the odious priests, their poor law guardian is persecuting every one who did not vote for him, rating their holdings too high and leaning very light on his friends. Hal had to go to John Hornidge about it, Tom Kelly being of course, under ban and having come to complain. Mary Dodson and many more were turned from the Chapel door at Black Ditches because they had not pennies to pay for entrance. It was shut in their face by Mr. Germaine himself and all they do is to change their chapel. Tom Darker says he knows a 100 would go to church to-morrow if they were not afraid of one another and of the little secrets told at confession. Wretched country.

MONDAY FEBRUARY 8. Hardly ever was more vexed than on hearing this morning of the folly of that nice girl Anne Fitzpatrick, whom I used to admire as much for her cleanliness and modesty and industry as for her beauty. She has never been quite herself since her handsome lover, Pat Hipps, the carpenter, jilted her for a little dumpy heiress with forty pounds and latterly annoyed her mother by allowing a shabby looking labouring lad, without house or home to dangle after her. Last Monday she said she was going to Mrs. Tyrrell's to have a gown made. Instead of that she went to Judy Ryan's where she was joined by Mary Dempsey and this beau—from thence the three set off for the young man's mother's where they remained till Friday when Anne returned

home to announce that the young man would not marry
her. When he was sent for he would condescend to take
her with twenty pounds. Old Mrs. Fitzpatrick stood
out, would give no money, sent off the man and kept
her daughter, but she will give in at last, they all do.
This is the common way of proceeding where the young
people know the old people won't approve of the match
they are making, this whole business is just a sample of
the *principle* of the *moral* Irish. The lad aware he had no
pretensions to be openly received as a lover, steals away
the girl, assisted by another girl and also by a relation, a
mother herself who could so easily have detained the silly
girl while she sent down here for her brother John.

15. Read the little Temperance tract sent by Aunt Lissy. If
all people kept their baptismal vows there wou'. be no
need of any human laws to govern our Commonwealths
and if all people could be sufficiently educated, probably
in some thousand or two of years we might reach this
perfection. But in the meanwhile with the higher orders
absorbed in selfishness and the lower plunged in vice and
ignorance any restraint on the most degrading and most
pernicious of their evil habits must operate beneficially
on their morals.

18. Waked by a light in the room which made me start,
it was Hannah with a candle, in a cloke, come for the
pass books for Paddy who was just starting for Dublin,
about five o'clock. We advised him not to go, it was so
boisterous, rain and wind so violent, but he went. In
the paper a violent letter of Mr. O'Connell's and equally
inflammatory speech of his son John's threatening the
English with another Irish rebellion whenever America
and France declare war.

19. Interrupted all day by visitors, Mrs. Hornidge and Mrs.
Finnemor, most beautifully dressed, had they been six
and thirty and going to a publick breakfast, painted and
made up and falsified in every way, they would have
looked very well on the stage by lamplight.

20. Such a beautiful morning. Hal off in great glee for a
fox hunt. No Paddy, what can the old man be about?
Made ourselves miserable all the evening because Paddy

had not returned. Hal began to think he had absconded altogether with cart, mare and goods for America, & as he dropt from the clouds here, whether he were a rogue or an honest man was problematical and this might have been a temptation beyond his withstanding. I absolved the poor man of all trickery but I feared he might himself have been tricked. Like other great men he has a failing—a woman can do anything with him and as in the course of these excursions he don't always meet with the best of the sex I feared his having been inveigled into some den while his cart was pillaged and we were calculating how we should ever make up such a heavy loss—in short we were most ingenious in tormenting ourselves and we really passed a most anxious evening, I could hardly play piquet, and Tom Darker gave us no comfort for about one o'clock he began to have his misgivings and Miss Cooper's consolation was that Paddy had broken the pledge and was lying in the ditch and that the mare would be sure to bring the cart home. At eleven we went upstairs, Hal, once more opened the window to listen along the road and heard them at the gate of the yard, it was such a relief, Paddy and the mare quite sober, all right, so we drank a glass of beer to their health!

21. Paddy came to deliver his letters looking so decent, so clean, so well dressed, my heart smote me for having doubted him. The nursery man had caused the delay.

24. East wind, stupid post. Election begun for the King's County, dreadful excitement, Priests as busy as bees and this time they must succeed for no Conservative ever before tried to rescue the people from the degradated state they have fallen into.

25. King's County election a perfect riot. All Sunday the priests were thundering from their Altars, so 70,000 ruffians assembled, regularly drilled, relieving one another and ill-using in every way Mr Bernard's voters, who, however, make an excellent show on the poll. A small body of police and Military unable to keep the peace. This will be the last *liberal* struggle. The Conservative wealth must prevail over the pauper radicals in the end.

FRIDAY MARCH 5. Sort of debate in the Commons concerning

Maynooth College. It is a perfect pest to the country, a plague spot whose contamination is daily spreading. If there is to be a papist college it should be upon a more liberal scale, greater funds, *lay* professors, men of science competent to instruct the pupils and it should be freed from the absolute controul of the priesthood. At present it is a nursery for bigots, they learn nothing there but a spirit of persecution and intolerance and political fury, the fools become enthusiasts in bigotry, the wiser become frantick for temporal power, there is no attempt made to cultivate the mind, improve the intellect, controul the temper and they have so managed that there is no one with authority to rectify this abuse of the nation's money.

The Doctor who came to dinner talking over this said it is surprising the spirit of enquiry among the priests themselves that has latterly been springing up and he goes much among them. And for the few Roman Catholic gentry, they are protestants in all but name and conservatives too; with the exception of the troublesome *tail* who being all men of broken fortune and few with much character find it suit them to live in a storm. Wrote to Ellen [Lucas] with a few more commissions and to condole with her brother John on the *bit* he lost from his arm at the Election; coat, shirt, *flesh*, all were bit out together by a ruffian, who is, however in jail.

22. Sweeps here, the same pretty boy again who was sold to the business by his mother for £1. Our master sweep was sold in the same way himself and he bears a good character and seems kind to his boys who are fat and healthy though nearly naked so that they must suffer miserably from cold, but climbing boys could not wear clothes, it is well the vile system is over. After this year no boy can be bound to the trade till he be sixteen years of age.

31. Heard that good Mr. Murray died last night about nine o'clock, quietly, he had been too weak all day to speak though perfectly sensible, he fell into a gentle sleep from which he never wakened. He survived his excellent wife little more than four months, they will be missed humble as was their sphere more than all the rest of the families in the neighbourhood, kind, worthy people.

THURSDAY APRIL 1. Mr. Murray is to be buried to-morrow, there is no idea who will be the new agent, Lord Downshire not being a man of any attachments except to his purse. *Tom Murray* heard he meant merely to keep a common bailiff here at an inferiour salary. Ogle Moore has written to ask for the house. Will it be given? Will Mrs. Moore like coming in to play parson's wife in the village so many miles farther from the gaieties of Dublin and nearer to clerical duties.

3. Application from Mr. Fenton for the treasurership to the roads vacant by the death of poor Mr. Murray, Hal had already promised William Murray.

5. Finished Anster's *Faust* yesterday; it is a very fine poem, beautiful passages in it, too wild in its construction to please me, a great deal too much mystified for me to attempt to understand, *German* being beyond my range. *Our* taste don't bear God Almighty sitting talking with different attendants and laying bets with the devil, so that the prologue offends; the moral was intended to be good certainly, but it is oddly developed.

6. Sent off the half yearly query sheet to the National Board and a bad account it gives of our success, eighteen pupils the average daily attendance; patience, the priest will tire them out by and bye and I will tire *him*. Took a drive this most lovely of days but called no where. Went round the hill and to Blesinton, which was full of the trustees of the road, Colonel Bruen, Mr. Greene, George Moore etc. etc. Mr. Fenton had few supporters. William Murray was therefore made, *acting* Treasurer for the present and on the 5th of May a Meeting will be held to settle the matter.

Tom Darker and John and Tom Kelly off to Baltinglass to register their votes, it was a hard matter to get them to do it, the Irish are so cowardly and have so little energy, things never can be better while people are content to sit still and look on at all the ill that is doing, the other side don't seem so inert. The priests whip them up to mischief enough. A queer mode of management but one that seems suited to their very limited understanding. Having borne a rent in John Fitzpatrick's coat these ten days I sent his wife a present of a needle and thread to-day. She is generally very tidy, he says her eyes are bad, she was with the Doctor about them yesterday.

15. Had all the world to see me at home, first the Miss Henry's, next Lady Milltown, shabbily dressed looking old and not well. She was very gracious, full of gossip and for a wonder not the least ill-natured. It is quite evident from her tone that the liberals as a party are gone, the wiser among them are all turning Conservative and leaving the ultras to their deserved fate the contempt merited by their very vicious principles.

She says they are beginning to think that all this long time Mr. O'Connell has been merely making tools of the patriots to fill his own purse, that his repeal agitation and his low rate of franchise and his plan for the farmers to value each other's land are almost signs of insanity. I really think it a mercy that he has got to this for he is now no longer formidable, these absurd flights have ruined him with all but the few vagabonds immediately belonging to himself and though they may yet keep the people for some little time in too great a state of unhappy excitement for them to attend to the business which will really improve their condition this won't last long.

Lady Milltown thinks Sir Robert Peel the greatest man of the age!! party spirit is dying away!! Baron de Robeck really has turned Conservative they say. He dined at Colonel Acton's and his agent having carried all his tenants down to vote for the Liberal Candidate the Baron forbade them and threatened all with ejection that did so. Lady Milltown says he has left them because they would not give him a peerage—maybe.

Then she had a great deal to tell me about the exceeding beauty, the sense, the talent, the *temper* of Prince Albert who is very fond of the pretty little Queen and very happy with her and has improved her greatly in every respect as is indeed very evident for we never hear of those indecorums now which were slowly but very surely undermining her character in the eyes of her people. She dotes upon him and however he may influence her in private there is no appearance of his taking the slightest concern in matters of Government

or any other matters not entirely belonging to himself.
She has shown great judgment in choosing such a man
from out of the whole world, and how clever and how
clear sighted must [her mother] the Duchess of Kent and
[her uncle] Leopold [King of the Belgians] have been.
Lady Milltown seems out of spirits, discontented, not
happy even in the expectation of company, poor woman
I do pity her, but like her I never can again.

18. Lord Downshire has come with his new agent Mr. Gore,
they came very late last night, half past eleven and sent
for Mr. Kilbee who was in bed, had to get up and dress
so kept them waiting. My Lord don't like to be kept
waiting. 'Hah, Mr. Kilbee—in bed, hah, you go early to
bed here Mr. Kilbee' 'People who pay so high for their
land, my Lord, had need to be early in bed and early
up', said Mr. Kilbee. Lord Downshire's is a character
intolerable to me, so weak, so vain, so pompous, so self
important. Not a bad landlord if he would be quiet about
it, though a hard one, nor an unkind master but so full
of himself he considers no one else and requiring a degree
of subserviency in all his dependants. The Doctor's story
of him was enough for me, he had given £10 to clothe the
poor of his estate here which brings him in £7,000 a year.
'Mr. Murray' said he 'how is this, I gave £10 to the poor
here a week ago and no mention of it whatever in the
papers, how was that?' To fancy a man, a rational being,
dictating those fine puffs we every now and then laugh
at in the newspapers about his trees, his charities and
his liberality, one can hardly suppose such a lamentable
degree of silliness.

20. Red cow calved yesterday, brown mare had a colt foal last
night the image of Major; four young horses and four old,
a nice stud and not one of them fit for use,—if I managed
my department in like manner I wonder what would be
said to me, my dear Colonel, eh. Sold all our lumpers[2] at
two pounds a ton, the produce of the old orchard, not an
acre, value upwards of fourteen pounds, set that against
the horses, Mrs. Smith!

2. One of the coarsest varieties of Irish potato.

21. All our cattle sick with this distemper everyone of them, it is not now fatal, nobody has lost an animal of late but they suffer a good deal and are very much reduced and thrown back by it; for fear the pigs should take it and so all our feeding be thrown away, we ordered both porker and baconer to be killed.

23. The Doctor brought the post down in the morning with a note from John regarding tenants in arrear which I answered by return of post. Now don't owe a shilling in the world except this thousand pounds to George [Robinson]. By living quietly for a while we have got over all our perplexities and shall certainly on settling accounts in May have a balance in hand, the beginning of comfort. I don't think we shall ever live up to our income again, all heavy expenses being over and the more land we get into our own hands the richer we shall be and the more valuable the property will become. So all looks very bright towards the future.

    There was a little scrap too from Aunt Mary [Bourne] enclosing Jane's extracts from the India letters. All perfectly well, [brother] John off at last by long sea to sail early last month, March, in the *Walmer Castle*. He is bent on living entirely in the highlands with his wife and children, determined upon it and very rightly. If his boys are to live on their inheritance hereafter they must learn to love their Duchus' in childhood, and his wife will better bear a Highland winter in her old age by recollecting how many most happy summer days she passed with her young husband in the beautiful woodland scenes of Rothiemurchus. He wishes my mother and Jane to live with him, but this my mother will not do. She has no love for the Highlands and she will never return there without my father.

25. Heard of Pat Farrell being nearly thumped to pieces by the priest the little Roman Catholic Curate, Mr. Rickard, a perfect little fury.

27. Had Pat Farrell with us in the morning. The Colonel had gone to him last night to see what state he was in and to insist on some steps being taken to put an end to these proceedings of this reverend firebrand who not

content with beating almost everyone he has anything to do with, maligns those he is offended with from the altar and has kept the parish in perpetual disquiet ever since he entered it. So several of the people who have been themselves ill-used have determined *they say* to sign a petition explaining their grievances and to send Pat Farrell and another man up with it to their Bishop. The Colonel wrote him a note to back them which I think a very proper one though it did not meet with the approbation of the Doctor with whom we sat an hour before going into the poor Murrays' auction. We looked at the plate and several other things and got Tom Darker to stay and bid for them but this day nothing we wanted was sold.

28. The Doctor came to breakfast and brought the post with him. We showed him the copy of the letter to Doctor Murray[3] of which he could not help highly approving, his objection is against interfering with their squabbles at all. The more tyrannical the priests become the sooner he says the people will tire of them, the more the priests beat and abuse and extort the sooner will the William Tell arise who is to prove to the poor ignorant terrified multitude that these furies are but men and may be resisted with impunity. There is much truth in this and the fact is that the people generally are beginning to feel towards their priests and *to speak of them* in a way they would not have dared to think of two years ago. Farrell told most injurious tales yesterday of them. At the same time the landlord interfering to protect his people never can be injudicious. What we want to lead them to is to consider him as their friend, the natural guardian of their rights and their comforts.

I heard some complaints of Miss Gardiner I must enquire into, such as her sending the children into Blesinton for messages and to gather sticks for her fire and asking higher fees than I had settled on, these were Mrs. Hugh Kelly's reasons for taking her children from school. Very

3. Daniel Murray, who the H.L. much admired, was R.C. Archbishop of Dublin from 1823 to 1852.

likely quite explainable but still I must look after it all. I shall have time next week to set affairs to rights. Now while the Colonel and Doctor are at their piquet I must go and make my preparations for Dublin. I don't somehow think that Pat Farrell and his petition will get there.

SUNDAY MAY 2. A rainy day the very best thing possible for the country, too wet however for church so I have time to set down that there was a very proper note to the Colonel from Bishop Murray saying he should in about a fortnight come to this neighbourhood when he should enquire into the very painful subject of the complaint against Mr. Richard.

9. Hal and I are reading at night Whateley[4] on the '*The Errours of Romanism*', so far most admirable, shewing that the *spirit of superstition* or *misdirected religious zeal* is inherent in human nature, as rife among the members of the reformed church as ever it was among the papists, taking different disguises in different sects, hurtful in all and to all and quite adverse to the purity of religious feeling inculcated by Jesus Christ. To me it has always appeared that we have changed *names* not *habits*. We are pagan idolaters still, have misunderstood the doctrines of our divine teacher, profaned His name, disobeyed His precepts and dishonoured the religion we only pretend to. But if the world continues to enlighten at the rate of its progress during the last five and twenty years, superstition will vanish in a few generations. Another startling kind of book I am reading is full of sublimities amongst its oddities. Carlyle on the French Revolution.

10. Tom Darker has entered with his accounts and I have Monday's work to do before settling them, he is selling about thirty pounds worth of old potatoes and the two calves we parted with immediately after their birth, brought one nine the other eighteen shillings. Went to school and found matters improved, twenty-six pupils, more coming. Father Germaine been to visit them, the

4. Richard Whateley was protestant Archbishop of Dublin from 1831–63.

first time for near a twelvemonth. All very orderly and
children doing very well. The removal of Mr. Rickard
will certainly do good, he was a vile political agitator,
ignorant and violent and bigotted, two years ago the
people would never have complained of their priest had
he half murdered them, they are grown bolder now and
I am glad they see their Landlord will stand by them and
that they find he can get a priest removed.

11. This is the road meeting and there are fears that
Mr. Fenton's party is so strong that poor William
Murray may not be made Treasurer, perhaps no loss to
him, the little fifty pounds a year might encourage him
to sit still with the brother in his curacy as in this cheap
country it would keep him alive in a chimney corner,
when if he is outvoted he will be thrown on his own
exertions for his bread.

I must not forget to set down all Mr. Verschoyle's
political news. A letter from Mr. Evans, the member
for Dublin, reports that the Queen is inconsolable at the
thoughts of losing her ministers, that Lord Melbourne
has over and over again entreated to resign, assuring her
they had lost the confidence of the country but tears,
screams, claspings of hands was her answer to which
absurdities of a headstrong girl he weakly yielded.

Poor girl she has many a hard lesson to learn and was
called too early to such dangerous distinction She may
hereafter turn out a fine character when *tamed* and one
don't dislike her attachment to the first set of people she
ever had to deal with, who escorted her from a rigorous
obscurity to the throne and first made her feel she was
somebody.

Thirty people at the road meeting and Mr. Fenton was
elected by a majority of three votes.

20. The news is that there is a majority against ministers of thirty-six upon Lord Landon's motion on the
sugar duties. We shall see by the evening papers. Vans
[Hornidge]says he dined at Baron de Robeck's yesterday
where he heard that all the Officials are packing up. Lord
Ebrington [Lord Lieutenant] said he should be a very few
days here now and they are hurrying the Queen's birthday,

making its celebration take place tomorrow instead of Tuesday as otherwise it could not in the hurry be kept.

I read aloud Sir Robert Peel's splendid speech all of which is masterly, one or two passages quite beyond the eloquence of these days and there is a fairness, a sobriety, an honest open English air pervading the whole of his business details and his censures of the present management and his exposition of his own intentions, which like cooling waters to the thirsty soul actually invigorate the brains which have so long been wearied by expediency.

27. John had the tenants in the hall for coolness, they paid well, two-hundred pounds and upwards in cash, a few begged for a short delay, but on the whole John don't think there is above a hundred pounds of arrears on the property, the people all thriving too, visibly, how different was the state of things when Hal and John began their management. And then they say no matter about Absentee landlords, it may be fine theory but it don't stand the test of practice.

I had to go to School to meet the Inspector, thirty-two children, very neat in their appearance, no parents, no visitors, no priest, only Mr. Foster and towards the end Judy Ryan, Tom Kelly stood at the gate for half an hour but never had the curiosity to look in. The children answered well, they looked clean, happy and up to their business, the Inspector was much pleased and said 'this is a very nice school, it is a pity it is so small. I really do think now it will get larger, these publick examinations must have a good effect.

TUESDAY JUNE 1. Miss Gardiner came for thread, in such spirits about our school, three more pupils, twenty-nine in attendance yesterday. I think we shall conquer the priest and I hear Mr. Germaine is to be sent off after his Curate as his conduct has by no means pleased his Bishop. He has been threatening Pat Farrell and talking very indiscreetly about denouncing him from the Altar etc. Farrell answered him very stiffly and at last told him he had better be quiet for very little would rouse him to take the same course with him he had done with his

Curate. And on telling the business to Tom Darker he declared that if Father Germaine ever attempted to strike him he really will summon him for the assault before the Magistrates. Would any one of them have said this or half of this, or made any sort of a complaint of their priest two year ago, indeed no; there is a wonderful change coming over them.

6. We were forced to unpack the cart though it was Sunday morning, the young ladies requiring their clothes and beef and fish and other stores having to be looked after, and the religion of this household not being at all of a ceremonious cast we had no difficulties about it. Mr. Cooke was here to-day to settle about papering the nurseries—the better day the better deed, the Roman Catholicks in this country make Sunday their great day of business.

7. Busy filling up the Census papers which are very complete as to information, the use I don't exactly know, the poor people here are all terrified that they were to have been kidnapped or pressed or murdered on the night of the 6th. Half of them were not to go to bed and had barricaded their doors.

9. My Lord and my Lady in London, he at his Clubs and his races, she alone in that great crowd of which she forms too insignificant a unit to be even noticed. The most melancholy of all solitudes, her name was among the mob at the drawing room, but at none of the parties, not even at those few where by rights she should be.

THURSDAY, JULY 1. Elections, nothing but Elections, the papers full of them and the post full of them and the people full of them, though here we are quiet being remote from any polling places and most of us busy with wiser things.

7. I went over to call on Mrs. Gore [wife of Lord Downshire's new Agent] and think her rather a foolish woman, pretty, nice looking, but a great deal too talking and by no means satisfied with a house in which the windows look on the street of a village and which has neither a conservatory nor a flower garden. There was a great fuss about education too but it may be mere manner, acting fine from the *town* of Kilkenny. An old mother

of Mr. Gore's lives with them, above eighty, a papist, the protestants are scandalised at her being allowed to go to Mass, while the papists rejoice in an Agent who has so near a connexion in the true Church. She has one daughter a nun and another married to Mr. Rowe the great Methodist preacher, of course converted by him from the errour of her former ways. Mrs. Gore talked a great deal about religious impressions, Sunday schools etc., in short it seems very difficult to stop her upon any subject, I could hardly get away.

8. Drove to Russboro'—My Lady had just come in from her drive, the carriage was turning away from the steps and she was standing on them, most graciously descended to meet us, invited in the children and Miss Cooper and poured forth all her wrongs and her injuries and her distresses of various kinds with her usual passion and insincerity. Poor woman! She makes herself very miserable and there is no help for her, she cannot cure her unhappy temper and nobody else will put up with it, so alone she must live. My Lord wheeled in and kept me another half hour, such a wreck! Who would be a gambler. So noble looking as he was, younger than me and broke down completely and they affect to hold every one so cheap, he quietly, she outrageously treating all as dirt but themselves and their clique. While those they despise merely laugh at the despisers and leave them there alone in their arrogance to fret at it. What they might have been had either of them been better brought up.

11. Mrs. Haughton writes there were great fears yesterday that the radicals would after all head the poll; the same news was brought to Blesinton by the car which comes in late; this will be sad. Hal off about one for Dublin to vote for the County Dublin to-morrow and County Wicklow Tuesday.[5] Shocking work in Carlow and the priests as busy as bees everywhere. Mr. George Moore told the Doctor that everywhere the prospects of the Conservatives are most encouraging; the Carlton Club reckon

5. He owned property in both counties and thus qualified for two votes.

on a majority of seventy. I would divide this by half and still be satisfied. Mrs. Ogle Moore has a son, a fine baby; she suffered much more than usual, but she got over her dangerous time better though she was for two hours in great peril, so exhausted at last that she said: 'Shall I live, Doctor?' He says some day she will slip through, poor thing. How curious it is that to some women the very purpose of their being should be in the fulfilment so fraught with danger. Other animals give birth of their young with an ease one should suppose natural to an occurence in the course of nature, but women almost always peril their lives when producing their children. It must be from the artificial lives we lead. Too little exercise to develop the strength of our bodies, and too many luxuries which further enervate them. The poor Doctor is still a prisoner Mrs. Kilbee hourly expecting her trial, then Mrs. Foster and Mrs. Gore,—population encreasing well.

14. Doctor called and had a long gossip for us of election news, priest interference etc. Lady Milltown also called, in a gracious mood with me but sadly out of sorts with the rest of the world. She really is totally deserted by everyone. No wonder they should both fly to Baden or any where else where they are not known, the mere change of place is consoling to those who have neither friends nor occupation. My Lord is gone to some races, my Lady goes after him on Saturday. Miss Sçavoy is gone too, the new governess, poor thing, arrives to-day little knowing the misery before her and the mother leaves the children with a stranger. She has begged of me to look after them which so far as calling occasionally I will do with pleasure but I decline all other charge.

16. Fine day, riding, walking, driving nearly the whole of it. Hal took a great drive, *ride* I mean about sixteen miles I am sure, called on half his acquaintance heard from Mr. Gore that in the Agent's accounts there is a regular entry against Lord Downshire for the expenses of his visits to the Murrays. Hal was quite taken aback, so opposite from all he had ever heard. At Edenderry Mr. Gore said it was the same and that in the little intercourse he had himself

had with him hitherto he had always acted liberally. Lord
Downshire said he is not understood in this country.

17. Dublin County is won, Mr. O'Connell is returned for
Cork. The intimidation going on in the South and
West is frightful, armed mobs seem to have possession
of the country stopping the voters, whose party they
oppose even when in the Mail coaches, beating, stoning,
imprisoning even murdering, it is dreadful that such
things *can be* in a civilised land.

Miss Peel married with the greatest pomp to Viscount
Villiers. Every body that is any body at the banquet.
Prince George, Princess Augusta, many of the Queen's
household and a large number of the leading nobility
and gentry at the marriage. Sir Robert Peel may be a
proud man, fortune in every way favouring him, or
rather rewarding his consummate prudence and temper
and integrity.

Went to school and found no scholars, this fever and
the several deaths caused by it having frightened all the
parents. Drove to Blesinton and found quite a levée at
the Doctor's, himself, the Colonel, Mr. Ogle Moore, Mr.
Finnemor, Mr. Gore, all having met to decide on the spot
for building our new Dispensary which is to have rooms
overhead for an infirmary or fever hospital, the contract
is taken by the mason who built the market house and the
scite is on the road to Naas a little distance from the town,
on this side. Mr. Gore seems to be a very different sort of
agent from poor weak Mr. Murray who had no energy,
no abilities and no *new lights*.

26. A letter from John announces that the tenants are many
of them after all our trouble getting into arrears, nearly
three hundred pounds owing on the property up to last
May which must not be allowed and therefore he will
come and distrain upon all those farms whose holders do
not produce cash immediately. It is quite unpardonable
in those that really have it, such actual dishonesty as
in Commons, Rutherfurd, Mick Tyrrell etc., and in
the others, it merely proves that they are not fit to
manage ground and should descend into the class of
labourers at once for all the rents on this property are

very low—1200 English acres 20 miles from Dublin producing but £770 a year.

7. Gloomy morning but no rain. Mrs. Gore better, she was in great danger again yesterday. I never saw the Doctor more anxious about anybody, really fretting. She was so ill and is naturally so delicate and the husband in such a state of misery about her, the six children too to leave behind. He came this morning looking quite relieved. There is going to be a subscription for Colonel Bruen, [the defeated candidate for Carlow] any sum however small will be accepted with much pleasure, none over £1 taken and whether a piece of plate or what will be presented to him they have not settled nor does it signify, the respect all the Conservative party hold their champion in will be demonstrated and indeed he is entitled to it for he has fought the good fight well.

The more I think over the unhappy condition of the people of this country the more convinced I am that *all* their misery springs from want of education, moral and intellectual, they get neither, either in their homes or generally at their schools and I should say the higher ranks are very nearly as much in need of it in every point as the lower.

Example in point. We went to Blesinton to-day to attend a Meeting of the Protestant Orphan Association, a most excellent institution of the utmost importance to the welfare of the country and the only remark it could call forth must be surprise that it is so lately established as twelve years ago, that it should be the only institution of the kind in Leinster and that its funds should still be so small. Two gentlemen connected with it came down to give information respecting its progress with a view to their statements exciting us all to greater zeal in our endeavours to aid it. We expected a pathetick appeal to our best feelings, a list of cases which had been relieved, an account of plans of education, expenditure etc.

What did we hear, the most furious declamation against the National Schools and other exciting political topicks without grammar, common sense, or proper application of words, from two unbearably vulgar creatures, one a Curate, not quite so bad as the odious Secretary to the Deaf and Dumb who obliged us the last. It was a most ridiculous exhibition, painful to reflect on as the amount of mischief in the power of these two mountebanks to create during their tour is incalculable. Mr. Moore was annoyed to a degree, Mr. Foster furious, it really might have the effect of injuring a good cause, indeed I should like to know more of the spirit which animates the Committee of the society before pledging myself to any further support.

At the Doctor's fell in with Edward, Vans, Mr. Moore and one of the Shehans, editor of the Evening Mail,[6] a most amusing and clever man, the worse of the fun of his youth I should say, he was on his way with the Recorder to his shooting lodge for a day or two during these political holidays.

28. A poor old body came to get help to stock a basket so I fitted it up in a way. Hal says they have a notion that if ever they have the merest shadow of a trade they will not be sent to the poor house, this trade then will not keep this poor body long out of it. John Hornidge is in the greatest fright ever was, he ejected a tenant and arranged with the man's brother-in-law, Hugh Kelly to succeed him and the night before last the house was burned, a bullock shot and a poor lad the care-taker would have been burned too had it not been for a chance passenger for they had fastened the door on him. John Hornidge was pale and trembling when he told his tale and he would not proceed home in the broad daylight without the protection of Vans and Edward.

After the Sessions yesterday Hal took us such a beautiful drive, he had to go to Elverstown to speak to Rutherfurd and we went in the car with him, he riding, poor Annie could not ride as the pony wants a fore shoe. We went all over the garden, the offices and the house all having a wealthy air for Ireland but bare looking to

6. Founded in 1823, the *Dublin Evening Mail* was a militantly protestant newspaper.

my foreign eyes. Mahogany tables in the parlour, beaufit with plenty of glass and china and an eight day clock, but a mud floor, no carpet, no curtains, bare walls. In the kitchen, two fiddles, no bacon, nor does he feed pigs, nor has he a dairy, he veals his calves and buys his milk, meat and butter. The back kitchen which in England would shew such comfort was here filled with turf, the oven a ruin, the way to the cellar blocked up, neither jug nor basin in any of the bedrooms but they were clean and airy and the beds seemed well furnished. A man that had such a farm in England would work just as hard as Rutherfurd but he would be fat and happy and there would be an air of plenty and of neatness about him that we must wait many a day before we see in this country.

31. Sarah arrived to see us. She had written to Miss Cooper announcing her visit and came about ten looking very well with a pretty, fat but very tiny baby. Indeed matters are not flourishing with poor Sarah. She and her husband can just make it out and that is all, the folly of servants marrying, particularly in this country where the wages are too low for them to support a family out of them, and then as in James' case the wages are not always forthcoming, that dishonest habit people have of living beyond their means. Misery to themselves and to all belonging to them. Thank God we shall never feel this. Both Hal and I would live on potatoes and salt rather.

TUESDAY AUGUST 3. An advertisement in the Dublin Mail that Mr. Calcraft has engaged several of the singers and will give eight nights of Operas the end of this month, Grisi, Lablache and others. Hal says we shall go up for them, I hope we may find ourselves able to do so without imprudence it would be such real delight to me, the purse will bear it better than the persons. We are both such ricketty creatures, so very little knocks us up.

5. Yesterday at Naas Hal went over the Poor House which upon the whole he thought well arranged. It is not yet open, will not regularly open till Wednesday next but they would take in any perfectly destitute objects now upon an application from a rate payer. They won't be

troubled much at first I think. Vagrancy seems to be quite the pleasure of these unfortunate idle creatures, begging their bit from door to door, hearing and telling the news of the country, sometimes faring ill, sometimes well, sometimes better, it keeps up a kind of excitement in them akin to gambling without which they are hardly happy in the absence of all other occupation. The only hope is that the farmers will not give.

6. Really quite tormented with little Caroline, she has taken quite a mania for dress and she clips and works at the bodies of her gowns till she can hardly stuff herself into them and patches on great bits at the bottom till her petticoats trail all round upon the ground and after her tour with Johnny on the wet days she comes in with a quarter of a yard of mud about her legs, her bonnets too she won't wear unless of the fashionable shape and she is such a plain little thing, she can only look well by being, very clean and very neat.

Wrote to Jane and gave her a little of my mind about this very foolish church business in Scotland. It is nothing but rank Popery under another name. An attempt by the priesthood to elevate themselves above the law of the land which certainly won't succeed and will most likely disgust most intelligent persons with the Presbyterian assumption that most undoubtedly does a great deal of mischief and so does its morose character. It hurts the temper and the feelings of the people, and as for the outward decorum of manner so much praised in the Scotch it is very dearly purchased by an arrogance, a sourness, a bigotry that we would not tolerate among the heathens.

8. Beautiful Sunday. Little girls looked so very nice in their *new* black satin shawls. Miss Gardiner, poor soul, in her folly went and spent all her saved money on ever so many yards of black satin turque with silk for lining and flannel for wadding, fringe, etc., in the forlorn hope that she would get sale for shawls by disposing of them at 2/—less than they could be bought for in Dublin. Finished the fourth volume of *Chambers' Journal* which continues to rise in interest and value and a most

valuable little work by a Rev. Mr. Abbott, an American, '*The Mother at Home*,' which should be put into the hands of every parent and every *Governess*, a class of persons more in need of instruction and education than almost any other.

12. Went to school, found seventeen children and every day now they are coming in again looking, poor things, very much cut up after this epidemick, took the opportunity of returning home with Judy Ryan's children, wishing to see for myself whether what I had heard were true and which the miserable condition of the children, the failure of the rent and other indications nearly proved. The dinner for the poor things was ready, a plate full of the small old potatoes such as John Fitzpatrick latterly very much grumbled at having to give to the pigs, neither milk nor salt. There is a good house, above twelve acres of ground once in fair order. Judy went from me fully clothed, clothes for her children, seven pounds in money, two pigs, two turkeys, crockery and hardware quite beyond any supply ever hoped for in her station and all which she really deserved from her care of little Annie and her general good conduct while with us. When her husband died he left her with a horse, a dray, a cow, and a pig and no debt, her spare room was constantly let to some of the tradesmen employed in the building of this house and afterwards to James and Sarah. Besides this an Aunt died and left her a great deal of furniture and clothing and it is said money; of all this there remains nothing, even her crops are sold off the ground, her grazing paid for in advance, there is nothing outside nor inside but poverty, a bare house, starved ragged children, unstocked land. What has become of it all is more than any one can tell, really eat and drunk I believe, by herself, her great big sister, her two lazy brothers, her old wicked mother and a whole crew of beggar nephews and nieces, her debts are many too. The Colonel and Mr. Robinson will probably eject her and very properly for not payment of rent, her dishonest mismanagement proving her quite incapable of holding land, but I feel very sorry for Christy Ryan's poor children impoverished to actual destitution, to keep for

a few years that detestable clan of Quins in idle plenty. The little forsaken baby I had put to nurse with Judy and which while money lasted throve so well I shall certainly take from her to-morrow or next day and place where her board will be more faithfully spent on her, the little creature has shrunk into half her size—really looks dying. The whole scene is most miserable.

14. Had to go to school with work etc. and to remove the poor little miserable child from Judy's wretched home to one not looking so decent but where I think she will be better minded—kept clean—made industrious and have enough to eat. She was at first saucy, but soon melted into tears, and exclaimed she wished she had taken my advice in time. She is indeed in utter poverty and has nothing but worse misery before her.

   A letter from [sister Mary at] Pau quite out of humour with everybody but herself, her children, and Monsieur Puyoo, père et fils, still enraptured with her 'Pyrennean home' in words, yet I *fancy* she is tiring of it, she has been near a year there, a long time for her to be content with any place.

15. Beautiful Sunday, full church, such a sermon, a whole chapter of Kings was the text, Ahab and Jezebel[7] the subjects, connubial felicity the moral in the unravelling of which he got into such a hobble that I let my veil down and sat quite in distress, there was no practical piety in this effusion nor indeed any piety at all, a kind of lecture of folly.

19. Beautiful day. Very busy preparing for the party to-morrow, boiling, baking, roasting, etc., to have enough luncheon for twenty-four people, though I suppose all won't come. So our number is complete. I will do my part to make this our first auction go off well. We shall see how the party succeeds, it is not easy to manage any thing cheerful in our neighbourhood.

20. Auction went off very well indeed, had our rooms all ready, table laid, all but the hot dishes served, every thing ready by one o'clock. There was a very good cold

7. I Kings, Ch.s 18 and 19.

collation of meats, jellies, creams, pastry, cakes etc., with a hot quarter of lamb and a hot pasty, a side table with vegetables, another with fruits, great plenty without being overloaded, all very nice. Ogle Moore and his sister Georgina, his wife and her sister and three children, the baby, Nelly and Edward; Mrs. Finnemor, Bessy and Louisa; Mr. and Mrs. Cotton and their two children; John Hornidge, Vans Hornidge, the Doctor, these were all we mustered.

John Hornidge was chosen Auctioneer and a most capital one he made, buyers were very 'shy' yet we managed amongst us to bid up some of the books pretty well. Altogether the Club will have twenty-seven pounds odd for the supply of the ensuing year which is more than we began with. We got our own book, Sir James Mackintosh for only a shilling or two more than half price. *Sketches by Boz*, his first work for four shillings, Sir Samuel Romilly for six shillings, Lockhart's *Life of Scott* for one pound twelve and six, Miss Casey, the monkey, bidding it up out of spite.

24. A grand event. I rode on Grasshopper, but had Frank walking beside me, felt happier after a while but painfully nervous at first, good natured Hal rode beside me, we went all round the hill, were out two hours and every body big and little laughed at me!

27. Delightful day. Exhibited myself and my folly [she believed she was pregnant] for a second time upon Grasshopper, going without Frank and suffering an agony of fear that should have excited pity rather than mirth. We went to Blesinton, to Tulfarris and home by the ruined cottage, I may call it now. We were out near three hours, but I could not screw up my nerves to a canter.

31. Old Mrs. Tyrrell was here in great glee having hope of work from Mrs. Gore, she has quite altered the look of my poor little foundling in this short time, the child has a happy bright air quite unlike her former stupidity, and is clean and fat; she will get a few thumps I daresay for that is cabin fashion, but she will be kept clean and be well fed and be brought up in habits of active industry. I gave my parcel for the 'orphan', queer kind

of orphan whose parents are living, to Peggy, and bid her tell Mrs. Quin to tease me no more with her stories, all the consequences of her own misdeeds. She deprived the son of her first husband of his inheritance to give it to the son of her second who is repaying her injustice with merited ingratitude. In managing her house she secreted a private hoard which to the amount of twenty pounds, or more she quilted into her petticoat and always treating her daughters harshly deserved that one of them should run away with a lover she disapproved of and carry this petticoat along with her. Still I am sorry for the old body, and for the seven destitute grand-children whose father should be where I am sorry to say red Pat Quin is, the Quins are a bad set, the whole race.

WEDNESDAY SEPTEMBER 1. [My brother] John [now] actually at the Doune, sitting in the library, walking along the passages, his children in our nursery and then wandering along the banks of the Spey, or in the walks in the plantations, our walk over the shoulder of the Ord to Loch an Eilen, shewing our cottage to his wife, all the places so well remembered, alas! not all the people. How these Highland scenes cling to the heart, what would I give to be among them again, shewing my children the lovely 'spot where my forefathers dwelt' to catch the remains of all the noble feelings of the Highlander before *steam* quite extinguishes the romance of that beautiful country; how different was the love of all our people for us from any sentiment of respect or attachment I have ever met since, and how certainly the recollection of past events and the ages of connexion between Chieftain and vassals, or rather clansmen, excited every warm and every noble feeling.

2. Sir Robert Peel sent for to Windsor, graciously received, ladies [of the Bedchamber] all resigned and Ministers too, Lord John's tone is very gentlemanly, Lord Stanley's reply equally correct, there will be no factious opposition.

I had a letter to-day from brother John, who is enchanted with Rothiemurchus all the changes are improvements, he has seen no place so beautiful, the plantations, fine woods, the young forest amply redeeming to the scenery, the effect of the old, he urges a visit from us, kindly and temptingly, and it could easily be done earlier in the season with time to prepare for it. Yet I am not sure that I should be happy in Rothiemurchus with any host but my father at the Doune.

8. The Doctor came to see after us and brought word that Lord Milltown has lost his match with Lord Howth, five hundred pounds and large bets besides, such infatuation. Really Lord Milltown must just be the laughing stock of his own vile set.

9. It is the greatest of pleasures to me listening to good musick. I can recollect alas! not Malibran, for I never heard her, but Grisi, Pasta, Miss Birch, Camporesi, De Begnis, *him*, *she* was horrid, Fodor, Naldi, Bartleman, and a dim idea of Mme. Catalani and Mrs. Billington, with Lodor, Cramer and even Salomon once when I was quite a child. My pleasures of this most enchanting kind seem to be over. We are out of the way of everything and were we near them there is asthma on the one hand, cough and fever on the other, quite in the way of any amusements except those quiet and very happy ones to be found either at our own fireside or in the open air of our mountains.

10. We are to have Lord de Grey for our Lord Lieutenant, violently objected to by Mr. O'Connell on account of his very protestant connexions. Lord Eliot as Secretary equally disagreeable to the *Mail* on account of opinions too liberal[8], manners too haughty; no Lord Chancellor—Sir Edward Sugden the most fitted by far would have been but for his wife, the follies of youth paid for most amply in mature age.[9] She was his cook and bore him several children before he married her, of course not presentable and he is weak enough to wish to present

8. Oliver Macdonagh (NH of I) describes the Lord Lieutenant as 'a right wing Tory with Irish protestant connections' and the Chief Secretary as 'a well-meaning liberal Tory'.

9. He had in fact been Lord Chancellor in 1835 and was to hold this office again from 1841 to 1846.

her. I think there is a coarseness of mind though in the man who could *marry*, entail as his companion for life so inferiour a person as one of Lady Sugden's degree must be.

11. Hal went to bed perfectly well, waked at two with asthma, had to get up and never threw the feeling off all night, it came on very badly indeed about seven, yielded to Stramonium[10] but returned even worse and did not leave him till noon when he took a light breakfast.

Mr. Moore came loaded with books for our Society and all *Chamber's Educational Course* for us, he talked away very agreeably, by the bye has got it into his head that we ought to go back to fasting and other ceremonies certainly enjoined by the rubrick but so long disused that a return would look very popish and be very absurd. My presbyterian education disinclines me to these observances. Lady Milltown also called, sat half an hour or more in great good humour though her Lord is in the midst of racing troubles and the entertainments they had provided for Curragh guests were spread in vain. No guests arrived.

Read *Chambers'* on Infant management, a most truly judicious work, drank tea in our own room with all the children, every one of us engaged with the little volumes of Chambers' Course. Miss Cooper took the '*Management of Infants.*' Annie the drawing books, Janey the '*Moral Class book*' and the '*History of Greece.*' I have my head just now full of 'infant education' and having studied it all the morning I gave the book in the afternoon to Miss Gardiner whom I sent for on purpose and held a long discourse with her on the necessity of educating herself by degrees as she is educating her pupils which with the books I give her and my assistance she can easily do.

How much real practical knowledge, judgement, temper, spirits, is necessary in the instruction even of the lower orders. What a serious charge then is such a family as ours, how much good or evil to themselves and the large

10. A narcotic drug prepared from the thorn apple (daturn stramonium).

circle over which even individual influence must extend
depends on the habits they are brought up in.

14. All went in to Blesinton on business, the Colonel to
a meeting to arrange a Loan fund, Lord Downshire
subscribed fifty pounds he was in the chair, the Colonel
fifty, Mr. Gore fifty, Mr. George Moore twenty-five,
Mr. Finnemor twenty-five, no others as yet, but papers
will be sent round to all. I went in to wait and met Ogle
Moore, the Colonel and Lord Downshire who begged to
be presented to me and indeed I think it very strange
he never called upon me, he is the only neighbour who
omitted that civility, pompous man they call him, but he
is beginning to find out that the airs of grandeur which
perhaps suited the style of the world in the days of his
youth are quite thrown away on this generation and on
me in particular. My old Highland blood laughs at his
new pretensions, he is very absurd and very weak and
very fond of money but not a bad kind of man.

19. My brother William's birthday. What a fête day this used
to be with us and what it might have been still had there
been as much good sense in the family as there is talent.
Sometimes when I think of the inheritance he was born
to and then feel he is now forty past, and has still to
endure some years of India, I do grieve over the waste of
happiness that mere carelessness has produced. To what
might not my father have attained had he kept his place
in his own country, his sons where would they *not* have
been, his daughters also, and his people, it will take more
than the next generation to retrieve a few years of folly.

22. Tried to get a kitchen maid for Mrs. Finnemor but fancy
I shall fail, the progress of civilisation indisposing any girl
who has a hope of doing better to take a situation where
the women servants sleep on a shakedown in the *kitchen*,
three together, bring all the water from the river, wash all
the potatoes for man and beast, have low wages, meat but
twice a week cut into rations in the parlour and sent out in
portions. They would bear this well in a farmer's house
and be glad to get the place but when with this low degree
in kitchen there is the utmost profusion in hall with great
finery at times and grandeur of position, always they

who practise such contradictions must be content with the refuse of the serving class who will besides never enter their shabby genteel precincts till squire of rank and honest yeoman have filled their households. How can the young people thus brought up be fit to mingle with the society their father's wealth would admit them to.

25. Finished an excellent work on natural physiology, part of Chambers' Course. Now that education has become *rational* we may expect to see people really wiser, better and oh how much happier, there could be no Mrs. Finnemors to torment us.

The Doctor was here in the morning to look after the Colonel, he shocked me with the history of the poor run over child. After the accident Mrs. Finnemor drove on to pay her visit as if nothing had happened, not waiting to see the Doctor nor calling on him nor on the child on her return. She left four shillings with the mother who watched her movements well and said to the Doctor it was very little like a lady not to have taken a little more trouble about the creature her own car had all but killed. She sent some rag and *a* loaf of bread and a message to the Doctor 'to have her mind relieved' but she has carefully avoided *employing him* to look after it, as carefully alluded to his *Dispensary duties* and though she earnestly asked of him what the family wanted to which he gravely replied 'everything from a roof over their heads to food, fire and raiment' there have been no results, these may come however, it is not the amount of recompense for an accident that can't be repaired that I am thinking of, it is the feeling of pounds shillings and pence that runs through her character that is utterly despicable.

Dear Janey and Annie if such a misfortune had happened to us should we not have been daily by the bedside of that suffering child, seeing ourselves that its wants were supplied and seizing the opportunity to develop some ideas of good in the parents.

26. I went to church with the little girls, it was crammed. Mr. Moore preached, I did not like the sermon it might have been given at the Chapel at the cross by the Priest, too minute an account of the Crucifixion,

painfully so, orthodox I suppose but not in unison with
my interpretation of the mission of Jesus. The *man* and
the sufferings of his *body*, not the divine doctrines he was
inspired to teach.

FRIDAY OCTOBER 1. Miss Cooper and I walked down to see
Peggy where we were annoyed by old Mrs. Quin with her
noisy history of family quarrels and I took an odd sort of
fainting fit and had to be brought home on the car, laid
on the sofa for the rest of the evening and carried up to
bed by the maids.

5. Hal really getting well which is lucky as I am like to be
laid up for some time to come I fear. I had hoped by all
the care I had been taking of myself with regard to diet
and exercise that I might go on as other strong women do
as usual without publishing my misfortunes to the world
six months at least before they need know of them, but it
seems all won't do, a bad habit in these cases is not easily
got over.

15. Such news, a letter from Jane, I am quite unfit to do
more than mention it, she is going to be married to James
Gibson Craig.

16. I could not sleep all night for the happy news of yesterday
and am still too confused to think of any other subject
or of that calmly. James has settled Mama is to live with
them. Every body speaks so highly of him, for abilities,
for worth, for business habits, and he will be very wealthy
and well will they both employ their wealth.

20. Such a season, God help the poor for I am sure man can't,
potatoe crop a failure, corn malting in the stooks, no turf,
misery.

21. Fine day. Tom Darker bought two pigs at Naas yesterday
for feeding, our potatoes being too bad to keep over the
winter, they were very dear as is all stock this year.

27. Bitter cold and dismal is the prospect before us, so early,
so severe a winter, no fuel, no harvest, corn still out and
malting, potato crop a failure, what will become of the
improvident poor of this country, in the Poor House some
must be driven to take refuge but it won't contain a fourth
part of the starving population and many will die rather
than enter it and many, many a decent family will suffer

bitterly and won't complain. It is all very well for such as we are. We may get less rent and be obliged to forgo some luxuries, some pleasures but necessaries we can always command in plenty, the worst evil to us would be to have to give up a workman or two and so throw industrious creatures out of bread, it is all very miserable.

28. Hal off to Dublin for india rubber hunting boots and many other little necessaries. The Doctor came to shew us his thumb which he had dislocated the night before on his walk home from Mr. John Hornidge's and set himself, they had dined at Mr. Lynch's and I think from the lateness of the hour Baron de Robeck being there he may have been a little bewildered, he swears not, it was a stone and a bad shoe.

30. A letter from Jane or rather *two* one to the Colonel and one to me, so full of happiness, dear good worthy Jane, how differently does this most auspicious marriage affect me than did your first, when all was sad around us, no ray of comfort anywhere and worst of all that was hanging over us was your sacrifice of your self in your very prime of life and with all your superiority of mind with wit and spirits and beauty to so old and so cross and so queer looking a little shrivelled up mannie as that clever worthy Colonel Pennington. I shall never forget that ceremony, for *I knew* all it cost you. I shall never forget all I suffered when you drove in bridal pomp from a door that closed on as much mental misery as ever wedding brought. It was as you said the dawn of better days, the year more of struggle and hope again lightened my poor mother's heart. My father's India judgeship carried us all from poverty deeper than was ever suspected to the far distant land where we found kindness and comfort and happiness waiting for us.

Old Peggy came up to have a gossip with me, to tell of the great price she got for her pig and the joy with which she hears of her new lodger, in short she would be the happiest old woman in the country if the cock turkeys would but look as plump on the dish as the hens. The priests are quarrelling among themselves and some of the people are quarrelling with the priests and there is a growing desire privately among some of the people to possess themselves of Bibles, so in spite of disappointments and vexations I do think better times are at hand. I have had a great deal of plague these few days with old Mrs. Tyrrell and her landlord who is not behaving well to her, but with the help of Tom Darker we have got all settled.

FRIDAY, NOVEMBER 5. Mr. Foster called to consult about the protestant poor on our church list, there are still eight on it, the farmers are objecting to the collection having the rates to pay besides. We agreed on speaking to Mr. Moore about each of the able and willing taking one of these poor creatures entirely for the small remnant of their days, as Miss Hall one, we one, Mr. Foster one etc. Also Tom Darker and I settled upon a plan for repairing the road to the bog next Spring. I am a very busy body I think, the Colonel may laugh and I may sometimes fail particularly where there are prejudices to fight against, still some good must sometimes be done and every little helps.

8. to 22. Sad gap in my journal, a whole fortnight this very day. Today I am writing at a table and find I am steadily regaining strength, though slowly and I attribute the whole to my frights on horseback, being at the time I began riding unfit for any agitation though I was not aware of this, so instead of expecting a little May flower I must, I suppose look for an April fool, the better suited of the two to an old goose as I must of course be called to be getting into such an absurd scrape at my age and after four years of rest. It is really ridiculous, and such a surprise besides.

23. Did rather much yesterday so do not feel so well to-day and am forced to keep the sofa. Peggy came up in great distress, her poultry house was broken into last night and my four fat turkies stolen, this sort of crime is very frequent this winter, fowl of all kind, turf, wearing apparel, even sheep, are stolen on all hands in this, which used to be reckoned a poor enough but honest country, misery is very rife, morals not taught, police idle.

The Prince of Wales has been born, a fine child, the Queen bearing his birth well, but a short time in pain and like me never for a moment ailing after so that from the 6th day no bulletin was issued. In no department of practical science does greater progress seem to have been made than in the management of the lying in room.

Our Lord Lieutenant is giving splendid parties, acting most judiciously, winning his way steadily, his Levée was immense, 1500 persons, all parties, the largest ever known since George IV. held one. They began to set down at eleven and finished at half after four. Many could only get their cards sent up, many were stopped on their road to town from want of conveyances, all being overfilled, the procession reached from the Castle gates to beyond Merrion Square, five guineas given for a pair of horses, two guineas for a bed. And there was a list of nobility to which our little Court has for long been a stranger.

O'Connell was there as Lord Mayor and was *agitated*, either by his strange position or his cool reception so much that he forgot to take off his hat. I see by the papers to-day that he is quite concerned for his omission and makes an ample apology, nothing being further from his intentions than any appearance of disrespect. His tribute Sunday, the last, brought him in Dublin alone £2,000. What does he do with these enormous sums, the repeal rent etc.

I have got to the 7th volume of *Chambers' Journal*, it is a library, and have gone through many of the little works published as his educational course, some numbers of the *Dublin University Magazine* with more of Charles O'Malley[11] of whom I am near tired in spite of the inimitable Baby Blake, '*Two years before the Mast*' stupidly interesting, and now am much taken with some stories by Mrs. S. C. Hall admirably illustrative of low Irish character in which there is so much good even great combined with serious evil and a perversity there is no overcoming in this generation at any rate.

We had a great party here last night down in the kitchen in honour of Aunt Jane's wedding. Upstairs only a glass

11. One of Charles Lever's early novels; the D.U.M. was seen as a strongly Tory, ascendency protestant publication.

of champaign round to the health of the happy pair, but
below a grand entertainment. Tea, coffee, round of cold
beef, slim cakes, bread and butter and a glass of sherry
each to those who were not teetotallers. The company
were the six house servants and the four outsides and
Paddy and Peggy Dodson. And talking them over Hal
and I began to reckon how many individuals we with
our small means entirely supported, it surprised us how
many we helped and there we stopt. Well spent money,
better employed than in dress or fine furniture or feasting,
for I am not yet a convert to the axiom that the *spender*
no matter on what is always a benefactor, I can't help
thinking there should be method in distribution.

26. The Colonel seized in the most unaccountable manner
with asthma, the worst fit he has had for years. Once
or twice the violence of the spasm was quite painful to
witness. We can no way account for the attack except
that drinking Jane's health in champaign and Constantia
might have deranged his stomach and the cold ride to
Donard hurt him afterwards. There we were, however, all
day a pretty pair, both perfectly helpless, he in his chair, I
on my sofa. The Doctor came to sympathize but he could
only preach patience, he had no cure for either.

27. John Robinson has arrived for the November rents,
looking well. Miss Cooper has settled his counting room
for him and the Tenants are waiting. John made us quite
happy in the evening by his account of the tenants, trying
to farmers as the season has been with the untoward
weather and mortality among the cattle, they have paid
well, are all forwarder than they were this time last
year and so decently dressed, clean, whole, comfortable
looking, many of them with good cloth body coats and all
good frieze coats, very different indeed from the ragged
crew that welcomed me to Baltiboys just ten years ago
this past October. It makes one feel very happy to see
such improvement year by year among old and young,
it is worth some personal sacrifice if indeed it can be
called sacrifice to substitute the substantial pleasures
resulting from properly fulfilled duties for mere selfish
gratifications.

28. All off to church in hopes of hearing Mr. Moore. And here am I useless to everyone, however, I think, read and reflect, lay plans for more active future days. Above all not to lose temper with the ignorant, keeping in mind how much stronger prejudices must be in those who have seen little, learned less and are naturally indisposed to an heretick and a stranger. John came up to our room after tea and talked very agreeably till bedtime. And we were all in high spirits, very different from last year when at this time before the rents came in we owed John upwards of a hundred pounds, and now it is the other way for we have a balance to that amount in our favour.

30. Unable to get up, Hal better, still he had to sit up for two hours in the night. I sometimes think I sha'n't get through rightly, these throwbacks are disagreeable, but I will do all in my power by patient obedience to rules to ensure the health and safety of the poor little creature that is trying mine and the issue is in God Almighty's hands.

WEDNESDAY, DECEMBER 1. I was very wrong to grumble yesterday when I can write, read and work really very comfortably, and am in no pain, even did all my accounts this morning, paid my debts, balanced my books and am all in order for another month or so.

From Mr. Gardiner I have a most miserable account of poor unhappy Mary. He has been in great anxiety, not without reason, and now though she is better the relief is but temporary, disease is there, checked for the present, but ready to proceed quick or slow according to the care she can be induced to take of herself. With a firmer character than Mr. Gardiner's to support her Mary might have been healthy, happy, deserving. As it is all her perverse dispositions have actually been fostered by his weak indulgence into inveterate habits of the most baneful tendency, and she who might have been the charm of all connected with her from her wit, her beauty, her grace and her natural kindness of heart only exists in a foreign land in broken health, low spirits, really the object of our pity.

A diseased craving for admiration is at the bottom of all her unhappiness, a growing want of excitement,

a gradual disinclination to home pursuits, a wilfulness
that would bear no contradiction all followed, tight
lacing, thin shoes, an exposed form, late and irregular
hours, a disregard of everything but momentary pleasure
combined with a system of rich and savoury and improper
eating such as in a woman is seldom even imagined, have
all ended in such complete derangement of the system
from indigestion that I do not see how it is probable for
her constitution to stand it. Wayward she was from her
birth, my father however controulled her into a creature
that was the charm of our young lives, poor Mary, when
I think of her in Highland days with her winning smile
and her graceful ways and her clear bright beauty I feel
she is not the same pure hearted being now, and in grief
I write it, is it a consolation to think constitutional mental
infirmity has much to do with it.

2. Hal a good night — I slept ill and was feverish and
   restless, to be expected with such an inactive life. A
   charming hunt, the Colonel home late in such spirits,
   rode forty miles.

3. A hurricane half the night, the meadows all flooded this
   morning, a fine day. Hal slept like a top all night, I
   pretty well considering, on the sofa again. Tom Darker
   sent me word he never knew the Colonel ride as he did
   yesterday, he thought he would kill the mare, he was in
   such spirits too.

9. This vigorous government has brought peace already,
   agitation now is such a mere farce that it must soon cease
   altogether, every one appearing tired of it, the [Repeal]
   rent too has been a perfect failure, smaller sums than usual
   collected in the most *repealing* neighbourhoods, none at
   all in some places, in others a refusal to allow of it. There
   is a great change coming over Irish minds most certainly,
   the most remarkable move being among the priesthood
   with whom alone any great change for good can originate;
   those of us who live for twenty years will see better
   times arising. In the meanwhile letters and pamphlets
   are [published] by priests and laymen, nobles and others,
   and the Executive doing its part well, getting quit of as
   much jobbing as possible, ten stipendiary magistrates

dismissed, twenty more to follow, the whole magistracy to be revised, the whole Poor Law scandals to be put an end to. This bad weather, and with me a prisoner to my room we actually live on the post, the penny letters are delightful, and the Evening Mail which always picks up any news going, the London papers say little.

11. Jane sends me an Inverness paper in which is a paragraph with which she is evidently delighted, rather a ridiculous effusion in praise of herself and in honour of her second nuptials with some flattery to my father in the Lord Downshire style half a column long. I am to send this on to Pau. Another supply has been sent to Aunt Mary and Uncle Ralph and I daresay half the world beside for Jane must live in publick. Great and good and noble qualities she has, her motives are pure, her actions benevolent and disinterested, her activity in well doing unwearied, but the world must know of it all and praise it all. Any woman of quiet delicacy, making a second marriage at forty years of age would have managed the business much more privately. There are hundreds of excellent women in these good days who do their duty more thoroughly than Jane and quite unobstrusively, but she is a fine warm-hearted creature, though a little spoiled by the doses of praise she loves.

13. In the Inverness paper was a much more interesting paragraph to me than the bonfire, an advertisement from a tailor in *Kingussie* for nine journeymen ensured constant work at Inverness prices. Thirteen years ago I don't know that there was even one tailor in the wretched looking row of houses called by courtesy a village. The first shop for soft goods had just been established, an untidy looking store where we all made a duty of buying some tea, ribbons and calico occasionally, the sale of the Duke of Gordon's large Badenoch property has effected this improvement, it has been sold in small divisions and has created a country neighbourhood; food for reflexion in this.

Hal a fine hunt with the harriers. All the rest went to call at Tulfarris and the good Miss Henrys had brought presents all the way from Wiesbaden for the children, parasols for the little girls and a toy for Jack, so kind in them to encumber themselves thus from such a distance, indeed to remember them at all, and it makes me take shame to myself for being so indifferent to the really kind friends amongst whom my husband has fixed. They all want much to make them really sociable neighbours, and the happiness of our circle would be materially improved could they all throw off a stiffness unknown to Highlanders and Indians, but elderly people don't alter their habits easily, we must only make the best of it.

THREE

1842

The first half of the year was spent very quietly is what she believed to be another pregnancy and this gave her time to write in detail about all she saw around her—in the family, or the estate and in the world outside. September she spent in Edinburgh and her journal contains a graphic account of how family and friends responded to Victoria and Albert's visit.

MONDAY, JANUARY 3. Such a blank in my journal. Since the 22nd of December—a fortnight all but two days—I have not been able to hold a pen to paper from the position in which I have been forced to lay. I therefore settled myself in bed with one pillow and one blanket—put out the fire which had been burning night and day—opened the door that I might not shake every time the lock turned—forbid any one to enter the room but Hannah—ordered her not to attempt to speak to me. Even, hardest of all, banished my dear kind husband, my constant companion and attendant all through this tedious confinement.

4. Such pleasant political news. All quiet in England, all getting quiet in Ireland. Mr. O'Connell no longer powerful, the government strong, the little Court quite splendid giving such an impulse to trade that all Dublin is in spirits. The religious world everywhere seems to be rather perplexing us, the Puseyites in England, the Puritans in Scotland doing as much mischief in those countries as ever has been done here; and there is always so much acrimony among religious disputants that the ferment caused by their bickerings is frightful. Perhaps the war with America which still looks very near hand may give these restless spirits something else to occupy them.

18. No use in writing daily in this stupid Journal. It is a

plague to get at my writing materials and the position is awkward and my brains a'n't always clear, and very little is going on. Fine weather, Hal hunting, children well, me myself but indifferent, well enough in health but always something going wrong with the poor baby—it will be a little wonder if it survive all its misfortunes; I don't expect it yet I will do all in my power to preserve it.

That crazy Mrs. Gore has during my illness been inundating my children with *tracts* which most luckily, dear little innocent things, they brought to me and I shall have them sent home again and not allow of any more borrowing or lending of books with such a methodistical family. I wish my children to draw their religious feelings from the New Testament where all that is harsh in the old is modified, not increased a thousandfold as it is in these mischievous productions where children sit in judgement upon parents, convert uncles and aunts, reform servants and preach and quote Scripture through every transaction of the day.

30. Hal was looking after the Loan Fund yesterday—it is doing a great deal of good. So many little tradesmen and even farmers borrowing to set themselves afloat and paying their small weekly instalment so regularly. When this has been fairly tried a while longer we are to have a Saving Bank in spite of the idle old set who would never wish to see change even for the better. John Hornidge was against the market; by the bye he is not well and young John has shot off his thumb pulling a loaded gun out of a corner of that regular magazine of artillery of his uncle's, the little back parlour which since the threats of a dispossessed tenant has been kept ready for action at a moment's notice.

I have just finished of grave reading Whateley '*On the Errours of Romanism*'—excellent like all his works, and am going on with Wesley's sermons in which there is much to reflect on to profit. I am waiting for more of Chambers' without whose gathered wisdom it really is quite dull to have to live. The Benefactor of his kind from this age to all succeeding. Those two brothers have done more for the welfare of their species than any of us their contemporaries are able to appreciate the amount of. They and Mr. Wilderspin[1] may reform the world.

SUNDAY, FEBRUARY 6. Since this day week much does not seem to have happened publick or private. No stir in the country whatever nor changes. I have had to take my little orphan from Mrs. Tyrell—she was too poor to do it justice. She would hear nothing against the character of a very ill-behaved young woman whom she had brought up and who quite imposed on her a *second* time—for some years ago this creature robbed her and left her. Miss Henry took her orphan away and placed her with Miss Gardiner which left Mrs. Tyrrell's ménage still more bare. All the money she had earned during the summer by her upholstery work seems to have been squandered by herself and this Mary and an object of a lame lover that the girl first disgraced herself with and then got to marry her. Miss Cooper found matters very bad when she went there—the lovers off with all they could lay their hands on—the only food in the house potatoes, the old woman in bed dying of starvation, so the child was brought away and given to Peggy where she has indeed fallen upon her feet and we send broth and bread to Mrs. Tyrrell till she is stronger and then she must manage for herself having brought herself to this miserable condition by her own folly. The child has made a good exchange for she is the pet of the house at Peggy's, who, having two lodgers, Paddy and Johnny Grace, has always plenty both of food and fire.

13. Miss Gardiner wrote to say she hopes to benefit by all she *sees* [at the Model School] in Marlborough Street. It all depends on herself for no particular pains is taken with her. There is no training especially for the teachers. Surely in eight years this most necessary part of a national school system might have been accomplished.

20. Sunday comes very quickly round again even to me that

1. Samuel Wilderspin (1792–1866) was an enthusiast for infant education and headmaster 1839–41 of the Central Model School in Dublin; this was where Miss Gardiner was sent to be trained.

am shut up in this state prison of mine. The two first large volumes of Mr. Alison's work in *ten*, a club book, rather terrified me—the Preface did not chase away the fear—and the Introduction from the bombast of the style so entirely disgusted me that twenty times I was tempted to let each magnificent period be the last I should try to wade through. However something or other has carried me on to the end of the third chapter and certainly since I first read Tacitus I have not been as thoroughly interested in any historical work. The style continues to be detestable—worse than Gibbon—but the master mind shines through the cumbrous language. Who could have suspected heavy ugly unmeaning Archy Alison of so much profundity of thought, such perfect enlightenment of mind.[2] In my day his aim was to be a man of fashion for which his large lumpy figure, his inexpressive countenance, little grey eye and scanty sandy hair, his want of ear in dancing and want of grace in motion most completely unfitted him.

The Colonel has had two very good hunting days—a good run each day—one of fourteen miles on Thursday. Yesterday he got a fall—his mare too eager in a leap sprang too soon, threw him over on a bank and fell herself into the water. The Doctor says it is merely a shake, and a shake won't do him the mischief it did to me. My rides on horseback were, I believe, ill-timed and I was so frightened all the time they must have hurt me but it was the jolt the day Frank obstinately would not yield the road to the car which ran against us and carried off our step that has laid me these three months on my back.

Government has not proposed but they have intimated that they may consider it judicious to propose to admit foreign cattle into the market at a considerable reduction of duty. This will be a great step in agricultural improvement. The large tracts of the best land which are now

2. Sir Archibald Allison (1797–1867): the D.N.B. (quoting Disraeli) suggests his plan in his *History of Europe* was to show that providence was on the side of the Tories.

half wasted as grazing farms will when less profitable in that trade be necessarily brought under tillage and thus increase the supply of corn, reduce the average price and better than all employ more people. Part of the too large profit at present realised by the grazier is owing to the few servants he has occasion to employ—much under the proper proportion per acre.

Dreadful news from India—a perfect massacre in Cabool[3]—all our troops cut to pieces—because our rulers were fools—not satisfied with the peaceful possession of our acknowledged and enormous territories, we must push a handful of troops up into the dangerous passes of a mountainous and but partially known northern country filled with a hardy people, and force on them for no reason a profligate sovereign whom they detest instead of a Prince of firmness and sense at any rate whom they preferred. Why we should meddle with them and their sovereigns it would be hard to say.

27. How very badly Irish women are brought up—they never seem to think of what is *right*, only of what is pleasant; Mrs. Moore's health had for some weeks been such as to make her sofa the fittest place for her, certainly her own house the only safe one for her to be in. But she must fidget about everything in the world—up and down stairs—in the house and out—even drive to Dublin to choose a dress for the Drawing-room and drive there again to try it on. And what on earth was taking her to the Drawing-room—a country clergyman's wife with six children, a very small income, six and thirty years of age and no beauty. Bad education, love of dress and company and having been brought to consider going to the Castle a mark of caste.

Probably going to the Castle is not exactly like going to St. James's; it is most likely rather the same as attending the parties of the Governours of Colonies and to a more

3. After the failure to impose Shah Shuja, the First Afghan War ended with the massacre here of the retreating army. The 'Prince of firmness' was Muhammed Akhar Khan ('quite a hero of mine').

general gathering, but in England no rational person goes to Court except those who would be missed were they absent. The Doctor says it was her mother's folly and that the old lady furnished the dress; but the butcher, the baker and the shoemaker who don't always get their accounts paid on presenting them would not have known this.

Politicks very dull—the *four* powers have ratified the slave trade treaty without waiting for France, which has made the French furious as if they were to be allowed to keep all the rest of the world waiting their leisure, content to postpone measures of importance to half mankind till these arrogant people should have somewhat recovered from their internal divisions and their pitiful jealousy of their neighbours.

And here is to end the month of February leaving me in exactly the same position as when it began and with little hope of relief for any attempt to sit up is invariably followed by evil consequences; so there is nothing for it but to make the best of it—make myself as happy as I can by following such employments as are suitable to an horizontal posture and lay up stores of useful information and good resolutions for the practice of more active times.

SUNDAY, MARCH 6. This last has been a bad week with me. I have been very ill and have come through another struggle much exhausted. I feel rather better this evening and I resolutely hope the best though certainly prepared for a tedious labour and a still born child. It is not in my power to ensure the life of my child or even my own safety but I am doing my duty. In these cases the failures are the exceptions. Nature intended children to be born and women to bear them and we dwell on the few cases of disappointment because they affect us from their rarity.

Very little public news. A very interesting Debate took place on a motion relating to the prison discipline of England—though much, much, is yet to be done, a great deal is doing. The separate system begun—and education, employment, reform, the governours and jailers and chaplains better chosen—in short the world

is enlightening and the effects of Christianity beginning
to tell—to spread—strange that 1800 years should have
passed before the followers of our divine teacher should
begin to practise the faith they have so long professed.
By and bye we shall get rid of those dreadful execu-
tions—that atrocious convict system and other *vengeful*
punishments. When shall we be rid of vice, when will the
higher orders set the example of acting on high principles
to the lower? Alas! the millenium is still ages uncountable
remote.

The debate on the Irish railroads interested me. Would
that these half cracked Irish would take the good advice
of the 1st Lord of the Treasury—give up their furious
party divisions and unite in developing the resources of
this fine country. Government will assist any plans for
its improvement though it is considered unwise for it
to adopt the Continental mode of managing all great
works itself.

All this time our little Queen is at Brighton seemingly
as happy as she should be—delighted with the place,
up early, out all day and herself, her children and her
husband all benefitted by the fine sea air. But what in
the world is the use of her to the nation? It is really a
very expensive head to the nation that one which wears
the Crown, of no use towards its government and for
other purposes might really be curtailed of much of its
importance for the world is gradually rising above Court
dangling and will not very long endure the extreme
etiquette required there. When we are fit for further
equality this magnificent remnant of barbarism will be
laid aside like other worn out institutions.

7. Jane Cooper is so taken up with her expected dolly and
all the little clothes for it that she has time for nothing
unconnected with the poor little creature that may be we
shall never see. We were like to have had it in a hurry two
or three days ago but after some suffering I got better. The
Doctor walked down to have a look at me—took away the
smallest bit of chicken I was going to dine on—also one
of my pillows and bid me not stir hand or foot for the
present; however I feel I am getting right again.

9. Fred Hornidge's father is to bring all his family home to Lodge Park this summer—he is quite tired of France though the ladies like it. In truth these continental schemes are mere dreams—people cannot be happy with nothing to do, and going abroad for *economy* one is precluded from that variety of change and amusements which can alone fill up the idle day. To *travel* with a purse full is quite another thing.

Lots of conjectures relative to the proposed system of taxation and all the Irish in a fright. I can't say that hitherto their exemption from any share in the burthens of the state has done either them or their country much good—probably a necessity for exertion might answer better and thin the ranks of the rollicking pleasure seeking, sporting, half idle, half gentlemen we are infested with.

There is a curious schism among the Jews. An enlightening faction following the march of mind are anxious to free themselves from a number of the more minute observances of the Mosaic Law which really are perfectly inconsistent with the usages of civilisation. This of course is resisted by the high synagogue party. Is not priestcraft the same in all climes, in all ages, in all forms of worship? Are there not divisions too among all the priest ridden. Two furious sects of Parsees—two equally desperate among the Mussulmans, and the followers of Brahma. God knows in the Christian Church our divisions are endless—from the earliest times of our era the Greek and Roman hierarchs waged deadly warfare and among we protesters against the errours of our Roman faith we have as many sects as there are regiments in our army, and all so full of hatred of each other, and all so absurd, so full of folly, disputing about things as nonsensical as are to be found in fairy tales and far distant ages distant from that religion which is pure and undefiled.

11. Rather an uncertain looking morning, bad for the steeple chace to which every human creature is going. That little imp Micky Whelan would to a certainty have been off to it without leave if the Colonel had not most wisely made a merit of giving it to him. And John Fitzpatrick,

my steady man with a wife, and ever so many children: James Ryan, Paddy the gardener, everybody that can get. Johnny Grace the youngest among them is the only wise one; he did not go last year, neither would he ask this, because his ewes are yearing. The Colonel and his steward and old Frank all off to the races, it is very harmless now that Temperance is in fashion. In the Commons Mr. Disraeli makes a very very long set speech about the Consuls—proposed a foolish plan—not listened to. It is strange a man who writes so cleverly should be such a dead weight in speaking.

So sorry to see the death of Kirkman Finlay, the prince of our Scotch merchants—none of his sons will ever fill his shoes—they inherit too much *oddity* from their mother. Ages ago when my mother was young and scouted the clerk of Uncle Leitch's partner, Aunt Leitch used to tell her she would live to rue her airs for that he would be one of the richest and one of the greatest men in the West country, and always kind to her and us. Jane who knew him well will be very sorry.

Such dreadful news from India. Sir Alexander Burnes really murdered and Sir William Macnaughton; General Elphinstone dead of gout from anxiety of mind—sixteen officers killed—others severely wounded. In the camp a month's provisions only. In the Town of Cabool none—the garrison determined to cut their way through the enemy and were butchered in the defiles almost to a man. 5,000 fell, the sixteen ladies, wives to some of these heroes are led away captives by the Affghans—to such a fate—millions upon millions of treasure have been wasted—and lives—how many thousand lives including a little band of the cleverest men in the service—to keep Shah Souja on a throne where he was detested and keep a better man from a people who loved him. And what earthly business was this of ours? Surely we have plenty of business and plenty of territory in India without entangling ourselves with this warlike nation inhabiting an almost impenetrable country at such a distance. If Lord Ellenborough can bring us decently out of such a mess he will be a cleverer man than half the world take him for.[4]

14. Sir R. Peel brought forward the Budget. A manly statement exaggerating nothing, concealing nothing, blaming no one, declaring the truth that for the last six years the expenditure has exceeded the income by little short of two millions annually. His plan may be compressed into an income tax to be imposed for three years, not quite three per cent on all incomes above £150. We shall be rich—Hal and I—nothing to pay for we drink no spirits and use no stamps and live in our own country and meat and bread and many of the other necessaries of life will be cheaper.

15. The Irish paper actually in an extasy with Sir R. Peel—no wonder for we have indeed got 'justice and more'. The speech itself the more one considers it the more wonderful it is—the indefatigable industry of the man—the clearness of his head—the depth of his calculations—the general soundness and liberality of his views—his honesty—his sincerity—his boldness—his calmness—are all unrivalled and stamp him the greatest statesman this country has ever produced since she gloried in Lord Chatham.

19. These quarrels about Church discipline and Church patronage are the disgrace of nations calling themselves Christian. There is no church by itself church. It is only wanted as an appendage to the State—a convenience for the better regulation of the morals of a country and when a set of priests set up to oppose the State or to affect independence of it they render the Establishment they belong to worse than useless. They make it a positive nuisance. The hotbed of strife and every ill passion instead of a nursery of virtue. How odious is priestcraft, how utterly opposed to the tenets of Him whom we pretend to consider as the authour and the finisher of our faith. I really can see very little difference between the Popish priest with his beads, his bells, and his vain repetitions,

4. He was appointed Governor General of India in the aftermath of the disaster.

the Anglican Bishop with his purple and his palace and his retinue of humble expectants and the arrogant presbyter with his unyielding severity assuming authourity over Laws and property and praying with closed eyes against the sin of walking out in the fields on a Sunday. They may just take their places beside the hypocritical Brahmin or the Tartar Lama to my mind but I suppose I must keep this mind to myself and my husband—the world must be a century or two wiser before it would be able to bear the truth as taught by our divine master.

26. The Colonel and I talked over our school and its teacher and we agree that it is unnecessary for Miss Gardiner to return to Dublin. It was not to accomplish *her* that we made the sacrifice of sending her there—her acquirements with my help are quite sufficient for the condition of the country round us. We wanted her to gain a little practical knowledge for which she has had time sufficient. She is thinking too much of herself, too little of the school on account of which all this pains is taken with her.

31. They have elected Hal a Poor Law Guardian; he had half a mind not to act but thought better of it and went to Naas yesterday with Mr. Hornidge where he met a great many of the gentlemen of our neighbourhood and two of them were chosen Chairman and Deputy Chairman, but there is so great a muster of low papists and they are so violent and so jobbing and so overpowering in numbers that it will be difficult to get matters properly managed in their despite; however time and perseverance on the part of the gentry may do much; the people are beginning to prefer their landlords to their priests privately and by and bye they may have courage to avow it.

I have bid Hannah not to let Lady Milltown up to me if she calls. I am not well enough to be amused with her folly, she would only worry me like poor Miss Gardiner who really was crazed for a couple of days. I could make nothing of her face to face so I wrote her a very quiet letter saying all that was proper and a great deal that was kind but yet firm in keeping her to her bargain, insisting upon the opening of the school now at the time prearranged explaining that this was a matter of duty with both her and me, not choice. She came down in torrents of tears on Monday and gave up the school. She was quite wild. I begged of her to consult someone wiser than herself,—Mr. Moore, her kind friend—no—nothing would keep her from Dublin. I did not feel well enough to bear this frantick scene so sent her to Miss Cooper who made just as little hand of this 'wild Irish girl' of twenty-five by the way. She was to be off in the morning.

This I put a stop to by Colonel Smith's advice who made me write as if she had no longer the school nor claim on me or on the Board, therefore requesting her to come down and deliver up her books before I wrote to announce my loss of a teacher. I fancy this opened her mind to her impropriety, for she walked down to Kilbride Tuesday to consult Mr. Moore and came to me yesterday so humbled I really felt for her. She will do all I wish—collect the children, class them, set the business agoing—only think of returning to Dublin should the authorities there consider it necessary—allow them to choose her substitute—remain here till the substitute understands matters—will give up her salary to her for the time—in short nobody could be more reasonable—quite unlike the hoity-toity lady who, intent only on her own advantage, thought nothing of breaking her engagements, neglecting her duty and leaving me to whom she owed obedience as her superiour and gratitude as her constant friend to close my school for three months longer at the very season it is most attended or to look to the moon for another Teacher in my present helpless condition. She is a fine creature by nature too, but a perfect specimen of her countrymen. Oppose them in any one thing and the world won't hold them—they don't understand duty—principle—self interest or rather self will guides them.

TUESDAY, APRIL 5. Hal had a letter from John Robinson announcing that Mr. Wynne grants a 999 years! lease of the Burgage banks, so we may begin and plant them this autumn and what an improvement that will be to this dear sweet pretty place which even while they are bare looks so well. His other tenants—Healys, Darkers, Kellys, etc. he has warned out—notice to quit has been served on all of them—they have been teasing him and thus he punishes them and will probably levy a good fine on those he may be prevailed on to retain.

The Doctor breakfasted here—sent twice up to me in the most violent hurry to be admitted but I knew him too well to put myself to the least inconvenience for him and when he was let in he gossipped a good half hour—all sorts of subjects but the last was the Colonel whom he pronounced to be the perfection of manly character, a conclusion arrived at by himself and Richard Hornidge in a late conversation. My own private opinion very nearly squares with theirs—nature meant him to be a very improved edition of his remarkable father *but* he is idle, very idle, and while quite a boy he was thrown away upon a regiment of cavalry in India which happened unluckily never to have anything to do or he would have made a name in arms for he loved his profession.

John sent me 'Emma' which delights me more than ever. Mr. Knightley is more charming than I even used to think him for he is exactly Hal—and I was alas! always reckoned like Emma.[5] The whole story and scenes and characters and sentiments are admirably true to nature and the moral so very good.

Yesterday Lady Milltown gave an account to the Doctor of the Kildare Club Ball. 'The most perfect mob ever collected—you did not know who you met—no moving—such swells—a coarser word she used—heat from the whim of having wax lights insupportable—rooms so beastly dirty—most stupid blackguard affair—sorry she had been prevailed on to go.' Baron de Robeck said to-day to the Colonel: 'Such a splendid affair as our Club gave

5. Jane Austen's opening description of Mr. Knightley is that he was 'one of the few people who could see faults in Emma Woodhouse and the only one who told her of them.' Emma, on the other hand, 'had a disposition to think a little too well of herself.'

the Lord Lieutenant. Nothing could exceed the arrangements—walls hung with chintz—wax lights so favourable to beauty—statues from del Vecchio—vases—greenhouse plants—wines of the finest—attendance admirable—900 persons, not mere anybodies—but all the
country gentry and nobility of respectability who had
come purposely out of their retirements—people who
had never thought of entering Dublin since the days of
the (first) Duke of Northumberland, (1763).'

6. Miss Gardiner was with me ever so long preparing needle
work—in great spirits for Mrs. Campbell will procure
a competent person to take charge of our school while
Miss Gardiner returns to finish her course of instruction
in Dublin.

7. Such a dreadful newspaper, I can't think of it without shud-
dering—the rumours of the disasters in Afghanistan were
very little worse than the reality. General Elphinstone with
the most extraordinary infatuation allowed Akbar Khan,
this subtle savage, who by the way, is quite a hero of
mine, to arrange the marches of the troops, their resting
places, etc., which of course he contrived should suit
the movements of the party he had ordered to intercept
them at a very difficult pass where every human being
belonging to this ill-fated division has been massacred.[6]
The Queen's 44th was out off to a man, they mutinied,
struck their officers, lost order and were destroyed. It
was a bad regiment—always in rows and scrapes when in
Dublin, officers very little better than the men and sent
to India for their sins. Can any amount of talent or skill
or treasure replace our Indian Empire where it was.

10. Such a beautiful Sunday. Mr. Moore preached to reward
them all for walking and giving poor Tom a rest after a
week of harrowing. Indeed I am not sure that he was not
drill ploughing to the great annoyance of Tom Darker
who don't at all approve of any change in husbandry. No
wonder they can't pay good rents here—besides having
too small farms they understand too little of the manner

6. There was supposed to have been only one surviver from
the retreat, a Dr. Bryden.

of cultivating it to be able to work near the full value out of the ground.

Mr. Moore sent me some religious periodicals published in Dublin for the purpose both of enlightening me as to Puseyism7 and of shewing me how very far from Christian are the body of Irish Churchmen. As for the *'Tracts'* I am a bad subject to try high church principles on the whole question with me being one of expediency.

13. If we are to do any permanent good in this country we must set to work and *educate* our *protestant clergy*. One could hardly have believed a body of men in these days being so very very far behind the age, and Dr. Whateley being rather before it he was not well selected for the see of Dublin; they won't learn of him; *can't*, they a'n't ready for him. Really such papers on National education remind one more of the days of John Knox and Cromwell than of any religious opinions of later days. It is this extravagant bigotted puritanism which is driving people into Puseyism. The farther from evangelical cant the better—think many.

18. Hal rode to Naas, Janey to Kilbride to bid farewell and on her way home she paid visits to her humble Blesinton friends, Miss Merrey, her dressmaker, Mrs. Grindon, her milliner, Miss Hall the Baker, Mrs. Farrell, the doctor's housekeeper, and Mrs. Foster. Little happy creature, you are getting dull now that the hour is come. You will find, my Janey, that there is after all no place like home; the finding this out from experience will be no trifling part of your education, and the being thrown upon yourself for a while is an important part. They will all be very kind to you [in Edinburgh] but you will miss Papa and Mama and Annie and Johnny and Miss Cooper, and you will often think of home employments, home pets, home happiness, for we are very happy, dear Janey, in spite of a little crook in the lot now and then.

19. They are off—were away before ten—Janey in good

7. Edward Bouverie Pusey (1800–82) was one of the founding fathers of the Oxford or Tractarian Movement.

spirits. I feel a little dull—not on account of parting with dear Janey for the propriety of her visit to her Grandmother and the use it will be of to herself make me easy about the mere losing her. My distress lies deeper.

My dear husband and I have hardly parted friends—he was for some cause unknown to me out of temper and therefore unreasonable and unjust and I instead of soothing made remarks which aggravated him. My nerves are irritable just now, but a little thought could have kept better order in my bodily economy. There is no excuse for a woman not exercising forbearance; it is very unwise too, for the reflexions of a good heart soon set temper to rights. I am therefore much dissatisfied with myself for my own want of temper and don't try to *excuse* it though I *account* for it. I am the more annoyed as he never recovers quickly from these misapprehensions and so his journey will not be a happy one. Little girls, let Mama's fault be a warning to you. No matter where the right lies, the wife is wrong who vexes her husband.

20. Mr. Moore sat more than an hour. We were so busy with our schools, our book club, our intended improvements in all ways that we forgot Dr. Pusey—just as well.

23. About 2 o'clock to our amazement Hal returned. I had a few lines from Jane in the morning to say he was unwilling to stay but that they would keep him if they could and I wrote to beg they would as I really thought a little variety would benefit him. Friday morning at seven Hal left Edinburgh. Jane and James lovers still—rather amusingly so considering their age. Hal likes him much, pleasant, gentlemanly, and quite nice enough looking. Jane is at the summit of earthly felicity. She thinks Hal looking remarkably well and Janey his image.

MAY 1. Sunday, most beautiful with a soft southerly wind. No one went to Church but the servants. The Doctor called and can evidently make nothing of me. No such case is in his books nor did he ever meet with such an one in practice—here am I walking about getting stronger, feeling pretty well, eating, sleeping, and with the same pair of stays on tyed to the same size as I put off in November. I don't know what to make of myself. Time will explain.

A note from Jane to the Colonel accompanied this happy letter to announce a shock—the death of Lady Cumming—Eliza Maria Gordon Cumming—how many, how very many hearts will throb at the news of the sudden death of one so celebrated. 'Judge (her) not' we who were better nurtured. How vividly I do remember *her* and *Altyre*. Its gay idleness, its mornings of active nothings, its evenings of indolent enjoyment, and she the charm of all, her cultivated taste improving all. Sir William's ready wit and cordial manner blinding us to his errours and his oddities, and the lovely scenery of the Findhorn adding its bewitchment to the wasted time. Lady Cumming and I were born within a week of one another. Sir William fell in love with her abroad whither he had gone to travel for two years as my father would not consent to his marriage with me till I was older, had seen more and could judge for myself.

5. Frank quite tipsy; sent with a message into Blesinton he returned in this condition after months of sobriety—poor old foolish man. After being so often forgiven, promising the last time so earnestly, he is incurable and what will become of him. I am sorry for him, he has many good qualities—so many as to make him in many respects a valuable servant, but he is a mere savage after all, with all the vices of ignorance and has done irremediable mischief in his department from temper and the love of whiskey. I cannot say I regret parting with him as he really is a supernumerary and an expensive one. One man servant in the house is as many as we can afford to keep—he should be a good one certainly; therefore if George don't brighten up very much indeed he must be made to understand he will have to follow the father.

6. An immense petition presented to both Houses of Parliament brought in on some sort of carriages helped on by ever so many dozens of people and carried off piece-meal after being presented. Violently ridiculously drawn up, signed by three million of men, women and children, Chartists praying to be heard by Counsel on their grievances. Their prayer was refused by a large

majority. After all it was a mere farce. What are *three* millions out of *twenty-four*.

There is a panick about the encreasing democratick feeling and democratick tendency of these later times which is surely unnecessary: during the French revolution that feeling was much much stronger supported by a much more influential class and much more enthusiasm shown upon the subject which at one period had become really formidable—yet no mischief ensued, and this feeble display by the very lowest orders only, more deserves pity than even anger for it cannot be denied that very great distress has long existed chiefly amongst that class and though the *cause* is in themselves, improvident habits, ignorance, vice, all conspiring to make and to keep them wretched; the remedy, an improved education, is too far off not to make one anxious to alleviate as far as possible the evils of a very miserable condition. This absurd claim for power for those whose extreme ignorance renders them entirely unfit to be entrusted with it can neither be urged by wise nor by good men, and so we may safely trust to the absurdity wearing itself out.

11. The Emperour of Russia has made an attempt to improve the condition of the serfs throughout his vast dominions but the proposal has been met with such ill will by his barbarous nobility that he will hardly be able yet to carry out his benevolent plans.

We need hardly waste our sensibility on the bondage of these soil tillers nor on the Slave miseries so feelingly depicted so long when this last report of the parliamentary commissioners on the subject of juvenile labour in our own vaunted country be reflected on. In the collieries of the North of England and East of Scotland and in Wales children from three years old are employed naked nearly to drag or push trucks of coal through passages in which they cannot stand half filled with mire, totally dark, where they labour till exhausted day after day, year after year, without instruction or change, badly fed and harshly treated—the details are actually horrible and have haunted me painfully this whole day. Parents carry their infants into these places of torture partly from the brutality resulting from their own cheerless lives, partly from the hope of gain, as their wages are encreased according to the number of victims they can supply for this unholy traffick. My God, what a race of pigmys both in person and intellect must be the result of such a childhood, such a youth, deformed limbs, stunted size, an idiot vacant stare harrowed the feelings of the Commissioners; reading this and recollecting the happy slaves in the Mauritius,[8] lightly tasked, well fed, well dressed and singing merrily without a thought of care, I cannot but feel that people are often deceived by sounds—the name of slavery—the name of liberty—have ideas annexed to them very very different from the reality. One can't advocate the system of one human being daring to appropriate to himself absolutely the possession of another, his equal in the eye of God. Yet the slave owner is seldom as depraved in the management of his gangs of purchased workmen as are the owners of our British Collieries in the case of their free labourers; nor did we ever hear of the lash of the slave driver being more cruelly applied than by the overseers of these bands of wretched children. It has turned me quite sick, it is dreadful.

15. One of the evenings Hal was in Dublin he went to hear Miss Adelaide Kemble[9] in the *Somnambula*—and was disappointed. She is not handsome nor graceful nor a fine actress; her voice is amazingly powerful and she does many surprising runs and feats of various difficulty, but he thinks she fails in expression and her tone is not sweet. The plot of the opera is most stupid and he is too new to Bellini's musick to like it. Now when I hear her I wonder what I shall think—probably much as he does. We are both most likely grown too old to like anything we have not been used to. Operas I did expect to retain a love for; plays I have quite outgrown, so has all the

8. The H.L. and her Colonel stopped off here on their return from India in 1830.

9. 1814–79: Charles Kemble's youngest daughter and the most celebrated English singer of the day—she retired seven months later.

world seemingly. All theatres are empty, all actors bad, but musick belongs to all ages—the most civilised as well as the most barbarous. I calculated upon musick always charming no matter who breathes the sound, yet I believe the airs heard in my youth please me best and I don't quite think I should be satisfied with much change in the way of executing them.

16. A great fuss about the Queen's masked ball—a most ridiculous piece of mummery to my mind—turning her Court into a Playhouse, descending from the calm dignity of her station into one of a group of maskers—putting a mimick crown too on poor Prince Albert's head, who must often enough fret at his position so near it; then in the very heat of 150 causes of irritation between us and those silly French to choose Edward the third and the recollection of all his triumphs over our exquisitely vain and sensitive neighbours, it will most assuredly put the whole nation into a whirlwind of fury hardly worth the price of the few ells[10] of brocade to Spitalfields.

17. Lady Milltown and her five children to tea; the Doctor dropped in at eight so we had whist in one room, romping in the other—plenty of laughing in both—for that is a most amusing woman, full of wit, full of fun, full of scandal, and not particular as to accuracy, her tongue never stopt for one moment; we played our cards certainly, but as for playing the game that was not possible. Story after story—jest after jest—husband—kindred—acquaintance—all served up with sauce piquante for our entertainment. By the bye in one of her newspapers is a furious debate in the French Chamber of Deputies on the insult offered to the great nation by the British Queen. All in commotion at the revival of such names as figured at Creci and Poictiers (sic). Alas! neither they nor we can blot the deeds of barbarous times out of our bloody annals, though we ought both of us to have reached a point in civilisation beyond which their memory should reach but as matter of history. How many unquiet spirits are still astir—the world

10. Scots unit of linear measurement, 137 inches.

how far behind still what steam must in a few years raise it to.

23. Waked really ill—one of my strange attacks. All attendants in a fright; old Peggy up making preparations not needed; for though restless and very uneasy for many hours I got better towards evening. How many games at backgammon Hal played with me because I could settle to nothing else.

25. Wrote to Janey and to Jane about Miss Clerk—the natural daughter of Lord Eldin who with the talent of her celebrated father it is to be hoped don't inherit the *temper* of the family, or the governess line will never suit her. I had rather send a girl out as housemaid or laundress, I think. Governesses are cruelly treated, but indeed they don't merit in general much respect; they are for the most part wholly unfit for so responsible a task. Any sort of decayed gentlewoman is shoved into the charge of the rising generation whether her *temper*, *health* and *intellect* be of that superiour quality alone fitted to struggle through such arduous duties. If they were what they should be their treatment would be suitable. Moral influence is the greatest of all influences—who can withstand it? Miss Henry sent me £1 for my lending library and wishes it every success but wonders who I will get to take the trouble attending it. She will wonder more when she hears I mean to take it myself.

27. Papa and Annie walked into Blesinton to buy at Mr. Dallen's new shop various things they particularly wanted. I gave them a £10 note to get change out of which this honest pair paid for all their purchases and returned me the balance—presents for the maids came out of it, doll's bedclothes, a pair of trousers, heaven only knows what.

John Robinson says in his letter that he goes seldom to the Italian opera not being able to stand the musick that goes down there; the worst style of that school, loose melody, meagre harmony, endless embellishments—just what Hal said of Miss Kemble and Bellini. But the German opera is delightful, and the Ancient and the Philharmonick concerts half craze him with pleasure; he seems to live most on instrumental musick—the

symphonies of Mozart, Haydn, Beethoven—that is he
delights in the full rich burst of the German Orchestra.
I am much of his mind. German musick alone satis-
fies me.

28. John Robinson arrived to collect the rents looking remarkably well—better than I have seen him for ages.
James Ryan and I have had a settlement of accounts;
altogether the schoolhouse has cost above £80 which
he gave me three years to pay. Both have fulfilled our
contract; he did the work well and expeditiously and I
have denied myself every other indulgence to keep my
word with him. If the children only attend, it is worth,
well worth, all it has cost.

29. Annie, the Colonel and John walked to Church this very
blustery day. George dined with us last night; he and John
each give £1 to the Lending Library. John says the tenants
have paid wonderfully well considering the hard times—a
very bad harvest and a very scarce spring makes money far
from plenty among them, yet they had it and came well
dressed and looking decent—thanks to Father Mathew
by whose aid they are a million times better off this bad
year than they used to be in more thriving seasons; he
also says that they are the most improving tenantry he
sees—the most improved also in the time—they are
indeed superiour in every respect to the ragged crew of
'ten years ago.'

30. Made out a List of Books for the Lending Library—an
easy task with the help of the Messrs Chambers, Penny
Magazine, etc. What times we live in—what strides the
world is making. Sometimes a perfect glow of happiness
comes over me when I think of twenty years hence. We
have party and sectarian bigotry to get over however
before any great advance can be made, and that will
take two twenties, I fear, though much of the extreme
uncharitableness. of feeling is already gone. As education
of the proper kind becomes general, all prejudice must
yield to enlightenment and the slowness of the process
should discourage no one. We don't want the rapidity of
enthusiasm but the sober conviction of rational intelligence and *Lending Libraries* are to be among our tools. I

am always sorry when John Robinson leaves us. I like him so much—intelligent, liberal, manly, active, industrious. I grudge him to the *flour factory business*, though the feeling is wrong. One of the means of improvement is the having superiour persons in all departments; they can't be lowered by their occupation and all depending on them may be raised by their influence towards their own high standard.

WEDNESDAY, JUNE I. I have been thinking whether it has been quite right in me to set down for evil as well as for good in this written exposure of feelings which I intend to be read by my children all my private opinions of people and people's actions, some of them very near and very very dear to me. My tongue I know often goes too fast, my pen too, I suppose, for it runs on over the words just as the tongue does. However, dear children, you may just remember this that whether what I feel be wrong or right it is my honest impression at the time; though I may 'nothing extenuate' I certainly do not 'set ought down in malice.'[11]

Miss Clerk is inclined to accept the situation at Russboro'. I have sent the young lady's address and all necessary information to my Lady who may now manage the business herself. The Doctor breakfasted with us; he is nearly knocked up with two dreadful days and a night attending a poor woman in agony. However she and a fine child are both alive. It is curious, among the ladies, this has been an easy season, among the poor women a very bad one. Many serious cases requiring surgical assistance, a rare necessity. I a'n't a bit frightened, what one woman bears another woman can bear. Skilful attendants give confidence; as for the pain it is so bad at any rate a little more can hardly matter—it is soon over too and leaves a blessing behind. Another little dear pet to love who will reward all the pain and all the care it costs if we have the virtue to bring it up properly.

3. The last few days I have really done nothing but receive morning visitors. To-day came Lady Milltown and her

11. Othello v ii 339.40

girls to finish the affair of Miss Clerk, poor thing, she will have a sad time of it I fear if ever she settles to come.

In the midst of the conference in came Mrs. Hornidge in the new landaulet bought for £20, dressed like the Hop Queen or the Queen of May—every colour—satin—cash-mere—silk fur—feathers and every kind of finery—long black ringlets—a regular object—there she stood, the grazier's wife, within a year or two of sixty as if she had been cut out of the world of fashion, and there stood the Countess, some fifteen years younger, in a chintz gown, plain shawl and poke bonnet. Lord Milltown has lost £4,000, gained in odd hundreds near one, so he has better than three to make out one way or another, and I fancy I am about as well able to make it out conveniently as he is; he has had within more than a chance of brain fever; lived for six weeks while calculating the odds on the Derby on seidlitz draughts and salad; looks dreadful, in the lowest spirits—promises to give up this madness; but so he has done before often and often.

We talked too about this second attempt to shoot the Queen and admired her courage as it deserved, though we agreed that the ignorant poor who are bad political economists might well lose temper at the luxuries and pageantries and splendour of a Court unrivalled in Europe upheld in their belief for the honour of a very useless individual while they are starving in thousands; out of work and hungry they reason ill—in full hard work they know their earning to be small—their indulgences few; is it any wonder some bad spirits among them become quite excited. This young man is too much a mystery as yet for any correct judgment to be formed of him or of his motives. The Queen had a narrow escape and the enthusiasm in her favour is so great just now that the sensation caused is quite extraordinary—a godsend to the idle Court loungers it will be—something to think of—talk of—in short to occupy them.

5. Just as we had dined Archdeacon and Mrs. Agar drove up. I was quite glad to see them—the country has not been like itself without them. Their strange old gigs and chaises and phaetons, the nondescript harness and elderly

leisurely horses were quite missed on the roads; and the pair themselves I missed them too—her comely, *sonsy* face and figure, his clever, odd, amusing conversation and perfectly gentlemanly manner. The Archdeacon don't get tipsy by himself but he drinks plenty and variety and the best, and for eating—*loads* of the best and richest and rarest—half cooked by himself—wholly served—for they seem to have but one bare-footed maid and Mrs. Agar's own attendant.

When people call, the Archdeacon takes their horses to the stable having no man to do it. When Mr. Fetherstone slept there the Archdeacon carried up his shaving water, took away his dirty boots; there was no one else to do it. In the tiny glebe house there are neither carpets nor curtains. On a side table are generally to be seen the half burned pair of tallow candles of the night before, the butter left from breakfast, a regular row of black bottles, full and empty. She seems to do little but patch her old gowns with a placid smile that never varies. Both are odd—decidedly—his family cleverly odd—hers foolishly ditto. Their wealth between them, for each brought a goodly portion to the joint stock, would be great for anyone—to them with their habits it is boundless; the strange thing to me is that he with a mind so full of ideas should be content with her society and that she without an idea and brought up in the busy frivolity of a London life can content herself with solitude. They seem perfectly happy—on the most agreeable terms—satisfied—both of them.

6. Still intensely hot. Hal nearly overcome by a very long walk with Mr. James Fraser, the *capability* man who came to give us a few hours advice. He was surprised at the beauty of the place which he had formerly seen to great disadvantage in bad rainy weather at an ungenial season. This day the whole country looked well; the planting everywhere has grown too and the new approach and other alterations, some of them suggested by himself, have all been well carried out and greatly improve the appearance of the place. The fields above the house enchanted him—the lay of the ground is so particularly

pretty and the views everywhere so fine—he says it will be a lion some day—a place to come and see.

I have no good eye myself for laying out grounds though I can beautify them well enough when the general effect is arranged for me; but I can quite understand the pleasure there must be in the capability of designing on this large scale and can quite feel the full beauty of embellished scenery. And the interest of the works while going on no one can enter into more completely. My whole heart is in Baltiboys—our own dear happy family—the pretty place—the people—the last the least improvable. Still progress is making even amongst them though Judy Ryan is not among the improving as her melancholy exhibition of this afternoon too plainly proved. Such total want of principle in a mind not naturally depraved is a curious fact in economical philosophy.

8. Never was there more truly summer weather. At least three weeks earlier the season is than usual, the crops everywhere giving fine promise of harvest with the exception of a few districts in which the oats have partially failed owing to the dryness of the seed-time. Yet the markets are extravagantly high. Oatmeal 18/6 the cwt; *lumper* potatoes 6d. a stone ; surely these unprecedented prices cannot last. They will half ruin our poor population should they continue longer. Everybody is buying, having all finished their own stores, and they have no way of earning the money to buy with.

The Doctor breakfasted with us and has given me food for reflexion for many a future hour. The moral of the tale, dear children, draw for yourselves. Here is the story. On Sunday evening Lord Milltown drove his wife here in his low phaeton little Henry sitting between them. In the rumble behind were the two girls and Edward—Russy on his pony. A happier, prettier looking healthier looking party could not well have been met. On Monday after breakfast Edward complained of pain in his head—vomiting followed without relieving the pain. A man and horse was therefore sent for the Doctor. Mrs. Farrell told the man her master was not at home, that he was however to be at Colonel Smith's about that time and by riding quick to Baltiboys the man might catch him. 'D—l a bit' would the man go—'he had done his message—what should he go scouring the country for, etc.' Why should he indeed. Did his Lord or his Lady ever consider him? Sick or well was he ever treated but as a bit of furniture belonging to their establishment? Would he have been permitted to take the slightest interest in their noble children? Wrapped up in themselves without a thought for others how can they expect others should care one jot for them?

Part the first being over, part the second begins. The Doctor had an intolerably hot walk from this house to the cabin of a poor woman in Burgage whom he found extremely ill, and a hotter walk home along the dusty turnpike road. With great ill-humour he heard of this additional fatigue—for not only does Lord Milltown owe him for five years' medical attendance, never having given him a fee since Henry was born when Lady Milltown was so alarmingly ill with inflammation, nor then even, but his manner has been occasionally so haughty, her airs so numerous, at times all condescension, at others so absurdly grand, that the Doctor who has no particular reason for enduring their absurdities has latterly withdrawn himself from any exposure to them. So far all well; why should he, a gentleman, more useful, more respectable, than either of these self-satisfied persons submit to treatment unbecoming to offer or receive.

But why did he let his own temper lead him into conduct as reprehensible. Angry with the parents, indifferent about the child, he paid less attention to the case than he ought conscientiously to have done—examined it hurriedly, prescribed hastily, quitted the house abruptly, paid no second visit in the evening. They deserved no better, but he was wanting to himself in lowering his own feelings to think of them at all; he felt it just as I feel it when the temper came round; yesterday morning the child was worse—in danger—and for hours—brain fever; he was shaved, leeched, cooled, physicked; the Doctor was right enough in requiring their carriage and horses to convey him through the heat and to ask for

them when not offered. I would make use of them without
ceremony on their own business—*always keeping my temper.* One don't expect this from their servants, but one
does from the Doctor; and Lord Milltown's hoity toity
proceedings, they are temper too. Moral cowardice—a
national failing—annoyed at his own conduct with regard
to the money matter he bullies it out because he can't pay
it out. And the poor child—what had so over-excited the
child? A very precocious boy of sanguine temperament
with the hereditary disposition to brain attacks—the
father's racing and gaming losses too freely canvassed
before him by both parents. The Doctor is very vexed
with himself, blames himself very justly and must have
suffered much while the poor boy was in danger; poor
dear child, one can hardly help anxiously watching his
recovery—yet why—what does life hold up for him
and his brothers—bad rearing—little education—great
notions—penniless—friendless—and this terrible family
complaint their only inheritance.

Fortunately such a spectacle of ruin is becoming
rare—the unworthy pursuits that have ruined Lord
Milltown in fortune and in character are little followed
by the rising generation; this history of the late 'Derby'
almost sounds the dying knell of the racing days—there
are no funds for there are no *pigeons.*[12] The sharks of this
age who to their ruin acted pigeons to the last can find
no prey in their turn; the young men turned out from
such a course of reading as modern College instruction
requires, have aims beyond the possession of swift horses,
minds above the low excitement of gaming. Newmarket is
forsaken by the rising race of gentlemen—it is frequented
only by the old stagers unfit for better things and the
tradesmen of London—the principal winner just now
was a great dry-salter and cheesemonger and he was
not quite up to the blacklegs—this spread of education
makes one however regret just one thing—the loss of
characters—individual characters—by and bye there will
be no Archdeacon Agars—even in Ireland.

12. Those who let themselves be swindled (OED).

9. Who should arrive yesterday afternoon but Dr. Eckford. I am really glad the weather is so very beautiful showing the country to such advantage—for during his last visit the cold and the constant rain gave him the worst possible impression of Baltiboys.

10. After an immensity of trouble arising from the dishonesty, trickery and attempted 'cuteness' of poor Judy she gives up her grounds this day, taking her goods and her youngest child with her; the goods I believe will not much burden her, every day decreasing the load. Stock she has never had. Hal gives her £10 to go off peaceably, £5 for her child, Jane her eldest girl is to be added to *my* family; the boy he takes himself and intends putting him apprentice to a good trade. So poor Christy Ryan's children, orphan children, have not been neglected by their Landlord. What a mother the poor things have; just at this moment they and she are starving—no money—no stores—no crops sown, not even potatoes, the land let for grazing till November *paid for in advance*, gone, and nothing for rent left. Even the May rent which James Ryan put into her hand as she was coming off to pay it, she subtracted £1 from; that, however, she *is* ashamed of and will pay. Misery certainly accounts for much worthlessness—want of principle brought her to misery; between all she has lost her respectability and my favour and totally degraded her own feelings; she was a superior being entirely when affectionate and merry and simple she nursed with care our little Annie.

11. Young John Hornidge called yesterday in a great bustle about some poachers who have been fishing the river with improper nets; he caught them on the Colonel's ground but it was too dark to swear to them. His Uncle is quite indifferent about their apprehension, ditto Richard Hornidge, ditto the Colonel; between ourselves—the day is gone by for the game laws.

   All arrangements with Judy completed; she has just been here to get a little money to purchase clothes, etc. for her *wedding*, having announced her approaching marriage to *John Doyle* in the bottoms, an ill-tempered, queer looking skeleton with some ten or twelve acres of ground who wants some thatch on his house, some stock on his land, etc. They may do pretty well for he is industrious, but it is strange to me that she would not rather remain independant. The Colonel has apprenticed Lachlan to Neale, the best tailor in Blesinton, bound him for seven years for £9; he clothes him for five years only and has made a bargain for the boy to attend school for two. I have given Mary to her great aunt, Old Mrs. Fitzpatrick, for £3 a year, I to clothe her; she is to go regularly to school and will be well cared for as the old aunt is a most respectable managing woman who brought up a large family most creditably.

14. There have been great riots at Ennis and elsewhere on account of the high price of provisions—scarcity I believe there is none, but the low class of capitalists who buy up the crop in the harvest sell it out usuriously high in the spring, actually driving a bargain with the necessities of a starving people giving credit at an increased rate where money is wanting and honesty known, thus keeping poverty in the cabins the year round. The mob as usual merely did mischief to themselves, destroyed some supplies, seized so little that subdivided it was nothing and conducted their outrage with so little discretion the police had to fire on them when a few were killed and many wounded. The police appear to have acted without sufficient authority and therefore have to abide their trial—they undoubtedly received great provocation.

Dr. came for his whist; he was riding in the morning with Richard Hornidge and saw at a distance our car with its freight returning from shopping in Blesinton and taking a tour to exhibit the best parts of the scenery to the *little* Doctor [Eckford]. Richard and the *big* Doctor had just had such a spectacle. John Hornidge's new old landaulet with himself in one corner, Bessy Finnemor in the other, Mrs. Finnemor bodkin—dressed!! never was such dressing; coachman, footman, old blind Bob and the lame gray—the Ballyward jaunting car behind with the four young gentlemen—all off for the Curragh! 'Mrs. Finnemor! Have you taken leave of your senses—are you mad?'—'That's what John

Finnemor says' screamed she in an extasy of happiness, and then ensued a scene of the usual half flirting, half romping, half impudent description that she and the Doctor so frequently enact for the edification of society. The woman is cracky there is no doubt of it.

Mrs. Tyrell came to offer me her step-grandson to support, and John Byrne our tenant, who is drawing our coals, likes the grass of our avenue for his horses which he turns in there after dark, leaving a boy to watch them and to take them away before morning—though forbid most positively to do this. Judy Ryan also declines paying a debt she owes for provisions supplied to her family while starving upon the faith of being paid honestly with the first money she could command.

19. I have written for Miss Clerk and really hope my part of the business is finished. There was not an approach on my Lady's side to any assistance towards the poor girl's journey. Lord M. is off to races at Newcastle; they all thought Dr. Eckford remarkably clever—of course so did I adding that he was odd, which she said was always the case with a genius; he is very good, kind, happy, contented, very much satisfied with himself but not offensively so—it merely keeps him busy putting everybody right from the ploughman ridging the potatoes through the rest of practical agriculture, the way of playing whist, the laying out of our grounds, the ordering of our dinners, down to my manner of blowing my nose and George's method of trimming the candles.

21. Too much rain going on for comfort—not a drop too much for the crops however which look most beautiful. Hal resolved on dismissing Mick—at any rate for a time; he was really so impudent when spoken to about going to the Review in Phoenix Park without leave that we hardly think he will ever settle into a steady servant and 'tis a pity for he is a most clever monkey. Mr. Darker thinks a little starvation may bring the young gentleman into a more humble frame of mind so we will try it and if he become penitent Hal will give him one more chance of doing well. Saw no one this day but Judy who came for her £9, the balance of her *bribe* I may almost call it.

She is to buy a couple of cows and marry Jem Doyle next Tuesday.

22. Such a thunder storm as is very uncommon in Ireland where thunder and lightning are rare and seldom violent. The flashes this day were blinding, followed so very closely by the thunder that it was startling. Richard Hornidge lost a bullock and George Darker of Trooper's fields a cow.

We had another storm too—by way of variety—from Tom Darker. What an odd country is this; what strange tempers the people have; what materials for a *novel* all round. I wish I could write one and bring in Judy Ryan, her character, dealings and second marriage. Mick and his review and his races should figure in it to a certainty. Hannah in a variety of excitable circumstances and as a crowning dish Tom Darker's *charge* of yesterday.

He has by no means seen with satisfaction the few roods of turnips the Colonel insisted on sowing—the drilled potatoes too annoyed him; some improved implements still more galled the festering wound of Irish jealous self-sufficiency. Yesterday in our walk we passed the women weeding these same turnips with their fingers—taking carefully up each individual plant not wanted and leaving a row about an inch apart to stand for crop. 'Only look, Hal, at the way those women are weeding the turnip field,' said Mrs. Smith in innocent surprise. 'Why, Mary, you'll be a year at that work; look here, have you no hoe? Well, get one from the garden—pull out lumps, weeds and all this way.' On to the drill I jumped and began very vigorously to do as I had seen done all my life. The Colonel gave her the measure of the spaces as no hoe of a fit size was to be had and we set Betty to follow to weed the tufts left by Mary, choose the best plant to leave and to fill up where there was any deficiency; the women were delighted; they saw at once they were in the right way.

I volunteered going for a hoe and was amazed at the check given by the Colonel's strange coolness to my precipitancy—not without reason did Hal look grave—I had never thought about Tom Darker, was little indeed prepared for the hurricane that burst from him; he gave up his place; he was thought unfit for it—he could do nothing his own way—he would interfere no more—he saw he was not wanted, etc. in a fury of passion that really surprised me nearly as much as the Colonel's perfect equanimity—neither look nor voice nor air were altered. In the calmest manner he awaited the subsidence of this deluge while the rest of us walked away.

Unhappy Ireland, how much have your wild children yet to learn? With such untamed passions how are they ever to be raised into that pre-eminence their talents and their energy seem to have destined them to occupy. And this is a superior man—honest firm—just—clever—attached to the Colonel and to the place, beyond, I thought till now, the petty jealousy that keeps back the progress of his country.

23. Poor Tom Darker—all temper—the jealous irritable feeling of conceit and pride hurt by interference really neither unnecessary nor unwarrantable, for excellent as he is and clever and skilful, he is still ignorant of many of the most important parts of his profession. Hal who truly values him, talked to him most kindly—told him how much we both prized him—gave him his due meed of praise but to say truth nothing but his due for he deserves implicit confidence; but he added the unpalatable truth that we did not consider him a first-rate farmer—thereupon arose a friendly discussion and it came out that *Scotch* methods, *Scotch* tools, *Scotch* books, and alas! the *Scotch* mistress, were the aggravating causes of all this absurdity producing the *Irish* jealous fear that I wanted to get rid of him to give his place to a Scotchman.

This is my reward for devoting time, thoughts, money, more than I can well spare to the improvement, moral, social and intellectual of this *strange* land wherein my lot late in life has been cast—for abiding here when a word, half a word, could have established my home near those who value me, for Tom Darker is not alone in his unkind feelings to the *foreigner*. Many a rub, many a scowl, many an insolence, has the Scotch Lady of Baltiboys had to bear from those depending on her for their bread—had not Johnny been born I really do believe they would have hated me. It is plain to me that a hope of being popular among these poor people had been at the bottom of much of my anxiety to do them good very nicely varnished over by an assumption of benevolence, otherwise Tom Darker's folly would not have vexed me. Such is humanity! It requires the spark of divinity to suffer calmly scorn and spitting. It is a good lesson in more ways than one. I had fancied myself grown very cautious in my manner of *hinting*, avoiding all collision with prejudice—or any hasty stride towards better ways—probably I may have been teazing poor Tom and others with my farming books and cottage economy and value of time.

George Robinson dined the day before at Archdeacon Agar's, a party of five. The dinner was roast beef, two roast ducks, three roast chickens, herrings, trout, soles, fricasséed rabbit, ham and eggs, pudding—pancakes and gooseberry fool, which two last the Archdeacon ate together out of a soup plate; the wines were few rather—port, sherry, Madeira, claret, champaign. The dinner is the grand business of the day, of *life*, with both Mr. and Mrs. Agar—half cooked by him, wholly served, for they have none but a bare-footed maid of all work. When the guests, always bachelours, at least always at the time without wives, arrive, they find only Mrs. Agar in the little parlour; the table already laid—five or six knives and forks to each cover—three or four wine glasses—one dumb waiter covered with bottles—another with plates. If anyone should cross the narrow passage a glimpse of a shirt sleeve may be seen belonging to a thin white hand in charge of some sauce boat or covered dish quickly passed through the staircase railing to the floor. The Master and maid then bring in some of the meats and the guests begin. Every now and then a knock at the door betokens a hot dish which Mr. Agar receives in exchange for any one done with; he also holds out clean plates for dirty ones and piles the dirty ones by his side underneath his chair, his table, his dumbwaiters, conversing all the while in the most delightful manner; sometimes he is humorous, sometimes grave, always clever; his appetite is very large; he pours down wine in quantities that would affect any one else considerably. After this he sleeps none—two hours is his longest stretch; often he walks out all night instead of sleeping, cracky decidedly.

Poor Tom Darker—he has turnip hoes going and weeders following and all folly over. The whole men are 'divarting' themselves with the little Doctor. He is for ever asking them the most searching questions, accumulating *facts* upon the condition of Ireland, and they tell him the greatest parcel of falsehoods that their fertile imaginations can invent, keeping as grave all the while as Venetian Senators in a stage play—the bystanders hardly able to keep their countenances; he is quite distressed at our extravagant way of living—so much meat—so much variety—a round of beef is making him quite unhappy—each day it is getting so much smaller, and though we tell him five healthy young people have to dine after us he is still annoyed at their appetites and thinks vegetables with a very small bit of *relish* should do here as in France.

26. All off to Church, with *Johnny*, his first Sunday. How will he behave? His little gospel of St. Mathew in his pocket to serve as prayer book, and his penny. Lord Ashley, who may be called the M.P. for benevolence, has taken up the coal mine slavery and is carrying a Bill to regulate the employment of children and prohibit that of women in all mines. Francis is sentenced to death for firing at the Queen; he is not mad but very wretched from dissipated habits and thought this a good way of providing meat, clothes and fire with lodging for nothing as the other half lunatick succeeded in effecting. Very, dull debates; party feeling dying away even in Ireland, rumours of a coalition again rife. What a blessing that would be.

Little Queen very gay, ever so many German relations having been visiting her, and now have arrived King Leopold and his Queen. It is to be hoped he may be able to put the French affairs a little to rights for us, enlighten that absurd country as to trading matters, and try to get thoughts of war out of their foolish heads.

A very pleasant walk in the evening to Tom Kelly's where *I* was received with rapture. So many months,

near a year, since they had seen me. They are models
of the comfortable small Irish farmer—rich with their
eighty acres of tolerably managed land, wallowing in *dirt*
and plenty. Such thorough untidiness. Beautiful butter,
three large cools worth at least £4 kept in the bedroom;
the children sleeping on straw laid on chairs; mahogany
tables inch thick with dirt, disorder all round, but good
new offices, fine cattle, splendid cabbage, with pease,
beans and turnips in a garden half destroyed by surface
water accumulating in consequence of the drain being
choked; the garden door too, was off its hinges, so it
was the more easily laid over a gutter full of filth through
which it would hardly have been agreeable for us to wade.
Tom pulled us all by the sleeve here and there to see his
different improvements, apologising in the old way for
the old deformities. Peeny the old mother is dying, just
at the point of death. A great loss in a picturesque view for
she was the most perfect, the cleverest Meg Merrilies[13]
of an Irishwoman ever existed—a race extinct with her.

27. Beautiful day—fine weather again; had to write to Miss
Gardiner with her salary, order Lachlan Ryan's clothes,
etc. By the bye we met his mother last night all pink and
yellow, very clean, very smart and very young and happy
looking, walking with the Bridegroom much smartened
up too. She has bought two cows, blankets, sheets as
well as 'cloading;' he is roofing his house and they are to
be married to-morrow. And Jack behaved scandalously
yesterday—would not enter the Church after all; he
walked boldly through the yard but his heart failed him
at the door; little shy monkey; his sisters were never so
bashful. Papa was very angry and in military fashion
punished the poor little creature for this constitutional
defect—the inheritance of his race, for Charles O'Malley
is quite right—an Irishman is essentially bashful and
blusters to hide his shame—a fact.

30. Dr. George came and had an interview with me the result
of which is that my cares are over; he has thought so for
the last two months. I have thought so for the *one*, so that

13. Queen of the gypsies in Scott's *Guy Mannering*.

had we been a little more explicit, a little less over delicate,
I might have been relieved from all my terrours and they
were great some time ago. It is a great comfort to know
that there is no more suffering before me, that a prudent
degree of care is all that will be necessary to ensure a perfect restoration of health and that a very serious complaint
has been got over so well. George feared we should both
be disappointed—was considering how to break the blow
little suspecting it was a perfect relief from many causes.
A most agreeable close to the month of June.

WEDNESDAY, JULY 6. Account day and quarter day so very
busy. Francis not to be hanged, only transported for life
to the most penal of the convict settlements. The Queen
actually shot at again by a humped back boy without an
assignable motive. Chartist meetings at the bottom of all
yet there seems to be no treasonable plots laid. Merely
excitable, reckless imaginations maddened by the rubbish
they heard there.

8. Judy as busy as a bee in her new situation, going to market
with butter and poultry like other industrious women.
The priest hearing she had been well paid for giving up
her land insisted on £2. for marrying her. She resisted,
paid but £1., battled the point with him and complains
loudly of his extortion. Changed times.

14. Went to school yesterday and was thoroughly satisfied, all
going on there to a wish. Children happy, animated, eager
in their business; Miss Gardiner a second Wilderspin
among them. It was well spent money and well spent
time that she passed in the training school. I feel sure
of success with the young through her means now.

Lady Milltown was here yesterday too with her four
youngest children and Miss Clerk all in high spirits. Miss
Clerk very little, very young looking and not pretty, but
agreeable looking, cheerful, gentle, and with an intelligent
expression; her French is perfection so all is sunshine
at present. Our young party drink tea at Russborough
to-night to take leave of Russy who goes to England with
his Mama on Sunday, perhaps up the Rhine, or to the
Spas afterwards, or home again, may be; who knows?
My Lord, perhaps, but not my Lady.

29. Mr. Graeme, District Inspector, paid a visit after examining the school; he is much pleased with Teacher and scholars and is to recommend Miss Gardiner to be raised to the second class which will give her £2 a year more salary. I told him all our difficulties; they are much the same everywhere and can be met only by patience.

TUESDAY, AUGUST 2. Another beautiful day, plenty to do though little to record; it would be one eternal history of domestick economy were I to set down regularly the details of our peaceful lives. Mrs. FitzPatrick has given me up little Mary Ryan, she and her niece Judy [Ryan] have fallen out. Certainly she is a dirty old woman though so clean looking, for the child who went clean and wholesome to her is covered with vermin, just as bad as Italy or Spain—horrid. No wonder the mother felt furious; then the retort courteous of the irritated old aunt about starvation and rags, etc., there must have been a battle royal; the poor child at any rate was worried enough between them. *Mrs. Doyle* must look about for a nurse for her child herself, for really I have not time.

5. The usual routine—business in the morning, a little work, a walk, a little reading, a drive, another walk, and the day is over. Last night we called upon John Young and his wife, relations of the Darkers who have four children at school. A very talking woman, very conceited, very ignorant, but very nice-looking, perfectly tidy in her person and with the cleanest house I ever set my foot in here-abouts. She is not satisfied quite with Miss Gardiner's mode of teaching. She understands she never thumps the pupils and they never will learn unless the master be severe on them. She now and then sends her directions what they are to be taught and how and to have them kept well to their tasks, no play—what does she pay for and slave for, etc? What a mine of patience it requires to deal with the ignorant.

This evening we visited poor Richard Gray whose wild daughter Kitty I never could tame, poor motherless thing. The old man is very ill—all about him very wretched, bare and untidy and dirty; no management, poor old creature. Our visits may not do much good but they can do no harm, so I will continue them as usual though I don't set them all down here, only when they suggest reflexions to me.

13. An agricultural meeting to be today in Blesinton. A branch of the Society established in Dublin. Marquis of Downshire in the Chair. It must do good, not at first as much as we may hope for eventually, but always something. The Rusborough children spent yesterday evening here. It was a 'Soirée Cuisinière, the company making their own cakes; it would be well if any employment producing half the pleasure were discovered to amuse assemblies of grown up people who meet generally but to weary one another; there was never a merrier party than those happy little pastry cooks, boys and girls yesterday.

The Agricultural Meeting went off well, plenty of audience. A sad maundering harangue from Lord Downshire of an hour and a half or more; then resolutions voted, officials appointed; Marquis President, Earl of Milltown, Vice, Sam Finnemor, Secretary. The dinner would be well attended, Hal thought; he gave his ticket to Bryan Dempsey!

16. Here at night in my dear little dressing-room, I am writing for the last time for some weeks. We really go to Edinburgh to-morrow.

Everything I am to leave seems dearer than ever; the place never looked so pretty as in our drive home this evening. After all if I were out of this country I should regret the people in it—many of them—most of them. Ogle Moore and the Doctor were here to-day while I was out to tell the Colonel that Burgage is to be sold—the cousin who bought it from poor ruined Mr. Wynne does not wish to keep it. What a romance it would be should it fall into the hands of the lawful owner again.

23. The Queen really and truly going to Scotland for a fortnight's play—to sail to Edinburgh in her yacht—hold a Levée and a Drawing-room in old Holyrood, and then take a week in the Highlands for Prince Albert to have a shot at the red deer. The nobles so eager to have her will remember her visit for many a long day unless money be more plenty in the rude North than it was in the time of the great Argylle.

26. Such a scene of misery as this day unfolded, or rather such a series of miserable scenes. Annie and I went to hunt out children for the infant class and every where almost we found people merely struggling for existence, some a little better off than others in consequence of better management, but badly at best and no seeming hope anywhere of better days, no prospect for the children beyond toil, toil for the bit to eat.

But all the wretchedness we found during our walk in the morning was nothing compared to the scene at Harry Kiogh's dwelling where I went after dinner to see his poor wife Betty, who is near dying after a miscarriage caused by overweighting herself with the turf she brought home on her back through the river, their fuel for the winter. It is an old cowhouse, part of a ruined building quite apart from all neighbourhood, has never been dashed inside or out, no window, no chimney, a sort of door that don't fit and some thatch by way of—the husband has built a rough stone wall elbow high to protect the bed from the wind of the door. I saw no bed-clothes, straw below, some sort of old dark cloth above; there was a pot and a plate or two and a basin and a spoon, the remains of a old dresser, four starved looking children, very clean, and the poor fainting woman hardly able to speak and not able to raise herself. She did speak and it was to give thanks! for returning strength and a job of work her husband had got which would bring him in 30/- pay, the rent 20/- !! for that place!! and leave a trifle to thatch over the bed!, and she had the fowl still and her four ducks and her pig that Tom Kiogh gave them last year, plenty of turf which she would soon be able to bring home and a fine crop of potatoes when they could release them, and please God harvest work would help them to do that if she were but once able to leave her bed.

All this I saw, but there are a hundred cases, aye more than a hundred worse which I have not seen. Is there no remedy for such utter wretchedness? Education alone won't do, the body must be fed at any rate before the mind can act. We can help Betty Kiogh, lead her to help herself as I have done by making her buy fowl for her knitting and then buying the eggs from her and making that money again clothe the children etc., but we could not do even this little to many, and who is to do it to all. My head turns when I think of it.

31. Here I am in Edinburgh once more, and not being inclined to sleep after all the excitement of the last thirty hours I will talk to you dear Hal just as if you were sitting beside me in our own pretty home for you will read all this when we are together again, or I shall read it to you if you are idle.

Well, you left me in a pleasant crowd, the queerest looking people that ever were packed up together in much less space than could agreeably hold them. We had a long passage, twenty-two hours full to Greenock the wind being against us the whole way and the tide, in the river, and the vessel the dullest of all sailers. It was a short pitching sea, of all others the most difficult to bear, very rough, worse than rough, quite uneasy, I who am never sick was sick to death and felt all the better for it. Annie and I and seven or eight more ladies without berths passed the night on the floor on part of a mattress with somebody's bag for a pillow, extra gentlemen occupied floors and tables in their allotted space and I suppose blessed the Queen for the crush as I did.

Yet we might have slept had it not been for a talking woman whom it suited to have the stewardess for her confidante in several very delicate family affairs of a melancholy description upon which she held forth for some hours, some bits from the Bible, pious ejaculations etc., all echoed by the confidante, all eked out the tales each to a respectable length. One of these tales was news to me and afflicting enough for it told me that young Mr. Fowler of Rosshire who was to be married to *her cousin* (and my cousin!) Eliza Grant of Glenmoriston was suddenly dead. I thought to myself that this magpie must be a relation of mine too. One of those Mathiesons perhaps, and that I must look at her in the morning with a view to recognition. She told us she had been twice married, the first time at sixteen and had seven sons all one after the other as quick as they could come, till she

was twenty-three, when she stopt and she never had any
to the second husband whom she called the Captain and
the Captain had sent her some punch which indeed I think
must have got into her head she gabbled on so.

Such a pair as daylight revealed! horrours, the dirtiest, filthiest creatures, he an old worn out drunkard in
appearance with coarse dirty clothes, nails an inch deep
of black, fingers, shirt wrists oh so beastly. She a mass of
faded flowers, all sorts of odious trumpery. I kept as far
out of their way as the two sides of the deck admitted of.
Which of my Highland relations this disreputable looking
couple belong to, what had taken them to Dublin and why
they don't wash themselves and their clothes I am sure I
don't know.

It is fully twenty years since I was on the Clyde.
I thought the scenery more beautiful now than then,
probably some of the young woods are stately timber now,
besides a few more houses built and grounds generally
better kept. No Scotchman need talk of the misery of
Ireland till Greenock, Paisley etc. improve, the *country*
is improving certainly, but I was struck with the stunted
look of the vegetation, shorter shoots, smaller leaves, less
vigorous trees, and the stature of the people, that again
surprised me. I took all the workmen for boys, so much
shorter are they than our handsome Irish.

We had to wait above an hour at Greenock so got the
luxury of washing combing etc., also a little refreshment
for on board the eating was disgusting, not to be touched
by a poor half sickly body like me. One train took us
in little more than another hour to Glasgow, another in
rather better than two to Edinburgh, these many changes
are disagreeable enough particularly as there is very little
time for them, but the expedition and the cheapness are
wonderful. Within a few miles of Edinburgh we heard
the Queen had not come the wind being quite against
her, yet bonfires were blazing on the Pentlands all along
the shores of Fife and a splendid one on Arthur's seat.

Before eight our funny vehicle, an Irish covered car,
only all windows, stopt before the handsome house in
York Place that Jane has been lucky enough to get

herself made mistress of. They were alone, at tea. I sent in Annie first, a pause, then Janey knew her and such a burst of happiness from the little creatures. It was all a scene till bed time, running here and there, talking, laughing, looking. Jane looks well but thin and no longer handsome. My poor mother woefully changed, very happy, most kindly cared for, every pains taken to make her comfortable, but she certainly has failed beyond my expectation. I am very very glad I came over to see her. James is very nice, the house beautiful, Janey grown tall, fat strong, unaltered in manner, still the simple child. The monkeys were too excited for sleep, so happy, darlings, with what pleasure I kissed them both together, then thought of Jack and came to my solitary room to write the events of this last day of August for you.

THURSDAY, SEPTEMBER 1. The Queen, nothing but the Queen; such a day as this has been, all noise and confusion and fuss and bustle, about such nonsense too. I should be dead in less than a week of such a life and my mother says there is always commotion of some kind going on here, the Queen only makes it a little more violent. The house is beautiful, filled with things of value and interest, Jane and James both clever, their way of living quite luxurious, plenty of servants, fine wines, good cooking, all handsome and handsomely done; yet would I rather be at Baltiboys where we have no finery and no variety, than here with all the grandeur. I long for my dear, quiet, rational home already.

We were wakened at half after six by two loud guns, the signal of Her Majesty's arrival, announcing that in two hours she would land. Soon after the Archers' bugle sounded through all the streets to summon this royal guard. We had breakfast over by a few minutes past eight, and set out for our stations—the children and I to a window of Mr. Thompson's office—Jane and James to the portico of the Institution just opposite; the crowd kept gradually collecting but it was too early for such a mass as had gathered in every direction yesterday. A few carriages rolled by, and some of the City Officials, the boys of Heriot's hospital and the City Clergymen in neat processions passed, at half after nine, a few dragoons turned the corner, then a few Archers, then a dark landau in which sat a gentleman, uncovered, a lady in a pink bonnet, very pale, both bowing most assiduously on every side, behind came five or six travelling carriages, a little van filled with boxes, a hackney phaeton, three or four gentlemen on horseback, a few more dragoons, they got through the crowd as quickly as they well could manage—and this was the Queen's entrée—the procession all had taken so much trouble, many come so many miles to see, never was such disappointment.

How the mistake originated it is difficult so early in the business to make out, a mistake it must have been somewhere for the Queen never could intend to outrage the loyal feeling of her people, and the discontent occasioned by the entire disarrangement of every preconcerted plan for her reception has spread and strengthened so rapidly than an explanation will be necessary to appease the feeling of extreme irritation universally prevalent. On returning home we found the Riccarton [the country house of James Gibson Craig's father] carriage . . . the wrath of this party seemed to be unappeaseable, with the ladies particularly, for they were in dread of losing their Drawing room, and all having ordered dresses the idea of not requiring them was almost a weeping matter.

From the strange privacy of the Queen's entrance a report was gaining ground that she had resolved to make this a visit merely to the Duke of Buccleugh, that no one else was to see her, that she was to dispense with all forms, in short—make herself utterly disgusting. Why not wait for the *Gazette* suggested James, it will be published before the evening, but no one would listen to him. The next callers were Lady Napier, one of her daughters and Lady Kinloch, all equally furious. They had ordered two dresses each, one demi toilette, one full dress after different newspaper reports, and were so angry at being now stopt on the look out for head dresses that they meant to punish the Queen for annoying them by not going near her at all. Next came an Archer, he had been drilling for six weeks and all for next to nothing; this early entrance was so unexpected, this royal body guard was not half collected, very few were in time to meet and escort Her Majesty. In short the whole business was a botch.

A grand barrier had been erected at the end of the New-haven road where the Lord Provost and Magistrates were to have been stationed with the City keys on a cushion, the Trades were to have appeared at different stations to give their welcome, the Schools at others, Clergy, Literati, etc., all had rehearsed their processions, but alas! the performance had excelled their powers of activity, for nothing appeared to stop the Queen. On she trotted to Dalkeith like any other lady, even the Duchess of Buccleugh miscalculated, for she was driving about the town looking for her royal mistress long after the little Queen had left it. The Duke, Sir Robert Peel and one Bailie had waited for her at Granton pier and brought her from it. She had no other welcome, and perhaps she was not sorry, for she had been deadly sick, had hardly slept, looked ill, and was very tired, but that would not pacify the mob, they were half inclined to murder her and wholly inclined to murder the Provost. Chartists were haranguing in the high treason style—in short a regular ferment.

What could the Bailies do; they very wisely followed the Queen to Dalkeith and asked an audience of her ministers. Their reception was most gracious, the whole affair had been a mistake, Her Majesty had every desire to gratify a nation she esteemed so highly, whose country she had all her life been so anxious to see, the appearance of which had already so perfectly delighted her and as some unaccountable series of accidents had prevented her reception being what it was intended, she would have the greatest pleasure in making a royal progress on any future day, and would put herself into the hands of the Town Council, convinced that their arrangements would be agreeable to her.

Nothing could exceed the extasy of the Bailies. Sir Robert Peel who had carried all the messages between the two high functionaries, the Queen and the Provost, with unaltered patience just suggested that they must not be too hard upon her as she had little time and much to do,

which was faithfully promised and the dignities in their
robes and their coaches returned in the happiest humour,
placarded the City in no time with the mollifying news that
there was to be a royal progress through the City upon
Saturday with a return to Dalkeith through Leith, which
trusty emissaries disseminated the Queen's affliction at
the botch, her extreme anxiety to show herself, her
admiration of the town and the sea and rocks and the
mountains, her gratification at the enthusiasm felt for her.
Good humour was restored in a very short space of time.
She was really pretty, she had bowed unceasingly, every
body was sure it was all a mistake. Then came the Gazette
Drawing room on Monday—could human happiness be
more complete.

2. The Queen was to be allowed this day to rest, but no rest
for her subjects, they must recur again to the misfortunes
of yesterday, of two days for they were sitting on Scaffolds
all Wednesday in multitudes when the East wind kept
her away from them and she being exonerated from all
the blame of the spoiled entrée, who was the culprit, he
should not escape the malediction of the whole nation he
might depend upon it, no skreen should shelter him. The
whole town was the whole morning sitting in judgement
on every one in Authority, some said it was Sir Neil
Douglas, he certainly fired the two signal guns agreed
on but it was his business when he found no stir ensueing
to have fired two more, indeed many people thought he
should have fired every ten minutes to let us all hear
the Queen was in earnest. Two guns did not waken
any one, certainly not the Provost for he never moved
till a messenger came to tell him the Queen had landed
and then instead of going to meet her he assembled the
town Council and by the time they had put on their
robes and made their speeches she was half way to
Dalkeith, he had indeed sent Bailie Patrickson down to
Granton Pier the night before, but the Bailie only went
to bed in the Inn there instead of in his own house in
Edinburgh and the honest man slept rather long in the
morning.

Sir Robert Peel was extremely culpable in not stirring

up the trades and the Schools and the rest of the pageantries himself, he ought to have sent messengers every where
and he should have arranged the day before for bugles and
cannons to play and to fire so as to explain her Majesty's
movements. Then what was the use of meeting at the last
hour, this was the time for action. The behaviour of all
the authorities was scandalous. At length the whole fury
of the whole Edinburgh world was concentrated on the
head of the Provost of Leith. The Queen on passing up the
firth despatched a steamer into the port of Leith to notify
her arrival for the purpose of informing the whole world.
And the Leith people in the sulks at her not landing on
their pier kept the intelligence to themselves taking care
at the same time to be at Granton to meet her. Still the
Edinburgh people must bear part of their burden. Why
did they not believe the guns which they knew were to
give them just two hours for preparation and why were
they not ready for any notice.

3. All night long the countless crowd paraded in multitudes through the streets and very early in the morning
they began collecting in the different situations whence
they were to view the progress of the Queen. She left
Dalkeith at ten o'clock. We had our old seats in the
window of James Thompson's Chambers, commanding
the whole mound, the best point I should say in the
town, the moving mob was magnificent, pouring from
every direction for hours, ever as she passed from one
spot dispersing to add to the mass assembled to meet
her at another, every window filled, every street an
ocean of human heads, other sight there was none. The
Dragoons could just be seen above the crowd and the
coachmen of the different carriages, the Queen's white
bonnet, her Prince's uncovered curls, the enthusiasm
was great, and to the amazement of my radical friends
at several different places there was three distinct cheers
'for Sir Robert Peel', they had expected a hissing! You
live in a small clique of your own said I to James and
you will not understand how the world is progressing, Sir Robert Peel is the most universally popular
man in the Queen's dominions. When he is cheered

here, in this hot bed of radicalism he may laugh at opposition.

An appalling accident which we unhappily witnessed damped all the pleasure of the day. Owing to the rush of persons to the corner of a scaffolding in the gardens just opposite to our window, the supports gave way and hundreds of persons were overthrown among the wreck in the most frightful confusion. The yell that burst on all sides turned every feeling into stone. The gradual disappearance of row after row of wretched victims made the head swim. I thought the town would follow yet could not keep my eyes from the dreadful scene; none of us were right in spite of effort till we heard for certain that no life was lost, there being no one *under* the scaffolding, and the trees in the garden breaking the fall of many, and the good sense of the sufferers inducing them to lay still till proper persons came to relieve them prevented the very fatal consequences that must otherwise have ensured, Dragoons were instantly galloped down to keep off the mob, doctors sprung up on every side.

As the poor creatures were raised from the melancholy heap they were revived, or bled, or dislocations set at once, many lives saved certainly by this promptitude, altogether the casualties were wonderfully few, not above forty or fifty hurt, not more than the half of these with broken limbs. One lady had both legs broken but they were clean fractures and will be set with ease. A few poor ladies who from their situation would have been better at home out of the crowd altogether are likely to be the most serious sufferers from the accident.

5. About the whole of the Gibson Craigs and every thing in every way belonging to them there is a want of ease, quiet elegance, refinement, every thing in short, that marks the highly bred. Greatness has quite been thrust upon them and they do not wear it as if used to it. But where there is no occupation of any sort, no way of filling up time but by the help of a very ordinary class of acquaintance, one not intimate with the occurrences of the clique feels the life stupid.

9. I really believe we were quiet all this day. I took a

long walk with the children up the head of Leith Walk
over the Waterloo Bridge and all round and about the
Calton Hill where are now splendid roads leading to very
beautiful rows of houses commanding the finest views of
the old town, Salisbury craggs, Arthur's seat, and the
ever changing sea, the High School is also new, and
the monument to Burns and the unfinished monument
to Mr. Playfair, a copy of the Colisseum which Sir
Thomas Lauder very wisely endeavoured to complete
by dedicating every separate pillar to a separate worthy
and so leaving the matter to time. A grand memorial to
the collected talent of Scotland, but his proposal met with
no support.

12. Dear Baltiboys, all the luxury of this house a'n't worth
one cheerful evening at home. All the busy trifling of
the day here is heavy work to those who are used to
the rational occupations of a country life. It suits James,
however, whose habits are fixed by long bachelour ways,
his office and his Club with sales of curiosities, dinner
parties and now and then a visit or a day's shooting in the
country is his settled round. Jane will make it suit her, but
I think she sometimes regrets her flower garden, her pony
carriage, and her riding, however, the company, and old
friends will make up for much.

13. I walked thro' the Princess Street gardens which are really
beautiful, laid out as far as the Castle walls including the
rocks and the green hill side as a pleasure ground, there are
shrubbery walks, and wild paths, and a long, long avenue
of fine young trees, fields, flower gardens, kitchen garden,
such a piece of beauty in a town must be unrivalled in
Europe. At home I found your letter dear Hal, you have
been very good in writing upon the whole, seldom three
days without a letter to some of us, full of news so near my
heart, for there is nothing like home. I am longing for the
country, our green fields, our woods, our river, my garden
and all my home occupations, the days begin and end here
as elsewhere, and I get through them, but not with any
interest though my mother's happiness in talking to me
and the great kindness friends, who have none of them
forgotten Eliza Grant, makes me very happy.

14. The Queen returned from her Highland expedition this afternoon. I can't interest myself in her proceedings, so very seldom set down any of the quantity we hear about her, her progress thro' the very beautiful part of the highlands she visited must have been a magnificent spectacle. She was received by the wealthiest of our nobility dwelling in palaces far surpassing her own, amid scenery unequalled, and the peculiar dress and the graceful *address* of the highlanders must have added an interest she would be quite unused to. She was much struck we understand, so were all the English part of her suite, with the manners of the highland gentlemen and the highland peasantry, so self possessed, so entirely gentlemanly in their grade from high to low.

15. One of Sir John Pringle's daughters has been at Taymouth with the Queen. She is the most troublesome little creature that ever there was in the world, ordering and counter-ordering without consideration the whole day. She will appear at luncheon at such an hour, then not till another hour, then have luncheon at some place during her drive, then have it in her room, which is the general end after every body has been kept half the morning upon tenter hooks. She never sits down for more than two minutes and as every one must rise when she rises the company are for ever jumping up and down like Jack in the box, she thinks she will be quite as sick on her voyage back as she was coming, for an appetite like her Majesty's very few of her subjects possess, the quantity she consumes in a day is surprising. A large Scotch bun, the richest that could be made, was sent from Dundee for her first luncheon at Taymouth, she ate several slices, so did the Prince, who has a German appetite too. They always breakfast together in private at eight o'clock, which was a great comfort to people, and next morning they sent for the remainder of the bun and *finished* it. My mother's furious with her early hours, the Archer's bugle wakened us all by six and at half after eight the Castle guns announced her departure from Dalkeith for Granton pier, the streets are crowded with people flocking to see the last of her. Certainly she has made herself very popular

by her visit which seems really to have much delighted
her. Whether the nobles she honoured will be equally
pleased with the long bills run up through their loyalty
is a consideration. It has done good to trade, given a stir
to every one and will be long remembered as an era.

16. We dined at the Grange, Sir Thomas Lauder's odd but
very pretty old place, patched up with the taste to be
expected from him. Lady Lauder is very much aged, Sir
Thomas quite broke down. Altogether I cared less about
this visit than I had expected, he is still so entirely taken
up with his crotchet of the moment, and she as invariably
delighted with whatever nonsense amuses him.

19. Dwarkanaught Tagore[14] told us that the Queen made
herself most agreeable to him at Windsor, he dined with
her and they played whist and she took him to see her
children and hid herself behind the nursery door to enjoy
their surprize, he says they are not pretty children, but
healthy, very plainly dressed, the little Princess spoke
to him and holding up his shawl said 'how pretty',
upon which he promised her one as handsome. He is
a very wealthy Hindu merchant, come here thoroughly
to understand our ways, he has long lived in the English
fashion, quite got over all prejudices of Caste, despises
the whole absurdities of his race yet never makes any
parade of his superiour intelligence, he is a well educated
man, very pleasing in manner and address, speaking our
language beautifully. In religion he professes himself an
unitarian. He has been of the greatest use to William in
money matters, through his means a great deal has been
done towards the payment of the debts, £15,000 this very
year. My father helps, but the property has all been made
over to William who has taken all the charges on it and
expects to free the estate in four or five years when he
means to return and to live upon it, he hardly thinks my
father will ever return.

21. Jane and I had a beautiful walk, we went to leave a note at

14. Dwarka Nath Tagore (1795–1846) was the founder of the
    ill-fated Union Bank of Calcutta whose crash so involved
    the H.L.'s father and brothers.

the door of Mrs. Siddons in Maitland Street, from thence thro' new streets to the Dean Bridge where I came upon the back of Murray place (sic) and the Terrace gardens belonging to it hanging over the water of Leith and St. Bernard's well, which in my young days used to be a walk of a mile into the country, then through new streets and new crescents and new squares, past Warriston to Stockbridge and up more new streets and more new squares where I had left a dead wall and gravel walk into that part of the town I remembered. We made a few calls on our route. It was my father's birthday, we had turtle soup, pheasants, fine wines and a game of whist for my mother.

22. A nice walk round the Calton Hill with Jane and James. We went to call on 'Tommy Thomson' and his wife and to ask them to dinner. Poor man, he has been under a cloud for some time, lost his situation in the Register Office, from having used the publick money for private purposes and been discovered by having his accounts called for before he had time to replace it, for his friends and himself affirm that he never contemplated more than to borrow it, he had heavy debts besides so that he must have been very culpably negligent in the conduct of his affairs as was too much the custom with those of the last age. His salary as clerk of the Jury Court is given up to his creditors and his friends subscribed to pay the Government, he also sold his library and all his valuables, James bought much and lately, on poor Mr. Thomson taking up house again, returned him all those books he had purchased.

25. We had no letter from you yesterday so were charmed most unexpectedly to get one to-day, the children were quite agitated, they screamed with joy when they heard you were coming. Dear Hal, what a dream about your unworthiness and my superiority. That I have quick talents I know, I could not fail to inherit them, but they are as nothing compared with your strict integrity, your honest upright morally courageous character, few neglected as you were could have become what you are, I am little more than dross spangled. We had a very merry

evening, managing among us to make my mother chatter and laugh all night.

There came to-day from a bookseller a prospectus of a new work to be published early in '43, 'The Queen's progress' with engravings of all places, persons, objects, connected with this remarkable event and a description of all that took place, by Sir Thomas Dick Lauder Bart., price, large copy four guineas, small two guineas, human absurdity, where will it stop. He is off on a tour in her Majesty's footsteps in order to ensure accuracy and encrease enthusiasm. With his head full of this rubbish no wonder he forgot to speak to me. James brought in a placard t'other day that actually had been stuck up in one or two places when people were looking for places to see the Queen drive through, the omission of *one* letter made it read thus—'three widows to let, with a splendid view.' I have kept it to carry to Ireland to prove that our very wise Scotch friends can make blunders.

26. In the evening we had whist for my mother and oysters and ale, the little girls sitting up to partake they were so happy. It is certainly a task to amuse my poor mother, she has not an occupation upon earth nor won't have any, she can't converse, merely talk scandal and listen to it and to very silly gossip with an avidity that is childish. All her feelings too are wrong. I had almost forgot there were evil passions in human nature, I have lived so long where none are either felt or met with and it jars against my temper to find suspicion, envy, spite, idle curiosity and unkind constructions all in full vigour, in an old woman too within a footstep of the tomb. Much, much mischief has she wrought during her life, much would she still do were she with those who would be influenced by her, or who did not scrupulously avoid attending to her. Jane is too blunt with her though firmness is absolutely necessary. James manages her beautifully and she does not like him. Poor woman, what a wretched education they all had.

27. Craig Crook has the same look it used to have but it is much altered, much improved. Walls thrown down, fields bro't in, trees grown, house enlarged, gardens beautiful.

Lor Jeffrey is very well, as kind and as clever as in former days, more agreeable from being less affected, his manner is quieter, he don't wish to astonish, don't care about being thought a great man. She is perfectly charming, without an accomplishment on earth, plain good sense acting upon good feeling; the house is small but very pretty, the new dining-room a large, fine room added in the best taste, the grounds kept with perfect neatness, every thing flourishing. We had a good luncheon and between eating, talking, walking, passed a very happy two hours, at the end of which we promised to dine with them on Thursday. A son of Constable's came in with the prospectus of Sir Thomas Lauder's folly, a very handsome young man, quite gentlemanly in manner, distinguished looking, he is happily married and is thriving as a printer and publisher. A bitter disappointment awaited me at home. A letter from you to say you were not to come for us.

Well—to recruit our spirits we resoled to go to the play. Murray has his company acting in the Adelphi, a small neat theatre where we found a fuller house than we expected, a very decent audience, tho' none beyond respectable tradespeople, the pit and gallery were crowded, the boxes held only a sprinkling. Miss Nicol is first rate, *Peter and Paul*, a piece in which she and Murray are near perfection, displeased me from the moral being to raise the lower orders at the expense of the higher, too much the fashion of the day with the mob. A nobleman is made, not only ridiculous from vanity and false pride, but he is a coward into the bargain, having deserted his colours when serving with his regiment in Spain. This disgusting person is brought to his senses by a bricklayer, who, notwithstanding that he gets drunk, is endowed with every virtue, one of nature's noblemen, who lectures to such purpose that the hero and heroine of the piece, rather a stupid pair, are married without more ado. Murray's acting of this rough diamond makes it all natural, but the principle is bad, catering to the evil feelings of the populace. This bad most depraving system was carried to such a pernicious height in a grand nautical entertainment which concluded our evening's amusement that we could not sit it out.

A Captain in the Navy commits such atrocities on board his ship that we were quite unable to lend our countenance to such an exhibition, in times too of such danger from Chartism and other liberal devices, and James says if such a system is carried on he will enter the playhouse no more. He was completely angry, and really will, I think, take steps to have such a dangerous excitement to passions one would by every means allay, stopt with speed. It is unaccountable how Murray, a religious man, can permit the acting of pieces so dangerous to the well being of society. If indeed it require the rousing of the worst feelings to fill his seats, then are the rigidly righteous correct in denouncing the theatre, none should support it, it becomes when thus conducted a very powerful engine of mischief.

29. I have determined on packing up, after your note of yesterday I must not expect you and I see you are not well and I cannot stay from you longer. Much more I have heard and much I have thought and felt and seen during my very happy visit to my old country, too late to-night to rhapsodise or sentimentalise or even gossip, for one o'clock has struck and I must be early up to-morrow for we must leave this house soon after ten, and I am quite tired packing.

SUNDAY, OCTOBER 23. Poor Journal! not one word has been written in it since the night before I left Edinburgh, more than three weeks ago. Long after midnight on Thursday the 29th of September, I finished squeezing all our property into our boxes and starving of cold got into bed for a few hours sleep, a very few for I lay long awake thinking of the past, wishing impossibilities for the future and the dreaming sleep which followed was short and I was early up and had all our packages corded before breakfast.

We took seats in a first class carriage which we had to ourselves and by a little after one reached Glasgow. A walk of half an hour agreeably passed the time till we started for Greenock with one companion, a respectable looking person who got out at Paisley after obligingly pointing out all objects of interest to us and giving us all the local knowledge he possessed, he seemed like a small manufacturer, yet he was well versed in the history of his country, always concluding his remarks to Annie 'as you've read, my dear, I'm sure'. On reaching Greenock we found our steam boat was not expected till seven or eight o'clock.

We had a dull enough evening in our dingy Inn parlour with its one window looking on a very narrow street. One object, however, brightened us up a bit, it was a bookseller's shop whence we procured some of *Chamber's Journals* and Campbell's poems for 2/6. Not till after nine did that weary steamboat come down the river. The obliging landlord, who walked down with us and our luggage, gave us over in so significant a manner to the Stewardess of the *Mercury* that we had choice of place and I chose the floor, Janey and Annie lay on a sofa together.

We got slowly down the Clyde, the river from the long drought being very shallow, in the dark too they have to be careful. We lost the beautiful scenery of course, but to recompense us, quite early in the morning when I first went on deck the Irish coast lay before us. We ran down it almost without motion the whole day and by five o'clock saw dear Papa upon the pier watching for us, he looked so well, no one could have guessed he had been suffering from Asthma, he soon had us landed, packed the little girls with the luggage on a car, and he and I walked after them to Gresham's, where we dined. Thus ended the month of September, one of great enjoyment all things considered, very pleasant to look back upon from many causes.

We left town at three in a new four wheeled two horsed eight seated car, set up between Dublin and Blesinton by Mr. Kilbee which rattled us home in no time. We picked up the Doctor, quite part of our family, at six and all walked to Baltiboys to tea to the surprise of Miss Cooper, who expected us to arrive in a much more ceremonious fashion, and thus after five weeks did we reunite for the winter as happy a party as ever gathered round an humble fireside. Dear little Jack was quite overcome on meeting Janey, he clung to her like the vine round an old tree, and when he raised his little sweet face he was in tears.

29. Little worth recording has happened during this month of October. Very bad news from Pau, poor Mary caught cold, an inflammatory attack ensued, so serious as to threaten a speedy end to her accumulated sufferings. She began exactly as I am going on, an eternal cold in the head, cough with expectoration, water formed with me last winter, and oftener than is agreeable I feel that I have a *heart*. She is six years younger than I am, so I have weathered on longer by being wise enough to do as I am bid. Shall I live to see these dear children men and women?

30. The Doctor brought a cargo of penny magazines for our lending Library. By the bye I have twelve subscribers no less, and Pat Ryan buys candles and has a reading every evening, Nowlan the reformed schoolmaster reads, Pat, his sons, his young brothers and James' apprentices forming the audience, the women knitting. What will Ireland be by and bye, are there not hopes, seventy children too on the school rolls, but they attend so irregularly, seldom mustering thirty of a day. We are reading one of the *People's* books ourselves of an evening, Stephens' *Travels in Egypt*, Syria, the Holy Land. A lively American with sound sense enough to make a very entertaining account of very ordinary incidents. There is a freshness in American impressions of the old world that makes their remarks very interesting to us ancients.

31. Here ends October and if I intend this queer sort of journal of mine to be at all interesting to us in our semidotage, when the fireside will be the better of the enlivening recollections of more active days, I had better write a little more regularly in it than I have done of late, and more particularly for at present full half of the impressions it would be as well to remember escape altogether any notice, and the remainder get but small justice.

NOVEMBER 13. Sunday, rainy, no church. Let me think of

what we have all been about this last week. On Monday
the Colonel took his little girls up to Dublin to see this
extraordinary skeleton of an extinct race of more than
gigantick animals found in the plains of the Missouri.
This wonderful beast stands fifteen feet high, an elephant
could walk under it, and if we suppose him when *in flesh* to
have had a scaly hide he would answer in every particular
to the terrible animal in Job, translated Leviathan but
which no animal known to our present world resembles,
though Commentators have done their best to satisfy our
scruples. Publick news there is hardly any, rather good
from India upon the whole, unsatisfactory from China as
usual, for whether we take a fort or let it alone it makes
no sort of difference, we are never a bit nearer our object,
if we have one, which is doubtful. And as there is not the
remotest chance of producing any effect upon that curious
people I suppose when we have spent money enough our
ships will be all ordered home. At home all seems quiet
except in the church, a few colliers seem inclined to riot in
Scotland but nothing comes of it. In England all turmoil
is over, trade in some places beginning slowly to revive,
markets low, weather fine, there is nothing to grumble at.
A few young *ladies*, one with bright eyes, female Chartists,
have begun to amuse the world with harangues upon the
rights of women 'Oo hort for to ave woices' in the state
etc. In Ireland we are all tranquillity, long may it last.
We may thank good father Mathew for it as much as the
Government.

We are reading in the evenings D'Aubigné's history of
the Reformation and much interested in it though the
affected style, the French dramatick effect style, hurts
the book which is also too lengthy, he begins too late
too, only with Luther. Besides our reading, the little
girls come to me every evening for drawing and French
alternately, each lesson enlivened at the end by a chapter
of Mrs. Marcet's invaluable grammar.

14. The little girls came at five for the lesson they are to
have on Sundays in future. Doyley and Mant's Bible
with its notes, introductions, etc. I am anxious that they
should have good early impressions upon a subject on

which the whole happiness of their lives depends and
being carefully instructed in the middle way, shewn the
impropriety of either extreme, guarded against the laxity
of worldly feelings on the one hand and the fanaticism of
the evangelists on the other, they may rightly understand
the religion of their country, and rightly comprehend their
own duties towards their God.

16. Wretched day, not cold however. The Dumbie was to go
to Naas to the workhouse, herself and her unhappy baby,
whose cries she can't hear and whom she has no means of
providing for. She lived up to her present age, thirty-six,
among the neighbours, earning her food and clothing by
her hard labour, occasionally assisted by kind Miss Henry,
the friend of all the destitute. She has been for the last two
years with the Pendars where this misfortune occurred,
she had been bringing in large baskets of potatoes from
the field about a fortnight ago and was suddenly missed,
looked for and found in the cowhouse with her new born
infant. Mrs. Pendar moved her to the hay loft, made her
some gruel, but understanding from the poor creature's
signs that she accused her, Mrs. Pendar's brother, James
Butler of her ruin, this woman about to become a mother
herself, on the second morning turned this poor creature
out on the road, hungry, dirty and naked, for the few rags
she had on barely covered her, and her baby was wrapped
in a coarse apron. She lay in the gripe of the ditch till dark
weeping incessantly when she made her way to her old
master, Dick Gray, about the poorest man in Baltiboys,
he took her in, shared what he had with her, Kitty shared
her bed with her, Anne Casey the pedlar who lodges there
washed her and cobbled up some old things for the baby.
There I found this poor victim of as disgraceful a sin as
ever the unbridled passions of man had to answer for.

I don't mean it to be right to take all ill conducted
persons by the hand, still we should do our best for them,
many are reclaimable, many are more sinned against than
sinning. That made me help Eliza Waters and has not
the result been good? The poor Dumbie was even more
an object of unmixed compassion. She could never have
received moral instruction, she could neither hear or

cry out and she slept in a loft with this man her only companion in it. Hal was indignant at the shocking story, he has tried all means to make these horrid Butlers and Penders pay for their unchristian conduct, but alas! the law can't help him. James Butler swears he is innocent and nothing can be done, the priest however believes him guilty and after an interview with the poor thing and her interpreters set him down in his book as the father of this unfortunate child, whom he christened Eliza Butler. I hope Eliza is not in honour of my few shillings and neatly made baby linen, a small stock of which I am generally provident enough to have by me, old flannel strengthened by a cover of calico, old chintz cut up and patched may be, remember this Janey and Annie, throw nothing away.

18. James Ryan came last night to change his book, he asked for one with drawings of the new agricultural implements in it. I hope he is going to make some, he did make one for the Colonel, a horse hoe and very correctly and this looks as if it had been approved of. We are reading Mr. Stephens' travels. While with our feet on the fender and the wind howling round us we read of delicious climates, beautiful scenery, interesting localities, we feel so dissatisfied with our rugged northwest that very little would sometimes induce us to cut and run somewhere or any where when comes the Grand Turk, the autocrat of all the Russias, the Plague, the Pacha, earthquakes, etc. to bring us back to content in the chimney corner. So all is best as it is I suppose though I fancy I could improve things.

Janey has just passed through the room, going off to ride with her Papa in her new habit, new hat, new green veil, very neat looking but not pretty, nor will she ever be pretty though she often looks pretty for a while and that is quite enough, I wish for no beauties. What did my sisters and myself make of the dangerous distinction, anything but happiness, a more careful education might have prevented much of the evil which sprung from the undue value we put upon our personal charms, but . . . these useful buts, the better the education the less need there is for beauty of form, beauty of expression being so much more interesting and the more the mind is enlightened and the temper controuled and the habits improved the greater will be this more perfect beauty.

The Moores go to Dublin on Monday about servants, having had two regular thieves plundering them in the most artful way for months. Mrs. Cotton had much the same sort of story to tell me, which · reconciled me to Marianne's cobwebs, Hannah's fancy for dishing turbots with their backs up, Mary's unwashed stockings, Caroline's large stitches, George's very moderate capacity, etc, etc., all tormenting enough in their way but so preferable to vices that I shall resign myself to put up with good principles.

20. A present from old Peggy, the back griskins of her pig which she has really killed. What a commotion such an event must cause in the little household, poor old bodies, it will be the most delicious bacon ever cured, but all the comfort that so small a weight of consumable material will give, the skin for a sieve, and the lard for kitchen and the bones for soup and the blood for puddings and the inmeats, a week's dinners, it will be a merry beginning of Christmas for poor Peggy.

There have been latterly admirable leading articles in the *Herald*. One a finely conceived stricture upon the profligate of the upper orders and a truly English panegyrick on the staid old country family nobility who, residing for centuries on the same property among the same tenantry, spend their lives in doing good. And certainly these peers of the *tattered gowns* are an entirely distinct class from the newly manufactured batches on whom they look down, as I well recollect, with a sort of quiet pride that is to be expected from the high minded of ancient race towards those who by no merit of their own are raised into a sphere beyond their capacity to support the dignity of.

A second article was on the absurdity of fashionable life, the misery of mind produced by alternate excitement and ennui where no end but the amusement of the hour was followed. A third is on the very scandalous treatment of the *working* population, first brought into notice by the immense fortunes accumulated by manufacturers totally disproportioned to the gains of those by whose humble labours this wealth was acquired.

Our population is encreasing, our means of providing for it not encreasing in proportion, too much property seems to have got into too few hands, too many mouths have too little to fill them, there is a want of energy, a want of principle, a want of knowledge, that knowledge which alone will make rich. Agitation being, we may say, over, there should be nothing to interfere with our national improvement, the press is beginning to take this better part, let us hope that good will follow. A better system of agriculture by which a greater supply of nourishment may be extracted from the ground seems indispensable.

And to this end, intellect, knowledge, and capital all being necessary, *gentlemen* must turn to the profession of farming now that Law and war are out of favour with the times, treat the earth they till, scientifically, employing and paying well the thews and sinews of those used to labour. A thoroughly educated man of sense with his younger son's portion could make as much of *acres* as the same sort of man now makes of lb weights, the produce of these acres, and thorough integrity will be found to be the basis of good fortune in both, *in all*. I can't but think too that ostentation will by and bye give way before good sense, people will rather see a row of neat cottages filled with healthy happy human beings than the same value of money shut up in silver dishes on their table, this may be fanciful, even inconsequent, for political economists tell us the more we spend the more we distribute our overplus on those who require it. Very well, spend away, I want to save up nothing, but if I buy one velvet gown for myself do I do as much good as if I laid out the price of it on fifty cotton gowns for myself and my friends. I should like this explained to me when you come to this part of my imaginings, my dear Colonel Smith, you may read me a Lecture.

24. The publick news is a French telegraph announcing peace with China, on very good terms, too good we fear to be true. And then I have some private gossip throwing light

on those miserable Indian affairs which I shall set down for the sake of acting Bishop Burnet[15] to posterity—*my own* I mean, not having any intentions of the publick at large benefitting by me in any way, and that makes me just add that it seems to me to be quite a breach of trust to amuse the idle world with *family* papers.

27. Yesterday John Robinson came to receive the rents, it was a very busy day amongst us, the tenants paid well, what is quite as satisfactory they were well dressed, looked clean, fat, happy, are perfectly contented with the times and are most of them bit with the spirit of improvement. Wish to improve their land, wish to improve their houses, wish to improve their children. They are now most desirous to have a boy's school on the National system. 'They see the old method was no good, the girls are doing so mighty well entirely under Miss Gardiner, and the little boys, that they all wish for equal advantages for their big boys, they are willing to *help* to build an addition to my Schoolhouse'. Pat Ryan is to collect the subscription, can this be true, after years of struggling with their prejudices, true enough, it is the fruits of *patience*, kindness, forbearance and the real wish to benefit them, the sincerity of which they are now convinced of. I am so happy, the seed is sown, and even were my days to be cut short, some hand will be found to cherish them.

I have had a walk to-day, the first for a long while, John Robinson, Annie and I walked to the labourers' cabins, all the rest went to church, brought back no news. There can be none for a long while we have had so much, so glorious too, peace with China after a series of brilliant successes and the storming of a fort at the last, nearly as fine a thing as Ciudad Rodrigo[16]—on such terms too. Five ports opened for free trade, a Consul at each, the officers of the two nations to be treated hence-forward

15. Gilbert Burnet (1643–1714) Bishop of Salisbury and author of 'History of His Own Time' (1723).
16. The key fort whose fall to Wellington in the Peninsular War opened the way to Madrid. These terms are those of the Treaty of Nanking.

on equal terms. The expenses of the war to be paid by the
Chinese, an Island (Hong Kong) ceded to us in perpetuity
etc. The odious opium trade, admitted on our part not
to have been authorised by our Government, is our only
concession, while Sir Henry Pottinger in a circular issued
for the natives, enumerates four or five serious grievances
on account of which they richly deserve the chastisement
they have got. Steam is altering the Chinese like other
nations. The bravery of their Tartar soldiers is quite
barbarick, like the Russians they disputed every inch,
were bayonetted on their posts, then like only themselves
they strangled, drowned, stuck themselves, their wives,
their children while their General had himself burned in
his chair, perhaps from a dread of no quarter from us, or
more likely from their own Emperor, who would show
no mercy.

SUNDAY, DECEMBER 4. A note from Mrs. Jameson to announce
'*Norma*', and a coffee maker on a *new construction* for
the Colonel greatly superiour to all those he has already
collected, but which I expect to place shortly by their side
on a forgotten shelf in a cupboard while we continue to
boil our very good coffee with the help of a bit of muslin as
they do in the West Indies! Mrs. Jameson's '*Norma*' is in
Duetts for Janey and me, very well arranged. Mrs. Moore
brought it me as a loan arranged for one performer on the
pianoforte, three or four of the airs are worth copying
from their gracefulness, and a march is fine, but there
is a very great sameness in them, nothing original in the
opera. Janey said of it so well that no one can know who
is singing, while in Mozart's operas there can hardly be
a mistake as to the appropriation of the airs. I am glad
to learn it however, to keep up with the day.

At church to-day we had Mr. Moore to read prayers,
Mr. Alcock, a brother of Mrs. Gore's to preach, to
a crowded congregation, every pew full nearly, such
a charm has novelty [but] the theatrical exhibition of
Mr. Alcock was by no means to my taste; the sermon was extempore, wonderfully fluently poured forth
with an immensity of gesticulation, jumps and thumps
and striking together of hands and a voice ranting or

whispering, a sort of bad imitation of *Kean* I said; *young Kean*, Richard Hornidge said, which I daresay is more near the truth. The inflated style of some parts was at strange variance with the homely expressions made use of in others; probably had the discourse been corrected and delivered with more decency, the French *retenue*[17] is the word, it might have been reckoned good; on the parable of the ten virgins, who really persecute me, everybody seems to preach upon it.

As it was the preacher and his sermon gave the most entire satisfaction to the congregation generally. Miss Darker whom we picked up on the road never heard any thing more delightful, all the maids were in extasies. So these sort of Congreve rocket preachers are of use. Once or twice he put me a little in mind of Mr. Irving,[18] whom I had the luck to hear before he went quite mad. A finer voice, a nobler presence, language quite sublime and a manner imposing beyond any one can imagine, except Mrs. Siddons as Queen Katherine in her trial scene, made this wonderful man all powerful over every faculty while his genius remained under the controul of reason. I shall never, I think, listen to such eloquence again. Yet in the sermon I heard from him he taught me nothing, it was not exactly the Christian *pastor* preaching.

5. Whether my hero Akbar Khan will retain power or no he certainly deserves it. We leave his country, which we should never have entered, now that the honour of our arms is vindicated, and they may all fight among themselves till they weary, the origin of the war will hardly add to our glory as a nation. We, boasting of freedom, attempting to force a sovereign upon a reluctant people, and such a sovereign, the most worthless of a bad race, and his opponent respectable. The opium smuggling trade the

17. 'Attitude, qualité d'une personne qui sait se maîtriser, contenir ses sentiments, éviter les excès' (*Larousse de la langue française*).
18. Edward Irving (1797–1834): the flamboyant Scottish preacher and orator who enchanted fashionable London when the H.L. was there as a girl.

immediate cause of the China war was equally disagraceful to us, for had we wished to humble the Chinese out of a multitude of offensive vexations we might easily have selected an honourable cause of dispute, however, all grievances are now to be redressed, the haughty nation has humbled its proud neck and we may be the means of introducing knowledge and real civilisation among its crowded population. There is now peace on *earth*.

6. Plagued to death with the servants, their loves and their hates and their delicate health but take care to appear totally indifferent. We have gone on so well so long that I am spoiled, and fancied we were to swim on for ever, but I fear there must be a grand break up. Cupid has been my foe.

9. A visit from Lady Milltown of such a length, all about John Robinson whom she is in despair at losing as her Agent. She would condescend to much in the way of explanation or apology so as he will resume charge, and she thinks this decision of character of John's part will be a warning to Lord Milltown not to interfere between him and the tenants again. I feel for her a little, for her poor children much v) have but this precarious income to depend on for their maintenance, for him I don't feel and both him and her will be all the better for finding out that they must behave themselves civilly. No one will in these days tolerate airs, still less from persons by no manner of means respectable in conduct, rank without wealth too will go but a little way in these days of common sense.

11. John Robinson came down to consult his brother and the Colonel about the Milltown business, wrote a note to me to be forwarded to *her* explaining as much as was necessary to let her understand why he could not act with Lord Milltown and leaving it open to them to do as they pleased. He has no objection to retain the Agency, provided he is not thwarted by his absurd interference always so injudicious as really to hurt the value of the property as well as limit his wife's income. His love for popularity being so senseless that the most undeserving idlers, by flattering his vanity, got their debts excused, while an industrious neighbour, too well

principled to invent falsehoods, struggled on in poverty, without encouragement. This vanity of Lord Milltown's is a totally different thing from the lenity of a good landlord, it may so happen that the very best tenant may be behind in his rent, the reason can very easily be discovered, it may be a misfortune, an accident or an inconsiderate outlay beyond his means probably on some improvement which would in future tell. To exact the rent to the day from a person of character in such circumstances would be as unwise, as it would be harsh, though as a general rule and for the sake of the tenant himself he should be very strictly dealt with both as to his rent being paid to the day and that being fully high for the value of the land. All human beings requiring a stimulus to exertion and the farmer almost more than any other man of business needing to employ more both of mind and body to enable him to do justice to his holding. To give need to any plausible tale without enquiry is generally to offer a premium for bad conduct, few but the idle and disorderly ever making a habit of thus cheapening their own merits, and in Lord Milltown's case to grant releases to persons whom he had put under the controul of another who was responsible for his dealings with them was quite an impertinent interference.

15. Lady Milltown had a long talk with the Doctor, whether she will manage her Lord, who sometimes is obstinate beyond belief, we cannot tell, John will not budge one inch, he will do their business on his own terms, no other.

All these days I have been busy *hours* every morning getting the things belonging to the kitchen cleaned, never was such dirt, such thorough untidiness, and a breakage that was truly provoking. All used to be thrown on Mary Dodson, who to say truth did her part well, but the stately Hannah has cost me a fortune herself. One can't expect better from creatures so badly brought up, people must I fancy have a little more than they actually want just to keep the life in them, before we can expect any idea of *comfort* to enter their harrassed minds. In this part of the country existence is such a struggle, it is hard for them to be humanized in any way. Little Catherine Redmond is a good case in point. The first two days that she came to scrub and clean after Hannah left no one could do better. Wait, said I, we shall see presently. Accordingly she began by looking sulky, proceeded to be dirty, then disobedient, and finally ran off home. Being one of my pupils habit has given me great hold of her. After she was caught again I spoke to her as she could understand of her mother's poverty, her own duties etc., and she is behaving beautifully again. The bottom of the whole was the wish for *tea* for her breakfast like the other maids! She, who has often and often had but one meal a day and that dry potatoes.

Letter from John Robinson enclosing Lord Milltown's two impertinent letters upon the last of which John resigned the Agency, their tone is so insolent that had I seen them earlier I never would have obliged Lady Milltown so far as to ask any friend of my husband's to subject himself to a renewal of such impertinence. I could hardly have supposed it possible for a gentleman so to display an arrogance of temper that must make it impossible for any respectable person to serve him.

17. A letter from my father in which he notices very favourably Margaret Gillies. It seems so short a time since we were girls in Edinburgh at the harp class. Her mother came from a *cabin* in the highlands, a very bonnie but perfectly uneducated lassie, soon after the marriage of my father, whose distant connexion on the wrong side, she was; that, however, was always a claim in the highlands.

How many of these romances of real life could be collected from the highlands. It is a curious fact, not only that so many highlanders, men and women, should have risen to the first station in different ways from the meanest beginnings, but that these fortunate parvenus should all of them have worn their honours so easily, with such true nobility alias simplicity that one might live with them for ever and never once suspect they had leaped over grade after grade and atchieved their greatness. Hal will laugh at me, but there is a quiet pride, a simple dignity about a highlander that marks the manner even of the peasant with high breeding, they are never elated by success, they deserve it, they are never cast down by misfortune, they will retrieve it, and they are all kin to their Chief.

19. 20. 21. Disagreeable days, no one out but the Colonel who is proving that his health depends almost entirely on his spirits, for he is occupied really and fully with the draining of some piece of ground, where wet or dry, windy, rainy, foggy, he stands the whole of daylight and no sign of asthma has he, the newspaper even is neglected.

I have my hands full, having so much more to do below since Hannah went, but it is so much better done that I don't grudge the time. Only I do wish they would not take the people from the particular business assigned them to do any odd job going and every job indeed I may say. The yard boy, hired for the sole purpose of keeping all without clean, and feeding the animals, and who has abundance to do in his department, quite as much as a very active boy can do well was supposed to be of no use except as a jobber; first he was taken here there and everywhere, next given a pair of horses to groom and their stable to clean. I had been really angry two or three times about dirty steps, messy yard, wondered the gravel round the house and the avenue could be allowed to be in such a condition, at length the skeletons of two turkies coming after a pair or two of indifferent chickens brought matters to a crisis. Andy confessed he had totally neglected the work he came to do, not even preparing the food for the poultry properly from actual want of time, so I sent for Mr. Darker and after shewing him that *at least* thirty shillings had been thrown away besides very great discomfort having been produced by this regular Irish method of any body doing anything he told me he had observed himself, and John Fitzpatrick had told him, that Andy could not get through all that was put upon him and that he would release him from stable duties. I suppose the lad himself liked the stable best and so did the additional work first and left his proper business to chance moments. I had promised to go through the stables to-day, which were all to be cleaned for me but I can't get out, they are kept disgustingly dirty, I do wonder how the Colonel can allow it; a curtain of cobwebs over every window, the same gossamer drapery all round the walls, every bit of iron rusty, of glass coated with filth, of wood inch thick of nastiness, nothing clean but the horses in our stable, in the farm stable not even the horses. It is very hard to get cured, *telling* is no use, one must stand and see every order executed or 'tis but a farce to give it.

22. Still gloomy, very damp, far from pleasant though mild. I have heard of misery this morning that would make it a dull enough Xmas were the sun ever so bright, and we can't relieve it, which is worse. All springing from the want of principle among the people themselves. This case of the Kellys' is similar to the Kioghs'. A widow left with land marrying again and casting off her first family for the sake of the second, giving possession in fact of her son's patrimony to a stranger. What to do with these wretched Kelleys, who should be where red Paddy Quin is no one can tell, the Poor House is their only refuge.

23. 24. Had to give audience to half the world, some humbly begging for a little help, some asking merely for a loan, some with bright faces coming for their earning left till now in my hands for fear it should be spent in theirs, some merely wanting a 'couple of heads of cabbage'. There are few of our own people who require anything, and not many with any claim upon us in real distress. A change indeed since we came among them, still life is a struggle with poverty too generally, and unless better farming prevail and some occupation arise for the employment of the surplus hands this must remain a miserable country for another half century.

25. Sunday and Xmas day, dark and rainy and mild, old Irish weather which we are to have till we drain our land properly. I have been reading Mr. Stephens on the subject attentively for the purpose of fitting myself to help the willing, but it is still difficult to me and will require more reading and some conversation with persons capable of explaining much that I don't comprehend before I shall be able to explain to others.

What a pity that the country gentleman was not a generation or two back brought up to consider his truly enviable position as a profession to which time, money and abilities should all be devoted as entirely as if his daily work were to produce his daily bread. What an amount of happiness for himself and others would have been accumulated, what an amount of *wealth*, one of the *means* of happiness, and misery spared too on all sides. It is doing now, even here, a little late, but the Irish gentleman is at last waking from his dream of idle pleasure, which never satisfied, which deteriorated his character, impoverished his resources, spread distress around him, and left him to drown reflexion in his bottle.

Contrast this melancholy picture of human nature, such as it must always be when not raised by high principle to a correct estimate of the duties incumbent upon each in his particular station with the intelligent, well informed, well educated father and friend of all belonging to him, able to instruct and to assist and to act himself as a model to others. With command of temper to bear patiently with the ignorant, to forgive much, to be content with small progress, to wait like nature for great results in a remote age from imperceptible beginnings in his own. How careful should his own education be to fit him for so responsible a condition, a moral philosopher, a well-read historian in the comprehensive view of the term, a good lawyer thoroughly acquainted with the laws and the customs, the religion of his country. Master of the sciences, for he will have to apply them all, his information cannot be too general, he will want it all, nor his accomplishments either for they will materially add to his usefulness, his moral character too must be above reproach, for upon it must he depend for his influence. The long and the short of it is that the better people are the better they do their business. Mothers, you have the destiny of the world in your hands, indubitably.

DECEMBER 31. Saturday and farewell to a happy year, for upon the whole notwithstanding some anxieties it has been a happy year. We ourselves all thriving. And by quiet living we have got before the world again. Our people are improving our children are daily becoming more companionable, our position here continues truly agreeable, affairs in general look much more promising than they did a year ago for *peace* has revived commercial activity and with the exception of the Kirk in Scotland, a little Poor Law agitation in Ireland, and some *Chartist* noise in England all seems likely to work together for good. It is a fine mild Xmas though not a healthy one, old people going off fast as is usual in *green* winters.

Little has happened during the week, rather more letters than usual but not much in them, the newspaper stupid enough too except that a report of an Agricultural Meeting at Belfast where Mr. Smith of Deanston lectured on this new mode of draining perfected by himself, an honest practical farmer, has quite enlightened me upon the subject, taught me as much as will be necessary to set others a going. They say, resolve to do anything, no matter what and it will be done. I mean to drain and to improve the property of Baltiboys, if I live a few years we shall see whether I do it. Hal laughs, so he always does, if he win too all will be well. Just fancy getting from eight to ten per cent on your outlay immediately and for ever. Little Jack, if you become a rich man you will owe it to your poor mother. Laugh as you please, Colonel Smith.

I am writing on for somehow I don't like parting with the old year. We are to sit up and drink it out in negus upstairs and punch below, but it is never a merry farewell do what we will with it, for alas as years run their course they seem to get shorter and shorter, leaving in spite of our best intentions too many things undone.

FOUR

1843

All the themes and threads of the first three years journalising reappear in this year but increasingly she and her husband are absorbed by the need to get their finances on a firmer footing in order to equip their children for what she regarded as their station in life and to effect improvements on the tenantry. The whole family therefore left in August for France; after a year in Pau and another in Avranches, the Smiths returned to a very different Ireland.

THURSDAY, JANUARY 12. We are reading in the evenings aloud and John Robinson has got us such a bargain, Miss Edgeworth's works in eighteen volumes for two guineas—invaluable where there are young people. With Miss Edgeworth and Mr. Chambers the education of a family would be independant of parents, the least fortunate in this respect with such assistance may turn out most worthily.

15. Poor Mr. Gore! What a loss to his family—what a loss to this country! Just and firm and kind, liberal, industrious, patient, steadily pursueing his plans for general improvement without frightening the ignorant by over rapidity; and with great influence over Lord Downshire, an influence gained by the value of *character*, he would, had he lived a few years longer among us, have altered the whole of his extensive charge.

22. Sunday The country looking well, the people in spirits, and here at least we know nothing of the turbulent opposition to the Poor Laws which is distracting the south. A war with France seems likely again, and as there is peace everywhere else we should soon whip that absurd nation into humility.

23. Lord Milltown and Richard have ended this their second lawsuit amicably in the same way they ended the first,

the least expensive in the end I really believe to Richard, who can well afford to pay a few hundreds for quiet and certain possession of his rights, and poor Lord Milltown will have a short respite granted him by this means on his road to ruin—how he goes on or gets on or holds on no one can conjecture.

31. Meetings everywhere about some alteration in our Irish Poor Laws; it is becoming more unpopular every day and is a subject altogether beyond my comprehension. This plan seems to do little good and to cost much—no one proposes a better—misery is encreasing. All an individual can do is to employ as many *workmen* as possible, and give as much spinning, knitting and needlework, in short any work that can be done *at home* and as they can afford, to the women.

SATURDAY, FEBRUARY 4. Mrs. Doyle (Judy Ryan) has a daughter just six months from her marriage. A poor young girl who, in her innocence, is drawn into errour, loses character for ever when her sin, for such it is, becomes known—this old widow, without excuse of any sort for her irregularities, because the man married her will merely shock her acquaintance for a week or two and be a decent woman afterwards. But she won't find me quite so forgiving. She had the want of decency to send to me for some medicine. I shall be a little surprised if she ever send to me for anything again.

9. The Doctor was full of poor Mrs. Gore's distresses. She mentioned to Lord Downshire her intention of leaving Blesinton last Friday; his answer conveyed his pleasure at the news—not that he would on any account disturb her, but he confessed he did not like this 'interregnum' and he thought the sooner the new Agent could enter upon his duties the better. After this she can't bear the idea of sleeping another night in the house. She has been looking for lodgings in Blesinton—none to be had. The Doctor has offered his house, which she seems to have a delicacy about accepting, and he wants to enlist me in his cause, so Hal and I are to walk in to the village this morning.

TUESDAY, MARCH 8. And the poor Gores are gone. They were

worthy people and though they had that twist in religious matters common to good hearts where the imagination is strong and the head weak, one could quite get over it from their excellence. It is merely the spirit of popery—the delusive hope that *penances* and *ceremonies* will prepare us for heaven—and where the temper is cheerful, less harm is done than one would at first sight suppose; the gloomy or the sullen become really pernicious under the influence of these so-called evangelical feelings filled with bad dispositions themselves and blighting all around them.

19. [The girls] must have a more cheerful companion than poor Jane Cooper, one who can enter more fully into their plans, associate herself with their occupations, accompany them in their walks be active and merry and busy with them and for them.

Poor Jane's spirits, naturally low, have become quite gloomy. Dear good creature, if it were only herself she should be nursed among us with affection to the end of her days; but she requires a room, the best room in the house, to herself, a maid night and day to attend upon her, for she cannot raise herself upon her couch without assistance. An extra washing for her every two or three days, high living, messes at all hours of the twenty-four, a doctor daily almost. And all this we could do were it all, or but for a time, but the Doctor can see no end to it. She may linger months, years—she may not get through one year—she may in time with care recover, but when or what may or what the recovery be?—always an invalid—probably a cripple. And we with our small means must have another governess, another children's maid—we who can hardly make the two ends of the year meet as it is. My own health being very infirm too and I going without the comfort of a personal attendant from the feeling that we can't afford it.

20. No news going. A hope of the Kirk of Scotland listening to reason—the refractory parsons are some of them giving in—Government has been quite firm, but very temperate and their exposition of the dispute has much diminished the Kirk's supporters. On both sides the argument has been conducted with perfect temper, indeed the whole

session has been remarkable for the gentlemanly tone of every debate. Would that such calmness could reach Ireland, where the violence of every feeling is displayed with the heat and the folly of lunaticks. All sides sinning alike, all parties, all creeds, and on all matters, publick, scientifick, religious, domestic. They will fight to frenzy about the placing of Jack straws.

I am sure I wish they would *work*—the servants at least—we should all be a great deal more comfortable; their frightful idle habits are intolerable. I at any rate will not put up for another month with their dirt and their gossipping and their utter carelessness and indifference to our interests. The very moment I am better I'll put an end to our discomfort. There is no enjoyment of life while one has to act slave to one's own servants. Catharine Redmond, the child from school, the only one in the house who knew the meaning of *order* had to be sent away for a dirty habit never cured in her infancy; besides she nearly set fire to the house reading in bed—burned all the bed clothes, and in the morning never told.

24. The dear Children's first sorrow—their canary bird is dead. He was killed by the cat, who had stolen into the room and concealed herself under the bed. So she had the whole night to worry her victim. It was hard to comfort Jack. All were in tears to Miss Cooper and Caroline, for Dicky was a great pet, so tame that he flew about the room, fed from their hands, sat on their heads or hands or shoulders. He was buried under a rose tree in a coffin and wrapped in flannel—a very melancholy procession of maids and children bore the loved remains to the grave, and the tears that fell were many and most sincerely shed. Nobody speaks of him, mirth is gone and the cat entirely out of favour—she was publickly whipped by the side of the cage and is banished to the kitchen.

Jane has written a very nice letter to Janey with an account in it of a Mr. Oliver who dined lately with them—the greatest and best farmer in Scotland—he began life as herd to his father, a small farmer; at twenty-one commenced his own education, learning Latin and all those sciences necessary for his profession; he attended the college at Edinburgh regularly, working hard in private to make up for previous ignorance. He is now turned of forty, is very intelligent, very wealthy and very modest. He rents large farms, makes £5 an acre of tillage, £40 an acre of grass—all which history we read to Tom Darker, he is really enlightening. Last Spring he was going to give up his place because the Colonel insisted on drilling his potatoes and having turnips. The other day he said he would do a job I wanted whenever the spring work was over. 'That,' said I, 'will be such an age.' 'Not at all,' replied he, 'sure we'll drill all the potatoes, they'll be done in a crack.' I was prudent and said nothing.

28. A letter from Mr. Gardiner earnestly recommending our removing before winter to Pau. Mary is pretty well. He thinks the climate so restorative, and living being cheap, masters good and plenty, society agreeable, scenery beautiful, he thinks we should do wisely in many respects to go there and that it would really set me up.

SATURDAY, APRIL 2. When we went to India in 24 the Highland Coach from Inverness to Perth which had been running for a few years three times a week began to run during the summer months daily. Our post bag was at first carried by it as a favour, but latterly a mail bag was officially sent and there were receiving houses at Kingussie and Lynwuilg—now these little places are post towns—the *Mail* goes that road the year through and there are besides two daily coaches. I believe if I were to return now to the loved land of my fathers I should grieve like my good Aunt Frere and exclaim that the romance of the Highlands was gone. 'Ah,' said she with a dejected manner when I was with her in '23 at Hampstead and was detailing with great glee all the improvements so rapidly proceeding there, 'ah, my dear, I remember when we could get nothing there but what the farm produced and the household manufactured. Sometimes we were without a loaf of bread, sometimes were without ink or pins or thread. There was neither shop nor market within six and thirty miles. It must be sadly like the rest of the world now.' I defy them to get a railroad through

Drumochter or a steam boat on the Spey. We shall be spared that humiliation though all the remains of feudal times are so fast disappearing.

Really and truly as my Aunt Bourne says the servants of these days almost drive one frantick. That brings me to two letters, one from her and one from Jane, who beseeches us instead of continuing to live in the scrubby way we do and hoarding up our income to leave them all fortunes, to spend our abundant spare money on a really accomplished Governess . . . a mere dream. I like to educate my children myself, considering myself much better fitted to form their characters and to judge of the proper period to cultivate their different faculties. I merely require a cheerful, good-tempered assistant to take the fag of daily instruction off me with ladylike manners and a judicious method of playing the part of companion to us all. I undeceived her with regard to our circumstances—I sent Jane an abstract of our gross income, the heavy charges upon it, the small sum that remained for us to live on, and assured her that so far from saving, we had a hard matter to bring the two ends of the year to meet, particularly as neither of us could be called economical. She with £2,500 a year, no child, and rich relations all helping, all giving, little feels the difficulty of keeping a family respectably on £600. Aunt Bourne begs me to get a sensible governess to assist me and in the prettiest way entreats to be allowed to send the Governess—in other words, her salary—dear good Aunt. She is always doing these generous things to some one, but I undeceived her, and proved to her that, small as our means are, we do dispose of them as to leave sufficient to bring up our children in the rank they belong to.

24. Two long walks with the Colonel—one to the school to settle about the new room for the boys, and we looked at the little kitchen we are building for Miles Byrne on our way home. The other was to Blesinton, which tired me a good deal. We killed our first stall-fed beef, and selling it at 4d. a 1b. and honestly charging ourselves with all expenses, made a clear profit of near £5. A acre of turnips and an acre of hay will feed four well, so that

style of farming would pay well; however, in this case, we had the butcher's profit also.

Aunt Bourne has written to me twice—such letters—She had laid aside £50 for the salary of a governess for our little girls and take it we must, apply it as we like; but she wishes, *entreats* it may be one means of inducing us to winter at Pau. She is very anxious about me, speaks most sensibly about the wisdom of taking things in time; argues so very justly about the numerous advantages of a change to all of us that I believe she will prevail. Much as both of us love this place, sorely as we regret living away from it, there are many reasons which make the plan desirable. Hal has made up his mind to it, I think, and I believe all he *well* considers he always decides rightly on. My kind Aunt then proceeds to say that though she gives a good deal of her income away, as I know, she yet saves a good deal, and that fearing my Mother would be slenderly provided for in the case of my father's death, she had made her will leaving the interest of all her little savings to my Mother for her life: at her death small legacies among us, and *me* her residuary legatee. Thus between the portion my father is to leave me and what my kind Aunt has willed me, dear Hal will get sufficient to provide for his two little daughters without encumbering poor Jack's inheritance.

30. Book day yesterday, but I forgot, so tomorrow those most amusing *Memoirs* of Madame Junot must go to Humphreystown. What a state of society that book discloses—what immorality, what frivolity—Buonaparte's Marshals might be brave, their young wives beauties— wit and luxury and pleasure did abound, but it was a Court of under-educated people, but superficially polished, not thoroughly accomplished, fortune thrust upon them, and very brilliant was their short career. Those that sow chaff can't expect to reap corn. They are gone—all—leaving little trace of good behind—they knew it not by sight or name—how could they practise it? Yet it is interesting to get behind the scenes even of a puppet show when the puppets were amusing, and these Kings and Queens of a day were most diverting

in their dressing rooms. Poor Rameau, my dress-maker, who was one of the femmes de Chambre of Pauline,[1] is delightful upon this subject—she saw much, but is discreet in telling.

SATURDAY, MAY 14. Now for a little review of the last fortnight that I may get clearly into my head all we are arranging. Having determined on going abroad for two years we have offered to let this house for that term, furnished, with the garden, orchard and good stabling and for a good tenant might throw a cow's grass into the bargain, asking £150 a year and the gardener's wages. It is a good house for a private gentleman even in its unfinished state; our three children and our four servants are luxuriously lodged in it. We are finishing the three rooms, the study, drawing-room and bedroom over it, that they may be ready in case of any tenant requiring one or all of them.

We shall sell the Jaunting car, all the harness and saddlery, all the riding horses. We hope that the sale of all these will pay our journey to Pau, and that the rent of the house with the Colonel's pay will be sufficient to keep us there. Then we can leave the rents of the Irish property to accumulate, as Tom Darker thinks the profits of the farm should nearly pay all the unavoidable expenses attending the estate. I have written to Mary to take for us for a twelvemonth the apartment they are just leaving for a more expensive one, to hire us a cook and a footman. We shall take Harriet, our own maid, with us, and we shall require no governess till we are settled at Pau. Mary knows of a daily one so good we may be tempted to engage her permanently.

There is a good deal to do with the boys' school to set agoing, thorough draining to begin, the house to get ready, and our travelling equipment to prepare—though this last shall be limited to a small stock of Linens for each in good order and those few etcs. which Mary says are not to be had in France—namely, needles, pins, tapes

1. Pauline (1780–1825) has been seen as the most beautiful of Napoleon's sisters; her racy *Mémoires* were published in eight volumes after her death.

and sewing cotton, Fry's cocoa and linen for shirt collars. All else is best got where one is living as it is wanted: the additional penny or two per yard for calico could not be equal to the carriage of an additional trunk. We shall therefore travel light, taking no plate beyond forks and spoons, nor books except for the schoolroom, nor house linen beyond the week's supply.

We shall all feel the parting, indeed the break up altogether is far from pleasing. We were so happy here, were doing so much good, all was thriving round. Twelve busy years have we lived here in the enjoyment of all that could make rational beings comfortable. The last three winters, have, however, made a sad change in me, the first passed as accidental derangement, the second staggered *me*, the third frightened *Hal*, and I am sure not causelessly. With Mary's example before our eyes it would be worse than folly to try a fourth; so no sentimental nonsense shall overset me, feeling our removal right, I will make it agreeable, so *couleur de rose* must brighten all.

One thing, no one need wish to stay in this country till it be a little safer to live in it. This Repeal absurdity sooner or later will come to bloodshed unless the signs of the times change greatly. The Government were endeavouring to let the folly die away, evaporate in nonsensical speeches at mob meetings, but the meetings have grown into such enormous assemblages, the speeches become so seditious that even without leaders these masses of rebellious spirits were looking formidable and the apathy with which Ministers were reproached by their anxious supporters has had to give way. As much to encourage the well-disposed as to awe the unruly, the Duke of Wellington in the Lords, Sir Robert Peel in the Commons, replied to questions, purposely I suppose put by Lord Rodon and Lord Jocelyn, his son, that the Queen and her government were determined to preserve the integrity of the Empire at all hazards and at all risks and that they were watching the mischievous agitation now deluding part of the people of Ireland with the most careful anxiety.

Sir Robert Peel's speech was exceedingly dignified. Not one unbecoming expression—calm, firm and perfectly conclusive—it will have immense effect, though of course Mr. O'Connell's plan is to bluster in great style. I cannot but pity a man of his talents sinking in old age into such contempt, Shakespeare's accompaniments of old age. 'honour, credit, troops of friends:'[2] stand to mock the decline of him who is Bankrupt in all sense. The English all wonder where his millions go—he don't get them—the figures of his various rents stand to ornament the newspapers, little more—those so ready with their names lend little more to the *regenerator*, and many names are set down without even the knowledge of their owners. O'Connell owes £40,000 to the National Bank and threatened to break them if they pursued him for it.

I remember believing this unprincipled man to be honest though mistaken, a patriot a little mad; but either he is the mere tool of a crafty priesthood or he fancies he makes tools of them for some selfish purpose of his own—the gathering a fund to supply his extraordinary extravagance, for he is a very ill-living man in private life—probably a little truth in both ideas—he has not the slightest intention of carrying the repeal: knows well it can't be done. Merely unsettles the common people, for no one else minds him, out of vice. The only one of our tenants who attended the immense meeting at the Curragh last Sunday was Pat Ryan. I am inclined to hope it was mere curiosity took him there, but it was a very foolish proceeding and will prevent the Colonel adding to his farm as he intended, as he could not for the sake of example select for such a mark of approbation the only agitator on his property.

I see old Sir Richard Arkwright is dead at eighty-six, I recollect passing part of a very pleasant day with him and his nice old wife at their pretty place near Matlock; the house was not large nor richly furnished nor were the grounds very fine, nor style beyond that of a country

2. *Macbeth* v iii 24–5

gentleman of three or four thousand a year. He met us at one of his mills, told us he would take his working coat off, a white one for the cotton dust, and follow us up to his early dinner—three o'clock.

I often think over that winter spent among the manu-facturing *gentlemen* of England. It was a surprise to one of 'gentle blood' to come among those who made no account of noble ancestry and yet with the feelings and habits of educated people conducted, as the 'Baillie' would say, their 'Wabster and Spinner'[3] business with attention and enjoyed the elegance of their homes none the less for having earned their luxury.

15. The Miss Henrys kindly brought the little girls home in their covered phaeton yesterday. John Hornidge Jr. called to return one of Miss Edgeworth's novels, which he has been three months reading; and the Doctor came to see his patients—he is still rather savage about the Pau scheme, but beginning to get used to the idea of losing us, though far from being reconciled to it. Certainly he will miss us much and we shall much miss him.

17. The estimate for completely finishing the house inside and outside will be in round numbers at the most £150, but this without chimney pieces, grates or *paper* in the two lower rooms or fine painting the wood in the drawing-room. We have made out that we ought to get £200 for what we have to sell, which will leave a balance the right way.

24. Hal is off to a Poor Law meeting at Naas. The agitators are doing as much mischief there as elsewhere. A note to Jane from Henrietta anticipates a rebellion in Ireland evidently, people in London seem quite frightened, very needlessly; it is possible, though not probable, that there may be a little bloodshed, but the whole thing is mere bluster that will die away of want of fuel. Mr. O'Connell's most ridiculous bravadoes prove that he is quite aware the game is up, but he sadly unsettles the poor deluded mobs he gathers here and there.

25. Forgot to set down that Hugh Henry came on Tuesday.

3. Baillie Nichol Jarvie in Scott's *Rob Roy*.

He staid luncheon only—seemed to think £150 more than people liked the idea of giving for a country house without any ground. We were told to ask it by several who ought to know the value of such property. A house is a house with the Irish—conveniences, luxuries, necessaries to the civilised, go for nothing with them. One large reception room for their occasional state parties is more prized by them than would be rivers of water.

27. We have I believe secured Miss Hart as governess. She knows we can't give her £50. She will come to us for anything we *can* give her, and she will be of the greatest use to us in every way—first on the journey, she having travelled so much in France, next with the children, who have been suffered of late to get too idle, last, to me, for she will take every sort of trouble off me. Should we get Margaret Fyfe also we shall really be set up—*paying for the same*—but what is money for but to make us comfortable, which we have never been since I became unable to attend to all domestick details and since poor Jane Cooper was laid up.

We are to give Miss Hart £36 without washing. Jane C. had £25 with washing which in her state of health has been very expensive to me; her wine and ale and porter have cost a great deal, her fire night and day at all seasons, the time of a servant nearly occupied attending to her, obliging me to put out needlework, and presents of little things to the Doctor on her account, have altogether made her costly enough, poor soul—not that I grudge it, but it makes me think that active, healthy Miss Hart will not be a more expensive governess. I am truly glad we are to have her, for I believe her to be an admirable person.

28. Sunday, John came yesterday but collected very little rent I am afraid. We shall hear all particulars on Monday. Times really are bad. Between weather, bad farming, dull sales and political perplexities we cannot expect agriculture to prosper. But they take advantage of the outcry many of them who might pay well enough. Some apparently the worst off have paid the best.

Mr. and Mrs. Moore and Miss Casey called, came to balance accounts with us. We had a consultation about our Book Club matters and resolved on spending the money now in our hands on more books, then calling all in and holding a lottery without any blanks, so to dispose of our stock and end the business. All agree it never could be kept a-going without the 'flapper' so till we return that and many another improving project must slumber.

In the afternoon, late, Lady Milltown called, despatched all our children out or upstairs, or anywhere to be rid of them while she unfolded really a vexatious matter to a friendly ear. My Lord has three Italian children whom he has educated in their own country, unluckily, under the wing of their Mother. The eldest of these, a young man of nineteen, appeared the other day in London in the Hotel where his father is staying to enquire what was intended to be done with him. My Lord appeals to my Lady and with all their titled friends, their rich connexions, etc. sends her to Colonel Smith and me for assistance. *She* is most willing to help the boy to *earn his own bread. He* seems inclined to put him in a higher position, half feels his way towards his being received at Russborough. *I* supported her view, for everybody's sake, more especially the young man's own, whose head has been already unsettled by folly imbibed somewhere, for on meeting a friend in Paris he mentioned being on his way to his *noble* father in England with great flourish, 'car, je suis Milor'. The ridiculous name Lord Milltown manufactured for these poor children is against him and must really be altered—*Mr. Fitzleeson.*

Many schemes were turned over which his want of *English* and English education and his age also render unavailable. Others were suggested feasible enough in time, for the present she has written to advise his being boarded in some decent lodging for a week or two while they try to get him as usher for foreign languages into some school where he might be taught other things for teaching what he knows himself, namely French and Italian. She says this sort of coolness is the only way to bring her Lord to his senses on the subject. She had always wished those children to have been taken from a worthless mother and out of a profligate country and brought up and provided for in respectable professions or trades in England. Now with heads full of nonsense, with faulty education and morals not to be certain of, what is to be done with them?

The Irish Lord Chancellor has dismissed those magistrates who have taken part in repeal meetings since the declarations of the Duke of Wellington and Sir Robert Peel, amongst them are the names of *Daniel* and Maurice O'Connell, and he has written I think an admirable, because so temperate a letter, a circular, to accompany the writs of supercession. The Colonel and the *Mail* differ from me.

The general assembly of the *Kirk* has met and been beautifully addressed by her Majesty and the disaffected clergy belonging to it have seceded—walked out of the hall to the number of near 100, been joined by their brethren in absurdity and have formed themselves into the free something or other—very calmly, more in sadness than in glory, the pride perhaps that apes humility. They have been regretted by the wise remainder in the same sober spirit; there is no acrimony anywhere. The ministers who have lost their parishes offer to do duty in them till their successors be appointed. The Commissioner bears full testimony to their merits as a parish priests and will make their fall as light as is consistent with the maintenance of the laws. He will if he can keep them hanging on the skirts of the Establishment though they are no longer of it. So the nineteenth century is an improving age. We may expect a *degree* of wisdom in reality from the twentieth.

29. Very busy morning. Carpets up, curtains down. Dusting, rubbing and scrubbing everywhere. Jane and Anne Cooper packing their trunks. John Robinson intending to be away early in the morning, made up his accounts with us before going to bed. The tenants upon the whole have done well, they are no more in arrear than they were on closing accounts last year—indeed a pound or two less, and they are most of them in more comfortable circumstances than I ever remember them. So that having 'kept their own' during this very trying period we may

fairly hope better days are coming in which all the well-disposed will thrive. Pat Quin, of course, paid nothing—he owes more than a year's rent now—his ground nearly ruined, his cabin a wreck; he will not be got out without trouble, though he *promises* to give up his land peaceably in November. J.R. owes us a balance of £50 before receiving these rents, so we shall get on well, though there will be a serious outlay for the finishing of the three rooms, doing the outside of the house and adding the little necessary furniture—£200 I should think.

MONDAY, JUNE 12. The evening being very fine we took a drive and found all the fashionable world in Blesinton—the village street crowded with carriages. Mr. Gilholy's door and shop quite Grafton Street—the monthly fashions had arrived—the Miss Smiths' muslin dresses had been finished according to the latest improvements and were there exhibiting to the publick. We bought some calico, then drove to school with our bundle to be made into coarse shirts and shifts and to enjoy the new map of the world just sent up and giving such delight to all those poor little creatures, many of whom pointed out the various parts very correctly.

18. Hal likely to get over this attack of bronchitis well. He was downstairs yesterday evening, played whist till midnight, he and the Doctor against Hugh H. and my brother *John*. The poor Doctor was so kind to Hal and has come down from the clouds so good-humouredly after all, put the leeches on himself, staid two hours by the Colonel's bedside, would not join us that night—was evidently ill at ease, but yesterday he had got over all his nonsense, he slid into his usual position in the family and was quite himself again. I wrote him a little note to beg of him to come to see Hal and with a few honied words gave him a smart tap or two well merited by his fit of absurdity. I am resting in my own room after the heat of Church and the drive to and from it, and Hal laying asleep on the bed beside me, I can only talk to my journal for company and set down in it what impression my brother has made on me.

It is better than I expected. He is not so eccentrick, so absent or so half asleep as they all led me to suppose, but he is odd, very odd, very pre-occupied sometimes in manner, silent, yet knowing what goes on, often pleasant, gentlemanly, clever, and must be reckoned on the whole agreeable by those who have time to wait to find him out, for he don't strike at first.[4] His appearance wofully disappointed me. I parted from a handsome, graceful, tall and finely proportioned boy, I meet an over-grown, indolent, slovenly man, ugly in face, unwieldly in person. His very features are distorted—eyes that were once good, sunk in surrounding fat, nose drawn up to a regular cock, cheeks falling on his collar. I was shocked, nor have I yet got over it; I look at him and think, can this be John? The Grecian Apollo—fifteen years alone should not so much have changed him. I should not have known him. He says I am little altered—older of course, stouter—more like my Aunt Bourne—still quite myself. I think he flatters.

19. John and the Doctor came back at ten, they had walked all over the Town, gone to the repeal meeting! dined at Hugh Henry's and were in high spirits. John begins to think the repeal agitation must end seriously—he had no idea of it till he saw the crowded room—the regularity of the business, the bag of money, the system of perfect organisation pervading the whole arrangements. What can O'Connell mean. I don't give up my belief for all this—it *was* mere humbug whatever events may force it into, on O'Connell's part at least, and the priests the root of the evil.

21. This morning Hal was off early to a Poor Law meeting at Naas. Great work in the House of Commons—this vile repeal. Shocking in any M.P. to say one word that could either excite the people or disturb the Government at such a crisis, but odious party spirit destroys all good sense, all decent feeling. If ministers could pay the priests and employ the peasantry they might quiet the country

4. Nevertheless, his career flourished and he became Lieutenant-General of Bengal and Governor of Jamaica.

for the present at least. Really these are awful times. Hal returned at seven in pretty good humour with his day's work.

24. In the evening, when we were wandering about among the flowers, Lady Milltown and her two daughters arrived. They staid three hours or more. She was most amusing—her Lord and she are rather at variance about Mr. Fitzleeson—he is still in England making his tour of the race-courses, while she is left alone without a penny in that Cathedral of a house.

O'Connell has so unsettled people that many dreading evil to come have given over the *instruction* of their families, occupying themselves with preparations for running off to America or anywhere whenever the outbreak threatens. Anne Henry told us, and she is from a very radical set, that O'Connell is in a great fright, pushed into measures he never contemplated, he has raised a flame he can't quench, they would turn on him and destroy him if he were now to recede. They are so excited by his promises and his eloquence that some boon they will have, or will fight for it. Sir Robert Peel will be a wonderful man if he weather all the storms gathering around him, for in his own Cabinet there are very violent disagreements about the management of Irish affairs. The Duke and a strong party being for measures *à la militaire*, which would be ruin. Sir Robert means to let the bubble burst and will not yield, and for the time he has conquered.

26. John and his wife off by one o'clock in a queer-looking post-chaise of Mr. Kilbee's, with a number of singular boxes on the top of it. We were all sorry to part, he is absent, indolent, eccentrick, but clever and gentlemanly and I believe a kind heart to be hid under that indifferent manner. Their plan is to see as much of Scotland as they can on their way to the Doune, which they must leave for Inverdruie by the 1st of August, as that vile Duchess of Bedford has this year the Doune again.

Mrs. John Hornidge had made us an apology yesterday for not having been to call on Mrs. Grant. So to-day about four she and Mr. Hornidge arrived. She was dressed! as no one ever was before except some figurante on the stage in a band of so-supposed youthful peasants dancing. We were strolling about just before dark when Lady Milltown and her two girls drove up to ask us all to spend two or three days at Russborough, and she would hardly take any denial.

27. It is disgusting the way the various oppositions try to embarrass the Government during this disagreeable Irish Agitation. Sir Robert will not interfere between Landlord and Tenant, but he makes a forcible appeal to the rigorous Landlord in behalf of the *ignorant* tenant, and he will never give up the Protestant Church Establishment in Ireland, the *bulwark* of the Union. How wise he has been to let the fiery bubble burst, for I still think Repeal mere nonsense, tho' the agitation of it is most mischievous.

29. How well the '*Herald*' understands Irish tacticks. O'Connell's various rents failing forced him on 'repeal', the best milch cow he ever tried, says the Colonel. The priests' influence failing makes them urge on any agitation that will keep the people's minds excited so still under their controul, without leisure to make unpleasant discoveries.

30. The Colonel has fixed for us to set out on our long journey upon the 1st of August. I therefore begin in earnest the preparations for our departure.

SUNDAY, JULY 2. Sarah, James and the baby came to bid goodbye to the family. Poor Sarah, she hardly looks as thriving as she reports, but she is not in beauty just at present, a second baby being near at hand. She says James just manages to clothe himself and pay the rent of their unfurnished house, which is very high—£7—she has to provide food and firing and her own and her child's dress, for his master does not feed James. She is very hard-worked though she has two apprentices; the payment for her work is very low, lower much than hereabouts. Sarah and Margaret Fyfe were glad to meet—our two first servants. I wonder which is happiest, the well-paid, valued housekeeper, fond of her employment and but lightly worked, well lodged, well fed and undisturbed by care, or the struggling wife and anxious mother, toiling for bare subsistence, deprived of sleep, of fresh air, getting on by hard labour from day to day, seeing little of her husband and not having time to fondle her child. Sarah would not change, she says.

3. I have been all the morning making a clearance in the nurseries and made a grand gathering of old shawls, handkerchiefs, gloves, boxes, books, rags and tatters, etc., the distribution of which to the needy caused great joy.

4. Such a tidy set of little creatures as came this day to have their school quarter's tickets signed, so clean and neat it is a real pleasure to see them and a grief to leave them. However we must live in hope of returning to all our happy occupations again better able to fulfil the duties of our quiet station.

9. Sunday and a summer Sunday, beautiful. All at Church. Mr. Moore preached. The village is full of soldiers, who are all busy enough just now attending upon repeal meetings, where some day or other they certainly will have work to do, for these mobs of blackguards cannot for ever be kept so peaceable.

O'Connell is beginning to feel himself in a 'pretty considerable fix', as the tone of his late speeches shows. Donnybrook too was a poor affair; no respectable person has yet joined him either, so he will have to decamp some dark night, for his tail will tear him to pieces when they find out he has been deluding them. They are so excited by hopes of blessings innumerable depending on 'repeal'. How wise in the Government to let the man ruin himself—he is evidently in despair because they won't attack him. What merit there is in keeping one's temper!

In publick or private life all hinges on calmness. We dined early, had a long drive, then a rambling walk. The children drank tea with us, and Mr. Titmarsh[5] occupied us till bedtime. He is delightful—Ireland to

5. Michel Angelo Titmarsh was Thackery's best-known pseudonym but the *Irish Sketch Book* was the first work to be signed with his own name.

perfection—there is no use in singling out an expression or an anecdote, or a page. Every line is truth itself—would that every Irish man and woman would read it and reflect on it, the book I mean which Mr. Thackeray, under the name of Titmarsh, has written.

10. To be a busy day. The trunks which were packed for the *Harp* are to be finished for the carrier in the evening. The stores required for the expected company to be ordered. Letters written. Lists copied, so goodbye little gossipping book for the present.

16, SUNDAY, Rainy—warm, soft rain, very good for the country, particularly where the hay is still waiting for the scythe, as with us. Let me review the week. What have we done? Progress considerable in the rooms; new boys' school nearly ready for roofing; three trunks gone to Pau; the carriage sold—for little certainly, but it was well to be quit of it; bacon and hams disposed of; farm looking well; school scantily attended owing to the bog—there is always something at every season put forward as an excuse for the irregular habits of these poor people. What has the world been doing? Nothing—and that same is a comfort. All is as it was a week ago. 'Lots of talking' only—and the tongue though sharp enough is a safer weapon than either pike or pistol.

I am much of the man's mind who has suggested that, having tried every other means of pacifying Ireland, coercion of every sort, concession of every kind, we should now attempt the effect of feeding the people; the idea has novelty to recommend it at any rate, and if the Highlander says true of the difference between a full stomach and a fasting, tranquillity might spread from the individual to the millions. It is agreeable to see the liberal spirit which is spreading among all this younger generation; it has made a great stride in advance of the last—business habits, economy of *time* and money, kind feelings, fair dealings, are replacing with the young men, the *sporting*, squandering, idling, niggardly habits of their fathers. *Castle Rackrent* will soon be a Grandmother's tale.

23. Sunday, very fine. None from the schoolroom would go

to church. All engaged to wander over the country with John Robinson.

Poor Mrs. Cumming of Logie, she is gone. I am glad that I made a point of seeing her several times during the month I passed in Edinburgh. When very young she was Burns' 'bonnie Leslie'. I think of her as the charming companion of young, happy days, when the Doune was filled with the overflowings of Kinrara in addition to its own ever-changing guests, and my father and mother young and gay and wealthy lived in a sort of brilliant dream in the romantick country our hearts still cling to.

30. Rain again. July is a sad hay-making month. There ought to be some change made in this part of our agricultural proceedings here to suit the seasons. Sown grass might be in the stack before these periodical rains begin and the meadow grass might stand till they were over by proper management one would suppose. No letters, but one—very short—from John with the bonds held over Michael Tyrroll and John Byrne for a small part of the very heavy arrears owing on their farms—the greater part Colonel Smith forgave and their good conduct since has been such as to induce him to take advantage of this parting to relieve them of a load these bad times leave no hope of their enduring without utter discomfort. How happy they will be, for though they paid little annually on account of it, it was a weight over them—a paralyser of exertion, though a necessary check at the time, as they might not have turned out worthy.

31. Poor July—our last month. Never can we be so happy anywhere else. Hal has a hard struggle with asthma this time; he owes it to his own imprudence. The only hope I have is in setting all my griefs down here, where his inquisitively curious nature will ensure his finding it and I may make some impression on paper perhaps.

FRIDAY, AUGUST 5. I emptied my own room of all that does not go with me, sorted papers, etc., and carried all down to Mr. Darker's sanctum. Went to school, which was very full and where I was very busy. Paid visits to Pat and James Ryan on our way home—they are both in the way of doing well moderately. Pat's farm is small but he is cultivating it in earnest; he is going to drain on the new principles directly. James has three acres in good order and his trade. Unluckily the carpenter line is overstocked, and the batches work for so little that the clever men find it difficult to get on; times, however, are mending. After dinner we drove round the hill to Jack Byrne's. I had to speak to him about draining too. He was not at home; nor anybody else in the country, I believe, for coming up Feather-bed Lane we encountered at least 150 people who had all been to see O'Connell pass; he had changed horses at Mr. Kilbee's on the way to Baltinglas, where he performs to-morrow. Blesinton was filled with a mob of the unwashed, but there was no enthusiasm among them we heard—mere curiosity for the most part.

7. Jack Byrne came about his draining—slow, but quite intelligent; he agrees to the terms willingly. The Colonel does not laugh at me now, he only smiles. What expression will his face wear when our labours have added a third to his rental!! He gave Byrne up his Bond, and lightened the man's heart of a load—how happy he looked. Kitty Ryan said to me yesterday, the old woman, 'Faix! were they all sich landlords as the Colonel, Mr. O'Connell might go whistle for repalers.' The old body has hit it. Old Michael Tyrrell came to see his Bond destroyed. How happy they must feel—so do we.

Drove to-night, met a teetotal Band—bad enough, and some jaunting cars returning from Baltinglas with really decent-looking people on them. —Police very tired.—And a few shabby carriages, one with four horses at the waterfall. Dan's entry into Blesinton was quite a failure. He sent horses from Dublin to some publick house—would not change at Mr. Kilbee's because he is no repealer—*drew up* the blinds, and drove quick through the Town, no one raising a hat to him. There was no crowd anywhere to-day awaiting his return.

8. Drove in early to Dublin. Got our passports for which we paid 10/-to the French Consul's handsome clerk.

Went to the National Schools on our own account and on Mr. Moore's.

11. Finished the principal part of my business. Inventories completed. All put away that is not wanted. Mr. Darker's room, his lists, his keys arranged. Wrote several Mems. for him. Saw some of the Tenants. Did other little bits of business, for there were bodies to keep going, work to give, and charity and lectures!

14. Packed the trunks for the journey; they go this night by the carrier. Too many people came to call. John Murray and Dick Hornidge took luncheon with us. Drove to the Cottons, Tulfarris, Russborough, and humble visits in Blesinton and neighbourhood.

15. A day devoted to Tom Darker. Interrupted by Mrs. Cotton, Richard Hornidge, old John Ditto, who dined with us, and Moores, old and young, who came for a couple of hours in the afternoon. A melancholy business altogether.

16. Off by eleven in our own car. One of Mr. Kilbee's carrying Margaret [Fyfe] and the luggage. Drove to John's office, then sent on the children; Drove to the railway, met John and on stepping on board the steamer encountered Mrs. Finnemore, her two daughters, an escort of beaux, the band of a highland regiment, a red deer, the Lord Lieutenant and all the Dublin world on the pier in full dress, enjoying the fine summer evening in mob style. We were away before six. Not too many passengers; beautiful vessel, thoroughly comfortable. The children and I had a cabin nearly to ourselves, one lady only being with us—a Roman Catholic from Tipperary—an intelligent, liberal, clever woman, and if there be many such, bigotry is at length departing from our unhappy land. Very different indeed was her gentle exposition of the times from what we had listened to a hour or two before from Mary and Eliza Browne.

17. Got to Liverpool by five—a dull, foggy morning. Drove in an omnibus to the Grand-junction-railway-station hotel. Dressed, breakfasted, read a good debate in the Lords, and were off in the train at eight. It was a hot, noisy day, yet I was less fatigued than I expected. The children

bore it very well. We were all glad of the half-hour's rest at Birmingham and the good luncheon provided for us there. An omnibus took us from the terminus to Baker Street, which we reached before seven o'clock.

19. Heat oppressive, Jack and I prepare for Oxford. Hal took us in a cab and placed us in a second-class carriage, which we found infinitely cooler than the grander first. A very decent set of people filled it, and certainly one sees more of life by thus mixing with the lower grades of our very curious society than is possible if we aristocratically preserve our distance from the mob. I met with great civility and a good deal of amusement. My Mother and Aunt were anxiously expecting us. They are both looking well—my Aunt particularly so, and they have chattered away all the evening in great spirits. Jack is much admired. He has behaved very well, poor little fellow, for it was a hot, tiresome journey and he must feel very dull without his sisters.

20. Too much engaged for Church. My Mother speaks less than she used to do, seems subdued, yet in fair spirits—her disease probably causes much of this, her extreme deafness helps, and her natural disposition, which discontents her with her present position, whatever it may be, prevents her ever being really cheerful. My Aunt, on the contrary, is thoroughly happy, always busy about something or other, a great chatterbox, quick and long-winded together.

23. Up by six, breakfast at seven. At the Vauxhall terminus in two cabs with all our luggage before nine. At Southampton before one. We walked from the Terminus in a drizzling rain to the pier, and through the toll to the *Calpe*, a little smart-looking vessel, crowded with packages and people. Colonel Litchfield took care of the luggage and Margaret. Miss Hart met us on the deck. We got ourselves settled long before starting, they delayed for the next train in hopes of more passengers, but, none appearing, we were off by three with only four gentlemen passengers, but the little cabin for the Ladies crowded with women and children. What a place for such a voyage! Three days and three nights at sea!

FIVE

1845

The Highland Lady continued to keep a journal in France
and on their return to Ireland in July 1845 she describes
in her usual way what greeted them at Baltiboys with the
same mixture of outrage, praise, disgust and optimism.
As the family settled back into the routines of responsible
landlords, and as she details how the lives of all on the
estate seem gradually to be improving, there is the irony
that this was to be the first year of the failure of the
potato crop that heralded what came to be known as the
famine years.

MONDAY, JULY 28. The Colonel has gone in to Dublin to-day
to see about all the various things our two years economy
has enabled us to purchase. We have seen nearly all
our neighbours already. Lady Milltown was the same
unhappy creature at heart; however, I will if possible
avoid vexing her and the best way is to avoid being much
with her myself and to keep the young people entirely
asunder. Her girls are very coarse looking, Barbara is
handsome, might be made to look well I daresay, Cecilia,
poor thing, is, I fear, not improvable, but they were
so disfigured by their extraordinary dress it is hardly
possible to judge of them. The Doctor says that they
are reputable now compared to the anticks she made of
them in the winter. He has dined three times with us,
but he don't come about the house as he used to do,
no longer young enough perhaps to scour the country at
all hours.

Our humbler neighbours so far as we have yet seen
are all thriving, a great change for the better since last I
went my rounds among them. Peggy Dodson has chintz
curtains to her bed and many other little indications of
well doing. Antony's foolish marriage to a young girl

without either money or sense, and his folly in quitting journeyman's work and setting up a carpenter's shop of his own in a garret in Dublin have vexed her much, still old Paddy is well and Mary in our service. She has no lodger now but Paddy the gardener who will probably soon follow his wife when he finds we have no house for her here. Johnny Grace is married. James Ryan has built a good two story house at the back gate with the workshop and timber yard adjoining garden and dairy. They have five children already. John Fitzpatrick and Miles Byrne have their joint tenement, very decent, each has a bit of garden, a yard, a bedroom and kitchen, and Miles has a turf house which John must also have. The wives of course did not agree, there will be greater peace now that poor Judy Byrne is gone. She has left three baby boys, poor thing, dying a few days after the birth of the last. Kitty Fitzpatrick has two pretty girls, one quite a little beauty, and a fine boy; great comfort in a humble way in both houses. If they would but keep their tempers how happy they might all be.

Pat Ryan has drained his farm well, tidied his farm-yard, and looks happy, the good humoured, untidy wife has plenty within and without and six ugly children still, having lost three by want of care. They have lent (sic) the two rooms James Ryan used to occupy to Johnny Grace and his managing wife, who have already gathered a good deal of furniture about them; he is much steadier since his marriage and looks almost clever, certainly happy, and there is a fine healthy baby eating potatoes at eight months old. The last visit we have yet paid was to Tom Kelly, where, as in former times we found amongst some dirt and great disorder, a flourishing farm, a full house, a well furnished room and kitchen and half a dozen as fine lively children as ever were seen. Little Mary grown a nice girl and the loquacious mother as thorough an Irishwoman as ever.

31. We have rainy weather, very rainy, which is unlucky for the hay and it prevents our continuing our walks, but it is good for the oats and it enables me to get the household settled. Janey with Mrs Fyfe went over the

inventories and we found a good deal more damage than we expected—things worn quite out and not replaced, much broken and many little articles altogether gone. George Garland has come back to us, looking wretchedly ill from overwork, he will soon recover with our quiet regular ways. We like to have the old familiar faces round us. I miss nobody from the outside work and we have still some bachelours among the labourers, two of whom, John Cairns and Andy Highland live in the back yard in a shed which must be made more comfortable for them.

The school had just begun to thrive, numbers having poured in upon the news of our speedy return, when the fever broke out amongst some of the children, Miss Gardner caught it and has been at death's door. She is now recovering, and when a little better must be sent away for a while till the infection is banished when we can reopen the school under the master. It will require a little attention this same school.

I have read nothing since we got home but Mr Guizot's lectures on *history* I may call them, for he takes the proper view of it and makes the proper use of it in his philosophical speculations on the progress of civilisation in Europe. We have been too busy for thought of any kind. I have written a good deal and one business I have brought to a satisfactory close. Miss Clerk comes to us as Governess. She has left Russborough with the best of reputations, not a word can be said against her, and in her favour a great deal is spoken in the way of moral conduct, good temper, and considerable abilities. We hope she will be an acquisition, keep up the practice of those accomplishments the girls have begun and be a clever, cheerful companion for them. The Doctor would not listen to my doing without assistance in the care of the children till March. The little girls seem half pleased and half sorry, but I shall take care that their present freedom remain uninjured. It is more a companion that I want for them than a mere teacher.

The king of Holland has now come over to England on a visit. These crowned heads can none of them stay quiet at home now that the fashion of running about all over the world has once begun with them. So as they keep us all at peace they may gad to eternity.

Sunday, AUGUST 3. I am going to make an abstract of all money matters which will thoroughly acquaint us with our position and will, I trust, prove that we can live most respectably here and save sufficient out of our income for an excursion every second year with the children. John Robinson had above £300 in bank for us on our return home, Mr Darker £130,—we have not been so rich for many years. We have come back to find all our old servants outside in their old places, and in the house three school girls as maids. Mary Dodson housemaid, Biddy Quin kitchen maid, Mary Ryan to wait on the girls. And Mrs Fyfe is charmed with them after the French maids, quite satisfied. We shall have an admirably appointed household. When Miss Clerk comes we shall be very comfortable.

6. On Monday I took rather too long a walk, Janey and I having gone over the hill called on old Commons whose smoky chimney sent us quickly out to the pure air again, and then on to Mrs Dempsey whose dirty, unfinished, unfurnished house looked as miserable as herself though there was an air of plenty about it too. Grief has worn the poor woman to a shadow; she has lost her fine son of two and twenty and her daughter Mary, not long married to Pat Fitzpatrick. I took a long rest there for the poor woman liked to talk of her sorrows, and then we entered a really wretched cabin, George Cairns's; there were children enough and they were clean, but there was nothing else, not even fire. The wife says they are beginning to thrive, I hope so for they seem to want it.

Hal and the girls went to Russborough yesterday evening, it was very stupid, the dinner long and dull, those silly games the only amusement of the drawing-room. The Duke of Leinster, good-natured, his Duchess noisy, his son rather nice, his daughter ugly. The girls were happy enough while in the schoolroom but they thought the drawing-room part very dull.

More letters from Jane, with private information respecting the employment of her own income. She has been devoting it for years to the payment of a particular debt of my father's, the Bond to Wm. Cameron. [Brother] William is now able to repay her so that in future she will be as rich as she has hitherto had the name of being. I think her income is £600. a year; she has been giving away half besides a sum of several hundreds and the original £2,000. I hope William may make the fortune he deserves and soon return home among us.

9. Jane writes to Janey to tell her that she has a present for her, worthy of a Godmother, a grandpianoforte! I am afraid my enquiries about my own have made her determine on this too handsome gift to her god-daughter. She has thought me ill-used; though she excused my father, she sends me his note explanatory of his affairs by which it appears that although the creditors at large will with William's help be paid off this coming October, £8,000 more is required to clear some private debts never brought forward. And he has suffered the interest so to accumulate, even on the £1,000 borrowed of Lord Lauderdale for John's outfit and chargeable on the younger children's portions, that were this not paid up, the £5,000 settled on Mary and me would be diminished by so much. I can't think it would really be affected as the sum of '£2,500 my daughter so and so's portion' is mentioned in the marriage settlement of both. But the tricks of the Law there is no comprehending.

15. We are really all so happy I half fear the arrival of little Miss Clerk may disturb us. If the abominable spirit of faction which is now agitating the place could by any means be calmed, our life here would be all sunshine, but with such excitable natures the people are ill to manage, both parties being violent, prejudiced, vindictive, jealous and so on to the end of the catalogue of follies, the fruits of ignorance. It is almost amusing to listen to the two versions of every tale. It is nearly impossible to guess the truth between them. The other day at Dempseys I was diverted with Anne's way of washing up her dishes, the large black pot on the fire with water heating *chaudron* [cauldron] fashion into which she dipt each vessel then merely wiping one and all with the same cloth afterwards. It was Adèle in her kitchen [at Pau] only the tidily dressed

French girl made a prettier picture than coarse, clumsy, slatternly Anne Dempsey.

19. Pat Ryan and I are very likely to agree about little Mathew as garden boy, he is a fine intelligent child, a good scholar fond of reading, fond of gardening and if we come to terms he shall have his trade thoroughly taught him. I like advancing our scholars, and that they may not stand still after they begin to labour, Mr McConnell is to have an evening class—a shilling a month the highest fee for three hours schooling. He has also undertaken the charge of the Lending Library, and will, I hope, prove a zealous and very useful assistant to us.

SUNDAY, SEPTEMBER 7. Certainly my poor journal must have fallen into disgrace for I am quite neglecting it. One excuse for such indolence is the life devoid of incident we pass in this our quiet home, another is the little leisure left in my short day for private pursuits unconnected with the family business, the last is the failing strength and spirits which disincline me to any mental exertion. Sadly changed is my active mind when to *think* has become difficult.

After first returning to our comfortable house I fancied myself greatly better. I breakfast at eight on a bit of bread and butter with a cup of tea, taking care not to omit half a wine glass of fluid magnesia the first thing if there be any uneasiness of head or stomach. I then get up and wash all over in cold water following this pleasant bath with good smart friction with a rough towel. After this the chest, spine and right side are hand rubbed by poor Margaret Fyfe for half an hour, then comes a dose of hydriocate of potash. The toilette is over about ten, then different family matters are arranged, orders given, work cut out, accounts settled and so on and then with bonnet and shawl and clogs and umbrella I descend for the day, which I pass in strolling out and resting in with work about, which I a'n't particular, or book fit for desultory reading, or a gossip may be with some incomer like the Doctor.

A little after one a bit of bread or a potato or a cup of gruel forms my luncheon, at two we drive. The Iodine has to be taken both after luncheon and after dinner which in any case is but a name. Tea is always welcomed, and then till bedtime we have work and conversation and often musick; at ten comes bed, half an hour of hand rubbing and a rhubarb pill closes my useless day.

We must all decay—'First we ripe and ripe, and then . . .' But I had hoped for a poetical decay, tired nature seeking repose in the calm of a green old age and this realization of Touchstone's Commentary[1] on our frailty rather disgusts any feeling of delicacy, the more so as a sort of selfishness grows infallibly upon anyone forced to incessant care of a suffering frame.

Publick events have been few. The Queen and her Prince seem to be very happy in Saxe Coburg, the houses of Parliament shooting the grouse, the ministers reposing, the repealers asleep, popery silent, but the Orangemen awake after their long slumbers. Their regret at the liberal policy pursued by the Government. We will trust that good will result from their folly; as regards themselves personally, their prejudicial intolerance places their characters very low in the scale of intellect. Really to read their arguments fatigues the mind almost to sickness. I never take part in these exploded vagaries now, merely listening and then turning the discourse.

10. Jane sends a list of pianofortes with prices which is to be returned to-morrow. She fears I ought to let Margaret Fyfe go to close her mother's eyes, the poor woman is really dying. The highlanders have such exalted ideas of filial duty that every other feeling gives way to this, therefore if Margaret decides on going she will go nor can we keep her nor ought we; great as the sacrifice will be on both parts it must be made but it is the most seriously inconvenient necessity that ever happened to annoy a household. I am fit for nothing, I must not even go down below, I can bear neither trouble nor vexation, on the contrary I require a great deal of care, constant nursing. The Colonel is often quite unable to

1. 'And so from hour to hour we ripe and ripe/And then from hour to hour we rot and rot.' *As You Like It* II vii 26.7

help himself or anyone else when the fit of asthma is on him. She waits on him too; after his suffering nights he requires attendance in the mornings, for when he is what he calls well maybe he has not lain in bed two hours and of course is little refreshed by sleep in his chair.

23. Spent two hours this morning in the schools. Miss Gardiner is getting on, she has twenty-nine pupils gathered with every prospect of her numbers encreasing, all looking bright and clean and happy. Only sixteen boys. Somehow Mr McConnell don't get them to look as cheerful as the girls; he is not popular among the people I hear, it is indeed hard to content them but as there generally is some foundation for mob fancies I must enquire further concerning him. I have no particular admiration of him myself. Our coadjutor met me there by appointment to talk over the way and means of encreasing the attendance, he is an enlightened young man, quite unlike any priest we have hitherto had in these parts and he and I are likely to agree perfectly well which of itself will much advantage the school. On our way home we called on James Ryan's wife; the new house will soon be very comfortable, it is conveniently arranged and a neat elevation greatly improving the appearance of our rapidly thriving little property.

26. Hal has gone into Dublin about various matters, so we are to have a dull time of it. He rode with Annie to Russborough, where they found Lord Milltown had won £1,500. That and her share of a Kilkenny property varying from £80 to £120 a year and some small legacy left him lately by an Aunt is the extent of their means; all else is under sequestration owing to his folly, which, were it not hereditary would be incomprehensible. The Milltowns are off for Boulogne, probably in the end to Paris. I am glad to have it to say that since I gave up the iodine I feel much stronger, can eat meat at the boy's dinner with a glass of Chablis after, enjoy my tea at six, and yesterday walked to Blesinton.

FRIDAY, OCTOBER 3. Miserable weather, we suppose 'tis the equinox. Sold our sheep pretty well, bought a few more so that three or four cattle between this and winter are

the only additional stock required. Another Monster
Meeting somewhere in the South, an enormous one.
In wretched Munster these mobs of misery may still
congregate. I doubt our busy population hereabouts
leaving their occupations at the call of agitation *now*. I
hope he may not put us to the proof, for we don't want
to be disturbed by such worry.

I have found out how it is the poor Journal don't
occupy me as it once did. Mr Chambers takes all my
spare time. I am reading up my leeway, two full years
of his well packed journals, the interesting articles in
which lead me on and on so that it is often an exertion
to lay the book down. It is not mere 'pass time' luckily.
A fund of practical wisdom is accumulating for the use of
my dear young charge upon which they draw perpetually,
particularly Jack during his happy hour before bed time
when the prints of his penny magazine, etc. are explained
at my knee.

4. We had our Inspector here yesterday with whom we
seriously consulted about the ill success of our Schools,
for though there are a good many children and their
progress is good, and their parents satisfied, the number
is so infinitely too small for the population that it is very
disheartening to see those fine schoolrooms so empty,
such competent Teachers so discouraged. There is no
disguising the fact that our Parish Priest, Mr Germaine,
does not aid the National School, he visits it twice a year,
writes formally in the report book that all is correct
and then he thinks his duty done. He never examines
a class, never takes trouble of any kind, and close to
his house, and near the Weaver's Square also are hedge
schools containing above seventy scholars each squeezed
up into a little room the size of a pantry and taught
by a succession of incompetent masters against whose
malpractices he never finds one word to say. His present
Curate seems anxious to assist me in every possible way,
but his last was quite an open opposer of our system,
and this has so unsettled the people that all this more
enlightened man's efforts have helped us little as yet.
The school-master suggested my writing to Dr Murray,

their Bishop, on the subject and as the Inspector highly approves of this idea I should put it in practice.

6. Another fine frosty morning brightening into a glorious day. We had a letter from Mr Caw yesterday who, warmed into recollection of Miss Lissy by Margaret Fyfe's eloquence, offers us his house of Inverdruie should we incline to visit the dear Duchus. I should so like a few summer months there and so Hal says would he, it is therefore not impossible that the month of June may find us on our way to the highlands! I shall think it a dream, nor can I think, even now, of the plan with calmness. I, who fancied every feeling of enthusiasm dead; but we mountain children never lose the love of fatherland; true as the needle to the pole our hearts turn ever to our heathery hills, the pine forests, the wild burn, the lonely loch and the deep feudal love of our people. 'Wherever we wander, wherever we rove the hills of the highlands for ever we love.'

8. Yesterday I went to the Schools—ten boys, fifteen in the girls' school. Was quite pleased with the intelligence of some of the children. The boys were standing in circle before a map of Ireland giving more than geographical description of it. The girls shewed me a large box of neat work. Then I went on down the lane to the river making various calls on either hand by the way, some rather satisfactory, others very very much the reverse.

10. I was interrupted in my recollections of my walk down the river lane. Cullens not at home, all tidy about their Lilliputian premises. Grays much more comfortable than I have ever before found them. Mrs Tyrrell away, her outer most miserable room let to a James Craig, a labourer on Miles, I mean Jack, Byrne's farm, his wages in summer 5d. in winter 4d. a day and his food. The winter half year having begun the young wife receives two shillings a week for the maintenance of herself and three wretched looking babies, out of which pittance she pays sixpence a week to Mrs Tyrrell and threepence must go for the husband's tobacco, leaving 1/3. for food, clothes and fire. Such a scene of misery my eyes have not witnessed since I once found as poor a woman, Betty

Kiogh, dying. An old dresser containing two tin cans, a broken spoon, a small crock, and a pot on the floor in which a baby just able to walk was dabbling was all the furniture, I could see. 'Where is the bed', said I. 'There mee lady'—'Where'—A wad of straw in a corner, a little pile of chaff near it on which lay folded a ragged single blanket—all, father, mother and the three babies slept *there*. 'And your husband smokes', I said 'spends 15/—or 16/—shillings a year on tobacco'. 'Sure mee lady only threepence a week! And he don't drink mee lady, sorra drop, the Lord be praised, a'n't it a mercy?'. I burst out crying for my nerves a'n't as strong as they once were.

This is a wrong system though it cannot be changed yet. A man should not marry on fourpence a day. A married man should not diet at the farmer's, a farmer should keep no married man whom he cannot give a house to, a girl should marry no man till they have between them saved enough money to buy their furniture. When shall we see these prudent rules in practice. Mrs Tyrrell too has no right to let part of her house being only in it herself on sufferance; she is a very hard Landlord too as all of her class mostly are.

My next visit was revolting from a different cause—dirt and filth and discomfort of every kind in and around the dwelling of Michael Doyle and Judy Ryan. They were in the bog, Jane Ryan literally, not figuratively, nearly naked, her large exposed limbs and chest burned almost black by the sun was in the field amusing an ugly dirty enough but perfectly well dressed baby. She helped me over a wall to the dung yard in front of the cabin which was cleaner than the kitchen floor over which I had to grope in darkness to the fire, carefully holding up my petticoats and stepping so as to avoid what the two fat pigs had been depositing on it. Beside these two beasts on four legs, two others on two, old Mrs Doyle, smoking, and lame James Quinn seemed to be in charge of a lately born infant and a wretched little nursechild both seated in the chimney corner. Energetick measures wanted here.

19. Colonel Smith dined with Mr Owen to meet Lord Downshire who without any appearance of talent he found frank in manner, cheerful, disposed to be pleased

and to shew that he was so, a great improvement on the particularly stiff reserve of the father.[2] We have had a delicate investigation and war with the clergy, and the grand pianoforte has arrived. Altogether the effect is of an orchestra, these two evenings we have listened with delight to the two little girls whose playing richly deserves this well-bestowed present.

The delicate investigation was upon poor Tom Darker's character, his morals and his probity both attacked by the evil-minded gossips abounding here as in other idle places, poverty, ignorance, and the accompanying jealousy of the prosperous, having really distracted the whole of Baltiboys. Poor Tom has been trying for long to bring matters to the point and at last he found a courageous man, James Carney, the mason, honest enough to come forward and state what he had heard uttered and attested, so there was a confronting, and a denying, and a bringing forward of books by which every insinuation against his conniving at dishonesty was disproved. It was quite a triumphant refutation after which there was a shaking of hands and we hope at last an end to the propagation of as malicious a set of calumnies as ever were invented.

The warfare has been about the schools. Father Germaine did not dare openly to condemn them but he has never publickly shewn any interest in them and he must privately have discouraged them or more children would have attended, fewer hedge schools would have been permitted, and they would not have been filled to crowding, seventy to eighty pupils while we had under forty. His former curates never concealed their aversion to National Schools, this Mr Galvin professes to assist us yet after his friendly consultation with me he went and set up a new hedge school *within a mile* selecting a master for it with the utmost care. Our Inspector said this was all nonsense, this struggling for years past against their secret enmity, so by his advice I wrote to Dr Murray who has given it them

2. The fourth Marquis (1812-68) succeeded his father who had died of apoploxy earlier that summer, when the Smiths were in France.

in earnest and sent me Mr Germaine's letter excusing his conduct by a most unfair statement distorting facts, the Archbishop accompanied this precious document with a second courteous note to which I made as courteous a reply.

Then comes an enquiry from the Secretaries regarding the unsatisfactory amount of pupils. I answer so as to let them comprehend I have the priest against me, and then I write to Mr Germaine himself as civilly as possible to assure him I have no wish to do anything inconsistent with the regulations or concealed from him, that if his charges against the Master be correct we should after investigation dismiss him, that I complain of the near neighbourhood of the new school but hope a meeting may set all matters to rights by giving us the opportunity of talking over everything, and I venture to expect either himself or his curate will agree to this. So rests the matter at present. Whether good will come of it I know not, certainly no harm, he may be angry for a while but he dare not say so and as his superiour will now look after him he must behave himself less radically. The Inspector says we never shall have a good attendance while Mr Germaine remains our parish priest.

26. Sunday, The month of October is running rapidly away, the weeks actually flying. The Colonel has been very much occupied with plans for the prevention of such extreme distress as the failure of the potato crop threatens the poor with. Just in Ba⌐tiboys there seems as yet to be no damage done but very near at hand this widespread disease has already attacked some large con-acre[3] fields where the poor man's supply for the next nine months may without active measures speedily taken fail him entirely. The potato once attacked is quite unfit for food, it rots away, infecting all its companions, but the farina the nourishing part of the root is uninjured even in the worst cases so that by scraping down the potato at once and making it into what they call starch

3. The letting of small portions of land (especially in Ireland), ploughed and ready to be sown.

nothing fit for food is lost. This starch or flour mixed
with a half of wheaten flour makes delicious bread some
of which we tasted to-day for Mr Shehan amongst others
has been trying this experiment and he sent us by young
John Hornidge a sample. Corn is an abundant crop, and
though rising in the market at present during this panick
it is expected shortly to fall, particularly if they open the
ports to foreign corn free of duty which we hear the
Government will do if necessary.

Hal fears the want of energy of the lower orders,
their idleness, and their ignorance, will prevent their
setting to work to supply themselves with this change
of food so he went to see Mr Owen on the subject
of establishing a scraping manufactory and perhaps a
bakery, and he found him quite ready to do everything to
lessen this calamity. Lord Downshire is equally desirous
to assist the neighbourhood as indeed he has shewn by
insisting on taking to himself the debts of the Loan
fund, unfortunate Mr Alley having helped himself to
the Savings deposited and to much more, for the money
originally lent by Colonel Smith and others to establish
the fund was gone too. This fraudulent conduct had so
much inconvenienced the poor who had trusted their hard
earnings to the Bank that the gentlemen had determined
to subscribe the necessary sum to pay up these debts, but
Lord Downshire won't allow them, which we all think
very handsome conduct.

Our next topick of interest has been my war with the
priest which looked very serious at one time. He took
no notice of my civil letter to him, talked very imper-
tinently of my *interference* in my own business! and
thundered away at the Chapel worse than ever. But the
week has much changed him, he has been in Dublin,
was sent for! returned quite amiable, wrote me the
kindest possible note, and we are to walk through the
parish hereafter hand in hand doing good and peace
ensuing! If he will be but quiet I shall be quite content.

27. Raw bleak day. Janey and her Papa have just come in
from their ride, they are going everywhere to teach the

management of diseased potatoes and to whip up my tardy scholars.

28. Another day of bad weather yet all get out but me, sick poor, destitute poor, and ignorant, idle, prejudiced poor oppress me. Relieve them I can't, instruct them I can't, but I can try, every little helps, and many littles make a mickle. Energy is so wanting among these Celtick races there is no inspiring them to help themselves, and there is no other help really availing. Mental force seems to be wanting, it will require a generation or two to reproduce any in beings so degraded. How absurd in me to feel angry with creatures so deficient yet their folly is so lamentable it is very hard to bear patiently all the evils it produces.

One contented man whose case would be hopeless were he as indolent as his neighbours has beamed like a bright light across the waste of misery. With six small children, owing a heavy debt, a bad house, land in bad condition, and his only cow dead of this distemper, he is cheerful in his hope of better times, 'With the help of God and *my own industry*,' for which addition to the usual mockery of resignation he shall have assistance where he does not look for it. The cow falling sick, he killed and salted her, 'and sure is not that a grand provision for the winter anyhow. And once the frost takes the taint off of the grass I'll get another, the milk and manure for the grazing, till the spring comes round, and it might have been worse, mee lady!' If this be not Christian submission where shall we find any, honest-hearted George Kearns will not thrive the worse for our conversation. Hal will respect the *self-helpfulness* so rare among our peasantry. He has three of his small children at school and when I told him in that case, he would only have to pay for two, the merry 'Long life to ye,' with which he jerked his sixpence back into his immeasurable pocket rung in my ear all the day afterwards. It is a pleasure to help such a poor man, it lightens the duty of helping the more debased, who lean on a reed when they lean on the casual charity of the benevolent.

We have now in Baltiboys but two families in distress, George Kearns, who will soon by his own activity be out

of it, and John Byrne, uncle to Jack, and old ailing man
with a wife rather more feeble than himself, an idiot
daughter and an orphan grand-daughter, all inhabiting
a single room hovel dependent solely on the labour of
one son, our workman Luke. The nephew is kind to
them but it is very little the small farmer can afford to
give, the son does all, gives them all £15 a year for this
household. Three other families not strictly belonging to
us we occasionally help. We must try and get rid of them
to the railways or the Poor House for they will never
learn to help themselves. Harry Kiogh who was rather
unjustly deprived of his farm by his mother in favour
of her younger son, James Kelly ditto ditto, and James
Craig whom I found the other day squatted down in
Mrs Tyrrell's kitchen. Of deserted children two only
are left on hands, Mary Ryan and Bessy Healy, both
now with old Peggy who is herself comfortable. Mary
Ryan did not do here without Mrs Fyfe so I shall keep
her at school another year and then get her a country
place. Old Peggy Nary seems to be growing young and
if little queer Katty Pheeny will lodge with her through
the winter I shall be at ease about our old pensioner and
the plan will be a help to the industrious little oddity who
goes about to sell our school needlework.

It requires constant watching to keep them all in
order—up to industry—in heart, and out of all the long
catalogue of miseries poverty is heir to. The school is the
foundation of all hope for their future. To waken up their
faculties is the only dependence we can have for another
generation of a happier kind. When I look back on the
condition in which we found our pretty little property I
can hardly believe that fifteen years should or could have
worked out so improved a state of things. Land neglected,
mud hovels ruined, farm offices wanting, proper fences
unknown, meat seldom tasted, rags for clothing, all in
debt, in dirt, in utter ignorance of everything,; this
was what we met the memorable day that Pat Lalor
answered my enquiry as to who were all that mob of
beggars, with 'Thim's the tinants.' Now we have larger
farms, larger fields, some good fences, much finer cattle,

a few sheep, even some turnips, five new slated houses, three of them two storeys high, good clothing, meal and bread and bacon and a 'bit of beef by times'. Draining a rage, planting, clearing, good schools, a night school, lending library, and much approach towards cleanliness. Fifteen years more and what may we not hope for.

30. The Colonel is off for Dublin. We were making great preparations for Halloween, kept here with much the same ceremonies as in Scotland. In the midst of fun of all sorts came poor miserable Betty Kiogh for meal, milk, flannel, etc, for her boy in typhus fever. All day we have been harrassed with the Blesinton beggars, who well knew the Colonel was from home. I gave them nothing, however.

SUNDAY, NOVEMBER 2. I am all alone in my room in consequence of a severe bilious headache. In the watches of the night I took myself to task for the over indulgence of my poetical temperament, so very much too highly strung for this working day world we live in, and I resolved by every means religion and reflexion can employ to endeavour to strengthen this *weakness* of character so near to *fifty*. So much misery results from this oversensitiveness, excusable, perhaps, in a *young* woman whose attractions may entitle her to attentions all her sex prize so dearly, but in an *old* woman it becomes troublesome. She can only expect to be endured on account of her usefulness in some respects, or out of gratitude for past merits, or out of the involuntary homage paid by well-principled minds to her experience.

All are at church, walked there. I question whether they will hear as good as sermon there as I have composed here for the edification of my Grandchildren!! Old Mrs Tyrrell came to me yesterday for advice in her distress, and I had no advice to give so sent her to John Hornidge. Her very ill conducted grandson has been lodged in Baltinglass jail for stealing a coat, he and Johnny Cooper were both concerned and Johnny Cooper has run away. If we could get the lad sent to a penitentiary and so after a while to the colonies it would be the best thing could happen to him.

3. The priests have been again abusing my Schools, this proves that they are becoming popular, otherwise these reverend gentry would have no need to interfere. I don't much mind them. The people are tiring of being so priest-rid, and they are beginning to shew it, resenting their interference, treating them with little respect and often flatly disobeying them. All working for good.

4. Hal went to the meeting at Mr. Owen's house to consult about fit measures for the relief of impending evils on account of the potato disease and it was settled that another meeting should be held this day fortnight further to consider this publick calamity! Would not this do for Boz.

Here is an overland from Bombay, despatched October 1st, arrived November 1st by the new route through Germany. The Governor General has gone to the Upper provinces, war appearing to be inevitable with some tribe or other. He will avoid this miserable necessity if possible, but my school affairs have taught me how nearly impossible it is to manage the ignorant except by force, gentle force if practicable, but it must be force, there is no other way of even doing them good.

Some of the dull old people hereabouts decline making starch of their bad potatoes, it can't be wholesome, if the potato be tainted the starch must be tainted and so unfit for food. We have explained to many the structure of the root and how the farina escapes when the fibrous part suffers, and wonderfully well some of them understand, by the help of the illustration of the honeycomb, others are quite obtuse and mean to sit down with folded hands to bear the Will of God, in other words relief from the benevolent without any exertion on their part.

5. A letter from Mr. Caw [from Rothiemurchus]¹ and thank heaven Margaret Fyfe sets out on her return this day. Not before she was missed, for the improprieties Hal discovers below and the inconveniences we are all put to above are really enough to fret the most patient. Therefore in future I shall set down all people's oddities to loose screws

1. See 16.2.48

somewhere, and I trust they will all be equally charitable to me, for certainly I much require their forbearance at times. Hal has just brought in two damaged potatoes, the first we have seen of our own for on our hill few have been found as yet. It is a dull misty day, surely the rising barometer cannot have been for this cold wind instead of a continuance of bright weather.

6. Another blustering day after a stormy night, however as there is no rain it will dry the potatoes finely. I have begun *to fag* at Chamber's Cyclopedia. A knowledge of our early writers is useful. I have no great *rhyming* turn, though poetical thoughts delight me. Those old conceits therefore and half barbarous metre give me little pleasure except as curiosities shadowing forth the better things to come.

8. A blustering night, but a fine day, riders and walkers all preparing, the ground alas! too wet for me. Hal busy arranging employment for the poor, and a hope expressed in many places on tolerable good grounds that the distress will be but partial.

9. Sunday, I am quite surprised at finding myself so much interested in our early writers. The one who has aston-ished me is Ben Jonson, I knew him not before, my reading never having lain among our Classick writers of the olden time. I have marked the bits which best pleased me, that if ever, dear girls, you look well through this useful book you may try your judgement by your mother's. Many of the sonnets are old friends learned from the songs and MSS. of my Grandmother, which struck me in my girlhood though I did not know their Authours. Sir John Suckling and Herrick of course were my old friends and my last of these times I almost think, for the reign of affectation is beginning, unless I find a few among the Scotch who hitherto have kept at a very respectful distance behind their neighbours.

11. Another foggy day, it a'n't the least cold but disagreeably raw. Mr. Darker much afraid of this second potato field. The first had hardly a bad potato so that he was unprepared for this.

12. Mrs. Fyfe returned loaded with grouse and tartan.

Mr. Caw sent by her a mountain hare, four brace of grouse, a blackcock and heath hen and a couple of ducks; he has, she says, his house full of work people preparing for us and is so lifted up with the idea of our coming to visit him that he is almost *fly*, all the people equally enchanted; there is to be a putting of the best foot forward all over the property to have all look well to us. I had to-day whole packet from India round by Edinburgh. William expects his coffee plantation to turn out very profitable speculation. He has made his [natural] son William Grant an assistant overseer on it and the poor young man is turning out well.

13. Still a heavy fog. Road sessions took the Colonel out early, while I was busy arranging a dinner party in honour of the grouse, for Saturday. The Doctor called and sat talking nonsense half the morning. *Half* the potatoes in this new field are tainted, some very badly.

16. In my reading I have met with no more poets much worth mentioning in this third period except, perhaps, Sir Thomas Aytoun, a Scotsman, author of one pretty ballad. Then come the dramatists where I am more at home and the prose writers where I am quite at home,—my father's well selected Library having early introduced me to these graver, and to me more interesting writers. The old Chronicles, the voyages, memoirs, philosophy, even state papers of that age were quite familiar to my childhood and never ceased to retain their place after their long line of successors became as fully known.

17. Hal is off for Dublin to register his votes. Mrs. Fyfe has begun to clean the house. Oh what an idle, lazy, dirty, indolent, indifferent set are the talented Irish. Talk, talk, talk, is their whole occupation.

18. I have heard of a marriage this morning which accounts for the untidiness of the house and all the other failings in Mary's department under which we have been suffering. The happy bridegroom is Barny Quinn, a very respectable good-looking young man in every way worthy of a good industrious girl like Mary, and were they content to wait a few years it would be a desirable connexion for both. As it is, they have saved nothing, they are both in

good places which on their marriage they will lose, and with the prospect of scarcity before them from the failure of the potato crop, without a house, without employment, they are going together trusting in the Lord! They need not trust in the *Lady*, for I can't help them, neither do I feel inclined, indeed they have settled matters so nicely themselves there is no need. Mary is to take her husband to her mother's, I am to give her the washing, Colonel Smith is to employ Barny, at out work first, by and bye in the stables, and they are all to be as happy as possible!

30. The last day of November, Sunday, and fine, that is not rainy, the wind is however, high, the air cold, a sort of wintry look everywhere around. Mr. Robinson came down yesterday to collect the rents, the Tenants paid well, were in good spirits, made no complaints, not even of their potatoes, were well dressed, so that altogether it was a most comfortable gale day. The potatoe failure has been much exaggerated, the disease is by no means so far spread as was supposed and the crop so over abundant that the partial failure will be the less felt, particularly as the corn harvest was excellent. But people were much frightened and this caused a run on the Savings Banks which might have encreased the evil, that too is luckily over so that the prospects for the winter are brightening. John Robinson said nothing could more fully prove the encreasing prosperity of the country than the multitudes whom this panick proved to have been saving, the very poorest looking people drawing out their fortys, fiftys, hundreds. The crowds were so immense and so excited that horse and foot police were necessary to guard their lives. It was quite a curious sight. He is in great spirits himself for all with him is thriving, his brother heard somewhere that he had realised already £15,000.

I have been reading my own works instead of any others, to Hal and the children and was quite pleased to find them so good. They have spirited me up to begin again, so I have actually written them a new story within these few days. Dear Mary, I read them her clever tales too. We were really happy while writing them though such desolation was round us. In our large, barrack room, an attick, during the long cold highland winter, often in the mornings gathering from the plantations ourselves and bringing home the additional wood necessary for our fire, for we wrote at night, after bedtime, with stolen ends of candles and bits of quick fir for light. And when the first forty pounds, our own earning, reached us, our extasy, I almost feel it yet, we bought some sheep, sent to Inverness for tea, sugar, shoes, wine and flannel for my mother, and then we told her how we were so rich. It was no present from our married sister, it was the value of our time and brains aided by the education my father had given us; this last idea had comfort in it, for that the daughters of a man of £12,000 a year should have to work for their and their mother's food and clothing had caused her a violent burst of anguish. Afterwards the whole affair became a play, we wrote beside her, read our first sketches to her for correction, giving her dull life an interest of the utmost use to her health, while the produce of our pleasant evenings kept her supplied with the few luxuries habit had rendered necessaries to all of us. My dear Aunt Bourne on her second marriage sent us a large sum of money as we had learned to consider seventy pounds. My mother's fifty pounds went for John's Edinburgh bills, our twenty pounds to the house. But we had not the same delight in spending it as our own forty pounds had given us. What a curious life has mine been.

WEDNESDAY, DECEMBER 3. Hal ill. Mrs. Smith not well. Weather cold, harsh, gloomy, blustering: sadly in want of something to cheer us. Women can always occupy themselves, but what is there for a man to do, in delicate health, in miserable weather, all whose pursuits are active? I have been as busy as a bee, spinning out my brains with the idea of some day turning them to profit, reading with a view to the improvement of the children, working my chairs, knitting Jack's socks, etc., etc.

7. Finished my 'fourth period' [of Chambers'] which has most extremely interested me; I have found that Locke, Boyle, and other philosophical writers of that period advocated those principles of education which are only beginning to be acted upon *now*; this should teach us all

individually patience in our endeavours to carry out our plans of improvement. There must be time even for the most admirable changes; yet we do everything quicker than in former ages—railroad speed comparatively.

8. There is a most wicked combination in Dublin among the shipowners and I suppose the coal factors, by means of which coals have risen gradually from fourteen shillings a ton up to thirty-five, a hundred sail in the offing are prevented entering the river to deliver their cargo, one or two only being admitted at a time to keep the price up. Quantities of vessels have gone to Belfast in consequence and the coal will be carted overland cheaper though in small quantities. The Mayor has no jurisdiction, nor can anything be done till the Meeting of Parliament; and this an unusually inclement season. Such unprincipled villainy, for 'tis the poor that suffer—the rich fill their cellars in summer.

14. Yesterday, Sunday, I walked to school the frost making the road quite clean, found Miss Gardener thriving; twenty-nine clean, happy-looking little girls. Mr. McConnell shut up having closed a few minutes after eleven, his pupils averaging from nine to thirteen. So he must go; I much dislike him. I have found him jealous, greedy, inattentive, though a clever, well-informed young man. The priest was so unjust to him that I thought it right to give him time to retrieve his popularity—in this he has failed; and being disinclined to him myself I was afraid a prejudiced mind might misjudge him; therefore I agreed with him to remain till Christmas that he might have a fair chance. He is not fit for the situation owing to his selfish character and shall therefore be dismissed.

But *the* news is that the Ministry have resigned: a split in the cabinet, and Sir Robert has felt himself obliged to execute his oft-repeated threat. What the country will do without the only common-sense head in it remains for time to show; it will require no common talents to steer our unwieldly vessel through so many shallows.

28. Sunday, Sir Robert Peel was recalled to power above a week ago, he was indeed but a few days out of office for Lord John could not succeed in forming an

administration. Too many conflicting opinions among his motley charactered, so-called followers, private piques, political variances, and the country evidently not with him.

I have been teased to death about the school. Mr. McConnell is odious, mean, tricky, careless, not what I call honest in money matters, nor morally courageous, yet I am after all keeping him till April to give myself time to find a good master and not to turn this ill brought up young man adrift; his night school is very well attended—forty pupils, very few day scholars—fifteen or sixteen. Miss Gardiner too is troublesome. It don't do to leave home for two years. They were all at church to-day in *my new covered car*. We have exchanged the pony carriage for this much more useful conveyance by the help of kind Mr. Owen who has got it quite a bargain for it is as good as new, having been but little used and only £26, the pony carriage will surely sell for £25 so we have managed beautifully.

31. This last year seems to me to have made an entire change in the character of the family; the Colonel and I have become two old people able for little of the business of life, and the girls have started up into young women so formed in their appearance that I constantly forget their childish years and catch myself fretfully annoyed at some exhibition of childish mind, forgetting that a higher development of feeling or intellect would be to be deplored, and that my study hitherto has been to keep them back, from principle. Unfortunately various circumstances have of late combined to bring them more forward than is desirable at their early age. I was writing this last sentence when little Jack ran up to ask to whom I was writing—'To you, you monkey,' said I; he laughing would not believe me. 'Some day you will find it true', added I, 'and you will remember the day and the words and all, long after this when Mama will not be with you.'

The last evening of 1845. Papa in bed nursing a fresh cold, I writing beside him, Jack tired of the long hours, waiting for twelve o'clock, had crept down to us for amusement, the little sleepy eyes betraying how much more happy he would have been in bed had pride not prevented his retiring to it.

Dear little boy, if I could but ensure the same pure feelings to you through life. Save you from the misnamed amusements of your class in youth—low, sensual, dissipations, hurtful to health of body and of mind, self indulgence in the lowest instincts of our nature, instead of the manly occupations, the fruits of moral vigour of character. Fox-hunting, steeple chacing, racing, these are hardly worse than waste of time, follies pursued by the idle, harmless maybe in themselves, but what do they lead to?—vice, despicable vices, at the best unfitting their determined follower from all the higher duties of his calling, the exertion of all the nobler powers of his mind and heart, more pleasurable as they undoubtedly are too. When I think of my brothers I tremble for my son. I would not have him wade through the mud which nearly choked both even should he cast it off as they did. There is something so very wrong in the education of our young men, a wrong bent given to their minds, really, I believe, from the impure ideas suggested by those classical authours so much boasted of as their best teachers. Nature is powerful enough without any aid from these exciting sources, and were she rightly directed could she debase all the warm feelings of youth as is done systematically. Eton, Harrow, and other celebrated publick schools nurse the vices which are matured at Oxford, Cambridge, Edinburgh. Diseased in body, vitiated in feeling, crippled in every energy of the mind, the husbands and the fathers of Britain prepare to transmit to posterity the consequences of their hardly censured crop of 'wild oats'. Let us give things their right names and call them sins, breaches of every law given to us by our Maker.

I won't let the old year by with only these melancholy reflexions. If ever anyone had reason to look back on such a period of time with satisfaction it should be me for our little circle in this wide universe has had but blessings to commemorate. All we love that are left to us well, our home thriving, place progressing, people improving, neighbours agreeable, children our comfort. Hal is not as young as he was, which is hardly extraordinary considering that in March next he will be sixty-six; for this age he is a strong man, active, cheerful and hardy; he must not expect to do all he has done. For me, my health seems to be gradually returning to me. We are certain of nothing and I still feel great prudence to be necessary, but with prudence I hope yet to see a few years and to pass them not uselessly.

SIX

1846

The first full year of the Famine, and her journals provide a detailed description of how the estates around Blessington were affected. The summer was spent back in idyllic Rothiemurchus and with her family in Edinburgh where she planned her literary pieces with Robert Chambers. The Smiths returned to a deteriorating situation with various haphazard schemes to retrieve the poverty in operation. October she crossed the Irish sea again for her niece's wedding but, in view of the challenges facing every class, as she wrote, with great reluctance. And the crisis was there to greet her on her return.

SUNDAY, JANUARY 4. Our New Year's day dinner downstairs was a very satisfactory one to the company, inasmuch as they had a most bountiful display of joints and puddings, with tea afterwards at discretion. We only used to have the men, but this year the thought struck us that it would do a great deal of good to ask their wives with them and Mrs. Fyfe tells me that cleaner, tidier, decenter behaved women could not be met with.

18. I have been reading only Chambers in various lines and Mr. Dickens's *'Cricket;'* I am inclining to James Craig's opinion that these writings are immoral. They certainly give false views of society, the poor are not so angelick, the rich not so demoniack as he represents them. As a class the poor have little sensibility, deep but rude rather than fine feelings and are equally incapable of conceiving the poetic ideas, as they are ignorant of the language he gifts them with; while the rich middling classes are not *all* brutal, though some individuals may amid their growing prosperity retain too much of the hard-heartedness they learned either from their own or their parents' poverty. The upper ranks, the truly benevolent, the untiring

friends of the wretched, he seems to avoid describing. It is wrong to widen the breach already too large. It is pandering to the bad passions of the multitude; and there is the immorality—some may be in fault, may well deserve the satirist's lash, but for the crime of the few we should not all be held up to reproach. The '*Cricket*' as a work is inferiour to the '*Chimes*,' both together are not worth the '*Carol*'. Yet 25,000 copies of the 'Cricket' were bespoke. Mr. Dickens is the Editor chosen for the new Liberal newspaper—name has slipt my memory.[1]

Politicks are sleepy enough. We shall know nothing till next week, a ravelled skein it seems to be. If our 'pilot weather the storm' he will be a great man. I was at school yesterday and was wanted there; many things require my weekly eye; still there was nothing very far amiss, the attendance good—32 girls, 26 boys. One of our little pupils is gone, dear little pretty Jane Fitzpatrick; the Uncle Tom, who had come from Birkenhead to spend the Christmas, took ill, and died in four days, no one thinking it worth while to call in the Doctor. I told them from their description of his case 'twas scarlet fever; they said no, so they waked him in form, Mrs. John Fitzpatrick taking her three children with her to the infected house, a place the size of the sofa, and keeping them up all night in the crowd round the corpse. Little Jane sickened the second day and was brought home in the cold morning air without one wrap about her. The school children attended her remains to the grave, her own class walking immediately behind the coffin. It was a touching sight old Peggy told us, and was extremely gratifying to the neighbours. We have old Peggy Nary dying, and not one human being can I get for love *and* money to go and nurse her, her outrageous temper has left her friendless.

19. Set up my repository this morning, whether it will succeed or no is a question. We begin modestly with one small boxfull in Peggy's little window. All is such uphill work in this country. The schools hardly thrive. The Lending Library has few subscribers. The Savings bank and the

1 It was the *Daily News*; see 23.11.1847.

Loan fund went to the mischief. The hospital is still unfinished. Will the Repository do better. We can but try.

21. Mrs. Grace ill, all but gone when the Doctor, for whom we sent a horse, reached her. Poor creatures, they suffer a great deal in those miserable-looking cabins with only the one room for the sick and the well. These excitable Irish! the husband came up to me with tears streaming down his cheeks, so agitated. 'John,' said I, 'we must act now, cry afterwards. Send off a man and horse for the doctor, and do you go home and bid the woman do as I tell you till he comes.' Then followed short directions. My dear father, how many owe comfort to you, for years I managed his dispensary, visited our sick for him, and when neither he nor our ten-mile-off doctor was at hand, prescribed myself successfully.

24. Twenty-nine boys in school to-day, thirty-four girls, all in good order. The master having now begun to behave himself, the mistress takes her turn to be troublesome; not by neglecting her duties, but by rendering herself unfit to perform them thoroughly, giving way to low spirits almost hysterically—the consequences of typhus fever, her tormenting mother and little tender anxieties not to be further alluded to at present.

WEDNESDAY, FEBRUARY 4. Politicks sleeping for the present, a strange state of things, out of which there is no seeing any way clearly. Sir Robert avows himself the most perfect convert to free trade which might be all very well if we could carry other nations along with us, and he only hesitates to abandon protection on everything till the country is ready for the step. He lowers the duty on corn year by year to extinguish it altogether in three years. The Tories are outrageous (sic), the topbooted gentry furious, the [Anti-Corn-Law] League not satisfied, nor the Repealers, yet it is supposed the ministry will stand the shock. We shall see.

6. The Doctor is going to a ball on Wednesday in Dublin at Mrs. McMahon's and Annie is teaching him to Waltz! and to Polka!, Janey playing to them. Gravely, for two hours this night he pulled the poor child about the room, charmed with the success of her instructions and his own

assiduity. One could not have believed it had it not been before our eyes, and he has just as much idea of dancing as a bullock, neither ear nor agility.

9. Fine frosty morning, bright sun. The girls had to manage the repository basket for me as the wind was too piercing for me to venture out. All my little books were gone except *one* on cleanliness, and the usual proportion of baby linen, etc. I am charmed at the books taking so well.

15. Mr. Owen was in raptures with the well drained field Tom Darker has just completed. All the slope of Judy Ryan's farm below the road thoroughly drained and levelled and thrown into one field, about seven acres. It looks very well certainly, cost about £36, well bestowed money on the labouring poor, and Tom Darker thinks that two crops will repay the outlay. Hal had an offer from Mr. Hanks for Pat Quin's ground, but has refused it, finding the management of land on his own account so profitable.

19. Sir Robert Peel's noble speech. Greater than ever, each event brings out this magnificent character. Party spirit no longer confines this high mind. The landed aristocracy are improved indeed since Squire Western's[2] time, but they have many a long stride to take yet ere they reach the moral standard of men much beneath them in worldly rank.

24. Having finished my '*Lairds*' I have actually written to offer them to the Messieurs Chambers. If they will encourage me as did the Editors of various periodicals in my youth I may make my £10 every now and then as easily as I did then and shall, I hope, employ it as usefully, though instead of supplying necessaries to my home, where, thank God, every comfort abounds, it will be used to cheer the humble hearths and rouse the dormant energies of the miserably wretched around us. Clothe some of the naked children at any rate; and this spring will be one of deep distress, potatoes are now 6d a stone and that unhappy creature Jemmy Craig's wife

2. The hard-living, virile, rustic bore in Henry Fieldings' novel *Tom Jones* (1749).

told Mrs. Fyfe to-day that she cannot do with less than ten stone in the week. Fivepence a week for her lodgings, three pence halfpenny for the husband's tobacco—where is the firing, the clothing, and what they call the kitchen to come from for these five miserable creatures, even though he is in the Colonel's work, for he is so weakly he cannot earn as another man. The idea of such a pair of incapables marrying without a home, without employment; it is really a moral sin, though they none of them comprehend its enormity.

MARCH 1. A rough Sunday. Hal in his room with asthma of course after his improprieties; the fit not a bad one, however. The girls none the worse of their fatigues, nor I either; Jack in gay spirits. We hardly ought to be so cheerful with starvation at our door here and that dreadful loss of life in India, wholesale murder on the Sutledge called a glorious victory. How many mothers, wives, sisters, and young betrothed will lay down this fatal gazette in agony of heart. We were not the aggressors and indeed in the present condition of the world, war in some parts of it is still unavoidable; the day will come however when such horrours will be no more, when the changes now beginning will have thoroughly altered the whole social system, when there will be no force on earth but the force of truth.

Hal and I, and I and Mr. Darker, have had long consultations about the best method of relieving the poor. Hal and Mr. Darker will have a finishing conference to settle the plan to be pursued which I will then note down as a guide for future times should any such melancholy seasons occur under the improving management of these more prudent days. With potatoes at their present price it would take 9/—a week to buy sufficient of them for the labourer's family; he can earn at best but 6/—and there are all his other necessaries, house rent, clothes, fuel, milk. The Managers who buy up the flour and meal and sell it out in the very small quantities the labourers can only buy, nearly double the cost price on the poor purchaser, and if they give credit, charge usurious interest besides—a system that ruins hundreds—a system that every landlord or master is bound to check as far as in him lies.

3. The doctor spent yesterday evening with us talking over politicks of course. And free trade is making its way it seems steadily, as the subject comes to be better reflected on. I was so imbued with my father's 'protection to agriculture'[3] that my head a'n't yet convinced of the wisdom of opening our ports to cheaper and finer grain than our climate will enable us to raise. Two such men as Lord John and Sir Robert are not likely to be wrong, people say. And when they have altered their opinions and changed their measures it is thought to be right to follow them. Mr. Cobden made an admirable speech towards the close of this tiresomely lengthy debate, addressing the aristocracy as they are little used to—as it would do them good to be oftener spoke to, for they do indeed live in a charmed world—a world of their own to which the real world without bears no resemblance. A few years more and all this must be altered.

4. No news by post yesterday. A perfect hurricane of wind and rain all day, a frightful stormy night: trees blown down, panes of glass blown in, such an uproar there was no sleeping; bad weather for the ploughing match which takes place at twelve in Lord Downshire's park.

5. Ploughing match very good yesterday. Upwards of sixty ploughs. An immense concourse of people, almost every-one in the country, high and low; the day though coarse, kept up very well. There came too a letter from the Messrs Chambers accepting the papers for consideration; vanity whispers that after reading they will not disapprove. What a pleasure this occupation will then be,—interesting in a high degree and useful where a large heart has but a scanty purse to back its inclinations.

7. Doctor again, to say he had dined the day before at the Manor and the people were all up in the skies about the

3. This was one of the topics, according to *Hansard*, on which as M.P. for Great Grimsby (1812–18) and Tavistock (1819–26) he spoke most frequently.

'ball.' Passing through Blesinton I put *My Father* and *My Brother* into the post and paid eight pence for them, Miss Boothby gratifying herself with a leisurely scrutiny of the address which seemed not a little to surprise. Mem: not to excite her curiosity again.

9. I believe that this first will likewise be the last party ever attempted here. In my weak health I am quite unequal to bear up against the fretfulness any plan not originating with himself causes the Colonel. I hope the little girls will be happy for their poor mother has earned their short-lived pleasure dear enough. I have no right to worry their father on any account whatever—duties to children, to neighbourhood, all must give way to the comfort of the master of the family. This dance indeed grew out of the fun of the young people assisted by the Doctor; I had little to do with it, having for some time back never given an invitation of any sort of my own accord and I was wise. Men who have managed bachelour establishments to near fifty have no idea of a wife's part in it. The women they think of are a kind of upper servants.

Poor Mrs. Gardiner died this morning. I went to see the poor daughter who almost shocked my composed Scotch nature by the vehemence of her affliction. It will be as short-lived, for these keen Irish feelings last a very short time. The expression of the countenance was so peaceful I took Janey in to see the corpse: the first sight of the dead body is so awfully affecting to all that I was glad of an opportunity of showing what all we love are to come to in this less than usually disagreeable form. A person too in whom we were not much interested, still it shocked the child greatly.

12. Our great day. That foolish Margaret has sat up all night making her confectionery that it might be fresh which will of course knock her up afterwards. We did nothing in the way of arrangement till to-day that the Colonel might not be put out of his way in the least, and we had all done before breakfast that there might be no commotion after he left his room, so that he was spared all annoyance.

13. Still the party. John had his harness room prepared for stable guests; superiour grades were to be accommodated

in the kitchen, Mrs. Fyfe carrying on all her refreshing operations in her own room assisted by Mrs. White and Mrs. Dodson. Everybody was well dressed, everyone looked happy; the rooms were brilliant, the musick excellent; two good performers playing the richly set modern musick on that fine instrument is as good as any band. After each set refreshments were served beginning with coffee and bread and butter; then tea and cakes; then light biscuits with negus and lemonade, a supply of which were then placed in the billiard room and the trays ceased. At twelve we had supper; everything cold but the game those very obliging young men John Hornidge and Sam Finnemore had been two days shooting for me over all the grey mountains in the neighbourhood. These snipes, woodcocks and teal were sent up in the silver covered dishes for the top and bottom of each table. We had besides raised pies, poultry, ham, tongue, and every kind of dried fruit, jelly, cream, cake and pastry; oranges too, and plenty of wine by help of which the spirits of all were so recruited that they danced on again till within twenty minutes of four in the morning, when all broke up apparently with much regret.

14. The doctor utterly crazed with this polka mania—indeed dancing mania for everything of the kind is much the same to him; the whole night he passed on the floor treading on the ladies' toes, tearing their dresses, setting the figures wrong, misdirecting all, and so furious at some of his orders in the moulinet being disobeyed that he quitted the quadrille in disgust leaving his partner standing there all forlorn. It is the most incredible delusion, his idea that he dances well, and his unwearied exercise of an art he knows nothing of and which in his youth he never cared for, being then of a composed character, fond of sensible conversation with people older than himself and enjoying a grave game at whist as his recreations. Now it is all jigging it with the youngest girls he can get, and there he whirls, stout, and heavy, and ungraceful, and grey-headed, out of all time, altogether so astonishing a spectacle that I begin to fear with Ogle Moore that it will end seriously.

15. A stormy Sunday. The Poles are making but little of
their insurrection. And the Americans are beginning
to swallow half of their big words about the Oregon
Territory, so probably in a little time they will make
up their minds to gulp down the remainder. I had a
letter yesterday from Mr. Robert Chambers, delighted
with my *Lairds*, but must consult his brother, will write
again in a few days; then he gossips on four pages about
an old Rothiemurchus housekeeper whom he knew in his
obscure youth and described under a fictitious name in
one of his early journals. I feel so clever, so grand, 'tis
an honour to the family to sit in the room with me!!

21. I got a note from Robert Chambers to say that brother
William approved of the *Lairds*, and asking for the third
part. It was ready and Hal put it into the post at Naas.
I must now set to work again, keep the press going.
I may make quite a little fortune if I am industrious,
brains paying better than fingers though a little of both
is good.

23. The Doctor brought us yesterday a printed paper, published by Government to teach the people how to use
the Indian corn flour. It will be very useful although the
Dutch oven part might have been left out, even a griddle
few of the poor possess, and to talk of yeast and butter and
eggs and new milk to perfect paupers is a sort of mockery.
Margaret and I can teach the porridge, the hasty pudding
and the common cakes from seeing them made at Pau
where the maize flour is much used. Unfortunately any
trouble is so disagreeable to the habits of our indolent
population, I doubt their taking it till actually dying from
want, any food they are unaccustomed to they dislike
equally, but the famine is coming, has begun in the plains
and must reach the hills, and though those immediately
belonging to our small knot of good landlords may feel
little of it, all around are already in misery, the poor
broom man among them who while walking up from
the gate with me, his load upon his back, told me he had
no work, no food, and was reduced to one meal a day,
himself, his wife & five children. Why will they marry
on nothing?

24. A milder morning. Could not sleep last night for thinking of the miseries of that wretched James Craig's wife and fifty others, who I daresay were sound on their straw under their scanty coverings and half open roofs.

28. At school there was no Miss Gardiner, she had gone off to Dublin in the early car without asking leave, or leaving a reason, hoping to be back by Monday, the little girls, such of them as had not returned home, sitting in a row in the boys' room. She is really unsettled in her wits and when she returns I must have a serious conversation with her, either bring her back to her senses or get quit of her.

29. The Colonel's birthday. I had bought him a square of rich silk for neckcloths, and I presented him with *Mr. Gray*[4] which I had only written the last line of just before his bell rang. It is a fine sunshiny Sunday morning and we must all get ready for church. I have a mind to wear my white 'velours épinglé à panache blanche,'[5] in honour of the birthday and the sunshine. There is no use in keeping our finery till it spoils in our wardrobes. By the bye Miss Knaggs has sent really pretty white organdie dresses for the girls, simple and tasteful and though too late by ten days for Mama's dance they will be all ready for the Blesinton Ball. If we ever have it.

30. Tom Darker sold ten more of our cattle for £10 each, he sold eight at the fair for £40, the worst quite young things, and he has the best to sell yet, as many as will bring in about £90 and all this for five months keep, making a profit of near thirty per cent. On the outlay the Colonel calculates, half yearly, the bad or dead half year too, so farming answers.

31. No word yet from Messieurs Chambers. I continue writing for them as it very much amuses me, and having had so flattering a reception I am in hopes of not being cast off just as the road has been cleared for my making a little spare money for *menus plaisirs*, probably they are

4. This thinly disguised autobiographical article for Chambers' portrayed how an Irish state not dissimilar to Baltiboys was improved by the new landlord.
5. Uncut velvet with a white plume or feathers.

waiting to see the effect in print. The musick of the German polka arrived just after dinner and the Doctor coming to tea the evening was spent in practising the new figure, the Colonel getting up to assist, just as busy as the rest of them after all the laughing he has had at the polka epidemick, and certainly the most promising pupil among the whole, not anyone of the youngest of them dancing within a million of degrees as well as this elderly gentleman of the last age who must in his Beau days have been no small acquisition in a ball-room.

WEDNESDAY, APRIL 1. We heard that Lady Milltown had returned home, herself, her five children, her maid, her footman, all packed up in one hired carriage. I hope she may be so occupied with her home for a few days as to leave me in quiet; I am determined, however, not to let her worry me as she used to do. Whenever she tired of herself she drove over to bestow her ill-humour on me.

5. At School, yesterday, I filled the report sheets, fifty-two in the girls' school, forty-two in the boys! the average attendance for the six months small—twenty-seven and twenty-one, the last three busy months not making up for the first three bad ones. Poor Miss Gardiner, she is really out of her mind, deprived of the little sense she ever had, so discontented, so disinclined to exert herself, so indifferent to my business, and so overcome by her own folly that though I have given her a month to recollect herself I have no idea that she will ever settle herself to be where Mr. Dixon is not, and he a clever, handsome, and very ambitious young man, seven years her junior, has, I understand, no thoughts of her, poor thing.

6. Wakened upon a fall of snow—the whole country as white as if one large sheet were spread over it. This accounts for the extreme cold of yesterday evening which really was almost intolerable. I could do nothing but crouch over the fire considering of a subject for Mr. Chambers, and have determined on writing a few more highland sketches of a humbler rank of life than my chieftainly lairds as a great deal could be told of the peculiar manners of this important class which it would be a pity to lose the recollection of.

20. We have been engaged with the miseries of ouŕ poor.
We have brought home some of the maize bread and
some of the maize flour which we all think delicious,
and very luckily, so do all those who have tasted either
about us. A little of this with Hal's potatoes and meal
sold at low prices will keep our own people in comfort
through these always scarce months; he is also going to
bring home some coals for sale on the same terms, as fuel
is not to be had in the country. All this care will prevent
much distress *at home*, but beyond there will be much,
more even than usual, for there is a less supply of turf
and potatoes than ordinary, and fuel and food that have
to be *bought* however cheap their price, are unattainable
by those who have not the money to buy them with.

25. The Doctor rode with Janey and a letter came to me from
Messrs. Chambers most flatteringly expressed enclosing
thirteen pounds for my *Lairds* and soliciting further
favours. The pay is not much, but enough for such
trifles. They are all in print in the three last numbers of
the journal. I am sorry for one thing. Robert Chambers
has told Mrs. Mair of this freak of mine, and as I have
no literary ambition I had rather no one had known of
my authourship beyond our mere selves.

30. Poor little Sarah is gone—our first maid. She died in
childbirth of puerpural fever which has been fearfully
fatal during the last year—leaving three sickly infants
behind her. Just sixteen years ago the poor thing came to
us at Malshanger after we landed from the *Childe Harold*.
What a long busy time to look back on. Poor Sarah, she
was a foolish thing whom there was no doing much with
or for, but she was a simple-minded creature and with all
her faults we liked her.

   If one could but give people common sense. There
is Miss Gardiner quite beside herself. Go she will, and
Mr. McConnell not giving the Inspector satisfaction I
shall dismiss both and endeavour to get a married
pair of superiour condition, reduced, if possible. Our
moving just at this time is really inconvenient, and so
troublesome just as the school was succeeding to have
all our hard work with it begin again. I like my *Lairds*

in print very well—to my amazement '*My Father*' heads the paper, ushered before the world too with a flourish of trumpets. It has however rather annoyed me to find that anyone knows 'who wrote it.'

SATURDAY, MAY 2. Obliged to take some notice of the transactions between Mary Dodson and Andy Hyland though sure of doing no good by it. This affair will therefore continue to plague me and I must lose a good servant, very difficult to replace, because Mr. Darker chooses to identify himself with a very impudent set of people of which clan of Hylands he has brought far more about us than I think at all just to the rest of the people. Mary will not stay where this odious young man is, nor can I expect it. Really they tease me too much.

3. Hal and I went into the Delanys—such a scene of misery. The two old people objects, neither of them able to move. She swelled and breathless on one side of the fire, he worn to a skeleton, crippled and deformed by rheumatick gout upon the other. They pay two guineas a year for their miserable cabin, which Colonel Smith this winter thatched for them; four pounds for the summering and two pounds for the wintering of their cow, not in money, but in their son's labour, who thus, at two and twenty earns sixpence a day. On the other hand John Hornidge, the landlord, says,—'I don't want the fellow; I keep the idle blackguard out of charity, sometimes I have work for him, more times I have none'. Idle!—who could be busy, underfed, under-clothed, under-housed, crushed body and soul by the extreme of poverty. The Messrs. Chambers have graciously accepted my last packet of papers.

4. What a good story I could make of that most impudent Andy's proceedings. Vicious though he be, there is a fearless insolence in his conduct that is positive heroism. He actually marched into my laundry this evening and when the maids shut the door in his face he stood whistling outside it for near a quarter of an hour. Maybe he will sing to-morrow week, I should not the least wonder. Having got rid of his pigs he then took to poultry and we had a whole tribe of his cocks and hens

strutting over our yard, dogs too at any time. I forbid him entering the house because he not only ate up any provisions he saw on the tables, but helped himself to pots, frying pans, spoons, dishes, anything he happened to be in want of, and as a climax helped himself out of the pantry to the Dublin bread and a whole tub of fresh butter just brought down from our tea. This is the honest, civil, conscientious, industrious boy, with whom all the keys of the yard are occasionally entrusted. He will find, however, that he has meddled with an edge-tool when he has meddled with me, and that the young girls under my care are not to be insulted with impunity. Mrs. Fyfe has taken charge of the poor old Delanys; Hal sent them a quantity of old clothes and a straw easy chair to which I have added a cushion. Mrs. Kearns a farmer's wife, brought us instead of their rent the most earnest supplication for food for the support of her family, she has one day's provision in the house!

5. Beautiful weather for the crops, showery and shady and sunny and sultry, they almost grow to the eye. The first reading of the Coercion Bill is carried by an immense majority—149, in spite of the vapouring of that very ridiculous faction of so called Irish 'patriots'; the Corn Law bill will now be proceeded with. Sir Robert has it all his own way, a regular dictator, and most luckily a wise one.

Mr. Smith O'Brien has been performing the merry Andrew part this session. Turn and turn about is fair play, he won't serve on any Committees but Irish ones and having refused to take the share of work allotted to him he is in charge of the serjeant at arms in a little room where he is locked up endeavouring to perform martyr in some nondescript cause, but as yet he is only laughed at. Legislate for Ireland! a nation of lunaticks! Reason with Irishmen! Everyone one of them stark staring mad from the peer to the peasant. At the publick works where the pay is 2/- a day, to men never used at the highest to more than a shilling, they have all turned out for advance of wages. On the railroads, being equally well paid they have collected all the disorderly women and other

profligates for company and run headlong into a career
of debauchery which will end in the miserable death of
hundreds. The Doctor made me shudder over the slight
allusions he made to what has already come under his
medical experience. The people are not ready for higher
wages, higher tastes must first be produced, otherwise
their habits are only lowered by encreasing their means
before they are qualified properly to employ them.

7. Forty-nine, Mrs. Smith. Last year in my own mind I did
not think I should live to see another birthday, this year
I begin to reckon on as many more as will permit me to
see my boy through the dangerous season of early youth,
then my work would be done.

8. The Doctor brought me a New Testament! curious man!
Then he made a clean breast of the ball preparations
setting the little girls half wild with the thoughts of such
a pleasure in prospect. Mr. Darker and I then had the two
disturbers of our peace before us,—a tragi-comick scene
out of which we could make nothing, though Mr. Dickens
might have filled a good long chapter with the queer
speeches, odd words, and violent tempers exhibited on
both sides, the lady shewing to least advantage decidedly.
I will be worried with them and their like no more, they
are both to go, and so shall all else who embroil the family
and don't choose to put up with Mr. Darker. He has
brought his troubles on himself by too much favouring
a particular set of people, Andy deserves punishment for
his bragging folly, his impudent style of manner, etc.,
Mary for her unmaidenly conduct, encouraging a man
for the fun of laughing at him and then telling falsehoods
to clear herself, and I have been wrong ever to allow such
low squabbles to occupy me at all.

9. More of this horrid quarrel, and Mrs. Fyfe has given up
her place because I won't take part with Mary. I have not
fancied her contented for some time back, indeed no one
can wonder at her taking an opportunity of getting out of
such a nation of evil-speaking lunaticks. It would require
great sense, great command of temper and a deaf ear to
all gossipping to pass quietly through life among these
uncontrouled and vindictive people. She has put herself

in the wrong too by becoming such a partizan, allowing herself to be so prejudiced as to become unreasonably violent in a wrong cause. I am getting strong enough to do without her, and her headaches and her temper, her high notions and her meddling detract a little from her many admirable qualities. Still she will be a great loss in the family.

10. A letter from Jane at last, all well, accusing me of never writing, hoping I am occupied with my '*Memoirs*'[6] which Janey Gardiner told them I was writing. Then comes such a compliment on these wonderful abilities of mine as makes me suspect she has either been reading or visiting Mr. Chambers. So the Colonel says in return for her pretty speeches she must be let into the secret. My Aunt nicknames me Madame de Sévigné, and the Colonel now always calls me Madame de Staël, and he will forget someday that we are not alone. Dear me, what an honour it is to belong to such a genius. I will make the children pay more respect to me I declare and as to the Colonel, if I am to be Madame de Staël he shall be poor Mr. Rocca.[7]

11. The Doctor dined with us, [then] came Lady Milltown with her daughters. *They* were very tidy in dress and frank in manner and made themselves very happy, *she* was in one of her affected moods, ringing her r's, talking grand, and in such a fright of a bonnet as would have deformed Venus. I have long ceased all delicacy with her, it did her no good, rather encreased her impertinence, so when she asked if my girls drew I let them go for their portfolios, and when she begged of them to play to her I did not prevent them;—Colonel Smith enjoyed her surprise Miss Clerk her mortification, I was pleased to see her manner

6. In addition to writing her lengthy journal and articles for Chambers' Magazine, she commenced at this time the memories of her first thirty years which came to be called *The Memoirs of a Highland Lady*.

7. Not the most appropriate of comments, for she married John Rocca in 1811 in the twilight of her tumultuous career some six years before her death.

at once become natural and I thought she bore the lesson very well. My Lord has returned. The Doctor's rudeness during this visit was abominable, he read a book in the corner without ever opening his lips and when she asked after his brother's family he told her Mrs. Smith knew more about them than he did.

16. Out again by six this morning for the purpose of whipping Miss Bessy. I must do it as no one else will. Not only has her disobedience to orders encreased, her wanderings, her fibs, and her sullen fits, but she has begun to help herself to other people's property: stealing to give away, thimbles, balls of cotton, from the Repository, a private store of these articles being found in a bag under her pillow. Old Peggy is not judicious with her, not firm enough to manage so clever a child.

19. Such a rainy day, torrents, and cold as winter. Old Paddy Dodson laid up—regular influenza—poor old man; the Doctor has seen him and we are all doing our best for him but it is like enough to go hard with him. George Kearns sent his wife again to ask charity. I told her the conditions on which she would be relieved, but she did not seem to like them!

20. George Kearns came himself and was very reasonable. If he don't shew us at Holantide [All Saints Day, 1 November] that he is thriving, he will at once give up his ground and turn with our help to something that will answer better. In the meanwhile he is to get meal, at the low rate.

21. A holiday—the Ascension. We walked round the hill meeting little groups of people in their best attire—better indeed than we once remember it, but oh, how far beneath what it ought to be and might. We entered some houses: the best were very miserable—as much from the low taste of the people as from want of means; the two Blacksmiths, for instance, earn each 16/- a week, nearly three times a labourer's wages; they had mud floors, no ceilings, little furniture, and were eating potatoes and butter. They squander their money they hardly know how—for they do not save it.

25. Beautiful weather. When I look upon this pretty scenery

brightened by a summer sun, the crops giving such fair promise, the wooded banks and the emerald meadows filled with fine cattle straying by the little river, and am then disturbed by those wretched quarrels between neighbours and servants and priests and folly, I feel with Lord Byron in Greece 'that all save the spirit of man is divine.'[8]

26. My Lady, her two daughters, and her two younger sons came to tea, the children happy and agreeable, their mother such a mass of affectation as to be almost intolerable, beyond merely ridiculous. Half her words French—lolling on the sofa—dressed for a ball—grand to the sublime! and to crown all quite youthful—somewhere about five-and-thirty, and this to me who have often compared ages with her in our early days, and know it to an hour from old Mrs. Wall who was present at her birth; fib after fib about Paris, as formerly about London. She must think me a fool, or else, poor thing, maybe she is only trying to cheat herself—neglected as she must sorely feel she is by everyone: her own fault, for she has outraged everyone. The children are really nice; the girls very awkward, very coarse, and none of them one bit more than mere children.

27. Went up Blackamore Hill, a large party, to eat our cold dinner on the top; yet such was the force of much combined attraction that the day passed very pleasantly. The panorama was worth climbing up to view, the eye reaching far over the hills at hand to the wide plains of Dublin, Meath and Kildare. All determining to drink tea here and dance the polka afterwards, we passed a merry evening, not breaking up till after ten.

One of the pleasantest sights of the day was our group of attendants over the fragments—men who never taste meat twice in a year truly enjoying what we had left of our luxuries; the saddest was one the Doctor and young John Hornidge called me to look at—a little ragged frightened boy, the herd of some cattle grazing on these uplands who

8. 'Where the virgins are soft as the roses they twine. And all, save the spirit of man is divine'. *The Bryde of Abydos* Ii.i.

had collected on a stone the *shakings out* of the table cloth, and who was piling up crusts of bread with one hand and holding bare bones to his mouth with the other—the impersonation of famine. Need I set out that we added more substantial morsels to his store—enough too for the morrow, and the Doctor slipt sixpence into the poor thin hand for milk hereafter.

29. Another scene of misery. The Doctor had got a note from old John Hornidge to go and visit Edward Shannon in the lane. My mind misgave me that the man was dying like his children of starvation, so when the riders departed, the Colonel, Janey and I drove over to see; the one room was very clean, almost tidy, except for a stack of furze at the foot of the bed—the fuel. The man was lying down ill enough, the wife burst into tears when I entered. 'Now God be praised,' she said, 'we are saved.' 'Oh Lady Smith, my jewel' etc. He had worked on when quite unfit for labour because his wages are stopt in sickness; he gets ninepence a day, but having two acres of ground and this miserable cabin so much is stopt for rent as leaves him but two shillings a week in money. He sublet his land to pay for firing, he sold his cow to pay his debts, and there he is with six children, five of them girls, and one an idiot. Their potatoes being done for a fortnight they have had in the family but one meal a day; no wonder the children had no spirit at their lessons. Yesterday morning they had nothing till the old grandmother Mrs. Delany sent them two *quarts* of meal from her scanty store. Biddy Shannon *made two* halves of this—one half gave them all a cup of *thick gruel* yesterday; to-day it was *thin* as she had to keep enough for a drink in the evening for her husband; the little girls wept bitterly. Oh how they bounded off for milk and meal when the means to get both were given them.

30. Sent broth to poor Shannon who will recover if well fed, the Doctor says. And must not pride have a fall? A *packet returned* from Mr. Chambers—two tales *rejected*—the Irish sketch and the Highland story. I think the subjects of both may perhaps be too delicate. There's an humbling catastrophe! My literary honours! Nipt!

31. Such a hot end of May—fiercer than ever anyone remembers of late years; certainly beautiful weather; crops looking very healthy. Corn Bill passed in the Lords by a good majority—forty-nine, I think.

TUESDAY, JUNE 2. John Robinson arrived to collect the rents, having given the people three weeks law on account of some fairs which were postponed. The tenants paid well generally, no complaints except from the sickness among the cattle some time ago which was a serious misfortune. The scarcity of potatoes is little felt by the farmers it being caused principally by the stocks having been kept back from the markets in the expectation of prices rising continually which system pressed heavily on the labouring purchasers in which class the failure of the crop had been the commonest owing to inferiour management. The passing of the corn bill has lowered all provisions already.

3. The Ball all 'knocked in the head' as the Doctor elegantly expresses himself. Ogle Moore has written to the Committee as 'your clergymen,' poor Mr. Foster declaring notwithstanding that he had no voice in the matter. Well, your clergymen in consideration of the misery of the poor, request that to put a stop to it the rich will give up spending, for this is the argument tho' given to us in many such fine words as luxurious amusements, generous impulses, every noun properly qualified in the superlative degree too, true grammar style. Thus appealed to, the Committee to avoid a quarrel *postpone* the Ball, but a coolness must ensue because in addition to the political economy being out of date, part of the note is very arrogantly written as if he had been violently offended and thought it necessary to castigate his flock whom he wishes to rule 'alla Roma.' I a'n't sorry, my delicate blossoms would have expired in the arms of some of their sturdy partners dancing all night in this weather.

4. John went by the early car. What an active man of business. We can't get him to take a proper percentage on the rents and he gets angry about it. We must make it up some other way, Hal was his good friend once, he says, when he was poor and wanted aid. Now he is the richest

of the two! I heard last year he had made £12,000. Well we are before the world too, half a year nearly in hands, quite sufficient for we don't want to save, the children are provided for.

26. Yesterday our highland cousins [James Grant of Glenmoriston and his family] left us to pursue their Irish tour. It was a wise idea this sudden thought of Glen's to look a little at an almost unknown part of his own country after having travelled half over the continent. He tells me to expect many changes for the worse among the people in 'the north' along with wonderful improvements on the face of the country. Old families extinct, old estates gone, old feelings decayed, and this free kirk movement completing the disruption of ancient ties; the seceding ministers having inflamed their flocks to old covenanter height. It is wonderful that no blood was spilt, it was very near it. And all for nothing, no point of doctrine was involved in the dispute. 'The spirit of popery,' secular power, the aim of an ambitious priesthood, ignorant, arrogant, and bigoted, as are all presbyterians from the very nature of their self-sufficient style, clinging to this the whole of those ministers who rode the rigging, *deserted their posts*—for in plain English this is the interpretation of their breach of duty.

James was astonished with Ireland, its beauty, its fertility, its fresh balmy air. Dublin a little London, all alive, so full of splendid buildings, fine streets and squares, beautiful well dressed women and handsome men. This place, this house, our way of living, and our business habits enchanted him. He was perhaps prepared to be pleased but he did not expect the civilisation, the polish, he found. 'Poor Eliza banished to Ireland,' he means to announce her as meriting the envy instead of the pity of all her relations.

27. Very showery weather during the last week. It began just this day week Saturday when our hay was all out laying almost ready for the carting but not quite, and had they set about the last tossing at 9 in the morning instead of 11, it might have been in small cocks at any rate before dinner, and had that obstinate Tom Darker

begun to cut it the day the Colonel told him or even the day before he reluctantly did do it, it would have been in the stack in proper time, of a good colour, without any making almost. As it is, all the men have been for days shaking and raking and idling amongst it when they might have been at other things. It is safe however and that's something.

28. A dozen visits from Lady Milltown, sometimes a mere call, sometimes to tea, her grandeur is quite laid aside for the present and, poor woman, she seems to be very unhappy, not without cause. He is borrowing on her Life again, a third time. In the end she will have no income left. What on earth will become of them? Poor Sir Robert Peel, or rather happy, to get quit of such bear-baiting as might have overthrown the mind of a less phlegmatick man. How we shall miss him, his practical head, his calm temper, his enlightened views, above all his admirable finance. Lord John will be a poor substitute.

29. We intended going up to Dublin to-day but it is too stormy. What changed times are these. Here is Ibrahim Pasha, the heir of Egypt's throne, in England with a suite, visiting all our Manufactories, all our publick institutions, dining with our nobles, living as a 'Christian.' Dwarkanoth Tagore is here again, and as for German, Russian, Danish Princes, they are popping in upon us in the most friendly way every now and then. The fruits of peace, of blessed peace, but will peace last. With Sir Robert Peel's Government end all my hopes of good for some time at least; powerful as the merchants have become all over the world they want sagacious statesmen to back them.

The Tories must see their day is over, their party defunct, their spirit laid. We could no longer tolerate doctrine so illiberal. For a time we shall be saved the anarchy of a growing democracy till men's minds become more prepared for the great changes advancing and which it should be the endeavour of this generation to retard as the world is by no means yet ready for them. But come they must as intelligence progresses, the present aristocracy must fall as the feudal system fell when its power is no longer wanted. Among themselves our nobles still foster the spirit of exclusiveness, fancying that the world at large worship them as they worship one another. But the world at large are beginning to think little about them, their acres still give them influence, but their titles are beginning to be less valued and their ancestry to be disregarded unless in the few instances where *character* adds its weight to ancient blood. There must be both a sinking and a rising before society finds its proper level.

FRIDAY, JULY 3. A long walk with Annie this morning to make a round of visits on as many of our poor as lay in one direction. It was no bad lesson for Annie though in general the circumstances of these poor creatures have improved so much since I first went about amongst them, that to my practised eye in misery they appear to be almost comfortable.

4. A great day at school—quarter day—and the *priest* with me, the young priest, the curate [Father Galvin], and I hope he is satisfied of my sincerity, for he seemed really pleased with all he saw—anxious to assist me, and made no objection to take charge of the children during my absence. They cheat him as they cheat me for half of them who discontinued school on account of the preaching never came near the chapel at all. He agreed with me as to the advisability of going on for this quarter as best we could and not putting in the new people till my return from Scotland.

After dinner Annie and I drove to Russborough where I had long owed a visit; I set out at four o'clock and did not get back till eight, so glad was Miladi to have a visitor. Annie was sent off with the girls to gather mushrooms. I had to listen to many complaints, a good deal of scandal, some fun, and a quantity of conjectures, political and otherwise; all this in the Library; then was walked out to see many real improvements in the grounds—a new flower garden, a hot house building, greenhouse preparing, iron gates projected. Brought to the Dressing-room for a cup of tea and to review the whole of the Paris wardrobe. All the caps were put on my head; all the flowers and bands and bows and

streamers and fringed ribbons and tissues and gauzes
and a little hat and feathers on my lady's; the bonnets, a
pale pink among them, were ferretted out of their boxes;
a *pink* glacée silk with two deep flounces, short sleeves,
low neck; a light blue satin equally low, a green and lilack,
a rose and white, a red and green, a deep blue, were all
paraded before me. Also a Limerick lace with two skirts
festooned up one side with bows and flowers; and she
must weigh twelve or fourteen stone and has become the
size of the house, and is one year younger than myself.
Then there were shawls, scarves, visites,[9] dessus[10] furs,
lace, embroidery beyond counting; more than two dozen
pocket handkerchiefs lay at one time on my knees, while
a pile of habit shirts lay beside me.

It was quite bridal array—and for what purpose? for
the poor woman visits nowhere; none of these things
will ever be on hardly as she herself acknowledges;
it is a curious passion under the circumstances. She
showed me some trinkets too, presents from him,—sixty,
seventy-eighty guineas. And in the last paper was his
advertizement to raise ten thousand pounds upon her
life annuity—the *third* insurance of the same kind, which
with the interest paid to the Coates after the lawsuit
with them went against him reduces her once handsome
income by one half. Such infatuation! How will it end?
And those children brought up so magnificently in some
respects. I was hard set to get away at all, I was in
such favour, and I had to bring some caps with me as
patterns. At the gate at Russelstown we met George on
the girls' pony sent after us, then Colleen, and we feared
a well-merited scold on appearing, but our tale was so
amusing we got off with a slight reprimand.

12, Sunday. Little has been done during the week except
such arrangings for our departure [for Scotland] as even
the short absence we propose necessitate. Janey has a
note from Colonel Litchfield; he will meet us at Glasgow
or Greenock on Wednesday. To-morrow we start—dear

9 and 10. A short sleeveless cloth and ladies underwear
respectively.

little home, again to leave you. I have no real pleasure anywhere else, much as we are sometimes plagued here. We must always remember that these are but an *emerging* people, civilising a little too rapidly to improve *equally* as they proceed. We consider them too much as if they were further advanced—more on a par with ourselves than it is possible for their intellect to become under many generations.

14. All our affairs being in most exact order the Colonel and I started in our covered car after breakfast at eight o'clock in a cool hour of a hot day. We reached Dublin before eleven, shopped, got our money in gold and English notes, picked up our children, saw Mrs. Haughton and Mary, and reached the *Mercury* a good hour before she sailed.

15. Tontine hotel, Greenock. There don't appear to be a single change in this little stupid town, the same narrow, dirty quay, crowded with a working mob as before. Colonel Litchfield not having kept tryst Papa and Jack are off to Glasgow by the train to look for him and we ladies are all going to give ourselves 'a good wash', a night at sea requiring some after cleanliness. It was a miserable little vessel and so slow a sailer. We had a state cabin the size of a common bed, for four of us; bad tea, a lack of salt, and knives, prices enormous, and a most curious assemblage of a very under set of passengers.

The sea being perfectly calm, the weather fine, and no one the least sick, the voyage was pleasanter than is usual. A foreigner, a young German, was really very nice; so much good sense in all his observations on all he had seen with a quickness which passed over nothing, and a quantity of information, and a degree of accomplishment rarely, alas! to be found except among foreigners. His appeared a different intellect, and it was, from the commonplace chatterers around us, who at first amusing soon became quite tiresome from the repetition of the same unmeaning gossip.

Our German friend spent some months last year between Pau and the Pyrenees so we wandered back among that lovely scenery and on to Switzerland and the Rhine which the Clyde much resembles. Then we had the world of modern authours for a theme, national feelings, prejudices, politicks, musick, English education compared with German, etc. He had been at school with Prince Albert who was clever as a boy and much liked and is pitied for honours considered dearly won by the surrender of liberty. He was betrothed to a young German lady when our Queen fell in love with him and had a struggle between love and glory—the deserted love followed him to England when he decided for glory and there were exciting scenes before she could be prevailed on to depart, Mr. Wessel's family are acquainted with her. So we had our gossip too.

The river Clyde gains every year in beauty as trees grow and pretty houses rise along its banks, the unchanging mountains remaining the finest of backgrounds. Still they look dwarfish after the Pyrenees. Our walk about the town showed us that towards the west it had much extended, a row of better shops followed by good houses running along a considerable way parallel to the river; but all thoughts of improvement in Greenock fled on our return to the inn where we found the Colonel and little Jack returned with Colonel Litchfield.

16. Breakfast over and we with our luggage on the quay before eight, ready for the steamer which came down from Glasgow. Between all passengers the deck was crowded and a high wind made it feel very cold particularly when gusts of rain came on. A tall young man walked down from the inn with a very pretty baby in his arms whom he settled in a snug bed made of great coats on the deck. Another younger child was watched over by a nice-looking young mother, two maids assisting. These were Lord Emlyn, Lord Cawdor's son,[11] his wife and children. It would have been a good lesson to many of our airified nobodies to see these young people doing almost everything for themselves, buckling

11. The first Earl (1790–1866) and his son (1817–1898) were both M.P.s—father a Whig (Carmathen 1813–21) and son Tory (Pembroke 1841–60).

up their parcels, unwrapping their clokes, counting their packages, attentive to their nurses. Watching over their children, all so simply, travelling without carriage or man-servant from London to Cawdor Castle. She was so neatly dressed in a black silk gown and coloured cambric bonnet, her cambric handkerchief and her valenciennes alone showing the luxury of her class. There were two little objects only fit for the theatre, two fine healthy boys, in kilts, hose, garters, low quartered shoes with buckles, velvet coats all covered with silver buttons of great size, bonnets, and huge sticks and plaids of shepherd's grey. We got quit of them at East Tarbet without finding out who were their foolish parents.

Rounding Taward Point was very beautiful, poor Kirkman Finlay's Castle looking really well amid the fine flourishing plantations now grown into handsome woods. The whole voyage through the Kyles of Bute, the mainland to the right, the chain of islands to the left grouping far away in the distance was beautiful; the mountains were finely shaped, the wooding in general rich and the fields fertile. It was curious to see the women packing the herrings at Tarbart, squatting by dozens round the barrels, gutting, salting, and placing, as quick as their hands could move. Loch Fyne is famous for the trade. After a run through part of it, we left our steamboat and were shifted into a very neat track boat which conveyed us along the Crinnan Canal twelve miles of a cut through the Mull of Cantyre (sic) leading us again to the sea in a space of time short after all tho' more than the half of it was spent in passing the nine locks required by the hilly ground. Another steamboat awaited us and more company. Lord Selkirk, his mother and sister joined us here. I think he is about as ugly a very tall man as I ever saw, but we all came quite to admire him from his beautiful attention to his deaf mother who could only be communicated with by means of a slate; the sister seemed equally dutiful and rather a pretty girl into the bargain in spite of sticking out teeth and a most singular dress—boots fit for a man, gloves suited to a hedger, short tartan petticoat and a coachman's cape. The mother was arrayed in much the same style so they are probably great walkers.

We got to Oban about seven, into fine scenery again, some of the bare islands having been our later companions, and by the Colonel stepping quietly on shore the instant we touched it he secured us very comfortable rooms in a little inn where we much enjoyed some excellent tea, bread, sweetmeats, new baked oatcakes and very delicious butter; the little village was crowded, hardly a bed to be had, three steamboats having reached it. We took a longish walk in the country round, and then paraded the street where the good-looking shops surprised us as did the excellent confectionery we found in one of them. But Oban is much frequented during the summer.

17. On board by five o'clock fine scenery but the mists hanging so low as quite to conceal the summits of the mountains, Ben Nevis only now and then showing us the 'cold shoulder' through a cloud. At Fort William we left our steamboat and jogged away very disagreeably for some miles in a sort of van or Dutch wagon passing in the rain Loch Lochy and Loch Oich and Locheil with the finely situated house at Glen Arkaig where the Chief of the Clan Cameron mostly lives. The other lands in Lochaber have changed masters of late years, [bought] by various 'little bodies', one of whom, a merchant in Inverness, has built a very pretty house just opposite to Locheil's with the waters of Loch Oich between them. All the better for the country is this subdivision of the ancient Baronies, but we must poetically regret the extinction of the old families.

We passed into another steamboat and into another carriage—a little one this time, which divided our party and we had a long drive again with a thick rain falling which prevented our seeing the old Castle of Invergarry, though the lower part of the Glen with its little racketting river and thickly wooded banks and braes made us strain our eyes through the misty air. At Fort Augustus we again entered a most convenient steamboat handsomely fitted up, restoring to us some degree of comfort on our journey.

We dried our shoes in the engine-room of the steam boat after keeping them on an hour very damp in the carriage, but it has not hurt us.

Passing the wild shore on Locheil purchased by Sir Duncan Cameron, the little odd Waterloo hero, who once wished for a 'tall lady', I was delighted to see it regularly allotted into small divisions hedged off from one another, a small cabin on each, and cultivation proceeding on all; he was always said to be a worthy little man though he could not please me. Loch Ness rather disappointed me. It is so fine, looking back on it from the other end as I had only ever seen it, that the banks on either side at the upper end seemed tame by comparison.

18. I had a little shopping to do [in Inverness,] so Hal and I walked a good deal among the streets of this clean little town. I did not see much change in it; there are probably more shops, new houses, etc. but all so like the old I did not remark them. We had much trouble in arranging our journey to Rothiemurchus; it was difficult to transport our large party. At last Mr. Grant of the Caledonian hotel suggested the loan of a mail coach which took us bag and baggage. In spite of rain I sat outside with the Colonels; changing horses at Moy, resting an hour at the Slough, and refreshing the same team at the bridge of Carr by which place the road, now shortened by three miles, runs, we took up the old hostler Willie at Aviemore to guide us and reached the boat at Inverdruie by five o'clock.

20. Monday. Walked direct to the Doune [her father's ancestral home], went all over the house, into every corner, opened the closets and the kists to show the children the reliques of past ages, explained all the pictures to them, wandered over the hill on the lawn which once was shrubbery.

23. A rainy morning preventing any out of doors excursion gives me time to think over the events of the last week. 'Tis but ten days since we left our distant home and how easily have we made out our long journey. It was quick and not very fatiguing and beautifully interesting, but far from costing little, though considering the distance and the numbers of our large party the expense was small.

From our own door to this about thirty pounds for eight of us—the Colonel and I, two girls, two servants, Miss Clerk and Jack.

As we were driving out of Inverness I watched well for all the places that I knew but recognised none but Castle Hill, very much improved. A change in the road avoids the dreary moor once so unpleasant to pass over; keeping the lower ground after passing Freeburn it turns up to the Slough from a fertile valley with fields, cottages, a bridge and newly planted banks on the brae of one of which stands the first free kirk we had met, economically built in the plainest manner with a very low flattish roof of paper and composition. This third road through Slough Mouich makes one wonder at the remains of the *second* and stare indeed at the outline of the *first* up which that a carriage could ever have been dragged seems a marvel. None of the cabins along the road have improved as I expected, though the face of the country has—larger fields, more of them, better crops, fenced in gardens and young thriving woods everywhere.

On quitting the woods near the Dulnen we came out upon our own hills every one of which I named through the rain watching for the Ord and for Craig Ellachie as if I expected to see the beacon fires of the olden time. McKenzie came out to us at Aviemore—the son, a nice looking little man; all looked neat about the inn and he has a bed of flowers beneath the enlarged window of the low parlour and his large garden beyond the road is in really perfect order. To guide the strange coachman to the boat he gave us his hostler Willie, the same who as a lad drove my mother, my sisters, William and me to Belleville nineteen years ago when we set out on our melancholy journey to India. Right glad he was to welcome me back for tears stood in the poor man's eyes. No one spoke; the rain fell in torrents. We entered the boat and were rowed silently across and thus I returned to Rothiemurchus. On the wall just opposite to where I am sitting hangs the excellent painting of my father. How it carries thought back to all the past so full of history; he is in his Judge's robes, pale and sad as was his usual expression when unoccupied, at the time I left him. He has become gayer since, I hear, reconciled to his condition, happy even, and it is fortunate. To have been born Laird of Rothiemurohus should have satisfied the most ambitious spirit. To have thrown such an inheritance away would, if reflected on, have brought *brown* hairs down with sorrow to the grave.

24. Walked through the young fir forest to the Loch and we took the offside of it till we reached the point whence I always fancied the scene looked best—whence Mr. Landseer has taken his celebrated painting, and whence an equally fine artist, of nature's own making, I believe, took one of his prettiest sketches. All my Uncle's framed drawings left at the Doune have been hung in the best lights by Mr. Landseer who greatly admires them. The High Street, Oxford, given to old Mr. Cameron and so prized by him, is the chief ornament of the pretty little drawing-room at the Croft.

We returned by the Milltown burn to the really pretty cottage built by the Government commissioners for the Clergyman upon what was once the Milltown moor, now a fine field of oats, with the manse where the old sawmill was, tidy offices standing back on the stance of the saw-miller's house, a small railed-in flower garden and the fruit wall of a fine kitchen garden, stretching along in front of the birch wood all the way to the bank at the polchar, the burn is carried by the roadside skirting the little globe and the Duke of Bedford has carried water from it in a pipe under ground to the garden, our garden, a most ingenious idea. Mr. and Mrs. Rutherfurd are very decent people, quiet and respectable, but not active among the people. He is a very bad preacher, I hear, in English, and very nearly unintelligible in the gaelick. Is the free kirk movement any wonder?

26. In spite of all the changes nineteen years have seen, many of the old friends of my youth are still here to welcome me back among them; the children of a few others are grown up full of the recollections of their parents; so that it a'n't all melancholy that has met me in the home of my youth. Almost all that has been done to the land

is improvement, draining, levelling, clearing, fencing, new roads, new plantations, fine crops where was only heather, green pasture on an old swamp, a young forest to replace the fallen. But the people have stood still, no schools, no shops, no doctor, an inferiour clergyman, the want of the resident landlord very plainly to be seen; they are far behind our Irish, not within half a century so much up to the times; their cabins too are worse, though the furniture in them is better; the moral condition of the people seems to have been altogether overlooked by my reforming brothers. They are *charitable* as it is called—at least John is—liberal with pensions, flannels, provisions, etc. but *raising the class* they have not thought of. I find them—the peasants—as ignorant, as bigotted, as unintellectual as I left them. And the free kirk movement is wondered at; landlords intent only on doubling their rents, great men jobbing their patronage among their connexions, a defective education for all classes, most particularly for the clergy. What can be expected but folly and errours from all?

We walked yesterday to the March beyond Kainapool, wonders in the way of improving waste lands; the bog and the marsh drained, the stony banks cleared, the labour of giants to appearance. William has given up farming; he buys in young cattle to sell again as we do, cultivating only as much as is required to winter his stock and he makes by this system as we do.

We are presently off to the kirk, a melancholy contrast it will be—nearly empty, when in days of old full as it generally was it would have been crowded on the return of any of the family.

Mr. Caw had Indian letters, one from my poor father which deprived me of half my night's sleep: he really leaves Calcutta with the March mail—to return, not here, for he is not offered a home here, neither will my mother ever set her foot on land no longer her own, nor to Edinburgh for she refuses to live there. To settle in the North, so changed as their position is, so few of their old friends remaining would really be adding affliction to their many griefs. Why must *we* live so far from them?

I would like to be to them in their decline what I was to them in their prime, the staff on which they leaned through many troubles.

28. Spent our morning at Kinrara . . . more beautiful than ever, the wooding so fine, the grounds neat, the drawing-rooms pretty, and our Kainapool improvements shewing to such advantage from it. We walked along the banks a mile to the Duchess [of Gordon's] grave, lost with its large obelisk in a clump of very fine evergreens extended to four times the original size by the good taste of her successor; the interiour of the clump is also well laid out in formal walks with vistas of the monument, the river, the mountains, altogether an interesting scene were it not for the absurdity of the inscription, a sort of catalogue of the worldly honours of her children, mocking her own dust, put up her own desire.

Her picture by Sir Joshua Reynolds in the blaze of her beauty, still hanging on the walls of her loved Kinrara is a much more truly affecting monument of her fame. I don't know why but there is not a spot in the world dearer to me than Kinrara: the mirth there in my childish days, the more stately gaiety introduced by the present Duchess in my girlhood, the young, the beautiful, the rich, the great, the noble, all well remembered as congregating there with recollections of gay equipages, merry laughter, crowds glittering every way in my young eyes, throng through busy memory whenever my thoughts return to it; and to find it desolate, the furniture faded, the books and pictures gone, yards empty, and the house let with the garden and shooting to half a dozen English Indians who come down there for six weeks in the Autumn.

We crossed the river at the Doune—all so pretty—such order around—preparations going forward for her Grace. As it was to be let there could not be a better tenant for she spends much upon the place and circulates large sums among the people, many of whom she employs—to many she is very charitable—to all very kind. There is good feeling in all she does. Within, the old pictures remain in their old places excepting some of the family portraits which she has *framed* and promoted to the walls

of the principal rooms. My father and mother are in the
drawing-room. So are the Spreckled Laird,[12] and his
Lady Jean, her own relation. Much comfort has been
added in many ways; and among her many handsome
easy chairs, sofas, ottomans, still stands the little low-
backed seat which was my grandfather's and then my
father's. The Duke always used it. On the mantelpiece
are the skreens we three *girls* were so praised for adorning,
Jane's penned sketches from nature of the blighted tree at
Loch Gaun, and Loch an Eilen, my pencilled landscape
backs to dear Mary's crow-quill figures, so beautifully
done; they surely should not stay there. I will go to the
Doune once more, before the Duchess comes, take a last
lingering look, then try to expect the future though I must
ever mourn the past.

SATURDAY, AUGUST I. I am glad to say her Grace of Bedford[13]
don't come north for a fortnight owing to the death of
her stepson Lord William Russell, whose remains are
probably on the way from Florence or she would hardly
be detained for this cause alone. All this morning I have
been occupied receiving poor bodies who come daily
with their little complaints as if I could redress their
grievances. Some small services I may render them,
but they must wait for real relief till one of the Lairds
come home.

2. Sunday, No church to-day luckily, for the heat is too great
for so long a walk. The sacrament is going on at Alvie
where the attendance will be small enough while a free
kirk field preaching in the Kinrara meadows will be a
gathering of far and near. I am a little disappointed in
Tom [Gardiner]—perhaps the vigour, the enthusiasm, the

12. This is one of the clues that hint about the extent of the
family's acquaintance with Gaelic; the 'r' converts a word
close to the English freckled into something altogether
more celtic.

13. Georgina, widow of the ninth Duke of Bedford, was the
fifth and youngest daughter of the famous Duchess of
Gordon who so influenced the H.L's girldhood. The
Doune had been leased to the Bedfords since 1830.

brightness of Irish character throws other natures into the shade. We are all thinking of home again, enquiring of one another when we may return to Baltiboys.

This day my father and my mother have been married fifty years. My sister Mary, the first child they lost, has been buried two. Her bones will lay at Avranches ever. Jane bustles away her happy life in Edinburgh. I am fixed in the Emerald Isle. My brothers fag in India for the same end—a comfortable return to Rothiemurchus and though more worldly minded men than I have learnt to think they should be even for their own happiness, their aim is worthy, and their characters, while pursuing it, are respected, their abilities fully acknowledged; they are attached to each other though they don't agree; they suit though very unlike in disposition. They will battle on, and they will struggle on, saving, speculating, *spending* with an extravagance incurable and which will keep them years, if not their lifetime, in the East. My father too: the vanity of station is still there or he might have ended his difficulties ages since and might consider now instead of repining at imaginary poverty that at his age fifteen hundred a year with my mother's *good savings*, some twelve hundred pounds to start with, is ample provision for their every want.

I have never felt it pleasant to reflect on the ways of any of them; it is not my affair; the past is gone; if ever any of them want me they shall find me as they left me; till they do, our own happy family in which mind and heart are exalted by feelings purer and higher and warmer than any known by more worldly natures shall be enough for the affections so little prized by those who long engrossed them. In all the many letters, folio sheets on their own affairs, I look in vain for one symptom of being recollected; more too did I think it right to set down much that has shocked me on becoming acquainted with the many complicated transactions of late years. Well, probably it is the same with all selfish and inferiour natures—defective education in fault.

6. Colonel Litchfield can't overcome his wonder at the habits of the highlanders—the manner in which they

all plunge into the water on every occasion seeming to get on as comfortably, clothed in wet as in dry, pushing the boats, leading the ponies, filling the pitcher, fishing with rods, the water comes the same to them as the land, nor do they ever take cold though drenched to the knee and marching on without a thought of discomfort. Then he thinks their throats must be lined with *proof* skin to bear the many bumpers of proof whiskey they pour down them. What must their heads be, for they really don't get tipsy. It is lamentable the way they give in to dram drinking; the high wages they get here are just thrown away; their families are little the better of it; whiskey, punch, parties, and a fight afterwards demoralise both men and women. There is hardly a young women in the country who has not stept aside, as they delicately call her loss of reputation; the Laird and Lady are really wanted home for nothing can be lower than the social morals of their people. Very far are they behind the maligned Irish. It must be so wherever Calvinistick tenets brevail. Unnatural restraints on innocent amusement produces the grave evils of general misconduct as to all those vices which can be quietly indulged in; forbid dancing, singing, sociable meetings, and other innocent entertainments, and the saturnine Bible reader will, like the kings of Israel, take to wine and women. I am glad to find them hereabouts tiring of the free kirk; the begging box comes round so often they are beginning to find it a tax—as formerly for church ministrations they paid nothing; they have seldom a preaching either here, and then only in the open air—altogether it is unsatisfactory.

7. I have had my levée—fewer than usual attended it—for nearly all have been here now, and the place is very thinly peopled. Jack is helping to pile the peats—the young ladies are making a shirt for *Johnny* among them; he fell in love with some coloured shirting brought here by a pedlar wife yesterday, and I who spoil everybody, the Colonel says, was coaxed to buy him a shirt of it. Said pedlar wife got ten shillings of my good money for she had such cottons and ribbons and laces, etc. that between caps, collars, and neckcloths, I soon had a long

account; how much happiness purchased for so little. In the evening we were to walk towards the Loch to make some presents of money for tea and sugar, to some kind old creatures who had sent us presents of fowls; *payment* of course they would not take nor dared I offer. We were in the Mill yesterday, the ghost only of itself; how busy I have known it: seven circular saw frames going; two upright *sets* of saws, logs drawing in, planks throwing out, a yard filled with timber, a mob of workmen. Now two saws going and but lazily; three men and a boy preparing some small wood for repairing the bulwarks. The forest being gone no mill work is ever done beyond what is required for fencing.

9. Sunday, Janey Gardiner is going to be married to Mr. George Gordon Mackintosh, the only surviving brother of Balnespick. It is well it is no worse was my first exclamation with a long breath after finishing the history of this rapid courtship. I saw at once from Mr. Gardiner's style upon what subject he was writing and with full knowledge of the young lady's susceptibility, the irksomeness of her home, and her expressed wish to have one of her own without delay, visions of rather questionable Avranches beaux unduly bepraised oppressed me; so that this respectable highland gentleman was a great relief.

The Balnespicks in my young day did not take rank exactly with the higher Lairds, for they were a poor branch of a great house and they had not continued to connect themselves highly; but they are unquestionably well-descended being near of kin in a direct line from their late Chief of what was once the most powerful clan in the highlands. What is of more consequences in these days, both brothers are particularly well spoken of, clever, gentlemanly, handsome, well-doing men. Aeneas the elder has made sufficient fortune in a mercantile house in Calcutta and has returned for good he told us the other day. George is in the Bengal Civil Service; he has served thirteen years already, latterly as Collector and Magistrate of some up country district; he has nine years more to serve—a short time Janey thinks *now*. And he has one year more to remain at home during the course of which we shall all have time to become acquainted with him. He is very handsome, turned thirty, and her father gives her to him with the most perfect confidence of thus securing her happiness.

11. Tom thinks his sister too young for such an important step; and he also begins to think he had better have accepted the Indian writership. We all told him so; so the Army has him. In other words folly and idleness are to be his portion. There is no army as a profession now—no wars likely hereafter except a little Indian skirmishing, and lounging through the garrison towns, Canadian forts, and the West India stations is a most melancholy existence of may be worse than frivolity to all but such first-rate characters as those who would make wise occupations for themselves in a dungeon or a desert.

So, Jack my dear, dream not of 'girding on your father's sword.' The progress of civilisation has turned all these murderous weapons into ploughshares and reaping hooks, and as you will have acres enough to experiment on with these sources of wealth and health and happiness to all who duly understand the employment of them, turn your thoughts to the arts of peace. Or till people are fed and warmed and clothed and housed there is little hope of elevating their feelings

14. We were sitting over the fire yesterday despairing of the rain ever ceasing when a heavy chariot with four horses driven by two fat men smartly dressed as postillions stopt at the door and delivered up little old Miss Macpherson[14] finely dressed in black satin, white cachemire and an open straw polka bonnet lined and trimmed with blue. Not a day older in appearance than she ever looked since I remember her, less disagreeable in person because more decorously attired, and not the least altered in manner for nothing could be more unpleasant. She did not seem the least glad to see us; she very faintly repeated her invitation to Belleville; she very easily received the apology I at once made for not now having time to accept it; she declined

14. The daughter of James Macpherson who claimed to have translated the poems of Ossian.

luncheon having engaged herself to dine with the parson;
she sat but ten minutes, the lady she had brought with
her as her companion during the drive having remained
at Betty Campbell's to be called for; and having lectured
'à la fanatique' on the free kirk which she supports, one
of the very few of the higher class who do so, and
contradicted every other word any one of us attempted
upon any subject to say, she started up and trotted out
as she had trotted in leaving us utterly bewildered with
her apparition. In the evening the two Colonels walked
with me to the West Lodge at the Doune, returning, at
the turn from the Milltown moor to the garden the heavy
chariot and four passed on home after five hours spent
at the Manse. I remember hearing Mrs. Macpherson say
that Miss Mac was only comfortable in the society of her
inferiours, as indeed she shewed by chusing the Kingussie
ladies as her companions; and since she became her own
mistress she has, I hear, limited her acquaintance to those
'bodies' whose deferential manners keep up her feelings
of grandeur among them.

The newspapers tell us that flogging in the army is
virtually abolished—restricted to fifty lashes and only
to be employed in the most flagrant cases subject too,
to medical controul and regulated by weather and other
causes. It was disgraceful to the service that such bar-
barian customs should have prevailed so long—in such
a refining age. We have begun, keep the schoolmaster
going, let him teach not reading only, but the doctrines
of the new testament practically—where then would be
the corner poutings, the dark closet, the wounded hearts
of children, the scolding, flogging, prisons, hangings of
the ignorant and therefore vicious adult. We have begun,
slowly, yet surely, and by geometrical progression we
must proceed. Did ever anyone utter an angry word
that it did not raise an angry feeling. Having sermonised
I may dress and walk to call on the Duchess who sent us
three brace of grouse last night.

16. Not being in the humour of journalising yesterday I never
once opened my writing case. On Friday afternoon the
Colonel and I went to the Doune. The Duchess having

gone to Glenfeschie and all else being out, we went in to look at the dear old library, now only a pretty drawing-room, very nicely furnished, full of comfortable arm chairs, books, pianoforte, writing-table. It has been new papered since the other day; more of the old pictures have been reframed and hung upon the walls; altogether it is a very charming room but how can I manage to 'look forward cheerily' when thinking of what was, and is, and is to be, its living furniture.

In the evening we had an infinitely gayer diversion. The people generally had a great wish both to see us all and to shew themselves all, leisurely, to us. They asked permission to meet and dance in the barn here. Some of the men dance admirably—better than any of the last generation, as actively and more skilfully and quite as gracefully, and the few who wore the highland dress, smart handsome lads evidently the beaux of the country, were attired magnificently—buckles in their shoes, fringe to their garters, velvet jackets, silver brooches, belts ormented, handsome dirks, purses, etc.—nothing could be more beautiful; there were but some half dozen thus accoutred, pets of the Duchess's; the expense of this superiour style is so great few can afford the outlay, and the simple belted plaid of former days won't content the young gallants of these; generally speaking the men looked more lumpish than formerly, the girls certainly not so pretty, but they were generally neatly dressed and danced very quietly. My girls were in pink muslin half dress; they caught up the Strathspey style after a reel or two and gave much satisfaction to their partners. I made myself very fine—Aunt Bourne's everlasting grey tabbinet, gold ornaments, French cap, Barèges scarf, and was pronounced to be just 'extraordinar like Miss Grant' still; Annie, 'Miss Grant hersell come back among us, so lively like, so jimp,[15] wi her bonnie smile and her head of hair,' etc. etc. The Colonel danced with the cook, Tom with the kitchen maid, little Miss Clerk with all

15. Scots—graceful, neat dainty (Scottish National Dictionary).

the barn and capitally; so it was a very merry night.
We left at one; others at two, the rest at five in the
morning. Of course the party became very merry after
our departure, for they commenced toasts, giving first
the 'family' generally, and then they individualised us,
so after that the dancing was glorious, though the maids
assured me no one was tipsy—only hearty, the translation
of which is that all got safe home.

To-day, Sunday, has been very amusing—I went with
some of us to the kirk, and heard a most silly sermon, and
counted forty of a congregation including the Duchess.
After the service [she] called to me to wait for her a
moment, when up she came all kindness, introduced her
family, and then walked on with us to Inverdruie; sat a
while there to make acquaintance with Colonel Smith and
then like the Captain's lady and the Laird's we walked
back with her. She is exceedingly agreeable, very much
softened since her Duke's death and very unwilling to
annoy Lady Rachel who don't approve of all her mother's
former doings.[16] She is a very interesting girl and she and
Annie took so much to one another, talking of musical
duettes and pony rides here and there that there seemed
mutual regret at the acquaintance being so soon to end.
'I hear,' said the Duchess to me 'that you are bringing up
your girls charmingly. Accomplish them as you like but
don't make fine ladies of them—that's a deplorable life,
useless and miserable, etc.' I told her there was no fear.

She gave me a very odd account of the Duchess of
Gordon who has gone really crazy on religious subjects;
then we talked over all the clans of the Highlands, all
their southern allies, all that had happened since the last
day I saw her when she carried off my Jacobite airs to sing
them at Invereschie. A loaf of bread has just arrived from
her Grace, she promised one when she heard we depended
on Forres and Kinguissie. She asked us to dine, asked the

16. Her husband, the ninth Duke, died in 1839 and this
    comment is presumably a reference to her relationship
    with Edwin Landseer, (whose Rothiemurchus painting is
    described 24.7.1846).

girls to an hour or two of musick and luncheon, in short
is all kindness.

18. Very rainy. I have been wearied nevertheless with humble
visitors, poor bodies, nor have I time amid my packings,
payings, last words, etc. to set down all my sorrow at
quitting dear Rothiemurchus.

I am teased very much just now by that little good
Miss Clerk. She has got her head quite out by this life
of pleasure. She chatters incessantly, cannot hold her
tongue, whoever is addressed she answers, whatever
remark is made she replies to. She has begun like
Miss Hart to entertain all the visitors and when as a
delicate check none of us notice her she sets to work to
converse with the dog in so loud a key as to startle one.
It is perhaps the air, great happiness, and nothing else to
do, but if it don't stop I must stop it, for such a jabber has
become intolerable. How difficult the governess tribe is
to manage: keep them at a distance they become sulky;
admit them into the family circle and they quite forget
themselves. So easily are underbred people spoiled. The
Duchess has just sent five brace of grouse for my mother,
and Lady Rachel has sent with them a pretty note of
regret at our departure.

19. Breakfasted early, filled Mr. Caw's cart, a melancholy
procession, and all mourned the end of so many happy
weeks. The coach came up soon and we packed in and on
it. The day was so very fine we did not think Drumochter
dreary. Indeed cultivation is stretching over the hill so far
on either side and so many shooting lodges are erected
here and there, that the extreme wildness of the pass
is gone.

Killiecrankie is still the finest bit of scenery I ever
passed through though too full of Elizabethan villas,
cottages ornées, and miniature castles to be as grand
as in its wilder days. Dunkeld is a smart little town
full of good shops, with grand hotels where bustle the
greatest dandies of waiters; indeed all along the road the
smart waiters and very smart chamber maids startled all
my recollections of freckled louts in faded tartan jackets,
shoeless, capless maidens with little English, and the

naked rooms and dirty crockery and smoke and mess
and discomfort attending their ministrations.

The neighbourhood of Dunkeld is choked with villa
residences; just beyond Blair too a little Cheltenham
has sprung up round the mineral springs at Pitlochrie;
verandahs, roses, trellises, green paint. I looked on the
prettily dressed up houses with amazement, reminded
by muslin curtains of France, among as fine mountains.
We dined at Blair handsomely. From Dunkeld to Perth
new farms, with their good enclosures, small gentlemen's
seats with their sheltering planting, redeemed the flat
landscape from its ancient insipidity. After the last peep
of Murthly Castle, where I might have reigned,[17] rising
from its wooded Terrace above the Tay, there used to be
but a dreary drive to within a mile or two of Perth. Now
all is under the plough. We reached Perth before nine,
very tired, and put up at an admirably kept hotel—the
Salutation, very large, very reasonable, a Bible in every
room and the civil landlord quite tipsy.

20. After an excellent night and a comfortable breakfast we
took leave of our dear Colonel Litchfield who wished to
see Crieff, Stirling, Taymouth, etc. as he was so near
them, and packing ourselves outside a three horse coach
we started about half after nine for the Ferry. I don't
know how often we changed horses, every five or six
miles, but we seemed to go slow, and not through
pretty scenery though all in progress of improvement
particularly the labourer's cottages each with its good
garden; it rained incessantly which threw a gloom over
the country generally, though it could not obscure the
beauty of Blair Adam which I remember in my childhood
a bare hill looking on bare hills all surrounded by swamps.
Then I passed it enclosed, drained, planted—now it

17. Although she does refer occasionally to her broken engagement in her Journals, this is the one occasion where
there is even a suggestion of positive evidence to identify
her betrothed, probably Sir John Archibald Drummond-
Stewart of Grandtully, Murtly and Logie Almond who died
unmarried in 1838.

broke on us a richly wooded fertile country filled with neat cottages. We crossed the ferry in a few minutes, and some of us having changed to the inside in the place of three ladies left near Kinross we took up an intelligent man, who is working some of the stone quarries near Edinburgh and has a large farm on his hands besides. From him and from our own eyes we have the melancholy fact of the entire failure of the potato crop.

23. Jane has got us really delightful lodgings—where? In my father's old house in Picardy Place. What a strange romance is life. I have been all this Sunday morning writing up my travelling journal so have tired my head too much for any Edinburgh impressions or any account of letters sent, or letters received; probably in the afternoon I may gossip again with myself.

25. I find it impossible to get a moment for writing. All is bustle without much business either. Sunday we staid at home writing, but the young people went to chapel; then in spite of a misting rain Jane took us a fine walk through the old Town, the meadows by Heriot's hospital, George's Square, back round the Castle, etc. I missed Robert Chambers to-day, but as we have written a note or two upon the subject we look forward to meet to-morrow. I have little time for I have my authourship affairs, Johnny Mackintosh to settle in a lunatick asylum, the schoolmaster business, an Irish boy to get into a garden, and an Irishman to get into a farm, other letters, and all amid perpetual visiting. I had best now seek my bed where my Colonel has been snug this half hour.

26. Spent this morning at the Grange and then to the Institution where we spent an hour very agreeably among some good pictures and a very interesting collection of statues, casts from antiques. On our way to the Grange we viewed the quadrangle of the College, and returning came by the new cemetery which Sir Thomas Dick Lauder receives a high rent for—£10. an acre for thirty acres; he hopes to feu for villas in its neighbourhood at a high rate also.

27. This is a marked day for me. My first interview with Mr. Robert Chambers. It was an appointment so I staid at home for him. He is a plain looking and

plain mannered man particularly unobtrusive, almost humble indeed, though quite at ease and pleasant to converse with. We talked over the Irish sketch which is in type and will appear in a conspicuous part of an early number. He calls it a beautiful paper. We then talked of the Normal Schools here and of my proceedings as to a Teacher, etc. and then he offered to shew us his premises which I had wished to ask to see but did not like as it might have looked like presuming upon our connexion. It is one of the Lions of the Town too. So the Colonel and I caught at the obliging offer and arranged to pay our visit to-morrow at three o'clock.

28. We spent a couple of hours in looking through [Robert Chambers'] establishment which he was prevented from shewing us by some other engagement. A very intelligent foreman however well supplied his place. We descended seven times to different storeys all occupied by the business which employs a hundred and sixty persons—neat and clean and healthy and happy looking working in airy rooms well lighted.

29. Walked with Colonel Smith to leave a card with '*Avranches*' at Mr. Robert Chambers's handsome house in Doune Terrace; he has written me such a quantity of notes and called so often that this civility was quite necessary. I also sat an hour with Lissy Mair who told me that he told her he hoped I should not get idle for that I wrote too well to be allowed to stop, etc. At luncheon we had William Craig, now a Junior Lord of the Treasury, just arrived from London where he left his ministerial colleagues busily occupied with Irish affairs—devising means to feed the poor potato-less people.

31. This is the last day of the month and the last day of our visit to Edinburgh for Colonel Litchfield went to Glasgow Saturday to see about the steamboat and took our berths in the *Vanguard* to sail at six Tuesday afternoon so we can leave by a late train comfortably. Jane called for us before one and took us all to Craig Crook to luncheon. Alas! I much fear I shall not see Lord Jeffrey again; he is changed indeed since my last visit. We walked in the gardens, up the hill, and on the terrace, and we looked

at the Firth and the view of Edinburgh again waiting as of old in a threatening day for some shifting cloud to allow the sun to light up the Castle. Another dream for memory. Edinburgh adieu.

WEDNESDAY, SEPTEMBER 9. Reading over my scraps of journal to the Colonel my head has filled again with dear Rothiemurchus, where I am sure I would gladly have passed the remainder of the summer had we not had our own pretty little home to return to. Upon the whole our visit there has been very satisfactory. I feel rationally convinced that no scenery in the world is more beautiful, no air so delightful; although much has been destroyed, much has been so to speak created. The people, though changed in many respects for the worse yet still retain their love for the family, all feudal affections are not yet extinct among them, they could easily be revived and will be when the Lairds come; their character will rise again when their best feelings are again in exercise, *if* William take the pains he ought to improve them.

Colonel Smith was almost equally happy during our stay in Edinburgh when he met at Mr. Craig's so many old friends of ours, kind and clever and disposed to welcome him heartily among them. Also our drives to those beautifully kept places through parklike scenery, such noble trees, such luxuriant fields, such neat habitations. He was delighted with the management of Rothiemurchus, the order, the method, the regularity, the tidiness, all so essential and so unknown in our own Isle. Our journey too shewed us equal care every where, of the land, with infinitely superiour attention to the people, the labourers having their neat cottages very generally two storeyed, with gravel round them, flower plots in front, good large gardens at hand; the farmers living in neat villas, ornamented in good taste yet forming a part of the steading. About Edinburgh all this was of a higher order including the fields where not one weed was seen near crop or hedge or roadside, nor broken fence, nor gate a wanting, nor any evidence of any lack of care. The master's eye it was plain was everywhere. Then at the Grange the charming house, contrived out of a set of old turrets, plainly but so comfortably furnished, full of evidence of good taste and perfect care, the three acres of garden ground so beautifully kept by *one man* at £30 a year with help only for a few weeks at spring and fall. At Bonally, a wilder and so a more interesting place two men keep a large extent of garden, shrubbery and mountain walks, one of whom has the stable to look after besides. He took fright at Riccarton where *seven* men have enough ado to manage the policies, so it was well we visited these more approachable places. Order makes all so easy, keeping each man to his own work, seeing that work regularly attended to, allotted both as to days and hours and never omitted nor ever left over beyond the time. The amount of work accomplished by *method* astonishes all, accustomed to the license of pallmall proceedings. Craig Crook has only one man and a boy large as are the pleasure gardens; but there is old Jamie for the greenhouse and for weeding the flower borders.

I liked Edinburgh better this time than I ever liked it before; and unless the High School retain the character it is now regaining under this most accomplished rector of German extraction and regularly *philanthropick* education, I should not care to remove there when Jack is fit to attend it. The society is better far than we could have anywhere else we could take him; the air suits Hal and me; living is cheap and old friends plenty—on my side at least, and Hal has none he much cares for except his Indian connexions who are no farther from us there than here. Masters of all sorts are good and reasonable and one certainly lives there in an atmosphere of talent.

10. On Sunday morning last the 6th, I looked early out of the window of my beautiful bedroom over the fertile valley with its background of mountains and foreground of rich wooded banks and green meadows through which the little sparkling Liffey wanders, and thought as the sun brightened the pretty prospect we had seen nothing in all our travels more satisfactory to the eye. After dressing and breakfasting my contentment nearly vanished for I discovered that Biddy had cut up a bedroom carpet into

long strips to cover the back stairs, and burned the handsome rug in the drawing-room in five or six places that very morning, she having unbidden laid it down; the parlour kettle she had been using in the kitchen in addition to the two belonging to her batterie, in short the less I used my eyes in her department the better. Without there was more comfort for Paddy had the garden and pleasure grounds in better order than I ever found them in before. Mr. Darker had done the filling up of the terrace remarkably well, the stable yard was clean, the gravel tidy.

All this on a fine day was very agreeable, but not a thing had we to eat; no butter nor eggs in the house, nor meat in the larder, nor poultry fat, no preparation made in any way for the food of the family. So I had to send here and there—a man to Blesinton, a boy through Baltiboys and a girl to Burgage to endeavour to make some provision for our necessities. It was rather careless, stupid rather, to have nothing ready. A cow has calved luckily, and fowls soon fatten on rice. Monday busy unpacking and to dinner in walked the Doctor whom they had told us was at Kilkenny, he was so glad to see us and truly we were as glad to see him for we did not feel any of us half welcomed home till his beaming face and hearty shake of the hand rejoiced us.

11. I can't hear of much change among our people: Ned Gray married, his wife brought home to the three acres of course. Old Mrs. Quin, the mother of Red Pat, dead. The whooping cough has been very prevalent, in some cases where fever was superadded, fatal. The potato crop gone, here and everywhere, the root I suppose extinct, and were we once over this first year may be 'tis so best, for the cheapness of this low description of food encouraged idleness, pauper marriages and dirty habits, and neither mind nor body could be fully developed upon such nourishment. Government is exerting itself nobly to provide useful work with good pay, therefore like last year the Irish labourer will fare well. All summer hands have been so scarce from the number required by the railroads and the new buildings that the farmers have

been paying from 1/6 to 2/6 a day with diet, good bread, greens, milk, bacon, pork, etc. yet no one is satisfied—all miss the potatoes. Even old Peggy is all lamentation, no other food is so strengthening. Poor old body she has been robbed of all her best clothes—her new cloke, two good gowns, blankets, sheets, and some money, a few shillings in a little bag the produce of my repository. A man and woman of pedlar appearance seen on the road suspected, but though they were traced to near Naas they have not been discovered nor as yet have any of the missing articles found their way to the pawnbrokers though as the police are on the search they will probably soon be heard of. Antony still lounging about the country, Mary, after some delay, in a low place in Dublin, the only servant with £5. a year wages. So her humble duty has been forwarded to me—there is no lady she would rather serve, if I want a maid she would return to me with the greatest pleasure, etc. But she shall see a little more of the world first.

Politicks seem asleep, thank God for it. The ministry are carrying out at home the same wise policy marked out by Sir Robert Peel who gives them his best assistance. Abroad they hardly seem to be acting so wisely. Lord Palmerston interfering foolishly in matters of no importance to us, as before, grumbling at this alliance of the Duc de Montpensier with the Infanta of Spain which surely need not concern us. Our Queen is at sea in her yacht, at Guernsey, Jersey, Plymouth, a very good way of passing her summer. She has grown unpopular again and Prince Albert is disliked extremely—mean, haughty, cold, exacting. It is hard for the great to please.

12. There seems to be quite a sensible Pope [Pius ix] reigning at Rome in these days—the new Holiness a youngish man—railroads, schools, draining, charity to all in need—he will turn Protestant by and bye; that must be the end of all Romanism some day, when the reformed must be purified afresh, made more like true Christians, real follow rs of him who was meek and lowly of heart. Anne Mulligan has come in Biddy's place and that unfortunate George has been a year married to Marianne Dizest. It is melancholy, poor boy. She is out

of place now, living with Hannah in expectation of her baby, he supporting her out of his wages. I heard she was married in Dublin but never guessed to whom, however such news flies, and when the Colonel taxed him with his folly he confessed. She is to go to service again and they are not to live together for some years till they have saved a little money—Perhaps.

20. Politicks quiet & people quiet too though without a potato. Till Christmas it is supposed we shall get on pretty well, work is plenty, wages high, but the corn harvest is light. The second crop of hay is as fine as the first which may cheapen beef a little, and the weather is beautiful, and, as the Musselman says, 'God is great'.

23. Wrote about the new schoolmaster, arranged the repository: which has realised but seven and fourpence halfpenny during our absence. Tom Darker is off to the Agricultural Show at Naas to make his observations and rouse himself to competition against next year. I am sure there are no such ducks there as mine, as there were no such peaches last year. Hal thinks his young cart mare would astonish the judges; we must become members against another time. Mr. Darker sold ten of the young cattle off of Pat Quinn's farm, the fourth part of the stock on it, and on these ten he has made a profit equal to the half year's rent, rather more indeed. I wish there was not a tenant in Baltiboys, there will not be many by and bye, no small holders at any rate. When potatoes are gone a few acres won't be worth a man's time to manage. What a revolution for good will this failure of cheap food cause.

25. The Doctor was a couple of hours with us, full of gossip. Tom Darker an hour, talking of the Show. We should have carried all before us had we sent our ducks, foals, yearlings, etc.; so next year we must really compete, and it will probably be here in our own Barony, for Mr. Owen has thrown up the secretaryship from the arrogance of the Kildare gentry which was too offensive for him to put up with. He is *hot, presuming, conceited*; very clever, very active, and acting for 7,000 a year; being young he should reflect on the per and contra [sic] and go more quietly about reforming old men long established in the

September 1846 261

country to which he has come a stranger. One slap he got from Kilbride, which I had hoped would have done him good, for he is worth improving.

Being much behind with my correspondents, I have been writing many letters; some on business, one about the school, Mr. Sullivan [the Inspector] having behaved unaccountably ill, forgotten our conversation, his promises, notes and advice; got me no master, and declined recommending one, and Mr. Cross, the secretary, says there are none in the training school who will be ready before Christmas. Here comes the famine too, the rain has spoiled the few miserable potatoes left, the markets are higher than they were ever known to be since the war, harvest work is over, the Irish landlords generally are bankrupt, three fourths of the land mortgaged to full value, with, therefore, nominal large rent rolls they have not a penny to spend in labour. From some hitch between the government and the Board of Works, no publick works are going forward, the ministry don't choose to interfere with the provision trade; so here we are, the peasantry starving.

26. This was the day for a meeting of the gentry, etc. in Blesinton, to consider the state of the starving poor, two or three hundred of whom collected in the village to learn the result which appeared to be simply that they would be looked after; at least I could make very little else out of the rambling account the Doctor gave us of the proceedings. The act of Parliament is so imperfect it don't at all meet the emergency, and it is supposed the collective wisdom of the nation must assemble without delay to amend it, for as it stands those landlords who have always done, are now doing and intend to continue to do their duty, will be assessed for the support of those of the lower orders who have been neglected by bad landlords, who again having never done anything for their people will get them all supported now as a recompense for their improper carelessness, the willing horse, in fact, having to bear the burden even till his back be broke. It seems however that there is some way of exempting oneself from this overweight by the landlord giving his own pledge to

employ all able-bodied persons on his property, or to see
them employed, and to send the incapables to the poor
house. Mr. Moore, Mr. Armstrong and Mr. Owen have
thus exempted themselves, and as we have not only all our
people occupied but three or four strangers in addition
we must get some 'voice' to speak for Lower Baltiboys
as poor Hal is at present too unwell to attend any of
the meetings. It seems very unwise in the Government
to refuse to interfere with the provision trade for the
capitalists are buying up all the grain to retail really at
an exorbitant price—two and eight pence a stone for
meal. I have known it a shilling, two and threepence
for wheatmeal. What labourer's wages can support his
family at these rates, and how can wages rise when there
are double the number of workmen that are wanted.
Something must be done for between the poverty of
the masters and the destitution and the idleness and the
recklessness of the people mischief will most certainly
ensue if matters are left to take their own course.

28. Tom Darker and I were the whole morning settling our
affairs. He has dismissed the two old men who for the
present have work elsewhere. James Doyle will most
likely get enough during the winter to support his family,
a brother in America having lately sent him £10, and
written for the eldest son to go out to him. James Craig
and his dirty idle wife must take their wretched children
to the Poor House, old John Doyle may want a little
help, so may Pat Quin's delicate mother, no one else. And
instead of raising wages, a bad precedent, the Colonel
with pleasure consents to give them meal at a low price
instead of selling his oats in the market, and to ensure
his supply lasting the horses will get none unless the two
working mares one feed each. Then we shall buy another
cow, and so have milk all winter to divide amongst them.
Thus we hope to get through this famine year, and being
able to pledge ourselves to the good work, Tom will go
to Mr. Owen and get us exempted from all care of our
neighbours.

We had then the schools to look after. Mr. McConnell
luckily consents to stay till Christmas, my distressed

condition moving his pity. I shall mind the people and the priest and the inspector and the board no more, this young man is as good or better than most we could get and perfection not being in human nature we must just make the best of him, keep a tight rein. Mr. Sullivan at any rate can't help me after all his promises. The fact is that these well educated young men being underpaid as teachers are bribed to give up their schools for better situations so there is a dearth of masters, and a surmise of the salaries being to be raised.

30. Has been a busy day. Between Tom Darker, Mrs. Fyfe, Paddy, the schools, and packing, I have had work enough. I never left home so much against the grain, I think. I am afraid the poor people will miss us. Lord Besborough and Lord John really seem enclined to help us but they have been overruled. Lord Palmerstone playing the very mischief, and our wretched peasantry are actually starving while these wischeads are battling how to relieve them. We have but a gloomy winter before us.

SUNDAY, OCTOBER 4. Oxford, Star Inn.[18] Here is a heading, and here am I all alone by myself in a very comfortable bedchamber, between nine and ten o'clock at night, a very nice fire burning, a little round table and an easy chair placed just in front of it.

We had nearly forty miles to go to Oxford [from Towcester] through such pretty English scenery that we quite enjoyed the journey. Rich fields, wooding, villages so neat, cottages so clean, flowers, cross roads, turnpikes. About Lord Southampton's the cottages were pictures, the little village at his gate a model. The paint and the bright windows struck the girls most and the happy air of the people, the children in groups a play, the good clothing, the air of comfort; it is very delightful to see such a peasantry after France and Ireland.

6. A very rainy day. We got a damp disagreeable walk down

18. She and the girls visited her favourite Aunt Bourne on the way to her niece Janie Gardiner's wedding in Twickenham.

the High Street in the New College gardens and home
by St. Gile's, but it was the fine stained glass window
in the beautiful New College Chapel, the cloisters there,
the handsome new Taylor's Buildings, the enlarged street
leading to Worcester College, the old Clarendon printing
house and the monument to the Martyrs. This last don't
seem to be exactly in good taste, to be ripping up in these
times those old sores best forgotten. Both sides in those
days had their shoals of victims to superstitious bigotry,
and if Cranmer, Ridley and Latimer suffered a cruel death
for their opinions under the ascendency of one prejudiced
sect, a host be resuscitated on the other side who fared
much like them when the reformers prevailed. They were
savages all, for whose deeds we should blush in silence.

From the little I have been yet able to see of Oxford
it appears to be rapidly improving as far as building is
concerned, not only publick works but good private
houses of which there used to be a great deficiency,
rising on all sides. These are necessitated by a large
encrease of inhabitants consequent on a change surely
for good in the wretched bad plan of English University
education. Quantities of clergymen, M.A.s come here as
Tutors for private pupils with whom they read or to whom
they lecture, and being mostly married they have infused
a little life and ease of manner into the dignified society
of this stately assemblage of D.D.S.

7. Visitors in the morning. Mrs. Buckland one of them;
the wife of the *Bridgewater Treaties*,[19] a very ugly coarse
mannered woman, but clever and kind and hospitable.
They are thought to be very eccentrick all the family,
particularly odd in the eating way, so that people don't
very much like partaking of their entertainments; they
stew up serpents and snails and worms, saying one animal
is as fit for human food as another and that these are
prejudices that should be overcome, these dislikes to
what we are merely unaccustomed. They could be found

19. William Buckland (1784–1856) the geologist and eccentric;
    his 1836 *Treatises* aimed to show the *power, wisdom and
    goodness of God* through science.

I daresay in clean England in the bye lanes and hedges. A very uncertain day, very showery. We did not venture out till after dinner when I made an unsuccesful tour among the book-sellers for some of Mr. Chambers educational works, not yet known in classic Oxford.

11. Still Oxford, Sunday, and nothing very important to set down. I took the girls to University College which we minutely inspected. The Common room furnished in a very superiour style to hertofore, where hang two of my Uncle's poker drawings, Henry IV. and V. very beautifully executed, having all the appearance of Sappia till the light reveals the deep burning of the shadows. The Chapel we saw too, with a stove in it quite new, my Aunt's old pew now used as a coal cellar. Another poker drawing for the alter piece, Christ blessing the bread, and near this on one of the diced flags of the pavement the letters J. G. with the date of the death of my excellent Uncle whose remains lay underneath.

I wished to show my girls, the famous tiger so broke through all the ceremonies of this ceremonious place, and ringing at Dr. Plumptre's door I sent my compliments to the Master with a request to be allowed to look at my Uncle's pictures. It was granted at once and in the most obliging manner and in a few minutes he appeared himself, shewed us all over the Lodgings, pointed out all the heirlooms left by my Uncle, told us he had endeavoured to restore all to the same chaste beauty as Dr. Griffith had originated, Dr. Rowley[20] having rather neglected the premises. He then took us over the garden and dismissed us with a collation of grapes from trees planted by my Uncle, a large basket of which followed us home as an offering to my Aunt. I never saw such a Head of a College,a complete overturn to all my old recollections of old, fat, vulger, pompous men in cassocks, filled with nothing but their grandeur. Dr. Plumptre is young, remarkably handsome, tall slight,

20. Her uncle James Griffith (with whom she stayed as a girl) was succeeded as Master by George Rudley (1821–36) and Frederick Plumptre (1836–70)

polished in manner beyond anybody commonly seen, actually courtly, and accomplished to a high degree. I was fascinated, no other word is strong enough to convey the degree of pleasure I felt in his society, I can't get him out of my head. My Aunt tells me he is as good as he is charming, and Jany has the good taste to remark on him as the very nicest person she has ever seen. Mrs. Bridges tells me that these *great people* are really descending to meet the times, that there is more ease of manner, less assumption of state, much less vulgar stickling for place, that many don't like their honours, few wear constantly their dress. The wives are more rational, altogether they are very different from the dignitaries of my young day. My Aunt regrets much of this, she is for keeping up proper distinctions, naturally enough perhaps.

18. Sunday, 5, Sion row, Twickenham. The most comfortable lodgings I ever was in, small though they be. [Mr. Gardiner] spoke very rationally about Janey's marriage, as a step he is reconciled to on account of her being motherless, feeling himself inadequate to the care of her, and satisfied with the worth of her lover he commits her to him in full confidence of her happiness. He had never any ambitious views for her, with her peculiarly delicate health he caught at the idea of India and he feels now as if a load to which he was unequal had been removed from his heart. I really believe all this and I believe that the whole affair is most fortunate; it might have been far otherwise. Never for one moment do I believe that she has regretted this precipitation, she looks perfectly happy, pleased with her lover, very much pleased with her character of Bride and all the little éclat belonging to it, and busily occupied with the necessary preparations; not at all averse to the affectionate endearments exhibited publickly before us all, yet quite self-possessed while enduring them, as if they were part of the necessary preliminaries, conducting herself as if at forty she were marrying for the third or fourth time,—so to my mind not in love, may be all the better.

George Mackintosh at first sight disappointed me extremely. Far from being handsome as Jane calls him

he is really plain, not tall, a clumsy figure, thick legs,
big hands, large shoulders, a great ill-shaped head with
a face fit for a giant, had he been six foot high he might
have looked well enough, but he is out of all proportion
for five foot nine inches. To redeem these defects he
has fine eyes, very fine teeth, a good complexion, pale
and clear, an agreeable expression of countenance and
a very kind smile. His manner though shy and quite
unpolished is far from awkward being unpretending,
his accent is thoroughly highland when the least animated and always in tone and mode of expression carries me back to Badenoch. There is nothing the least
striking in his conversation, no wit, no observation,
no reading, no reflexion, nothing to remark on one
way or another. But in the love his family feel for
him, the respect his character is regarded with and
the actions depending on himself with which any of
us have become acquainted, we feel that a good and an
amiable and a sensible man is to be the future guardian
of our Janey.

Mr. Darker has written in good spirits, no want of
work or food about us yet. The Colonel thinks of
borrowing some few hundreds from the Government
and draining the whole of his property; the terms are
very advantageous for the borrower, 3½ per cent., repaid
by instalments in twenty years, while the profit on the
labour will certainly not be under twenty, often more.
It is an excellent idea, likely to produce present quiet
and future wealth, for in fact the Landlords of Ireland
as a body are paupers with incomes barely sufficient for
their maintenance and the payment on the mortgages
with which their estates have descended to them heavily
encumbered, so that funds for improvement there are
hardly any in the island. This visitation of providence
will thus be the means of prosperity to our nation by
bringing forward the help so much wanted without
which we must have grovelled on for ages through
turmoil and poverty and misery, and with which we
may hope all of us of this generation to see plenty
and comfort in that dear land 'where all but the spirit

of man is' lovely.[21] Some of our neighbours mean
to adopt this borrowing plan. In the meanwhile the
Barony has cessed itself in upwards of £4,000 to provide immediate employment for the peasantry. They
begin with the roads which are to be made passable,
hills lowered, swampy bits drained, new cuts where
necessary. My schoolhouse will benefit and I hope the
road to the bog. Perhaps it will be a better year for
the poor than they have ever yet known, of essential
use in many ways; they must starve or *work*, no bare
existing on roots with idleness, their food will be of a
better kind, invigorating to *mind* and *body*, they *must*
learn decenter habits. Their small holdings will become
valueless to them, their children can't be suffered to hang
on at home idly when every mouthful has its price well
felt. Oh! it may be the dawn of happy days,—God
grant it.

21. Dear Janie Gardiner, there is an end of your young
girlish life, the trials and the troubles with which your
business path henceforward will be thickly strewn have
now opened before you. God grant you strength to bear
them and give you a kind and tender and steady support
in your husband. He appeared to more advantage to-day,
looked better, talked more, he may improve still further
upon acquaintance, at any rate it is our part to make the
best of him.

26. We got a newspaper today to see what the world is doing.
Provisions continuing to pour into England from Ireland
and yet the famine said to be pressing there. I can't
believe it, for besides that both food and work seem
to be plenty, it could hardly be that if people were
really hungry they would refuse task work which from
the Lord Lieutenant's proclamations they must in many
places have done, claiming for daily wages, in other words
leave to idle. They have got it into their heads that being
in distress they are to do nothing to get out of it, but are
to sit comfortably down and open their mouths to be fed.
Like cousin Bartle [Frere], I can't but despise a people so

21. One of her favourite Byron quotations (see 25.5.46).

meanspirited, so low-minded, so totally without energy, only I attribute it to the want of animal food; there can be no vigour of mind or body without it. Lady Blakenay was giving me some Irish gossip, she assures me our neighbours Lord and Lady Milltown are quite shunned, he is considered a blackleg, a regular cheat, often by signals from her, and her impertinence is no longer tolerated.

TUESDAY, NOVEMBER 3. Mr. Bax took the girls and me down to Westminster, where we went through the Law Courts and saw the Judges sitting in their wigs and the Counsel pleading before them and the Attorneys buzzing about and crowds of clients and idlers around them. We then walked all over the new houses of parliament, no small journey, then into Westminster Abbey, then over Westminster bridge in hopes of seeing the front of the new buildings, but the high boarding, which skirts the footpath, prevented our getting a good view.

4. Bartle [Frere] and I had four young ladies to carry to the Concert at Exeter Hall. It is a fine room, very large, very lofty, very well ventilated. There were 500 performers in the Orchestra, a few of them professional people to keep order, a good leader, Conductor, Organist and some more, the rest Chorus and all are the trades-people of London. What a change is coming over John Bull.

The first part was a miscellaneous selection, all sacred, a Te Deum and Jubilate composed by Prince Albert I thought magnificent, Bartle prefers Handel but there is no need for comparisons. The 2nd and 3rd parts consisted of an Oratorio of Spohr's, 'The last judgement' which I think were I to hear often would be likely to take great hold of my musick heart. I never understand new musick, not even a new air of an old friend, and Spohr is quite a stranger to me; yet one quartette near the end needs no repetition to be enchanting.

11. On Wednesday the 11th early in the morning, we filled, locked, corded our six boxes and after a family breakfast started in two cabs an hour too early, the mail train not leaving till 10 o'clock. At Birmingham at one o'clock, we were met by Colonel Smith and Colonel Litchfield

whom we could not persuade to cross the sea. We reached Liverpool at 6, and had plenty of time to establish ourselves comfortably on board the packet as she did not leave till 7.

12. Landed at 6, only 11 hours, after a perfectly smooth passage, left town early, picked up the Doctor in Blesinton and found my darling blooming, taller and stouter and rosier and improved in every respect by the care of that good little Miss Clerk.

27. Political news rather dreary. We are embroiled with every foreign court, the merchants at home are all dissatisfied, Exchange has fallen instead of its being so much in our favour as of late, we shall have to export bullion to meet deficiencies, the ministry are a set of incapables, there is no manner of doubt about it, but who is to be had in their stead. Nothing can be more deplorable than their Irish measures, they are positively demoralising the people still further than their own bad feelings had already accomplished.

Then such jobbing goes on. John Hornidge shifting almost his whole band of labourers on the publick, some of his smaller tenants among them even though their holdings are much above the value below which relief is limited to. So others are following this laudable example, saying, 'Why should we keep extra hands and pay for our neighbours too.' Richard Hornidge therefore sends eight men, Mr. Cotton four, Mr. West four, to be provided for by the Barony. We keep our large band for the present but we will try and diminish it by getting permanent situations by degrees for those we dismiss.

John Robinson has been down receiving rents. The tenants have paid very nearly as well as usual. Some require a fortnight to pay up, others will persist to owe the hanging half year. A few who should do better owe a year. One or two owe more, we therefore in earnest proceed with them. About £160 is due. All will be in time recovered little by little except poor George Kearns's encreasing arrears, he must go, and at once, for his own sake, it would have been better had he gone years ago. Redmond has paid no rent these three gales [biannual rent audits,] nor Cullen, the old man and woman have gone off to England to a prosperous son, the youngest *boy* has settled himself and a wife down in the cabin with its acre without leave from any one and thinks it extremely hard he is not to be allowed to remain.

Upon the whole we have no reason to be dissatisfied with the conduct of our people these pinching times, they will require a steady rein, kind words, encouragement, in many ways, and thus proceeding I think we shall get over the season better than most of us. Money will be scarce enough, by the time the Christmas bills are paid there will be no great stock remaining, but in February comes the pay again, we will save in every other way, and if need be I can apply to Jane who will gladly lend to feed the hungry. In the meanwhile I shall borrow from the girls the remainder of Colonel Litchfield's kind gift. Besides their chains they got themselves stays and nice silk dresses, the odd cash they are to have for pocket money, and the sum remaining is for the savings Bank, I can use it now and repay it in better times.

I often wonder how with so small an income we manage to make the two ends meet, for our expenses are not household, latterly not stable, but masons, carpenters, plumbers for ever and for ever, improving the property certainly, but unproductive labours none of them repaying the outlay. Now this half year £140 went back to the tenants in allowances, a hole in a bare £400, then deduct the defaulting rents another £100 at least and but little remains for the family and labourers. Were it not for the E.I.C. we should be hard run indeed.

I have proposed to Colonel Smith to allocate his income for the future and he rather approves. Let Baltiboys keep itself, improve itself, and supply us with what we want of its produce. Give me the half pay and Elverstown and they shall do all the rest, pay the Dublin bills, the house servants, the governess, and our own personal expenses. By this plan I think we should almost feel rich, there would be £400 a year for certain purposes and then it would be my fault indeed if I could not make it comfortably do.

29. Sunday. The grounds covered with snow, a hard frost all
yesterday, a storm at night of thunder and lightening,
and regular winter to-day. Fine healthy weather, but the
starving! those who have bad shelter, scanty fire, little
food. God help them for man can't. Were we to divide our
all with all we could not ensure their comfort for they have
ruined dwellings, they have laid in no fuel, their clothing
is but rags and provisions are at triple price.

Such a miserable creature as besought Janey and me
yesterday to buy a straw basket that she might carry home
a supper to four children and a husband who had fasted
with herself since the night before. *He* has got upon the
roads but will not be paid till the pay day nor then in full
as the overseers are obliged to keep this bridle over these
wretched idlers, and how to subsist these two days the
half distracted creature knew not. 'Oh Lady Smith, my
jewel' said she, sobbed she rather, 'Sound may ye sleep on
your feather pillow for all belonging to you is in comfort.
Long life to his honour, for it is he that's the father to his
people. If others were like him and looked to their own
there would not be this famine in the country.'

The Colonel was rather satisfied with the Meeting
yesterday, preparatory to the Presentment Sessions called
for the 4th of next month. They settled the amount of
Cess to be levied for the next three months, a twelfth
of the income of the *quarter*, I suppose, our proportion
will therefore be about £20, and they will try and have
it profitably expended if possible on reproductive works
such as thorough draining, but before entering on such
a responsibility as a Government Loan for this purpose,
Hal thinks he must have fuller information on a matter
which appears to be a good deal complicated. The labour
act, the drainage act and the Secretary's letter, all having
to be rightly understood and reconciled if possible with
the orders of the Board of Works, none of them seeming
to our plain capacities to run well together.

My impression is that we must each pay our proportion
to the whole, that unless reproductive works be engaged
in we may consider the money thrown into the sea, that
the more we rescue from this engulphment the better for

us in the end, and that if we borrow at 3½, and must get 7½, and may get 15 per cent, in the long run the borrower must be the gainer. Supposing the Colonel borrowed £100, and hired a gang of labourers and commenced thorough draining, his own fields we know would repay him, his tenants merely paying him as they paid me, 7½ per cent added to their rent for ever; the gain is certain, and they will gladly pay 10 per cent now that they have proved the advantages of the system. The hitch is, that the 'form' a'n't sufficiently explicit about the liabilities of the Electoral division either as a whole or as to the precise liability of the different individuals owning the lands in it, but Mr. Owen will probably be able to explain this. At any rate a lawyer will and Hal is going to town in a day or two.

I have made up my mind that the distress of the poor demands a large sacrifice on the part of the richer, and it must be our business to prepare for this and to give up luxuries to meet this. 'To feed the hungry' is a duty that cannot be shirked and Hal is not inclined to shirk it. He will find his whole family anxious to second his right intentions willing to bear their share of the difficulties, and as Almighty God never fails to fit the back to the burden, by His blessing we may hope to get through this season of trial using the means we are but the stewards of to the best of our abilities in alleviating this great distress. The young, the aged, the weakly, must suffer, let us do our utmost, for the able-bodied though employed can't earn sufficient for their support while provisions are so unnaturally high and this brings on the question whether the Government have acted right in declining to interfere with the markets. Extraordinary cases require extraordinary treatment. Abstract principles are probably correct and in future years may work for good, but having never acted on them hitherto we are not prepared to receive them, and one shudders at stepping over mounds of graves in the experiment at this time. At the present prices it would require 21/s a week to support a labourer and his family, he earns 6/, 7/, or 8/, at the highest. What must be the result?

FRIDAY, DECEMBER 4. Colonel Smith has gone in early to a consultation with the Government Commissioner and two or three of the wisest heads in our Barony, previous to the great gathering at the presentment Sessions at 12 o'clock. Between the mistakes on one hand, the jobbing on the other, and the unprincipled representations of the people, we are likely to pay dear for our benevolence.

6. The presentment Sessions were held on Friday. Mr. Fraser called here afterwards and made me understand the proceedings better than I should otherwise have done. The money already voted has been very carefully expended even with all the jobbing, and as this will be particularly watched there are funds sufficient to meet all charges till March. We therefore are called on to do nothing more for the present. With the usual hanging on spirit of their country, the whole people of the district were crowding to seize their share of what they look on as fair plunder and fancied was Government money, regardless of the fact that their rulers and landlords were coming forward only to relieve the *destitute* by employing labourers whose work was not wanted and whose wages it was a serious tax to have to pay, every man with a pair of arms rushed to the roads where they scrape away in herds, lazily, carelessly, and almost uselessly. Men with several acres of ground up to twenty, or thirty even, mangers with their stores full, families with a good sum saved, sons of parents in comfortable circumstances all represented themselves as starving, and leaving their proper employments came craving for the bread belonging to the *poor*. Hal has a list of men who sent asses to draw gravel, all of them able to *give* relief instead of requiring it, some of these asses bought, or *hired cheap* from those whom it was intended should have had the benefit of them. Many of these cases having been reported and the farmers beginning to comprehend that wherever the money may come from now they will themselves in the end have to pay their share of it, and that the fewer at work the less to pay, we hope the ferment will subside and things by and bye resume their ordinary level. If provisions fall, which looks likely the distress will be much relieved. Still the

sick, the weakly and the aged must be assisted, not more than usual however.

Parliament not to meet till the usual time. February rumours of a very divided Cabinet—embroilments abroad, dissatisfaction at home; no one can yet see any clear way out of many difficulties. It is a bad ministry, but where to get a better, unless Lord John and Sir Robert could coalesce. Great changes are however coming surely on. Besides the baths and wash-houses now established in many large towns there are lodging houses arranged where the inmates have separate beds, every convenience for comfort and decency, water, light, a kitchen in which they can cook their own provisions and all at a most moderate charge. Then attention has been called to the ordinary dwellings of the poor which have already been improved in many places, and this must spread, and wages must rise, for the days of serfdom are over. We are opening the minds of the lower orders and we can't expect that intelligent human beings will be content to live on like the brutes, merely protected from the weather and coarsely fed. They will civilise like the upper classes and God grant it may be soon.

Another striking feature of the times is the quiet agitation everywhere resorted to for the redress of grievances, instead of Wat Tyler and Jack Straw with their armed mob dealing death and meeting with the scaffold, we have the 'pressure from without' freeing trade in the shape of deputations of gentlemen insisting on alterations suited to the times. Corn is free, tea will be free or nearly so. Education too is coming before the eyes of publick opinion. Woolwich and Hartford and Eton and Heriot's Hospital with many more have had their iniquities dragged to light with a determined hand, and the consequence must be, reform. If each of us would but do our duty in our little sphere, what a happy world it would be.

15. Letters from Jane, several within these few days. She has got the place in the Riccarton gardens for Mat Ryan, at least Margaret Craig has kept it for him, he is to go on the 1st February. She had evidently forgotten William Darker for whom Mr. Innes had given me to understand

he should have had a vacancy ready last Martinmas, having been now reminded of the matter she will speak again and get the young man if possible to Phantassie[22] by seed time.

17. Mr. Owen has just been here with a Mr. Hazlitt, who is sent by the Irish Linen Society to engage the proprietors and farmers in the south to cultivate flax for them. Native growth is the finest, spins finest, he shewed us some thirty hanks to the lb. twenty hanks beautiful, *hand-spun*, the trade is so brisk just now they have demand for much more than is grown at home, and have the last year sent 4 *millions sterling* out of the country to Belgium, Russia, Egypt for the raw material. If enough of acres are sown in this district the Society will send an Overseer to direct the cultivation of the land and the preparation of the crop this first year, & they will buy the produce merely scutched. If the small farmer will employ his wife and daughters in spinning it, they will buy the yarn. If it could but succeed, here's employment for women, profit for men. The expenses on an acre are about £6, the produce unspun should sell for £40, where proper attention has been paid, say £30 for three or four months only for turnips, vetches or rape can follow the lint crop, which if sown early in April should be reaped early in July.

We had snow yesterday, all gone to-day. The Poor Houses are full, therefore now I believe in the destitution cry. The people are starving I believe. Cold and nakedness and discomfort of every kind they are indifferent to, provided they can fill their stomacks, stuff them rather with the lowest quality of food, its bulk is what they look for, for years the failure of the potato crop has been expected, yet no preparations were made to meet this coming evil. They have no forethought. If they get a shilling they must spend it. They can't make 11d. do and save the penny, they have no store for the rainy day, then when it comes they rail at all the rest of the

22. The estate of Sir Thomas Dick Lauder's son-in-law, Alexander Mitchell Innes.

world for not stepping forward to their relief instantly as if they deserved the quicker aid because they never helped themselves. There is no energy, no honesty, no industry among them. But this wide spread calamity must rouse them. Already good effects have been produced. The Poor House will improve their habits, the dearness of provisions has driven many of the idle hangers on at home out into the world to earn the food no longer to be had by grubbing for it. So we must live in hope that happen what may things can never again be so wretchedly bad as they have been.

20. Sunday. Milder weather. I got out yesterday and again to-day. The Doctor has dined with us and says the famine has come, is in every house on Bishop hill, Pinmaker's hill, Holywood and the Radcliffes mountains. Every neglected property in short, the Poor House is full, 1100, where there never was 200, and sheds erecting for hundreds more; the price of provisions is so enormous, three times the wages would not give sufficient food to a family. After Christmas soup kitchens must be set up.

We have been trying rice and find it liked so have sent for a further supply although we cannot get it so cheap in a small quantity in Dublin as it could be got in Liverpool or as we hope to get it shortly from John Robinson, who has been written to by a London house on the subject, they offer it at from 13/6 to 16/- the cwt. We are paying 24/- and even at that price it is the cheapest food to be had. Old Peggy sells it at 3d a 1b. and sold a stone a day the two first days when few knew she had it, so we have ordered 2 cwt, and we will order a ton if necessary, and buy coarse beef which Peggy can make into soup to sell at cost price or below it where needful. We must all do our utmost, share our all. Mr. and Mrs. Moore called yesterday and my Lady and her girls in red clokes and black beaver gypsey hats and feathers cocked up behind like the cobwebs to catch flies. Lunaticks from Bedlam. She was not in good humour. Wanted us all to go and dine and neither we nor Moores would go.

26. Lots of letters but only on business, all requiring immediate answers too, and there's Mr. Rutherfurd with that fine

farm and these high prices owing a year and a half's rent,
We sent to him for money and got £20, and we desired to
have £30 more in a week or two. By and bye I shall apply
again for this sort of thing won't do with sons flying about
in jaunting cars, riding races and keeping hunters. There
never was a worse manager than that poor man, of farm
and family, working himself to death, too, all the time.
The ground covered with snow, cold in the house great,
out of doors the young things are laughing merrily as they
run round the shrubbery on the swept gravel.

27. The snow being hard enough the girls have walked to
church, where by the way they seem to have become very
fond of going. Dismal looking weather. We got this week
the sequel to that very clever novel by Alexandre Dumas,
the *Chateau d'Yf*, which I consider quite equal, in many
scenes superiour to, Walter Scott. This continuation is
called the *Comte of Monte Christo*, written with wonderful
power, dramatick to a degree, engrossingly interesting,
but too rapidly put together for some of the incidents to
follow naturally, some of the characters to be properly
worked out, and the horrible is too frequent, and the
morality detestable, false feelings throughout. The end
is wrong, badly atchieved, the life of the hero is a lie,
he utters falsehoods by the dozen and acts the part of
a demon, making his own heart as depraved as those
he punishes, then he sails away to begin a new life of
happiness, leaving the only two persons who have shewn
a conduct founded on principles of virtue, to a future
almost of despair provided for them by his means. This
style of romance makes one comprehend the authour's
'additions to Shakespeare'.

I am amused also rather with a disjointed sort of book
called *Memoirs of Lady Hester Stanhope*[23], by a vulgar
mean-spirited man who lived with her at odd times as her
Doctor; he makes her out to be a clever violent-tempered

23. Charles Lewis 'Memoirs of Lady Hester Stanhope as
related by Herself in Conversation with her Physician'
(1846). She, for the D.N.B. was 'eccentric' and 'a beauty
of the brilliant rather than the handsome order.'

woman, grown imperious to insolence from want of a check of any sort to her fury; and quite mad like most of her family. What he supposes the world will think of him who endured her impertinence patiently himself and permitted a series of insults to be accumulated upon his family by a person he evidently did not respect, he is probably indifferent to, money being most likely his reason for thus violating private conversations, exposing the circumstances and the frailties of his patient and offering up his own character as a sacrifice to his necessities.

I am reading much less than usual this season without well knowing why. The state of the country really fills our minds, we think of nothing else.

31. The end of a happy year, the last day of poor 1846 during which we have had as much pleasure and suffered as little pain as could possibly fall to the lot of humanity. Except that the Colonel and I are growing old we have little personal to complain of. We are neither of us robust but by being prudent we can avoid any serious ailment. The children are well: not pictures of rosy health, but sufficiently strong to get on well, not wonders in any way, yet all three amiable, engaging, nice-looking and talented; our household comfortable: our people the same although starvation is very near us: and in our connexions we have been spared any sorrow. At my age in a changing world people should be prepared for losses. I am beginning to understand the possibility of feeling that one has lived long enough—once so strange a thing to hear of. Mind will weary as the bodily powers decay, rest will be welcome to the aged. For the present however I mean to keep myself young a while. I have much work to do and I must not let indolence unfit me for my labours. Farewell 1846.

SEVEN

1847

Throughout this year the 'frightful reality' of the Famine
was to be 'seen in every face'. The Smiths' lives were
dominated by their responses and the *Catalogue Raisonné*
of every family for whom they were responsible on the
estate provides the individual details of hardship or
survival against the background of government debate
and the activities of the local Relief Committee.

MONDAY, JANUARY 4. How the years pass, coming round so
quick as to be almost bewildering, and the months, and
the weeks and the days and the hours. We had a dull New
Year's Day for having given money to all our people as
better for their families this very pinching season we
had no kitchen parties; upstairs only the Doctor who
dined on hogmanae and sat till midnight to welcome in
the new year.

5. The Colonel and I propose dabbling a little in the
provision line having it in serious contemplation to
establish a store for the purpose of supplying the poor
at a reasonable price. We have begun with rice which
old Peggy retails for us at 3d. a lb. getting a ready sale
hitherto. By and bye we shall have it for them cheaper
as John Robinson has contracted with a London house
for a supply to arrive in April at a much lower rate than
we can get it now. We are also thinking of adding a little
Indian meal to our stock; unfortunately in all our range of
offices there is no storeroom for grain, etc. but I think we
could manage to make one. The repository continues to
thrive quietly. Whenever the poor women have a sixpence
to lay out on themselves or their children they go there
for their clothing, but of course this hard year they have
less to spend in this way than usual. The schools are all to
begin again. We hope we have at last procured a family to

suit us. An elderly man, married, with daughters capable of undertaking the charge of the female children. Miss Gardiner went very nearly out of her mind when she found she was really dispensed with, and actually thinks she has been very harshly treated, turned out of doors in fact because after the fifth resignation she was taken at her word. She has by no means given me satisfaction for some time past. We can't fail to change for the better. All the 'Busy Bee' fully occupied, for this honey-making insect is all alive again. It is delightful to feel useful once more. Unfortunately I can't go about much out of doors, but I manage to know what is doing.

New Year's Day being fine the girls and I paid many visits and all the houses we entered showed much humble comfort. Would that all around us were the same. However charity must begin at home, quite certain of not ending there. Example does much and as we can't assist all we must only continue to look after our own and be content to distribute elsewhere the crumbs left by those who have a right to the bread. We are giving milk and soup to all our workmen and soup to all our sick or aged. Margaret has a large pot of soup ready every day at one o'clock and a list of persons to whom she has to give it. Each gets a quart every second day. At present we have to give twelve quarts daily. The workmen have milk on the day they don't get soup, and we must buy another cow for we are running short both of milk and butter. Upon consultation with Mr. Darker the Colonel adopted this plan in preference to that of raising the wages. The poor are such bad managers, they spend their money very foolishly and in the matter of food which supplies the strength on which the breadwinner works, the women are so ignorant, so indolent, that they are utterly incapable of preparing a comfortable meal. They have not fuel indeed to cook one, nor pot nor pan nor griddle nor crock to prepare one in, most of them at least. Patience! Better days will come. I have always to look back to encourage myself to look forward. Thinking of what we found gives me spirits to hope for what we, or at any rate our children, may see.

8. I called in on Miss Gardiner who seems at last to have found her senses, or rather being employed packing her goods has no leisure for folly. She was neither tragick nor comick nor unreasonable, but busy, so perfectly rational. I shall have a deal of plague with her successors of course; however she was herself but a burden to me for some years, and a great deal of useless trouble I took with her for she by no means rewarded my care, her character being of the weakest sort. Still she was a much better teacher than I have any hope of meeting with again. Dr. Tighe Gregory sends us a very good account of Mr. O'Keeffe, but I require so much that other people don't think about, that I am preparing myself for some months of strict management.

9. We are reading aloud after tea Miss Edgeworth's charming tales. I had several purposes in beginning them. One was amusement blended with instruction; another the hope of leading the girls to wise and useful and elegant pleasurable occupations; another the belief that clever little Miss Clerk will benefit by the educational hints so profusely scattered over these truly rational volumes. I find myself so embued with her spirit that it amuses me to find what an *automoton*, so to speak, she has made of me. Unconsciously, I have been all through but a specimen of her principles in action allowing for the imperfections of her humble instrument, and this proves the utility of filling the *young* mind well. As children we lived upon her writings and certainly our after habits have been most materially influenced by them.

12. Alas! the famine progresses; here it is in frightful reality to be seen in every face. Idle, improvident, reckless, meanly dependent on the upper classes whom they so abuse, call the bulk of the Irish what we will, and no name is too hard almost for them, here they are starving round us, cold, naked, hungry, well nigh houseless. To rouse them from their natural apathy may be the work of future years. To feed them must be our business this. Baltiboys is in comfort, few of our people in real distress, some in want of assistance and they get it, others in need of nothing. My habit of going constantly about

among them keeps me pretty well acquainted with their condition, but lest I should miscalculate I am taking the whole estate regularly through at this time. Two days of visiting introduced me to no distress, only to two cases of *struggling*—that expressive word. I mean to make a *catalogue raisonné* of our population to leave among our family archives as a curiosity for future squires and a guide to us now.

Hal has killed a beef for our poor and we make daily a large pot of good soup which is served gratis to 22 people at present. It is ready at one o'clock and I thought it quite a pretty sight yesterday in the kitchen all the workmen coming in for their portion, a quart with a slice of the beef; half of them get this one day for a dinner with a bit of their own bread; the other half get milk and the cheap rice we have provided for them. Next day they reverse the order. The Colonel is giving them firing too; so they are really comfortable; there are twelve of them and ten pensioners, old feeble men and women, or those with large families of children; some of them no longer living on our ground yet having been once connected with us we can't desert them.

So far well; but beyond our small circle what a waste of misery; how are we to relieve it? Such a dense population squatted here and there upon neglected properties, dying with want, wretched every year, but ruined this. At the Relief Committee yesterday it was resolved to institute soup kitchens at proper stations for general relief, to be supported by subscription, each subscriber to have a certain number of tickets. I think the gentlemen doing this, the ladies must combine for a clothing fund. The rags are scarcely coverings for decency; beds and bedding there are none, among the mob, I mean; such misery crushes hope, yet hope I will. 'Hope and wait' as was Dante's motto.

I am going to send you dear Aunt Bourne, my January journal for I really have not time to write you the sort of letter your love for me and mine deserves. And to enable you to comprehend our busy life I will describe my day. How different from the painful invalid day of last year.

Wakened by a cup of tea at half after seven. Bathe in cold water, dress, without a fire; down by a quarter after eight, to keep tryst with Jack who meets me then with his lessons. We work together till nine, I knitting the while the little triangular pieces for a counterpane; whichever little girl is housekeeper for the week comes down at nine to make breakfast and while the tea is drawing they all go up to the schoolroom to prayers, then call in Papa and so we all gather to our pleasant meal, after which Jack takes some warm milk to the cat, Annie the crumbs to the birds who actually know her; Miss Clerk other little remains to Rover. At ten all set to work again. Jack goes up to school. I have an interview with Mrs. Fyfe, another with Mr. Darker, and then I write for the post; then receive any applicant, tidy the drawing-rooms, by which time it is near one o'clock for a good deal of business is included under these few heads. On fine days I am out till four, walking, each walk having its object. Middling days I take the little covered carriage and pay visits—a job I hate. On wet days I have all these hours for my own private occupations the only authourship time I now have, and the weather is so fine just now that I am doing nothing in that line. At half after four all dine; afterwards if the Colonel have finished the newspapers in the morning I play backgamnon or piquet with him. If the papers are still to read, I can sew, mend or make or work for the Repository. At seven we go to tea, and then I read aloud till ten except on the two musick nights when I work. At ten we all retire, but as I sleep little, I sit after undressing for an hour or more by the fire reading, or knitting warm petticoats for the wretched. Of course visitors morning or evening change this routine. As every walk has its object, the schools, a farm, the repository, a sick call, etc. so every day has its business: the storeroom, or workroom, or accounts, or garden affairs, provision stores, etc., etc., making an agreeable variety of occupation.

Who would exchange for this rational furthering of the improvement of our race, the life of the town fine lady? Or will any young woman brought up in this higher style of employment ever sink into the party giving idler? I

am sure I hope not. To learn early the wide difference
between society and company will raise the most joyous
female mind above great crowds, fine clothes, and silver
dishes; they may be found agreeable accompaniments,
but they will not be considered essentials. And those who
have been accustomed to the interchange of cultivated
minds while living with a few chosen friends will hardly
stoop to be *satisfied* with frivolous *talk* for we can only
converse with the enlightened.

We have been unable to get on with Mr. Dickens's
Christmas Love tale. Mr. Owen who lent it foretold this.
To make amends No. 1. of Howitt's new journal[1] in
which Mary Gillies is to write we found very interesting
although too radical. It is to be the mouthpiece of the
new movement. That movement must be. As the great
barons of old, their oppressions, feudalisms, charge and
power have vanished, so must our present institutions
fade before the power which must prevail—Truth. We are
raising the lower classes in mind, and they will themselves
raise their physical position. They must ascend and we
must meet them but cautiously, gradually, or we shall
convulse society as in the days of rude revolution. And it
always strikes me that this liberal school are for hurrying
matters; if some of the higher ranks know little of their
poorer brethren the poor less understand the rich. And
these good Howitts and Smiths and Foxes, etc. are a
little visionary; they are unacquainted with the great;
they are miscalculating for the humble who will at
least require *three generations* to educate out of their
present low feelings. The leaven remains longer than
they reckon on.

13. I shall set down here the result of my present careful
survey of our people as a good mem; to have beside
us. Walk the 1st: To old Paddy and Peggy Dodson,
pensioners in a good cabin near our gate which we built
for them; two rooms well furnished; a good garden; their

1. William and Mary Howitt left the *People's Journal* in
January 1847 to found their own *Howitt's Journal* which
they intended to be a focus for radical ideas.

two children off their hands: Antony a carpenter, Mary housemaid at Rusboro'; pension eight pounds a year. Peggy keeps the Repository and gets a penny out of every shilling's worth she sells; also keeps the cheap provision store, gets a penny for every stone weight she sells. An orphan girl is boarded with her for whose keep she gets four pounds a year; I providing clothing. We give this family soup one day, milk the next, dripping every Sunday.

James Ryan the carpenter, a good two storey, slated house with four rooms, a closet, and dairy, workshop, shed, yard, three acres of land, one apprentice, one journeyman, a boy, a maid, wife and five children; one boy and two girls at school, two little girls mere babies. All comfortable here, neater than the general. Two cabins together on what was Judy Ryan's ground. The stableman John Fitzpatrick in one, the ploughman Miles Byrne in the other, two rooms a large garden a yard each, Miles a turf house; wife dead leaving him three boys and a nurse child, a girl now at twelve years of age managing his most tidy household under the aunts, as she calls them, Mary and Betty Hyland who look in every day these good women have also taken the two baby boys home leaving Miles only his eldest son, a clever child at school.

John Fitzpatrick's wife is neither so clean nor so tidy as her little neighbour but she has plenty in the rough, and but three children, one girl at school, two little boys, babies, and a nephew of her husband's, the child of very distressed parents whom they have taken out of charity. The wages of these two men seven shillings a week with milk or soup daily. Pat Ryan a small farm of thirteen acres in high order; the lower part drained on the new system, fully stocked; poor looking house with three rooms, plenty of rude comfort, stables, sheds, etc. A wife, a mother, a half idiot brother; three boys, one Mathew in our garden just going as apprentice to Riccarton: the second assisting the father, both attending the evening school; the third a first-rate boy at school; the little girl at school. Nothing wanting here. A cabin at hand is occupied by our herd and our gardener, one room each, no garden; wages seven shillings. Paddy White, the gardener, has an industrious wife, no children. John Grace, the herd, a pattern of a wife and two pretty little baby girls. Both families get soup or milk daily and are very comfortable.

Next farm, ninety acres, Tom Kelly, an old man now, with old untidy ways; married at fifty, a girl with a hundred pounds who has made him an excellent wife. They have a large yard, new good offices, a garden, house of three large rooms, and seven children, four boys and three girls; the four elder ones at school; plenty here but in an uncomfortable manner and the worst farming though the rent is never behind; no draining, no turnips, not sufficient stock. Hal means to resume about twenty acres of the low ground to reclaim himself as this stupid old creature can't be moved to exertion and we shall have a world of plague to get back the possession, both husband and wife acting tragedy when informed of it although they got this addition to their old holding on the express understanding of improving it.

Here ended my first day's survey which I consider very satisfactory both as to the present and future, for Tom Kelly will manage fewer acres better as he will not diminish his labourers and they are too few for the size of his present farm—two old half useless men and a little boy, all of whom he gets at half wages, with a niece as maid-servant. His little daughter, one of my pets, manages her younger brothers and sisters. The herd and gardener want each another room, one house more in fact, with garden ground, but this is no year for building even a cabin—ten or twelve pounds at the cheapest to be decent, and all we can raise must go into the soup pot this miserable season. We ought to have the lodge for the gardener, but that would cost much more. Patience.

Walk the second. Next poor George Cairns—almost a fool—simple as a child & really almost as innocent, evil not in him nor good either. It is him we have taken his ground from although he has not yet given up possession.

We are waiting till we get a place for him as sawyer, the trade he was bred to, and we give him leave to retain the house for his family till he settles elsewhere; he has let his house of three rooms go to ruin, ditte the crazy offices, bad at the best and few of them; he has not a hoof on the land, nor a hen even; the hay is in small cocks on the meadow just fit for manure; fences all broken, no gates, no furniture, but decent clothing, a good bed, fuel, and corn enough to feed wife and six children till May; four fine boys are at school; a cousin lives with them who for reasons of his own has tried to prop them up these several years, but it won't do; two years' rent owing now, and the ground destroyed. They will be rich on their guinea a week, sawyer's wages, and this is utter misery; besides the wife may do her duty to *George* Cairns better when separated from the cousin *Charles*.

Close to these wretched people is a thriving farmer on the same quantity of land about thirty acres—Bryan Dempsey,—a reckless, ruthless, vapouring, '*cute*', model of the bad style of Irishman whom I can't feel interested in for his want of principle; two sons, two daughters, one man and an active wife compose his family; slated house with three rooms, and decent offices, clean and rather orderly, but no 'English neatness.' On again was Tom Kiogh doing well on twelve acres, but all in dirt and filth and wet; his once beautiful wife a regular old beldam, dirty beyond idea, yet all her clothes were good; her four fine boys were well dressed; three of them go to school. There was a new press, new shoes, great coats, tea things, yet the whole looked wretched from the filth. It was the dirtiest house and yard we saw, not excepting Garrett Doyle's a little above on the hill. This smart young man has a large farm forty acres or thereabouts and his fields are in good order; but his yard is knee deep with mud, offices mere ruins, house little better though the old mother keeps plenty about it. Three men and a nurse child grown up into a servant maid compose this establishment which will never be more comfortable while the old woman lives. Dempsey's was by far the neatest household we saw this day; his daughters who were kept assiduously at school while they were young have acquired habits of neatness there with a perfect knowledge of their needle which has enabled them to improve their humble home. The good new house too aids them; dry and light, they see their way and their labours of cleanliness are not in vain. A little grandchild here is going to school.

Walk the third. Down the lane towards the King's river on the right a small cabin of three rooms, warm and clean with tidy furniture, good bedding, a neat small yard enclosed, cowhouse and pigstye. Here with one acre of ground a decent labouring man has struggled through his laborious life and reared a large family in the days of pigs and potatoes. But times are changed. James Cullen and his dear old wife are past seventy years of age; neither can work as they used to do, and the acre of ground for which they have paid no rent for the three last half years is an encumbrance to them. Still I doubt their giving it up but by and bye I shall try though one can't be hard on the old couple. He has always made a good deal of money by preparing turf in summer for which he gets a ready sale in winter. I think of setting him up as turf merchant to the district, by lending him in spring the small capital necessary to buy a stretch of bog, an ass, and small cart; he is near the bog and the new system of farming coming in will leave the active farmer no time for cutting his own fuel. This old pair are on the soup list and James having work at his brother-in-law Michael Tyrrel's, they will get on pretty well; they would have got on quite well but for their youngest son who married against their consent, brought home his wife, robbed them right and left, and had to be bribed to leave them, the Colonel giving a pound to be rid of such a scape-grace.

To the left a better cabin and very neat yard full of manure made up properly; a cowhouse, stack of corn and hay—the produce of three acres which old Dick Gray is to keep while he lives—no long term of tenure apparently for he is in bed in a very bare room, laying upon straw, full of pains and aches, his eldest son beside him in an equally hopeless state. It was quite affecting.

John Gray had been working in Liverpool under a mason to whom his elder sister is married, neglected a cold, and came home to die, poor lad, I fear; the youngest son Ned took the opportunity of these troubles and a bad season and our absence in England to get himself married. I found the wife pinned up behind a blanket in the wide kitchen chimney and recommended her and Ned who was thrashing *in the kitchen*, to provide themselves with a more permanent home as soon as convenient for that they were quite too many here an unmarried daughter Kitty being the best manager for the old father whom with the sick son we added to the soup list.

In more wet and dirt and filth and misery than we had yet seen we found the next little farmer Michael Doyle, a fine looking and very hard working though low feeling man who for his sins and for her fifteen pounds, married the widow Ryan, my Annie's nurse. Her three children, two she has had since this marriage, a nurse child of course, all seem to squat on the floor of a very small kitchen, for we saw no stools, chairs, tables, nor any furniture but a crazy dresser with very little upon its shelves. She stood to receive us in her cloke having but one gown which was washing; all the children nearly naked, the husband very bare; no way of getting up to the house but over a broken wall, or up to the door but over the dung hill. She would not let me into the bedroom and then she told me they had turned it into a cowhouse and the reason the floor was so bad was that the cows passed and repassed through the kitchen. Twice I have succeeded in improving this most slatternly Judy, and twice she has fallen back when my watchful eye was removed. I will try again—her and the husband together—rouse them if possible for they want but method to be comfortable. They have near eight acres of land, two milch cows giving her *now* four lbs. of butter a week which she sells in the market for eleven pence a lb.; a pound she keeps and all the buttermilk; they have two young heifers coming on, and he has promised this year to sow an acre of turnips. They have still eight barrels of oats; he will want three for seed; he promises to *change* this at the market, to sell three of the remaining barrels, oats are very high now, twenty-four shillings a barrel, and to purchase with their price, rice and Indian meal to mix with the oatmeal his two left barrels will give. As he has just recovered from a long illness, six weeks of typhus fever which took all their spare money, the family is put on the soup list; he has had a meat dinner daily since he was able for it, and is so grateful that I hope he will oblige me by setting to work in earnest to encrease his comforts. I ordered the second girl and two little ones off to school, leaving the eldest whom we have well educated, to help her mother and mind the baby.

Close at hand was another small farm about the same size with a low bad house, very dark having no window in the kitchen, but it was a real pleasure to enter so decent an abode. Manure at one end banked up, cowhouse with four cows in it *never let out, feeding on turnips*, large turf stack, very clean kitchen, bright fire, dresser well filled, wall hung with polished pots and covers, meal chest, table, and two neat chairs brought from the bedroom and wiped with a clean cloth before being offered to us by a young pretty woman in appearance like a tidy housemaid who was churning when we came in. She was a mountain beauty with a little money and is seemingly a prize to Pat Fitzpatrick who was a widower with one child when we went to the highlands. Nothing wanted here but praise and some little present for an encouragement. It was a real scene of humble comfort.

Close to the river rises the new two storey slated house just built by little Michael Tyrrell, the largest farmer on the property having close upon a hundred acres; a thriving man with a wife deserving of him; the offices are to follow; in the meanwhile the old steading serves the turn; the daughters of this house are all well married, the sons in trades, except the youngest Philip, who will worthily succeed his father. Last summer this fine old man when busy in his hayfield told us it was his birthday—seventy-six. This day I found him in his bed where he has lain three weeks with influenza, declining he says, in want of stimulant, said I; so I set the wife about a bowl of broth for him, ordered him a cup of tea, bade him get up in the evenings, and promised to call again in a week when he would be well enough to show me all he had been doing with his farm. We walked five miles before getting home again, dodging here and there added so much to the distance.

15. Three more walks will I think finish my examination of those families connected with us, and perhaps introduce us to many much worse off and who poor creatures shall have all the help that we can give them after *our own* are served. We called in Blesinton on the Doctor who is better but still in bed. The Colonel went up to see him and thinks him ill enough, quite overworked these wretched times; fever and dysentery among the people, distances so great, wet feet, fatigue, grief for the wretchedness that all our means can't overcome, most of it the consequence of the character of the sufferers who will be many generations yet before they rise to that higher perception of their duties which can alone ensure their greater comfort.

20. What would this country do without him? Where should we get such another friend and physician, devoting every energy to his professional duties? I have heart again now to relate my wanderings among the wretched, how wretched. Can strangers believe that a whole country would consider itself fed, on *one good meal* a day; could they manage a light supper besides for their children, three turnips and a pint of meal would quite content them for this latter purpose. Yet if all did as we do—*looked to their own*—there would be no distress. But this system of public relief is an *unjust mockery*—nothing else.

Walk 3rd. The distances being now greater I was able to take fewer houses on my round. I went up the hill again first calling on the Widow Quin who being left some years ago on her husband's death insolvent with a large and very young family and she an ailing woman, the Colonel relieved her of her land, forgave her seven years' rent, gave her the stock and crop to dispose of and left her the house and garden for her life. All her children were employed as they were fit for work and

she has certainly done better than if she had retained
her ill-managed farm. All her sons are in good places,
one of them with us; her daughters married except one
who lives with her and takes in washing. I put mother
and daughter on the soup list, times being so hard. Two
of the daughters are very well married; the third made
a wretched one; she took a sickly labouring lad who
is often laid up, but to whom she has brought seven
children. They live in the mother's cowhouse where she
had no right to put them and thus settle a whole family
of beggars upon us, but we did not look after things then
as we have learned to do now. It is the most wretched
abode imaginable, without window or fire-place; mud
for the floor, neither water nor weather-tight, nor scarce
a door, all black with smoke, no furniture scarcely. Yet
times are brightening for the nearly naked inmates. A
brother in America sent them at Christmas ten pounds
which paid their debts, and bought them some meal and
fuel, and their eldest son is to go out to this kind uncle in
March. They have no business where they are, the man
not belonging to Baltiboys, but there they are through our
negligence so we must take care of them for the present.
I gave the poor woman a quarter's school fees for four
of the children and put the family on the soup list, and
when we come to the clothing which we must do for the
very poor, she shall not be forgotten. Nothing could be
cleaner or neater in the rude way only known here than
the Widow Quin's comfortable three-roomed cabin.

The next visit was to a cousin Red Paddy Quin with
a good farm which affords him every comfort from his
good management; his wife lately died in childbed and
her baby; he has two fine boys, the eldest at school, a
little tidy girl as maidservant; two men, and plenty of
everything. Little Paddy, a copy of Jack: with his boots,
frieze great coat, and cap! and quite familiar with me from
our school intercourse, and only seven years old, insisted
on escorting me to the next house on the hill, the abode
of another old pensioner, the plague of my life though I
am very fond of her.

The widow Nary wants a few months of eighty, and

there she was as brisk as a bee darning her stockings in the doorway without spectacles. As we provide her with everything in the world she wishes for I merely called in to see how she was. She has found a decent little pedlar woman who was 'long in the army' to live with her, the only person she ever yet kept a second night with her, and the Colonel and I were so relieved at getting any one that pleased her, to look after her, that though this old campaigner has a son, we consented gladly thus to domicile them—the rather, that the son is a pet of mine, a dwarf, blind of one eye, marked deep with the smallpox, quite an object of ugliness, who working everywhere during the busy months, merely at boy's wages, always contrived to save enough for school during the winter. There he learned to net, by which trade he is now supporting his mother, her pedlar business being but slack now that every penny is required for food, as I know by my Repository at which we now sell nothing. Last year it nearly paid the expenses of the female school.

I came the back road home over the hill, down past the quarries and through the farm yards, looking in at the new room we have just contrived for the two men who sleep there to watch the cattle. I bought the furniture from Miss Gardiner, had it repaired and I don't believe any of the better farmers even possess as many comforts. We have eight bachelour labourers who all know they leave us if they marry. As they are they rich on their 6/- a week getting their soup or milk daily. Twelve out of door servants, four at 7/-; eight at 6/- makes a hole in small means, but this year we must keep them. Ten is our ordinary number. They are a truly decent set, grateful in earnest for their good places.

Walk the 4th. Along this side of the hill along the road behind the rockery, past the Darkers' excellent house where I did not call knowing well that all there was as one could wish. Northerns, protestants, well educated, industrious, they are a credit to the country. Of the two bachelour brothers John manages the good farm of ninety-six acres; Tom is the Colonel's steward and bailiff at a salary of fifty pounds. Two maiden sisters take charge of the house, etc. Amongst them they have brought up five orphan nephews and nieces, the children of two brothers who died beggars. It is the eldest of these nephews whom I have Sir Thomas Lauder's promise to get to Phantassie as an apprentice under his son-in-law Alexander Mitchell Innes, who bought this famous model farm belonging once to the Rennies. We have taken great pains with these children, indeed with the whole respectable family; lending them every book that was good for them and how their minds have grown—the women and all—prejudices and follies and affectations vanished, replacing gradually by good sound sense, without the odium of teaching either. It has grown somehow on them all through Tom Darker's constant intercourse with us.

The next farm is in a bad way—a great annoyance to us, though owned by a most respectable woman the Widow Kelly. We have still a few of those miserable little patches of farms of 7 or 8 acres not having been able to get rid of all of them so many subdivisions having been permitted during the negligent days of my brother-in-law and his careless agent; but this is the only farm we have, not our own, which we can do nothing with for it is let on a lease of lives to a middleman, who sublets it to the Widow Kelly. She is a managing woman struggling on with twelve children on her sixty acres, very decently; but she is not improving her ground or her style of farming, or if she did we should not benefit, and she is letting the offices go to ruin. She has five children at school and plenty to feed all with; five acres of this leased ground are let to Bartle Murphy up at the top of the hill close by the moat which once defended one of Cromwell's watch towers. The Colonel has planted all these furzy fields and Murphy has the charge of them at a small salary without which he must have been begging, the five acres having ruined him: his potatoes gone, his two cows dead of the murrain, nothing left of all his labour but a cwt. and a half of oatmeal. There are six children, four at school, one at the breast, where, poor thing, it got nothing, a scanty breakfast and a turnip supper not providing much supply for it. All was very neat here and the clothes of the family of a better description than usual. The wife however broken-hearted; it hardly raised her spirits to have her family put upon the soup list.

My last visit this day was to James Carny the mason; he is doing well on his farm of twenty-three acres; has it well stocked, lives in a good three-roomed slated house with a pretty wife and four children, two of them at school; his trade has hitherto kept him easy, but no one is building this year, so he has had to part with his men, his wife with her maid, to leave enough food behind.

21. Mr. Owen is beyond first-rate—a blessing to the neighbourhood. As agent for such large estates as Lord Downshire possesses here his power is great, and most conscientiously is it exercised, and his knowledge of the duties of his profession is so perfect, his energy, activity, thorough-going, so different from the jobbing expediency system hitherto pursued that he cannot fail in a few years morally to revolutionise the district; he has the young man's fault—not perhaps an undue opinion of himself, but too little patience with the errours of his older associates amongst whom he has come a stranger and for whom he don't show that respect in manner, due to their years at least, if not to their characters.

Would we had more like him faults and all. George Moore does much good, gives abundant employment and looks after the comfort of all his people. Ogle Moore, as far as his small means go, exercises them fully. Mr. Armstrong likewise. Richard Hornidge also, but there we must stop; the other resident landlords get on in the old way, the lowest wages, little work, no help in advice or otherwise; they may throw about a few pence when much importuned by beggars, but they will take no trouble—they will not do *justice*. And there are large tracts of land belonging to absentees filled with squatters—all paupers—among whom a shilling is never spent, and who with the neglected peasantry of the indolent Landlords are all thrown upon us the willing horses. I don't know what will become of us before spring.

We have no right to look to richer England for help,
no right to expect the government to take charge of
our private affairs. We have brought our miseries upon
ourselves; a long series of improvident management
results in ruin. We who suffer may not in ourselves
all of us, deserve this severe affliction, but we must bear
the consequences of the evils permitted by our ancestors.
The young race, rising, are aware of this moral retribution
laid upon their generation; they bow to it, are preparing
to meet it, to retrieve it, and no doubt the country will be
raised a century the sooner from the frightful apathy into
which all classes seemed to be sunk. But deeply must the
nation suffer, and all that individuals can do is to work in
their little circle to mitigate the misery.

24. We were all the evening busy with the debates upon the
opening of Parliament. It is of less consequence in these
days what tools of governing are used; the sub officials,
who are never changed, manage all the routine business,
do all the work in fact. and the ministers must yield
to the all powerful publick, pass just such measures as
the people—our true sovereign—chuse. We shall see
what they will do for Ireland, or rather what they will
make of Irishmen; if these could be induced to mind
their business, to do their duty, to look after their own
affairs, and to depend alone upon themselves, trust only
to their own exertions, this naturally gifted country might
become the pride of Europe.

It's nonsense to talk of good landlords as the rule; they
are no such thing, they are only the exception. In my
walks about this little locality have I not found evidence
against them that would fit me for a witness before a
Committee of the House, on the causes of Irish misery?
When I pass the limits of our own ground nothing meets
me but wretchedness. The other day when looking for
a family we thought it our business to relieve, in the
Weaver's Square, where no looms are to be found now,
every house I entered on my search broke my heart. The
particular circumstances of this afflicting year have much
encreased the misery, for the little farmers having no food
to spare have dismissed their servants; the men leave their

ground untilled, the women have eat their poultry, sold their pig, so do not want the help of a maid; thus young men and girls are returned upon their poverty-stricken parents, while between want of seed and want of hands to sow it, the prospects of a harvest are blighted; all rush to the roads which are rendered by this unprofitable labour impassable; there are two or three at hand actually shut up by the diggings and shovellings going on upon them, and we are to pay for this waste, and for our ordinary and extraordinary expenses out of diminished funds. From Lord John's tone we hope they don't mean to tax the land with this misapplied million. If they do it will be very unjust. All exclaimed against the scheme, as useless in itself, preventing useful work, and loosening the few remaining relations which yet attached the employed to the employer.

31. Sunday. At the present time with the assistance of the Government loan the people here-abouts can just struggle on, scantily fed on two meals only a day, that is a man can feed in this poor manner himself, a wife and *two* children; where the family is larger his earning can't suffice; but then generally there is a son in this case grown up enough to earn an additional trifle so that *famine* here there will not exactly be; but they will soon all be nearly naked; not a penny have they for clothing, or fuel, or house-rent, and the small farmers are almost worse off than the labourers as they are not given work and their very few ill-cultivated acres yield them too little to support them. They will be starved out of these miserable holdings—that is one good result of these melancholy times, though much suffering will precede the change.

The promised debate on Ireland came off with a degree of quiet unusual on Irish affairs; the House seemed overwhelmed by the magnitude of the evil. Some nonsense was spoken of course, but the feeling on all sides was kind. The Government acknowledges the errour of the road plan. Still what could be done at the moment, during the winter season? It don't intend continuing these works, nor interfering with the natural relations between the tillers and the owners of the soil, nor endeavouring in any manner to influence the markets. It confines its measures to taking off duties, lending money to the farmers for seed and to the landlords for improvements. Lord John emphatically says: 'not to be squandered in Paris or Naples but to be employed under the superintendence of resident landlords in works which will repay the cost.' How any person with the full use of his senses can approve of these degrading petitions for English charity or even tolerate such libels on the social morals of their countrymen is to me a marvel; or how any man can shut his eyes to the fact that gross neglect of the duties inseparable from the possession of landed property is at the bottom of all this misery, the continuing cause of its extent, the real evil of which this famine is but a symptom or a consequence, I can't comprehend. We ought not to have accepted still less have *begged* the purse from England. Involved estates should be sold; luxuries should be given up; absentees should bring their money home; the idlers should turn to work; all ranks should exert their utmost energies, should depend on themselves alone, for they do possess the means of relieving themselves.

MONDAY, FEBRUARY 1. I have taken my last walk through Baltiboys; there were four houses to visit. The neat cabin of the Hylands; the old mother in it still alive nursing her grandchildren by the fire, her other descendants all employed and so the family in comfort. Pat Farrell our other carpenter plenty to do in his good shop; three acres of land helping to employ his sons at leisure hours; a managing wife with by far the neatest furnished house in the country; Jack Byrne thriving on a good-sized farm sixty acres; his wife a daughter of old Michael Tyrrell's in the Bottoms, quite a pattern, with four fine boys, three of them at school; the old mother-in-law, a maid, two men, nice new two storey house, parlour below, very tidy bedrooms above and a large well managed farm some of the fields in which he drained under our guidance. His old uncle in the little cabin near the river was our last visit; he was sick—laid up from cold having tried to work on the roads to help to support his good little old wife, an idiot daughter, and an orphan grandchild, poor Luke's earnings not sufficing though he is a yearly servant with us. Some help was wanting here so it will be given and the family is put on the soup list.

I did not visit old Commons knowing him to be very comfortable, with a niece and nephew doing all they can for him and he such an oddity that there is no making anything more of him than suits his own whim of the moment. In the Weaver's Square I looked after the few who for old connexion sake have some sort of claim upon us with a view to help them when occasion serve, and in the meanwhile give any little assistance in our power. They were all very wretched living in miserable half ruined huts under hard middle men for landlords with but the government shilling a day hardly sufficient for the decent maintenance of a single person. The Widow Quin and the poor Craigs were added to the soup list. On the Burgage side we assist Kitty Colzean and the Delanys. The people in the Lane have no claim on us. The Hylands don't want help, and the Redmonds are of suspicious character; yet we must not see them starve.

11. Our relief committee has been very active—above eighty pounds subscribed without the absent landlords. Ogle Moore and Mr. Owen joint secretaries went up to Dublin for supplies and I heard to-day they were distributing at cost price or less where tickets were purchased for the purpose of thus assisting those in most need. All the Protestant clergy are coming forward actively giving time and money with zeal in the charitable endeavour to lighten this appalling calamity. Not so the Roman Catholic priesthood—at least not by any means so generally. Mr. Germaine not only refused to superintend the stores at Blackditches himself but prevented his two curates from undertaking the care of them. All which is *telling* among the people. A Roman Catholic mother took her baby to the Protestant clergyman at Tallaght to have it baptised by him and on his remonstrating, remarking that its father also was a papist, she said she meant to rear her son up in the reformed faith—that times were changing—and that by the time her son

were a man it would be more advisable for him to be a protestant.

It really seems as if our common distresses were drawing us all closer together, producing kinder feelings among us, soothing sectarian asperities, renewing the old attachment between the upper and the lower ranks. God grant it, for if so the blessing will be unspeakable. This is a revolution as complete, very nearly as awful, as the French one. Produced by much the same first causes though ascribed to the secondary which has been but the agent—this failure of food. Pleasure seeking, wrapped in *self*, unfeeling for others, the higher ranks by their neglect of the lower stifled every kind sensation in the ruder breast, engendered evil passions, contributed to the recklessness and the idleness they now deplore and encouraged the bigotry they now see the worst effects from. The lesson is hard on all—it is not all learned yet, and great must be the sufferings, entire must be the changes ere we settle to better things. The newspapers are beginning to point the moral of the tale; sales of horses, hunters, hounds, jewels, plate, houses to let; there must soon be lands to sell; then we may look for the brightening. The columns of servants out of place are widening, the appeals from shops for custom encreasing. The Government talks of lending money for seed and for improvements but it has yet to come and will it avail with bankrupt landlords. Lord Mountcashel rates the income from property in Ireland at thirteen million, the charges on it at ten and a half. Sales must be forced on us.

16. No news stirring—nothing going but misery, nothing thought of but the relief of it. As an occasional variety anxiety is changed to momentary anger by some deception practised by the worthless on the kind feelings of their neighbour such as a family dispersing its members to gather an undue amount of alms, or women borrowing extra children to swell their train of wretchedness; this is our daily fare. The Doctor came to see us on Saturday looking very much better, and Hugh Henry who was spending a couple of days at Russboro' walked over one morning to call, thin and miserable and out of spirits.

What a curse to him has been his independence—indolent by nature he can contrive no occupation for himself beyond hunting, billiards and card playing; and he is deserving of being far better employed; he should marry some sensible woman, intercourse with whom would in a short time supply the deficiencies of his ill-conducted education.

17. Quite a surprise came upon me the other day by a letter from my father. He wrote in good spirits just after returning from his excursion to the Neilgherries. He had steamed to Madras, then by dowk to Bangalore where he remained some time with John. On to Octacamund to Sir Lawrence Peel[2] whose guest he was. He is full of his return home, hoping to settle near Edinburgh and to find my Mother fit to enjoy a cheerful old age with him in spite of my warning voice; he is so sanguine. William and Sally well; John's reputation much encreased by the ability he has displayed in the difficult business which happily for his health has kept him so long in the beautiful Mysore country. So the family may hold its head up.

23. Lord George Bentinck has lost his motion by a very large majority—upwards of one hundred. It appears to have been ill-considered. Government to borrow at this time sixteen millions of money with an Exchequer much exhausted and a gloomy future before it, for the purpose of embarking in railroad speculations [in Ireland,] a sort of enterprise always better left to private management.

We are a great deal more comfortable hereabouts since our Relief Committee began to act; their sale of provisions at cost price keeps starvation from every door though it may not exactly give plenty to every house. Clothing however must be looked after for they are all naked or much the same, in rags, and scanty ones. I am going to look after our own people in this particular—to take charge of their gardens having sent for seeds, and to get the dung heaps

2. Lord Chief Justice of Calcutta (1842–58) and therefore concerned with the Union Bank scandal which was about to break and in which the H.L.'s father and brothers William and John were deeply involved.

removed from the doorways have the manure dug in to the gardens, where there are any, and buy it and carry it away where there are none. I shall try and undertake an anti-tobacco mission though with little hope of success; however a beginning should be made; the poor are very extravagant, no better than the rich; human nature, full of frailties. Self is the Devil, figuratively and really—the drop of evil we have to war against. That's better gospel than we hear from the pulpits.

28. Provisions are rising every market. Thus the large farmer is doing well, his produce selling for three times the prices of an ordinary year, his consumption though more costly still very fairly proportioned to his profits. The small farmer is ruined, he must eat his corn, sell his stock at an unseasonable time because he has no fodder and therefore leave himself penniless for the coming year. The tradesman has no custom whatever, people buying nothing but food; he must live on his capital if he have any; if he have none, he is bankrupt. The Labourer can just keep four individuals alive on his earnings—two scanty meals a day, no fuel, clothing, house rent, and near a fast on Sunday. Where his family is larger and no son big enough to help with work they must be very near starving.

The large proprietors must be content with half their usual income and it must be spent share and share upon their people, very little on themselves; the lesser proprietors will suffer more as they have fewer luxuries to dispense with. Where there is debt there must be ruin, that is land sold to redeem the mortgages, whole or in part according to circumstances; the world to begin again with age, disappointments, children, clogging exertion in the lower station to which they will be reduced: where there is no debt there will still be years of difficulty, no rents from the little farmers, the rents from the larger ones fully required for the cess, the taxes, the head rents, the rent charges, the government advances to be repaid, the government drainage loan to be repaid, the sickly and the aged to be assisted, the able-bodied to be employed, the poors rates, the relief fund, and the regular labourers, leaving little indeed for the support of the proprietor's family or for the purchase from the poor ruined small tenantry of the patches they will have to give up and who must be assisted in their emigration, or trade, or whatever new line of life they turn to.

After a few years we of this class may hope to be comfortable again—more comfortable than before—for our tenants will be few and those will be thriving; the land in our own hands will be great and that is a sure fortune; and we shall be more skilful in our management of it, and it will produce us may be tenfold its value now; but in the meanwhile we must suffer privation. Were it not for the half-pay earned as Jane wittily says by the sweat of the Colonel's brow (under his helmet in India) we should really be totally ruined; this will keep us up till better times, only that the new poor law frightens us.

And by the bye poor old O'Connell is dying in London—really of a broken heart—ashamed of having been purchased—ashamed of the taunts deservedly levelled at him—vexed at losing his influence—friends—fame—and name—with those he so long deluded for the advancement of his own family and a small pension to himself.

SUNDAY, MARCH 7. Well how is this fierce month beginning? Very like a lion. Cold north-easterly winds, not much bright sun, sometimes sleet, fine dry roads for walking, fine dry fields for ploughing, fine dry air for turnips keeping. Things rather better than worse, though the times are very trying; one can't help feeling very anxious. The misery is great, its relief unattainable, its alleviation difficult, for the markets are still rising.

Last Sunday young John Hornidge called and this is all the visitors we have had for ages. People are quite disspirited by the wretchedness round them. The relief works are to cease as soon as the roads now in progress of amendment are completed. What is to be done with that immense army of disbanded workmen is not known. The Government measures are not as yet fully developed. Some new Irish poor law bill has passed the Commons but we don't yet know its details, nor is the Loan to

proprietors for Improvements yet ready to be acted on.
The terms however we understand–principal and interest
will be paid up in twenty-two years at the rate of 6. 10. 0.
per annum for every hundred pounds borrowed; estates
to be liable for the debt as a first claim on them. Whether
part of the improvement will be allowed to be the buying
out of the small holders we do not know; if it won't we
must borrow privately for this purpose as they can't stay
and we can't wish they should.

Cairns has found this out; he yesterday gave up possession to the Colonel of his house and farm; his house
is restored to him for the present till he can arrange his
plans; he wishes to emigrate to America and the Colonel
is to assist him—with twenty pounds, but perhaps a little
more. The poor man has gone up to Dublin to make his
enquiries carrying up a letter to John Robinson who will
direct him and gather for our benefit all the information
possible upon the subject as probably others will follow
this wise example. Old James Cullen is to give up his one
acre and turn his attention to turf cutting; his married
sons talk of America. Young James Doyle has gone; his
uncle Barny Quin who is in a good place at Tulfarris talks
of following him; his other uncles mere day labourers
have no ambition as yet to better themselves; but time,
example, cold and hunger may teach them wisdom. Little
Mat Ryan is quite happy at Riccarton; he made out both
journey and voyage well; was very kindly received, has
been in York Place and his friends here are really satisfied
that the boy has done well.

Miss Gardiner has become under Matron in a Lunatick
Asylum from which happy abode she is teasing me with
notes I don't intend to answer. She is abundantly silly;
very selfish and so excitable I should not wonder if she
ended her days as a patient in the ward she has charge
of. A letter from Robert Chambers who is in London
very angry with Ireland whose necessities have prevented
the repeal of the tax on paper; the mercantile world are
beginning to tire of so expensive an appendage, and to
incline to leave us to ourselves to fight out our own
quarrels and to rely upon our own resources; he has sent

my papers to his brother in Edinburgh for approval. As they are both on Irish subjects perhaps they have not hit the time. I am sure I have forgotten a quantity of things I should wish to have set down. I must exert myself a bit and chronicle my small facts daily as I used to do, or this will be no longer the faithful family legend I intend to be of use to our children and grandchildren.

9. Discovered another feature in the overwhelming distress of the times—the relief don't reach down to the very lower class it was intended principally to succour. Most of the labourers are in debt to the hucksters as deep as those hucksters would let them go—a week's provisions is the ordinary extent. When they get their pay therefore the little shopman at whose counter the change is given pockets it in payment for the last score while the poor victim contracts a new one to keep his family alive, his money going but a little way either for all provisions are from 6d. to 10d. a stone dearer in these places than at our relief stores. The thing don't appear to have struck anybody, nor is the remedy easy; the only one that appears to me likely to succeed is to oblige the pay clerk to provide himself with change, then to put into each man's hand his few shillings which he can then spend where he pleases. To the one or two in whom we are interested we have advanced them the price of the supplies for which we gave them tickets; next pay day they will be out of the huckster's debt; they will owe us instead and they are to pay us by one shilling weekly, still leaving them an odd seven shillings in hands. Hal must represent this matter at the next meeting and now I shall turn my attention and my essay money to the clothing of those connected with us.

12. The farmers can't get a labourer to work for them even at fifteen pence a day; they prefer the road scraping at a shilling; on this they can just live and the delight of idleness overbalances the odd 3d. though neither they nor their families have a stitch of clothes left almost. What a people. Another generation at least must pass away before we can hope for much moral improvement. At present in plain words they are all mere beasts; they

have none but animal propensities. And do what we can
with the children of such mere brutes we can very little
advance their feelings; the scene at home counteract the
discipline of school. Patience!

Mr. Robert Chambers being in London sent my papers
to the Committee of learning in Edinburgh who have sent
them back to me as extremely interesting but unsuited to
the journal. A sad descent for my vanity d'auteur. The
subjects were Irish and they are angry with Ireland on
account of our necessities having interfered with the
government's intention of remitting the tax on paper.
Leitch Ritchie[3] writes to me, a bad authour to my mind,
and a bad judge of authours of course!

Relief Committees continue. But the various funds
contribute to our locality nothing; the people are very
patient, satisfied with having food and very little labour
for it they are content with little fire and no clothes and
are 'trusting to God' for the future. The Parliament
goes on talking nonsense; the government struggles on
doing little.

21. Mild weather—a good deal of rain which is excellent for
the newly sown corn. Sickness has now begun among the
poor, inflammatory attacks, dysentery, influenza, fever;
there is food sufficient for the greater part of them,
they are worst off at present for clothing; but we fear
starvation cases must become frequent here as elsewhere
all the small holders of land having been turned off the
publick works—the most destitute class of any; their
ground not being sufficient either to fully feed or to
fully employ them so that they get indolent, reckless,
discontented and miserable.

We are getting on better than was expected. Paddy
Quin has paid up his November rent; Rutherfurd £35
of the £120 due then. His two sons William and Joe
are very anxious to go to America; they see they are but
losing time working for their father, but they find him as
unmanageable as ever; unwilling to part with them, no

3. The Editor of *Chambers' Journal* and (admittedly according
   to Chambers' *Eminent Scotsmen*) a 'talented writer'.

money to give them, not even paying them wages now and with no prospect before them at his death but of working as day labourers.

These new Irish poor law measures are before the Committee, not likely to be modified to any purpose. If the proposal to render each proprietor responsible only for the destitute on his own estate were carried, as we who have been for years doing our duty think only just, they say it would make bankrupts of all the South and West where ages of neglect have caused the congregation of multitudes of paupers more than sufficient to monopolise the mortgaged revenues. Let these ill-managed properties be sold then, say we. Ah but the votes! Ministers can't afford to lose one ally from the respectable class supporting them, so we must make up our minds to expect nothing for some years from our Irish acres. If we can keep them together we may think ourselves fortunate.

I can't get well, so the doctor has me again and I think I shall get on after a while: that delicate stomach of mine is irritable to excess, the liver idle, bile abounding, no getting exercise, and the influenza hardly gone. What a slight hold have I of life; how small a matter would end my 'high imaginings,' my hopes for these poor people, my anxieties for my children, my little 'world'of cares and duties, not always well attended to though always well intended.

There has not been a new book in the house since *Monte Christo*. No one thinks of aught but the poor, feeding the hungry, clothing the naked, relieving the sick. We have nothing left in the old linen way, and I have bought and *made* quantities of coarse clothing, the women waste the stuff so when they get it unmade; they have no scissors either most of them—a pair upon an average to every half dozen houses; the girls who are working so neatly for us have none either; they bite off their threads. As making presents to people so gluttonous that to gorge themselves with food they deny themselves every decency is hurtful, I shall deduct the price of a pair from the next payment—presenting scissors and balance together. It will be generations before such characters are raised to even a low standard of respectability.

29. My good dear husband's birthday. How well he is—better than we have seen him for years; so strong, able to walk for hours daily, to encounter winds that would kill me. To-day he is gone to Blesinton as is his almost daily custom now, to look after the poor; there is also a ploughing match in the park which he will probably look at. Lord Downshire has been at Mr. Owen's these ten days, very good-natured to everybody, charitable to the poor, admirable to his tenants, affable to all, but very stupid, a great hulk of a man weighing sixteen stone at eight and twenty.

Hugh Henry was at Tulfarris all last week for the hunting generally contriving all the time to pass an hour or two here. We think Annie the attraction; he pays her such attention, a thing quite unusual with him. Were she older I should say she had made a conquest. The Colonel is very fond of him; indeed so am I, and I wish to rouse him up to an employment of his abilities worthy of them. But he 'atchieved' his independence too early for his profit; he will enjoy life his own idle way at present at any rate, and by and bye his good principles, his gentlemanly feelings, will tell as they should in the development of the higher parts of his character. He seems through the agency of his brother to be doing his duty faithfully to his dependents; he is about spending £2000 on emigration.

The girls have gone to school for me. A large attendance of pupils, I hear, bad as the times are. Nurse Flood is going to board her two youngest children with James Ryan that they may attend it. It is really thriving. I am at home to give soup and meal tickets and to dispense some clothing; my fund for this purpose has been unexpectedly replenished by fifteen pounds *to come*—five from James Craig, five from Aunt Bourne, three from Jane, and two from my mother. Mrs. West gathered fifty pounds or more, but then she begged. I never asked for a penny. Hal and I resolved to look after our own little as we had to do it with, for none of the English money has come our way. The distress in the south and west appears to absorb all relief and hardly to be relieved by the assistance they get so liberally for the papers are filled with deaths in hundreds from starvation; that has never yet happened here but if they don't hasten the new relief measures it must be expected that it will happen whenever the publick works cease as the farmers are employing as few hands as possible, less than they ought, by many.

30. The Poor Relief has got into the Lords and the clause about affording outdoor relief to the able-bodied is causing a very lively discussion. It appears to me that with the peculiar disposition of the Irish this measure will ruin peasantry and landlords but others seem to believe that it will work in the most effectual manner to improve the country by rousing the indolent of all classes to pursue actively the only means by which their own interests can be eventually benefitted. If this prove a true prophecy we shall none of us regret the difficulties of a few years. Matters can hardly well be worse than they are.

O'Connell is on his way to Rome to die: mind gone as well as physical powers. Curious character. Restless, ambitious, needy, and clever, he brought himself into notice from motives purely personal, caught a little of the spirit of the breeze of patriotism by means of which he hoped to reach some comfortable haven and using the priests as tools when he wished to end his course, they the slaves so far, turned upon their master whom they thenceforward ruled with iron power, and latterly he is said to have sorely repented the mischief they had done between them. But he could not stop. Money was the cry—it must be had, and though all we heard of was by no means really received, large sums certainly were collected and shared equally between the agitating priests who enforced their payment and the Liberator who was the ostensible tax gatherer. O'Connell was not much enriched, his staff was enormously expensive, so was his press, so was his family. Well the turmoil is now over. Unmasked he is sinking into an unhonoured grave, almost execrated by the populace he deluded. He dare not show himself in the Emerald Isle he would be torn to pieces. And the priests have lost instead of gaining by their turbulence. The people are actually tiring of them, losing confidence in them, failing in respect to them. We shall see great changes: those of us who live a few years.

THURSDAY APRIL 1. Dreadful weather, colder than in winter, ground white with snow both to-day and yesterday. I can't get out to look after anything but I had Miss O'Keeffe with me; her father will bring the books down and settle affairs for the past quarter; she has latterly had forty-five scholars in attendance.

Some of the poor are beginning to feel almost approaches to famine; the relief works are contracting the old measures closing, the new not yet arranged so there will be a few weeks of difficulty. Aunt Bourne sends me her five pounds to-day, and Mrs. Bridges sends another. Extreme kindness this: they are totally unconnected with Ireland and have already contributed to the general fund. We shall find this assistance truly seasonable for truth to say we were ourselves nearly run out. It is impossible to see people half naked and to know they are half starved too, without supplying their necessities, be they well or ill-conducted; poor ignorant creatures they are acquainted with nothing but misery: that they know well in every form of wretchedness. I shall catalogue our necessities and relieve them by rule for I dare not trust to feelings. My daily levée is a scene truly painful though they are on the whole patient and on the whole not encroaching, but they are destitute, dispirited, helpless, without the power of rising into better circumstances. Mind and body alike without energy for the most part. Some few shew more spirit but they are exceptions.

The new poor law bill is in course of operation, that is preparations have begun. We are separated from Blesinton; Lord Milltown, John Hornidge, Richard, Mrs. Cotton, the Colonel, Weavers Square and its neighbourhood, Black ditches, and the Ratcliffe Mountains with all their miseries—quite enough for we have three or four absentee landlords and one or two middlemen with swarms of paupers crowding the deserted properties. Here enter Lord Downshire and Mr. Owen.

2. Good Friday. We found Lord Downshire very agreeable: plain in face, heavy and large in person, quite unpolished in manner and neither brilliant in conversation nor courtly in address; but he is kind feeling, kind acting, kind judging; he has good common sense, an agreeable affable manner, and he is entirely interested about the business of his property which he seems to understand perfectly. He was greatly disturbed by a report in the newspapers of an assertion made in the House of Commons by a Colonel Rawdon[4] on the authority, he said, of a resident Irish nobleman, to the effect that our half barony of Lower Talbotstown was amongst the most wretched of all the distressed districts. A statement perfectly untrue and which accordingly the Marquis has written to Lord George Bentinck to contradict formally immediately after the Easter recess. He encloses a well composed letter from Ogle Moore to himself denying as secretary to the Relief Association that there was the least foundation for such calumnies. Both communications give credit to us all for our exertions—the fact is that Holywood must be meant, Lord William Beresford's wretched den for pauper squatters; his neglect pauperises the whole Dunlavin division.

We had the Doctor again to dinner and whist. To-day all have walked to Church but Jack and me. It is bitter cold; a north wind, and there was snow on the ground in the morning. The showers of snow and sleet and hail all yesterday were incessant. Mr. Henry I believe goes to-day; he would stay if he got any encouragement. He is I think twenty-eight and should know his own mind, but we will make sure he does. So we will not at present encourage further intimacy much as we both like this most agreeable and clever and handsome young man—my prime favourite in spite of faults.

6. To-day we have had Cairns with us; he decides on sailing on Saturday from Dublin, the Colonel pays his passage.

4. John Davidson Rawdon, M.P. for Armagh City (1840–52).

The poor man is unable to sell his furniture among the neighbours, little as he has of it, nobody has a penny to spare from food. The Colonel therefore buys it, and some old iron, and the manure heap this will make a clothing and provision fund for him and he is to have five pounds as a present that he may have something in hand on landing. William Darker was to have set out for Scotland to-day but the torrents of rain in the early part of the morning prevented his journey on the open car and we have no close conveyance on this road now. Mail, caravan, even the long car gone. It is a great thing having got this fine young man to such a farm in East Lothian. I feel sure he will profit by all he sees there for he is steady and diligent and very fond of his business. It is well to have some pleasant reflexions these miserable times.

8. In this Poor Relief Bill which as yet we have not seen there have been two clauses inserted by the Member for Dublin, Mr. Gregory, one of which precludes the holder of more than a rood of land from being in any way assisted. This has set my mind at ease about the Ratcliffe mountains; the hordes of beggars there are all small farmers so we need not dread their numbers. In fact the name of relief to the extent proposed is all that there is to fear; the paupers of Ireland are not the labourers; they struggle on in their own miserable way as well as their low state of habits and feelings admit of, there are hardly more of them than are required even now, under this idle system of husbandry; there would not be enough were the land properly cultivated. The beggars are the small holders, entitled to no relief, and so we shall gradually get rid of them; they must give up their patches and take to labour. I am anxious to see the Bill for I feel pretty sure its provisions are in the main good and that the Colonel's anxiety is causeless. Townland division would have been more just than Electoral but there are clauses, I understand, to protect the conscientious. It will bear very hard upon us who do our duty but we must make the best of it. Some will be ruined; we shall rise again, it is to be hoped in a year or two.

Cairns is off to-day, begging to the last. Cousin Charles

goes with them—unable to part from the children particularly from one boy by some strange accident the perfect image of himself. George half asked me to lend money for the cousin's passage, but I declined, refused also to ask the Colonel or Mr. Robinson; so a friend has come forward for the purpose namely George Cairns himself: seven pounds he produced from the secret drawer in his chest, and I have no doubt there is another seven pounds or more remaining, for he has paid no rent these two years, and in September he had forty pounds worth of hay, in January thirty-six barrels of oats, and as six with the cow would abundantly keep the family most likely he won't land in America with only the Colonel's five pounds. Such a set—'tis worth all they have cost to rid of them.

We walked into Blesinton yesterday the Colonel and I to see about our bread. To please Ogle Moore who set up Jo Agar in the vacant bakery we ordered our supply from this respectable protestant; he was very civil, gave us good bread, but was uncertain in delivering it. In short the scheme did not do; he has baked none these three weeks since a Rathcool man set up in Blesinton from whom Agar has been buying for his customers and charging us all ¼d. a loaf for serving us. I therefore considered it would be as well to deal with the new baker direct and save the farthings. Irish probity is a curious commodity—about on a par with its industry.

9. Tom Darker went to Dublin yesterday with his nephew and took the opportunity to call at the Board of Works and acquaint himself properly with drainage proceedings. He is in high spirits with the result of his consultation. We think it will cost about a thousand pounds to drain that side of the hill alone, but as we have twenty-two years to pay it in, by yearly instalments of six and a half per cent, and as after the second year there must be a profit upon the work of ten per cent and there may be one of twenty or upwards, the speculation is good. It will give a deal of employment and so lighten the rates. My Aunt sent the other half of her ten pounds yesterday, so all our people will be in comfort.

The Colonel has been writing to Lord John Russell about the injustice of rating the proprietors by Electoral Divisions six or eight or ten of them together, all to pay in equal proportions towards the support of all the paupers in the Division, instead of by townlands, each landlord burdened separately with his own, by which arrangement the good would reap the benefit of their care and the bad would be deservedly charged with the maintenance of the beggary their neglect had fostered. It is a very temperate statement of his own case as applicable to many others, resulting really in the ruin of the good landlord for the moment and the merely temporary relief of the bad. I want him to consult someone before sending it but he is so confident of the justice of his plea that he don't seem to consider further reflexion necessary, as if they don't notice it, there is no harm done, and a plain country gentleman setting the truth before an honest man may lead him to reconsider the government plan.

10. Great good news: our district is relieved from the Ratcliffe mountains; our Townland is rated by itself, and, bad as one or two of the landlords are, so many of us are good that we can very well manage all the poor now left with us. In regard to the outdoor relief to the able-bodied, it is to be given in such a shape as will certainly ensure us from much mischief resulting: a pint of soup and a biscuit to be consumed on the spot by the recipient *once* in the day—just to prevent starvation; none can be carried away except on medical certificate and as Tom Darker so justly says there is as much trouble in this and less profit than in work and there are besides few pauper *labourers*: the really distressed are the small holders, and they are exempted from all relief.

11. Sunday, The post yesterday brought a letter from Anne Hay McKenzie. The distress in Wester Ross is so great that Cromartie can't afford to introduce Annie this season. Instead of a house in town, the drawing-room, gaieties, and all fashionable expenditures, he must feed and clothe the hungry and naked, provide seed and employ labourers. This will give our Scotch friends some faint idea of our Irish sufferings. When in that

scantily peopled district large wealthy proprietors feel
themselves cramped by relieving this slighter degree of
destitution what must we have to bear in our densely
populated wildernesses belonging to bankrupt landlords;
heavy indeed will the relief rates fall on the solvent few.

13. A fair in Blesinton yesterday—a new one set on foot by
Mr. Owen. We sold eight heifers for fifty-three pounds; a
falling off from last year's prices but still the profit is very
fair. It has been so unusually severe a winter the cattle
have not thriven as in ordinary seasons, and the spring
is so late, so ungenial the sheep and lambs are feeling it.
We have lost a ewe and five lambs out of our small stock;
the big fox on the hill helped himself to two of the lambs
however. The Doctor dined with us yesterday and won
three shillings from me at backgammon; he had spent
three and sixpence at the Repository to please the girls
and was charmed at being thus reimbursed while I, who
had worked my fingers sore making the things found it
a little hard to pay for them besides. Well I'll live to win
double stakes may be.

15. I am almost sick of the dishonesty of these poor miserable
creatures. In every way, in all classes, lying, cheating,
defrauding, concealing—every sort of underhand meanness is practised among them. Here has come to light
such a tissue of evil as really disgusts one—how can it be
otherwise—brought up in sin and sloth for the purpose of
struggling through misery we are absurd to expect correct
principles from so low a state of morals; patience—one
had need indeed to be made of it, to endure life with
such surroundings. Mrs. Farrell the provision dealer and
Mary Craig the starving purchaser tell the same story
very different ways. All I can make out between them
is that the merchant selling on credit with little hope
of speedy repayment charged about double the value of
the goods she sold, while the buyer, catching at present
relief troubled herself very little about the acquitting of
her debts in one place or another being just as ready
to go on borrowing as to go on eating, and both ladies
trusted to me to bring them out of their difficulties.
My intention is to leave them in them: they are both

shrewd enough and if there is any loss anywhere it is well merited.

16. The Colonel and I walked to Rathbally yesterday. We went this side the hill, up by Widow Mulligan's and so along the Common, round the Quaker graveyard and climbed the gate at Mr. West's new entrance as we found it locked: I wanted to ask where Mrs. George West had bought all her charity clothing. Widow Mulligan had to be scolded for her selfish folly in refusing her son to the police where he would get ten shillings a week and clothing, at least the uniform, 'because who would support her.' As herd to Mr. Hanks he has five shillings a week and a house on which mother and daughters seem inclined to keep him and themselves starving for they have no energy to do anything for themselves; the mother was three weeks knitting a pair of socks for the poor American priest who came back here in rags, and has now been a month making three pairs for Jack. Peggy seems equally destitute of activity. Mary seems more like Anne our kitchen maid and so extremely neat in her appearance that I hope Mrs. Hornidge to whom I sent her on the chance, may take her as housemaid. In the Weavers' Square we had pleasure in visiting John and Dan Byrne, the smiths, in their tidily kept cabins; both have got good managing wives; their *little* sister Nancy Doyle all of whose children are bigger a good deal than herself seems to be very poor; her husband is discharged from the roads, only working odd days with the farmers; her son is still employed and on his wages the family is subsisting. Hal left some substantial comfort behind him and I have promised the poor little ailing *wify* soup she can drink for the relief mixture her stomach is too delicate to bear.

We walked on through much appearance of wretchedness, dirt, ruin, rags, but I must say that I never saw the people look so well, so fat, so clear, so lively. They always complain let them be ever so well off, and they eat such enormous quantities it is not easy to supply their appetites; a two lb. loaf many of the men finish at a meal. German stomachs!

Jane tells us our young farmer, [William Darker], had arrived; she kindly gave him his dinner and good advice and speeded him on his journey; she thought him a fine intelligent lad but fears there is a leaven of foolish pride that may disincline him for the abasing himself in order to be exalted. I hope not, for on this subject I spoke to him also. Tom Darker brought all the rest of the heifers back from some fair he went to—no buyers. I must buy—another cow; we have no butter to signify and what we get in the market is quite uneatable; there never was nor will be so determinedly bad a manager for the wants of a family as that excellent T. D.

23. At the last fair little business was done; meat is up to a price hitherto unknown—eight pence and ten pence a lb.; poultry not to be had; bread stuffs are falling. So scarce a time I never knew. We can get nothing. The publick works hereabouts are over; the new act not yet in operation, distress therefore prevailing. As the two hills they were cutting, one at the schoolhouse, the other in Featherbed Lane, are unfinished there is to be an application made to have them set on again which will employ the idle hands here for a week or two. So far we have come through very well; our district is favoured beyond other parts of this miserable country. The worst feature in the condition of it is the utter want of probity in the mass of the people which the necessity of sifting individual cases has brought us more thoroughly acquainted with. It surpasses belief. How can permanent good be done with a population so demoralised. One don't know where to begin, how to arrange any system that can work by any possibility so as to improve rogues, liars, ungrateful insolent idle sensualists. I could not have imagined there existed in these days people so low in their feelings, so gross in their habits. Nothing will rouse them but the pain of hunger, they are incapable of comprehending any other sort of suffering and that they have here hitherto been saved from experiencing. Yet I should not despair; we have had none of this extremity of vice among our own people; the evil drop is there but it is diluting; they are patient, thankful, diligent by comparison, and

much much more decent in their homes than any others I am acquainted with. Mr. Galvin is a real blessing; he preaches upon the moral virtues, tries to instil good principles, praises England, the help it has given, the good it is aiming at; he encourages a spirit of industry, and checks the idle love of wakes and patterns and gossipping. But the people are pretty near sick of their priesthood; it is wonderful how rapidly they have been rising of late years towards more enlightened religious feelings. And this famine assists; the heavy *dues* are now intolerable their Protestant brethren paying none; relief all comes from Protestant gentry, the Roman Catholicks have been very deficient in tendering aid, generally. The two parties have however been brought very much more together by the affairs of the poor whom they have to relieve and the result will most certainly be of use to our social position.

Our *Director General* of the Poor Law Committee a fine good-humoured gentlemanly boy, a subaltern in the Artillery [Captain Brandling], who has the office of Government Inspector for this district has rather mismanaged his business. He arranged his committee in the pretty little cottage he has brought his girl wife to where they are living so comfortably on the £1200 a year we have to raise for them and not taking the trouble to ride over here and being quite a stranger, he has misnamed John Darker calling him George so that he can't act; left out Colonel Smith who next to John Hornidge is the largest proprietor of our small union; and put on Mr. Fraser who does not belong to the country at all but is merely on a visit to his sister-in-law Mrs. Cotton. Lord Milltown is going up to Dublin in a fury about it in the teeth of a dignified epistle from that old twaddle my cousin Sir John Burgoyne[5] who wearied out by the same sort of absurdities elsewhere has announced that he will positively not interfere in the change of any appointed members of relief committees. He has had to

5. Inspector General of Fortifications from 1845 and appointed a Relief Commissioner 1847.

do it though and he will have to do it again so he need not bluster.

The Doctor has begun to know us again; he has been popping in of a morning and dining in an evening as of old—brimfull of gossip of course. It is a truly unsociable country; however this year no one seems to feel inclined to give a bit to any but the poor who have without any doubt thriven on this new system for never did the lower orders look so fat or so clear or so alive since I first came among them.

SUNDAY, MAY 2. All going on pretty comfortably notwithstanding a serious mistake about the employment of the people. They idled so shamelessly upon the roads that the funds which were ample failed before the jobs were complete; this was talked of (the Irish live upon talk) but not otherwise attended to, consequently the bands were dismissed suddenly; the men went in mobs to seek redress, got shillings here and food there and after *five or six* days the Committee met, struck a new rate, presented for the completion of the works, sent their minutes up to Dublin where the Board will forward them to the Treasury which will consider them, pass them, return them; then an advance of money will be asked for, granted, and the labour will begin again; no day is however yet fixed and twelve have already passed since all means of earning a subsistence have been denied to our paupers.

We provided ourselves with bread which we deny to no applicant; the few who have asked for it have convinced me that there is not the extreme destitution here that is talked about; the people are such inveterate beggars that there is nothing they want they won't ask for—even those in decent circumstances; it is therefore plain to me that there is not the scarcity of food pretended. Mrs. George West finds the same. While she gave money her door was besieged; when she changed to bread the numbers dwindled to a very few really hungry. Good is steadily progressing though slowly. Large families which in the days of potatoes would lounge on in listless poverty all together, neither sons nor daughters ever keeping places that were procured for them by some exertion, now have separated voluntarily. All are dispersed trying their luck, as they call it—putting up with work, wages, hardships, they would not formerly have brooked for half a day.

The young men too are beginning to look for situations in the police. We lose Pat Hyland for this purpose and so shall save a servant as Christy can take his place; Lawrence Mulligan also; he don't belong to us yet we have taken a sort of care of him from his having been steadily at school for many years and belonging to very decent parents. Mr. Hanks, his late master, is hard in all his dealings; not the worst of landlords yet far from good—neither kind nor liberal—and rich, a miller, one of the most flourishing of trades in these times. We have lent the poor lad the needful which he can repay by instalments and made him a small present besides.

Hal did not send his letter to Lord John Russell; the new division rendered it less necessary as did the two saving clauses in the relief act; he wrote to Sir John Burgoyne about John Darker but has had no answer nor has the mistake been rectified.

The Lord Lieutenant's illness and the cause of it, is occupying Dublin. It seems the drunken scene at the Ball was not confined to *two* actors: their name was legion, all women whose tea and negus had been drugged by the Aides de camp for their own especial amusement, the company at St. Patrick's night not being select, a sort of Easter Monday at the Mansion House society with whom these highly finished young gentlemen thought they were justified in taking liberties. Some were carried home by the police in covered cars, two on stretchers. The two ladies of condition partook in mistake it is said. Where all their male relations have concealed themselves, whether they have heard of the jest, or been silenced, is not made publick. One would think Shillelaghs had given up growing in the land when a hundred were not broken over the backs of such *blackguards*. The Lord Lieutenant has been recalled. He was much liked. A little gay, well-bred old man, extremely agreeable, and no more immoral than the rest of the unthinking set he belongs to—a thorough Irishman.

3. Very much interested in the debate in the Lords on the new Irish poor law bill. It was opened by Lord Lansdowne in a luminous speech explaining the provisions of it. Nothing can be fairer; I have little doubt now of its working well; the onus will fall on the land certainly but on the *occupier*; the farmers will thus be driven to employ more hands; as they must feed their number they will find it best to get labour from them in return; thus their system of husbandry will improve. Truth to say at present they know nothing of agriculture, very little about stock either except just to choose the best description of cattle for summer grazing on their fine pastures.

Lord Stanley makes a speech equal to his former one on the same subject; he undoubtedly knows more of Irish affairs than any one of the publick men who meddle with them;[6] his own property is admirably managed; his opinion of the country generally is accurate as far as I can judge. I admire him for standing up for his class—the Irish Landlord is in no essential different from the Irish peasant—his superior position has raised him in many points above his labouring countryman but the character of their race is common to both. The same carelessness or recklessness, call it which you will, the same indolence, the same love of pleasure, the same undue appreciation of self, all more disagreeably prominent in the *lower* nature because further debased by the more degrading consequences attending extreme poverty, and unredeemed by the brilliant qualities which refined habits set off to advantage.

It is the greatest mistake possible to argue upon a presumed difference of *disposition*, the difference is in *condition*. And to array the one class against the other, to insist that the Landlords are always crushing the peasantry, and the peasantry always rising against the

6. He had been Chief Secretary (1830–3) and, as the fourteenth Earl of Derby, he was to be P.M.

landlords, is mere prejudice: there is no opposition at
all between them, they agree remarkably well. The upper
ranks pursue their amusements without reference to any
other human being, merely giving a volley of curses to
anyone that comes inconveniently into their way, the
lower ranks admire the style of these diversions, imitate
them as far as they have the means without the slightest
idea of being oppressed or even neglected.

The Landlords that are not popular are what we should
call the good ones, who look after their affairs, insist
upon value received for value given, who will neither
be cheated of time nor property, and look well after
the habits of their unruly dependents. Patience, all are
educating together. Starvation is helping and by and bye
matters must mend for as a race they are wonderfully
clever people. Poor creatures, in this their grub state
they are very disheartening to deal with; just now they
are all ill. I sit writing here with castor oil and laudanum
beside me and generally have to give two or three doses
away of a morning; no deaths hitherto from this disease
alone though it has carried off a few ailing people.

4. A whole essay upon Rothiemurchus [from my brother
John]. He don't think I have judged fairly in saying
everything had been done for the place and nothing for
the people. I may have expected improvement among the
latter incompatible with the peculiar circumstances of the
property, but the very tone of his remarks proves to me
that he has not a just idea of the duties of landlords in this
respect and that from want of reflexion upon the subject
he skreens his neglect under an ironical disparagement of
the present movement in favour of the 'million.' I shall
write him an essay in return which may awaken such a
mind as his to a higher perception of its capabilities. It is
a pity to find a man of such talent yielding to the vulgar
prejudice of ignorance being either bliss or virtue.

My father wishes *us* to join him at Florence the end
of October there to pass the winter with him and my
mother! The Colonel will decide unassisted by a word
from me.

5. Mr. Graham passed here on Monday last to make his

observations upon Lacken where a National School is wished for; he is delighted with the O'Keeffes; no wonder; they are models for their class; so contented, so humble, so industrious; he without and she within leaving nothing to be wished for in these departments. Their schools clean, orderly, well-regulated; all that is useful taught well; in fact their acquirements are exactly suited to the conditions of the people. The girls are made to do the household work in turns; the boys to labour in the garden; the old man has made already quite a well ordered domain of that wilderness, while Mrs. O'Keeffe's plain furniture well kept, and her clean windows, and her bright fire, give an air of cheerfulness to her rooms they never wore in former days. We have made a hit certainly; just the people one would paint in a novel for the village schoolmaster's family. The average attendance of boys is still small—twenty-six. Girls—forty-six.

6. The girls and their Papa rode yesterday, called at Russborough. We have taken my Lady into favour again, poor woman, she had got so beyond absurdity that it was quite necessary to let her feel she was of no sort of consequence to anybody. It was done without a word merely by leaving her to herself. She fretted and fumed to the Doctor but he never heeded and when she tired of solitary state she came out all smiles again. She is very much to be pitied. He is at Chester races, and she has not a farthing nor the hope of one.

The young labourers hereabouts are all trying to get into the police. None will be taken who cannot read and write; this will speak to some of the parents surely, show them the necessity of school for their children. William Scarfe, a protestant, was appointed, required only his equipment; amongst us we contributed the money; *he has spent it* otherwise and is now writing begging letters to a brother to entreat his assistance which if granted may avail so unprincipled a lad as little. Larry Mulligan, Anne's brother, we have lent the necessary funds to, to be repaid by small instalments. Pat Hyland we must do the same to, though he ought to have saved out of his wages; but this improvident habit of depending on one another prevented him from doing what was right to himself or conscientious to his master. He made no gathering for his entrance into the police though he has had it in his head these three months; he has been going about in rags which is very disrespectful to us who pay him more than sufficient to keep him in decent clothing, that every penny not required for food may go to the family of beggars he belongs to, two or three of whom might earn if they were so enclined. As far as we are concerned this system shall be put a stop to; it is bad in every way for everybody.

7. 1797 was born Elizabeth the eldest child of my parents. 1847, how old is the infant now. And what cause for thankfulness have I not in still reckoning my father and mother among us; only one of their five children gone; the two aunts who watched our infancy, Mrs. Bourne and Mrs. Frere still living; even Uncle Ralph left to us; and for fifty I am really wonderfully active mind and body; no need of spectacles, no grey hair, no imbecility of any sort beyond the occasional weaknesses of infirm health; even that is improving.

9. Sunday, Fine weather the last few days. Westerly winds with soft showers much wanted for the season is alarmingly backward. The temporary relief is going forward keeping the people alive certainly but in idleness, therefore in discontent; the reason given for this experiment is to force the occupiers of land on whom these rations are to be levied, to employ the proper quantity of labourers—one to ten acres—three times the present aggregate. In the meanwhile we have mob riots in all the less civilised districts, general grumbling everywhere the people now beginning to insist on a *right* to be supported; they are to marry, smoke, amuse themselves, beg, borrow or steal, and *insist* upon a maintenance. Charming people, high-minded, active, honest. There are crowds of them who have been receiving relief as destitute all winter now coming into the market with cartloads of sound potatoes for which they are receiving extravagant prices and the 'greatest of praise' from their equals; 'think of that now! there's cuteness.' The want of probity strikes

none of them. It requires unremitting watchfulness to keep farmers and tradesmen in decent circumstances from appropriating a share of the relief stores; they apply unblushingly for everything going, anything.

Margaret tells me that when refused both bread, tea, soup and a long list of petitions they will descend to beg 'a little taste of salt' with the smell of tobacco so rank upon them that even in the open air their near affinity is unendurable. Some of the most respectable of our very limited class of yeomanry are selected as members of the committees. While they imagined that the landlords only were to be taxed for these relief funds, they took very little trouble to scrutinise the lists of applicants; now that they find the rate is to be levied on the *occupiers* of land indiscriminately they are scrutinising every claim, most jealously, full *half* of the names given in have been already cancelled and every meeting the pen is drawn through more.

We are converting Jews in Jerusalem, Roman Catholicks in Germany and at home, building healthy lodging houses in our great towns for our labourers, opening our eyes by means of the astonishing discoveries in chemistry, a science only quite of late begun to be studied with a view to practical utility, and shall improve in every respect in consequence. It is very interesting to live in these days, to watch the changes for good going on quickly and steadily all round us.

13. The Lords are altering our Poor Relief Bill, amending it hitherto by several saving clauses; it is indeed difficult to manage Ireland. Such an extraordinary slippery people—high and low—all such unblushing jobbers in their different lines—depending too on anyone but themselves; the higher seeking for place and getting it by pure patronage, the lower doing their business by fawning and cheating. Jem Doyle whom we employ out of charity, disinclining to work one rainy day went to the relief stores, much astonished to find that being in service he could get nothing when he preferred idling. Jem Quin whose manure we bought and unluckily did not bring entirely away filling up his heap with mud, grass,

rushes, anything he could gather to encrease the bulk, etc., etc., etc.

15. A note from Mary Gillies. She has sent off my '*Thoughts*' in a rapture and hopes to tell me both that and my '*School*' will be valued. I must try and make a little money somehow for a private purse these pinching times I can't do without. We have sold our cattle well and have plenty of money to stock our ground for the summer, so that we shall do pretty well with the help of the pay.

18. Anne Mulligan told me that her mother is turned out of her house, allowed a month for her removal and there is the poor ailing woman after serving Mr. Hanks faithfully, herself and her husband, for twenty years, set adrift in her old age without one human being taking an interest in her. How fortunate that the son has got into the police. After the first month's outlay he will be able to assist her; the daughter here can help a little, and I will contrive sufficient plain work for the two daughters out of place as will keep them in such necessaries as they will require beyond the relief dole of a pound of Indian meal apiece, for to this the poor humbled woman has bowed her high spirit. She was to go yesterday evening to Mr. West for this purpose. I went to see her and advised one daughter immediately to take any sort of service that offered since Mrs. Hornidge after her many delays has decided not to have her, and proposed to the mother to take a room merely, which she will get for six-pence a week; and by selling half her furniture for she has a great deal more than she will now want, she will provide a little fund to meet difficulties. These middle rank landlords are very hard; their conduct it is which gives the bad name to the whole class.

There has been another letter from William Darker—an excellent one; he is very happy, quite reconciled to his lonely room; the people where he lodges are so kind to him; and to his situation where he is evidently learning a great deal. He is astonished at the size of the fields [in East Lothina]—the cleanly husbandry, weeding so carefully persevered in; the tidiness, the regularity, the extent of the business; he describes all in a sensible manner like a young man who will profit by all he sees. Mat Ryan in his more humble way makes equal use of his opportunities. I do indeed hope that these two young men have been so judiciously selected that they may return to be the means of greatly advancing their generation. If they could but rouse their countrymen out of their slovenly habits, cure their indolence in a degree even.

22. A meeting yesterday which did not end well. The relief now afforded at a great expense is but a mockery—one pound of dry meal a day to adults, half a pound to children without any sort of kitchen; it may keep them alive a few weeks, but in the end a pestilence must ensue; the quantity is not sufficient and the quality is defective. The recipients do nothing for it; it is a present we make to the idle. At present a ton and a half of Indian meal is the consumption, £24 per week. Mr. West and Mr. Fraser were here on their way to Blesinton and they and the Colonel were to stand by one another to insist on soup, or a nutritive slop of some kind being added; but they could not carry it; perhaps they will by persevering. Their proposition however to get the Union out of the Government's hands as Lord Downshire effected in his district would have been listened to better but for John Hornidge. The Relief Committee undertaking that there shall be no unemployed able-bodied man in their locality the Board of Works would interfere no further; young Mr. Brandling would write no more impertinent orders and all those reams of paper and the time consumed in filling them with the great expense thus incurred would be saved to the ratepayers; to effect this each landlord must honestly take his share of labourers; it would be a much cheaper plan, and we should get something for what we give; but Mr. Hornidge who employs very few servants would not hear of it.

The people are in a deplorable condition; the willing horses must help them, and 'fear not but trust in providence.' I found our Jem Doyle's family in but a melancholy way yesterday, and the grandmother the widow Quin, little better; dysentery has got amongst them. I have a difficulty in supplying ourselves with meat at present, let alone the poor; the meat is up to tenpence and a shilling in the markets; beef not to be had; mutton very scarce. We are to buy another cow and give milk instead of broth in future, except to the sick whom we must nourish with a share of what we have. If an epidemick break out the Colonel says he will pack us all off out of the country in a moment. But I must write, write for bread and not for my amusement, so good-bye journal, and let me turn with resolution to my tale.

26. Poor old John Hornidge shot himself yesterday—not dead—but very severely in the thigh, just above the knee; he will carry about little pistols in his pockets and he is extremely careless in the loading and the cocking and the placing of them. Not many months ago he narrowly missed hurting himself seriously by one going off in some unexpected manner in his parlour and one would have thought this hint sufficient to have made him cautious—indeed he did say he should have a small pocket made on each side of his easy chair for the purpose of keeping the 'lads' in, these dangerous times; still out he goes armed like a bandit. In getting out of his carriage the deep pocket of his great coat in which he carries some of these firearms struck against the side of the carriage and off went the pistol. It is a mercy that the bone of the leg was not broken—or that Mr. West who was helping him to alight was not killed.

The relief committee was put quite into confusion; Dr. Robinson sent for to the river where he was fishing. A man of Mr. Owen's was mounted on one of his hunters and despatched to town for Mr. Porter who arrived about eight in the evening when the two cut out the ball; some cloth still remains in, but there is no appearance of the *joint* or even the bone being injured. Still such an accident at his time of life and with his habit of body may be followed by grave consequences; he can't be pronounced out of danger for a week at least till they see what turn the inflammation take; so to-day he is altering his Will, in as great a fright as ever man suffered under for never breathed there mortal man so terrified with the idea of Death.

28. The Colonel, Tom Darker, Jack, and George driving, all set out yesterday morning for Dublin with maps, plans, calculations, surveys, all ready for the Board of Works. It was a beautiful day. When they were off I went to the Redmonds' having heard that they had been refused relief by some mistake and so were starving; it was not so; they were only near it. Mick has been working these few days with James Ryan. I have hired Fanny to weed the flower beds and then I expect to have other work both for brother and sister. This affair settled I next gave a character to Mick Whelen as a clever handy boy in a stable, which he is, and sent him off to Dublin to Dycer's where he might answer well—the sort of license of a livery-stable suiting with his free and easy style of conducting himself; the lad cannot really keep his senses together when he gets comfortable.

He was to take a small parcel to Mrs. Foster on the way, and this mean puts me in mind of the way he served Mr. Foster once; he was living with them as a sort of boy of all trades when he was quite young and was rather in favour for his readiness. Mrs. Foster one day was confined and during her recovery little fidgetty Mr. Foster was very busy every night shutting doors and windows; he had closed as he thought all and was sitting up composing one of his eloquent sermons when he fancied he heard more than one voice laughing in the kitchen; he had shortly before left the only maid asleep on a shakedown in the room with her mistress. Again he heard a tittering and listening more attentively felt convinced there was company in the kitchen. The scene he lighted on there would have done for Boz. On a round table before the fire were set two wine bottles cross cornered each holding a dipped candle; round it were seated four persons with cards in their hands playing at spoil five:[7] Master Mick, a gentleman of his acquaintance, much such another as himself, and two young ladies inadmissible in good society. 'This' as

7. A round game of cards said to be 'spoiled' if no player wins three out of a possible four tricks (OED).

poor Mr. Foster said, 'in a Christian minister's house!
Outrage to all decency! Offensive to every moral feeling!'
He never thoroughly got the better of it for the season. I
am anxious to get the little 'varmint' out of the way as he is
excessively amusing and had latterly taken it into his head
to help to educate Jack—'insense him into the manners
of a gentleman'—for which purpose he ransacked his
memory for all the pretty tales his respectable father
had related to him of the 'olden times' cursing in
most approved fashion during these recitals. Luckily
we discovered the intimacy early and put a check to it.

Mr. and Mrs. West called; sat hours; talked very
pleasantly, and took a bread and butter luncheon. Poor
law business almost entirely occupied us; he desired me
to have poor little Andy Ryan buried at once, the house
fumigated, etc., and begged me to take charge of a general
lime washing throughout Baltiboys. We the willing horses
must draw the weight; it must be moved as much of it as
possible and neither farmers nor graziers will share the
trouble—the *expense* they must share and their conduct
will encrease the amount without their getting anything
in exchange for it. Mr. West has advanced a hundred
pounds for provisions already; no one has proposed to
help him and he and Colonel Smith have bought up
most of the cabin manure. What a mean set are the
rest—short-sighted too, even for their own interests.

My girls and little Miss Clerk walked home with the
Wests and so round by Rusborough where though kind
to them my Lady was in the worst of humours. Between
her disfiguring nose, the Marquis of Drogheda's intended
marriage and the *utter* ruin of their circumstances, the
poor woman has griefs enough to mortify her. She has
begun to hate her husband and to dislike her son—tells
that the one swindles and the other drinks—which she
should have the decency to avoid exposing.

After dinner I walked to John Darker's and he wrote
up to forbid any wake, to order the funeral this morning
and then a general cleansing—all which was attended to
by these unfortunate parents; they have now but three
children left of ten, and their only girl will hardly long

survive for she is a wretched looking little creature. Between constitutional delicacy, the great dung heap at their door, the mother's carelessness, and the father's aversion to go in time for the Doctor they have lost a fine clever family. This was a particularly talented boy of twelve whom we intended to bring up as a national school teacher; he went to the fair of Naas, caught cold on a neglected stomach and not attended to got gastrick fever ending in suffusion on the brain; he died in strong convulsions yesterday morning.

29. A letter from Colonel Smith saying Mr. Mahony out of town so the papers regarding the property, which he has charge of, could not be got, and the Board of Works can grant no money without seeing them. So they all come home to-day little the better of their journey! O'Connell died at Genoa of congestion of the brain; the news came a week ago and not a being alludes to it; it was scarcely noticed even in the newspapers.

30. Sunday, All came home last night. John Robinson and I had a long private conversation on the state of our affairs—on the whole not unsatisfactory. He is so kind himself, so desirous to return the assistance once given to *him*, insisting that if there is *debt* it shall be to him not to tradesmen with whom Colonel Smith's credit is so high. I can tell nothing positively till after to-morrow when we shall see how much rent we shall be able to collect. Many that won't be able to pay much now will probably manage to clear themselves by harvest; others must be dealt summarily with, pensioned or otherwise disposed of. We certainly shall have a struggle to get on during the next four months, for it is impossible to dismiss any of the labourers or under servants as long as we can by any possibility feed them; neither can we diminish our relief. On ourselves we never spent much; nevertheless we must contrive to spend less. And in earnest will I set about it. One newspaper, John Robinson says, makes a fuss about the Liberator's decease, no responsive echoes however swell the strain. A shower of rain would have caused infinitely more sensation.

WEDNESDAY, JUNE 2. Alas! Poor John Hornidge! Yesterday

morning at eight o'clock he expired; sunk gradually from
about the same hour the day before, his mind wandering
occasionally, reviving towards the last when he talked
to Mr. West who had been reading with him of the
probability of his attending the Relief Meeting of that
day fortnight. Hal's oldest friend, the gay companion of
his young giddy days, near neighbours, in the yeomanry
together, and the same age. *Irish*, and jobbing, and
questionable as some of his principles and practices
were, we shall not look upon his like again—the race
of such as he, is gone, full of kindness, full of fun, full
of talent, clear-headed in business and useful beyond
all others in his neighbourhood, with all his faults he
abounded in merits. Nature made him a superiour man,
want of education and the prejudices of his times and
nation prevailed over better feelings, at times. He will be
missed while any who remember him live; he can never
be replaced; the void he has left, never can be filled; he
is quite unapproachable for influence here. Alas! Poor
John Hornidge! We could have 'better spared a better
man.'[8]

8. Such busy times. Not a moment for journalising; delightful weather, crops all looking well, people very quiet,
either better able to live on what they thought a scanty
allowance during the heat or learning to dress their
small meal more productively, for they are very quiet;
no beggars wandering about at all as formerly. The
principal dread latterly has been of fever, following the
dysentery consequent on ill cooked food and restriction
to one only kind of nourishment, and induced also by the
dirty habits of the whole country, the dung heaps at every
door, the stagnant pools, the damp floors, the inability to
buy soap this year, and the disinclination to make use of
any if they had it—all require the imperative order of
the relief committee enforced by the power of exacting a
heavy fine or in default a month's imprisonment, in case
of non-compliance with it.

I certainly got a great fright, not only with Andy Ryan's

8. Henry IV part I, v: 100.

death, but on the way to Blackditches at the Carrolls'
publick house and at the filthy Scarfes' every inmate was
seized; however they are all off to hospital, such lime
washings are going on and other purifications that the
pestilence seems checked. A fine cool wind too has been
blowing all round these healthy hills, and it is intended
to change the food—give half rice and half Indian meal,
cooked—1 *pound* of each furnishing when properly made
10 *pounds* of nutritious stirabout, exceedingly good, and
sufficient for a meal for four working men. We made
some yesterday and to-day I have copied the printed
recipe to distribute, and mean to have it further spread
by the school children each of whom shall write a copy
to carry home. We made in like manner copies of the
white-washing order and pasted them up in several
conspicuous places. They are all allowed, with their
families, to keep their rations while in the bog, cutting
their own turf; this ensures comfort next winter, and by
the time this work is over the hay and the turnip weeding
will be on.

Matters look brighter for the lower orders—the upper
are well nigh ruined; the best of us cannot recover this
over-whelming calamity under many years; the improvident, a large class, are utterly bankrupt; swept from their
places, they must be, with families unprovided for, habits
unfitted for business. What an amount of misery; all their
own doing and so the more wretched. Now the other day
at the gale here the rents were almost paid as well as usual;
they are never so well paid in May as in November when
old scores are generally cleared off, and at this time there
is a delay asked of six weeks in a few cases for even the
lesser sum ordinarily paid now, and what is strange is that
two of the larger farmers are the defaulters: Little Tyrrell
and Rutherfurd. It would seem as if they were not yet
capable of managing a hundred acres—not sufficiently
skilful; they seem to be richer on thirty: Fifteen to thirty
they manage to be very comfortable on; but when they
have to employ labour for which they pay, workmen
beyond their own familes, they don't get on—too penny
wise for large dealings. Hal got £130 in money; £70

will be paid in July, and the arrears will probably be all cleared off in November. It was worth spending on them to be thus repaid.

9. Thursday last was the day of poor John Hornidge's funeral, Blesinton was crowded, bright and sunny day, such as the old man used to enjoy when driving along to the Sessions where he had reigned as Chairman so many years, glancing a proud eye as he passed in his high phaeton over the Russelstown woods and meadows covered with the cattle he had such pleasure in calculating the profits on.

10. Howitt's journal is conducted with great ability; its contributors are for the most part very talented and sprung at once from the people; they startle the quiet upper ranks but those of us who reflect must feel that such minds will not bear much pressure on them; they must rise to their fit place and we must meet them or be overpassed. We may count the bubbles now but when the fermentation encreases they will rush up in force irresistible when room must be made for them or they will take it all. It will soon be the aristocracy who will have the lesson to learn; their order in its present form must pass away like other feudal usages no longer wanted.

14. We are in hopes of getting quit of a couple of men outside. Pat Hyland is promised the next vacancy in the police and we shall not replace him, and when the lambs are sold we shan't want James Moore and the harvest then beginning he will get work elsewhere. One thing must be insisted on with the rest; they must not employ Colonel Smith's money to support their relations; they get wages not only to feed but to clothe themselves and till their appearance is decent they have no right to give any money away. The moment one member of a family gets into service all the rest suppose they have a claim on every penny thus earned, consequently all our servants in and out go half naked, ragged, dirty, run in debt if they can, that the demands of their relations may be satisfied. Said relations, most of them, content to lounge on in idleness at home while the working member can be applied to. With the maids I have put a stop to it, refusing any

advances, keeping their money and laying it out for them in clothes; they come so bare it takes fully two years to collect them a plain wardrobe; they have often given these clothes away, but as I continue keeping the purse till I have made up the deficiencies I generally tire them out. There is a looseness of habits as of principles runs through the whole characters of these unsettled people that won't cure in our day; however I shall undertake our own men for I will not submit to their rags and tatters.

It is odd how little stir there is about O'Connell's death. As little about the approaching elections. The world is weary of politicks. No distress here, not a beggar to be seen.

21. The Doctor has been lending us some volumes of the parlour library, containing extremely well written novelettes any one of which would have made the name of its authour celebrated some few years ago. One of these tales is particularly important as a real true representation of the common fate of woman. It is a mistake to *finish* with the marriage of the heroine. This important *change* is in fact the *beginning* of their history, the practical employment for which all that went before has been but the preparation for. While her beauty remains unfaded, while her character can still charm by its novelty, she may be indulged with a lingering lover-like husband. After that she must educate herself to become his best friend—not to expect that the time of man is to be frittered away by the side of woman, or to fancy that she can remain the only object of his every thought. She must accommodate herself to his habits, enter into his pursuits, bear with his infirmities, watch that she may not offend him with her own, and look for her reward in the confidence he will place in her, and the feeling that she is doing her duty.

26. A Mr. Sullivan has come to verify our survey of the lands to be drained, so we shall soon have a band of poor men at work. £1200 Hal has asked for.

30. We have very hot weather. Began to mow yesterday, about three weeks earlier than if it had been natural meadow and so shall have the hay *in the hagard* before the rains. Surely

this year will *teach* the Irish that in agriculture at any rate they had *all* to learn. The Relief Committee will not assist Dick Gray. The Colonel has forbidden my doing so. He is an obstinate old man and will starve before coming to terms; they have none of them any principle.

We fear Mr. West will throw up the Relief business. He is already a hundred pounds out of pocket by it, nearly the whole of his time consumed and he has had considerable annoyance besides from the interference of Monsieur à mustaches [Captain Brandling]. No one else will undertake the trouble so they must pay for its being given to the Government Commissioners. Colonel Smith, Mr. West, and Mr. Fraser, and one of the Darkers have alone attended the meetings for some weeks. What people. What melancholy prospects for another generation. Indolence, sulk, irritable dispositions, all to be got the better of in every individual almost, throughout the country before we can hope for any permanent improvement in the race.

Just what I have been convinced of for years. The nation is uneducated, and here is my own dear boy, my Jack, with whom such pains have been taken, the curse of his race is on him spite of the good dash of Norman and Saxon blood he owes to his mother. Idleness in him hath made its masterpiece, he can neither rouse mind nor body when the fit is on him; let but one single cross occur to him and from that moment the blight of discouragement falls like a moral palsy over his feelings; he can rise above no difficulty, redeem no errour, he sinks into listless despair, thus turning *one* slip into *utter ruin*.

My dearest child, if when you read this you should not already have educated yourself out of a weakness which will involve you in endless troubles, begin then, from the moment these warning words of the mother who doted on you, meet your eyes, resolve to conquer the indolence, the irritability, the *feebleness* of your nature.

SUNDAY, JULY 4. We have been driving out in the evenings on the few roads left passable by the relief works. Curious thing to begin such extensive alterations in every place and finish none. I have the comfort of possessing one single pound note towards the family expenses, the remains of ten pounds of borrowed money which must be repaid when some of the rents promised to be paid up during this month, come in. A good deal is owing but we can't expect all. There are lambs to sell, but there are weekly wages to a large amount and the butcher, besides the Dublin bills for flour, groceries, etc., and I am sure I don't know how to meet any of them for those horrid Howitts have sent me no answer yet.[9] I must spirit up and try my friend Mr. Chambers again. This miserable year too, when the world knows that as a nation we are bankrupt, that as individuals we are ruined—not to understand that ready money is wanting. We have good prospects fortunately—fine crops. The hay is all cut, at least the sown grass, and will be all made to-morrow—about three tons per acre, thirteen acres, at a cost of about nine shillings per acre, value four pounds a ton; there is a great deal of meadow hay besides, a little here, some on Kearn's land, which won't be ready for a month. We now begin to weed the turnips and the mangel wurzel, hay made in four days, when did such a thing happen in Ireland?

7. Been balancing my books for the last quarter: 'tis to a fraction, and note book and purse and copper bag all empty—not a farthing in hand, pleasant result, cheering prospects; the first time such a thing has happened to me in this happy home. In my father's house my poor mother had this to bear often, and I, for her, after her health made it necessary to conceal difficulties from her. We are to have some money paid us to-morrow—much is owing—but what is our little arrears to others, who are actually ruined? Some whom we know by name, without the price of food—Ogle Moore without one penny but what he has borrowed; Milltowns done up. He has been lucky enough to sell some racers well and this enables them to go off—where, we don't know,

9. Their Journal, started in January 1847, was only to manage three editions, the last of which was received on the 26th July.

perhaps near at hand, just to get rid of all superfluous hands at Rusboro', and then return to look their altered circumstances boldly in the face, for they will live cheaper on their farm here with no house rent to pay, than they could ever do on the Continent with their encumbering title. The young people have *all* had the small pox and got over it very well.

12. The Queen has been at Cambridge installing her Prince as Chancellor, grand doings. She is going to Laggen to Lord Abercorn's Lodge with all her Court for the shooting season, and before that is to yacht round her islands—can't sit still, poor restless young creature. Our *poor* business in an odd way—this out door relief will *not* do, many prefer their rations to work, as it was foretold they would. Another experiment is to be tried in August. Got some money thank heaven! A small balance from two of the tenants, and sold wool and lambs. This little fund will keep us going for a month, when the pay comes.

14. We had a cousin Graydon here at dinner yesterday, and who staid all night. Alexander Graydon, of Newcastle, a rough specimen of the old hunting, drinking, skying, kind and witty Irishman. Amusingly full of ridiculous stories of his wild youth—quite aware that the present age is far superior—thankful that his sons will not follow his steps. He seems however to keep a very Galway style of house and to have near run through his means, much in the manner there practised. He has got one of these Government jobs to do—valueing some of these roads they are picking at through people's lands all over the country—probably none of them ever to be finished. What will become of us by and bye, who can say? This out-door relief has put the finishing stroke to the resources of the upper classes, and the immorality of the lower—none care to work now—they are fed while idle. Crowds apply for meal who are in no need of it. We are quiet which is a comfort, but the storm is but delayed.

16. A new Inspector is appointed to our district, who of course gave up near five hours to his business. Will this continue? He paid us such compliments that both Teachers and Manager must feel quite gratified. He told

me he had as yet no school like this of ours; so clean, airy, cheerful, good rooms, tidy children, so judicious a system of management, it is a pattern! Miss O'Keefe wants further education but he prefers her as she is, to the conceited things brought up in Marlborough Street, and the father is beyond perfection with his pedantry, and his attitudes, and his whole soul in his profession. It is a bad year for my purse or it should all be better. Still with the help of the Repository the girls' school has not cost me a pound note this half year, fuel and all I am but some twelve shillings out of pocket. The boys' cost four pounds ten shillings for the poor Teacher would have starved had we not advanced his year's salary of one pound a quarter for the pauper pupils. Very cheering this, and we shall do better yet it is to be hoped.

18. Sunday, Mr. Wynne must sell Burgage, he has offered it to Colonel Smith, and we should both like to repossess this fine bit of very improveable land. Not having ready money, however, makes it a much less profitable business so that we must calculate narrowly and take sound advice before entering into any arrangements about it. These are bad times for land speculations. The Poor Rates are heavy enough now, and we must expect them to be heavier—far.

Called at Rusboro' yesterday evening, did not go in, met on the gravel, in our open carriages, my Lord very gracious, my Lady very cross. They only *talk* of going away, the means it seems are wanting, but they wish to change the air with the children, after the small pox, for a few weeks if they can manage it. Poor people, we can't help pitying them, though they don't deserve it, they have such low dispositions both of them, and act so very absurdly.

The Doctor lent us William Carleton's '*Black Prophet*,'[10] very fine, very truthful, very wretched, showing the

10. Carleton (1794–1869), coming from Tyrone peasant stock, is singled out by Thomas Flanagan (NH of I) as 'expressing for the first time in English a civilisation that lay behind the hedges.'

miseries that cannot be remedied under several generations—never—while the Roman Catholick superstitions
prevent the spread of true religion. Presbyterian bigotry
keeps back the Scotch in the same way, Methodistical
cant the English.

21. We went yesterday into Dublin. One thing was satisfactory; all the way the improvement in the style of farming
was very visible as also the houses, cabins, gardens, all
are quite superiour to what they once were even to what
they were last year, but on getting into the suburbs of
the town only melancholy evidences of the distress of
the nation were to be met with—every second house to
let—of those retreats where the Dublin tradesmen lived
with their families, neat small places with carsheds beside
them, little gardens in front and green fields behind.
I began to count the number of shops shut up as we
advanced and got to twenty-six by the time we reached
the entrance of the busy part of the City. The shops are
deserted. One or two we had to enter, we were alone in,
few shopmen either, there being nothing for them to do,
and they offered us their goods for anything we chose to
give them, like cheap bread to those who cannot earn its
value. This was useless to me. I had to lay out the least
possible sum required by our necessities, so had to look
on what was tempting with the same eyes as would one
dying of hunger on a heap of diamonds.

26. What was my surprise on looking thro' the packet of
Howitt's journal last sent, reading on, article after article,
to stumble upon my '*Thoughts on Irish Charities*'. It reads
very well and is very good. Those journals of Chambers
and Howitt are very delightful. They fill the mind,
exercise it, occupy it. One wants no other society—what
will these people make of their readers, the least attentive
of them. Never was such an amount of good seed scattered
and surely some will fall where it can take root.

WEDNESDAY, AUGUST 4. The Elections are making very little
stir except in a few particular cases. Mr. Macaulay
has lost Edinburgh. In Wicklow we are to return our
old members, Colonel Acton and Lord Milton. Lord
Kildare is secure, from family influence, but really his

supercilious airs deserve defeat. He would not solicit a vote. And the first requisition to him, got up by the retainer voters not being numerously signed, he would not even answer it. The day is passed for such vulgar assumption, these are no longer feudal times.

The ministers have had another blow. Sir John Cam Hobhouse has lost Nottingham. I fear a very radical parliament will be returned. The strength of the people, now educating, is enormous. Up is heaving a force our bulwarks of mere canvas can't resist. On will come the flood and unless we can absorb it as it spreads, it will rush through and overwhelm us. 'Tis folly not to see it, not to prepare for it. But the aristocracy is blind, as the French in 1780.

Jane is much disturbed at the result of the Edinburgh Election, for which she was totally unprepared. She lives so completely in a *set*, who closing their eyes and ears to everything not agreeable to their peculiar prejudices, are unable, clever as they are, to see the world as it really is. Mr. Macaulay is personally unpopular everywhere. Unrivalled as an orator, very talented as an Authour, he is not thought to be a good man of business, he is not even trusted, while his unsociable manners, penurious habits, and supercilious address, have rendered him rather an object of general dislike than of admiration.[11] He and Sir John Cam Hobhouse are considered to cause much of the unpopularity of Lord John Russell's administration, though his own want of firmness assists. He has very evidently not a large enough capacity for his position, honest and hard-working though he be.

Mr. O'Connell's remains are being paraded all through Dublin to-day, up and down every street in the town like another St. Swithin, well rained on too. His body lay in state in the Marlborough Street Chapel with a glass window in the lid, over his face, a peep of which was given for twenty shillings, and there was no want of spectators. Hitherto all has been peaceable, although the Election was going on.

11. 'too thorough a Whig to please the radicals' (DNB)

9. Dick Gray has just been here to ask for more relief. He has not got it. Phil Tyrrel has no money, as promised, neither has Rutherfurd. These two last have large farms, one hundred English acres or more, it must be bad management in both cases, for the Tyrrels are but three in family. Gray has his seven acres too cheap, he will not give them up, so he must take the consequences. John Robinson spent yesterday with us, rain all day. Dublin very well. Tradesmen and merchants failing. O'Connell's funeral extended in length two miles, two and two a-breast few carriages, no gentry, priests and mob and the family. There was no demonstration of any sort. All passed off quietly, and the glass window in the coffin lid was a hoax. The one pound was paid to only touch the coffin. The Elections were quite uninfluenced by this bit of priestcraft, they created more interest but caused little stir compared with former times.

13. Mary Gillies much approves of my '*Hannah White*' she has forwarded it to the Howitts, and as they don't seem inclined to make use of my '*National School*' she is going to get it back, and send it elsewhere, so I shall get up a Charity Fund against winter. We have very heavy rain just now, which is far from good for the ripening corn. The mummy wheat looks excellent, twenty-seven heads from the *two* grains. It has been too damp for Lady Gardeners of late, besides I am busy preparing a highlander for Mr. Chambers. A most curious event, unexpected, and most exceedingly opportune, the quarter's pay arrived to-day, and with it £35.6.4! Deccan prize money! earned thirty-three years ago! Half of the poor Officers present in those engagements must be in their graves. Certainly this sort of thing is "atrocious."

15. Yesterday, being a beautiful morning, and there being several little things to do in Dublin, Papa, Mama, and Jack got up at half after five, breakfasted, the girls getting up to see us off, drove to Sallins, and there took seats in a railroad carriage. Beautiful line of rail, neat station, handsome carriages, fine rich country all the way to Dublin by Hazelhatch, Celbridge, Lucan, plenty of gentlemen's seats. A wonderful promise for

harvest which is already begun, several fields were full of reapers. We got in an hour nearly to the terminus, an immense building, though not so extensive as the Company's factory, a mile from the end round which they have quite a village of neat houses for all the various people they employ, some of whom are quite gentlemen. The clerk, who took our tickets, had the manners and the *hands* of high breeding.

The publick relief is over. It was never contemplated to carry it on beyond harvest, indeed few have been receiving assistance of late, comparatively, there being plenty of work for those who choose to go and look for it. The class who can't earn is no larger than it ever was, it is now thrown upon the Poor Law guardians, who at their meeting on Friday last, instead of electing relieving officers to take charge of the several districts, as they were called together to do, fell into disputing, about a set of jobs they had a mind to perpetrate. They wanted to join large districts and lump the pay, thus making a good income for a *son* or a *nephew*, who would have been physically incapable of getting through such an extent of duties. Mr. Owen and others battled the point and gained it. The seventeen divisions of our Union are to be paired, two and two, the *three* smallest only going at the end together, and Mr. Owen had the address to join Blesinton and Baltiboys, so we shall get on comfortably, for with our many ordinary works and our extraordinary draining and our better description of landlords, we are by no means *swamped* with paupers, even though part of the mountains, Shannon Harbour and Weavers Square are included. Colonel Smith is in the list for the draining loans gazetted yesterday, still we can't begin, so for this next month till the next Poor Law meeting we shall have to give a great deal of help, that even with the Deccan prize money! we can ill afford. Still, we think the times are mending. Land property must be sold in those miserable parts of the country, where the landlords have been keeping up false appearances, living like wealthy men while drowned in debt. And the equally improvident tradesman must publish his insolvency, break and lie and cheat no more. The whole people, so to speak, have been existing on credit, make believe, there was nothing real about far more than half of them.

Carleton has written an Irish Glenbervia really truthful, called '*Paddy Go Easy*', the hero we can pick up his like by dozens, but the heroine, I fear exists as yet but in fancy. I am sure in this country we might look long and never find her. However somebody must teach or the story could not have run. It shows how correctly we have both painted from nature. Many traits in my *Luke White* are so like those, that had I not written my tale before reading his I should have believed I had copied him.

16. The Colonel went off early again by six, to reach the railway in time for the train to Athy. Quantities of voters at the Station. He saw all his Kildare acquaintance and when he left, Mr. Bourke[12] was at the head of the poll in every booth. However, as the Election will last for a day or two the repealer may pull up, so many have been returned where no such result was expected. We called in on Peggy Nary, who is going to turn her lodgers out of the house, having at last quarrelled with them. I don't on earth know what to do with her. She is going to white wash her kitchen! she says—herself—no one else would do it to please her.

We then went on to Jem Doyle's. Most wretched it all was, though very clean, he must go to the Poor House, he and his family. He has an ulcer on his leg, which will prevent his working for weeks, and they will starve during this month, that there is no relief going. I shall also send Bessy Healy there, her habits of idleness, lying and thieving seem incurable. And to spend money on a girl who will never turn out well, at least as she is, seems folly. Old Peggy can't manage a clever wilful child. Widow Mulligan is also starving. So are the Widow Quins and fifty more. They must be forced into the Poor House for they cannot otherwise be supported. They are the meanest feeling people ever were, they will accept of

12. Chief Secretary of Ireland three times; sixth Earl of Mayo, 1867; Governor General of India 1868.

charity from anyone, live on it in idleness, but they won't go to the Poor House.

21. The Queen is fairly in the Highlands. Sailed up the West Coast, on to Fort William, thence across the hills to Laggan, at the junction of the roads a little above Kingussie she was to be received by the Badenoch and Rothiemurchus men headed by Cluny, Sandy McIntosh and twelve more in the full dress go from our Duchus. Mr. Caw should denude himself for the occasion The Daily News says not badly, that in certain of the Indian islands the natives uncover the head and shoulders as a mark of respect. In the country of the Gael they expose a different part of the person.

26. The Queen in and out and round all her lovely islands on that fine Western Coast. The weather beautiful. Crowds uncountable attending. It really seems a wise thing to do. Unconstrained happiness for herself, much good to the bulk of her subjects, although such of the nobility as help to entertain her must smart under the honour for many a long day to come. There is still too much state about it all for these rational times.

29. Sunday, Delightful weather. Mild and the crops so fine. Every able-bodied person employed about here, or might be, did they choose to work; there are however a few who prefer receiving alms, actually sit still doing nothing, trusting to the compassion of anyone inclined to feed them. The new poor law practice will soon set all this to rights.

Very little stir about politicks in these days. Dislike of the ministry seems to be the only feeling very much alive in the public mind, a dislike of some individuals, and a want of confidence in the whole. No wonder after the deficiencies of last session, foreign troubles, and home distresses. The Queen of Spain and her husband don't get on. In France there has been the most horrid murder: the Duke of Praslin has murdered his wife, and in the most barbarous manner in the middle of the night. These wretched great! The aristocracy has indeed need of a reformation. The Duc was not a faithful husband; he was not even decent in his gallantries, choosing as his mistresses the governesses of his children.[13] These French manners are very demoralising. All their habits are at variance with virtue. Amongst our own aristocracy it is very much the same. They are all much to be pitied, for true happiness they know nothing of.

Our little Queen is at Laggan. Cluny received her at the head of three hundred Highlanders,—McIntoshes, Grants, and McPhersons. Why he played first fiddle, can't say, except that no one else would take the trouble. Sandy McIntosh headed the Rothiemurchus men. I must write to him for an account of the proceedings. The Duchess of Bedford went up to Ardverikie to receive her, and then returned to the Doune, it is said to prepare for a royal visit—and the Laird so far away! The beautiful Duchus! 'That lovely spot where my forefathers dwelt.' McAlpine would have right royally received her, and proudly he would have stood upon his native heather. It is all so changed now. I grieve over this importation of Southrons, who with their gold steal from us the hearts of our followers—divide them with us at any rate doing them little good, and as I thought when there, some evil. Well, my time is nearly over. Soon the progress of things will vex me no more, and the little while still to be given to me should be devoted to my duties here. A busy practical present instead of the poetick past.

SATURDAY, SEPTEMBER 4. A few spare moments trying to please Mr. Chambers have altogether kept me too busy to give any time to the journal. My *'Highlander'* is much admired, but the end did not please. Formerly I had to take away ever so much of the middle, and now I had to put ever so much more to the end. I believe it to be an improvement however, indeed I liked the *tale* in its first dress, but this shortened sketch may be more suitable to the journal. Leitch Ritchie sent it me in type with a flattering note suggesting the change required. No word from Mrs. Howitt.

13. He battered his wife to death and succeeded in taking arsenic during his trial; this was widely seen as a condemnation of the traditional ruling classes.

17. All off early to Glenbride, some on ponies, some in buggy, some in clarencette. Dinner at Lord Downshire's lodge, a sort of picnic supplied by Mr. Owen and me. The gentlemen shot over the moors, the ladies tried to reach the source of the King's river but got such a ducking in the attempt that there was above an hour's fun drying ourselves at different fires, dressing in any stray dry garments at hand no matter whose, etc., etc. We came home here to tea in much the same order as we went and danced till near midnight.

21. Tom Darker was at the fair of Naas yesterday which was worse than Rathsalla, nothing offered for anything. All our sheep and cattle came home as before and everyone else was in the same predicament. There is no grass in England, not much in other parts of Ireland and the turnips look very bad everywhere, they have not bulbed at all. This prevents the cattle jobbers from speculating. Our grass is fine, our turnips good, so by keeping our stock over we must be fully repaid by the high prices we shall get in spring or may be at Christmas. In the meanwhile we get no cash and the rents may be uncertain. Some say this will be a harder year than the last. It is well the Colonel sold poor Major or we certainly should be in a straight. £54 10 0 he got for him.

23. Janie Mackintosh would give much to have a cousin with her. She wants a companion. Her husband is a kind protector, a safe guide, very sensible, very amiable, very fond of her, and very judicious in his management of her, for she is much improved in many ways since she came under his direction. She looks up to him and I think she loves him with a sort of filial love; she is certainly anxious to please him. But she married too young. She has read too many French novels, and she imagines she is putting one of them in action. All unhealthy, all dangerous, even though there is perfect confidence between her and her husband on this strange subject. Were they to remain in this country I should tremble, for George Mackintosh is a man of business, whose relaxations are the sports of the field, a good dinner, a bottle of wine, a dish of gossip, for he has no other conversation—a little scandalmongering

in a good-natured way, and love making with his little wife set upon his knee and his great shoulder-of-mutton hand round her slight waist. When she plays or sings he falls asleep; he has read nothing so comprehends none of her clever allusions; he possesses no accomplishments, wants the capacity indeed to learn any. When she has her heart and mind full of ideas, no response meets her from his, and already she feels this painfully. Poor dear Janie, she was educated for a higher destiny, yet she has got worth, sense, affection and affluence. It may turn out well.

SUNDAY, OCTOBER 10. Little in the papers but failures. Cattle dealers in Dublin have gone and caused immense distress, in fact paralysed the markets; not an offer for a beast of any sort at any of the late fairs. Banks, merchants, brokers, agents, all are bankrupt in all places. John Robinson has lost seven thousand pounds by bad debts, trusting people who have failed to pay; he must pay the millers who sent him the flour he so imprudently parted with out of his former profits, his capital, and learn wisdom by this shake. He hopes to recover about half this sum when the affairs of some of these firms are wound up.

Janey and I walked to church this morning, the rest went in the carriage. We saw everybody, talked to many, and received four letters. One concluding the draining business which the Colonel will therefore be enabled to set agoing immediately much to the relief of the country round us for we shall employ at least fifty men.

17. Sunday again—the 17th. I hardly know how the week has gone—not a creature has entered the house but the Doctor. We have been as quiet as possible, indeed the country generally is very dull; people are oppressed by this frightful amount of bankruptcies, almost everyone either themselves or their friends affected by some of these numerous failures. Then the winter prospects look very gloomy. The destitution is expected to be wider spread than last year for the very poor will be very nearly as ill off while the classes above which then relieved them are all this year in serious difficulties. No money anywhere; the little hoards of cash and goods all spent and

nothing to replace either. The ministry says the land must support the people on it. Half of the country having been left untilled for want of means to crop it while a million of money was squandered in destroying the roads, much of it finding its way into pockets full enough before.

The Queen has ordered the begging box to go round all the English churches for us! Sir John Burgoyne, head of the Poor Law Commission, writes to the Times newspaper! to entreat charitable subscriptions for the starving districts. Mr. Trevelyan, the Secretary to the Treasury, sends this precious emanation forth to the publick with some little addenda of his own to the same tune. One would suppose stones were scarce in Ireland and her rivers dry when no one hoots such drivellers out of the country. We want no charity. We want a paternal government to look a little after our interests, to legislate for us *fairly*, to spend what we should have properly among us without jobbing, to teach us, and to keep a tight rein over idleness, recklessness, apathy. It is plain these people can't do it. We must all begin and call again for Sir Robert Peel as we did some years ago, for the state of the Empire is unpromising. We can't get our money out of that weary board. All forms had been complied with and it was so announced; the Colonel went up on Wednesday to receive the sum promised hoping to bring it back and to set the people to work directly.

24. Three weddings on hand—great fun. The only cheerful events expected in the country for no winter ever opened upon us more gloomily. It bids fair to set in early and with unusual severity. Every newspaper brings large additions to the long list of bankrupts; the whole mercantile world is affected by the pressure on the money market. Banks have failed everywhere. Manufacturers, traders, brokers. We can sell nothing, and though a bountiful harvest has filled the country with cheap provisions, no one can buy. This in England, Scotland. The Highlands is much worse. What then must Ireland be, dying only. It is beyond ruin in the South and West. Here we shall get on better, we hope; it is the paradise of the green isle this Eastern coast of Wicklow.

The Colonel received yesterday the first order on the Treasurer of the Board of Works for his drainage money, so he will set on thirty men at once; such a gleam of comfort. I have money to last ourselves till the pay comes again in the middle of next month; but I can't pay poor Miss Clerk her half year's salary. I have given her five pounds to account merely. The Colonel spends nothing; he sold his horse to help us; gave up the Deccan prize money he had intended to build the lodge with, and I have put off paying the girls the money borrowed from them last year. No word from my editors either on whom I reckoned for our school.

31. Sunday and last day of the month and a cold thoroughly rainy day. John Robinson walked in about noon; no one went to church. He came down about Tom Kelly's farm. These are not times to dispossess tenants that pay so well even though they be slovenly farmers. I wish the Colonel may hear reason in this respect.

Draining business still at a stand. Some necessary plans not yet executed. Was there ever such an office for delays? Since June we have been in communication with it. These plans are promised this coming week. Tom Darker made a fruitless journey this last one for them. We anticipate a very gloomy winter; rents but ill paid, sickness, sorrow, . sales backward. Everything is cheap enough were there money to buy with. But nowhere is there any. Even literary productions are at a discount. My friend Mary Gillies can't dispose of my *School*, nor has she heard anything more of my story. Our reforming Pope has turned out a black sheep: he opposes the new Irish Colleges in toto, and don't approve of our National Education. I suppose we shan't take much notice of his folly. The Roman Catholic Bishops have been to the Lord Lieutenant with a memorial upon the distresses of the times with a suggestion amongst other things of reviving monasteries to assist the poor. The answer is considered a masterpiece—a regular slap in the face most politely given—a very rational and very courteous resumé of all points, and a little good advice to end with. As far as we can yet judge Lord Clarendon is really a clever man, thoroughly just and also enlightened.

NOVEMBER 7th. Sunday evening. This has been a more eventful week than the few preceding. We have begun the draining; thirty men the Colonel has employed. The plans arrived yesterday with a few very simple directions and a very long account of the various soils upon that part of the property. It is a pity they delayed so long in that tiresome office for two months the best suited to the purpose have thus been lost and all these poor people struggling all the while with misery; it seems there are large sums of money missing and one of the under officers of the Board is lodged in jail on suspicion of having embezzled for his share about eight thousand pounds.

If the Landlords would take advantage of the Government Loan and begin to improve their properties by employing the labour of now idle hands, there would be no need of much charity. Things look very gloomy in other parts. And another dreadful murder. A Major Mahon, a man of large property, who had been doing great good[14] but looked for his own: it is a frightful state to have a country in: more failures still; matters far from mending anywhere, Parliament is to meet immediately.

Now I must chronicle my troubles. Those tiresome servants: they are the true plagues or our lives. Mrs. Fyfe has given up her place. For nothing that I can make out. I can't see that she has one rational cause of complaint, one reasonable annoyance in her most comfortable situation. It is hardly possible to believe that a woman in her senses would give up a place she once considered her home for life because her master found a dirty pig bucket in the kitchen the odour of which perfumed the house, and insisted it should be cleaned. This 'insult' she could not put up with. I have for some time back found her very

14. Major Denis Mahon of Strokestown, Co. Roscommon, had been much involved in assisting his tenantry to emigrate to Canada; it was suspected his ships were not sea-worthy and that has been seen as a reason for his murder.

hoity toity when interfered with. These are times which make retrenchment of every useless expense necessary.

8. Mr. Darker's plans seem very good; he has divided his men into five gangs, six men to a gang, so that their work is easily supervised, changed, or their numbers added to; he thinks another gang will include all the unemployed, the Colonel being resolute to take no discharged servants. They, the farmers, are actually beginning the same tricks they played with the publick works last year, relieving themselves of their labourers of course to the detriment of their farms; penny wise and pound foolish. Tom Kelly leads the way. We had such a scene with him and his 'cute' wife. Mr. Robinson had to come down to arrange matters. We must keep our eyes upon them for they are a nice pair. There is no such thing as truth or honour or conscience in this country—high or low all alike speaking generally. These half savage people are little better to-day than they were a century back; the good times we must hope are coming.

14. Sunday, Wednesday last the 10th we went early according to promise to the auction at Kilbride Manor of household furniture, all the farm stock had been sold before and 'twas for the benefit of Ogle as his mother has given up to him everything she was entitled to, except her bare jointure. We had agreed to buy a little, to help matters, to bid at any rate. We wanted furniture for our last empty bedroom. The Doctor required furniture for his drawing-rooms. However this day nothing in our way was sold. Stables, dairy, kitchens, and servants' rooms only were got through and the things were all collected in the yard where was a large crowd of the farmer class buying as fast as the articles were put up, and paying for old things the full price of new. We had a nice luncheon at the Lodge which is stuffed full of the bits of furniture from the Manor which they did not like to let out of the family. A valuable library for one thing which arranged in handsome cases makes a pretty room of the parlour.

Thursday we returned to the auction again and found it quite unnecessary to purchase for charity sake. Although there were neither ladies nor gentlemen among the crowd the farmers were there in plenty. The scene was highly amusing. One man with a little two-roomed cabin bought an old set of dining tables to hold sixteen people. Another paid thirty shillings for a rosewood sofa table much the worse for wear. A third bought a console with faded pink linings, a broken marble slab and very slight bookshelves with gilded rails, and a fourth a gentleman's dressing-table full of drawers and pigeon holes. Chests of drawers sold for any price. All this though not saying much for the prudence of the people looks well for their rising tastes; they are beginning to appreciate the decencies of life.

Does it not also seem as if there were no lack of money among the class generally. All is paid for before being carried away; there was no lack of thirty shilling notes, which have not been current these two years as they are no longer issued. Mentioning this at Ballyward where we dined, Mrs. Finnemor told us a story of old John Hornidge and a tenant who owed him some years' rent. He held only a few acres and he came with the usual apology and the usual excuses, large family, bad times, sickness, etc. He had three pounds to give *on account* which no way lightened the arrears, but he had done his best—fumbling into his pocket he produced three *notes* which on Mr. Hornidge examining them proved to be *three ten pound notes*. He took them gravely, pulled out his books, made out the man's accounts clear, and then handing him a small balance informed him of his mistake and that he now did not owe him a penny. What a scene for a novel.

I called on Lady Milltown to congratulate her on her Lord's good speech at a meeting of Landlords in Dublin where they deliberated and will do no more. It is impossible to get uncontrouled tempers to act together. She gave me a curious book to read which has much diverted us all. An '*American Stranger*' a woman of fifty, educated, used to decent habits, comes to Ireland to judge of its condition. She drinks no fermented liquors, no tea, no milk, eats no flesh, walks her tour for the most part, sleeps in the cabin lodging houses in dirty beds, sometimes with dirty bedfellows often in a crowded room, dresses in mud boots, a polka coat of the newest fashion, a velvet bonnet, a parasol, carries a basket on her arm with a change of linen, wears a belt underneath the polka attached to which are two bags full of testaments, and in her gown she has pockets filled with tracts. She reads wherever she goes and attracts large crowds by singing hymns. She is not quite mad—only an enthusiast, and too imaginative, too quick, to be quite correct in her facts or her inferences.[15]

21. Sunday, Little publick news stirring, Lord John *put out* from Glasgow University of which he had last year been chosen Rector. These honorary dignitaries always hold the office two years; there is no former instance of the re-election failing, it was always gone through as a form merely; the result of this year must prove even to the stubborn Scotch that there never was in this country a more unpopular ministry. The state of the country is frightful everywhere but here we are quiet enough as yet.

   Friday our great people came, and very stupid it was, my Lord better a good deal than for many weeks past, my Lady good-humoured. Politicks, poor relief, agriculture, the ruin threatening the upper ranks, and the steady uprising of the classes below us formed the subjects of our varied discourses.

23. That Daily News is an excellent paper. These two last have been most interesting. One had a bit about the Scotch landlords, their encumbrances entailed on them along with their estates now encreased beyond the value almost of their properties, and, so, when the rate of interest rose with the pressure on the money market, resulting in the ruin which has already overtaken Islay and is impending over all. Much like Ireland. Also a character of Napoleon from the master mind of the American Mr. Emerson, the very best that ever was presented of this impersonation of the spirit of his times to the world he so abused. The next giving a full report of a most interesting literary meeting at Liverpool on the fifth anniversary of the opening of the Athenaeum; Archy Alison, President, whose carefully prepared speech

15. This was Asenath Nicholson whose *Annals of the Famine in Ireland* was published in New York in 1851.

is worth being got by heart by young and old, equally with that extraordinary Mr. Cobden's burst on the moment and Mr. Emerson's tribute to Saxon firmness.

When such sentiments are uttered, applauded, echoed, there can be no fear of a country, although in all likelihood a new class will soon be called on to conduct its interests. The old sapless trunks must be cleared away that the young vigorous plants shooting up so thickly round may take their places. Will it be a quiet change? Yes—and gradual—and some few with ancient roots, lopped and pruned, will remain where they have stood for centuries, to assist, to foster the new. Lord Milltown had a long talk with me on these subjects; he is well alive to the supercilious arrogance, the inanity, the egotism, the ignorance of his class, and yet he falls in with their follies.

24. I am glad to say that our good Mrs. Fyfe has returned to her senses. It would have been inconvenient to me to part with her this winter for I am not strong enough for active household cares; the girls are not experienced enough to manage for me so that I am well pleased to keep her for the present, although I would as soon be without her as far as feeling is concerned. I must contrive quietly to gather up the reins a little, take my own way, resume a sort of superintendence gradually, and at once and decidedly put an end to any disputing of the Colonel's will. He shall be master in his own house. She cried, apologised, excused herself upon her health. The Doctor says her nerves are very irritable from the state of her stomach. In future when I see a squall preparing I shall give her a pill!

25. Letter from Mr. Robert Chambers advising me to try the fate of my *Irish Tales*. Mary Gillies sent me back *Hannah White*—the Howitts were so long in using it, and money is so very long in coming from them she advised my trying elsewhere.

FRIDAY, DECEMBER 3. Lord Clarendon is a trump—no truckling—even handed justice meted to all. Where a murder has been, such a force of military and police will be sent and *kept* at the cost of the locality as will cause a change in the hiding system now so shamelessly pursued. The late vigorous proceedings have much checked the barbarities practised. To arm these half savage Connaught men is something like arming New Zealanders.

I was near forgetting that our school Inspector called yesterday—so pleased—he says we are a model. How pleasant it is to see that our management fills the Board with the most perfect confidence in us, and is daily improving these poor people. Our flower plot he highly approves of, and the rule of no child touching anything. We made a hit when we got these people. The attendance in both schools is now large, the night school only middling.

4. Such a commotion in the family. The Colonel has been for some time past dissatisfied with the way in which his horses were shod. The smith was frequently spoken to, no improvement took place, one after the other the horses all went lame, recovering always immediately when their shoes were taken off. The last long drive we took, Grasshopper was dead lame so the Colonel forbade the carriage or the riding horses to be shod by John Byrne any more and sent for another blacksmith.

Well, the first time Perry came to work all went well. But yesterday he said he must give the job up he had been so threatened & such calumnies had been circulated through Baltiboys regarding his ignorance of his trade. The very same feeling that leads to murders in those parts of the country where the vindictive propensities of the people are not kept under by *resident protestant* gentry of high character. The Colonel is not a man to be frightened: he settled matters summarily enough, announcing that he should employ what tradesmen he pleased and that if his servants attempted to annoy any such as he thought fit to send for, he could change the servants just as easily as he had done his smith: that he had not taken the farm horses or the general work in iron from John Byrne *as yet* thinking him sufficiently skilful in those departments, but that if he heard another syllable *falsely* derogating from the abilities of Perry, from that moment he should dismiss Byrne altogether. Everybody has since exculpated himself from having taken any part in these malignities and I hope the mischief is over.

The Baltiboys people are so interconnected, intermarried, that in offending one we offend all and up they all start as if no one had a right to act towards any of them but just as the whole junta please. I was once served much the same on changing a laundry maid and had to announce that sooner than take the old one back I would wash the clothes myself, before any peace was given to her successor.

8. Monday, John Robinson arrived to meet the tenants to whom we had given all this extra time on account of the fall of stock. The rents were admirably well paid; no larger arrears upon the property up to the first of last September than there were to that date the year before; four or five owe no hanging half year; a few are a few pounds behind but they promise to make this up by Christmas, even Dick Gray. There was a good sum in allowances, but John got £180 in money, and £40 is to come to him. We were in his debt £76, for which reason he would never send down his accounts. We owed him £61. in May so we have not increased it much this half year, and now he is paid and he has money in hand for any demands and we have not a tradesman's bill unpaid except the running account with Hanna the Grocer which he will settle for us at Christmas. I doubt our getting on to May without borrowing from him again but we must try for he is pushed himself as I know by his having taken all our savings, the children's and mine, out of the Savings Bank.

We must live very prudently to bring ourselves even with the world again. That once accomplished we should be extremely comfortable for people with our moderate habits make a small income go a great way. John Robinson said trade has not yet the least revived; the ruin is entire; the whole mercantile world shook, and the landed interest of course suffering elsewhere as well as here. Are not we fortunate or rather are not we rewarded for all the care we have taken of the trust confided to us. Hal may hold his head up with the best of them though he don't send puffing articles to the newspapers. As John says this is the blessed result of years of duty well performed. Our tenants are a credit to the country—never excuse the Irish landlords after this. They might do as we have done. We found a nice mess when we came home from India: rags, ruins, quarrels, and six thousand pounds of arrears.

9. Mrs. West gave us really most frightful accounts of the state of the disturbed parts of the country. Major Mahon's cousin, and her cousin, Ross Mahon has received several threatening letters. Those gentlemen who remain in Roscommon have kept a guard of police about them, armed themselves and their protestant servants, and worn shirts of chain armour.

And there sits our government politely giving time to all who wish to reconsider their intended measures while the best men in the country are being murdered. The Roman Catholick clergy could without a doubt check these atrocities were they so minded, in many instances at least, perhaps not altogether for they can but follow the people in some respects, but except in this diocese they rather urge them on to crime, turning everything into a religious aspect, affecting to believe and of course teaching that the exertions, the charities, the assistance of protestants during the late times of suffering were for proselyting purposes; and their ignorant flocks relieved for the present from the pressure of want, forget their obligations once so fully recognised and forget the apathy of their own priesthood last year so indignantly reprobated.

The Doctor came in yesterday morning with bad accounts of fever and other exterminating diseases here. He had come upon a wretched group, a woman and children cowering over a smouldering fire in a plantation at the back of Russborough where they had passed the night—all ill—he got a cart from Lord Milltown and sent them all off to Naas. But sickness is so prevailing he has come round to the necessity of fitting up our Dispensary as a fever hospital. If the gentlemen will subscribe for a nurse and provisions and fuel, we ladies will manage the bed and bedding and linen. Colonel Smith offers ten pounds, Mr. West ditto. Richard Hornidge and others don't see the necessity of any such measure. As the Doctor says: 'in a Christian country—Christian people.' They have need of the parable of the Samaritan to be repreached to them.

23. Monday, I took the dear little girls to Dublin. We went to Gresham's and finding from the waiter that Mr. and Mrs. Charles Kean were staying in the hotel and acting we went with John Robinson to the Play. It was not badly got up as to dresses, scenery, mob enough, but the acting was horrid. Charles Kean is a caricature of the father—less, harder, squarer, a more sepulchral voice—all defects exaggerated; he would do for first murderer.

Christmas Day. Another drive for me. We brought the Doctor back to dinner to talk over all events. The murders of the higher orders seem to be over; the farmer class are however very brutally assassinated and a great many outrages are still committed, the priests still foul mouthed, the country in a *revolting* state. Lord Clonmel has been threatened which is coming rather near us, and Lord Crofton and some others have left the country, which is a pity; the French nobles over again—just what these incendiaries want.

We were all in blue bonnets at church to-day! My lady asked me for one and I gave her a dozen, for she began all airs, talking grand, undervaluing everybody and I told her she was wrong and made her confess it. Such nonsense—a brewer for their ancestor, a blanket weaver for one connexion, a silk spinner for another and then to look down on the son of a silversmith. 'He can never be noticed by the aristocracy.' 'I can't see any aristocracy hereabouts' said I, 'they all appear to be to be just like these Wests, sprung from the people and none the worse of it,' etc. etc. etc. So she had a taste of highland pride to digest her folly with.

28. The Colonel and Annie rode to Kilbride Manor, Janey and I walked to Rathbally. We had a round home through the Weaver's Square where we had humble visits to pay as I am beginning my Christmas inspections. We heard a miserable account of Kitty Gray's troubles. A most tedious labour—unkind father—no help sent for—and

fears for the unhappy girl's life. The Doctor being in Dublin I could only send for the wise woman, James Ryan's wife undertaking the management of the business for me.

30. The last day of the year—the happy year 1847, I may call it so for no serious affliction has occurred in the family. Many arrangements for good have been made among us, and the poor people particularly depending on our ownselves have come through these troubled times so far without much suffering. Better hopes seem rising for future years—the famine having roused the energies of this clever race. Nothing else I believe would have spirited them up to exertion indispensable to their decent comfort.

In all Baltiboys we have no destitute family; a very few distressed. Dick Gray who from drinking, gambling, company-keeping and children reared amid these vices is the most so and we will not help him for he will not give up his land nor till it properly nor live reputably, yet he has done wonders for him this summer. Mick and Judy Doyle are more uncomfortable looking than really in want; they owe nothing and as they have by hard labour made a good deal of money their dirty sloppy ways are their own choice. The old Byrnes are poor enough; they went on the old system and having spent in their youth have nothing in their age, but the labour of their son Luke; he has four mouths besides his own to provide for. Clothes must be out of his power. Pat Quin is not so deserving of assistance because there are other brothers and sisters able to assist him to support his mother. One sister is indeed an object—the blind woman married to the lame Jem Doyle. They had no business to marry, no right to squat themselves down in that cow house, but there they are and God help them. I have not forgot them this Christmas. They and the old Byrnes must be looked after. Mary Ryan having left the Poor House I am done with her. She is sharing the misery of the grandmother—another mouth for the lame uncle to fill, and so be it; they must take their own way, reason is lost on them.

EIGHT

1848

This was the 'year of revolutions' and she comments fully
on how Europe, England and Ireland (with threatened
upheavals and State Trials) were affected. The Famine's
dire effects spread but Colonel Smith's drainage schemes
employed some of the destitute. She spent much of the
summer in Edinburgh (where she learned of the death
of her father, at sea, on the return from India) as the
family begin to learn the full extent of his and her
brothers' involvement in the fraudulent dealings of the
Union Bank of Calcutta.

SUNDAY, JANUARY 9. I never had fewer letters than this
week, no books to be had either, but the last volume
of Chambers' Journal which is improving again. My
'*Highlander*' figures, and a sad affair by poor old Miss
Edgeworth, they should not have let the dear little old
lady expose her failing intellect, she who had shone with
such beautiful brilliancy. It made me really sad, like the
dotage of the iron Duke, between old age and epilepsy the
brain of that wonderful man is shattered and here we have
a letter of his to Sir John Burgoyne (twaddle) *published*
invoking death before the fearful *tragedy* which owing to
the defenceless condition of our coasts, and the use of
steamboats, he foresees will be enacted on our southern
shores by the French on their way to settle for the night
in London.

The English Roman Catholicks unable to tolerate
longer the shameless conduct of the Irish priesthood have
come nobly forward to denounce it. Lord Shrewsbury's
letter is really fine, utterly fearless, he tells them all
their misdeeds, accuses those that merit it of falsehood,
equivocation, tergiversation, agitation, want of Christian
charity, of pastoral duty, etc. They never got such a

castigation from an heretick as from this true son of their church. It will open the eyes of the few Roman Catholick gentry at any rate, whether they will see the better after, who can say.

15. Sunday, Our out o' door works are progressing. Richard Hornidge has begun draining with his own money so employs another good band of men, still numbers are idle and the Doctor tells us that influenza and fever are so general as to produce much distress. The fever hospital is a great blessing, already there are nineteen patients glad to be received there, not as in former times preferring to die at home and to infect their whole family. The expense will come off the county at large and what an amount of good results. First the patients are surrounded with comforts, and get hourly visits from the doctors, next infection is prevented from spreading, then fuel must be bought, provisions must be bought, washerwomen hired, nurse tenders paid. Poor Mr. Payne, the apothecary gets a guinea a week for his double duties and the Doctor gets £90 a year. They are all so satisfied with the results hitherto that they are thinking of branch wings for wounds, etc, a general hospital in fact. Time and patience.

The commission is very busy, three murderers to be hanged, twenty-five convicts sent off from the dock without communication with their relatives, ironed, handcuffed and escorted by military and police to the railroad direct for Dublin under charge of our old friend Captain Seymour, who was to deliver them to the vessel awaiting its miserable cargo in the roads. The wailing among the mob was dismal. It is hoped the effect will be as expected, the suddenness of the shock strikes terrour.

Some of the Tipperary boys were suspected of having travelled to these parts, if so they did not abide. However, some busy bodies in the other half of the Barony thought it a good opportunity for bringing themselves into notice, so they published that owing to the disturbed state of this district they considered an encreased police force necessary and they should therefore attend in Blesinton on a day named for the purpose of swearing in special constables. Mr. Owen saw no necessity for any meeting in this perfectly peaceable district, Tipperary boys might have passed through but they had not staid for there was no one to harbour them. Lord Downshire had no rebellious tenants, and in any case those resident gentlemen who had hitherto so prosperously managed the business of their locality felt themselves quite competent to the continued discharge of their duties.

23. Pray heaven the Calcutta National Bank may be enabled to meet its obligations. I have had two packets from Jane grieving over the folly of my father and my brothers, the extent of whose ruin was not fully known to themselves when they announced the first crash.

24. Jim Doyle, the son of those miserable people upon the hill who went out last year to a kind uncle in America writes home that this uncle met him on the quay and had two suits of clothes ready for him as people must be well dressed in that country and has put him into a factory where his wages are 20/—a week. Now will any of the family starving here have sufficient energy to try and win a smile from fortune there. And will the poverty-stricken parents let this well doing lad alone or let him really help them by sending by and bye for a brother or a sister. I fear that neighbour-like they will try to draw all he can spare from him to help them to exist in their wretchedness, and they are so wretched, so very nearly destitute all of them, we can hardly wonder at the pauper family clinging to and draining a prosperous member.

25. Getting on pretty well with the subscription for the Hospital linen. Mr. Foster has undertaken to go the rounds with it. A letter from Jane who had been dining with Mr. Dickens, very underbred man, but not affected.

30. Sunday, So busy these few days working for the fever hospital that no writing time was left. I am also vexed about our affairs. There were so many heavy Dublin bills to pay during this struggling year we had to borrow to discharge them. We have so many idle horses that we had no oats to sell. The markets were so gone that no stock sold at all. Tom Darker has had therefore to come upon the half pay for the current expenses of the farm,

labour, smith, carrier, etc. This has left me penniless. I have not one pound towards the ordinary demands of the family and the first of the month approaching. The Quarter's pay will come in a fortnight but I am afraid so much of it is fore-stalled that very little balance will remain and we have the biting spring months before us and not a shilling to the rescue until May. Well! the stout heart is the more wanted, the brae is stiff enough, God knows. The 16 Numbers of *Dombey and Son* yet published we have finished to our sorrow, the reading of a Number aloud every night kept up our spirits finely. Our good Doctor elected Surgeon to the newly established Dispensary in Ballymore. He has done all the duty for long; he will really be comfortable in his decline of life, £100 for Blesinton fever hospital, £90 Ballymore, £70, the interest of £3,000, his savings, how hardly earned, and his practice among the upper classes.

31. Six inches of snow lying evenly over the country. Except that it stops the outwork we ought to be glad to see it to keep the ground warm, purify the air, and drive fever away. Spite of the worthlessness of our fine peasantry one can't help grieving for their sufferings. We, in this district never would give any out door relief while there were vacancies in the Poor House at any rate; at Ballymore they gave it and it was abused beyond idea. The Government Commisioners have put a stop to it, taken another house in Naas and refused all aid except under what the people consider imprisonment. A report got about that only the able bodied would be forced into the Poor House, that the aged, sickly, etc, would be relieved in their own homes; crowds therefore presented themselves to the Doctor to beg certificates of decrepitude, hale and hearty men and women assuring him they were suffering under every ill that flesh is heir to. This description of consciences last year, when only the able bodied were accepted for certain relief works, were equally anxious to make themselves out in the rudest health whatever infirmities they had. They are all again beginning to beg, of course, because some are so foolish as to give. We are little teased, we never refuse a bit of bread, we never give anything else, and

they leave us in quiet, for it is money they want, pennies for tobacco and snuff and tea and whiskey.

John Tuam[1] has at length answered Lord Shrewsbury, a perfect volume, I can't tell how many columns of rubbish, unreadable, no argument, no reply, coarse abuse from an ignorant, vulgar, low born, lowbred, bigotted despot, of an accomplished nobleman. These poor creatures, the Irish priests are living three or four hundred years behind the age, and no gentleman ever entering the profession, they are such a set of 'surpliced ruffians' as really disgrace the country. It was a bright thought to send Lord Minto[2] to Rome. The Pope knew no truth about Ireland.

TUESDAY, FEBRUARY 1. It was a bright day for poor Lord John when he thought of sending Lord Clarendon to Ireland, 1,300 gentlemen at the Levée. Such a Drawing room as Dublin Castle has not seen for very many years. Quantities of dresses interested the girls from their knowing the wearers. The monkeys would like well to be among the bright throng. To me the whole thing is ridiculous—however, when such things are, even the wise must conform to custom; so I should not much wonder some day when times mend and years fall on, Annie, to find myself marching away under my feathers, sweeping past Lady Somebody in advance of two very happy little daughters. They have been reckoning up to me the list of their acquaintance at this drawing room, and recurring to the Court dresses of other days as worn by their Aunts when they were presented.

6. One only visitor this week, Mr. O'Connor Henchy, fresh from Levée, Drawing room and Ball! All very splendid, all very crowded, and on *tick*, for money was never scarcer. We hear dismal news from Galway, thousands dying there, it is bad enough here at Ballymore, and the

1. John MacHale was the Roman Catholic Archbishop of Tuam in Connaught from 1834 to 1881.
2. The son-in-law of the Prime Minister, Lord John Russell, had been sent on a diplomatic mission to Italy where he met Pius IX.

creatures will not enter the Poor House. Thirty-one in our fever hospital yesterday, they won't allow that they are getting well that they may not be turned out to misery so soon. We have a dismal spring before us, I fear. For lack of money ourselves we have sold our two fat Kerries, they cost £5, sold for £15, the profit must be £5 fed only five months.

I have been engrossed by an extraordinary book of that flighty Mr. Carlyle's, '*England Past and Present*', he dare not go to *future*. It is full of *truth*, full of fire. I had almost said from heaven, amidst much trash. He speaks to us words we must listen to. Class legislation is over, the times have grown beyond it, the world is meant for all, and *all will* have their share of it. I had marked many extracts for my journal but have lost my texts, for the Doctor who lent it has carried the book away to try and do good with it elsewhere, waken up some sleepers if possible.

7. The Colonel brought a young Mr. Dennis home from Church with him, son of an old Mr. Dennis near Baltinglass, nephew to the Saunders's, cousin to Mr. Tynte, Lord Aldboro' etc. He is satisfied with a place of Surveyor under the Draining Commissioners, and he came here in the place of poor Mr. Sullivan who has been taken off by typhus fever, with 100 more, 1000 more! He had been at the Levée, 1,300 people, Drawingroom 1,600, Ball 1,200, no jewels, they are gone, but handsome dresses and apparently hearts as light as if the owners were not encreasing their debts, and were surrounded by a prosperous instead of by a pauper peasantry, a dying peasantry I may say, for the sufferings of the last eighteen months are telling daily upon the miserable crowd who have been for so long struggling with privations. Begging is becoming general again. The markets are falling, corn 8/6. and will be lower. Rents indeed, shall we live, my God what a spring is before us. I hope I am in a gloomy mood and see terrours where there are only difficulties. Yet everyone who thinks wears a long face.

8. A report that the income tax is to be raised to five per cent. Ireland included. For a wise purpose we might bear

this better, but if the reason of such an additional burthen upon those nearly ruined already be to add to our too large military force, this miserable ministry should be turned adrift. All rational persons should join with all their power to prevent such a cruel encrease to our difficulties. I don't see how we in Ireland can meet it. We in Baltiboys must descend a few more pegs. Governess, carriage, hunters, are gone already. Butler and housekeeper must follow. These luxuries can be done without, and after a while we shall hardly miss them only it frets one to feel that we give up our comforts for a political folly.

10. I believe I have never mentioned [Mr. King], this addition to our neighbourhood. He is a young man very much in fashion on account of his expectations, the father a man of large fortune, brother or Uncle to Lord Erne, lives in Merrion Square.[3] This is the only son, less spoiled than one would suppose from the fuss made about him. A little, goodlooking young man with agreeable manners.

15. [Janey] is much admired both for air and beauty, very young, just beginning to educate herself, her home is happy, her prospects fair, why should she lose her best years by marrying before her judgement is sufficiently ripe to choose well. Dancing, riding, etc. suit her present age better than household cares. Annie with noble generosity enjoys her pretty sister's success, and she will have her own yet, when two years more have formed her. She is now graceful, lively, clever, very attractive to many, with a fine figure, eyes and teeth that will redeem the aristocratick nose by and bye when the complexion clears. And for abilities my own daughter Annie, there will be no lack of them.

16. Lord Shrewsbury has sent John Tuam a rejoinder; too lengthy, tiresome, but hitting still harder. The Pope has sent orders to the Bishops to put an end to these scandals among their clergy, to forbid politicks from the Altar. A meeting of dignities was held in Dublin, kept very

3. James King was to marry Annie less than two years later; his grandfather had married the eldest daughter of the first Earl of Erne in 1783.

quiet though, to consider of an answer. That good old man Archbishop Murray in the chair, who spoke his mind plainly, backed by the propaganda. Now all will go right. Give those vulgar creatures rope enough and they are sure to hang themselves. While they were as they fancied persecuted, at any rate kept down, they had their partizans to plague us. Now the well educated of their own flocks help us. How wise to bide the time.

Mr. Caw[4] confides all his affairs to me. He will be the better of making a clean breast of it for he was really brooding over his misfortunes. He has lost just half his hard earnings, and is annoyed by advances made for John and William which they cannot fully repay at present. They have each sent home more than half their debt, the rest will come, for their incomes are handsome. An idea that John is to be acting Auditor General as he was before. William has certainly been speculating disastrously, though he will not own it.

21. They have brought in the new Landlord and Tenant Bill, very cumbrous machinery. I hardly think it will work or pass without much modification. Italian revolutions progressing, Swiss over, Bavarian over, French beginning. Times not mending with us, trade of all kinds very dull. The Board of Works in a nice mess; sums embezzled by the Clerks, by the men most relied on. The three Commissioners sent over from England to take charge having been negligent in the extreme, quite inattentive to their business, signing blank cheques, looking over no books, no papers. Sir John Burgoyne and Colonel Jones are the two delinquents, Mr. Griffith having less to do with the money matters.

26. By the bye there is such an émeute in Paris. The discontent has been long encreasing, confusion in the chambers, noisy demonstrations, a press to suit, reform meetings, at last a monster reform banquet with procession prepared

4. He was a trusted confidant of the Grant family who lived at Inverdrui on the Rothiemurchus estate; his 'misfortunes' sprang from his investing in the ill-fated Union Bank of Calcutta on the advice of the Grant brothers.

which caused a concentration of troops and was just at the last prohibited. The mob rose, scenes of violence, bloodshed ensued. But the military prevailed and the report is that the agitators are annihilated. We shall see.

They are curious times, interesting, even amusing as we look on them by our own fireside. I often think when the Colonel is sleeping over the Newspaper in his easy chair, and I look round on the prettily furnished, cheerful drawing-room, with all its comforts, its bright hearth, the lamp upon the little table, the children all engaged in different ways, those children who have never yet given us one serious uneasiness, that in this world wide, a happier family party could not well be found. What are the few troubles of our quiet lot when there is such a fund to draw on for support under them. Being prudent, we have felt the money difficulties of these two bankrupt years much less than most others. We have been able to help our poorer neighbours to a greater extent in consequence, no small comfort, and if times don't mend we can cheerfully bring our habits down to meet them, conscious that no one suffers loss by or through us. I wonder, dear children, whether you will smile over our family history when you come to this record of bygone days.

29. A fine end to February. Louis Philippe de-throned, that is to say he abdicated. He went off in a *Brougham* 'tis said, escorted by a guard, where to is not yet known. The old King seems to have taken fright rather quick, he was off in a hurry. After seventy, those in authority should resign their power into stronger hands; the fireside, warm slippers, and an easy chair are best fitted to the few years of failing faculties then left them.

This news must have some effect in England where we are very nearly ready for a similar revolution. The higher classes cannot be allowed much longer to live in idleness principally from the proceeds of the labour of the middle ranks, enjoying peculiar privileges unearned by any merit. The taxes fall heavily on the working members of the community. Their large amount is necessitated by a bad system of Government. Expensive dignitaries, otherwise idlers, sinecure places preserved for the support of

Cadets of noble houses, absurd army not a quarter of it wanted for home defence, offence should be impossible, heavy colonial charges which we should do well to get quit of, by throwing off into independance most of our gigantick offsets. And added to all these extravagancies, the pride, the hauteur of this self adulating order renders them personally offensive to better men.

A great change must come. If we are wisely ruled it will be a quiet one. If we go on as we are doing it will be violent and to some of us annihilating. This income tax is making a great commotion, petitions against it from the whole island, in very strong language too. 'Tis the old story over again, a deficit of more than three millions, with nothing available to meet it. There is outcry everywhere, without and within.

THURSDAY, MARCH 2. Yesterday's news from France confirms the universality of the revolution. Every post brings in the adhesion of the provinces to the Republick. The Tuileries is turned into an asylum for indigent workpeople. All the carriages of the royal family have been burned, the horses roasted and *eaten*. The mob has been hitherto kept in order but there is no saying how long such an excitable people will bear command particularly with their democratick notions so alive.

3. The provisional Government seems to feel itself very strong. It acts with calm decision, is obeyed at once, so that order is gradually being restored. There is to be no *death* for political offences, merely degradation. If things go on in the same reasonable way, the revolution will have been effected with wonderfully little mischief. They had quite a right to depose their King if he did not govern them satisfactorily, and if tired of monarchs, as we all shall be by and bye, they choose to try a republick it is nobody's business to question their wisdom. We have happily learned by experience that our British interference with Continental politicks does no good to others and brings much evil upon ourselves. The ministers have wisely announced to both Houses that we are neither to meddle nor make with the internal arrangements of our French neighbours. So long as they let us alone we are to

let them alone. They don't like us, they have burned our Indian mails, insulted our railway labourers, attacked all English ensigns in Paris, but this is only the mob; these excesses have been severely reprehended. One good has resulted from these startling events. The detested income tax is abandoned, at least its encrease and economical measures are to be seriously pursued. To relieve us from present difficulties they talk of raising the penny postage to two pence.

10. The King of Prussia has followed England in acknowledging the Provisional Government, other Continental powers not yet declared. The new powers in France going on steadily, all affairs there as calm as if nothing more than ordinary had happened; for the present therefore all looks well. There have been serious riots in Glasgow. A meeting in Edinburgh wherein a resolution was passed by acclamation praying the Queen to dismiss her ministers and call *Mr. Cobden* to her Counsels.

12. Sunday, Very fine. All quiet here as yet. Riots in London, Manchester, Glasgow and Edinburgh, but mere mob riots, no purpose in them, nor any leaders, hungry people wanting food and there will be an encrease to their numbers for the French are sending all the thousands of English they have been for years employing in different trades, back to us. Such is mob rule. One lives in a fever these times longing for the post. The whole continent is so unsettled and we ourselves far from being at ease at home. Our Roman Catholick clergy have been most exemplary in their pastoral charges, no allusion to politicks. They dread French influence which has of late years been very inimical to a priesthood.

14. I have been expecting these few days to hear from Jane, not so much about the riots, for it was a mere mob, though in large numbers, as about the Union Bank of Calcutta. Our Indian news speaks very tartly about the management. It began with a capital of a million, seven eights of which have disappeared. All other creditors will be satisfied, but the shareholders, my two brothers among them, will receive just an eighth of what they put in. I want to know whether they will be liable to one another

or will just put up with the loss. The Directors are accused of being non-entities with the exception of two, Mr. W.P. Grant and Dwarkanouth Tagore[5] who did as they liked in defiance of other parties. Also too much money had been lent to one or two favoured Houses whose insolvency has of course ruined the Bank. I hope we see the worst and that a couple of years longer in India will enable all to make up for this. William is not a man I should like to have any dealings with—speculating, arrogant, and I am afraid selfish.

15. A long letter from my father yesterday, a disquisition upon Ireland shewing how opinions can change. A coercion bill of his framing would be effectual indeed and the only way after all of taming savages.

A visit from Lady Milltown, and her daughters, very gracious, talking *sensibly*, but a little maliciously. She feels herself and her Lord being so overlooked, so vapours a little. He has gone to join the repeal association and make a speech!

19. Lord Milltown is delighted with the exhibition he made, his speech, his reception by the motley crew, and the puff in the repeal papers. He has been busy all this week composing another oration which he will deliver to-morrow, 'and so' says Mr. Foster, 'the poor gentleman will amuse himself now that he has no money for Newmarket'. My Lady must give up Dublin after this escapade of my Lord's; the more easily as Dublin had long since given up her. She won't be missed either among the peeresses. They throng to the castle now. Unlike the Normanby days when she and the Baroness de Roebeck figured in a line a piece, unsupported.

A letter from James Gibson Craig tells me Mr. Caw will have to pay one thousand pounds to the Union Bank besides the loss of all the money which made him thus liable as a shareholder. So my brothers will not be quit for their shares only. They will have to help to make up the deficiency. Mr. Caw could have sold his share a few years ago for six thousand pounds, he will have about two

5. See 19.9.42.

hundred a year left to live on. He would have thought this riches once.

21. Janey and I went about visiting the sick. So many poor people ill, it is frightful. Old Mrs. Delany dead, a good woman, the crippled old husband still surviving but very feeble. Pat Ryan just going. The fever hospital not quite so full, only twenty-two patients, but the cases much more virulent.

26. French Government going on steadily, things more settled, yet the mob very difficult to deal with. All the powers have recognised the new republick, only one or two have made reservations. So we may hope to have got over this crisis, congratulate ourselves on a lull at any rate.

In Britain mob gatherings went on in a few towns but the mania soon passed away without any mischief, beyond a little glass breaking. A life or two at Glasgow. In our green isle the mountain brought forth not even a mouse, a crowd but no riot. St Patrick's day passed over without even the show of a meeting. One was appointed for the following Monday, last Monday, at the North Wall which did take place and several thousands of the merest rabble were harangued from a platform in a high treason style which was listened to very coldly.

The physical force section make no way that is certain and therefore I am sorry the three truly contemptible leaders have been indicted for their seditious speeches at their Hall where they figure away once a week of an evening, supported by a newspaper, the most impudent that over attempted to disturb a nation.[6] They were held to bail and then returned to their vocation to preach 'down with the Queen, a republick for ever! fraternity with France,' and every conceivable folly. They must be cracked. The 'Morals' as that rebel Paddy the gardener calls the O'Connell set, keep quite distinct from these lunaticks. Were there more talent among this faction,

6. These were Smith O'Brien, Thomas Francis Meagher and John Mitchel who had started the *United Irishman* in February 1848 openly to preach revolution.

more probity, they might be formidable, for no doubt our grievances are many and no redress to be had for them. As it is however, they only make our country more ridiculous.

SATURDAY, APRIL 1. [Sister-in-law] Henrietta's mother, Mrs. Parker is dead, from the effects of chloroform. Mr. Parker lost twenty thousand pounds by the Union Bank, and being a shareholder has a large sum to make up, by this twelve months, twenty pounds on every share, a *fifth* of the sum wanting. I am afraid to *think* of these affairs. All last week after the Mail arrived I was in a dream of misery. The Colonel and I have talked matters over so often that I am becoming more accustomed to the dishonour of my brother's name, and can hope some further explanations may remove much of the obloquy from him. Still it has been a heavy blow. The dear little girls were disappointed at not getting to Lady Blakenay's Ball, but how could I shew myself.

2. As far as I can understand those Union Bank affairs, a system of swindling expedients was entered on, which added exasperation to the irritation of the ruined creditors. Whether their claims will ever be liquidated, who can say. A Committee has been appointed which says that Mr. W.P. Grant had not dirtied his own hands, though he can't be acquitted of conniving at the misappropriation of the funds entrusted to his watchfulness by others, or at least of not knowing, as he should have done, what they were doing.

I don't believe any merchants are honest, they are a set of gamblers, very clever men of business when their speculations succeed, fools when they fail. And they could easily play upon William who is speculating himself, was trained in expedients, educated among money difficulties, without any wholesome horrour of debt, and is besides so self sufficient and so arrogant that he won't bear any interference and so sanguine that he never can believe anything he has to do with can go wrong. Such a character is easily managed where people find it worth the trouble. It is a very unfortunate business in every way. My father had money there with which he intended to pay certain debts not entered in the general schedule, luckily what he had reserved to come home with he had sent to Coutts; neither of my brothers will ever be able to leave India. They must borrow to pay up this first dividend, after which there will be four more to provide for. Was there ever such madness.

5. So busy preparing '*Pau*' for Mr. Chambers that the poor journal is out of fashion. I took up my travels again that I might have better occupation for my head than that Union Bank which there is no use in thinking of. Few incidents are happening with us. Whether the calm will last, who can say. The misery is great, the struggle is universal, the discontent wide spread. In the country parts little mischief is dreaded. The larger towns may be turbulent and God help the rabble if they rise, for the Government is in earnest. The '*United Irishman*' is mad, recommending rifle practice, giving directions for the shape of pikes, the size of muskets, the sort of bayonet necessary for the coming combats. The smiths in Dublin really are at full work night and day, but Colonel Browne, our Fouchet (sic),⁷ knows all they are at, his detective police bring him the most accurate information so that the poor fools are all in the net and will be dragged to light when the fit moment comes. French affairs look very middling, mob rule completely. Lord Normanby is leaving Paris. The rest of the Continent still in confusion; Sicily independant, Venice a republick, Warsaw in flames, some Kings abdicating, others granting liberal constitutions, and all the high powers who run away taking refuge in England.

7. Letters from many places, all with good news. My father leaves India on Monday, just twenty years after reaching it. Dublin all military and only just in time for the pike making was going on by night and by day, muskets were arriving by thousands from Birmingham, even small brass cannon, and the rifle practice was regular in many towns, a cap on a stick representing Lord Clarendon and shot

7. Chief of Police for Napoleon 1799–1810 and, somewhat unusually, for the different regimes 1814–16.

at till well riddled. The Lord Lieutenant's determination has over-awed the agitators, the unexpected answer given by the French to their ridiculous deputation has quite depressed them, in fact the rebellion has evaporated. Papers have been sent about by the Government for signature by all those who intend supporting it, the result has been entirely satisfactory. The poor law is to be revived so our grievances may in time be redressed.

9. Sunday, Mr. Lamartine made a nobly liberal reply to those three crazy men, refusing fraternity with any *section* of a kingdom he hoped to continue in strict amity with, he would never interfere in internal disputes, etc.[8] It has quite sobered the Irish whatever it may have done to the English agitators. More troops are landing, quite a fleet at Cove.

Mat Ryan has behaved so ridiculously he has lost his place. There is no helping these half cracky people, I had really thought him a sensible lad. He wrote to Baxter to say he could not return unless his wages were raised; he an apprentice, nineteen, served *one* year, learning such a trade without any premium paid. An Irishman here is glad of five shillings a week without one extra, six shillings is good wages, seven shillings great wages, a wife and family are supported on these fees, rent paid out of them. This impudent boy had six shillings, lodging, bed, fuel, milk and vegetables!

10. The day of the Monster Chartist meeting in London. It has been forbidden by proclamation but the mob is determined to assemble. The utmost precautions are being taken, troops, artillery, special constables and barricades. Mr. Butler told Mr. Foster that Lord Milltown had saved this country! Little mean sycophant; good Mr. Foster came to ask us how. There is strong speaking everywhere but as yet little acting. The French reception has sobered them. But the times are sadly unsettled.

16. Sunday, After a truly anxious week, indeed an unhappy

8. Smith O'Brien headed a delegation seeking support from the head of the provisional government, the man of letters Lamartine.

one, I will set down all in order now that we are something
recovered from the agitation of all our little trials, in hopes
at some future day of looking back upon them without
bitterness. First for publick affairs that I may get up the
steam a bit. The monster Chartist procession in London
last Monday was a failure. The Government deserves
the utmost credit for the vigour with which they have
met this first open attempt at rebellion. The petition
was announced to have been signed by two million of
'unwashed artificers'9. They should publish a list of
these humbug signatures, it would do more than anything
else to check the whole democratick monomania; throw
ridicule over anything and the game is up. Mr. Smith
O'Brien spoke republican in great style *in the House*
and was set down! properly! He will not open his lips
in a hurry again. All this has quieted Ireland. Every
precaution is taken to prevent mischief till the new law
be passed, when the authorities will be enabled to deal
so summarily with these audacious broilers that they will
soon retire either to Botany Bay or obscurity.

Having accomplished all this our Government must
then redress our real grievances, and then neither here
nor in England need we fear a revolution now, for all
the property and the greater part of the intelligence
of the country are against any discription of tumult
though a very large proportion of influential men are
determined on reforms much required in almost all
departments; many of our institutions from having stood
still in their feudal grandeur while all around them was
being liberalised and utilitised, are behind the age. We
hear that much of this will be gracefully conceded. One
very good idea for us is a National Council in Dublin to
manage all local matters while the Imperial Parliament
will still decide imperial questions. Some change there
must be, for the present system works very badly. With
the best intentions they manage very ill for us in England;
we may fail at first ourselves, but being more interested
and better informed, and feeling it all, we must improve

9. *King John* IV ii 201

in time, and we cannot do worse for ourselves than they over
the water do for us. The English Chartists are quite as
bloody minded as our confederation, violence equal to
Messrs. [Gavan] Duffy, Mitchell, etc. When people have
nothing to do and very little to eat we must forgive
their follies. And how to employ one half of our over
population these paralysed times is the question we all
ask without the hope of an answer. And this brings me
to one of the causes of this last week's distress.

[After the discovery of the attempted break-in of Col.
Smith's old camp table protected by a Bramah lock], we
sent for Mr. Darker, merely told him an attempt had
been made upon the lock of the cash drawer and bid
him go up and examine it. He came down and said a key
had been introduced which did not fit, which had been
broke in trying to turn it, which must have taken some
strength to do, that then an attempt had been made with
a carpenter's pinchers to pull out the part left in, that a
chisel and a bradawl had both been employed in various
ways and that something like the point of a penknife was
sticking in the barrel of the key. Who had been in the
house, no one, not a creature, upstairs or down but James
Ryan who had worked here all Tuesday from nine till five,
alone in the schoolroom, all of us out, the maids washing,
and George occupied below in sight of everyone.

The Colonel, Jack and I went off to Blesinton to consult
Mr. Cradock [R.I.C.] and the more it was talked over the
more suspicion rested on James Ryan. He is in the habit
of going all over the house repairing everything, no one
would be surprised to see him in any room, or coming
out of any place, he might remain any length of time
in any place without exciting the least surprise in any
of us, and this was a job which altogether must have
taken near a quarter of an hour to accomplish. He is in
the habit of walking about the house without his shoes
not to dirty the passages, so that he is never heard except
by his knocking.

We brought two of the police back with us. The
Serjeant said a tradesman's hand had done the deed,
a hand practised in the use of tools, and that the tools

used were good ones. No stranger had done the deed but one who knew the contents of the drawer, the ways of the house, had the privilege of entering my room etc. Everything tends to criminate James Ryan. He was sent for to saw out the lock, quite composed he appeared, pale, subdued, entirely silent, no surprise, but no trepidation. The investigation finished, in the evening came the Doctor to talk over the mysterious *burglary*. In every way he turned the subject, named each person who by possibility could have worked fearlessly away upstairs in my bedroom with these edge tools for a quarter of an hour without a probability of detection, their motives, objects, wants, etc, etc. And poor James Ryan stood for culprit again.

Proof we appear never likely to get. In every way we have examined the servants without a sign of guilt appearing in any of them. All suspect James Ryan. Mr. Darker suspects him, nay is sure from a knowledge of his character and his difficulties and his opportunity, and his acquaintance with the cash drawer that it can be no one else. His changed manner almost satisfied me, the Colonel also, and those who have seen him since the discovery say he is an object of pity, gone to nothing, hardly able to stand, and inattentive to anything said to him. Unfortunate man, why not ask a loan, many a time he has had one given him from that very drawer. To try such a thing with us who made his fortune, he helped to build this house, he has worked for us ever since, we trusted him, I am afraid, too much, for a man don't *begin* a career of thieving by means of a false key, it is only after many successful smaller peculations that this sort of serious felony enters his vitiated mind. It has shocked us so much, it is such a disappointment, it is such a loosening of our trustfulness in our dependants. These are wretched times, the hardship of them induces people to resort to plans they would have abhorred in better days, tradesmen especially are so unemployed they are in danger of starving; then why not ask his indulgent landlord for help, was it ever refused him.

Mr. Darker knows the poor creature to be in serious

difficulties. The other day I went to see his sick child
when he told me two strange things, one that he would
be right glad to make its coffin, that he would be glad to
make all their coffins, at their ages they would die in a
state of grace, and what was he rearing them for, sorrow
and hardship, which was all they were like to meet with,
and that if he could compass the few pounds he would
emigrate to a certainty for he was starving here! I saw
him on that suspicious Tuesday when he was so long
in setting the hearth stone in the schoolroom. I thought
him uneasy, restless, unable to look at me. He must then
have just finished his fruitless attempts first to steal our
money and then to hide that he had tried to do it. After
all is the poor creature worse '*according to his lights*' than
the talented Directors of the Calcutta Union Bank. Alas!
nothing that we hear of that sad business brings balm to
wounded feelings but in 'the deepest hell a deeper still
seems ever to be revealing'. Jane tells me all the money she
advanced to buy up Rothiemurchus debts and so enable
our brother to purchase out my father's interest, is gone
for the present. She has William's bond, that is all, his
promise he has broken for she only lent this sum, for a
certain purpose and for a certain time, long over passed.
How careless in him. He had never meant to wrong her
but delayed and so can't right her. He never meant to
wrong any one yet speculated with the money of others
and ruined himself and them.

18. The Chartist petition was introduced to the House
as weighing five ton and containing seven million of
names by Mr. Feargus O'Connor who also announced
that he had to get the assistance of four friends to
help him to carry one division of the five packets.
The proper Committee having taken charge of this
weighty document reported that it weighed not quite
five cwt. that the signatures amounted to nearly two
hundred thousand, that there were seventeen thousand
women's names among these, that there were innumerable
forged names, countless false names, many indecent and
blasphemous ditto. Several sentences of obscenity lower
than the streets and whole pages written in one hand.

The bubble has burst, no danger from such a managed affair, too low for fear. We hope this may do us some good, however pikes, rifles, blood, *republick*, repeal is too tame now, were all the rage last week among the confederates. The high and mighty leaders *talk* bigger than ever. We shall soon see the effects of the new law and of their trials. The Doctor took Jack up to Dublin with him yesterday. It is filled with troops, no danger apprehended. I went to school yesterday and must resume an active superintendance for it is not as I wish it to be, particularly as regards the infant class; all neat and clean and orderly.

Poor wretched James Ryan committing himself more and more deeply by foolish talking; having recovered from his first terrour he is now trying to prepare his defense by uttering a tissue of falsehoods, and insinuating the criminality of other parties. He came down to see Mrs. Fyfe, told her he did not know where I kept my money! that he had tools would open any lock! that this and that had been said, that never was said!—in short a melancholy making of bad worse. If I had had doubts before this would have confirmed my suspicions. Poor unhappy man.

26. Mr. Gardiner writes very amusingly about the Chartists, he was a special constable and is savage with the Duke of Wellington for giving all the credit on that memorable day to the military. He is looking forward to what will surely come, the downfall of our aristocracy, the sooner the better say I. We do not want anarchy, or mob rule, or undue influences, but we must have justice, a fair day's work for a fair day's pay. Mr. Leitch Ritchie sends me £6.6.0 for 'Hannah White' and has forgotten the *Highlander*, so I have reminded him of it. No need these times to let a penny slip honestly our own.

30. I have heard from Jane who is very anxious though resolved to hope the best . . . thank God William is weathering the storm. He had been consulting with Lord Dalhousie, [Governor-General] Sir Lawrence Peel and others about my father, so he has not lost caste. He has been negligant, even sanguine, arrogant, unscrupulous,

but not dishonest. He will recover character, he will get on, but, I feel that he is fixed in India. He is not only ruined but he has heavy debts to pay, sums that will tell hard even on his good income.

FRIDAY, MAY 5. The Doctor tells us John Lester has bought part of the Duke of Buckingham's Irish property for sixteen years purchase. This news ruins Lord Milltown and Ogle Moore, all they had to depend on for release from their difficulties, was the sale of their estates, twenty-five years purchase they had calculated on and it was the least that would have benefitted either.

14. Publick news is flat enough, Irish agitation over, Parliament very stupid, very dilatory. We want our bankrupt lands sold and they give us polling booths; we want employment for a starving people, and they extend the franchise. Matters therefore far from settled, the upper ranks blind and deaf to all that must take place if they don't go on with the times. Abroad, France seems settled, Spain and Portugal far from it, Germany in confusion, Italy worse. The Pope threatened with the loss of all his temporal, much of his spiritual power, his clergy want leave to marry, etc.

15. John Hornidge brought us the *United Irishman* yesterday, all alive again. Last week no printer would work for these madmen, they have found someone it seems to spread their treason this week. Actually asked Tom Shehan for the loan of his presses! it must have been full. A letter to the Ulster men is really full of sense however, so are the strictures upon the reports of the Agricultural instructors, full of point, of wit, of reason, sometimes false conclusions, and all done to suit his purpose, yet it would be well for our Statesmen to reflect on these articles, and on Mr. Cobden's honest prognosticks, otherwise there will be a struggle in earnest before long.

One rather grave incident in these thickening times is a Meeting of *Protestant repealers* in Dublin, tradesmen and professional men of the middle classes, calm, clear, steady men of business, thoroughly in earnest and not in the least excited. Men who six months ago treated repeal as the wildest of all crazy chimeras. There really seems to be nothing else left for us. This centralising of all things in the City of London quite at variance with the domesticity of all our institutions, making a sort of Paris of it, must have a Parisian result, sooner perhaps than all these addlepates look for. Lord Clarendon wants to get away from Ireland.

He says, a Military Lord Lieutenant is necessary, which makes *me* think their policy all wrong together; we want food, work, our own people employed in our own business, sales of bankrupt's lands to men with sufficient capital to improve them, and a better system of education for the *higher* orders than it is the custom to give them, or else let their *betters* take their places.

By the way we have had a fine business to-day with one of the lower orders. Mr. Bryan Dempsey refuses to let his farm be drained; refuses to let our gang of drainers set foot upon his fields; refuses to let the Colonel's carts cross his ground with stones from the quarry to the field on what was Cairns's land, which we are now draining. I don't know the law myself, though I do know there is a clause in the Act of Parliament especially inserted for such contumacious cases. I thought we had had a copy of the act but I could not find it; so I sent to ask Mr. Owen to come to advise me, as we could not tease the Colonel with such vexations, he would have got angry and then a coughing fit would have come on. The Doctor when he came said I had done perfectly right that the Colonel must know nothing about it till he gets better.

Tom Darker has acted very sensibly, he suspected evil last week when on telling Dempsey he should soon be with him, this half ruffian answered he should like to see when. On being told the probable day he replied with an oath that he would dare any man to cut up *his* ground, or words to that effect. On Saturday Mr. Darker went to tell him the operations would begin to-day, when he got outrageous. I don't know all he said, threatened violence, spoke most impudently, 'like a drunken blackguard', vowed he did not care, no one should touch his land, not attempt it, nor *should it stop there*; he might as well die for one thing as another and he would die for that. He

laid a sovereign no man should dig a sod on his ground
but himself. Tom Darker called two witnesses to prove
the threatening and then told him, he says calmly, that he
had done his duty in informing him of his landlord's plans
and that he had better take care he did not go beyond
his in his way of taking this, that he meant to have no
altercation with him, and so he walked away. To-day he
sent his nephew with the workmen, directing them not
to resist this madman, but to proceed to Cairns' ground
if they were prevented beginning on Dempsey's, which
of course they were and he was quite prepared to proceed
to violence had they not retired so prudently. The carts
too, our carts made no attempts to brave him; they will
draw stones from the old quarry till we have consulted a
magistrate.

Whatever may be advised for the present, my own
opinion is that the Colonel will take the opportunity of
serving a notice to quit upon this most troublesome man,
now that the feeling will be universal against him. He
would be a good riddance for his character is detestable
and I believe detested. But he is dangerous, for though
too great a coward to commit murder himself he would
hire an assassin as soon as he would a labourer. He has
no lease so that his ill got land can be taken from him
easily. Honesty is the best policy, even in a worldly view.
The seed of the righteous are indeed rarely seen begging
their bread. I can't make out what Dempsey wants or
means. He would be benefitted by this draining like the
rest of the Tenants, his land improved, himself and son
and servants and horses employed, and any little mischief
caused by cart tracks, etc, would be paid for; it seems like
a fit of frenzy.

Lady Milltown was in a gracious mood when she called
today, poor woman, her purse full. Her Lord won two
thousand five hundred pounds by bets and racing; they
are furnishing a house they have in Stephen's Green
against next winter. The girls look so happy; so do mine
with their new bonnets coming to-morrow, the Waterfall
party next day, and their kind Colonel Litchfield's generous present to them. The year of the famine on our

return from Scotland to all the difficulties here, having unfortunately spent our ready money, quite unsuspicious of the need we should have of it, the Colonel determined to borrow enough to lay in provisions, keep up a large band of labourers and aid every charitable purpose set agoing. He got two hundred pounds of Colonel Litchfield which we hoped to pay at twice in a couple of years. But 1846 was no worse than 1847, hardly as bad. We had no power to save a penny. This year looks better, still the prospect of fifty pounds to spare is distant, so we or rather *he* thought of another plan,—borrowing from Peter, the Doctor, to pay Paul, the Colonel, Peter having money he can't these times put out to use: so said, so done.

But the Colonel won't receive it, sent it back to the girls if we are too proud to take it, and in such a way that we cannot refuse him without inflicting pain. So we have put it in the funds for the *trousseaus*! bought stock for these brats, and the funds being very low they have within a few shillings of two-hundred and forty pounds stock for their two hundred. We shall repay the good Doctor by small instalments which we can manage without difficulty. He is delighted to be able to help us. What true friends we have got, kind and generous and attached to us sincerely.

31. On Friday last [the Colonel] drove us up to Cuylbeg, a private picnic, so very pleasant. The day was beautiful, the air delightful, Mr. Shehan's lodge very comfortable. We dined in his only hall, out of which all round open the small bachelour bedrooms. A good kitchen behind, attentive servants. After dinner *our* piper attended, for we are taking up a Chieftain's state, and played Quadrilles and polkas.

Mr. Owen's interview with Mr. Dempsey had a humanising effect upon that savage. Finding the law against him, all knowing as he thought he was, he submitted, ungraciously enough, announcing to his neighbours that having vindicated his *rights*, he permitted matters to proceed. We have taken care to spread the true version. Mr. Robinson will settle things on Saturday. He has also Ryan affairs to look into. Poor Pat Ryan thinking his elder son provided for as a gardener has left his bit of a farm to the only other son left alive. The mother is quite content, Jem is much like herself, good-natured and thoughtless. The grandmother, a managing body wants Mat to be master. There's another affair besides. A little orphan girl to whom old Commons owes four pounds; she can't get a penny from him and she wants an acknowledgement of the debt from him minus one pound, which she requires now, to dress herself neatly before going to Miss Gardiner as her maid. Miss Gardiner is at the head of a school again, I don't know where.

Foreign affairs very complicated. Several little risings in France, all put down; Lamartine and the moderates still in power. The Emperor of Austria fled to Innspruck in the Tyrol, some Archduke managing Vienna. Dreadful massacre at Naples, two thousand people mostly of the higher orders, men, women and children, murdered with the utmost brutality by permission of the King, who rather than grant the new constitution invited the Lazzaroni [beggars] to join the soldiery and suggested their plundering the town. The pillage lasted eight hours till put a stop to by a threat from the *French* admiral. What was the English Admiral doing, not interfering, we having had enough of *meddling* in Spain. That miserable creature Lord Palmerstown is to resign it is said. Will they all go? heaven grant it, but not a bit of them, they can't afford it having nothing to live on out of office, and no one envies their places.

I have yet our State trials to gossip about. Mr. Meagher was acquitted by one dissentient Juryman. Mr. Smith O'Brien by two. Out and out repealers with strong constitutions, Roman Catholicks too, who would not give in. Mr. Mitchell was found guilty,[9] sentenced to fourteen years transportation, carried from the dock to the steamer which immediately set sail, and he has left his native land for ever. He is consumptive and little hopes

9. The charge in the first trial was sedition; ten days later Mitchel was tried under the recently passed felony act and found guilty by a packed jury.

are entertained of a frail frame bearing up under a mind harrassed both by grief and excitation.

Janey and I were in Dublin yesterday. We went up to choose lodgings, the Doctor thinking a little change would much benefit the Colonel, the Colonel wishing to give some advantages to his children. The town was quiet, the people quite depressed by the condemnation of Mr. Mitchell and the suddenness of his immediate removal. Considering all things the verdict caused little excitement. A slight blustering among his friends within the Court, and disturbance but no rioting without. He bore his sentence manfully, retired calm, entered the van, ironed, with quiet dignity, proceeded unmoved to the steamer, and waved his hand quietly before descending to the cabin where he might relieve feelings of deeper grief than any of us can imagine.

The monomania he had yielded to being passed, the reaction must be very painful. A clever, illregulated genius, the type of his countrymen. He ran away with his wife when a girl of fifteen; made her as wild as himself, for she wrote in that newspaper some of the most seditious of the articles, and he has left her now with five children, all beggars, for a felon's property is escheated to the crown. Her furniture has not been taken from her, the printing establishment was of course despoiled, and a subscription has been made for her among the rebel crew already amounting to three hundred and fifty pounds, of which Lord Cloncurry [Lord Milltown's stepfather] contributed one hundred. Now will the movement end, or is it but the beginning of many troubles. That the country is ill ruled, much oppressed, not attended to, unjustly taxed, none of us can deny. Will the English right us. Can we Constitutionally right ourselves.

SATURDAY, JUNE 3. John Robinson arrived to-day. He did not receive his full rents although we gave them a month's law. Two or three are to pay up in a few weeks. We had a deal of business to settle. Mr. Dempsey, Redmond, Pat Ryan's farm, and the little orphan girl of the Lawlors. Only chalked out the way for so many ins and outs could not be settled in a moment. Then the draining accounts were very troublesome; such a complication of little details to be reduced into a clear summary. However, this practised man of business soon had it all in order for Tom Darker to complete. The exactness of that conscientious man is really above all praise. A *good* Irishman, or Irishwoman beats the world, as they say themselves. Of course, the same abilities which misdirected, work only evil, must ensure the best results when guided by good principles.

SUNDAY, JULY 2. We liked our three weeks in Dublin extremely and can readily believe that in a good house, properly arranged, we might live most agreeably there. At present we know few people, but many of them are of the best, through whom a more extensive acquaintance might easily be attained at no greater expense than we could afford if we let our country house. However, all this is for after consideration.

We never found our pretty country home looking better than on this return to it; John FitzPatrick makes a good under Steward, all is as neat as it used to be untidy and I think the difference between his wages and a boy's will be fully made up by the care he will take of all property. James Ryan must be employed as usual, there is no proof against him. As he is not happy we hope that by and bye he will emigrate to America from whence such cheering accounts have arrived, that many are preparing to follow the prosperous example this very season.

Amongst them is the little Smith, or rather the least of the little Smiths, Dan Byrne, and he and his decent wife take charge of Mary Lalor whom we are going to send to her Uncle. Mrs. Fyfe bought all her equipment while we were in town. I had five pounds for her and old Commons four pounds, left by her father for the purpose of fitting her out in life. We must advance Commons's money and we must lend John Byrne eight pounds to buy his brother's interest in half an acre of land; and we had four heavy bills to pay on coming home, and Dublin was not visited for nothing, so it is as well that Jane sent over her twenty-five pounds, otherwise I must have borrowed for the Edinburgh journey.

There is owing on the property about two-hundred and fifty pounds, I remember when it was one thousand, and of this Mr. Rutherfurd owes the one half, so we sent for him to bring some money. The son John, the eldest, came and talked very reasonably and will bring some on Wednesday and try to get out of debt. The times are hard on all. Pat Ryan's widow is to manage her farm till her son James is of age. I think there will be more emigrations, they are beginning to find life here is not the life a human being is made for. Dempsey and Redmond have had good lectures, whether they will keep their promises time will show.

And here enters the Doctor with *such* a scheme. He is going to give a Ball! in Kilbee's deserted house! on Wednesday, in honour of Janey!!! She is eighteen to-morrow and we had promised her a little dance, but her Papa's continued invalidism prevented it. So I do believe that this kind creature could not bear she should be disappointed.

6. All yesterday in Blesinton decorating the Doctor's rooms, arranging the supper, etc. Home to dinner, then dressed and off early to prepare all for the company. The rooms were lighted by sconces, the two dancing rooms, and there were candlesticks and lamps besides. A cloke-room with every toilette convenience and a fire; a tea-room, coffee, tea and cakes served there, and during the evening trays of lemonade, *iced* and sherry cobblers were handed about. A quadrille band from Dublin! about forty-seven people, almost all the neighbourhood and some rather distinguished beaux additional. Beautiful supper with champagne! confectionery from Dublin. Broke up at four, broad daylight. The Doctor received his company most kindly, managed all little arrangements very adroitly, and was as happy as man could be. Everybody was in good humour, all seemed determined to thoroughly enjoy the evening, all but one or two whom nobody minded.

9. Sunday, 24, York Place, Edinburgh. Before sending off to my dear Colonel all the minutiae of our journey I must make up a little lee way to prevent the poor journal from being disconnected. The day after the

Doctor's Ball, Thursday, we were very busy, packing
and otherwise preparing for our travels. Amongst other
matters we had to arrange the affairs of the Repository,
and while we were at work old Peggy amused us with
the comments of the country upon the Ball as she heard
them from those who were of the crowd that patiently
stood near the whole night gazing in at the windows.
All agreed that the politeness of the gentry in leaving
their proceedings open to the publick was deserving
of the highest of praise, it was the Doctor's good
nature they were sure, and just to be expected from
him. Some of the dances none could understand. Two
mountain men did not know what on earth the quality
were doing, whether they were dancing or just running
about divarting themselves, but there was one time that
they all ran off and huddled theirselves up in a knot
and the gentlemen divided to one part and the ladies to
another and then they met and linked and came up very
purty two and two together; not a bad description of Sir
Roger de Coverley. They could not quite make out either
what was meant by the gentlemen standing up before the
ladies and holding out their arms and the ladies ran into
them, and they took them round the waist and whirled
them all about the place, that was queer divarsion, and
so think many decent people.

It is a melancholy feeling leaving home, and we had
nothing to cheer us in our prospects, for a lowering
sky, a small steamer, and a crowd of passengers promised
anything but comfort. We shortly found too that of all
dull sailers ours was the heaviest, and while pondering
on this down came the rain, pouring unremittingly
for four hours. We sat it out on deck protected by
our own clokes and umbrellas and some additional
waterproof wraps obligingly thrown over us by some
of the gentlemen. The wind was quite in our favour,
this made our passage very smooth, but all the breezes
in the bag of Eolus could not have driven that tub across
the water; She did not reach Greenock till nearly one
o'clock.

10. Yesterday we saw my mother for a few minutes before

going to Chapel, she admired us particularly, so beautifully dressed. You were quite right, Colonel Smith, to insist on the handsome cloke and bonnet. The cloke was felt, pronounced both by milady and her maid to be the best silk, the bonnet was Parisian, the gown a beauty. Oh it was much to be wished that my sister would dress as I do, but even then she would not look so young,—so we are in great favour.

We found poor old Mr. Caw in the hall as we were going out to chapel, and he waited for our return, and ate bread and butter with the girls, gave them half a crown each to buy pins, then sent them off while he opened a very heavy heart to me. No need to say on what subject, nor what was the sort of news, the least said the best, would that I could avoid the thinking of it. Jane's loss is seven thousand pounds, Mr. Caw's five thousand, but these sums were honestly lent and invested. Other sums, from very struggling people too, were, as the owners thought, spent in the purchase of shares, but no entries have been made of them, and W.P.G. appropriated twenty-thousand pounds of the U.B. funds of which there is no account. He has been excluded from Government House, so they heard here. Mr. Caw thinks he cannot retain his situation if these reports be true. We are anxiously awaiting the next Mail. We dined at five. Miladi did very well in the fish and chicken line and remarkably well in the port wine way—three large glasses, which set her into a deep sleep during which the girls escaped and I read the last report of the Edinburgh ragged schools.

By the bye, Dr. Gillespie called, as he does daily, not a day older, he told me they had manoeuvred admirably to make that very foolish Donaldson's hospital of better use than the inconsiderate founder intended. It is endowed for the education of the children of the poor and not *excluding* any, the Committee intend always to *prefer* the deaf and dumb, for whom there is no pauper asylum. This is surely a very allowable *contrivance*. Heriot's hospital is getting out of its rules in much the same way. Their funds being much beyond their wants, they have established assistant *day* schools in almost every quarter of the town, but they have had to get an Act of Parliament to enable them to do this.

11. The girls and I went out to the musick shop in Princes Street to order the Tuner to come to the pianoforte, then into a shop to get ribbons for the girls' bonnets in lieu of those spoiled by the rain, then we went on to Moray Place to Mrs. Tytler.[10] On our way home we stopt at a chemist's for some toilette necessaries, all of which we found cheaper than in Dublin. I must tell you that Mrs. Tytler, stimulated by some of my stuff shewn to her in confidence by my mother, has begun to contribute to Chambers. An article on Indian life, a very good one, in the last part you have, is hers.

14. Friday. Yesterday I read the newspapers to my mother as usual and had just finished when Agnes Cathcart came to go with us to the Princes Street gardens. It was a very pretty sight. The fine town new and old, the Castle and the Castle rock and the beautifully laid out grounds filled with a moving crowd of well dressed people. Numbers were there whom I knew by name at least, but so altered as to be otherwise as strangers. Fat, waddling old ladies whom I remembered fairy-like girls, heading lines of daughters not half so handsome as their mothers had been. Scorbutick-faced skeletons, who were once plump and comely. Agnes and I agreed that we two had worn the best, which is satisfactory to ourselves at any rate. Some of the women were very good-looking, the *young* girls extremely pretty, all much dressed but not with the good taste of Dublin. The men are quite inferiour to our handsome Irishmen. In air and manner both sexes here are far below the Green Isle. The girls were enchanted at this admission on my part.

Mrs. Tytler spent part of the evening with my mother and me. She is very angry with William Chambers and *his Juvenile Library*, for he manages this work, originated it, and highly approves of Miss Edgeworth's rubbish

10. Anastasia, second wife of Patrick Fraser Tytler, (1791–1849), author of *The History of Scotland, Lives of the Scottish Worthies*, etc.

with which it begins. Mrs. Tytler's—'*Alfred in India*' is an attempt to give with baby life in that country some account of the ways of elder people, and William Chambers has taken out so much, put in so much, made her alter so much that she no longer knows it or cares for it, indeed considers it spoiled, but she will pocket her ten guineas. Mary Gillies is preparing the next one, and my mother wants me to write one. I used to be so successful in *telling* stories to children. Maybe when I am quiet at home again in the winter I may set about that and some more articles for the journal, which last almost pays better. These brothers have not been the least shook by the times; too prudent, too conscientious in their dealings, they returned their income at seven thousand pounds. Each brother has a beautiful house in the fashionable part of the town. One has a dozen children, the other none and *he* publishes the little books.

15. Mrs. Tytler and her daughters drank tea with us in the evening, Janey and Annie doing the entertaining in the playing and singing way, Grandmama being extremely vain of their performances. Mrs. Tytler's conversation was anything but pleasant, for she had been visiting in Fife and Perthshire, where almost every landed proprietor is bankrupt. The Lairds of Scotland really seem to be in a worse condition than our Irish Squires, and for the same reason,—a reckless extravagance one condition of which has been inattention to their affairs, a seizing on money at any cost for present necessities, shoving off the repayment to some indefinite future, shrinking from balancing accounts. Walter Campbell of Islay failed for *six hundred thousand pounds*. The House of Gibson Craigs, Dalzel and Brodie lost not one penny by him, too canny for that.

16. Sunday, and broiling. It was so hot yesterday we did not go out till quite late, just before tea when we strolled for an hour in the Queen Street gardens. These beautiful shrubberies at intervals all over the town are blessings as well as beauties, yet Edinburgh is quite *airless* at present, the first time I ever found it so. Mr. Caw was here yesterday too, I had near forgotten although I shall

not easily forget what he came to tell me. Mrs. Wynch's money, eight thousand pounds had been on my father's advice lodged in that Union Bank and she commences a prosecution against him the moment he lands. He must have implicated himself in some way in the transaction for James Craig proposes a compromise, an annuity out of his pension for the present. There is wheel within wheel and no comfort anywhere. Mr. Caw is of a gloomy cast however. I can't at all understand these complicated affairs, all I can make out is that there is little chance of much happiness for my poor father and mother during these their last days.

18. The girls and I made a call or two in this close neighbourhood, and then walked out to Shrub Hill, the very pretty Villa Tommy Thomson and his nice wife live in, surrounded by beautiful grounds. A niece from Ireland is staying with them. The three girls seized on each other by a sort of free masonry. I have not seen ours look so happy since they got here. All the world was going to the play last night. Mr. Dickens and company were to act *The Merry Wives of Windsor* and a dozen other things; full value for the raised prices—half guinea, boxes and pit, gallery three and six. All the seats but five were taken on Saturday, and none of the set good except Dickens himself who, they say, will have to end upon the stage, his extravagance has been so great, he has not a penny, spent all his gains on Champagne suppers, eating and drinking and dressing with an under set of rattling vulgarities.

My mother is beginning to feel anxious; she is really very patient, but far, far from happy, having picked up somehow, in spite of her deafness a great deal it is a pity she has heard. She is quite aware that my father dare have neither house nor furniture of his own. She would give the world to live with us *if* we did not live in Ireland, I don't think she would object to Dublin as a sacrifice, for the good of her granddaughters whom she is bent on producing at the Castle. She told me that in spite of kindness for which she ought to be grateful she hates this house and has become heartless, spiritless, in it, *submissive*. It is dull certainly, and she cannot be so much made of as she likes. Poor woman, I really grieve for her, my father's arrival, or *non arrival*, will end all her troubles. I feel for her loneliness from my own. Every hour of the day I am thinking of what you and little Jack are doing, fancying where you are, wondering how you get on, and every night I lay awake in *my own room*, every bit of its furniture before my eye, little Jack's bed where my sofa was, and his dear sleepy face and your *snore* all alive in my mind. When shall we be all together again. We are of course happy everywhere, that depends on ourselves, but *quite* happy is another thing. The girls and I work in the study here till half after twelve when I go up to my mother's breakfast, a walk and visitors occupy us after that till her five o'clock dinner. Tea at seven. The girls then go down to the pianoforte to play and sing, for it is light till after ten in this northern latitude, and this is our daily life.

19. We heard from you by the late post, and though I don't in general particularly like the plomber's bills at this present time, I am glad to hear of one as both you and Jack will be most happily occupied in that dirty business, you will not even long for us while all those pipes are arranging.

I am just thinking how right you have always been about the Orange men. At last they have to be turned to, and in spite of ill-usage they respond. Still I don't regret the trial made of equality of confidence, it must have proved to all reflecting persons that the Roman Catholick Irish are inferiour in morals, in principles, in conduct, in intelligence, and I trust that henceforward they will be left in the low estate suited to their low character, for it really endangers the country to put them on a par with their fellow subjects. The worthy will rise out of the mire, and be very easily distinguished. But that wretched priesthood should be silently kept down *or* educated.

Another subject of my thoughts is my mother,—the impossibility of keeping anybody happy who is so idle, her fingers are useless to her, she never employs them in any way, she cannot read for ever, so that her avidity for news is insatiable, and she is thus an almost intolerable burden to herself and all round her. It is quite lamentable her idleness of mind and body, for her reading is all novels, her talk all gossip, and a bit of malice in it too. A most unsatisfactory state of mind is the consequence. What a companion for my father!

Major Mair says that business with Mrs. Wynch is this:—My father and William were left by her husband *joint* Trustees, the sum was nine thousand pounds. William invested it in his abominable Bank, and they proceed against my father, the only one they can catch. He ought too in equity to pay the interest of eight thousand pounds, left in that Bank till he should remit it home for the payment of debts never brought forward by some of his creditors, Mrs. Cooper among them. What will become of them?

20. Thursday, I am beginning to be fidgetty about that ship, not a line by post yesterday. The *Hardwicke* is teak built and a heavy sailer rather, still the wind has been so fair she ought to have been in. We have unpleasant reports here of some men of consequence, nobles and others, having been discovered to be in league with the repealers, determined indeed on proceeding at a fitting time to a disunion of the Empire. I can't believe in the insurrection idea at all, think it all talk, on which our dear countrymen live. You will be glad that this failure of a Session will really give us our Sale of Estates bill as it will tend more than all the military to tranquillise the green isle. What our active idlers want is employment; *that* will give them food and likewise act as a sedative to diseased brains. We must allow that this wretched ministry has been harrassed every way, and has not after all stood the baiting badly.

20. We took a cab and drove out to Craig Crook. The drive was beautiful and the place was beautiful and our welcome was quite affectionate. Lord Jeffrey will be released from his duties in Court to-day, and we are, if possible, to go out for a long morning next week. Everybody here thinks a great deal of '*Vanity Fair*', a good and an amusing work by Mr. Thackeray, 'Titmarsh', in the Dickens style, but very inferiour.

Mr. and Mrs. Dickens and two very ungainly associates

Messrs. Lewes and Forster, were [there] on Sunday.
Mr. Dickens, handsome and pleasant but not well bred,
Mrs. Dickens very nice indeed. He has hitherto been in
the power of the booksellers, and the little they gave him
he thoughtlessly spent, but having emancipated himself
he means to reform his habits!! His gains did not *all* go
in foolish living, he has been very generous to his wife's
family, who were much in want of his assistance, and he
is besides very charitable.

22. Saturday, Why do you not give me some Irish news,
truths. Here we have the rebellion broke out, Carrick
on Suir [Tipperary] in the hands of the mob. Why
did they not shoot that priest. Districts proclaimed and
Lord John at last aroused and announcing the necessity
of Dictatorship powers for our Lord Lieutenant. There
really does seem to be some grounds for alarm.

24. Everybody here is talking of Ireland, everybody delighted
at the energy of the Government; though roused rather
late, their measures will be effectual for I can't help
clinging to my notion that the agitation is mostly all
talk, that is, that they may meet and arm and shout but
I do not myself dread their acting, beyond a stray mob or
two doing mischief. It is, however, wisdom to crush all
this wickedness in the bud. That must be the first step,
but to preserve the 'integrity of the Empire' they must
afterwards treat us more justly. 'Give our ain fish guts to
our ain sea maws' and relieve the encumbered properties.
Then when money can buy labour we shall do. Transport
a few priests also, that is essential to break the charm their
reverences fancy invincible. My mother is in a fever to get
you and Jack out of Ireland, I suppose you will be safer
there now than even before. How gallantly the Commons
responded to Lord John, carrying his measure through
all its stages by acclamation in a few minutes. The day
after to-morrow the Habeas Corpus Act is suspended
throughout Ireland.

26. Wednesday, We drove round by Duddeston (sic), Mrs.
Macpherson and the Duchess of Gordon had been sitting
with my mother. The Duchess thinks Janey like me, the
same beautiful coloured hair. We drank tea at Miss Cox's

in the very handsome house in Rutland Street, which her Uncle, the celebrated Dr. Combe[11] has left her, with ample means to keep it. I went for the purpose of meeting George Combe, the author, and his handsome and charming wife, Cecilia Siddons, the youngest child of the great actress.

Among the company was a very old friend of mine, Mr. Simpson, the *Lecturer*, the originator of the publick baths, and fifty other blessings for the labouring classes. He is so happy at the success which has attended his benevolent efforts, and he tells me that some of the Free Kirk madness is dying away, particularly the unchristian sabbath rigours to which advance in civilisation Mr. Combe's writings have mainly contributed. We had a long and very interesting conversation, for he is very educational, he was much pleased with our little girls, and gave me many hints for the advantage of my boy. As my own sentiments are very much like his, I liked his advice extremely.

I had a much longer conversation with Mr. Combe on the *mind*, the *heart*, the *intellect*, Ireland, Irish, higher orders, spread of Education, means to be adopted to raise us all to where we should be were sin no more, by sin, meaning our own departure from those laws, moral and physical which can never be broken without suffering ensuing. Effect following cause throughout nature, etc. etc. A child could have comprehended him. He will produce a moral revolution as surely as the sun ripens the harvest. I could have listened to him for a century, it was like having another sense conferred upon one, or a film removed from eyes very anxious to pierce through darkness. He is coming to call upon me and to bring me some books which may be of use to us in our poor attempts to enlighten our people. I never spent a happier evening.

29. Saturday, Such a paper full of Irish atrocities as I have been reading at breakfast quite prevented my

11. (1788–1858), he wrote much of moral philosophy, education and phrenology.

finishing my roll, I had to drink more tea! to drown my sensibilities, and when I had got to the bottom, it was actually all contradicted, turned out to be a 'base and malicious rumour' fabricated for bad purposes by a set of Liverpool confederates.

This morning has arrived a scrap of a note from [my cousin] Eliza Cottam with a fragment of a sort of novel, or novelette, the most commonplace trash that ever was penned and which I certainly will not compromise my judgement by even offering to Mr. Chambers. It may do extremely well for Miss Camilla Toulmen's *World of Fashion*, it is just like the trash she has to publish along with her own rather superiour writings. I will see if I can get a communication established between the birds of a feather.

30. Sunday, Mrs. Bell called for me after breakfast yesterday and took me to her infant school, and then to her Repository; both on such a grand scale that I felt quite humbled. My poor basket at Peggy's and my infant *class* faded almost out of recollection. Mrs. Bell, left a widow without any child of her most unhappy marriage thought herself marked out as it were for the duties she has undertaken. She has *time* to devote to them. Next, in this most charitable country she had but to mention her scheme to ensure supporters. Donations, annuities, were offered at all hands with assistants anxious as herself in all good works. I have got many hints from her, but I don't expect *help*. Our Irish ladies are too busy with themselves to bestow much thought upon their neighbours.

31. The end of July, and the *Hardwicke* apparently just as far from us as ever. It seems there have been dreadful storms in those Indian seas, quite a hurricane at the Mauritius. The *Fox* has, however, come safe in with Lord and Lady Tweeddale[12] and the wind continues westerly.

Mrs. Tytler came in to tea. She and William Chambers have not at all got on amicably, everybody says he is very troublesome to deal with, quite different from his

12. An old social and political friend of her father who was governor of Madras, 1842–8.

truly amiable and much cleverer brother, my friend Robert.

Mr. Howitt has not passed through the Bankrupt Court very creditably. He is an ill-tempered man and don't act altogether correctly. The wife is an *angel*. She bears with him, helps him, does almost all the work, has hitherto kept him up in fact, and to her he must now look for bread, as no one in future will have any dealings with him. I shall send Jack Mrs. Tytler's '*Alfred*' when it comes out to-morrow, and by the bye will you pay Jack one shilling glove money, he always gets this sum on the 1st of every month. You see I run on from one thing to another, whatever is in my head, just as if we were really talking together.

There have been a great many Chartists taken up here without causing the slightest tumult. Meetings have been held too on the Calton Hill, which although so close to us, we never heard of. I fear this rebel organisation is wider spread than we had thought of, better arranged and by cleverer heads. The north west of England is in an unsatisfactory state. Smith O'Brien quite mad. We have him here openly defying the authorities at the head of ten thousand rabble, somewhere up in the mountains; but the Lancers headed by Habeas Corpus will soon end his crazy career. I don't fancy there is any fear of Wicklow. I am very anxious to be back with you. It has done me good, this separation. I value our quiet home, our modest station, my husband's good name, and his honest principles, more than ever, and am quite confirmed in my rational inclination to seek for nothing brilliant for our daughters. Happiness is to be found only in a middle station.

Mr. Caw has heard from James Craig, to whom poor William has stooped his once haughty head and written to say, that he will receive by the *Southampton Mail*, copies of his Correspondence with the Chief Justice which has not been considered satisfactory. Some questions are to be put to him in open Court and upon his answers depends his place. He anticipates the loss of it, talks of appealing to Parliament, the Queen in Council, etc, but we know

this would avail little and will not be. The Ceylon Estate
has been pounced on and the rents of Rothiemurchus.
The few trees fit for the axe in that once fine forest,
about nine thousand pounds worth. There will remain
for William and Sally to live on the interest of her six
thousand pounds, which was luckily settled on her. Poor
dear Sally, what she will have to go through, what she
must have gone through, for her eyes have been partially
opened at length. James is in despair. Between the father
and son he is almost overcome, no daylight through the
gloom for either. Don't allude to these wretched affairs,
the poverty part of which is the least miserable. The ruin
is complete, fortune, character, station. All gone for ever.
You may suppose how welcome Mrs. Tytler was to me
as I could sit silent while she talked. I long for the mail,
yet dread its arrival. I tell the girls the truth, but I don't
dilate upon it. I tell them that the faulty education of
former times is bearing its fruit, that pride and temper
prevented their Uncle from acting uprightly and that
encreasing difficulties entangled him as he pursued his
crooked course, till ruin overtook him. He is more to
be pitied than blamed, for I can recollect his youth. An
angel could not have escaped corruption.

TUESDAY, AUGUST 1. I am actually at my desk before breakfast, having been waked by martial musick, the soldiery
I concluded, parading in honour of the Chartists, who
were to have had another of their meetings on the Calton
hill last night. When we were returning from our walk in
the nursery gardens we saw several of the Artillery quietly
moving towards the scene of folly. It has probably passed
off as others have done, without anyone hearing much
about it. Sunday night there was a great battle in the
Cowgate between the police and the navvies, but the
authorities triumphed. My band turned out to be the
musical gardeners heading a procession of their trade,
sent free by railroad to Glasgow to spend a day in the
Botanick Gardens there.

I got your nice long letter of the 29th yesterday. You
are beginning to weary in earnest, and indeed we can't
wonder, it is very dull for you all alone. Still you are better

off than we are. You have light cheerful rooms looking out on flowers, trees, meadows, river, mountains. All green and bright and lovely. We live in very gloomy rooms, in a low dull part of a city, looking out on hot pavement and deserted houses. You hear birds chirp and cattle low and scythes whetted, and we hear a few carts rattling over the stones and the eternal whistle of a rail-road, the one to Granton, the station of which is close behind York Place and has very much, I should say, lessened the value of property in it. Nothing can be imagined more incessantly annoying. I tell my mother she may rejoice in her deafness.

My first employment after breakfast yesterday was writing such a letter to Mrs. Cottam as should not only not offend her, but encourage her to continue her literary career unaided. I have no intention of doing her work. It is the family habit to sit with their hands before them and open their mouths to be fed. I delicately insinuated that she must take a great deal more pains with her compositions, that they were not suited to the Edinburgh periodical press, but might do for London. I daresay she won't be pleased. The stuff she sent me had been scribbled on without rhyme or reason, and I am quite sure she has no notion of ever requiring to take more trouble; she is just a plague.

We went out to buy a few prints for my school as patterns for the young ladies to prepare a whole series for me and then we took a hot walk, a very hot walk which I don't think did any of us any good, and we returned to a Levée my mother was holding in the Library. There were Miss Dalzel, Mrs. Macpherson, and Mrs. Gillies, all sitting in judgement on '*Alfred in India*', which Janey had run up with to my mother on our way from the shop where we had bought it, to the nursery grounds. It is extremely good. I read it between dinner and tea, and not knowing what it was as Mrs. Tytler first wrote it I am quite satisfied with it as corrected by that fidgetty William Chambers. Mrs. Gillies came in again in the evening to read us a chapter or two of a novel she is writing, also a bit of a story of humble life which she has finished. She reads remarkably well, but she writes inimitably. Wit, fun, good sense, dramatick scenes, and clever conversations, in Miss Austen's style, but more sparkling. She is not at all inclined to publish which is a pity, as so much instructive amusement is withheld from the world. My girls are too fond of the Polka, a prohibited dance among the 'unco guid' in this seat of refinement and delicacy.

This empty town is to begin to fill to-day, for the Agricultural Show. All sorts of farm produce, a promenade in the Zoological gardens, a ball, etc. I say little about all these gaieties, for I don't feel that I could enter into them, or indeed that it would be decent to appear at present in publick. The girls are by no means very keen about it all. The Scotchmen are so ugly, so heavy, so ungainly, their Irish eyes see them all askance., and the flaunting dress and the hideous dialect of the women indispose them to any acquaintance with the race. They certainly don't shew to advantage after Ireland. I have no wish to change my quarters, but there are many admirable people here, much to admire, much to copy, and were it necessary I could live very happily in Edinburgh *for a season*.

2. We went off after our singing yesterday in high spirits with Mrs. Bell to the Examination of one of the out Infant schools, belonging to Heriot's Hospital; a detail of proceedings would not interest you. The children were all of the labouring class, very creditable in appearance to the care taken of them. They went through their little exercises very nicely, the teacher is crack, Scotch for first rate, by no means equal to Miss Gardiner, but quite good enough. There were too many hymns and psalms and scripture expositions, but this suits the genus of the people.

The afternoon post brought me two letters from Jane, one full of scraps, some of which you will get, and a note marked *'private'* for me. Here are the contents in short. The Press announces William's suspension from his office by Sir Lawrence Peel, who was affected even to tears on delivering his judgement. William appeals to the Queen

in Council against this decision. William has written to
Bartle Frere to say he intends coming home to plead his
own cause, he is sending home by this mail, papers to
be printed and circulated. Mr. Caw has been here this
morning with the *Calcutta Star*, and the *Hurkaru*, both
of which I have laid before my mother. The intelligence
has had no sort of bad effect upon her. I even think the
excitement has been useful as occupation. The Scotsman
makes no allusion to this event. My sisterly affection
pleads hard for my *brother*, but my judgement and my
conscience say the *man* has erred. Alas! This mercantile
speculation jobbing has been all along pursued by all
in high position in India, uncensured till it fell on us.
Winked at till it became unfortunate. There will be a
strong phalanx of friends at home, but can they act
the conjuror's part if there have been more amiss than
judgement. I hope Counsel's opinion will be taken on
the Case before it is hazarded so publickly.

3. Thursday, I don't know when I have thought so little of
you and Jack as during these two days. What do you
think of the rebellion now? All those little man milliners
at Pim's, Captains, under tailor Colonels. Poor Smith
O'Brien must be mad. I see Wicklow is proclaimed. If
there is likely to be any disturbance near our hills you
had really better come away. I don't fear it myself, still
I am sure Redmond, Dempsey and some others are up
to any mischief, though perhaps too cowardly to aid a
failing, we may say a fallen, cause. The manner in which
the Government have pounced on their prey just in the
very nick of time is worthy of all praise. I was inclined till
this morning, to think they were making too much of the
matter, but they seem to know well what they are doing.
The disaffection we knew to be widespread, we did not
know it had been so extensively organised. Poor Smith
O'Brien spending five pounds to feed his army with bread
and milk! and routed by fifty police. It is very creditable
to that body, requiring no military aid. Really the times
are very exciting at home and abroad.

I feel a little more at ease to-day as you will see by the
subjects we are discussing together. Kind old Sir James

Gibson Craig came yesterday to see me and was closetted
with me half an hour. He had carefully read Sir Lawrence
Peel's judgement and he says that upon his own showing,
it is incorrect, the premises do not warrant the conclusion.
All here agree William could do nothing but what he has
done. If he felt his motives to have been pure there was
no other course before him. Sir James says he shews to
advantage all through this last act of the unhappy Union
Bank tragedy.

But back it all comes to my mind as so wrong from
the beginning. How could an Equity Judge have *time*
for mercantile affairs. How could a man of sense peril
a certainty for these chances. How could an honest mind
stoop to the chicanery of gambling trader's arts. No, dear
Hal, excuse it as we may, he is much to blame, and he
must suffer for it, he never can be exonerated entirely.
He has been cruelly used, made the scapegoat for a vile
crew of debtors and creditors, all alike unworthy, whose
clamour has terrified the weak Chief Justice and which
has brought ruin on him and on those quiet claimants
equally, who deserved better, for his *recorded* wish was to
work to relieve all. The other side argue that a judge must
be spotless—Alas! this is true, but it has never been yet,
and this money jobbing in India has been the invariable
practice of all hitherto. It is therefore unjust to *punish* till
the habit has been broken. Well we had some comfort.

6. Sunday, Eleven o'clock at night. All quiet in this sober
house so as we are likely to be busy to-morrow I must try
and write up my journal to-night, the history of an age it
seems to me. I was in this room on Friday between three
and four o'clock wondering whether the Irish post would
bring a letter to me when little Janey opened the door.
She was so deadly pale she startled me. 'My love' said
I 'what is the matter, what has happened.' 'Oh, Mama,
the *Hardwicke*, very bad news. Aunt Jane has come, Aunt
Jane and Uncle James, they are in the study.' I was
downstairs before the child had well finished. I knew the
whole. My poor father did recover for the first few weeks,
but he was very feeble and in the frightful storms which
overtook the ship he began again to suffer. On the 15th

of May he took to bed, on the 16th there were no hopes of him. In hopes of soon reaching the Cape they watched his remains ten days, but on the 26th were obliged to commit the body to the deep which has been a great grief to us, for in four days more the vessel made the land.

Who was to tell my mother, Jane was totally unfit, even James shirked it. I came in and kneeling down beside her took her hands. 'Mother' said I very sorrowfully, 'Jane and James have come.' 'Who have come' said she quickly. 'Jane and James' I said again clasping her hands and kissing her, 'and no one with them, and the *Hardwicke* has come.' She looked at me for one moment, such a look, paused. 'My child', she said very low and very slowly, 'I never expected him.' Old highland days came back upon her and she wept for the first time abundantly.

She will quite get over everything like grief. There will be tender recollections of young days, she will cherish his memory, she will make an idol of his name, and she may have moments of sorrow when opening his papers, and so on. But she will be very happy, and having now nothing either to hope or fear she may live for years in better health than we could ever have looked for. I am sure I thought that this would kill her, at least I thought so till I saw how she took William's ruin.

William's party is strengthening, not that anybody attempts to justify his proceedings, but they consider him to have been very unfairly, very unjustly used, singled out to appease a clamour. In his private affairs my poor father's death considerably relieves him. His life was ensured for £20,000 in behoof of certain Creditors, the last he owned to. They will now get this and the high annuity paid for it, £1400 a year, all the rent of Rothiemurchus is released. Wood can be cut to about £9,000 worth, another help. I think things look better, it will ever be a grief to me, my dear father's lonely voyage and lonely deathbed, in that solitary cabin on a stormy sea, feeble in body and depressed in mind.

We are all grateful that he has been spared the knowledge of William's unfortunate situation, spared the hearing of the suspicion against his character, the utter ruin

of his fortune. Spared the distressing scenes which were
awaiting him in London where if he even escaped a jail, he
would have found his prospects worse, much worse than
when he began his Indian toils twenty years ago. Even
his pension to be sacrificed. Were it not for the memories
of our youth we should feel less, for of course this long
separation had estranged us from our father. With me
he had kept up little connexion till quite latterly that he
renewed it in the hope of coming home.

11. The Duchess of Gordon was sitting with me half an hour
in the morning. She had seen Lord and Lady Tweeddale,
both looking so well no one could well believe they had
been six years at Madras. But what she wanted to tell me
about them was the shock it was to Lord Tweeddale to
hear of my father's death. He was absolutely silent, then
slowly uttered the word 'Rothiemurchus' in an accent of
sorrow quite from the heart. When his rough nature is
moved the feeling must be keen indeed.

12. A curious day indeed. Mrs. Tytler arriving to sit with
my mother, the girls and I went out to shop. On reaching
home, the door was opened to us by Jack! nothing ever
so much surprised me, and there was the Colonel in the
dining-room. Jane's letter could not be resisted. He left
Baltiboys yesterday morning, spent the day in Dublin,
left by the steamer at six, and reached Edinburgh to-day
at four.

Sunday the 13th. The Colonel woke so refreshed
after an uninterrupted night's rest. He had no remains
of asthma. We all went in a mournful procession to
church, the kind sisters from Riccarton sitting in another
pew, likewise in black. They came in to luncheon, and
afterwards the Colonel, his children, and I walked to the
Dean Bridge, along Queen Street, returning by Moray
Place and Heriot Row. He thinks he never saw so fine a
city. The freestone with which it is built, the plate glass
so common in the clean bright windows, the shining
knockers, numbers, I mean, and bell pulls, the white
steps, the pavement of the streets as clean as kitchen
floors, and then the views of all the beautiful surrounding
country. An American writer described Edinburgh in the

magnificent language suited to the style of his country as a 'City of palaces, seated in Paradise', and I really don't think the bombastick enthusiast was very far wrong.

17. Rain. The girls have returned from Riccarton loaded with presents. We have nothing to do but to finish packing our trunks for our journey to-morrow. We have arranged to leave this by the eleven o'clock train, as the *Ariel* leaves Glasgow at two o'clock to-morrow.

21. Monday, Baltiboys. We left Edinburgh really with regret, all of us. The girls had been happy, little Jack had been happy, and the Colonel had been well and so able to enjoy his visit. The very kind friends and the very beautiful scenery and the very clean town had made an impression on all the Irish hearts. My sound *head* had put me into good humour, besides that, after all, old scenes and old friends and one's own relations and connexions, warm an old heart long separated from family ties, though, indeed, I have seen more of my own people than many married women, having often gone over among them. Poor Jane, looking very sad accompanied us to the railway station, James too, and Mr. Caw!, who took that opportunity to empty his pockets of ever so many articles of plate, on all of which he had had the Grant crest engraved that the Smiths might know who to thank for them. We left at eleven, reached Glasgow at one, were on board and off by two, and had a pleasant two hours' steam down the Clyde to Greenock, where we remained an hour to bid adieu to fine weather, for we had a dreadful passage. Short pitching sea, wind right against us, rain all night, ports down, dead lights in, shipped some heavy seas, and were wretched, stifled with bad air, sick and miserable. Instead of landing by ten, the *Ariel*, swift as she was did not make the quay till half after three on Saturday. It was a horrid voyage, odious vulgar passengers, and a baby!

22. We reached John Robinson's office at four on Saturday very much wearied, hired a carriage and got home to tea on the only dry evening they have had here among our hills for weeks. The weather has been truly wretched, Tom Darker says, St. Swithan belying his sun-shiny day and having taken his full toll of rain during his six weeks

sway, which however, end to-day, so that we may now hope for a change that may save the rest of the harvest. The potatoes are gone as a crop, the corn much of it is mildewed and the hay partly uncut and partly lying in the swathe under all these heavy showers. The cattle are not thriving up in these mountains generally. Prospects for the winter are therefore gloomy enough, still there is time for improvement if matters don't get worse.

25. The weather clearing a little these few days, but still showery, no change for the better as far as the harvest is concerned, nor is there a turf dry enough to be carried home from the bog. Very dull, somehow, life appears to me to be just now. There has been so much suffering in it lately, and I ought not to feel so much depressed for all in our own little happy circle is happy. The downfall of an ancient house, the slur upon a noble name, grieve me more perhaps than vain things of this nature should do; nature will however prevail and a highland heart feels more than a philosophick head can altogether approve of.

28. We know not indeed what a day may bring forth. Poor dear little Janey has again broken her collar bone, and a number of enquiries have already been made about her. The humbler class of her acquaintance all coming to see after her. Many of them in a dreadful fright, news flies so rapidly, particularly ill news, and it is so invariably exaggerated. I fear my day is done, for instead of the firmness which formerly characterised me I trembled too much to be of the slightest use, and finally I fainted.

30. We were quite surprised yesterday afternoon when the door opened and Bartle Frere walked in. He had come to Dublin on business so stretched a point to look at us and seemed unfeignedly astonished at the beauty and the comfort of the place. It will be a very dull visit for him, the Colonel so asthmatick, and poor Janey laid up.

31. Bartle Frere went off this morning at seven o'clock by the coach. Good-natured, obliging creature, he amused himself without tormenting anybody, and spent a great deal of time with poor Janey, reading to her etc. But where these good Freres have lived, or how, or with

whom, or what they have read, or more puzzling still what they have managed to avoid reading or hearing, is a kind of mystery to me. Their ideas belong to the times of the Crusades, so that we who are up to the present age really cannot comprehend their undeveloped minds.

FRIDAY, SEPTEMBER 2. There was a meeting of proprietors yesterday in Blesinton to consult about alterations in the Poor Law which will render it less oppressive. Certain preliminaries were arranged and another meeting settled. We wish to have the Unions smaller that we may better know what is doing in them, the workhouses encreased so as to be within reach, which now they really are not; some industrial or reproductive labours carried on in them, and Town land rating if possible, that land properly managed may receive its due reward and land neglected bear its punishment. Sales will be forced by this means and justly.

I have been quite occupied this week back with Mr. Combe's *Constitution of Man*. How often have some of the matters he treats of occurred to me in indistinct idea. He appears in some respects a little fanciful; he does not carry me altogether into all his notions, but the system is convincing, the grand fundamental rules or laws can hardly be denied by any one in the habit of reflecting on creation. What a world of happiness would open to us, did we act accordingly.

3. William's creditors have refused him leave to quit India till his account with the Bank is adjusted. I hear he is the largest debtor, owing it, some say ninety thousand pounds, some say the half, take either, and what a tale it tells, rash presumptuous William to believe that evil doings could ever come to good. Acquitting him of all intention to defraud, what can be said of the judgement of the trader who so perils his credit, or of the honesty of the man who thus borrows money he has no possible means ever to repay. He excuses himself thus.—Had these speculations succeeded, and one year they did, for he is reported to have cleared forty thousand pounds one season by bill transactions, he would have made himself and all concerned wealthy. He never contemplated a

failure. Our family seems inclined to occupy the tongues of the world with the scandal of its affairs.

10. Had my dear, absurd brother's judgement been equal to his intellect, his early adversity would have settled his mind upon a wiser employment of his great talents. He would have steadily saved the overplus of his fine income, he would have possessed now some forty thousand pounds unincumbered, he would have succeeded our poor father on the Bench, thus securing a retiring pension; he would have returned to his beautiful home in the prime of life, and what has he sacrificed this certainty for? The chance of wealth greater than any rational man would wish for, any childless man could properly enjoy. But he is not all to blame. His education was thoroughly vicious. A spoiled childhood, a publick school, the low dissipation of college, a habit of debt, a scramble for money all round him, a very unhappy home, and the means not forthcoming to give him his profession. 'No man's enemy but his own' is the falsest axiom that ever was propounded. How much misery, to the innocent, *must* spring from the faults of their progenitors.

14. Annie and I are busy with that tiresome school. Kate O'Keefe is every way inferiour to her elder sister, keeping no order, being neither tidy nor cleanly, in the children's appearance I mean, for she is very neat herself. And she has very meagre literary acquirements. We must only watch her well till Miss Maria have finished her studies, and then send her up to be taught too, for with so many infants we must have two teachers. It is next to impossible to manage the Irish. They so soon get their heads out, they have no honest principles and they are idle, very idle. These girls have taken to dress and try to borrow money to buy lace veils. I must put a summary stop to these proceedings.

17. Sunday, It seems more than a week since my last entry in this journal and yet it is but three days. The week has been favourable to our farming operations, the hay is all safe and the corn nearly all cut, the crop of both good. I wish I could say the hay was in the haggard, but good Tom Darker progresses very slowly, he has wasted two

precious days and £2 notes in these hard times piling it all up into tramp cocks in the fields. I enjoyed the good laugh Mr. Owen had at him to-day for such old-fashioned extravagances out of which it is next to impossible to drive him and the Colonel quite chuckled when I told him of the discomfiture of this worthy old bit of obstinacy. We have had a good many visitors as usual. John and Dick, the Doctor for ever, Miss Owen and Fanny, Lady Milltown and daughters, Mr. and Mrs. Moore and a car full of babies. Lady Milltown told us her Lord has determined on taking advantage of this new act to sell a considerable part of his property—the Head rents, which the occupiers may be inclined to purchase at a higher figure than the market price. His debts, she told us, were eighty thousand pounds. I knew them to be last year one hundred and twenty. Poor woman. She told us they had dismissed all their expensive servants, had economised in every way, for they have no income but *hers* and that is heavily encumbered. I believe they have a bare fifteen hundred pounds, and what is that to a gambler. She is softening by adversity, and was altogether more rational and much less disagreeable than ordinary.

Another affair has been occupying our attention, and that is the Poor Laws, a most vexatious subject. They have been diminishing the number of relieving officers and we have lost Joe Agar and are left at the mercy of a disreputable man near Naas, against whom, however, we have sent in so strong a petition that the gentlemen seem to think the appointment cannot be confirmed.

To assist the times the rebellion has begun again, a second edition in small, a little rebellion bursting out from the Slievnamon mountains just to be crushed like the former. The first accounts were wonderfully alarming, but we did not believe them, and Mr. Owen, who has just returned from the scenes of the delirium told us to-day that 'tis a sort of guerilla thing. Outbreaks for plunder more than anything else, consisting of a few hundred desperados who rush down from the hills and retreat again, headed by a brave and bold madman, daring enough for better deeds Doheny, who has hitherto

escaped, being caught.[13] It is supposed the other outlaws
are with him. They have plenty of food being supplied
by the farmers or helping themselves, and they amuse
themselves in their fastnesses with gymnasticks after
feasting, General Doheny being celebrated for vaulting
over a number of *assess* at a bound.

19. I thought it high time to pay a visit at Russboro',
so walked there with Annie yesterday, passing John
Hornidge *unshaved*, busy grieving his reapers. We were
rapturously received, no figure having moved over that
gravel for months and months, poor wretched people.
Their tempers are worse than their circumstances and
apparently as irretrievable.

She had given way to a violent outbreak the very evening
before. Young Sussex Lennox had come from Cecil
Lawless to invite them all to a picnic at the Waterfall, which my Lord *refused*. He had got into one
of his surly humours and certainly by her account
behaved rudely to everybody. At last my Lady began,
and stopt neither by prudence nor decency. She before
his children and their cousin displayed his character
in all its deformity before him, accused him of every
vice, upbraided him with having ruined her and them,
not only in fortune but in happiness, that she had
borne too much, would bear no more. Her girls should
not be inclosed behind those hateful walls because of
pride his birth and poverty gave him no title to, etc.
etc.

They have not spoken since, they look miserable, they
will but make all worse by such indecorums. He, cold,
selfish, unscrupulous had the advantage of a cool manner
which in the end of these quarrels ensures him the victory.
She is merely mad and very vulgarly ignorant. I pity the
children from my heart, and am always relieved to think
that I have been the means of benefitting them all through
by indirect advice to their strange mother, on which she

13. But he escaped again and reached America, where he
    was joined by John Mitchel after his escape from Van
    Diemen's Land.

has frequently acted, and by securing them three or four years of Miss Clerk.

We were in the beautiful grounds, so neglected, in the gardens where no one takes pleasure, in the *new* hot-house only valued for its grapes, and in the kitchens, which now being nearly empty, are in good order. They have few house servants left, but the stables are still crowded. It all looks very miserable.

21. The Island of Islay to be sold with all dependencies. What Walter Campbell's other property is worth I know not, but this island containing between four and five-hundred square miles, has a rental of near twenty thousand a year, rent to the crown not quite five-hundred pounds, other charges about one thousand pounds. In fact eighteen thousand a year clear and a little kingdom of riches and beauty. Lost, no one can tell how, in the merest follies, ostentatious hospitalities, squandering for low popularity hunting, nothing really tending to good ever attempted by that piece of weak vanity whose debts amount to half a million! if we except the building of his handsome house and a large staff of servants. Stowe is not emptied yet. What treasures it contained. The Rembrandts have sold well but not as such pictures used to sell. The cellar was not large, the costly furniture went beneath its value, the plate, such as displayed much workmanship, went off at great prices. Many a downfall will follow this beginning. The order is rotten, it is time it were like other worldly things swept away, its elements dispersed to form new combinations.

23. Lady Milltown and all her children here yesterday. The quarrel is made up. She is, however, aware that he has dissipated the entire of his own fine fortune and the greater part of hers and a sort of calm disdain of him has taken possession of her. There is no excusing him, so I don't try it. I limit my small modicum of advice to making the best of it. Adversity is improving her a little. She really bears the want of money, the want of company, the want of change, much better than could have been expected.

26. We had that little silly Mr. King here yesterday. I was very

glad to see him, and having carried him in to the Colonel, pursued my walk with the girls. My Colonel is better but not well. Burgage is in the market, and he seems to me to have very much set his heart upon purchasing it. We have tabled over the scheme, and to me it seems a bad one, but I have no business head. Had we the money ready it might do all very well, but to borrow the money leaves a very small profit out of rents not altogether secure while a large head rent must be always ready. He will, I hope, consult a lawyer before thus encumbering himself with what may prove an annoyance. At our age we want repose. Work and speculations are for the young.

27. This evening our kind brother-in-law, good Mr. Gardiner, goes down to Southampton to receive William and Sally, who are expected to arrive to-morrow or next day, the overland being due to-morrow. He has arranged to bring them back with him to Twickenham, from whence William can easily manage all his business in town. May God help him, for I fear man won't and he has been cruelly used.

The Doctor came to us yesterday evening. He had been walking about all the morning with Lady Downshire. She quite delighted him, getting over stiles, jumping ditches, facing the hills in her plain shawl and good thick boots. These rational characters being new to Ireland.

Doheny has escaped to France. The Mail says that all documents relating to these trials have been sent over to the home office, so many mistakes were made on the former ones, and that a sound English lawyer is here watching the Attorney General. A papist and a repealer and an ill-tempered stupid man should not have been raised to such an appointment. Why are they afraid to dismiss a creature they have no confidence in.

29. The Indian papers say that a meeting of the shareholders of that abominable Bank took place on the 7th of August, for the purpose of determining whether William should be placed under arrest, or permitted to leave the country. Mercifully and *wisely* they allowed him to return home, he having made over the whole of his property to the Bank. His house and furniture in Calcutta, his coffee plantation

in Ceylon, which *may* retrieve all, if well managed, and of course the rents of Rothiemurchus whenever the claims already on it are paid up. He therefore returns penniless.

His debt to the Bank is published in the same paper—seventy-two thousand pounds. This is the fatal point; how could he incur it, for what, except the Ceylon property about which we know nothing, there is nothing to show for it, but that absurd wall of such enormous extent over the mountains and round the woods of Rothiemurchus. Well! he must apply himself to some honest way of earning his bread, since he can borrow no more money with which to speculate. He is very clever, very active, very plausible, and possesses indomitable energy in carrying through the pursuit of the moment. Sally has three-hundred pounds a year, and he must learn to live on it. Abandon his extravagant habits and try to come out of all this misery a better man.

Lady Downshire was not at home when we called. She spends the whole day out of doors, riding, driving, walking, alternately, in all weathers. To-morrow Mr. Armstrong gives a déjeuner at Kippure after a grand ceremony—the laying of the first stone of a bridge over the Liffey, near a dangerous ford where many have been drowned. I hesitated about going, as to me my own self, it is at this moment really painful to have to go anywhere, among strangers particularly, but as none of them will go without me, a mistake I think, and very far from a kindness, I must bear it as best I may, for the sake of the dear girls who expect so much pleasure in this friendly gathering.

Well! we really had a day of it, forty people besides *mob* assembled at the ford. Lady Downshire laid the stone, presented with a silver trowel on a silk cushion by Mr. Armstrong; hurrahs quite deafening, then four horns played *God save the Queen*, then Mr. Armstrong read a speech, more hurrahs. Lord Downshire replied. Horns played *See the Conquering Hero*. Ten gentlemen were each presented with red and blue cockades, thus constituted Stewards, to keep order. Then all the carriages drove to

Kippure. Horns played the *March in Figaro* and *Away to the Mountain's Brow*. Sheep well belled met us on the lawn. Arrived at the door, horns played *Home sweet home*. A longish interval of conversation, then the banquet, very well got up indeed, hot and cold, stout and sweet, fruit, flowers, champaign. My Lord handed me to the left of our host, my Lady being on his right. We had a good song, retired to the drawing-room, several good songs, coffee, tea, and then adjourned to the Barn where all, high and low mixed in the *Social dance*, as it will be put in the newspapers where we expect to see a flaming paragraph composed by Mr. Armstrong himself; he always puts himself and his doings in the papers.

WEDNESDAY, OCTOBER 3rd. On Sunday we all went to Church which was full, of course, for the Marquis and all the female part of the congregation very smart. We went in to the Owens and had a pleasant half hour with those really nice people. I begged of Lady Downshire not to think of calling on me as I was far too rational to expect it and she thanked me cordially but for all that they came, between four and five o'clock having also been at Rusboro'; they put off going there till the last, purposely, and Miss Owen would not go in, though poor Lady Milltown went all down those long steps in the rain to invite her. She then made a world of apologies for *not knowing* Mr. Owen had a sister residing with him, would do herself the pleasure of calling on her directly, etc., etc. Still there sat Miss Owen in the car. We talked this and many another amusing incident over, and then Lady Downshire said she should like to build a cottage in the Park and come here every summer for a month or two. What good they would do, for they go everywhere, look after everything, see everyone. They are truly rational people full of kind feelings and totally without affectation. She is not handsome though tall and graceful, but she grows very pretty when she is talking. We have really the elements of a most agreeable society in this little neighbourhood and somehow or other neglect to cultivate it; not *we* indeed—we did our best to bring our circle together—but it seems to be impossible to make them sociable—all so very much occupied with themselves, they quite fail towards others.

4. The English Chartist leaders are transported for life. Our treason trials are a bad concern. The Government have determined to cushion the charges against the priests; this causes gaps in the evidence, suppression of papers, etc., all of which is thoroughly scandalous besides being a great mistake, timid policy never answering. Mr. Whiteside takes abundant advantage of all these errours and will, they say, save his client Smith O'Brien. It is a pitiable business, turns these partial arraignments into a farce and will make our insolent priesthood rampant with a vengeance and keep the poor peasantry still more under their bigotted rule.

10. A long respite to the journal. We have been so very busy at home and so much has happened abroad, that I had no time to set about writing down all the quantity there was to say. Smith O'Brien found guilty but very strongly recommended to mercy. He has indeed been the poor dupe of his overweening vanity—the stalking horse put forward and deserted by the real conspirators, and the whole movement appears to have been aided by the Government for the purpose of making sufficient stir to keep themselves in their places. Spies and detectives urged matters on and then at the fit moment gave the word to pounce on the fools they were humbugging. The evidence against the priests is kept back because it would interfere with the intention of paying them as clergy. Already a great outcry is raised in England about this.

11. Smith O'Brien sentenced—the traitor's death. He exhibited the peculiar calmness of insanity repeating his conviction of having acted a patriot's part, while all else were overcome with emotion. Poor Smith O'Brien—he is a noble goose, and he will suffer while the priests, Hughes, McDermott, Machale, Crotty, etc. and the Chief Justice Pigott's son with many others go scot free. Whiteside did not conduct the defence well. It was a sort of Old Bailey insolence instead of high ground. The Jury have behaved throughout admirably, so has Judge Moore; there are many more to try. Horrid times. What idiots these men

were to believe that with such means they could subvert
an empire, to trust to a Roman Catholick people and their
priests, wretches who backed out in time whenever they
began to be frightened.

We have our hagard so full—an enormous hayrick and
there will be a second. Eleven large stacks of oats. Our fat
kerries are well sold so I hope we shall do for the winter
gloomy as it threatens to be. They talk of equalising the
poors rates, making all Ireland pay for all Ireland. Why
not all England too? If they won't help us let them leave
us alone, let us manage ourselves. It will have to come
to that. I think so—I that used to laugh to scorn the
word repeal. They use us so abominably. They now do
this—they strike a rate—so many can't pay, so they strike
another and so on again and again retaxing for ever the few
who have money or honesty, till ruin overtakes all.

12. I am really at a loss how to manage matters in this strange
country. I rang the bell to order a certain number of
bottles to be packed to go in the cart to-night to Hanna.
No one answered which always makes me angry. Just
as I was on the point of ringing again Janey entered
rather excited to say she had just seen George and Pat
mounted on the two young horses leave the yard at a
good trot, cracking their whips and laughing, on their
way to join the cub hunt at the Covert above on the
hill. I sent for Mr. Darker; he was on the hill too.
All the people on the stacks standing idle. I sent for
the three: two only have come—Pat full of excuses but
humble, George a little insolent. This is all found out
to-day but I am led to believe that such sort of things
not unfrequently happens. Idleness, artifice, chicanery,
of one sort or another going on in all departments. I have
so very often and for so long a time found any alterations
in these respects impossible that I have entirely given up
all interference—living more as a visitor here than as the
mistress, but I should think when it comes to hunting
with the young horses some notice must be taken of such
proceedings. We may not get better servants by parting
with these but we can hardly get much worse and the
punishment in these miserable times may frighten the

rest into more propriety for a while. The very moment any of these people get comfortable they lose their senses. It does not do to be always on the watch for errours but a little stricter discipline than is practised here is very desirable.

13. My mind is certainly beginning to feel all the years it has been exercised; it is four or five days since I heard from Jane that her niece Annie Hay Mackenzie is engaged to be married to the Marquis of Stafford, the eldest son of the Duke of Sutherland who with his still beautiful Duchess made all the advances. The Gibson Craig side are delighted. They are fond of rank and are charmed at being thus allied to it. The Sutherland fortune is immense already—a hundred and fifty thousand a year or so. There is an immense family to be provided for out of it however and there are incumbrances—so there are on the lands of Cromartie. How can people get into debt with such incomes? Our poor Irish hundreds! How pitiful they appear beside these princely revenues; yet we are very happy in our little way, and what more is wanting. Yet I do think it would be better if fortunes were a little more equalised—none so very large—none a mere subsistence. Perhaps a sort of moral understanding may grow upon the world as its wisdom progresses which will induce these large accumulator*ees* after a certain handsome proportion has been ensured to the future head of the house, to divide the rest among the younger sons in perpetuity, not leave them as they do now, either beggars, or quarter them upon the country as soldiers, placemen, etc. A sort of medium between our over wealthy few and the French absurd equality for all men. Certainly we want some setting in order all through all conditions, for take us generally we are in a wofully bad way at present, most of us.

19. We are to have a hard winter and no fuel in the country; so much rain during the summer prevented any turf being dried or much being cut. The people are also beginning to look very ragged, they have bought no new clothes since the potatoes failed all their scanty earnings being required for food; the children are half naked. We must

do something for those who come to school—it is pitiable to see them.

A curious letter from Mr. Doheny from Paris where he is safely arrived telling in very plain language, although a Roman Catholick, that the defection of the priests caused the ruin of their cause. He felt it useless to prosecute the revolution with such influence against him, and he would not have proceeded so far had not this same influence been with him up to a particular moment.

All this painful business adds to the gloom of this miserable season. The Poor Houses are already filling, many taking shelter there who paid their rates last year. Some farmers with capital left are emigrating. All the South and West is, so to speak, left untitled—preparing the proprietors for the Poor House.

A pleasant scene has just taken place in Scotland. The Duchess of Sutherland summoned in all haste to the deathbed of her father Lord Carlisle reached Perth from Dunrobin on a *Sunday* and was refused permission by the railway clerk to seat herself in one of the empty carriages in the mail train. The pious Directors don't allow of any *passenger* traffick on the Sabbath. Has not Christianity yet to be taught? And are not these unco'guid Scotch very very far from having the faintest idea of its charity. Works of 'necessity and mercy' the most furious Calvinists of old considered cases of equal exception to their rigid rules as were David's shew bread[14] and the disciples' ears of corn. This madness outrages decency. It may do good—open the eyes of these arrogant bigots who fancy themselves alone to understand the way to heaven.

25. Lady Milltown has gone up with her Lord to raise fifteen hundred pounds; foolish, foolish woman—so much the nearer to beggary; he took to bed till she consented, put a warming plaister on his stomach and had the Doctor daily; she will pay ten per cent for this, and then the ensurance on her life besides. And nothing *can* save

14. These are the twelve loaves placed every sabbath by the altar and eaten at the end of the week by the priests alone.

him, and she is ruining herself, the only stay of the poor children.

Our Treason trials are not quite over. A writ of errour is to be moved unless the Attorney General refuses it. A nice way the Government will be in should the result be an acquittal of the prisoners. Lord Clarendon has completely lost himself by these late proceedings; he has hardly a supporter left as far as we can hear.

30. Bartle Frere told us that in his late journey in the South of Ireland the beauty of the country generally, and the perfection of a few isolated spots where good landlords had created a little paradise contrasted painfully with the desolation of the scenes en masse. This season too very little cultivation is going forward; the peasantry are either in the poorhouse or gone to America; the farmers ditto; the proprietors ruined. It was quite melancholy to look on. The poor law is partly in fault but by no means entirely; the potato failure is the determining cause, but the character of the people is at the bottom of the distress.

What then can we say of English rule which has been over us for so many centuries and still leaves us so very far behind in the race of civilization. Cousin Bartle thinks that with the present style of population little good can be effected. We must have a new description of upper ranks who will be better models for those below them. The destruction by poverty and famine of the present generation is therefore a good feature in our deplorable case; the numbers will be thinned and the orders replaced in the gross by better men.

In the steamboat and railway carriage he had Mr. Whiteside[15] for a companion and found him very pleasant. This clever Irish barrister has written a very lively book of travels in Italy where he saw the Pope and I hear hit upon his character well. His liberalism was all a mistake—led to where he had no notion of going for he is every inch

15. James Whiteside (1804–1876), who defended Smith O'Brien, was later Lord Chief Justice of Ireland 1866; his *Italy in the Nineteenth Century* was published in three volumes in 1848.

a high Churchman and meant to consolidate the power of his priestcraft by basing it on the love and strength of the people. He objects to our Irish Colleges; they will probably get on without his sanction; how pitiful of us to bend before him as we did. The old wife in the hills is right. We do indeed want a Cromwell.

31. The Doctor brought us very good news from Mr. Lynch who was told by one of the Poor Law Commissioners that it was decided to separate *us* from Naas, to separate *him* from Baltinglas, and to join *him* to *us*: a charming union. All interconnected, all lying along together, no part too distant to be superintended, and no great amount of pauperism in the district. I only hope it may be true. It would greatly relieve us. We deserve to be allowed to remain as we have made ourselves, independant and comfortable. We have spent much time and much money and much energy in faithfully doing our duty among our own people, all of us, and it is certainly only fair to let us benefit by it; it was very unfair to swamp us with the neglected districts of our neighbours. We can have our own Poor House and superintend it; make our own wise rules and so support none in idleness. It really takes a weight off the mind.

The farce at Clonmel is over. The prisoners made very fine addresses—fit for any stage. Mr. Meagher in particular was quite eloquent, talking of his young life, etc. knowing well it was in no danger, strutted in gallant style. Meanwhile the Writ of Errour issues; all are transferred to Dublin to await the result; if unfavourable there is an appeal to the House of Lords—a second edition of O'Connell's acquittal. In Mr. Duffy's case the bungling has been greater. I believe he can't be tried at all on the present proceedings. Was there ever such a set of nincompoops. As there was no rebellion but of the government's own hatching no one can find fault with their using the giants they have themselves made as it best pleases them. But to keep us all for months in such a worry, and saddle us with such thousands of troops and encreased constabulary is really utterly abominable. As

we bear our burthen why not load us? But will there be
an end of discontent?

The kind Doctor has undertaken to get Pat Hyland into
the police upon the 1st of January if in the meanwhile he
learn to write, and read writing, currently. This saves my
authority and advances the lad. When arranging this, and
a master and mistress and chaplain for our Poor House
that is to be, Annie asked whether this was what was
called jobbing in other places! 'Exactly, Annie,' replied
I, 'when persons unfit for the situations are thus through
interest placed in them.' Very ready in Annie, and very
ready indeed in Mama, and it is just the truth. Interest
would get Pat into the police without insisting on his
writing or any other qualities. And till these base doings
are given over we need never expect the world to go
on rightly, however earnestly we all devote ourselves to
improve it.

SUNDAY, NOVEMBER 12. The weather continues unpropitious;
very cold winds, quite preventing the Colonel from
stirring out and the ground is too wet for the plough,
yet there is hardly any sickness in the country even
amongst the poor, a singular thing at this season with
little food and no fire. Driving about, the many unroofed
cabins give additional desolation to the wet and dirty
lanes. The moment the Poor House receives the inmates
the wretched dwelling is destroyed so that a return is
impossible; quantities are still even at this season going
off to America, many of them with plenty of money in
their pockets! And we miss them not. This winter will
surely make some room.

19. Ogle Moore called on Thursday to consult about our
poor law memorial. A deputation went up yesterday
by appointment to have an interview with the Commissioners. Ogle Moore, Mr. Armstrong, Mr. Finnemor,
Mr. Owen, Richard Hornidge. I am sure I hope some
good will come of this for we may all be ruined if things
go on as they are doing.

It is the intention of the Government to root out the
present proprietors of the soil en masse. They wish to
finish them; perhaps they are not wrong, for as a class

they have failed altogether to do their duty, but why crush the few righteous with the many erring? The English capitalists are waiting till the glut in the market still further reduces the value of land; it can now be had for fifteen or sixteen years' purchase; they expect it to fall to twelve. This will annihilate our present aristocracy. Those of us who can struggle through will in time rise from the ashes fresh and vigorous, but how few there will be and how much must we first suffer. I think Mr. Moore is more dispirited than need be because his own affairs are in such a desperate condition. Still we must all prepare to look the evil in the face that penury may not overtake us unawares. *We* have no debt to speak of. We have a fair stock and horses sufficient to cultivate more land than we now have in our own hands, and three hundred a year good from the E.I. Company, so that I cannot see *want* before us. A reduced style of living may be requisite and what the worse shall we be of that? Many parts of the country are quite deserted—inhabitants all emigrated or in the Poor Houses, none left to till the ground and the landlords totally ruined are without capital to manage it themselves; without skill either maybe, or energy or will or all together. Certainly nothing of all this is to be seen here. I cannot help thinking there is much exaggeration in these reports.

22. The Doctor gave us half an hour yesterday just after arriving from Kilkenny before returning to dine with Mr. Owen. He gives a melancholy account of the neighbourhood of his brother-in-law's mills; the gentry all 'cleared out' as he terms it, farms given up, gentry off no one knows where without a penny; farmers to America with several years rents in their pockets; peasantry unemployed and ripe for anything. Mr. Lester never walks out unattended and both he and his companion carry their pistols in their hands ready locked. The desolation is awful, but when these bankrupt lands are sold, will not industry and capital set all to rights.

30. I don't know when I have been so long without entering the various events of our quiet lives in this journal—just because there was so much to put in it. To-night however

none of these interesting particulars can be set down
for it is late and my Colonel being well has resumed
his place in this charming room of mine and as he
is already in bed I must not keep the light burning.
But alas! November is ending very sadly. The whole
Continent in a turmoil—battles and murders and flights
and ruin—in almost every country in Europe. At home,
though we are spared these horrours, discontent is very
general, misery is very wide-spread, and the weather is
dreadful. Sickness has laid a heavy hand on Great Britain
and the Doctor fears it is beginning here. We wanted but
this to complete our wretchedness. The Poor Houses are
chokefull and there never were more poor abroad; the
rates are becoming heavier without lessening the destitution of the lower orders while they reduce to the verge of
want every class above. A pestilence must overtake us.

SUNDAY, DECEMBER 3. John Robinson has arrived, having
given the tenants extra time, more on his own account
than theirs, for I hear they are to pay well. I hope so,
for by a statement the Colonel and I made out we get
of *profit* from our landed property but one hundred
and twenty pounds; last year owing to backward rents
but forty-eight. This however clears all outlay even to
workmen's and outside servants' wages, leaving us our
farm of one hundred and twenty acres to support the
house-hold, the stable and the stock, and then we have
three hundred and twenty clear, of pay, besides the
occasional sale of a horse and my scribblings. As John
Robinson says who is so well off in these times; he
feels sure there is not such another *well to do* property
in Ireland; it is very small and we live on it.

Foreign affairs are very bad—murder after murder
everywhere. Poor M. de Rossi![16] We knew his brother
at Pau. Master of the fox hounds there! The Pope was
besieged in his palace and has fled. All the potentates
are flying about in distraction. At home here in Ireland
nothing is to be seen or heard of but wretchedness.

8. We have got our third drainage loan without the Surveyor

16. The murdered Chief Minister of Pius IX.

thinking it necessary to look after us; they deduct eight pounds odd however for expenses. Mrs. Doyle came here on Saturday last with her tale of destitution which I can well believe is entire seeing that she has five children at home and a cripple for a husband, an incurable; she is blind herself and her only grown up daughter hopelessly lazy. I told her we could not help her nor the farmers either; she must go to the Poor House towards which this little estate pays ninety-six pounds a year and sends hitherto no paupers to it. One old asthmatick woman receives a shilling a week outdoor relief and that is all we get for the large sum we give. She told me they would take no more into the Poor House, it was full. The Colonel rode into Blesinton, got her an order, hired a cart to convey them, and they set on the carter to beat him and would not hear of the Poor House. As they can't earn and won't starve they will steal waiting an answer they have a hope of from the son in America, whose industry they are willing to tax for the support of their own idleness and meanness, for their low feelings and unprincipled selfishness prevent their seeing how utterly depraved is such conduct. I will not sanction such want of principles and have forbidden her applying again here. At the same time I hate the Poor House. A sink of vice: idleness finishing to corrupt the miserable inmates; but when people have brought themselves down to it, they must put up with it. I begin to think a pestilence in this darkened land would be a mercy to it.

12. A Sligo steamer bound for Liverpool put into Derry from stress of weather and landed seventy-two corpses. The crew had shut down the hatches on the miserable steerage passengers, all emigrants bound for America, and suffocated half of them. Captain, etc. are in jail. Murder after murder in England. Pope fled to Naples. Emperor of Austria abdicated in favour of his nephew. A thousand emigrants per day still leaving our Irish ports, most of them with money. The runaway farmers have learned the trick of thrashing out their corn by night, leaving the straw neatly cocked, selling off stock and furniture and bolting, with heavy arrears due to the ruined landlords.

15. Unceasing storms. Probably the wind saves us from a pestilence as the air is particularly mild and so loaded with moisture as to be very oppressive. I have been quite unwell these few weeks. Can no way keep myself up. I get plenty of letters but somehow they are stupid. I fancy it is myself that am stupid. Our family distresses, our pecuniary difficulties, the worry of all their tempers, reach on my nervous temperament, but I must recall my philosophy and not allow these things to discompose me.

    The servants are all on good terms again. Comfort unspeakable; really while the two heads were at daggers' drawn there was no living in the house with them. They have both such irritable dispositions. He is idle and vulgarly impudent; she uncompromising and jealous; however at present all is harmony. Tom Darker has arranged some further economies—very necessary. Pat and the hunter will save between them forty pounds good. Soubahdar went for thirty pounds only, and was worth double, but on the day he was sold four hundred horses were entered, and five were bought, and Lord Milltown has been offering Russy's hunter for twelve pounds.

20. Received yesterday from Mr. Ritchie fifteen pounds for my five *Pau* papers and for Mrs. Cottam's *Anecdote* £1. 11. 6. Poor pay, after all, for there was a deal of work in them—at least as I write—really carefully.

23. A most curious letter from the Secretaries of the Education Board calling attention to the want of requisites in our schools, after all the correspondence on the subject closed above a month ago when at last I received the supplies I had demanded in September. Didn't I give them a pinch of pepper in reply. Some clerks must get through a sort of routine in these offices and the well paid Secretaries trouble themselves very little about the business.

31. The end of 1848. Were I in a moralising mood what a *pamphlet* could I write of all the deeds and doings and feelings and changes of this most eventful year. But I am indisposed for any mental exertion—overcome probably by the weight of materials, for there never were more teeming times.

NINE

1849

Against a background of the Famine continuing to
hurt all social classes, this year traces the continued
downfall of the two Blessington landed families most
grievously affected, the Milltowns and the Ogle Moores.
Their disgrace, and the equally desperate situation of
her brother William, do not exclude all the regular
happenings of a busy neighbourhood much enlivened
by the visits of the Downshires. Life goes on.

MONDAY, JANUARY 8. I don't see that the misery of the
country is at all encreasing, it is only spreading. None
of the lower orders need suffer for an hour, the Poor
House is open. They bear a great deal before they will go
there, hunger alone drives them into it, so that those who
are out however wretched they may look are not as yet in
want of food. The upper classes are now suffering, the
farmer class a good deal, the landlord class a great deal.
Every day we hear of the ruin of additional families, of
course among those who had been improvident, either
themselves or their ancestors, yet who managed to live
and let live till these unjust poor laws came to overwhelm
them. That *we* have so far escaped is owing entirely to the
Honorable East India Company's pay, small though it
be, for the little property having but a debt of £1,000 upon
it would yield but a bare £100 a year for the support of its
owner after all the charges on it were paid unless we were
to dismiss all the servants and labourers. We are tight
enough as it is and must try and lessen our expenditure
still. One labourer the Colonel has dismissed and he has
only a helper in the stables at labourer's wages, Pat having
accepted the reduced situation till the 1st of March when
he goes into the police. We shall also try and sell another
young horse, their keep is very costly.

14. A social revolution is inevitable. I agree with Mr. Cobden[1] and heartily wish him and all like honest reformers success, the Aristocratick element unduly preponderates in the constitution and must give place to an infusion of healthy democracy, to set the machine on its balance again. What are the Lords but feudal Barons? What are the Commons but their kith and kin? What are the Army and the Navy in their extravagant extent and most costly arrangement but provisions for their Cadets? What are the Colonies but refuges for their castaways, the church but an opprobrium on our Christian profession? And for all these idle supercilious ignoramus's the working publick is taxed, heavily taxed, not in their superfluities, in their luxuries, but in the very necessaries of life. Matters cannot go on thus. There is too much *power* in the middle classes, the real strength of the state, to endure longer such misgovernment.

The Californian gold is filling the world with wonder. The most dreadful crimes are already being committed on that plague spot of the earth, all rational industry is abandoned, a crew of wretches cover the surface of this extraordinary treasury most of whom spend in the vilest excesses their easily earned riches. It is supposed the quantity of the ore is so enormous that it may in a year or two affect the money market. I am sure I hope nothing may happen to throw us back into the despondency we are just beginning to recover from. Trade is reviving, this will re-act on the land, and if we can get rid of some taxes we may breathe again even in Ireland, for our numbers are thinning, there will not be so many poor to provision another year. They say there will be still fewer to provision them as the farmers are all emigrating, leaving wide tracts of land untilled. Well we must hope, despair won't mend matters.

My last paper on Pau reads very well, it is clipt but not injured by the editorial pencil, and I must write on. We

1. Richard Cobden (1804–65), founder of the Anti-Corn-Law-League; she had become very sympathetic towards his views on society.

are living now upon that £15, not another penny in the house can there be till the pay comes in February. I had to refuse Mr. Darker any help to pay his wages yesterday, he must learn to feel that his farm employs too many, the labour on it and his own salary quite absorb the profits, that and the stable, it is not the house, yet the house I would willingly remodel and now that I am stronger take any amount of trouble myself, provided suitable retrenchments are carried through in other departments. A woman's candle end savings are worth little and they frequently destroy all family comfort. It is the luxuries that tell in every way, one of these dispensed with renovates the domestick system. Upper servants, fancied wants, indolent habits, can all be dispensed with and no real happiness sacrificed, but there must be two to the bargain.

21. I was shocked at our own school, no rosy cheeks, no merry laugh, little skeletons in rags with white faces and large staring eyes crouching against one another half dead. How can we remedy it? No way; how feed sixty children? if we were to coin ourselves into halfpence we could not give a meal a day to one hundredth part of our teeming neighbourhood. The poor little Doyles so clean, so thin, so sad, so naked softened my heart to the foolish parents. They are on our own hill, although not our own people, they must not die of hunger. If I could manage to give a bit of bread daily to each pauper child, but we have no money, much more than we can afford is spent on labour, the best kind of charity, leaving little for ought else, people not being quixotick enough to deny themselves the decencies they have been accustomed to for the support of those who have no claim upon them, who little deserve help and who would not be really benefitted by it, only a temporary assistance it would be resulting in no good. These philosophick views are right doubtless, yet when I see hungry children I long to give them food. One meal a day I hear is the general rule among this wretched population. While they can get that they will not hear of the Poor House. Yet there are 1300 in it, and crowds turned away for want of room.

I am laid up with a sore toe! The joint of the great toe where sits in state a bunion, has enflamed and is very painful. Sir Francis Baring made First Lord of the Admiralty, Sir James Graham was sent for all the way from Cumberland but refused every office, so went back again, nonsense to try to patch up this ricketty set. Cheese parings won't help us, check the large bills for luxuries, leave us enough to eat. Still carry out proper economy everywhere all right, but no penny savings when we can improve our condition by striking off thousands. Wouldn't *I* govern the state, and can't govern my own household! We are fools all. 'Tis my toe makes me moralise, I wish it did not *shoot* so.

FRIDAY, FEBRUARY 2. Tom Darker after reflexion and consultation with brother John will take our farm whenever the Colonel may see fit to give it up. We were merely turning the idea in our minds, thinking that it might save us much bother and perhaps a little cash for really between the wages and the stables all the profits are eaten up. So we are glad to know that as we get older if disinclined for the burden of business we may be able to relieve ourselves from it. We are going to make a proper calculation pro and con.

3. Such a Queen's speech as this day has reached our Irish eyes has surely never been exceeded for folly by any of the long line of insipid predecessors. Lord John very indignant with Mr. Cobden and yet he will have to bow his aristocratick head to the blacksmith yet, for retrenchment is resolved on.

6. It is quite plain that we have no hope of getting rid of little Lord John, but the Company are likely to be extensively modified, some say strengthened by the Peelites. It is plain there is no good opposition, a set of sects each with its crotchets none likely to unite for any wise purpose. It really matters little who is in power now. The clerks, the true men of business, are never changed, and the intelligence of the nation at large through the press keeps the ministers in order, who are mere gutta percha people easily squeezed by the thumb of the Messrs. Cobden etc.

8. The two Houses of Parliament have appointed committees to enquire into the Poor Laws, heaven knows what
they will make of it, nothing till too late most likely. The
remnant of the farmers will have emigrated, and the last
of the ruined Landlords will have sunk before this sort
of humbug will report their doings.

14. I am reading '*Jane Eyre*', [published 1847 under the
name Currer Bell] and am thoroughly occupied with
it—pity that the extreme warmth of the love passages
makes it unfit for the girls, as there is a vigour of moral
purpose in it, a healthy resolve to do right at whatever
cost, which makes the character of the heroine admirable.
Still she is not womanly—drawn evidently by a male pen.
The interest of the book is sustained absorbingly, the
occasional eloquence is inspiring, all good, superiour.
Mind is making giant strides in these days. What will
the world be in a hundred years.

15. I have finished '*Jane Eyre*' in which I was regularly
absorbed. I should like to buy it to have it to read it again;
in parts it is sublime. The moral appears to me to be, that
a man prefers for his wife a woman not only content to
be utterly obedient to him, but proud of having him to
obey, full of energy to execute his commands, promptly,
wisely. With a mind to comprehend his, to follow up his
lead, if need be to whet his arguments. Above all to be
uncompromising in morals, honest, upright, truthful, the
letter of the law, no sophisms; and for the rest, beauty,
grace, taste, even *delicacy*, can be very easily dispensed
with. It is not exactly a picture to my mind, yet it is worth
reflecting on.

19. A grant of fifty thousand to feed the West of Ireland,
which it is calculated will last a month or barely.

21. Now for a tale. The party for Monday appeared to swim
gallantly on in spite of one or two apologies—but—'twas
a lull before a storm. Mrs. Wills came beautifully dressed,
Mr. Wills really grown presentable, the Doctor very gay.
The dinner was very good. Coffee was all right, tea laid,
but the urn was not to be had. Ring, ring, ring, and call,
call, call, nothing of any use. At last Jack descended to the
kitchen and after some delay up it came. The next event

was the real actual fainting of Mrs. Wills from having eat *crab* at dinner, and she never recovered this crab all the evening, spent most of it up in my room with brandy and water, etc. Mr. Wills walking up and down wringing his hands in despair.

Next event was George quite drunk, could not lay the supper, could not understand what was said to him, would not go out of the way either. I tried to get him in his room, not a bit of him. Sent the Colonel to him and then the Doctor and between them they took him off and got him a little quieter. The maids laid the table, the company waited upon themselves and all did pretty well. At last all were gone but the Doctor and Mr. Owen, whom we had asked to stay for fear of another outbreak, and there was a fearful one. I found my girls as white as two corpses, comforting Jack in tears. George had got a pistol, had pointed it at Jack in the passage on his way to the kitchen to shoot Mrs. Fyfe, which he most assuredly would have done had the pistol not been locked most providentially. 'Life for life', said he as he held it to her ear. He looked, they say, like a demon. Not being able to cock either barrel she had time to fly into her storeroom where she cowered down behind a sack and was found after a search more dead than alive, quite cold and weak, and shrunk into half her size. The Doctor said it was the Bride of Lammermuir precisely. It took an hour to revive her during which time George had been seized and turned out of the house first and yard last, he going off pretty coolly, giving up the pistol to Pat. The Colonel had some time ago, quite unknown to me given him this pistol to protect the house with, being unaware of the dangerous temper of the man. What an escape we have had from great misery. He told John Fitzpatrick yesterday that he 'meant to do for Mrs. Fyfe' and that providence had saved him from being a murderer and suffering a murderer's doom.

My God, what an evil thing is a vindictive temper. Here is Ireland and the Irish exemplified, jealousy of the foreigner, hatred of the conscientious overseer, all benefits forgotten or absorbed in one irritable feeling.

Uncivilised indeed are these excitable people. Margaret has earned this dislike however. She was jealous of him, aggravated his temper, her own being so imperious. We were wrong to have kept them together after their last outbreak. For our own accommodation we did it, they are both such capital servants, so we have suffered, for this is an unpleasant affair take it any way; ruin to the man, and not good for this high tempered woman to have had right on her side so entirely as a finale. We have resolved to do without a manservant. By relieving the housemaid of her laundry work she can very well wait on us, and there will be so much less washing, that a woman one day in the week to help Mary will be sufficient. The kitchen maid also will have a room the less to clean. John will give us an hour in the morning to clean shoes, knives, etc. And we shall save by these arrangements about forty pounds a year. I hope therefore the diminution of one-hundred and fifty pounds which John Robinson recommended will be very near carried out. We are now certainly reduced by one-hundred pounds, and not before it was time.

I was feeling very hampered, and Lord John is only patching up his poor laws, a clout here and a darn there; the *principle* from which we suppose we all suffer so much, remaining intact. There is to be a rate in aid, but only of sixpence, as thus—An electoral division, when rated beyond five shillings can apply for aid to the Union, when the Union is taxed beyond seven and sixpence it applies to something else, when that reaches nine and sixpence, the country at large is taxed the sixpence. Beyond this ten shillings compulsory aid will not go, but it certainly will soon reach it. And the remaining ten shillings has to pay rent, rent charge, head rent, tithes, cess, dispensaries, charities, and support the family. It is as if lunaticks were legislating. Whether the proposal will pass remains to be seen, there is little outcry as yet about it.

26. Mr. O'Connor Henchy called. He was just returned from France. All perfectly quiet. Louis Napoleon steering his way with great ability, an anti-republican feeling gaining ground so steadily that he has every chance of remaining

President for life. They make game of the democrats at the theatres amid shouts of applause. Mr. Henchy thinks the Pope will do better shorn of temporal power and that the Jesuits are too inconsiderable to get much support for their opposition puppet, though they may try to set him up. He also said that a Roman Catholick clergyman of his acquaintance, who was in fact sent to Rome by Dr. Murray to undo some of the mischief perpetrated by Dr. MacHale, allowed that nothing could well be worse managed than the affairs of the territories of the church. There could be no surprise at the turn matters have taken.

28. Tom Darker tells me the farmers *will not* pay the rate in aid. In Ulster this feeling is universal. It has reached Leinster it seems, and once begun this opposition may spread to all rates for the system is quite unjust. Little Lord John will make his exit upon its consequences is my firm belief. The *principle* is faulty that there can be no doubt of.

The brother of old Commons whose life was last in his Lease, is dead and Commons has given up possession peaceably. The Colonel will not alter present arrangements till November, which will give the nephew the present crops and time to look about him. Half a dozen years more and there will hardly remain many Tenants to plague. This old body owes a year's rent. Old Paddy Dodson too looks to be dying. No one knows his age, but it can't be far short of ninety, if not more. He was a grown man in the stables when the Squire died near sixty years ago. They live to a great age these people.

We expect Tom Gardiner directly, any day after tomorrow. He will remain till towards the 14th when Lady Blakenay has a Ball to which we are to be invited. *Pau* permits of our going. *Soubahdahr* is helping out the daily bread. So long as we can shuffle on till the cattle are sold we shall then do gallantly for the rest of the summer. The Ball would be a slight expense but for a gown and cap for me. I have no mourning full dress toilette, however black satin is always of use to an elderly gentlewoman. I feel a good deal better this day or two. Bitter beer and magnesia be thanked.

FRIDAY, MARCH 9. Must have been utterly forgetful of the next generation ever since this wild month of March began, as not a single entry in this faithful journal will my descendants find up to this date. My time has been scandalously mispent for I have neither written journal, nor memoirs, nor essays, nor letters but on compulsion. Darned no stockings, made nothing for the poor or the repository. Read only to amuse myself, stories out of *Chambers' Journal* and '*Town and Country*' by Mrs. Trollope, who is really a very underbred woman and she makes people act in the most inconsistent manner, yet writes so cleverly that the reader is, in spite of feelings, interested in her characters.

On Monday we were truly astonished by the door opening and Lord Downshire entering, the Doctor for his companion. He has run over on an agitating mission, to try and get up petitions against this odious rate in aid. He won't have much trouble, there is quite a fury against it, such determined resolution as makes one tremble for the consequences. Such an unjust proposal. When a property can't pay its rates and other burdens why not sell it. Why keep its pauper possessor and all depending on him hanging on in a state of misery and then insist on industrious neighbours supporting all these beggars. The rate itself is so small it is hardly worth noticing as a grievance if it were fair to levy it, or if it would do permanent good, or even prevent present misery; but nothing of the kind, the principle is faulty, tends to level all property, destroy all energy and finally involve us all in ruin. Lord John wished to carry it out at once before hearing evidence but was *outvoted*, and his opinions afterwards much modified by the examination of two of the poor law commissioners. This is our Prime Minister, this is legislation. God help the country, man won't seemingly.

Lord Downshire dined here Tuesday and was extremely agreeable, made fun of the want of a servant, handed round the dishes himself. The Doctor changed the plates.

Tom decanted the wine, the Colonel and the dumb waiter between them performed the part of butler perfectly, and the dinner being well dressed, the claret good and plenty, all did well.

10. The rate in aid has passed the first reading by a very large majority. Our petition against it has every name in the country, and all I suppose of no use. Sir Robert Peel has a plan which really seems to hold out a prospect of relief hereafter, he proposes that Government should purchase the insolvent properties in the South by which means the mortgages would be redeemed and the proprietors might probably have a surplus after paying up the rates to retire with to a colony, and Government might resell in smaller portions to such capitalists as incline to turn their energies landwise. Surely something must be done for universal bankruptcy will otherwise ensue. England is even now suffering, overrun by hordes of Irish beggars.

Lord Downshire's letter in the paper as champion in resistance of the rate in aid. What will happen, who can tell. Hereabouts they may refuse to pay it, but they will let it be levied; police, or at any rate military will collect it easily. In the north what they say, that will they do, and bloodshed may follow.

14. All up early. Imperial packed. Breakfast over. A fine though dull morning. Off at nine. The preparations were Irish enough. I had to go to see the carriage properly cleaned; John had to leave his pigs to drive it, dressed in George's old livery, and no trowsers being forthcoming, the Colonel poked out an old pair which were most gratefully received. We went to the Shelbourne on account of the situation, found it comfortable enough, though dirty, not dear and the people civil.

17. A beautiful St. Patrick's day. Lord Downshire made a very violent speech at the Down meeting about the rate in aid, a very unwise one. He wrote the Doctor that he quite forgot the one he had prepared, got nervous and spoke at random.

20. I shall forget that Ball if I don't begin upon it. We were early enough to see all the show. The entrance hall was lined by a double row of the old pensioners

and Prince George entering the same time we did, they presented arms to him which was a pretty sight. We were received in the anti-room where was a table spread with refreshments, tea, coffee, negus, lemonade, champagne, ices, sandwiches, cakes and white soup. The long drawing-room soon filled and then the door was opened into the old men's hall in which one thousand people found room enough to leave abundant space for dancing. It was lighted by three rows of chandeliers, eight in number, containing in all one-thousand candles. The recesses of the bay windows were lighted by lamps and carpetted and filled with sofas, charming, cool, retreats for many a quiet flirtation. The recess of the folding doors held Kelly's quadrille band. Two regimental bands were in the gallery. The supper was quite splendid, in the large dining-room, no seats; the company went in divisions and always found everything as at first. I heard the champagne alone cost one hundred pounds. The Lord Lieutenant walked up the immense hall at eleven, followed by a poor enough suite, and Court, yet it was all very pretty. The company stood till he was seated on the throne, Lady Clarendon beside him. All around were Duke and Duchess of Leinster, Marquis and Marchioness of Drogheda, Earl and Countess of Milltown, Clonmel, Portarlington, and their belongings with half a dozen more. A good display of diamonds, glittering Aide de Camps, etc. *The* Beauty was Miss Henry, next Miss Coddington, then really a crowd of pretty, well-dressed girls. Janey and Annie looked as well as any of them and were declared to be the best dancers. They were also about the best dressed—in white, very simple. They danced all night being in great request in the 40th regiment, and came away with regret between three and four in the morning. Tom danced with Janey in the grand quadrille which opened the Ball just in front of the throne, Prince George figuring in it. He danced the following waltz with Annie and then they were fairly launched.

21. I am perfectly tormented with that school again. Flighty old man, mad to marry his daughters, flying all over the

country with them to fairs and dances and wrote to ask my leave to give a Ball in the schoolroom. The attendance of scholars has of course fallen off very much. The few times I have been able to get there the rooms were nearly empty, the business going on in a most slovenly manner. They have got too comfortable, and grown careless, so they must go. Luckily I can get rid of them very readily, for the Inspector has a second time reported unfavourably of them, which has half deranged the remaining wits of this crazy body. They are like other Roman Catholicks of their class, neither honest nor upright.

22. Yesterday the girls and I walked to Russborough. A happier party never chattered away a fine spring day. My lady is satisfied with the success of her daughters, *they* are unaffectedly glad to be in society. Janie and Annie, though so much admired do not *clash* in any way with them, not being beauties, and not sitting on the red benches. More than all my Lord is not racing, and has received some rents. It was pleasant to see that poor woman so happy.

31. *The* Debate on the rate in aid not concluded yet. Mr. Twisleton,[2] when examined before the Committee gives as his reason for throwing up his situation 'his disapproval of the rate in aid', he anxiously recommends diminishing the size of the Unions making them as small indeed as is practicable, and giving no out door relief except in extreme cases. So we have lost a good friend. A letter from George Garland requesting 'sobriety' to be added to his discharge—for want of which word he has missed some good places.

WEDNESDAY, APRIL 4. The Committee in the Lords have thrown out the rate in aid, a majority of thirteen to seven condemn it as impolitick, insufficient, unjust and without a precedent; exactly the truth. Sir Robert Peel makes the most statesman-like speech even *he* ever uttered, the effect has been proportionate. He votes for the rate under the circumstances, but as a mere expedient to gain

2. Edward Twisleton (1809–74) chief Commissioner for the Poor Laws in Ireland (1845–9).

time, then opens out upon the whole subject in such a masterly manner. They little know the truth in England. So ill-used a people as the Irish don't exist, and these poor laws have completed the ruin of us. 'Sell the bankrupt estates', says Sir Robert and every other honest man.

5. Mr. Bright makes as clear-headed a speech as Sir Robert, goes even deeper into the subject which he apprehends entirely. He is really eloquent too; he denounces our own faults and follies, shews the way out of these difficulties and then *gives it* to that little fool Lord John, whose head really seems of late to have entirely left him. Not one single remedial measure can that shallow brain propound. Charity on compulsion given by the industrious to the idle is all this wretched substitute for a statesman can think of as a way of scrambling through another season of hunger, disease and death. It is a bad account of the temper of the Times when such a poor creature is allowed to remain Prime Minister. No brave English heart left among us.

6. Good Friday, and we have to walk through this high wind to church for the horses are harrowing. A second calf this morning but not a heifer. I heard from Mr. Gardiner yesterday about our money business. My idea about that Malshanger deed was correct. Described to us falsely, offered to us when my mother, who had resisted it, was at Oxford, Mary and I were cheated into signing an agreement [just before the Grants sailed for India] which might have left us penniless. One reads of such things in novels. Had my father out of his large Indian income paid regularly to Lord Lauderdale³ the interest of the borrowed thousand pounds, the word of promise would have been kept, not a farthing ever having been remitted, the accumulated interest now amounts to another thousand pounds, and so becomes a lien on the whole property. James Craig's plan is for Mr. Gardiner and Colonel Smith to pay up this sum out of the income, as far as I can understand it, in four or five years this will be done, and then we have the original sum clear. I suppose it will be

3. This was James, the eighth earl (1759–1839) who headed the whigs in Scotland with whom her father cast his lot.

the only good way of getting out of the scrape. The whole transaction is little better than swindling, humiliating to upright feelings. One more sinful act added to the many, shewing how far the first step into the wrong will lead us, who have no other guide but our own poor pride. The less I can think of Grant doings the better. In changing that high name for the humble one my honest husband gave me, I have been rescued from a web of falsehoods of all kinds, and have really *lived*, enjoyed the good of this fair world which is only to be done in an atmosphere of probity. I am ashamed at my Colonel having to hear of these crooked ways. Pride of birth indeed, I feel as if I were myself tainted.

9. A letter from Jane—it is nonsense to try to beat about excusing people who are totally inexcusable. I am in the habit of looking things in the face courageously. I can account for my father's conduct from the difficulties of his position, the natural timidity of his character, and his selfishness. I can excuse all this from his bad education and the unprincipled society he had been thrown amongst. But I won't agree to call all the chicanery and all the deception and all the careless disregard of others, practised throughout this dirty business as only a 'pity'. The deed is done and can't be undone and we must make the best of it and keep it all as much to ourselves as we can, for truly it is little creditable to the family, William having behaved just as ill as his father. Having betrayed his sisters into the scrape it was his bounden duty to have looked well after the yearly arrival of that interest, and to have told Mr. Gardiner and Colonel Smith of the claim, to have been open and honest, in short, what he is not. It makes the heart ache to think of what these two talented men might have been.

12. Fair as well as market at Blesinton, plenty of sellers but no buyers. Ewes and lambs from twelve to sixteen shillings each pair, a fat bullock six pounds. Yet hope is reviving for 'tis rumoured that the rate in aid will really be given up, and the company to whom the line of packets between Liverpool and New York belong have signified to Lord John through one of their influential Directors

that it is their intention upon the completion of our Irish Great Western railway to remove their station to Galway, with the concurrence of the principal Liverpool merchants. This will at once make the country. Poor Lord George Bentinck. If his sensible railway scheme had been adopted instead of that million wasted on idleness, these sad mistakes one after the other, we might already have emerged from our troubles.

18. A bad Fair at Naas, none of our cattle sold, nor did much stock change hands. The weather is such that no graziers would think of buying and really I don't believe there is money in the country. The respectable emigrants have carried away it is said about three millions which used to be the floating agricultural capital. James Craig writes to tell me that our Aunt Bourne *not advances*, but *gives* one-thousand pounds to pay up the accumulated interest due to Lord Lauderdale and thus release our portion in Kinloss. My Colonel will therefore get one hundred pounds a year as promised him till the estate is sold, when he will receive the two-thousand five hundred pounds settled upon us and our children at our marriage. James and Jane write such an account of the confusion and difficulties and miseries in which all Rothiemunhus affairs are involved by the crooked doings of both father and son as is frightful from the evils thus entailed on those who trusted to them. In charity we must suppose them to have been mad.

23. Two months too soon our coals are done, or nearer three, for thirty tons well managed are ample for the comfort of the house and always were sufficient till this year. Last June five ton remained in the cellar, thirty-one ton were added, and we brought with us from Dublin half a ton remaining over from our little store at the lodgings. As usual Mrs. Fyfe tells me—'We shall soon be out of coal ma'am', when she has one day's consumption in the house. Good, well-meaning creature, no worse housekeeper ever tried the trade. I shall in future keep the key, give out what is proper, and if she don't like the plan she can leave us. *Less* than her wages would give us a good man servant, and the saving in coals, candles,

sugar, would quite make up for other economies. I kept the house cheaper.

24. The coal mishap has been quite a hurricane. I am rather mollified since the mighty lady admitted to the young ladies that she had been much to blame. It would have been both more respectful and wiser to have allowed this to her master and me. The organ of self-esteem must be preternaturally large in her otherwise diseased brain, for she is up like a sky rocket whenever she is found fault with or even interfered with. Quiet woman as I am, I emit the spark when much enforced, and she is really with all her valuable qualities by no means an agreeable servant. I have much to put up with, my own easiness of temper being in fault originally. It don't do to be too yielding even in indifferent matters, particularly when there are arrogant or encroaching dispositions to deal with.

25. Off early to the Curragh, just in the rear of Lord Milltown's carriage, in which was himself, his lady, their two daughters and two younger sons, six of them! I was in hopes this first experiment would satisfy my girls and that this stupid place would never be thought of again, but quite the contrary. The day was fine, the only fine day we have had for ages, the races were really interesting, no heats, merely matches, so that the horses were no way distressed. There was a good deal of company, some ladies and quantities of gentlemen and mob enough to look well, riders careering about the course, etc.

26. Mr. Irwin, the Board of Works Surveyor, came to-day to inspect the draining. The best, most carefully planned, most thoroughly executed and cheapest done of any he has had to look after, and by no means an easy piece of ground to lay out. He was so much surprised to find the superintendant was a lad of eighteen that I am in hopes when we are done with him we may have a good chance of getting young George Darker under the Board. Mr. Irwin said they had very few young men capable of executing such a job, high as they paid them. Nothing like a good education joined to habits of industry and good conscientious principles, the best part of all training, the part I am sorry to say mostly left out in this country.

28. Politicks queer enough though dull. They are in a shaky condition these precious ministers of ours; what will come of it all time must tell. Death and starvation in Ireland at any rate, progressing rapidly. The roads are crowded with wretched beggars from the south and west, famine too truly depicted on their miserable skeletons, hardly concealed by rags. How thankful I am for the fortune that has placed us here.

30. Our good old Michael Tyrrell is dead, at seventy-nine or more, and hale and active to the last. He was going with oats to Dublin when he felt ill enough to turn back, took to his bed with cramps and died in a few hours, very like cholera, the priest thought. A better old body never existed. He leaves behind him a very worthy son

What will next month do for Ireland. The rate in aid little amended, has passed the Commons. A Bill is brought in by the Solicitor General which may save the country. In plain words he gives up the encumbered estates Bill of last year as impracticable, besides being useless, and adopting Sir Robert Peel's plan of a Commission, to avoid the Court of Chancery. Bankrupt properties will be sold without delay and a parliamentary title given to the purchasers which will perfectly secure them. This will relieve everybody, the ruined proprietor amongst the rest. If we can but get men of principles and education and business habits into the country happy days are yet in store. And no matter whom we are to thank for the boon, Lord Downshire and Ulster I verily believe. Our Hampden! for he certainly frightened them into serious consideration of our case.

FRIDAY, MAY 4. John Byrne came with rent due—twenty pounds, a lift, for all we had by us we have lent to the draining and no word of repayment yet. Such dilatory doings. Old Tyrrell had died without a will, so all the chattel property can be claimed by all the children notwithstanding his having given each their portion. He luckily owed a year's rent or more so the Colonel can seize the whole and as they will see that if they force a sale very little would remain over, they will probably agree to be equitable and leave the stock with the man intended to get it, particularly as they are decent people.

Tom Darker wanted to persuade me the schoolmaster was improved, he had had a supplicatory letter from him about starving and so on which had touched him. I went unexpectedly and found nothing altered, none of my orders attended to, and every one I met complained both of father and daughter, so I did not regret having dismissed them.

11. Drainage money has come. Pay will soon come and rents, so we shall breathe again. Redmonds gone, yet after getting two pounds and all the fittings and fixtures of their cabin which they sold without difficulty Mick blustered, quite frightened old Peggy and no wonder, for he is a clever and most vindictive man.

12. The Doctor took the girls a long walk yesterday and then dined with us. He was very anxious about a case of cholera, number three if old Mick Tyrrell died of it.

13. Sunday. The Colonel who was in the fair yesterday was much struck with poor Ogle Moore's downcast looks and shattered appearance altogether. I fear he is in very serious difficulties, such a family and so little certain income, and they say worse times coming. Well we must prepare for them and be ready to help one another.

We are reading 'Tremaine' [or *The Man of Refinement* by Robert Plumer Ward (1825)] in the evenings. My reason for buying it was to put a little inclination to finery out of our dear girls' heads. They would like to enjoy all the elegancies of life without *earning* this luxury by any trouble on their own part. They will be more respectable and much happier in cheerfully adopting the employments suited to women of our station. There is no need to be vulgar, or mean, or narrow in any way because we superintend the affairs of our household. On the contrary, there is a refinement visibly felt in every department of a family where a lady manages the details which the best housekeeper of a lower grade never can succeed in reaching. So my pets you must work.

14. Fine weather for farm work which gives one a little hope for the future, otherwise the condition of the country looks hopeless. Crowds of famished beggars everywhere.

19. Tom Darker sold our cattle very well. Mr. Owen and Mr. Lynch bought them, from knowing, I suppose, that they had been carefully looked after during the winter. Certainly the times are hard enough. Tom Quin, the carrier, is almost ruined by having advanced money for the little shopkeepers up and down the country as was his custom, and he cannot get repaid. He spent a day going from one to the other and out of fifty-three pounds due, he received seven and sixpence.

20. Such a mess about poor old Tyrrell's affairs. Part of his farm, nearly half of it, is held on a lease of lives, one yet unexpired, his eldest son Mick's, who can of course claim it, indeed whose it now is. The remaining portion has lapsed to the Colonel. Thus Philip, to whom it was promised, who has lived there, managing it on the faith of inheriting all, his brother's and sisters having received their portions, finds himself nearly penniless, entitled to nothing beyond his share of the personal property after a third has first been deducted from it for his mother. All this for want of a Will.

23. William and Sally have a beautiful day for their first peep of our green isle. Here has been Mr. Moore on all sorts of benevolent business which I have not now time to think about, though I have promised to help him.

31. John Robinson came, so the girls took charge of their Uncle and Aunt. We had a very bad rent day, little money going, some of those who should have paid did not pay, others who were hard enough pushed brought what they could, more is promised shortly, but it is a chance whether the poor creatures will be able to avoid considerably encreasing their November arrears. The times are very bad indeed and little chance of their mending. No price for anything. Tom Darker bought the summer stock for nothing, year olds £1.17.0, two year olds £3.5.0—and so on. Who could rear animals for such sums. That House of Parliament is infatuated.

SUNDAY, JUNE 3. We have been very fortunate in our weather. It has been delightful ever since my brother and Sally arrived. The country is looking its best, and they are quite charmed with it, fully alive to its peculiar beauties of verdure, luxuriant foliage, wildness, etc. Our house and way of life have also peculiarly suited people fond of the country, tired of the town, and disposed to be pleased at finding so quiet a refuge from the anxieties which have been so annoying to them elsewhere.

Here no one alludes to business, not farming business. We are careful to avoid allusions to exciting topicks and so William is calm and cheerful and happy, more like his own old self, Sally says, than she has seen him for many a long day. The old leaven is there, however, and would work in earnest if once set agoing. He would not bear opposition or reprehension or advice even, and were he to engage in any business again he would just get into another set of difficulties. Order and disorder and speculate and change and cut and carve differently from anyone before him, in short gamble with hundreds as he has done with thousands, for it is his nature and he will not alter it.

I have talked over this with Sally and she sees its truth and the hopelessness of his ever settling down to a comparatively inactive life though a small income would be quite sufficient for his *wants*, his habits being inostentatious, very domestick, very simple. To live as we do and in a much smaller house would quite content him, but then he would speculate and ruin himself again; so their little dream, or rather *her* little dream of a farm and quiet cottage here at home can never be realised. We must hope for his re-instatement and send him back to India to lay by sufficient to acquit his private debts and trust to his being permitted to compound with the larger creditors. If they put him by and bye upon the Bench we must be satisfied, and give up the Laird at home for our time.

We have had a bad rent day, and though more will be paid at nows and thens, before harvest we need reckon on on little more from the land than will pay the charges on it. Luckily we have the pay, and at Martinmas my mite comes in to help us. Times look bad enough, they may become worse here, if the support of the more wretched parts of the island reach us as expected, not only by the rate in aid, but by raising our own rates to the maximum ten per cent as must happen when the destitution spreads. Well, we have had warning. *But will the Union last.*

9. We spent this hot afternoon seeing the sheep washed in the pool at the Darkers' rushy field. These country affairs quite delight Sally, as for William, his old farming propensities have returned in full force upon him. Very little would settle him *here* in this fertile island if he dared indulge his wishes. His case has arrived and a few hopeful lines from Bartle with it, very temperately stated and if as stated I should suppose unanswerable.

10. Dear little girls, when you are in your turn Mamas and read these old journals of your departed mother, will you smile at the recollections of your happy ball days, or will it be in wonder at such fleeting pleasures having so entirely interested you. At your age I would not have it otherwise. Youth is the time for dancing joys, and precocious wisdom is unnatural. You are two dear, unaffected, pretty, graceful creatures, and so long as you don't marry for a few years more neither your father nor I will ever prevent your moderate gaieties. Bad as the times are, the five pound note is ready for you, it will furnish horses for the Review and all.

And this reminds me that William has been reading the Pau papers all night, half laughing at the first he never stopt till he ran through them all and he seemed really to like them. Sally must have told him for I did not, knowing how he despises modern *proceedings*, he is however, getting wiser in spite of himself, learning that the world is improving in its own way at its own pace and that he must humble himself to keep up with it. What a fine nature spoiled, yet so much good is remaining, he wants but to be thrown with superior people to become very superiour himself.

16. The Doctor and the Owens dined here, a very pleasant evening. Mr. Owen so happy and no wonder. William seems more and more enamoured of this country, he and Sally declare that if the Appeal is unsuccessful they will take a small farm in this neighbourhood and never regret their end.

17. Sunday, I have staid at home to rest myself. What

with the heat, the company, the picnics, the Review
and Ball to-morrow; poor William's anxieties and our
own embarrassing affairs together with the preparations
for a complete change in the household consequent on
Margaret's departure, I was a little overdone. So I
took my breakfast in bed, bathed and dressed leisurely,
and am now going quietly to read the sermon Ogle
Moore preached last Sunday, which so much delighted
everybody.

21. Quite a commotion caused by the arrival of the post;
an invitation from Sir Edward Kennedy to a fête at
Johnstown on Monday. No dresses, what could be done.
Papa and Jancy sct off to Sallins, got into the train, did a
deal of business in Dublin and were back here to tea. We
walked to school to meet the Inspector who was delighted
to find the O'Keeffes were dismissed. He had a long talk
with me. Times are changing people wonderfully.

25. About two-hundred people were assembled altogether
[at Johnstown]. In the study and adjoining morning-
room were plenty of seats and there we all staid to
see our acquaintance till half after three when dinner
was announced. Sir Edward and Lady Milltown led the
way, William and Lady Donoughmore followed, two
such immense women for such little men, the rest of the
company fell in as suited them. No entertainment could
have been handsomer. The band of the 71st Highlanders
played on the lawn where a large marquee was pitched
in case of rain. They played well, the piper occasionally
relieving the wind instruments, looking very fine marching about in his toggery. Lounging about to the Band was
very pleasant. Many sat out for the air was quite summer.
About seven they tried to dance in the house, but the
crowd was so great they removed to the lawn and there
a quadrille of sixteen couple looked beautiful. Waltz and
polka followed. It was quite a *Watteau*, the dress of the
present day being really picturesque with or without hat
or bonnet. We left at eleven, or soon after, leaving about
half the company behind us. The poor Leesons were
dragged off by their crotchety father before nine, just
as they were beginning to enjoy the only dance allowed

to them, the quadrille. Our girls never sat out the whole night. Their dresses were very pretty, they looked very nice and I heard them admired more than they have any need to hear of. We were home before two.

26. Up rather late of course, and so busy talking over our party that we cared less than usual for the post though there were packets from both Jane and Sally. The girls were charmed with their partners, some of whom were Carbineers! I had my successes too, for the handsomest of all these exclusives sought me out, asked for an introduction and took me to dinner! to my amazement! I could no way account for such distinction, even with the help of the mantelet!4 till after some desultory conversation my exquisite informed me he had letters to us from cousin Bartle! for my friend was a Forster! son or nephew to one of the old firm, Forster Cooke & *Frere.*

29. The clouds are gathering steadily and will pour their contents down upon us as soon as ever Tom Darker begins to cut the hay which has been ready for the scythe this fortnight. He will then, Irish like, complain of the weather and grudge the expense of the hay harvest and regret the injury to the crop. Well, he is better than he was in these respects, we must live in hopes of further progress.

I am teased out of all patience by the O'Keeffes, the old man has written me letter after letter, always the three quarter pages filled with his long senseless words, none of which I have answered. He then tried Mr. Darker, and then the Colonel with equal ill-success. This morning comes a ring at the bell and on the door being opened there is a row of little school girls, six or seven of them, no more, to present a petition written by Miss O'Keefe herself, highly laudatory of herself, quite in the father's style, representing that these seven little girls would break their hearts if their excellent and talented teacher were to leave them and entreating me to keep her for their sakes if only for six months! and their seven names, poor little

4. A short, loose, sleeveless cape. .

bodies, signed to this rubbish much against their wills as I well know. I asked them who bid them sign—'The mistress', Do your parents know of this, 'No'. Pretty sort of people to improve the characters of the rising generation.

30. Those poor people the Reades had taken such a deal of trouble to have everything nice yesterday but it was very stupid of course. They had asked all their acquaintance, however only the Johnstones came. A cold collation with claret, etc wound up the affair. We only got home to tea. The Colonel did not go, or he would have been put to the blush for his health was drunk as the 'proprietor who had done most good in the district during this season of distress'.

Such work as we have had this day with those O'Keeffe's, not the poor old man, he has, I am very glad to say got a school at Clane with a better house than he had here he says and an acre and a half of ground attached which he well knows how to make the most of, he was a little annoyed at my displeasure about the books, not one of which remains entire, a shelf full of disjointed leaves is all that remains of the free stock, and he tried to hold himself irresponsible for the destruction of them, but I would not let him. But when in consideration of all he had done to his garden, etc. we made him a present of his cow's grass he got into good-humour. But the wife and daughters were mad, sorry, poor creatures, to leave their pleasant home, and to lose so much income for they have nothing in prospect, so to ensure a little cash, Miss O'Keeffe made a demand for four pounds ten shillings, her school the last year not having been so lucrative as the first year by so much, and she considered me bound to make up the deficiency, talked of the rules, the Commissions law even, and her belief that she had had a lady to deal with. Very saucy indeed; the mother was worse, so I turned her out of the room and soon with quiet explanations brought the daughter to reason, the old father quite ashamed of them. We all parted friends, the women were merely excited—à l'Irlandaise.

TUESDAY, JULY 3. Was little Janey's birthday. I could afford but a poor gift—a cambrick handkerchief and embroidered habitshirt and cuffs, ditto to Annie without the handkerchief.

4. Forgot to set down the splendid results of my first churning, eleven pounds all but an oz. 'You see' says Mary, 'it's all the want o' company. Thim was iligant gentry, but they drank a power of crame.'

6. The girls and I walked to Russborough yesterday when the Colonel went to ride. I had heard that Miladi was very ill so bad as to have had to send for the Doctor late at night. This 'quits all scores', poor, unhappy, friendless woman, how glad she was to see me, she begged me to stay on and I did till our dinner time, I had not the heart to leave her. She is very ill, feverish, bilious, excited and wretched. They are penniless, their creditors have begun to lose patience, they are without a hope, I never felt so much almost for anyone. Who can reckon faults where there is such distress. She brought such a fortune and now to be reduced so low. She has no friends, no energy, no fortitude, no occupation, no temper. What a subject for such heavy misfortunes. Her Lord was keeping her too low, and he can't soothe her, and really very little would make her a lunatick, there is the beginning undoubtedly. She gossipped herself into better spirits, laughed as of old and ate two peaches and some broiled chicken while we talked, which did her a deal of good. I promised to go back to-day, but it looks too rainy. The four girls were very happy together talking of the few parties they go to. And the expected Drawing-room by the way which is a most annoying business.

Tom Darker has been in with me this morning, pleased with his own transactions in the fair but very doleful about the country, two year old Kerrys for twenty-five shillings a piece. We sold our wedders well, to Carpenter for thirty-three shillings, making a profit of seventeen with the fleece, the grazing however to be deducted, since October. I bought two pigs, high rather, pigs 'is riz' in the hope of potatoes continuing their present show. The Cess collector told him he is minus full half his due, he had not the heart to collect it from the miserable people.

How will this end, somebody must pay it. What a state of things.

8. Such a broiling walk to church with the Doctor. And by the bye I think we must have the carriage for church, the train of Beaux encreases both in size and in pertinacity, in spite of the Doctor's manoeuvres, who tries to distance everybody. We had new potatoes at dinner, very good and very dry—artichokes, cherries and strawberries.

9. An auction at Russborough of all the horses and mares and foals—twenty-two. Each was brought out by its own attending groom and *paraded* before a very small crowd of buyers, it was a *parade* indeed for his actual stable servants are reduced to eight, the rest were the labourers, white jacketted for the occasion. There was no bidding, a colt was sold to O'Connor Henchy for thirty pounds, a filly to Mr. King for fifteen, a brood mare with her foal to a dealer for forty pounds, and considering the times these were fair prices for the description of horses was not very saleable and half of them were foundered or spavined or aged.

10. Great discourse about the Queen's visit [to Dublin]. Go, all agree that everybody must, but very very ill can any of us afford it. And surely the Queen has chosen a most unhappy season for her first visit. It may put the nation into good-humour perhaps, but it will fearfully encrease debts and difficulties. A little present hurry for future cares. However, once in a way we must 'make an effort.' Make up our minds to it and go through it gallantly.

14. Lord Downshire has written such a kind letter to the Doctor begging of him to help with the preparations ordered for a Ball and supper to all his tenantry on the 6th of August, his birthday, concluding with his earnest hope to be 'soon amongst you all again'. The Doctor is enchanted, excitement kept up, for this quite new subject has started up just at the proper moment. It will do a deal of good to our rapidly declining country this six weeks of Downshire expenditure amongst us. Our girls are as extatick as the Doctor.—Such dancing prospects!

There are two cases of cholera started up here, Jack Byrne is one, and a bad one. Cholera never spreads in the mountains nor has it often been fatal in high ground.

17. We are not to grace the royal festivities. The Colonel was undecided for some time, but on calculating the cost, he thinks it would be not only inconvenient but wrong in these times to incur such expense. I don't agree with him, I think our duty to our daughters requires this effort from us, and that we keep them beneath their proper position by not presenting them among the society they ought to belong to, for it is not only the court they lose but every entertainment made for her majesty, at none of which they can appear. Perhaps he is right, at any rate he is the master, so there is no more about it. I may be too vain or too ambitious, former recollections interfering with the poor Officer's wife; while he may err on the other side, having never mixed with the world in his early youth and going out to India before he was capable of understanding the fitness of forms at home. He is also extremely shy, I am not pushing, both too proud and too indolent, but I know my own place and I should like if possible to keep my girls in it. But it is not to be. They had set their young hearts on it, having now a large dancing acquaintance among really nice people and they had been settling their dresses with the Lady Leesons, who are full of it too. It is a good trial—and so Adieu.

19. About twelve the Doctor arrived here, brimful of gossip. England looked rich and happy though filled with Irish, but the towns are going to the 'deuce'. Trade very stagnant, factories closed, masters emigrated to the Continent, workmen to America. Markets wretchedly low. John Hornidge got four shillings less for his sheep at Liverpool than he could got in Dublin, and others who proceeded with their cattle to Manchester got even less there. The Doctor left Stockton at half after eight yesterday morning and reached Blesinton at the same hour this morning, —nine hours only in crossing from Liverpool in one of the new steamers.

23. Such commotion this day in the little town of Blesinton. Instead of arriving next week as the Marquis of Downshire had pre-arranged, a letter came this morning to say

he and wife and children and servants and governess and secretary and all appurtenances would be here on *Wednesday*. The whole country is astir, for the tenantry, three hundred in number are to meet the carriages on the boundary of the property, on horse and foot, and escort the young heir into the village, which is to be illuminated from one end to the other in the evening. In truth this good landlord is much beloved and well worthy of every mark of respect from his people and indeed from his neighbours, for no man could be more really good-natured.

24. I am writing after breakfast again, my journal and I being quite on the most friendly terms just now. I have none else to speak to, and women must chatter. Ogle Moore is in very low spirits, no wonder, if all I have heard of his difficulties be true. His heart is in that home of his, his vanity likes the *name* of proprietor, his indolence suggests delay, flattered by delusive hope that something will turn up through some unknown channel to help him through without painful exertion on his part.

25. No letters again to-day, the papers filled of course, but after the fashion of Hamlet's book.[5] There are such preparations for Lord Downshire in Blesinton and all our servants, old and young going to see. My occupation at present is sorting two years' feathers, filling up the bedding, and now to-day begin the preserves. Happy country life, the pleasures of which my girls don't yet see. At this moment disappointment about the Drawing Room has vexed them more than any other they have yet met with. Many will be disappointed, for the Queen by her Chamberlain's proclamation don't come to meet her people one bit. She confines the presentations to the aristocracy, and will receive none not introduced by those who have attended her court at St. James's, alas! for the Castle train, few will bear the scrutiny of Lord Breadalbane [Lord Chamberlain].

26. Mr. King dined with us yesterday; having got the best intelligence concerning the Queen's movements he good-naturedly came here to acquaint us with all

5. 'Words, words, words,' II ii 191.

particulars and most kindly offered us a window of his father's house in Merrion Square, which is on the line of her entrance procession. He made another push for the Drawing-Room and failed as Dick, the Doctor and Ogle Moore had done. The young ladies walked till ten o'clock in the Avenue, —informing the young plantations of their griefs. It is a hard enough trial yet all these things are good for us. I feel it as much as they do, because I think it a great mistake and one likely to effect them by its consequences, but it is right to bear it cheerfully and it may be a proper decision after all. The Colonel is seldom wrong when he takes the trouble to think. It may be best for our girls to remain in an humble station, they have not fortunes to warrant their abiding among the great; so my dream of vanity and ambition vanishes without leaving any particular oppression of spirits behind. The girls themselves have really had a pouting fit about it, for the first time in their lives as far as I have observed, nor did I see it now till Jack pointed out to me a certain grandeur of manner, paucity of conversation and air of resignation to ill-usage which very amusingly was assumed to punish contumacious parents. The Doctor made matters worse, for he is so absurd about these children that he thinks them fit to sit upon the throne beside Queen Victoria herself with all the nobles of the land at their feet.

The girls and I went to see the Marchioness [of Downshire]. We found her looking very pretty, and she was very affable, quite kind in her manner, her Lord the same, and we saw the children, two very ugly boys, but rather a nice looking little girl, tall of her age. My Lord goes to Belfast to help to receive the Queen there, my Lady to Killarney to avoid appearing at her Court here. Both think that Colonel Smith is quite right to keep us all at home.

27. The Colonel and I dine at Ardenode to-day to meet Archbishop Whateley, a bore rather, though I want to know this oddity now that we are connected with him. We came away the first, about eleven, very tired of it, yet the Archbishop was worth the drive. He took me to dinner and I made him talk which he did well when once

set agoing and between his goodsense, his egotism, his vanity, his kind feelings and his extraordinary attitudes and quite unrefined manners, he was really an amusing study. I don't care a bit for Hebrew roots, still less for Sanscrit, nor do faulty interpretations or translations of difficult scriptural passages interest me either, yet he made these somewhat crude subjects matter of really agreeable conversation, and seemed not a whit annoyed at having to teach and not to learn from his Auditor. A demur about attending the Drawing-room in many quarters! So few have connexions who have been at St. James's! Her Majesty is in disgrace, and I am coming round to see the wisdom of my husband's decision. We have no portion in such *state*.

30. [The Ogle Moores] agree to come and live in the old hotel in Blesinton provided Lord Downshire will properly repair it. They will let their own pretty cottage with or without more ground and make by this about one hundred pounds a year, while they will save near another by buying all they want in the market instead of cultivating their forty acres at an outlay of two horses and four men. He will give up the Kilbride parish to a curate, or altogether if it can be dissevered, and sell his property the moment land rises, so relieve himself of a load which is breaking his heart. And after the move is made he will be so much happier, doing his duty, knowing his income, and living amongst us all instead of only with his bees and roses. In the middle of our serious conversation Lord Downshire called and stood gossipping a good half hour and engaged us all to dine with him to-morrow on a fine haunch of venison. Ogle Moore however, recollected that he had to go to Dublin. In the middle of our early dinner came Lady Milltown to see how many would go and dine with her—nobody, but the girls and I went to Russborough to tea, and found the evening very pleasant although my Lady was most extremely cross.

31. Another bright day with interrupting showers, and the girls and I have to go to school to prepare the rooms and presses and do what we can with the remnants

of the books for the new schoolmaster Mr. McDarby, comes to-night and opens school to-morrow, undertaking both boys and girls for the month of August. He is an intelligent young man, a native of Athy, educated in a National school from the beginning and trained in the Teacher's class in Marlborough Street. He was never a probationer, nor a third class teacher, but at once started second class and got two removes in one year. He taught two years in a school of Lord Stanley's at Doon and brings a high character with him from the Agent on that estate. He has been the two last years at Stratford under a *priest*, which though a Roman Catholick, don't suit him. I am sure I hope he will suit us for the advantage of these schools is incalculable to all the neighbourhood about them.

Our female teacher is to be Fanny Macdonald, a protestant, brought up in the orphan asylum where she was placed by the Moores after the death of both her parents, from fever in one week, an event which took place while we were in France. She is well educated in all respects, but her needlework is first rate, quite an extraordinary talent she has for it. She will however, require a month in the Infant Model School, for she has had no experience of Mr. Wilderspin's class and gallery teaching. I mean to give her a junior school entirely, all the little boys of the first class and girls of the first and second, the girls of the third and fourth classes shall be taught by the master, only coming to her for their sewing, and as I am going to receive the fees of the pupils myself and give the teachers fixed salaries the money part will be easily managed.

Mrs. Lynch most kindly volunteered to speak to her husband's Uncle, Dr. Murray, the Roman Catholick Archbishop of Dublin to issue his orders to our tiresome Father Germaine to give over his underhand practices. So I am in hopes of this new attempt succeeding. A great change is coming over the people and I do think if we have efficient teachers we shall not want scholars. If I could raise my Repository into something more of a shop, I might make more of it and between it and my brains, which I shall be able in future to dedicate to this most important object we may do more than we have ever yet done. I will try again. Begin with spirit, 'never say die', like the magpie.

We dined with Lord and Lady Downshire. All very neat, very kind, and the quiet style of waiting of those well trained servants makes the business pass off in such an orderly manner, with so little fatigue that none of it seems any trouble to anybody. The dinner itself was bad, not well ordered and anything but well cooked, the *name* of a man cook is one thing, skill is another, and certainly very little was shewn by this 'artist'. The evening was stupid enough. The Doctor and John Hornidge were the only additions to the party. My Lady has not much to say, there was no musick, no cards and the room is very small. My Lord chatters away at a great rate and very pleasantly, he is very full of his Tenants' Ball which he hopes we will all honour.

WEDNESDAY, AUGUST 1. All the morning in the schools with the new schoolmaster, a funny coxcombical concern very well pleased with himself and very well able to teach too. Coming home to an early dinner in hopes of thus stopping the Colonel's asthma, found the card for the Tenants' Ball including 'Master Jack.' Talking of the Queen last night, Lady Downshire told Colonel Smith that she is still most violently in love with her husband, he quite indifferent about her; a cold, quiet, not a clever man—a nobody. Her temper is very violent. She is not the least pretty now, nor by any means agreeable, never for one moment disqueening herself. She never descends from her high estate, nor suffers any one else ever to forget it. Lady Downshire is dreading this Drawing-room full as much as we wished for it. She most kindly offered to present us which would indeed have been a creditable introduction to the world.

2. Took a drive. Went into Blesinton to see all the cooking going on in the old hotel,—four bullocks, twenty sheep, lambs, hams and five cwt of plum pudding all preparing there under the charge of an old messman, quite up to the thing and very much delighted with the bustle and his guinea a day.

4. Most of the day in school, all right so far, but Irish and a Roman Catholick our new master has his little aims and ends and his own little ways of reaching these. He has an attachment and makes me the confidante and his beloved being a clever teacher, his hope is to get her here. We should have liked a married couple, but not knowing of all this underplot, he simply describing himself as a Bachelour, we had engaged Fanny McDonald and if she answers we must take her. The priests will not favour the school, said as much to Mr. McDarby, so we must apply to the Archbishop.

7. All very tired after the Ball which went off pretty well, one thousand five hundred tenantry and peasantry dined in the old hotel, the five rooms upstairs each contained two tables laid for forty or forty-four, the élite of the company, three rooms on the ground floor similarly arranged were for the second rank, and all the mountaineers were at fourteen tables in the vaults. The large room, now undivided, was prepared for dancing, but it being insufficient each room turned into a ballroom after the supper, pipers and *fluters* being plenty. The schoolhouse was used as a ballroom by the labourers, and in almost every publick house there was dancing, besides an immense crowd about the bonfire in the market place, which mob, owing to the rain, got very unmannerly and tried to force their way into the hotel. Numbers succeeded, making a rush every time the door opened, though two gentlemen and two yeomen were stationed in the passage to prevent them.

The rain was extremely unfortunate as it prevented all the fun we Selects had promised ourselves in visiting the different places of amusement. The gentlemen indeed braved the weather, leaving the *few* ladies collected in the market house to enjoy the excellent musick of Kavanagh's Band without any chance of dancing to it, for they were wanted to keep order in the hotel, carve for the awkward, serve the drink and so on, and they served too much drink, as long before mid-night there was hardly a sober man and long before daybreak there were hundreds drunken. It was wonderful that no accident happened among them; the gentlemen and a few others kept order. *Our* party was hurt by the Queen, so many had gone in to seen her enter Dublin. She was enthusiastically received, showed herself most gracefully and abundantly and was in high good-humour. She has grown very fat, was much sun-burned, and too plainly dressed to please the Irish. As she did not come in state there was no procession to signify. The illuminations must have been quite spoiled by the rain. To-day she visits all that is worth seeing in the city.

8. Miss Merrey came with great fun about the Ball. The dress of the mountain ladies, the manners of the mountain gentleman and such matters. Lord Downshire sent Janey a ticket for Mrs. Dodson & Company, meaning our three younger maids; they were sent home by the Doctor at four in the morning, the rest of the sober remaining till seven, the incapables were some put to bed, some sent to the police barrack, but all got off unreprimanded it being judicious sometimes to be blind and deaf.

The Ball was opened by a country dance, the Marquis and Janey, Lord Sandys and Mrs. Tynte, Jack and Lady Alice, and so on; and a while after, many gentlemen having vanished and the time hanging heavy, Janey and Annie were persuaded by their partners, Dick and Mr. King, to run over through the rain to the hotel. On their return their report was so amusing that the Colonel and I ventured in the rear of the Doctor, who made room for us by elbow work, for the crowd on the steps was very great, and in the passage greater, and in the ballroom fearful. There I met Lord Sandys, who carried me through all the supper rooms up and down and the mountaineers took us two old bodies for the young Marquis and Marchioness and cheered us lustily to our great entertainment. Tom Darker was doing the agreeable to Miss Kilbee, big Mr. Boothman to Miss Alicia Darker, too much to drink everywhere. The passage was one mass of bodies when we got back, and the door being left for a moment, the rush of entering mob, some regular ruffians, was really alarming. I got into a side room and as soon as the priest and John Hornidge had made a clearance the Colonel and I came away, John shouldering off the crowd in grand style and I holding by the skirts of his coat. The Marchioness, though dying with a headache when I came back to the market house went off to the hotel, where the poor thing danced among all that heat and *odours*, looking 'in her white dress like an Angel'. She was *carried* by John Hornidge and Mr. Wolfe over to Mr. Owen's house, where she went at once to bed.

9. Our fête is slightly alluded to in the Mail to-day, the Queen fills the paper. Nineteen hundred to be at the Levée. Jack is off to the Review with that good-natured Dick, who called for him at seven, the Colonel is not free enough from asthma to venture. Mr. Percy the new secretary was with her, not a well bred man, for he made me no bow at the door where I found him holding the horses, he must be a Smithson, not an old Piercy. I left this consultation to see a woman with starvation on every line of her haggard countenance, encountering with her husband and five children this lingering death rather than the pestilence of the Poor House. 'Sure,' said one of these decent objects to me once, 'if our children die in the ditch with us God will take them as Angels to heaven; they can only go to hell after the wickedness of the Poor House'; too true I fear.

12. I have this day put off the mourning for my poor father, whether exactly the year since it was put on I know not, but my things were worn out and would hang together no longer. I fear our dear mother will soon claim the same sad respect, for she is not keeping up as well as formerly. I wish it were more my disposition to dwell on the present and the future instead of for ever living on the past. There is nothing worse for the character than thinking over the poetical remains of what is gone, for the dark clouds which were there as elsewhere never remain in the memory, all the dreams of former days are bright and tend to throw shadows over actual enjoyments. Then there was something in the highland position, the Chieftainly state and the wild scenery and the feudal feelings, all so highwrought, that existence elsewhere is tame in comparison. —A dream indeed,

it all went with my father. William has doubly lost his inheritance.

The corn is laid, the blight has appeared on the potatoes, partially, and the trampers are stealing them night after night, seldom now calling for bread. What is there before us.

Heard in church to-day that last week went off brilliantly in Dublin. The Drawing-room frightfully crowded, but owing to the presentations at the Ball the night before, the Queen made quicker work than she was able to do at the Levée. There were three dinners at the Park, followed by an evening party, a Ball and a concert, then the Review and Drawing-room, after leaving which her Majesty embarked for the north. The Leesons were at the Ball. The Queen was in high good humour during her visit, everything went off so well, no mistakes, no annoyances, and brilliant weather. Her Prince is a sad stick, not even appearing to be interested at the Agricultural Show, where he merely walked about with a very indifferent air and left as soon as might be. He is a young man very much to be pitied to my mind.

14. In the middle of our early dinner came Lady Downshire and Miss Owen, they sat a full hour on account partly of a heavy shower and partly of a picnic the Marchioness is arranging for this day week, and wanted the help of our experience to expedite. Instead of our two households, the scheme has spread to every other, a regular gathering—thirty-nine people, no less, promising to be a very nice party.

17. We drove yesterday to Russborough and saw all, in high good-humour. Lord Milltown had been given the entrée at the Levée, privately, on account of his infirmity, they were all asked to the private ball, and Lady Milltown was one of the two Countesses among the twenty selected guests who dined at the Queen's table. Lady Milltown thinks nobody handsome and no woman well dressed, but her girls told mine it was one blaze of beauty and perfect toilettes and they heard the English suite were amazed at the *air* of all, person, costume and manner alike distinguished. Lord Downshire did

the honours of the north and found her Majesty most gracious.

Dick spent the evening with us. We found him at the river, a nice figure, fishing. We laughed away two or three hours, the Powerscourt picnic, the Bachelours' Ball and *our own* our subjects. The Colonel and I think we must give something, we owe so much and it would be a good opportunity to indulge some of the neighbourhood with a near view of *nobility* to have a little dance now when the certainty of a Marquess and Marchioness would secure an Earl and Countess and suite. We were a little startled however by the sum total of our first rough list of guests—one-hundred and fifteen people!

19. Sunday, Mr. King came home with us to our early dinner and was really very agreeable, I am quite getting to like him, he is much improved and will improve still further; his position at present is uncomfortable. He began farming as a profession in better times, his father then making him a handsome allowance, thus backed he built at Annesfield, bought horses, and so on. The father's fortune being in money all lent on mortgage on land near Kilkenny has failed him, he had lived extravagently and had no reserve, he can give the son nothing, has had to leave his good house in Merrion Square, his fine villa at Howth, and has gone with his wife and three daughters to some quiet part of England. And how much of the fifty thousand pounds will be available for his family, who can say these times.

22. Such a journey [to Powerscourt], fifty-two English miles. The lawn was extensive, the wooding beautiful, the views all the way up so pretty; then we passed the neat church, then a sort of dressed farmyard, and then came out upon the house, the *Custom House* on the Quay at Dublin transplanted to the country. I don't myself like this style of architecture, too formal, nor can I endure these palaces with their stiff gravel terraces amid the natural beauties of trees, fields, hills and ocean; but the place as a place is fine, the house as a work of art, handsome, and the interiour of it a shew and a shew only, for no one

with simple happy tastes could endure to *live* in rooms so gorgeous.

23. Powerscourt is very beautiful and we saw it to great advantage, house and grounds having been put in order for the Queen. She had intended to visit it with a view to selecting it for her residence on her future visits, but time failed her. I am certainly not intended by nature to live among the great for I could not exist at Powerscourt. I could not settle myself with my book or my work in any of those splendid rooms, nor can I fancy anyone enjoying existence in these golden fetters. No opening window leads to flowers, a long gravel walk on a stone terrace must be traversed before a shrub or plant is reached. Satin dresses, satin shoes, scents and ceremonies belong to those courtly rooms, the toys of the child and the occupations of a rational being would be equally out of place there. The beauty of the scenery is spoiled by the many villas which the near neighbourhood of Dublin has crowded the ground with.

26. Lady Milltown drove to see us yesterday to settle finally about the Seven Churches. She was in high glee, very amusing because so clever, but desperately malicious, jealous, and foolish. She really makes life a very unhappy business so ill-conditioned is her mind. I shall keep my distance if possible for she is less safe than ever, yet with good in her. Dick and the Doctor to tea, this Ball perplexing them. They have eighty acceptances and many more answers yet to come. We are filling our house for them, every room engaged and a dinner at four o'clock for all comers, on the eventful day. The moors are in fine order this year, equal almost to the highlands; eighty brace Mr. Shehan's party got in four days. Lord Downshire had good sport too, quite unusual in these hills. *We* are living on game, Lord Downshire, John Hornidge and Mr. Shehan keeping my larder full. To-morrow the Seven Churches. It will be stupid enough, and I had rather be at home where we have quantities to do in the way of preparing for all this house full but we are in for it, and dare not now decline, Lady Milltown being so jealous.

27. Very busy with Monday's work, then off to the Seven Churches, all but the Colonel who did not dare to venture. It was a lovely day and a very pleasant party quite unlike what we expected. There was a good and a merry dinner, a lounging walk, a tea, a boating and a charming moonlight drive home. Lord Downshire was my Beau during the ramblings, and for most of the hilly road home and very pleasant he is, altogether it was a highly agreeable day. Lady Milltown behaved wonderfully well and did her best to make her party go off well. At one time she was disposed to be a little hoity toity, but nobody minding her she sobered down, her girls manage her admirably and as for the conduct of Edward to his father, it is so unobtrusively devoted as to be beautiful. They are the best children in the world.

30. There never was a more successful hit than the Ball. It was admirably managed and went off in high style. John Hornidge opened it with Lady Downshire, who was splendidly dressed,—brussels lace over pink satin, a string of pearls round her head, lappets at the back, such a necklace, four rows of large pearls fastened in front by a quantity of fine diamonds nearly covering the neck. She danced away all night. Everybody was in good humour,—lights, musick, refreshments, supper, company all superlative. I was quite revived by Mr. Owen's champaign.

SATURDAY, SEPTEMBER 1. Went to school found no encrease of pupils but the few in attendance all neat and clean and the improvement in their reading, etc. very apparent. Poor Mr. McDarby is in bad spirits, the priests never having been near him and on a visit he paid to them, Mr. Germaine did not appear and Mr. Murphy very honestly told him they preferred the hedge schools as more manageable and less *instructive*, much learning being in the way of people who had their bread to earn by labour. We have discovered too that Mr. O'Keeffe is Mr. Germaine's cousin—still, we will persevere—time and patience will do much for us. But it is indeed hard to do good in this country.

2. A curious discovery made by the Colonel. He has been a

full Colonel ever since 1829 though only gazetted now. It is an unusual thing to promote retired officers, yet he is not the only one thus distinguished. An artillery officer is raised a step in the same way, but not so far antedated. The Colonel only retired in 1835, he was then unknown to himself a Colonel of six years standing. *Quare* is he not entitled to the encreased pay of his rank since 1829. or at any rate since 1835, he ought to look after this.

I don't quite know what to make of Mr. King: or indeed whether to like him or no—he is clever and lively and pleasant and gentlemanly, with right feelings apparently, though he does wrong sometimes like other young people. He is an only son and has evidently been spoiled. But I can't make up my mind about him; he seems too good to be discouraged if his attentions have any meaning; if they have not he deserves banishment for he is making our dear sweet Annie very remarkable, singling her out on all occasions, and whether her heart be touched or no, her vanity must be flattered for he is very attractive and these sort of things should be avoided if possible. Were I once satisfied about his character, either for good or evil, I would know what to do; I hear ill of him, but see little to find fault with except too devoted attention to Annie and a suspicion that the amusement of the hour is his only aim. As my child's happiness is mine, I shall talk him over with her; I don't think she is the least compromised as yet in any way, and try to keep him as much at a distance as I can for another year at least; but it is difficult to manage him. Come he will, meet us he will, and he makes his way with us all in spite of our determination to be guarded. Mrs. Finnemor told me that the whole country is ringing with his assiduities. Ogle Moore hinted at the same, the Doctor was open and angry. I told them all there was nothing in it, that he had no serious meaning, neither had she, which was fortunate as we would not allow her to marry under twenty. Then why allow him to hang about her, say they. How can I help it without rudeness, said I. He is not the only admirer: why so fidgetty about him alone? The Doctor who knows young men well, says there is a deal of good in him. Still he don't exactly like him. Annie must be left to herself; she sees others and must make her choice by and bye.

An opportunity occurring I told Mr. King to-night that Annie was not yet seventeen, and that we had determined on not allowing either of them to marry till they were turned of twenty; he seemed much struck, and it may have the effect I wish. The world would think me mad for he will have a little money, and he is very highly connected. but these things though very desirable do not come first with us.

3. Not much to enter to-day. A very busy Monday, so large a washing. Catherine the little kitchen-maid has given up her place. She was quite happy and contented on Saturday, and this morning was full of complaints, discontent, sauciness, considered herself entitled to cook's wages, etc., had been here three years nearly and was no better than when she came &c., her sister could get her a place in Dublin any day. The creature is mad. I could not make it out; but Tom Darker has explained: her father, a sensible man, is in Dublin, the mother is a fool and *tipples* and she wants the poor girl with some mistress who will not look after her wages. So we will leave the affair till the father's return, I taking it in the meanwhile very coolly. I believe it is quite impossible to do any good with this generation, there is so much to contend against.

6. Electrified the Doctor by the sight of the pretty service of breakfast china the Colonel has bought. Times improving! We could not have dared to attempt any purchase of more than necessaries the last three years. Yet the fairs are duller than ever. All our stock came back from Rathsallagh without an offer being made for a single beast. And whether Sir Edward Kennedy will send for the filly is to me extremely problematical. Tom Darker refused his offered thirty guineas—foolishly, I think. When a horse is not wanted it is a pity to be at the expense of feeding him. My little cook has recovered her senses after getting a good lecture from her great aunt Peggy.

7. I laid out one pound in books, all *Chambers'*; his publications are so good and so cheap; the three last monthly

parts of the journal are very good. My *Pyrénées* figure so I must set to work again. The Doctor tells me Lord and Lady Downshire are coming to look at our underground storey with a view to fitting up the vaults in the hotel for their servants; they will make a very comfortable house of that—with two really fine publick rooms in it; and what a thing their residence here even for two months only each year will be for the district; and they are such agreeable people too. That unfortunate George Garland has lost this good place he got, his drunken habits returned after all his sufferings and all his promises and the pledge; there is no hope for him, nothing but ruin before him.

9. And a dull cold Sunday. Surely the weather will not change—procrastinating Ireland. Our corn was fit for the sickle a week ago, and good Tom Darker would have been fidgetting at it with no more than our own half dozen labourers if the Colonel had not made fight. He hired another half dozen yesterday and is to have a band of twenty to-morrow. Annie has not been quite herself and these cholera times attacks of this kind always frighten one. The mortality in Dublin is frightful, in all ranks. Even here up in the mountains there have been *two* fatal cases; a third the Doctor has no hope of the patient being elderly; a fourth, a younger person, he thinks may recover. The symptoms are exactly those following some deadly poison taken internally and he is positive are caused by poisonous properties in the air acting on the nervous system affecting those otherwise prepared by accident or neglect to receive them. I hate this Ball at the Mansfields' on Tuesday and will not go if the weather is bad, unless they are all quite well. The Doctor is no use in these cases for he always sides with the girls, really from not having the courage to disappoint them.

12. A most capital Ball at the Mansfields': fine house, splendid supper, good musick, pleasant company; altogether a very happy evening although that little torment Mr. King, as usual made himself and Annie so remarkable that I am persuaded half the room considered them engaged, and he takes his own way in so determined yet good-humoured a manner that there is no out-generalling

him. But a stop must be put to these exhibitions. All the
maids inspected all the party, and then we set out, the
girls in their blue dresses.

At the door of the Library where we were received
stood Mr. King and Mr. Chetwode with open arms!
and never again during the whole course of the Ball
did these their ladies fair require the mother's wing.
They passed from one happy partner to another being
engaged half-a-dozen deep. Janey seemed to be most
in favour with the military, Annie had more civilians;
they are both however the fashion to such a degree that
I feel certain people think they have fortunes; the Colonel
having been so long in India, and then our having but the
three children it will most likely be supposed that there
is plenty to give them. So there is in a quiet way, but
nothing worth hunting after.

It was an amusing party to me, introducing me to the
better rank of Roman Catholicks, and very nice they
looked. One of the best features of our improving times
is the greater sociability of sects and classes.

13. A succession of visitors and very grand ones too. The
Doctor, Dick, the Lynch's, Lady Downshire and Miss
Owen, Lord and Lady Milltown and the two ladies
Leeson. The Doctor far from well; waked in pain, took
mulled wine, opium, and tincture of rhubarb, and came
out here to have his spirits raised. The girls and Dick
kept him merry and we made him eat curry and drink port
wine at our dinner; he is much afraid of the cholera which
is the worst part of it, as all one's nervous energy is wanted
to resist it. Lady Downshire came with the plate and other
things she had borrowed of us, she had them all counted
from a list, like any other honest man's wife and was in a
fidget about a fork of Mrs. Finnemor's which had gone
astray. We had it safe, so she went off quite relieved. Lady
Milltown came to hear news of the Ball; turned up her
nose at all the names, all details, shewing all the while she
regretted having sent their apology. Unhappy, envious,
proud, dissatisfied creature. The poor girls, natural and
good-hearted, everybody is sorry for them. Mr. Gilholy's
sale ended to-day—the bankrupt sale. All at a low figure

of course. At the conclusion the poor drunken body brought out the drunken wife and insisted with the auctioneer on her being canted; there was no bid. Irish fun even in ruin. What a curious people.

15. The great news I had to tell my journal was about the alteration in our arrangements for the poor. We have got it all our own way, are separated from Ballymore and Naas. Blesinton, Baltiboys and part of Holywood put together. Our rates will be nothing. Our Poor House industrial; it will quite reform the district which the present abominable plan was completely ruining. Which of these creatures would work if they could get one meal a day and idleness.

20. A note from John Robinson—times very bad indeed, and if the potatoes really fail utter ruin will be the consequence—misery far beyond any we have yet seen. We have a poor look out for the winter I know—no change for good at any rate. Worse and worse matters seem to be getting and what will be the end who can tell.

27. The day of fastings and humiliation for the cholera was unluckily fixed by the Bishop of that diocese for this 26th so one hundred apologies to Mrs. Archibald's Ball were the consequence. And such a farce these humiliations. Better be up and stirring—take our brooms and sweep away our filth, and our barrows and clear away pestilence, and feed the poor, and give them pure air and pure water, and at least a share of the good things meant for all, and raise their minds and bodies out of these cess pools we leave both in; then we should hear no more of cholera nor of half the other ills we bring upon ourselves by our slothfulness.

MONDAY, OCTOBER 1. Last night I was reading the life of an old friend Francis Horner, which the Chambers have published in a condensed form on account of its value as an example to other young men. His industry was indeed praiseworthy but it appears to have been wasted on very unnecessary labour frequently—he surely often began at the wrong end so found a tangled skein, and very often fagged at what he need not have ever entered on, at least so *I* think with all the improvements of this age familiar to me. The father and mother are seen to advantage in the son's memoirs—they were stupid old bodies to the world—and a pair of twin sisters were horrours. The brother Leonard was pleasant—however the whole set were dull affairs in my young eyes. I remember my father expressing astonishment at the start Francis Horner made about the time he got into parliament.[6]

4. If things go on as well as they have begun we shall have a full school soon and a well taught school. Fanny Macdonnell is a merry kind-mannered girl, clever in teaching and the most beautiful needlewoman. I hope and trust these two young people will not disappoint me. The Priests have evidently heard from their Bishop; both of them came to visit the schools and they surprised the master by praising—tone in fact quite altered—yet very sore on thus being obliged to yield. Of course, the spread of knowledge must frighten them—human nature requires objects of interest and the astute Roman Catholick Church has deprived her ministers of all save the aggrandisement of their order *collectively* for as individual each has little power, merely the wretched ambition of keeping ignorance in fear. They must give it up however—follow their flocks who will not much longer follow them.

6. Bankruptcy is overtaking us all; still sagacious people say that after a year or two more of struggle, the prudent among us will more than recover former comfort. In the meanwhile on marches ruin rapidly—in the South and West it has left little behind it, and here it comes close upon us in this the garden of Ireland. The system of carrying off the crops during the night in order to avoid the payment of rent has become quite general in the South and is even approaching us. Mr. Reid is the first victim—he is deservedly unpopular, yet it is a horrid dishonest revenge.

6. *Memoirs and Correspondance of Francis Horner* M.P. (1843) edited by his brother Leonard (himself a well known geologist): he died aged 39 in 1817 and is remembered as a political economist.

It has lately struck me much that the cheapening of our requirements, even in the necessaries, the *food* of the labouring is a mistake. A cheap market in a commercial country, appears to me to encourage improvidence and imprudence. In the potato days of Ireland the *poor* rushed into the most reckless marriages, economised nothing, thought of nothing, prepared for nothing, improved in nothing. The entire failure of their cheap food has checked marriage and all the train of ills following this unwise piece of profligacy, which is the true epithet of a pauper wedlock.

Finished the *Life of Horner* and liked it better towards the end and liked *him* better for as he saw more of the world he warmed towards it. Excellent sound upright man with such complete want of imagination—he never could have interested me. I don't like this new fashion of telling no story, but giving old journal & old notes and letters never meant for the publick eye by way of portraying character. The letters of men are dreadfully stupid in general and these of Mr. Horner's don't redeem his kind. The brother Leonard who edits the *Memoirs* was lighter in hand as a companion but of severe cast also. I thought neither of them agreeable though well knowing they were worthy. Francis really was beginning to shine in publick life, Leonard though clever scientifically, failed as Master of the new London University. I forget what he turned to afterwards.

17. Such an interval of silence, Saturday was Mr. Finnemor's funeral the Colonel's last yoeman friend—we were at the house by 9 o'clock—there was a very large crowd of all ranks, 25 gentlemen's carriages, some of them from Dublin—a breakfast in the parlour, refreshments *without* spirits in the kitchen—scarves and hatbands for the upper rank, all very unostentatious and very respectable. The train extended a mile and a half. I staid with poor Mrs. Finnemor till after her sons returned. Mr. Moore had done much to compose the poor woman by his little exhortations as much as by his prayers which were all extempore and beautiful. Time must do the rest, these outrageous sorrows soon subside. They are very shocking

to the reserve of my nature, an ungoverned display of feelings that should be sacred, annoying to all beholders, and totally unfitting the sufferer for remaining duties.

John Robinson arrived soon after I got home, he staid only till the next evening, but he saw old Rutherfurd and seems satisfied that he at least contemplates no fraudulency, but I have my doubts. He will owe £18, more than a year's rent by the 1st of November. He acknowledges to having kept a daughter and her 6 children for 8 months and to have equipped a son with goods and money for America. He has just started with his daughter whose husband is so flourishing that the whole family is bit with the wish to follow, and the best thing for all parties would be that they should go, but then not as a thief in the night. Now Tom D. has positive information from an eye witness that old Rutherfurd's carts were employed in the nefarious corn carrying of the son William, and one of the rates collectors told him that he had seen the Colonel's name as a defaulter in young Rutherfurd's books, although he had undertaken to pay the Elverstown poor rates to himself as Collector. Luckily Mr. Robinson made him give a receipt for the sum and we have the receipt which will bear us harmless—but if the facts be so, what confidence can we have in such people. The Mother brought up her family badly, she is a low born, low bred woman and has ruined them all.

I asked Mr. R. for his account current so he brought it. We had been obliged to ask him to pay some bills of a trifling amount so I suspected he was in advance but had little idea how much. He did not get from the tenants this half year sufficient rent to pay the burdens upon the land, and what he has disbursed on our own private account has been out of his own private pocket—£75—Am I never to get out of debt—this has been quite a thunderclap—it will be repaid him in November, but then the next half year brings its liabilities again. What can those proprietors do who have no income but from their land? We have the blessed pay—£320—quarterly to the day we get the 4th part of it and we shall have my £100 after next month, upon this we must manage to live and never touch the rents till times improve. Probably the farmers will by degrees throw up their farms, and then under our own management we may make the land pay something more than the regular charges on it.

23. Lady Milltown, Mrs. Butler, and the girls were here on Saturday to hear our news and to talk over Lord Cloncurry's imaginings [Lord Milltown's step-father]. The vain old man has made an amusing book though probably not a very veracious one and he has taken a good many liberties with names and family histories. His genealogy is incorrect—he does not belong to the respectable Lawless's he claims descent from; his grandfather was nobody knows who, his father a wool comber and got on by talents, chance and industry. I sent her the book yesterday as they can't afford to buy it, and it was not sent to them. Lady Milltown is very angry at figuring in it; Edward Lawless very much annoyed, and several persons who consider themselves aggrieved by his representations have forced him to make apologies in the newspapers. He is well used to that for many of his own letters in these Memoirs are in the same strain for the same cause—first a bluster, then a rebuke, and next regrets.

28. Mrs. Finnemor looks particularly nice in her widow's weeds—quite young and pretty, for everything unbecoming is discarded from the mourning of these days—the plain black gown, the shaded hair and close white cap are really attractive—a hint to elderly ladies to dress themselves as nearly after this pattern as is practicable.

We had a visit from John Rutherfurd the son, to say payment of rent was out of the question, but that his stock and crop were there and a proportion of their value should be the Colonel's after a settlement about the Lease which he will, with pleasure, give up to him. He is resolved to go to America and the sooner the better—the father would rather stay, but the son seeing in that case nothing before the old people but the Poor House means to take them with him. The first week in November, the brother William, his wife and the two little Kelly's the grandchildren start, with, in my idea, a good sum of our money, and in February the rest propose to follow. We shall easily get Elverstown let to a gentleman. It is a pleasant size, land in good order, very pretty and very well situated and a house which very little would put into a very comfortable condition—quite large enough for these times. So that we shall in a year or two I hope come well out of our troubles.

We may be thankful we are so well off—grateful for our small independant income and satisfied with our own conduct in having so well retrieved the little landed property that it will certainly provide for its own liabilities and perhaps begin after another year to give us something over as formerly though only by degrees, and when we think of some of our friends—the Milltowns—the Ogle Moores—I feel that we are mercifully dealt with. The Steward and gardener are dismissed from Russborough—nearly all the labourers—and two maids—they must live on six hundred pounds a year and the farm. The Moores have two hundred and forty pounds for their income, all else being swallowed up by the interest of his personal debts. The property will not pay its own liabilities so it can give him nothing—his living he has encumbered most improperly by ensuring his life for a sum borrowed to relieve pressing difficulties—he has bonded debts besides, for he is acting like a madman. With this two hundred and forty pounds and eleven children they are keeping seven women servants and 4 outside men, and permit themselves every luxury and indulge in lives of utter indolence, neglect every duty, and say *in tears* 'What can we do'. Mrs. Moore knows of every debt except the one to the Doctor yet she makes no exertions, gives up no indulgence, and he pets her up like a spoiled child. One feels ashamed of both of them, only we must recollect how very badly they were both brought up. What vicious sentiments they have always heard, what questionable habits they have always seen, and in Ogle's case I really believe his brain is not in order. My children laugh at me for calling every one mad who acts madly, that is ill, but is it not madness to do wrong knowing right. In this case the family weakness clings to poor Ogle . . . and the pride they are all puffed up

with. People of their condition! With just four ancestors
they can name on the father's side and zero on that score
on the Mother's—like Lady Milltown and her peerage!
bought in Mr. Pitt's time, by a Brewer!

SUNDAY, NOVEMBER 4. All our thoughts with Kilbride. The
Doctor went down on Thursday and had the dreaded
interview. I *believe* that all is divulged now, but Ogle had
been open with nobody, yet must we forgive him. *She*
has had a general idea of difficulties, since the father's
death, as connected with the landed property—no notion
of any private debt till the morning they drove here, but
even then the amount was concealed from her, and it
was not till the hour approached for the appearance
of the principal creditor, who had insisted on an open
conference with Miss Casey included in it, that Ogle
could bring himself to tell her of his debt to the Doctor.
She was very pale, extremely affected, wept a good deal,
but was firm in advocating the utmost retrenchment
for the purpose of clearing her husband's honour. She
has only two hundred pounds a year. Miss Casey, who
makes common cause with her unhappy and *I think*
ill-used sister, has the same income, and gives them
one hundred pounds for her board. They have also the
cottage and thirty acres of ground rent free. After all
sufficient for people accustomed well to manage small
means and whose habits had been properly formed to
their position. But to *them* this is beggary, still they can
have no more, his tithes must be employed in paying off
his heavy debts to the Doctor.

They have many pressing tradesmen's bills both in
Dublin and Blesinton. The plate, the pictures, the books,
the carriages, the surplus stock and surplus furniture are
to be devoted to this purpose without delay, and an
auction will be called immediately for their disposal.
One man without, Mick Manders paid by four acres
of ground and one pound quarterly—one maid of all
work within, and Mick's little girl, a child, to keep the
baby, are all the servants that this stern but just adviser
permits their retaining. Mrs. Moore is to receive and
to pay all money—Mick to manage the land—Ogle to

attend to his parochial duties which he has never even attempted to do yet. She offered all her trinkets but the Doctor refused them thinking her entitled to all that she can call her own. He has bid her keep them to fit out her sons.

They both shewed honourable feelings—every wish to do right—to make sacrifices to work—to give up errours, but can they do it? Four maids and the three men are gone, there are three maids still and the nurse among them, with whom to part will be very difficult for she has brought up nearly all the eleven children. However, she is to go, she is not strong enough for hard work and her wages are very high. The whole three have been much to blame—Ogle for exceeding his income, for spending extravagantly, for borrowing recklessly, for concealing his embarrassments from his Wife, from petting her up like a baby instead of treating her like a rational being, and worst of all for breaking his solemnly pledged word to the Doctor whom he has besides used most exceedingly ill, I really do believe from thoughtlessness though it would be hard to convince the lawyers were they consulted, of any man of sense shewing such lamentable ignorance of business.

Mrs. Moore ought to have seen her husband was out of health, out of spirits, she ought to have asked herself whether their income warranted their expenditure she ought to have attended more actively to her family, she ought never to have yielded to her most unseemly habits of self-indulgence. Her children were frequently in rags, she had no lists of their clothing, no catalogue of furniture, no house book of expenses, she never bought an article, she never saw a bill. When shirts or shifts or shoes or bonnets or tea or rice or beer was wanting Ogle was told, and Ogle ordered. Was it difficult to foresee the end. Why did not Miss Casey foresee it. How could she be insensible to what was going forward. Her part has been to foster pride, to adminster to vanity, to encourage frivolity, but she is redeeming herself, she has come forward like a true noble-hearted woman. They may not do right, it is very hard to change the habits of a life time, but they all mean right, and this honesty of purpose will bring them help.

Now shall we apply the tale—we have encumbrances—we have exceeded our income—we indulge in luxuries, in these times we have no right to—nine horses—and their attending men—we might do without the gardener and the Laundry maid and we will if I cannot get the stable retrenched in, and I shall have another very serious conversation with Tom D. who in respect of horses is an Irish fool, and one penny of our British money he shall never have *from* me till this extravagance is done away with—horses and labourers absorb the whole produce of this large farm. It is not the house as he always tried to make believe it was. Our twelvemonths' butcher's bill was six and thirty pounds with half the time twelve in family—he must make his two ends meet for we of the household will no longer be over-weighted.

9. Such harrassing times. Between our own distresses and our friends', it is really difficult to keep up our spirits. I have had no time for the journal some quiet half-hour I must run over matters, they will tell a tale for other years. By the way Miss Eliza Cook accepts the '*Junior Clerk*' with a most flattering note of thanks and hopes for further communications.

10. I am sorry to have to note in this truthful journal that the day I went down to Kilbride I found both Ogle and the wife very much cooled down about their Auction. They really see nothing they can part with but their plate and pictures; they have little extra furniture, no hoards of trumpery; the harp she wishes to keep to teach the girls to play duetts, the violincello he could not get the value for, the brougham would fall to pieces on any other road than the road to Dublin with him inside. And three maids they must keep, the cook and nurse remaining at twelve pounds a year. We must wait a while and then talk sense to *her*, a thing she has never heard yet. She mentioned some of her retrenchments to me and asked my advice which gives me an opportunity of opening the subject. She will find she will have to make greater sacrifices than folding up her table cloth, tidying her room, and hanging

up her towels to dry for next day instead of throwing them on the floor after once using them. *He* must wear darned stockings too, I rather think.

On what pretence could people so humbly born have been reared in such highly magnificent notions? *I think* that when *she* knows all, at least as much as the Doctor and I can tell her, she is so thoroughly honest she will do her utmost to keep *him* so. He will shrink from what he has brought himself to, and he watches the Doctor and me as an insane person watches his keeper lest we should contrive to speak to her alone; but we will contrive it—never fear; they are all in wretched spirits.

Our own affairs with those swindling Rutherfurds came off well; they assisted the seizure well pleased to prefer their landlord to the Poor Law Guardians, and after our claim is satisfied he will make over the remainder of his property to the other Bail who is well nigh ruined by this roguery of the son's. Rutherfurd will then be left with little here, so we hope he and his family will follow the missing money to America and allow us to let Elverstown to some one who will pay the rent to us. Commons has been very troublesome and there he is up in the old Cabin, himself and the niece and the nephew and all keen to go to law about his claim for the value of these Buildings for he won't believe that he is mistaken on this subject, neither will he let our herd, Johnny Grace come to live on the farm, but all the stock and crop we took at a valuation for rent he has allowed us to remove. The Colonel has been very good to him, had all this property overvalued, and has promised to buy the remainder and to give the old man their value in money; also to make the nephew a present of twenty pounds to set him up in the world—I am sure I don't know where it is to come from, and to allow Commons ten pounds a year as long as he lives, and the old oddity actually asked for four pounds a year more for the niece. I don't believe we shall ever be quit of them. Mr. Darker however undertakes in a few days when they have cooled upon it, to try and put all to rights.

We have had the schoolmaster's doings to divert us.

He offered when he came here to marry anybody we liked that could bring good temper and her fair share of income with her. We had no desire to present him with a wife so he acknowledged an attachment to a young female teacher whom he wished us to engage for the School. We had got one, so he picked up an acquaintance with Ogle Moore's laundry-maid, a fine handsome woman, a widow much older than himself with a child for whom she wants a permanent home. By her account he represented his as the very thing for her, a permanent situation, well paid, house and land from the Colonel and an estate in the Queen's County. She on her part, as he assured me, deposed to money saved, furniture ready, and an unbounded admiration for his *spirity* manners. On being mutually undeceived regarding these vapourings, all the affection has vanished and the matter is off as quickly as it came on; but I am afraid he is a flighty fool, very soft on the women. He has been beating the boys too and has written such rubbish on being desired to give this practice up. I shall try to improve him, poor conceited creature, for he really teaches well.

16. John Rutherfurd was here yesterday in great distress. I don't see any way for him out of his embarrassing position, any honest way. Even if we gave him time he could never meet his engagements, his best plan would be to give up Elverstown, pay the Guardians a first instalment, and from America, where he will be sure to thrive remit the rest. He acknowledged having given the brother Jo both our money and the Union money, intending to repay it out of the fortune of a rich wife he was engaged to, the rumour of his difficulties made the father of the Bride break off the match so as he touchingly said 'I done myself all ways' And so will it ever be when the ways are crooked. The Colonel advised his going up directly to John Robinson to lay the whole truth before him and he let me write to say he had no objection to stop the sale and take as much stock as would pay up the rent at a valuation. There will be little left, even after a high valuation and fifty-seven pounds odd must be scraped up before six months for

the Guardians. The brother William also owing them
sixty pounds. He and his wife are at Elverstown not yet
ready for America. They are turned out of their farm still
owing rent, although much of the crop was recovered by
the Landlord.

17. Best part of the day taken up with Rutherford's affairs.
A letter from John Rutherfurd about them, then the son
came and then we had to send for the father. They appear
inclined to deal fairly at last. Whether frightened into it
or no we can't say, but so as they can avoid the scandal
of a seizure they will give stock and crop at a valuation
like Commons, and they have had *some bad debts* paid
them, sufficient to clear off the arrears! We need only
help ourselves to the half year's rent. The Colonel is very
lenient with them.

24. A fine day at last to cheer us, a bright sun. It really was
too depressing to be groping about under that dark sky
while the gloom of increasing poverty was paralysing all
mental energy. Wretched land, what sufferings the most
meritorious of its inhabitants are undergoing, all more or
less stricken and no prudence on the part of the wiser able
to secure them against the pressure of the evils resulting
from the want of principle of the improvident. All share
alike in the general bankruptcy. I often pray that my
senses may be preserved to me, and that my health of
mind and body may stand this struggle, and aid me to
preserve an invalid husband and our dear children from
much of the real poverty round them—they miss their
luxuries—necessaries they still have and will have, our
British money will ever secure us a sufficient supply of
them—but the want of enough to help to relieve others
is a painful part of these unhappy times. To keep our own
people from starving absorbs all there is to spare.

28. Another dark east wind day. Poor dear Mrs. Owen can't
keep herself warm in Blesinton though such fires burn
all over the house as have seriously frightened all the
economical Irish lest the whole united income of the
firm should be expended in coals. She can get no veal
either without sending to Dublin for it, nor fresh pork,
and the little dealers' fish basket which used to be ample

for all our doors now never progresses beyond hers. To bring a woman of the lower order of gentility who has in her life seen nothing beyond the home comforts of the most comfortable north of England, here to the untidy dirt and *fun* of most uncomfortable Ireland was the very greatest mistake ever made. Her life has been passed in managing to admiration her house and kitchen and in talking over all the interesting details of this occupation with a swarm of tea and cake visitors, the little crowd of a little town, varying the anecdotes of this society with her needleworks. She never walks, she never rides, she drives indeed in her pony carriage, just a cut above Mrs. John Hornidge and her tub, and having no conversation, no one cares to try to talk to her and she is quite incapable of comprehending our dashing ways the fun, the wit of all classes fall on a very dull ear when addressed to hers, and the intellectual flights of the upper classes just amaze her. Her husband's sisters are quite beyond her, and so they seem to think, for none of his family come near her. I shall be very sorry if they go, for her clean house and methodical ways might much improve this poor country and such an Agent as he is Lord Downshire would hardly get again. But he has lost favour both with my Lord and my Lady—his loves—his marriage—his nonsense afterwards—his carelessness about their visit and the Auditors' dissatisfaction at the dilatory proceedings about the accounts which have never yet been made up, altogether have influenced Lord Downshire to alter the favour with which he once regarded his clever Agent. The want in the character was always there and 'tis a pity, for the good heart and the good abilities are of little avail with such unsteadiness of purpose.

SUNDAY, DECEMBER 2. The same most utterly abominable weather—rain for ever, so dark one can hardly see, and quite chilly, though not cold. We had the pleasantest rent day yesterday that we have had since the famine year. Not only did the tenants pay well but they looked happy—no complaints, no demands, no shuffling—a half year's rent and a pleased air in giving it, was offered by all but three who will pay up the difference by Christmas. Some even paid a portion of their arrears. They say it is the draining which has brought them through; money in hand for labour they had no call for, and time given them, and care taken of them, and kindness shown them. They couldn't but do their best. And I believe they are right. We deserve their attachment and I really do think we have it. Old Commons too has grown quite reasonable—will give no more trouble and is grateful for what is done for him. The nephew quite pleased with his present, is going to take a small farm near at hand and begin the world on his own account, keeping the Uncle with him. Paddy the gardener was waiting for me to-day, below in the kitchen to know his fate, and he did look happy when told there was no need to part. Poor Mary the laundry-maid too, she will get a reprieve so there will be great rejoicing in the kitchen. Jack is to have new clothes, the Colonel a new pair of pantaloons, and Mrs. Smith a new bonnet. It is to be hoped the family won't grow extravagant on this sudden apparition of riches. It will do little more than pay our debt to John Robinson and the dues on the land, but to be even with the world again is comfort unspeakable.

10. We have killed a very well fed porker and sold a quarter to the Owens and given a quarter to the Moores, and the Colonel would like very much to eat up a third quarter himself. I doubt the Doctor permitting him to have even a chop. Lord Milltown lent me Curran's *Life*[7] by his son which I remember made a great noise when it came out some thirty years ago; he chose it out of his library as a good book for Edward and looking into it could not lay it down again so thought the Colonel might like it, and he does, we all do; we began to read it aloud this night and were all quite interested.

Xmas day. Frightful chasm in the journal.

Mr. King came to spend his last evening with us on Friday. He has left his hunters to be sold and has gone on a long visit to his father. I think him a shallow pate, with some cleverness, a deal of good in him, but he has

7. John Philpot Curran (1750–1817), a famous Irish judge.

been so badly educated and has lived with such a vile stile of people that in spite of his gentle blood, I never wish to be more closely connected with him.

Jane's news is not altogether pleasant. My mother's claims on Kinloss are considered by the lawyers to be superceded by the proceeds of the insurance which gives her within £5 of £400 a year. Her jointure as the widow of Rothiemurchus is limited to £100 a year and the house of Inverdruie by the Entail, and William having given it as his opinion that my father intended the insurance to cover that also, she declines consulting lawyers on the subject. She has ample for her own wants without this, and to spare, for James Craig will not allow her to pay the board she used to do when her income was larger; he takes now only £150, excellent man, and my dear mother, good generous woman, she gives £50 a year to Mrs. Grant of Yarmouth, my father's worst used creditor, and £50 a year to William's most destitute victim, I suppose, Mrs. Camac.

Alas! Alas! all the misery, the wide-spread, crushing misery caused by two kind-hearted men who neither of them ever missed an opportunity of serving a fellow-creature. Benevolence was largely developed in both characters. Strict principle was entirely wanting. Controul over any impulse neither had. Nature, or rather selfishness, governed both unchecked, and fearful have been the consequences. My father was by far the most amiable man of the two. I am sorry to think so ill of William; but he continues to act so differently from what we feel an upright conscientious mind would prompt him to, that I have little faith in his future conduct and am reduced to pity and to excuse his many failings. If he be not reinstated I know not what will become of his poorer creditors. I must turn this over in my *brains*. Mrs. Grant Yarmouth must never want while I can help to earn her bread.

31. Shouts of joy ascending to my quiet fireside from the dining room announced this morning the return of the Doctor. He has past most of the day with us having much news to tell [of Hillsborough]. Jack is living at

Russelstown almost enjoying in his own way his holidays. After a whole long morning spent in shooting, hunting rabbits or coursing, they dine heartily and spend the evening very happily, all of them sleeping sound till tea enters at 9 o'clock.

Very different was Hillsborough! The Downshires live in regal state. Servants innumerable, silent as the grave, let you want for nothing, plate to no end. The cook shining, eating all day, dinners to twenty, hot luncheons, breakfasts beyond perfection, immense house, corridors and staircases and passages with bedrooms so luxuriously furnished, and all full. Besides which company staying there were crowds arrived to the private plays and the ball and the concert; many pleasant people and some beautiful girls. My Lord a very kind host. My Lady too careless to do the honours well generally. Both made plenty of the Doctor, who certainly enjoyed his visit much. Yet the philosopher carries the day; he says he would not lead such a life for twice the fortune, so unsatisfactory, so fatiguing, such a parade of wealth added to ceremony to get vain mortals one day nearer to the grave.

I have another way of thinking of all this, the good it does, the tradesmen employed—the servants required; the provisions consumed. The use in the neighbourhood, enlivening society, polishing it, improving it in many ways and bringing people together. I have no wish to act the princely host, but I should like very well to belong to the courtly circle when good feeling guided the proceedings of the centre of it. We miss that sort of *palace* in this country, there is no one to reign over us, so we get cross and stupid and *savage* and some of us impertinent.

Poor Lady Milltown came to talk over her troubles which have become a heavy load, how heavy she knows not luckily, but what she does know has much disturbed her, and her Lord's ill-humour and selfishness and unkindness are increasing with his difficulties. She minds him less than she did; still he has the power and the will to use her very cruelly and hers is not the nature to soften his. She likened him to Mr. Quilp,[8] which was a cut indeed. I should have thought such a lapse unpardonable, but she says it brought him to his senses. We had a long talk about their affairs which she hopes to see improve by Russy's management when he comes of age in May. While that wretched father of his lives nothing will go right. What will another year do for us all; the Evening Mail dreads it.

8. The evil, and deformed, persecutor of Little Nell in *The Old Curiosity Shop*—'an elderly man of remarkably hard features and forbidding aspect, and so low in stature as to be quite a dwarf', (chapter 3).

TEN

1850

After a visit to her mother and sister in Edinburgh in January (it coincided with the death of her father's old friend Lord Jeffrey, the last link with the great days of her girlhood in the capital city of the Enlightenment), the rest of the year is dominated by her incessant writing of articles to help assuage the constant distress and by Annie's engagement and marriage in December to James King. The year ends with the resignations of both Agent and Steward; so there is much work ahead.

WEDNESDAY, JANUARY 9. What have I been doing since we bade adieu to the old year? Trying to get rid not only of influenza but of a slight attack of liver which quite did me up for a few days; nursing my poor Colonel through first a bad cold and since a turn to bronchitis; copying another '*Conversation*' for Mr. Ritchie; preparing '*Bordeaux*' for Miss Cook which is ready and must go to her; netting tidies by the fire, and reading Chambers' new edition of Paley's *Evidences*, or rather his natural theology with extreme delight. The girls have a reprieve the Doctor not thinking me fit to travel to Edinburgh this week.

13. Sunday, A week of winter—hard frost over snow and a dark sky which is so gloomy, but the weather is seasonable and healthy and very good for the ground. The late mild winters were very unfavourable to fertility, they also hurt the cattle causing most of the diseases which have been so fatal both to stock and crop. We who house our beasts and have a plentiful supply of turnips and mangel for them rejoice in this bracing cold.

I am just now deep in Dr Arnold's life. His views are peculiar—I should scruple to say correct, though honest and fearless. In his system of education there is too much study, too long a time each day employed

in study I mean, and the ancients occupy too much of
this. He rests, a pioneer—a help to future improvement
sufficient of course for his day. We travel these intellectual
high ways so slowly—yet have we in this our age done
much. Arnold, Whateley, *Combe!* and to assist these
great floods, a whole host of little brooms to sweep away
the rubbish broken up by them.

20. Sunday and in York Place, Edinburgh. On Tuesday last
the 15th, Janey and I set out on a most unpromising
morning. The Colonel was not up so did not see the
snow. Jack and Annie attended to us and Mr. Darker
and all the men and all the maids, and as we passed
through Blesinton the Doctor's glowing face beamed
over his window blind with an astonished expression.

We breakfasted leisurely at John Robinson and then
departed in a car. It is a curious thing that a pretty
little house like that, gilt rod below the cornice in the
drawing-room, conservatory off the staircase, etc., should
have no indispensable convenience within the house. Out
to the garden through the snow, or rain as might be, lay
the disagreeable way to the most abominable hole ever
entered. None of the family find this unpleasant; to
me, it excludes me from ever profiting by their kind
hospitality—so easily do luxurious habits spoil us.

We had neither sea nor wind, and very few passengers—Janey and I alone in the state room. Nobody sick,
but such cold I never suffered from. The ladies had no
stove nor feet warmers nor any comforts, and the eating
was truly abominable. We tried only the tea but could
not drink it; luckily we had our own bread and wine.

22. Just this day week we left home—it seems a month at
least, having been so full of incident. Janey is playing
the pianoforte and I shall journalise till Mr. Ritchie
makes his appearance to whom I have written to ask
an interview—this reminds me of yesteday's doings. We
popt into Mrs. Gillies near five o'clock to please her
butler but we made our way upstairs and were received
with rapture; there I heard such flattering things as have
puffed me up with conceit for the rest of my life.

William my brother! raved to Mrs. Laing about the

Pau papers. She in astonishment read them and shewed them to Mrs. Gillies; they carried them then to Lord Jeffrey who calls them the gems of the journal, wants to know why there should be secrecy, they are papers to be proud of, *admirably written*! etc., etc.; he asked whether I had written any others. Such as they knew of they mentioned and he read all. 'Ah!' said he,'I never knew Lizzy, yet I am not surprised.' After this I may hold my head up at any rate to Leitch Ritchie and make my terms. However joking apart I really am glad of this testimony to my powers because I shall feel more confidence in my abilities and set to work with renewed vigour to employ them, as the proceeds can be so very usefully expended in our poor country. William has written to me; he is coming in to see me 'not knowing when we may meet again.' The Appeal comes on next month, and here, certainly nobody is sanguine as to the result. A Mr. Fulton goes about telling everyone that he put twenty thousand pounds into that odious Union Bank of which sum no entry has been made. Mrs. Wynch has the same story about her three thousand. If all these come out and are true how poor a chance has the Appeal. I wish it were all over—settled any way—and that we knew the worst.

25. Mr. Ritchie was glad to see me as it saved him writing about this new work—'*Papers for the People*'. for which he thinks me qualified to write; he is a very gentlemanly little man, good-looking with a fine forehead, and very pleasant to deal with. He thinks Mrs. Cottam improving very much and says her last contribution with which he *heads* the next number really good—as good almost as mine in the same style from which it is copied! It is really a great thing that she can thus earn a little money and occupy herself at the same time, and the creature has talent of a kind too, but so encumbered with rubbish that *I* can hardly ever get at it. Scribbling is common enough but good writting is even in these days rare judging by the absurdity of much that even the Chambers's give room to, in their, the best periodical of the day. By the bye Currer Bell is a woman, a coarse clever masculine woman—the daughter of a *clergyman*, some say the grand-daughter of Nelson

through *Horatia* whom it is proposed the nation should provide for to perpetuate the remembrance of the great blot upon her great father's fame. If so the morals of Lady Hamilton still influence the blood. A second novel has come out [Shirley], much inferior to *Jane Eyre* in interest and infinitely more outrageous as regards the decencies.

27. Sunday, My last entry was made on Friday morning since when we have been thinking of nothing but Lord Jeffrey. He fell back again, fever came on again, encreased, as did his weakness; he sunk from hour to hour and last night a few minutes before six o'clock expired. The dear friend we have loved all our lives who made our young days so happy—whom all the world admired and *spited* in his brilliant vigour and all the world admired and venerated in his maturer years. I believe he leaves not one enemy behind him. The more healthful tone of his later mind added to his own happiness and ensured the love of all his race.

What will Edinburgh be without Lord Jeffrey. Even in these last years when he was always ailing and often ill, he was the soul of his large circle. The best Judge upon the Bench, the kindest safest friend and adviser, charming as a host, delightful as a guest, and in his home with that dear wife of his, his daughter and her husband, and the grand-children all about him with the few remaining friends of his long life at times beside him it was a picture of true happiness such as a great man's fireside seldom shows. He died with his physician's fingers on his pulse. The world while books remain can never lose sight of the genius of our day, the friends, the clients, those who acted with the clever lawyer and the upright judge will never forget *the man*; the few to whom he gave a share of that warm heart will ever cherish his memory as one precious link between them and goodness.

The post was rich this evening. In this good town they are far too good to carry about letters on a Sunday but the post office has compassion on the anxious and delivers all letters that are there enquired for. The best note of all was from you my dear sweet Annie you little merry cricket. All with you well and seemingly very happy—but my

conceit makes me fancy you would none of you be sorry
to have Mama home again; poor Janey does not much
like my approaching departure. If I know and feel that I
am fit for my journey to-morrow, the next day positively
I go; if I think I am unequal to it or the weather be unfit
for the venture I shall not be so imprudent as to risk a life
that is valuable to all of you. Also my *mission* is not yet
accomplished. I have a novel yet to write—and so says
Leitch Ritchiel!

29. We have been greatly annoyed by a letter from cousin
Bartle asking Jane for money to fee Counsel, the junior
counsel, Sir Frederick Thesiger[1] takes no fee. Jane has
none to give. She has been ruined by William's speculations. She lent him three thousand pounds—gone;
bought Mr. Cameron's bond two thousand five hundred
pounds—as good as gone; is guarantee for seven thousand pounds, with only the rents of Rothiemurchus, part
of them, to reimburse her, and she pays about a hundred
pounds a year to poor annuitants of the estate, who would
be going about begging if she had not compassion on
them. James has near six hundred pounds out of his
pocket, little debts of William's he was ashamed of; and
fifteen hundred pounds is owing to the Chambers for
money advanced and work done, much work too never
charged. My mother, after her allowance was to come
through his hands, never received it, she had to live on
her savings from the annuity my father had remitted
regularly. What remained of this little fund she divided
between himself and two of the most to be pitied of the
creditors. Out of her four hundred a year she gives one
hundred and fifty for her board, etc. etc.; fifty to Mrs.
Carmac, fifty to Mrs. Grant Yarmouth, and keeps but one
hundred and fifty for dress, washing, books, her maid's
wages, her doctor, and her private charities. He says she
is not entitled to her Rothiemurchus jointure. So he can
look for no help here. Worse than all this, William Craig
says he met Sir Frederick Thesiger who spoke as kindly,

1. A very distinguished lawyer (solicitor-General and Attorney-
   General 1844–6) who became Lord Chancellor in 1858.

as warmly as ever, but has not the same sanguine hopes
about the issue of the case. He had trusted to William's
statements, and they are not borne out by facts.

There was a nice letter from dear Annie yesterday and
another to-day; they begin to want me home but all are
well and seem happy and though this fine morning I
wish much I were on my way to them I feel alas!
that though better I am hardly yet fit for the journey.
I breakfast in this pleasant room, served so neatly, in my
dressing-gown, in an easy chair, by the bright Scotch
coal fire and on a fly table is set the tray with such a
fine Damask napkin upon it, and a small silver teapot,
a small silver sugar basin, and a very small silver cream
jug containing such rich cream, and a tall slim covered
silver jug with hot water; china plates, delicious bread
and butter and Pentland honey. 'Tis the house of luxury.
These Edinburgh houses are particularly warm—warmer
a great deal than any I have yet lived in; they are large,
airy, substantially built, and the coals are so admirable
the heat is quite delightful.

30. The post this morning has been very amusing—a packet
from Oxford. The precious letter from Leitch Ritchie is
sent on its rounds. It is really flattering, but still more
kind than flattering and contains such judicious hints that
I have copied all the part intended to be useful to the
authour. Poor unhappy jealous E.L.C.[Eliza Cottam] she
has had to take a pill and is quite unhinged in consequence
of a paper on geology which she wrote in three days
having been returned to her by L. R. as unsuitable,
with a note of admiration of my *Mrs. Wright*,[2] who has
she says turned his head, and so overshadowed all her
pretensions—the truth being that he expressed himself
quite satisfied with her abilities and pleased with her
improvement and that I did my best to fortify him in
his opinion also putting in a touch about poverty which

2. She wrote several series of amusing but pointed conversations between this worldly-wise lady and her tenantry; the
views expressed are very similar to all she writes about
Baltiboys and Blessington in her journal.

I knew was one sure road to a heart acknowledged to be of the kindest.

One kind heart putting me in mind of another, James has been by request to see Mr. Empson. [Lord Jeffrey's son-in-law] They are all very calm, disposed rather to be grateful for having the 'light of *our* day' vouchsafed to them for so many years beyond the term, for dear Lord Jeffrey was seventy-seven, than to murmur at having had to give him up in the fulness of his fame and happiness. He has died very rich. House and furniture in Moray Place, furniture at Craig Crook and upwards of sixty thousand pounds—so it is said. James being one of the trustees of the Will must be at the opening of it, so we shall know correctly not that it is of much consequence, there is plenty of fortune for the few who are to inherit it. It is a great topick of conversation here; what will be the after proceedings of the bereaved family, where they will live, etc.

31. James gave us a long account of the funeral. All the publick authorities wished to attend but as it had been Lord Jeffrey's wish for as little display as possible this compliment was declined. About sixty private friends followed the hearse in sixteen mourning coaches to the new cemetery at the Deane Bridge where he himself had chosen his resting-place. Jane has walked there with him and looked at it. There was a long string of gentlemen's carriages, and a large crowd of the lower orders. The property altogether is about sixty thousand pounds, not the money only. All made by his own bright head and busy hands—for a harder working man never lived. Besides what he has left, he lost some money by Constable's failure and about fourteen thousand pounds in the American Funds, and he spent a great deal in building and improving at Craig Crook.

TUESDAY, FEBRUARY 5. I have a deal of leeway to make up so had best set to work this rainy morning and be done with it as I have quantities of business upon hands. James has taken a great deal of trouble about Mr. Moore's pictures and books—indeed he has quite interested himself in this unfortunate man's distresses. He wrote me a long letter in the humbug style, his true feeling at the moment I am sure, deploring his folly, announcing his amendment, and detailing most judicious plans—it really affected all who did not know him. The Doctor and I together *may* keep him up to these wise imaginings—however I doubt it. I was right to leave him in his hoity toitys: they did not last long. I knew his necessities would not let them, and he has now applied the second time for assistance and again it is ready for him. His four books will bring ten or twelve pounds; his two pictures fifty pounds; the spoon five pounds. I told him this and sent him a list of old books likely to be in an old collection which would also be worth something considerable, and I also gave him most particular directions about the packing.

Now for my journey. All ready by our usual breakfast hour on Friday the 1st and very sorry to part. A cab took us in five minutes to the terminus where I was made over to Mr. Campbell of Craig: he had come up for Lord Jeffrey's funeral and was returning to Ayrshire when we met him on the platform; he has danced with me before now so we travelled very lovingly together. Two gentlemen and one lady came on board and we all sat round the stove to read while the boat glided easily down the Clyde. She moved at two—made Greenock at five, and found there so much additional cargo that we were one hour and a half detained to take it in. What would it have been without our cargo of malleable iron from the Carron Works, furniture in the rough from Stirling or thereabouts, going to Dublin to be finished by the neat fingers of the Irish—potatoes, many tons of them and bales of soft goods. I was not the least sick, but the raging elements as the poets say depriving us of light or air, the ports requiring to be shut and the skylight lowered, one of my worst headaches attacked me and condemned me to lay still in my berth all the weary twenty-seven hours we were fighting out our tedious way.

Scotland had well speeded the parting guest, Ireland failed to welcome the coming one. Had I landed on the Wednesday as first arranged, the carriage would have been on the quay, and faithful Dick! along with it.

On this dark and very dreary Saturday night, no one expected me. The adverse winds had detained the mails, and although this made but a few hours' difference in Dublin, it made the difference of a day at Baltiboys. Even had our letters reached in time, who could have waited on that dismal quay, till nine o'clock at night to watch for me? So there was no help at hand. I sent a porter for a covered car. At last came my own turn and glad enough I was to climb to the deck and to scramble down from it and to be half pulled and half pushed up the steep ladder near the paddle wheels, and to cross the dirty gangway by the galley, and so to use the humbler means of reaching shore. I drove to John Robinson's office in case any message might have been left there, but finding none went on to Elvidge's hotel. There was a slight demur about admitting an unknown unprotected female arriving with so little luggage in a hackney car near midnight. However nothing daunted I gave my name and in an instant came an outpouring of attentions. A good bedroom, a bright fire, tea, my book and afterwards my bed consoled me for all sorrows. Next morning I dressed at leisure, had a cup of tea, got a covered car, and paying five shillings for my entertainment, drove merrily off that quiet Sunday morning for the Wicklow hills.

6. Jane's enclosures were highly ridiculous: notes from Madame de Cotta, who has written to tell Mr. Ritchie that I wonderfully admired him and also informs us that he fell in love with me—the one I suppose about as true as the other. Of the indecorum of thus communicating private opinions to those not intended to hear them, she appears to have no perception; on the contrary she indulges in very unladylike jokes about the probability of Colonel Smith's wife running away with the Editor of *Chambers' Journal*, and proud of her wit, requests this ingenious hit may make the tour of the family connexions, an excursion my rather dull fire is at this moment preventing. It is absurd to take any heed of the follies of so ridiculous a little self-satisfied piece of impertinence. I am sure I am glad I am out of the office of Corrector of her rigmaroles,

though indeed L. R. told me her '*Forty Years Ago*' is really clever.

He has given me plenty of work. Subjects for the Journal for the *Papers for the People* and even for the *People's Library*. Miss Cook wants a Tale and Jane wants me to take the Light Literature 'oar' in the *Edinburgh Review*. I doubt my ability. Mrs. Gillies would be the one for that. I will try all however—do my best—take pains and work hard. We must do something for the present aspect of things is frightful.

The draining being over the same distress exists as before it began. We have kept the people in our immediate neighbourhood alive these two years and now they must die, or beg, or steal, any thing rather than the Poor House which however must be full for we give no outdoor relief in this Union and our rates though lighter on us than they were last year are still heavy. Sheep are beginning to disappear. We have lost one, which considering all we have done to lessen the distress is a bad sign. Sam Darker lost five sheep, Mr. West two, one of them a prize for which he gave a high price. We must be careful in our expenditure as probably the few small tenants we have may be induced to emigrate if assisted. Lachlin and Mary Ryan are gone—to New Orleans—with a large party of friends, Mary under the charge of Kiogh the tailor's son and wife. We paid all her expenses and most of her brother's; he had a little money, the Doctor gave him a suit of old clothes, the Colonel did the remainder; Annie superintended the whole affair and did it all properly. Even in a business point of view this is a £10 profitably laid out. These orphans who have much plagued us will cost us no more, and they may act as pioneers for their numerous relations.

How cheap my journey was to and from Edinburgh: Steam-boat fifteen shillings each; first class train five shillings, cabs and porters and stewards five shillings more; eating need be nothing, most persons carrying a basket of provisions more suited to a delicate appetite than the abominable preparations of the pantry and galley. I brought eight pounds home with me for my

Pyrénées, and found two guineas from Eliza Cook. So I have begun my school breakfast to the paupers and bought some calico.

Went to Kilbride and indeed both husband and wife look miserable. *She* looks starved. He says he is now determined to do right. My business was to look over the catalogue of the books, mark such as are likely to sell in Edinburgh, and get the pictures measured. And to set *him* to work to write for the press. I arranged all the material part for him and have only now to push him on to make a beginning; he will run along of himself afterwards, interested in the occupation and pleased with the receipts for it. And he has the brains, and an extremely agreeable style of composition. I have given him for his first subject *Society in Dublin* past or present, of all ranks, handled in any way he likes, and have put up for him this night my *Lairds* and Miss Jewrie's *Chateau Life in England* as a kind of hints to him. He can fly higher by and bye. What a godsend another hundred pounds a year would be to them.

17. Sunday, Actually ten days since a single entry was made in this journal. Yesterday week, Saturday, I don't remember what we were doing. Sunday we went to church and for the first time for ages not a human being called here afterwards although Mr. King! has appeared again. There was a meet at Blesinton yesterday. The Colonel and Jack had a famous hunt, brought Mr. King home to luncheon, they all ate like hunters! and then decided on dining about an hour later, Mr. King going home to dress. He was very merry—made us laugh a good deal being full of amusing gossip without any ill-nature, and now and then a bright hit—but that is all—he has read nothing, thought none, seen little, lived in a frivolous set and has no taste for musick or any other accomplishment. This is all my home news—no great store—for never was anything so hopelessly dull as this poor wretched country. The Magistrates have been sending people to jail for sheep-stealing—the two McKayes for our sheep and a man of the name of Pearson who stole three or four, and three wretched girls who took two from Dizest;

plundering is going on all round us, fifteen hundred in the Poor House, yet we are infested with beggars. More of Lord Milltown's plate gone to be sold, and peers and gentles going down down down never to rise again.

24. Sunday, The servants in and out all behaving well and all content, yet the outdoor ones barely living; the draining done; no work anywhere except for picked workmen. God help the people; the roads are beset with tattered skeletons, that give one a shudder to look at, for how can we feed or clothe so many. Eighteen children get their breakfast at school. Miss MacDonnell has made bibs of the calico to wear in the school which improves the look but hardly the comfort. We must manage some shirting and some soap. It is all most wretched. Mr. McDarby has been so impudent—ignorant perhaps and selfish in consequence; he would neither go to live in the schoolhouse nor let anyone else into it—even locked up the room on my telling him that I could not let it remain uninhabited. I had to get the Colonel to demand the key. I then told him I considered his conduct highly impertinent and that such presumption would not do with me. Miss MacDonnell for whose lodging at James Ryan's I was paying, has gladly moved into the schoolhouse retaining the good old Cullens in the kitchen but I fear we shall have to give up the schools: so few scholars pay fees few can; clothing and eating are with many nearly as difficult to provide for; never were such times.

A gleam of comfort has been shed over this misery by the Acts of the Encumbered Estates Commission. It began its labours in October and here in February have begun the sales: the first a private sale, two farms bought by the tenants in possession, one for twenty-seven, the other for twenty-five years' purchase. The next publick—a bidding before the Commissioners—occupying eleven minutes, the conveyance made out in an hour, the money to be paid down and the little property bought at twenty years' purchase. We hurried down to tell the Moores for this was in Mayo on the borders of Galway. Kilbride will surely get a year or two more, and the head rents go still higher. Lord Milltown too went off to town at once in good spirits for some of his creditors are forcing a sale on him, and at these prices little matter.

28. With the first volume of Disraeli's '*Tancred*' ends all the cleverness. The hero a little mad in the beginning turns into a fool at the end and we have to accompany him to the East among Jews, Arabs, Mount Sinai and heaven only knows what; all that is stupid and improbable.

The Colonel walked with Annie and me. We went to James Ryan's to leave a message; to school—thirty-four girls; to the new fence between us and Dempsey; and visited three of our old women; poor creatures they think themselves comfortable and so they are by comparison but it is all very wretched. Made up a little bundle for one of them which that good Miss Macdonnell carried home. She is now in the schoolhouse living and will soon have her bare room neat, she is both managing and tidy. I declare the starving children look better already.

Annie had a long walk with the Doctor early, and he and I had a long conversation about our poor. He has been at his own cost sending some young people out to America and we are helping the Grays there. They have given up possession of their miserable holding quite peaceably. The old man asked nothing; threw himself on the Colonel's liberality and said he had a few bits of good furniture to sell which would help him. The manure he considers due to the ground instead of the half-year's rent; so the Colonel will give him five pounds and one pound to that wretched Kitty if they will take her with them.

A letter from Annie Need still hopeful about William, but I am not. I think the Judges would have decided at once could they have given sentence in his favour, but one result is certain, that his character comes out unsullied from this ordeal which was more than I expected. All those abominable calumnies have been refuted and any errours there are, are errors of judgement. With this we must be content.

TUESDAY, MARCH 5. A long walk to school, etc. We meet Mr. King every day; he goes in for the post; he dined with us Monday invited by the Colonel. I disapprove of any attentions in that quarter but cannot prevail to have them discontinued. It really annoys me much. I like the young man but I don't think him deserving of Annie. His friends expect money with his bride which indeed he would require. And Annie has seen so few that her judgement is not at all sufficiently formed for any decision she makes now to be likely to satisfy her maturer taste.

16. Nothing particular: no doctor now to hear our news as formerly. For weeks he has hardly been near us, and when he does come his visits are hurried and he appears little interested in our doings. Mr. King called of course; he favours us with a view of his handsome bright countenance pretty frequently; and really I believe he is a fine creature, capable of becoming very superiour to what he is.

17. Sunday; great meeting at church. Mr. King dined with us. Dick popt in to tea. Settled all matters relating to our wonderful week in Dublin.

18. St Patrick's Day Ball.

23. Annie made a great sensation at that Monster Ball. I could hardly extricate her from her mob of partners and get her off at three in the morning. The presentation was not formidable. Tom went with us and escorted us up the great staircase at the head of which a card from each of us was taken. We were then shown through an anteroom into the throne room where about fifty more soon assembled. It was very cold and we had a long wait. At last doors opened and twelve aides de camp entered two and two, four chamberlains with white wands two and two, their Excellencies, twelve young ladies in ball dresses two and two, a few elder ladies plentifully jewelled. They formed in a group before the throne and then all the company to be presented who had been placed in a double line under a gallery were handed forward one by one to receive the proper salute. We walked on to the opposite door and soon rejoined our friends the Grattans who had secured excellent seats near the entrance so that I saw everyone that entered the beautiful hall. The procession of the little Court was very pretty; it moved up to the head of the room where a carpetted space before the throne was

reserved for the party accompanying their excellencies. The Ball was begun by a long country dance to the tune of 'St Patrick's day in the morning' all the fifty couple danced faithfully down by Prince George and the Marchioness of Drogheda. The Duke of Leinster and Countess of Milltown next; three or four more titled couples, Lady Cecilia Leeson among them and then Tom and Annie.

I never had Annie near me again. She danced every dance of every sort, Mr. King kindly taking the principal charge of her. Mr. Chetwode was there, and so many partners she knew, and so many people I knew—altogether it was very pleasant; five refreshment rooms were open, a lounging room, a card room, a second dancing room and a pretty conservatory most pleasantly cool. I never enjoyed a party more. Indeed our whole week in Dublin was one continued pleasure. We were closely attended the whole time by Mr. King; he was at the Hotel on Monday almost as soon as we were having engaged a very nice brougham for us for the evening. He brought a bouquet with him for Miss Anne. Mr. Sheehan at dressing time sent her another greatly to the amusement of Miss Merrey who had again accompanied us as maid and very useful she was. We had Guillaume again for Annie's hair which he dressed beautifully. She looked so handsome in her feathers. Tuesday Mr. King dined with us. Wednesday we found him at the Exhibition and he went in with us to the Museum. Thursday he dined with us and went with us to the opera having got our tickets for us and chosen our seats. Mr. Sheehan followed us there by the bye and was most amusing. Friday ditto, substituting Play for Opera; and on this day he brought a bouquet which was sent upstairs with a note! All my precautions vain. I shall never keep Annie unmarried till twenty.

24. A memorable day in the Annals of this family. May God grant it prove a fortunate one. Annie had tried to keep her secret, dear little soul, while in town as her lover wished it but it came out so innocently to her own loved and loving mother. Mr. King had made his proposals on the night of St Patrick's Ball and dreading me wished to enlist the

Colonel on his side to help him to face me. So after church to which we did not go he came here and asked Annie in form of her father. He has been very open, very honest, very gentlemanly, in the whole affair, and the Colonel who really likes him has accepted him conditionally—there must be full consent on the part of his parents, and they must wait a little while she being so young. They had most unreserved conversations on business matters and must have another parley before sketching out means for the present and settlements for the future. And then we wait for Captain King's approval. So the Colonel wishes the young people to keep apart till the lover hears from England; he dined with us and seemed very happy, and dear Annie's heart is evidently much in the matter.

25. A visit from Lady Milltown. 'So Annie, you are going to be married!' How in the world does this woman hear everything? She then began to me, and when I told her it was not settled, that her Papa thought Annie too young and we also wished to know something more of Mr. King: 'My dear, I can tell you everything about him. Irreproachable character! Highly connected! Lord Lorton's family, cousin to Lord Erne, Lord and Lady Drogheda, Lord that this and tother and all rich. Such a match; people might spend half their time in Dublin and not hear of such an one and you to make it out all so quietly in the country!!' I don't make it out to be quite so magnificent as all this, but it is a very good connexion and there is money enough for our moderate views. Better than this the young man is amiable, does not want for sense, and has improved very much in many ways since he lived more in the morally healthy atmosphere of this house.

Tom Darker who has for some time had his suspicions on this subject delicately hinted them to me to-day and told me that for the love he bore us he had been diligently looking after him and any young man more correct could not be found; and shrewd and managing, yet liberal when necessary. From this interesting theme on which we talked long, we proceeded to another! *his own marriage*! and [his sister's] Alicia's. Alicia is engaged and will marry her young Boothman as soon as he can get a farm. Tom Darker is not engaged, nor will he speak to the elder sister Boothman till he can get a farm which must be here or near here for he could not bear, he says, to leave the Colonel, and I am sure we should do ill enough without him. My brain is quite confused with all these changes.

28. Of course we are all of us almost entirely occupied with dear Annie's affairs. Mr. King (as she says) has written to his proud and rather money-loving father to ask his sanction to a marriage with a young lady of the name of *Smith* without a fortune! Her little dower of £2,500 only £1,000 of which can be given down hardly deserving the name of a fortune. We are moderate therefore in our requirements—a subject we have hardly touched on yet though we have considered it ourselves. Both the Colonel and I are agreed that the young people beginning on little is no matter, provided that little be secure; nor can we demand a large settlement but we must have one—a sum for children, and a jointure in case of widowhood. If Captain King really have the fortune imputed to him he will have little difficulty in agreeing to our demands. What he inherited from his rich Indian father I know not; he has but one brother, a clergyman, and one sister, our Miss King who has twenty thousand pounds. It is therefore unlikely the Captain should have less. He married a Miss Tottenham—an *heiress* highly born. Our Mr. King is her only son and there are but three daughters. It makes me a little fidgetty. My Colonel is proud too and will not let his child enter a family that would not welcome her, and that child's heart is so engaged that were a stop put to matters now, it would go nigh to kill her. She has seen too much of her lover and thought too long about him to give him up on account of fatherly differences. I anticipate some cross readings and can only trust as often before to time and patience.

Tom Darker is to have fifty-one acres on the other side of the hill—all the scattered bits we have purchased from different little tenants; he is to pay a guinea an acre and still remain steward here. Where he will *house* Mrs. Tom is yet uncertain.

SUNDAY, APRIL 7. Our Schoolmaster, poor young man, came out of the hospital and has had to return to it. He is totally unfit to resume the school which I shall therefore give up as a bad job and save my pocket thereby. There are very few boys left on our side of the country; there will be few men soon for they are pouring on in shoals to America. Crowds upon crowds swarm along the roads, the bye roads, following carts with their trunks and other property. We have forty children as yet in the girls' school; but really I don't think there will be half that number by autumn.

I am busy correcting the *Calcutta Journal* and copying it out fair for the press; it is a long job. Ogle Moore is setting to work in earnest. I think his brother James's letters from Melbourne might be turned to account now that there is such a rage for the Colonies.

Our little Annie is occupying us; she is very happy and the lover is very near heaven—not quite at the gates as the father is still too ill to be spoken to although better, and the mother don't conceal that the want of money is a disappointment to herself and will be hard to reconcile him to. The aunt has however given her consent most cordially and she and the sister Arabella will in a little time bring round the parents. The week has passed happily to the young people; they have met three times, and to-day they spent most of the morning together. And certainly the more I know of our son-in-law the more perfectly I like him. He will improve rapidly when strengthened by the good sound principles of this house—though all his own feelings are right, honest and gentlemanly. I do think my dearly loved Annie will be safe in his hands and that they will be happy together. And I was a good deal prejudiced against him—too readily believed malicious tales, and perhaps looked too high for my daughter—expected some model man to drop from heaven in honour of her. The Doctor is inexplicable. Mr. King is in high favour with him—such affectionate greetings, unreserved conversations upon all subjects but

the one and presents of the finest cigars. He speaks to
the Colonel about his health rather kindly, and when he
and I meet he don't bite me, though he says as little
as possible. Annie he don't notice; he looks ashamed
of himself, restless, unhappy, and very ill. I must help
him out of this silly fit.

14. Sunday again. We have not had one visitor but Mr. King
who comes every second day and stays till we turn him
out. He is selling butter and trying to sell horses meaning
to get quit of three and keep but four—two hunters and
two between the farm and the *carriage*. We must try and
convince him a *car* will do.

Mr. King tells me that his father hitherto has made
him no fixed allowance but allowed him to draw for
about three hundred a year; if he would make it certain
four hundred we should be quite content, and we would
give Annie fifty pounds annually the half of our claim
on Kinloss, on which most surely for a few years they
could be very comfortable. The two estates on which
all the money is mortgaged are to be put up for sale
very shortly, under the new Act; probably old Mr. King
may himself purchase one of them. His wife has also
some landed property; and there is a very fine house
in Merrion Square and a villa at Howth—plenty heaven
knows! for all the family. Mr. King seems to think there
would be no difficulty about such moderate settlements
as we should ask for. So I hope before Christmas all things
may be settled happily and in the mean (time) the two who
are going for good and ill together are becoming better
acquainted and I must say that our greater intimacy is
very favourable to the new member of our family. I
am sorry it is all so very much 'talked of. Everywhere
it seems to be *the* theme. Mr. King and the Colonel have
been separately congratulated by everybody.

21. Mr. King is a nice creature really. Peggy highly approves,
has given her consent, first because he is our *aquals*, one of
those old gintry such sort as used to keep company with
the Squire; next, because he's quite the gentleman spakes
as civil to herself as the rale quality ever does; and last
and most particularly because he's clane. Miss Anne will

have every comfort with a husband so clane. Paddy was always a clane poor man and she had had great raison to be thankful for it. Mrs. Wright or somebody should get hold of that. I hear that lady's conversations have enchanted all my friends; they do read very well. Ministers have had a majority this week on some question. All the church bells should be set ringing and it may go down in the chronological tables as one of the remarkable events of the day. Pity I can't send this wit to Punch. We have got the first volume of Macaulay's history—'tis like opening the eyes of the blind.

We have had a grand reconciliation scene with the dear good absurd Doctor. Last Monday I made a third attempt, wrote him a third note and boldly broached the subject; this brought him out, in horrid temper though, and he preached away full of prejudice; there was no bringing him to reason, and though we parted friends I feared there was a sad end to real friendship. Indeed he was not to be justified. That day Ogle Moore called to talk him over—accounting for him, excusing him, apologising for him and counselling me. So the result of this kind friend's interference here was that Annie wrote an affectionate note which arriving after judicious interference there, produced an equally tender answer and yesterday an interview that finished the affair. His little foibles had all been rubbed against, most unwittingly indeed, but very sorely, and the malicious world ever ready to spread evil had not let such quiet people as us alone, or spared the high-born and successful lover. There is the whole affair, and since the Doctor has agreed to laugh at it as we do, so it will rest, doing no more harm to anyone. But how very meddling all the country have been. Watching our every movement, blaming us all, furious with Mr. King for nothing that I can see, miserable about us, all as unnecessary. None of us believing it to be requisite to send a trumpeter round to announce the facts, first of Mr. King's attentions, next of Miss Anne's respondings, then of the proposals, and last of the acceptance, with a supplement concerning the aunt and the father!

TUESDAY, MAY 14. Another long interruption. This being

a rainy day of soft balmy showers much wanted by the country I have found an hour to recall the most 'remarkable events' of our quiet lives. May be had I written daily, trifles might have appeared important enough to merit notice, but to look back on nothing strikes me. Publick affairs as queer as ever. Markets dull, people ruined; the better sort emigrating with money, leaving the Paupers of all classes at home to starve together. It is melancholy really to walk along the roads the day before the steamer sails for America: such crowds following the poor wretched carts with the rickety luggage in it, all the women in tears, all the men surly, and yet they leave want behind and have hope before them. A ray of hope beams now over all. The Dublin and Glasgow Steam Packet Company have advertised the *Viceroy* our old friend, to sail from *Galway* to New York on the 1st of June, the Railway Company assisting the enterprise. Should it succeed we may breathe again.

17. I think that this day two years my poor father died. Worse news has come to-day—poor William. The Doctor walked down and chatted pleasantly for a while and then came the post—a note from Mr. Gardiner reporting that miserable sentence of the Privy Council. Sir Edward Ryan[3] read the judgement. After clearing William's character as to the duties, etc. of his office, they find him 'deserving of dismissal on account of his connexion with the Union Bank because he first was a party to the framing and signing of deceptive reports; and second that he was concerned with six other partners in borrowing money of the Bank on their personal security for the purpose of keeping up in the market the price of the shares, considered imcompatible with his high situation as Master in Equity, next to the Judges themselves.' Besides those concerned there were not ten people in the Court. What matter? it will be blown about widely enough, crowed over by the malicious. And we must bear it for it is true. Who will believe that clever Grant was

3. Chief Justice of Bengal and from 1843 to 1865 he heard India appeals to the judicial committee of the Privy Council.

deceived by sly Beckwith and must not Grant suffer for
trusting another, deserting his duty in so doing, yielding
to flattery, indulging in arrogance, and worst of all, lax in
money matters from early youth, rash, and self-sufficient,
madly fancying evil doings could turn to good. It is very
very wretched—overwhelming to him and to poor Sally,
any other publick employment being now out of the
question.

25. Our cows are milking much better since our people were
told the doings of Mr. King's dairy. Really that managing
County Antrim woman of his makes a fortune for him.
She makes each cow rear two calves, sometimes three,
and she expects besides five pounds of butter per week
from each when but little cream is wanted. He churns
twice a week and sends off the butter when a thirty pound
cool is filled to a dealer in Dublin who gives the head
market price for it; then the calves at a year old bring
from £2.10.0 to £3.10.0 apiece and certainly don't cost
much after weaning. Dairy husbandry so close to Dublin
might pay well.

SATURDAY, JUNE 1. John Robinson busy with the tenants.
They are not in good humour—the times are against
them and Tom Darker's getting that ground has incensed
them: they say they are all to be put out to make room for
the Darkers. One good effect of this pique is that they are
doing their best to keep themselves in. They paid really
very well. We received about half the half year's rents,
but more will come in the course of a month or so; the
principal defaulter is Rutherfurd who has not brought one
penny. No tenant save him owes a year's rent. Some few
owe a half year; others are short only by a few pounds of
paying up to the term. We ought to be quite satisfied.

22. My private talk with the poor dear half neglected journal
must wait a wee. The *Indian Journal* will occupy my
writing time for a full week. Also *Mrs. Wright* must talk
a bit, and there is a deal of needle work to do, mending,
and no one to do it. And the houses to put in order—old
servants going and new coming—always a plague.

I have not attempted church, Sunday though it be. All
else are gone, the Colonel having threatening letters to

shew to Mr. Owen, sent to Tom Darker in consequence
of his having taken that ground; it has raised a most
unpleasant feeling among the people, one that it will
be difficult to allay; the transaction was a mistake, but
we must not now let them beard us. The Colonel and
I had talked over the proper steps to be taken on this
threat of insurrection in our kingdom and Mr. Owen
quite approving of our idea of addressing the assembled
tenants I have this evening set down on paper what the
Colonel proposed to say to them, made a rough sketch of
a speech which can be altered if necessary. It will make
the greater impression when they can read it afterwards
themselves and most assuredly the dear Colonel would
forget the principal part of his wrathful denunciation
were he to trust it to his memory; he will tell these
gentry that one and all must quit should harm of any
kind happen to any of the Darkers. They are a most
odious people. They seem incapable of rising out of low
vindictive evil feelings. Not a man in Baltiboys is the
worse for Tom Darker cultivating these patches on his
own *account* instead of on the Colonel's. What business is
it then of theirs? There is another sore subject with them
which I can better understand their ill-humour on—the
drainage loan; though the redeemed land puts many a
pound into their pockets they can't abide paying a few
extra shillings for this. I wish they were all in America,
I know.

30. We have been quite plagued with all the servants' doings
these some weeks. Marianne latterly would do no work;
it was no use coaxing or scolding, she was perfectly
insubordinate though always obliging to us above, but
a regular vixen below. At last she could not controul
her way wardness and point blank refusing to clean
the stairs she had to go at an hour's warning, and we
moved up Biddy Hyland from the kitchens where she
was assisting during the company time, to try her hand
at house-maiding. She has done wonderfully well. We
replaced her below by Anne Byrne, lazy, stupid and
dishonest. She stole eatables and wearables and hid them
in the stacks not daring to take them home to the decent

grandmother and Uncle Luke. We got rid of her and did without, the house quite full all the time, eating going on all day, and Mary with quite washing enough and seven cows. It then came to the time of Catherine's departure to seek better fortune in Dublin. By good luck I heard of a very respectable woman and good cook who had lived years with the Cottons and the old Major; hired her, and here she is, laughing at the work which so oppressed the other spoiled things and really likely in every respect to suit us. And on this arrangement being completed there comes out a love tale, Catherine's regrets, and a scene of sobbing, and a history of the most malicious slanders propagated by this evil-tongued people. So I had to get in Pat, hold a sort of agreeably delicate Court of Enquiry and open a new era in Irish History. Witness an engagement between two young persons to marry when they have saved sufficient money, and Catherine stays here as housemaid so I hope our troubles in this department are over, but we have been most extremely uncomfortable for as always happens the opportunity of a press of business was taken for the meditated changes. Catherine too must needs go to Dublin to set her parents' hearts at ease about her conduct and inform them of her intended marriage. She will return tomorrow when we hope to be once more comfortable.

WEDNESDAY, JULY 3. On the hill in the morning looking after the new cottages. We shall make them very tidy; then walked with Tom Darker all over the upper part of Judy Ryan's old farm which he is bringing into fine order, and laid out a plan for Common's ill-used acres. The Colonel had terrified me to death about my school declaring he would close it and fill the house with police and he actually wrote and offered it to the magistrates so I should have been obliged to write also and say that I could not agree. Tom Darker will settle it; the Colonel as usual had taken up his notions too quickly and fancying from something the Serjeant said that the boys' room which I had offered them a loan of, now that it is not used, would not answer, he determined at any risk to get the police here; it seems the Serjeant did not disapprove of the room at all only said the force sent to it must be unmarried.

Mr. and Mrs. West rode up to call just as we were going to dinner full of plans for the summer,—Giant's Causeway in the North, Cattle Show at Cork and a month in Roscommon besides. How people scrape up money for such vagaries these times is matter of wonder to me, and how the parents of four nice children can leave them to servants and go wandering about for no reason but pleasure is a still greater amazement to those who are brought up to do their duty and find their happiness at home. Letters come as usual; not much in them. Mr. Ritchie is a trump. I sent him two papers of the *Calcutta Journal* on Thursday when Annie and I went to town. He writes me on Saturday the day he received it, to say it had already gone to the printer's, so it must have arrived just in the nick of time; it really is so clever I don't wonder he thus hails it. Jane will be so pleased. I must send him some more and get him to publish it weekly while it lasts.

5. Sir Robert Peel died on Tuesday night. Such a loss—the world don't feel it yet, nor won't for many a long day. Never was there such a stir made about any accident, the lower orders crowding round the house like the upper ranks—the file of carriages and the mob vying in numbers; bulletins had to be furnished to the policemen to read at different places to satisfy the publick. And all of no use, any more than Lady Peel, a weak delicate woman who could not be told of her husband's danger nor be allowed to disturb his last moments; he took leave of everyone else. The intellect of that man—so ripened too. It is impossible to foresee the consequences of the want of him. There has not been such a calamity since the nation lost Mr. Canning.

9. A message of condolence is to be sent from the French republick to the family of Sir Robert Peel, an honour without a precedent. And a poor man's subscription is begun limited to a penny, to raise a monument less enduring than his fame.

Envy, jealousy, malice, evil speaking, hatred, lying,

and all uncharitableness, fill the minds of our wretched peasantry. Fancy that fine boy of Jack Byrne's having been used by his father as his instrument in this letter business—made to write the two threatening notices—it has almost been proved against him and the police expect to bring it quite home to that house. How I do wish we had not one tenant in Baltiboys. It will come to that probably. And if we do not live to carry it out, do you keep it in mind, dear Jack, to get all your land into your own hands; graze it, till only what the cattle require; house and pay your few servants well, and grow flax to employ their women.

14. Mr. Ritchie has sent me five guineas for the four published *Conversations of Mrs. Wright*. The school deserves working for, it is getting on very well. And so are the new servants. The cook is a very decent body—an excellent plain cook, quiet, and steady and cleanly and of an age to keep the rest in order. The parlourmaid understands her business well, and is never heard in the house. She is a daughter of Gyves the nailer in Blesinton, widow of old Norton the Sexton's son, and her children are dead. The cook is worse than a widow for she has a drunken husband who leaves her their three children to support. Catherine makes an active little housemaid, and Mary after a few battles consents to use the new churn, and instead of butter once a week taking her and two men two hours to bring, we have butter three times a week made by herself alone in something under fifteen minutes.

21. Sunday again. Our chief business within has been preserving fruit, a small proportion of the immense crop of small fruit actually over-running the garden. The farm looks as well as the garden. Such corn and hay and potatoes as we have not seen for many a day and difficult to get people for field labour. Eight turnip weeders after searching the country and we have to take them off to make the hay. Two mowers only; so here is the rain before that heavy crop is safe; poor dawdling Tom Darker; he is an honest man though, and we can't have everything. The markets have fallen again, the cattle markets and very much too—20/—to 50/—a head. We sold our last

lot of lambs wonderfully well considering—17/6—only
1/6 less than former prices; others had miserable offers;
many thought it best to bring their beasts home.

I should have liked to have kept Annie a few years
longer unmarried. I should have preferred a higher order
of mind as the companion and *guide* of hers. I should have
liked more easy circumstances for that young creature's
brightest years; but regrets are vain, the thing is done and
I am relieved by a better acquaintance with my son-in-law
to find with some weaknesses, plenty of brains, a kind
heart, a cheerful temper, and the manners and the feelings
of a gentleman. If God spare my life I may be of much use
to both of them. Annie is too much in love just now to
think very clearly, clever as she is. A year of matrimony
will form her character more quickly than would have
done my few more years of home and perhaps with as
little pain for I do not blind myself to the home she
feels it to be, dull, for young spirits to mope in—two
old ailing people, indisposed for society or any change
even, the one soured in temper by bodily infirmities and
always irritable at the best of times—the other nervous
and weakly; often worried; often vexed and too often
shewing it; I have not firmness for the part given me to
act. I have not sufficient activity either, and I am quite
aware that I sometimes lose my temper however flattering
my friends are on this point, and my spirits too give way
sometimes; so the poor children may find home fail them
and hope to change for the better in leaving it. I think had
we amused them more, we should all have been happier,
and we might had we been managers.

Our actual income *now* is nine hundred pounds, five
hundred of which is spent outside this house. On the
remaining four hundred pounds we live: butcher, baker,
grocer, wine merchant, chandler, carrier, wear and tear,
house servants' wages, Jack's dress and education, the
girls' pinmoney, the Colonel's pocket money, mine, our
little journeys, charities, Doctors' fees, extras. Four
hundred pounds a year pays it all with the addition
of the garden and dairy; but then I pay nobody for
doing my work. I do it myself or the girls do it; and

I buy no luxuries till we are plentifully supplied with necessaries. I look after everything, see that there is no waste, no losses, no destruction, and when people within don't do their work well, they go away and more active servants replace them. That abominable stable, that mob of idlers, poor Tom Darker among them, walls built and thrown down, things made and *altered*, failures, neglects, etc., etc. I suppose it is always so unless there be a *young, active, skilful* MASTER! at the head of affairs.

THURSDAY, AUGUST 1. Still fine weather. Tom Darker dawdling with the hay as usual. I have made him buy calves as he chose to sell ours and we are rearing one to every cow as we used to do for whatever milk they may drink it is all gain to us who had more than we wanted and only gave it away. The potatoe disease has begun again, partially. A whole field touched here and there but generally only in patches as if the blight had swept across particular portions and hitherto only the leaves and stalks are affected; it has not yet descended to the tubers.

The Session of Parliament is nearly over. I have lost all interest in politicks. We must go back to the primitive arrangements of the days of the Judges in Israel. Every man must do that which is right in his own eyes, for nothing of any sort is done for us. Such an imbecile ministry, such an absurd set of little oppositions, no man rising anywhere above the common herd.

4. Sunday; rainy, blustering day. No events yesterday. Lord and Lady Downshire have arrived in Blesinton with the intention of remaining two months, a bother rather to us and such like but a boon to all below, for a deal of money is circulated by the requirements of the family, also every encouragement is given to improvements by these really good people. A sort of energy seems given by their presence to all the country.

Mr. King is in great despair. The sale of these estates is postponed till November. The Commissioners have an immense press of business and their holidays and can't reach the first of these two properties till November I the first week in the month, though. I don't see any harm in waiting; the young people are very happy and the lover is spending nothing so he will have his Michaelmas rent the readier.

6. I have written to old Mr. King. The sales of these estates being postponed we can't remain thus in the dark, and this is a good opportunity for the approach to this oddity. I have let him know in the most civil terms that the connexion is by no means particularly agreeable to us and that nothing but the determination of the young people induced us to accept it; also I let him know that we think Annie's fortune a very good one and that all together we consider the gain on the side of his son; so neatly put together all this is that it sounds the most civil address in the world. Annie is quite satisfied with it. She just wished the matter placed in its true light. These old Irish aristocrats are so puffed up with ignorance.

Little Miss Merry was here altering gowns, brim full of Blesinton gossip. How the marquis had arrived unexpectedly and found nothing to eat—no servants arrived—Mrs. Owen in her room—Mr. Owen away—the Doctor out, so he got Charlie to do him some rashers and eggs on which he dined; next day came the Marchioness straight from Germany and after a kind greeting, my Lord went back to London to fetch over the children and in the morning my Lady went up to Dublin to shop. Really these flighty ways sound queer to quiet people.

We are getting our new cabins very neat, but they are all very tiresome, not at all lime enough in the floors and old shabby windows that won't open with only four panes in them. We must have hinges put to them at any rate; and the demand for a 'little scrap of a flower border' shall be complied with—gladly. This is owing to Lady Downshire's move; the neat gardens already blooming before so many of her cottages, and perhaps her intended flower show and premiums have spirited up her neighbours; the country is improving, there is no manner of doubt of it; and the potatoes are failing again; to sight and smell the disease is all round us.

9. We were at Russborough yesterday where it is the fashion of the moment to talk big. They all looked so well—in

deep mourning for Sir Joshua Meredyth. Poor Lady
Milltown, what a weak woman she is in some points.
She is so anxious to make herself out years too young,
therefore very angry with the newspapers for mentioning
her father's real age; he was indeed very old, and she
is old enough as all the world well knows. Nobody is
ever deceived by these silly attempts—few care—and
the ill-natured laugh and comment. Madame de Cotta
is making quite a fortune of her writings and she writes
so fast—eight articles at this moment dispersed in three
periodicals.

12. Oh, the days when I was young—the merry days when
I was young—the brilliant highland days, dogs, ponies,
guns, gamekeepers, in fact the grouse shootings—all
the glens alive—all the houses full—a regular bustle of
pleasure. My poor girls have no fun; their life is really
dull; nothing can exceed the utter stupidity of this neighbourhood, besides the Colonel and I are intensely stupid
ourselves; he never cared for anything but hunting, rather
indeed avoided society and I was too well pleased to be
quiet, to attempt to counteract his indolent shyness; then
our income is small and two thirds being spent outside
the house very little was left for within, so Annie has
married early.

We took poor Mrs. Foster a drive on Saturday; she was
so delighted being unable to walk just now. The Doctor,
she says, frequently drinks tea with her; he is in wretched
spirits, sometimes cries, sometimes furious; the loss of his
money and his Annie have touched his brain, she and we
begin to fear; he has always been very implacable when
his crotchets were interfered with and getting *old* don't
improve that temper with a vain man; there is desease
of the brain in the family, he has a niece now quite mad
and unless he struggle against these morbid feelings, they
will at last overthrow his fine mind—that it is touched for
the present, there is little doubt—his conduct throughout
this strange infatuation of his has been so inexcusable. A
disappointment to me to find such a temper and so little
true heartedness where I had believed so fully in both;
alas, people are never known till they are tried. All looks

bright in the sunshine. There is a degree of impertinence too in such conduct from an inferiour that alters my whole opinion of the man. There let it rest—another cloud in life—a mistake which has been painful to discover.

13. Lord and Lady Downshire returned our visit yesterday—they were riding—both quite well and in good spirits, anxious in every way to do good.

17. Dear little Annie very unwell; a violent attack of spasm in the stomach with disagreeable accompaniments, had to send for the Doctor not exactly knowing how to treat her. Poor James Ryan we fear is dying, a complete breaking up it seems to be; an abscess, Loss of power in one arm and a skeleton with glassy eyes; no one can look worse; seven young children and these hard times.

18. I pitied him [the Doctor], he looked so thoroughly uncomfortable, so much ashamed of himself, and truly I did not help him for I cannot affect to feel for him as I used to do. I consider him to have behaved so extravagantly ill to the kindest friends ever man had. Our short conversations were merely professional therefore.

25. Sunday again, for I have not been in a journalising mood. Annie recovered slowly. I had a bilious attack myself and have been suffering acutely from toothache the last few days. Lord and Lady Downshire are keeping the country alive, I *hear* for we see little of them being quite out of their beat; they are very kind and very good and are doing good; their horticultural show turned out wonderfully fair for a first attempt—it will do very well next year and really proves the art of gardening to be more than beginning here among the lower orders. Our Darkers got three prizes. We were none of us there; everybody else was, and grand dejeuners at the three great houses, the Marquis's, the Agent's, and the Doctor's.

FRIDAY, SEPTEMBER 6. Sad blank in the Journal. I have been ill and I have been busy and I have been anxious about the Colonel and about Annie's marriage, and about money matters and so had no mind to amuse myself, all my writing time was spent on the press! and I must work hard for a few weeks as there is plenty given me to do and money is very scarce with us. Such a stable! and that odious Rutherfurd owing a year and a half's rent; no chance of a farthing of it, but the certainty of another half year's loss after ejecting him before a successor can be settled in his good farm.

7. Wednesday I went up to town with the Colonel and Jack to see them safe off by the steamer for Southampton en route for Jersey. The Colonel has been so unwell, a change was really necessary for him, and as I did not like his going alone Jack went with him. It will do the boy a deal of good in every way.

There were few Cabin passengers but a shipload of Australian emigrants, decent looking people well supplied with luggage whose Adieux to the crowd accompanying them to the Quay was a miserable scene to look at. Tears, sobs, screams even, with hystericks and fainting. To their class the parting is final and though utter desolation is left, and hope shines bright before, the moment of separation from kindred and country must be painful to agony. I felt lonely enough as the vessel moved away, the poor Colonel leaning forward on the rail as the easiest posture for his asthma, and little Jack in the grey shooting coat too short in the sleeves for his growth standing by the helm looking wistfully after me. He has been too much with me, depended too much on me, he must now be prepared for his solitary battle with life, he will fight it gallantly or I am much mistaken. It was amusing to see the sort of charge he took of his father, his activity in looking after the portmanteaus, the head was higher by an inch.

8. We have had a hermit's luncheon of fruits sent us by Lord Downshire, Grapes black and white, Peaches, and Nectarines—very kind in him. No news in the paper. There has been so much of late that the world is resting. Louis Philippe is dead and buried temporarily near Claremont; more sensation in France concerning this event than was expected for the wise old man had some hold of the affections of that fickle people. Also this submarine telegraph having answered between France and England, it will be tried of course between England

and Ireland and then we shall become of consequence as the first and last point of communication with America.

I am beginning another series of *Mrs. Wright*, two more conversations are off, and all the *Calcutta Journal* which has been particularly alluded to in the newspapers as brightening up the last month's part. *The Love Tale* has gone to Miss Cook who accepts it thankfully. She don't pay high, but every little helps.

I had such a long letter from old Mr. King. I like him but he is very odd; he has spent some money on 'that youth' his son and seems unlikely to forget it. And he don't propose to do anything very handsome by the young couple, but he will give enough and leave him at his death plenty; he would like the marriage to take place as soon as possible, which will, I think, be in November. We could hardly get all ready sooner as I began no preparations till this formal consent arrived and there will be no money forthcoming on any side before that time.

17. Really a weight of business of one sort or another. Many letters to write and fifty thousand things to attend to have made me again neglect the journal. I am just finishing the fourth of a second series of Mrs. Wright after which I must set to work in earnest to the *'Clans'* if I can scrape up time from the trousseau now actually begun. We have cheerful letters from Jersey altho' the Colonel had not quite got rid of Asthma, or rather had brought it back as is usual with him by an absurd dinner of *veal* cutlets and *ale*.

Ogle Moore tells me the Doctor is broken-hearted, rude to every one, thinks *I* have cruelly illused, deceived and scorned him, that he is a persecuted martyr, and so, Cigars and their accompaniment are actually killing him. Yet he has ordered new clothes for the wedding. It is a melancholy monomania for which at present I see no cure; he has innoculated Mr. and Mrs. Moore with the idea that we have all been to blame towards him and that *I* am the most offending party. Unconsciously I am sure. We never know ourselves, but I feel as if I had humbled myself and wooed him more than was exactly requisite, out of regard to an old and a well-meaning but

very injudicious friend and out of compassion for the
infirmities of a good man's temper, a temper uncontrolled
either by Christian principles or good breeding. I resent
nothing—I pity—but I can't go on with a succession of
reconciliation scenes followed by undiminished rudeness.
Unaccountable to me, so I leave the subject.

22. Sunday, Mr. King came rather late to tea last night. A
process server of the name of Tom Lees had been, in
the discharge of his duty, set upon by men, women and
children at Humfreystown bridge and cruelly-beaten,
mercifully not wounded although some of his assailants
were armed with pitchforks and reaping hooks. Lady
Downshire and Miss Owen were driving home from the
moors in a jaunting car and came upon this frightful
assemblage enough to frighten any woman and it did very
much excite her but she drove on for rescue, sent some
men off whom she was right, as it proved, in trusting
and, meeting Mr. King, stopt him to consult further,
the result of which was that she went on to Blesinton for
the Police and he returned home to send off a man and
horse to Holywood for a detachment from thence. I shall
be anxious to know the consequences. Lees can identify
several of the rioters. These unhappy people are just
becoming as ill-conducted in this neighbourhood once so
peaceable, as they have long been elsewhere. A gathering
of three or four hundred is no longer uncommon to cut
and carry off crops in the night, ill-use keepers, and
in all ways defy decency. And neither the Government
nor the magistrates take the slightest cognisance of these
outrages. A spirit of discontent is brewing all round us
and must end in something unpleasant if not checked.
The girls and I have been paying visits among the
tenantry and I don't at all like the tone of some. I
would gladly improve the condition of all but am more
inclined to help the hopeful than the desponding and we
must, if possible get quit of the sulky.

The Baltiboys tenantry have not paid badly considering
the times. Rutherfurd's conduct is scandalous. He owes
a year and a half's rent now, and the half year we took
in kind was not worth half the money it represented.

We shall eject him in November, at the loss of the winter's rent for no one will come in upon a farm at that season here though it is the proper time to enter on husbandry. Two hundred and thirty pounds odd is no joke to lose in these struggling days. The poor old man would gladly go to America to his sons whose roguery seems to be prospering with them and as the Colonel will leave him what property he may still have he could take near a hundred pounds out to the firm but the wretched woman, the cause of the downfall of this decent family, declares she will not move; she may indeed stay here but not at Elverstown.

Old Lady Downshire[4] did me the honour to call here the day before yesterday with the young Lady, I was not in but the girls received them and liked the visit. I determined not to erect her into a Queen and pay obeisance to a perfect stranger. The late Lord never called upon me when I first came her although the Colonel waited upon him. The Colonel therefore never went near him again and I never took any notice of her when she afterwards came to the old Murrays! I did not want the acquaintance. If they did, it was their place to make it, and in this, it has ended.

24. Called yesterday on the Dowager Marchioness and found them all in the garden busy with their various improvements and very nice they are making within and without. The Dowager is a most pleasing well bred woman, very superiour in manner to the young Lady.

25. Poor old Rutherfurd will not give trouble. Besides being well-meaning himself he has a sensible friend an Attorney who is giving him good advice. It will end, I hope, in his taking the Colonel's liberal offer by accepting of which he may carry about a hundred pounds to America. The old woman, of course, is against this as she has been against every thing else that was right. He has paid dearly for the false step.

30. We had a very good sermon from Ogle Moore and I

4. Maria, daughter of the fifth Earl of Plymouth, was only seven years older than the H.L.

think the collection would be very fair for a poor country Church. I saw notes and gold on the plate John Hornidge brought to us for our four half-crowns, next year I will double them for the purpose is worthy of all help. At present my purse is very low.

And now I must go and arrange the matrimonial affairs of Pat and Catherine who lead off the hymeneal dance this autumn. Our matrimonial affairs have all gone on swimmingly. The Bride has bought with her savings bed-clothes and bedding—a little crockery, and she has an excellent wardrobe. Besides this she has her month's wages in her pocket and a present of a pound note from me. Janey and Annie are dressing her up very smartly for the ceremony. She has ordered her cake, a barn brack, and is going to Naas to buy tea, sugar, and a cap. Pat is brought rather unwillingly up to the whipping post, he had thought to be allowed to amuse himself tenderly till he was tired of it and rather winces at being pounced on by 'the mistress' and made to marry the girl whom he had compromised—his relations too who have been living upon him are all opposed to the loss of his ready shilling and he being quite a gutta purcha sort of man vacillates between pretty little Catherine and the trammels of matrimony—he however is in for it, so he does the thing handsome—he has *near* a month's wages to get. One pound I gave him as a wedding present, plenty of clothes, two jugs, a mug, and a kettle, and he goes to Naas to buy the ring of real gold to the delight of the Bride. His father, a piper by trade has shown himself much more reasonable than the rest of the respectable family and is to play at the wedding for nothing. Also as he lives on the bog he has whispered the probability of presenting some turf—so September ends happily to one couple at any rate.

WEDNESDAY, OCTOBER 2. I have made up my mind, Hal consenting, to have our dear Annie's wedding a family affair. All the servants and labourers and tenantry invited to receive her back from Church and to wait to speed her departure from the happy home of her childhood to the one which we may hope she will find still happier.

I will have refreshments in plenty for the crowd and a piper to set them dancing, which dance our small Bridal party can go to see, it will help to pass away the afternoon and yet avoid the appearance of a regular entertainment. We cannot ask all our acquaintance, and a selection would certainly give offence were anything like a ball attempted. We shall therefore merely invite our intimate friends and our nearest neighbours. What an undertaking even this is.

I forget whether I mentioned in my last month's journal that we have had good news from Mary and Lachlan Ryan, my memory so famed once, is alas! failing me. These two catches are both in service, have been ever since their arrival. Lachlan his board and a pound a week—Mary, her board and lodging and a pound a month. The letter was from Mary to Annie, saying how happy she is; both she and her brother had had the seasoning fever but were quite recovered and only anxious for their friends to follow them which I really think they most wisely seem inclined to do. Nancy Fox's two sons have sent her home money from Cincinnati where they are both doing well. The numbers gone are quite countless, and the countless numbers going are beyond all calculation, yet the wretchedness left is dreadful, although some are comfortable enough—more so a great deal than these servant classes used to be, so that if the priests would let them alone, or what would be much better, go ramping on in earnest and disgust them, Ireland might yet hold her poor head up.

6. Our cream of the post was the most affectionate letter from Aunt Jane to Annie enclosing her fifty pounds towards any little comforts wanted in her new home. The child is spoiled among them all. I hope to God her young bridegroom may be worthy of her; he seems to have a fine honest nature—to be kind, affectionate, liberal and he is talented enough but has not been subjected to the best influences; he is improving in every way, and will improve further now we have him to ourselves.

Publick news is very far from agreeable; that absurd

Tenant League⁵ quite unsettling the country, threatening us with troublesome times and little rents. Then the Roman Catholic clergy are determined to check the progress of education and popery is striding on to power in England fearfully. Burglary and murder are as every day occurrences about London as crop lifting and murder are here. And no one takes any notice of either.

We are very unsettled in our own home here with this marriage of Pat and Catherine. I am glad to know it will come off on Tuesday for really there is no existing among these scatter brains. Last night in to the drawing-room thundered Ellen loaded with cakes and other delicacies and thumping down upon the table two great bottles of whiskey, she shouted out that these were the gifts of Catherine's parents to the wedding. On her head she had a new cap purchased for the ceremony, flying off at the back from her coil of black hair—altogether she looked crazy with her dark flashing eyes. I thought Mr. King would never recover it, he laughed so immoderately. The girl really is wild from her kind untutored nature. The Hyland family having found resistance impracticable have given a gracious assent to these nuptials. Mary Hyland lending her house with its *three* apartments for the occasion.

10. Such a queer man as the Colonel is. Walked into the drawing room yesterday as we were reading our letters. With poor dear darling Jack too ill for me to think of anything else till he is better.

12. Jack going on well—he was up yesterday for three or four hours—the doctor very kind in looking after him. The boy did not feel quite well in Jersey but Dr. Eckford would not give him any medicine. In London again he was suffering a little, and then the Colonel, tiring of town at that dead time of year, of his club where he knew nobody, of his solitary lodgings, determined suddenly on starting for home. The Colonel really looking well

5. The Irish Tenant League was founded to agitate for changes in the land law.

and certainly much roused up in spirits. Jack like a corpse—he frightened me.

13. We drove to Ballyward yesterday and settled the affairs of the Bridesmaid amid such sunny smiles as chased away all clouds from the latterly heavy brow. Mr. King's old fashioned class prejudices gave way—this will do much to soothe the jealous irritation of the neighbourhood. Also his condescension on Catherine's marriage has made him quite popular with that class. He went in, going home, danced, drank healths, took tea and cake in the inner room, and gave the Bridegroom a pound.

Dr. Eckford sent each of the girls a handsomely bound polyglott Bible, and some rules to me for preserving the Colonel's health—just so much waste paper, alas. He has never owned any rule since I have known him, but the whim of the moment and I have less chance of guiding him now than ever, for he remembers nothing beyond five minutes if so long—he has lost much on his journey, borrowed money which must be repaid, having taken sufficient with him. Well, I am glad he is at home—warm and quiet and calm at any rate, if not cheerful.

18. Got twenty-four pounds, nineteen shillings from the sale of Rutherfurd's hay, and also fourteen pounds, odd, from little Tyrrell, balance of rent due this three hundred and nineteen pounds, seventeen and ninepence; a hundred pounds for Annie, a hundred pounds for Janey laid out in sheep for the present. Fifty pounds Hal is to give Annie in her hand and fifty pounds the wedding entertainments will cost, leaving the nineteen pounds for the dresses of Janey, Jack, Nelly Moore, the maids and new liveries. What an expensive business it is.

Also I have received nine pounds, sixteen and sixpence for two more papers of Calcutta, and two more of Mrs. Wright, Messrs. Chambers giving no more for that wonderful woman's clever hits than they do for their rubbish, highly as they appreciate her 'rare talents'—but it is really a great deal to make of one's brains, so easily too, for there is no great labour in *her* at any rate—the Journal took up more time—and those *Clans* I never shall get on with till this wedding is over. My money drawer looks so full, I feel almost like a Bank Director as Chubb's patent key turns the lock—I mean to keep a private purse! So the nine pounds sixteen and six is added to the fourteen pounds, I have repaid myself, and put away as a sacred deposit among my few remaining trinkets, for I am dividing them nearly all with Janey and Annie. When a woman has married daughters to wear them, she should give ornaments up for herself. The rings I keep for Jack's wife.

This is a cold frosty morning and we have had to send poor Rutherfurd cold comfort on it, in the shape of an Attorney's letter. He will stick by his ruined farm keeping himself a beggar and seriously inconveniencing us, when he might carry a hundred pounds in his pocket to America, and end his days in comfort among his prospering children there. A wretched fair yesterday at Naas—sold one beast out of seven, but for a good price. Sheep dear to buy, and ewes heavy to sell—really the times are kittle.

24. The Colonel quite well, enjoyed his hunt yesterday though they had no sport, only the ride. Rutherfurd here this morning so anxious to be allowed to shuffle on and I see no way he has of living, let alone pay his rent, and the surety money above all. He must go to Mr. Robinson and answer a few of his questions. The consequences of the weaknesses and the follies of the young man are visiting heavily the declining years of the old one, and so it must be—Jack, my child, remember this.

31. Really and truly the last day of the month—who would have thought it? The time is flying away frightfully fast. We got Chambers yesterday with two more of the *Calcutta Journal* reading so well and two of *Mrs. Wright*, excellent. More money will be coming directly. I am putting it all away, with thirty-five pounds, Hal has got for the poor chesnut filly, that we may have a little beginning to a reserve again in case of accident, the last has stood us in such good stead. Grandmama is to send Annie a clock for her drawing room chimney piece, Cecilia and Joanna something for her writing table, Uncle James some books. On the King side nothing has yet arrived but two sets of

harness. One set for a pair of carriage horses, the other for ponies—all most beautiful—crest plated buckles etc., for people with an income of £300.

Poor Mr. Owen has got into a scrape—he repeated remarks made by Lord Downshire and Mr. Sheehan upon each other to the parties, quite thoughtlessly without an evil intention in the world but it has set these two fiery spirits by the ears and there is all the to-do in the world about it. If people would but keep that little unruly member quiet how much more peaceable we all should be. Set down their thoughts in Journals as I do! and take very good care of whispering even to reeds.

THURSDAY, NOVEMBER 7. A great movement has begun in England at last, against the insolence of Rome. John Bull will never bear such assumption nor such a near view of popery. The Colonel thinks it all for the best—that had they gone creeping on as for the last few years, they might have made a progress difficult to check, but having betrayed their designs so soon we can the more easily put a stop to them. The spirit of popery is such that that church can never be trusted; they will force us back to modified penal laws and nobody can say that this severity will be undeserved. This movement will open many eyes. Neither national schools, nor national colleges are yet deserted in spite of papal denunciations, and *minds* will surely come very different out of them from what they go in.

11. So busy we have all been, Saturday Annie and I went to Mr. King's residence in Merrion Square. The sisters so glad to see us. The Papa came in and like an actor on the stage made a parental speech but received us cordially. After a while the young people departed and I had to endure one harangue after another for two mortal hours. He meant it all most kindly, this is his manner. He complimented me on Annie's appearance etc., and said many obliging things and none disobliging and as far as I could understand his intentions through their enveloping words he means to act kindly by the young people but by no means liberally according to my idea of what a rich father should do

for an only son. However I think he will give frequent presents.

19. Took leave in Merrion Square; called on the Lady Crichtons who had called on me; very nice women. Papa King in a set speech presented *Annie* with a carriage; a beautiful one I understand, built by Hutton and run for only a few months; the gift of the harness was therefore not inappropriate.

24. I am expecting to hear from Mr. Cathcart the lawyer to-day whether he will be ready with his settlements. They are very fair, that is all. Two hundred and twenty-five pounds a year secured on the King property to James and Annie and the survivor and their children after them and a fourth of the sum of five thousand pounds settled on James and his sisters, the children of this marriage will also have. On our part the interest of Annie's money secured to her and him and the principal to their children at our death that is the whole interest at our death, seventy-five pounds a year only, during our lives. The young couple have therefore three hundred a year from all of us their parents, during our lives. James is to have fifty pounds a year besides as Agent and there will be occasional presents. Also Humfreystown has been revalued at one pound per acre less, and Mr. Lytton the Master in Chancery in charge of minors will reduce the rent accordingly, so they may do very well; they have plenishing sufficient to start with and I really think they will be very happy; they will have much to make them so, and as for little trials, *this* world is intended for them.

TUESDAY, DECEMBER 2. Heavy rain. We were making lists and packing the Bride's finery. John Hornidge dined and Dick came in the evening and Mr. Mrs. and Miss King dined too and of course James. We had really a very capital dinner for them, plenty of champaign and such good claret that the old gentleman drank quite enough of it. Larking waits admirably; all went off as one could wish; musick and dancing and every body very happy. Papa King made a long speech to me in a corner upon the excessive propriety of all arrangements and Mama King took Annie on her knee and kissed her tenderly.

4. I forgot to say that the Colonel and I called on Mr. and Mrs. King on Monday, Emma and Annie with us. To-day he and Annie and I had to go to them again with Mr. Cathcart who came down with the settlements and a stormy day we had, as I was quite prepared for the breeze having freshened the evening before pretty considerably.

On taking leave I mentioned to old Mr. King that the papers were to be brought down and asked him whether he would sign them where he was or at our house. He got up a gale in a minute; he could sign nothing without the sanction of Mr. Hallowes; he had named no trustee; such affairs were not to be arranged in a minute; he felt himself ill-used, taken very short; he must decline affixing any signature, etc. What he had been about he and his lawyers no one can tell; it was odd of his man of business not to prepare him for the finishing ceremony, settle the trustee, and inform him that settlements were signed before marriages and were useless unless signed. All that was left for me was to repeat my civil speech and to say equally civilly no settlement no marriage: that he could reflect before the morning and let us know whether it would be necessary to send round to the invited guests to put off their attendance.

The son was in such distress, and we concocted between us an addition to this threat that the reason of the delay would be stated to our acquaintance. Either this fear, or a good sleep, or recovered temper or something had the proper effect for this morning I got a note to say all was put right. Mr. Cathcart brought a letter from Mr. Hallowes, as credentials, and Richard Hornidge being summoned the gentleman began; they were three hours reading and commenting and had to say a few hard words to this queer old man but in the end he did all that was requisite naming Mr. Verschoyle's brother, a clergyman, as trustee on his part. Annie behaved beautifully, composed but very quiet.

5. Thursday, Long to be remembered I fervently hope, and indeed believe, as the happiest day of my darling Annie's life. I could not write one word upon the day nor the

day after. I am writing now on Saturday near midnight when all bustle is long over, all the guests gone, all the house asleep, and I am making up my leeway that this faithful chronicle of my day may have no omissions in it of consequence. I will describe all the wedding at length again as a curiosity for future generations. Just now we will proceed with the simple diary of events.

And now for the Wedding. Ingram arrived the night before with his van, his cook, his nephew, and three porters; he established himself in the housekeeper's room and more of them all we heard nothing.

8. Early Thursday morning we were all up. Annie had slept well, was in great spirits and good looks. We of the family breakfasted in my room, the other company each in their own particular! The Bridesmaids were dressed by Miss Merrey and Miss McDonnell and then they dressed the Bride who reclined according to rule to have her hair dressed her shoes tied and so on. Janey did her hair. Louisa Hornidge put on the wreath and veil and I fastened in *the* pearl ornament. Her pretty gown fitted perfectly. All were collected in the church before our party joined them. Mr. and Mrs. King went on alone; then Miss King and Miss Hornidge, then Mary Jane, Jenny Aylmer, Arabella and Johnny Gardiner; then the Bridegroom in his own new carriage with his own horses taking with him two Bridesmaids Matilda and Emma, and the two Best men, his tall cousin, Mr. Fowler, and little Jack. Last went our carriage with Papa and Annie, Janey and me.

All the servants were collected in the hall to God-speed us, in their new dresses; a little mob outside the door, a great crowd at the gate over which they had erected an arch covered with evergreens enlivened by bunches of coloured calico tyed up into flowers. All respectfully silent, no sound heard but the muttered God-speed. Blesinton was all alive, the church filled to crowding, a sea of heads. We were obliged to force our way through the mob at the door and up the Aisle; on either hand were ranged the wedding guests all falling in as was proper. The Colonel with Annie on his arm walked straight up to the

Altar where Mr. Moore was waiting within the rails and James and his two best men without. The six Bridesmaids followed two and two and then the general company. The service began immediately, and how impressively it was performed. Everyone was affected. Dear Annie stood there quite composed but very still, bending down from all eyes so gracefully so modestly while he proud and happy yet grave supported her by his steady bearing. It was soon over being much shortened, judiciously; and then I slipt away, drove home in Mary Jane's car and was thus ready to receive them. After the signing, the Bridesmaids produced their prettily decorated basket and pinned the eight favours on—none else are given in an Irish marriage. Then the Bridegroom led forth his Bride and as he placed her foot on her own carriage step, loud pealed the bells from the steeple and away flew the four gallant grays now harnessed to it, the postillions dressed in blue jackets, white cords, and large favours in their hats. Larkins had given every servant employed a similar favour and as carriage after carriage rolled off with its gay inmates the scene must have been a very lively one. The cheers they say were deafening, drowned the bells.

At the bridge at Burgage all our people met the train when quickly unharnessing the grays they drew the Bride's carriage up the avenue to the door, the crowd running beside it, James and Annie bowing all the way and scattering handfuls of silver. I was on the steps and kissed them both as they alighted when 'God bless yez all' burst from the little mob and very nearly overset me. The rooms soon filled for of our forty-six invited friends thirty-eight attended. I never saw a prettier entertainment. Ingram had done his best, the eatables were excellent, the ornaments so pretty, and the plate equally so. The Colonel gave quantities of Champaign, and the cake which had been displayed in the drawing-room the evening before now handsomely figured at the head of the table. It was a right merry repast, everybody so happy, everybody so hungry.

When the Bride's health was given by Richard Hornidge, Tulfarris, old Mr. King responded in a far shorter speech than he ever made to me, but it was a very good one. He congratulated himself on receiving into his family so amiable a young person, so beloved in her neighbourhood and belonging to parents so deservedly respected; he assured the friends around him that he could promise her married life would be happy as his son possessed all qualities essential to their mutual well-being, and he took gladly this opportunity of thanking the neighbourhood generally for the kind reception they had given his son when he came a stranger among them, assuring them that it would always be gratefully remembered by him and his etc, etc. After we ladies retired the toasts grew many loud and furious and the gentlemen rejoined us in great good humour.

Our next move was through the house as the Scotch say, up to the school-room where the tables were laid for all the tenantry; in the corn room adjoining the tradespeople were served, the labourers and servants finding places among either. All the provisions were laid on long cross tables; the carvers were the three Darkers, two Boothmans and Carpenter the Butcher. Six little boys acted as waiters and admirably. There was a quarter of Beef fresh and salt cold, and two hams and a whole sheep hot, bread and vegetables in abundance; for drink milk and water for the teetotallers and beer and ale mixed for the more jovial portion of the company. All looked so decent, so neat, so very happy, it was quite a pleasure to pass among them on to the hay loft where the rest of them were dancing. It was lighted by sconces all round the walls, benches all along, and evergreens to fill up all the loopholes. At one end a fine evergreen bower with A.J.K. and at the other end ditto with a crown and V.R. We stayed to see some capital dancing and then came down to cut the cake. It was such a beauty, such a size, and yet scarce large enough for the company behaved scandalously; cut off big hunches five or six pounds weight and hid them behind the books, behind the pillows, behind the curtains, under the chairs and sofas, leaving so little for family use that Arabella [King] was quite angry and seizing her opportunity whipped the poor remains off and ran and locked them up. After this we set to dancing; then had tea; after that more ice, that left from luncheon with cakes, pâtés, fruits, etc. The Barn company also went to tea. Six barnbracks, fifty loaves of bread and a tub of butter, and then most of the fine guests who remained went up to dance again with the people.

Our company were all gone by ten o'clock. The Barn had coffee at one, danced on till six, then had a tea breakfast and dispersed. The Bride and Bridegroom left at four p.m. She changed her white brocade silk and veil for her shot red and blue, her white terry velvet bonnet and feathers and my white India shawl and she looked so thoroughly ladylike. I had avoided taking leave. Papa could not let her go without his blessing and perhaps the little burst this occasioned would do neither of them harm for she had been too composed to be natural and both required relief. The gallant grays carried them off like the wind, Richard Moore throwing an old shoe after them for luck which he had prevailed on Jack to fetch for him.

Throughout the whole entertainment not a mistake occurred, no noise, no offence, no breakage to speak of. During the nine Company days including the wedding feast, two tumblers and four wine-glasses were our damage, and three cracked tumblers in the Barn. There was no whiskey, tea in plenty and beer at dinner; this temperance accounts for the unalloyed pleasures of the wedding feast. In the Office below we had cakes and wine for the better order, the Darkers, Boothmans, Merreys, etc., They partook plentifully and after joined the rest dancing away with the merriest; and Tom Darker subtracted some of the beef and ale for a little supper for this same party, most thoroughly enjoyed by them; such cheering as they all gave us when we passed through their rooms, such a shout as they set up for Annie on her departing, and all through Blesinton and all along the road it was the same: a running fire of shouting.

And so ends the wedding. My dear darling Annie is gone; we shall know her as our own no more, but if she be happy why should we regret her so early being called on to fulfil her destiny. God ever bless and keep her.

12. Janey and I have been very busy settling the house, it was much disarranged, part of it extremely dirty and the servants so flighty it has been a difficult matter to get them back into their regular routine of work. That good Ellen defies my powers of governing; she must be a little wrong in the head. The thirty-eight people we had at luncheon on the wedding day were the following:-

Mr., Mrs. Richard Moore	Mr. Sam Finnemor
Mr., Mrs. Ogle Moore	Nelly Moore
Mr., Mrs. Owen	Miss Owen
Mr., Mrs. Lynch	Miss Casey
Mr., Mrs. King	Mary Jane Finnemor
Edward Moore	Jenny Aylmer
Dr. Robinson	Louisa Hornidge
Dick Hornidge	Miss King
Mr. Fowler	John Hornidge
Richard Hornidge	Three Miss Kings
Edward Hornidge	Janey Smith
Edward Leeson	Johnny Gardiner
Harry Leeson	Jack
Mr. John Finnemor	Colonel and me *and the pair*.

All these attended the ceremony except the Lynchs who availed themselves of our proposal to avoid it, not that they had any scruples but they must have asked leave of their Bishop and had a bother about it. Lord and Lady Milltown and the two girls came after luncheon was over and remained a couple of hours; he was in town and came down *he said* on purpose; she waited for him which made her so late, but I think it was half airs. My next list must be of the wardrobe,—a very neat one but very small and very plain it would seem to a fine lady.

Eighteen shifts
Eighteen pairs of drawers
Three pairs of stays
Three flannel jackets
Three flannel petticoats
Six under petticoats
Six Cambrick petticoats

Six corded petticoats
Eighteen night gowns.
Eighteen pairs of stout stockings
Eighteen pairs of fine stockings, silk and thread
Eighteen plain pocket handkerchiefs
Eighteen fine pocket handkerchiefs (six very handsome)
Eighteen collars and chemisettes
Eighteen pairs cuffs and sleeves
Six tuckers
Twelve pairs of shoes and boots
One pair of slippers
One pair of goloshes
One dozen white gloves
One dozen coloured gloves
Six pairs of dark gloves
Muff and boa—sable
Large warm cloke　　　　　White calico dressing-gown
Warm dressing-gown　　　　Cloth shawl
Flannel dressing-gown, blue　Chintz jacket and petticoat
Cloth pardessus　　　　　　White jacket and petticoat
Chintz dressing-gown

Three morning dresses:
　　Shot silk, green and red
　　Cachemire embroidered groseille
　　Grey cloth jacket and petticoat trimmed with cerise

Three dinner dresses:
　　Black velvet
　　Blue glacée silk with two lace flounces
　　Dark ruby tabbinet

Three evening dresses:
　　Limerick lace with two slips, one white, one pink
　　Net embroidered in green
　　Silk barèges pink and brown

Three bonnets
　　White terry velvet with feathers
　　Violet satin trimmed with black lace, etc.
　　Mouse coloured silk lined with pink.

The wedding gown of white brocade silk besides, and the best of all her old things: a couple of bonnets, a couple of shawls, polkas, pardessus, three or four gowns, etc.

Her books, musick, nick-nacks, writing-cases, work boxes, etc., we have set apart for her and shall send them to her new home as soon as we hear she is expected there. Her presents have been so numerous I really shall hardly remember them all; they are none of them of much value with two exceptions, and few of them use ful, but they are pretty little remembrances from kind friends:

From my Mother, a handsome French clock for the drawing-room chimney piece.

Aunt Jane, *fifty pounds*, to be spent in comforts for the house.

Uncle James, ten volumes Boswell's Life of Johnson, new Edition; nine volumes, Tytler's History of Scotland, both well bound.

Margaret Gibson Craig, a pearl hoop ring.

Cecilia and Joanna, an Ormolu Owl inkstand.

Mrs. Macpherson, a Scotch pebble brooch!

Mrs. Coxe, a landscape enamel brooch.

Mrs. Tytler, a glass ruler.

Mrs. Campbell, a blotting-book, her own work.

Mary Tytler, a letter case, ditto ditto.

Mrs. Haughton, a set of pearls.

Mary Browne, a beautiful prayer book and bible bound together, clasped and edged with gold.

Mrs. Gledstanes and Louisa, a set of bog oak ornaments.

The two Miss Henrys, an Irish pebble brooch.

Richard Hornidge, Tulfarris, a gold pencil case with a seal on which is engraved 'Annie.'

Lady Blakenay, a turquoise brooch.

Harriet Gardiner, another ormolu Owl.

Louisa Gardiner, an ormolu match box.

Mr. Gardiner, a gold brooch.

Aunt Bourne, the Cameo bracelet.

Mrs. Bridges, enamel locket with brilliants.

Uncle Ralph Hastings, pebble brooch.

Eliza Cottam, two or three charms.

Aunt Fanny, the veil.

From dear Johnny Gardiner a pair of real Turkish slippers.

Miss Hart, a purse.

Bartle Frere, Five pounds.

Anne Frere, a book tray.

From the King side, old Mr. King gave the carriage and a hundred pounds, besides paying wedding expenses.

Mrs. King, two solid silver branch candlesticks for four lights each. A damask table-cloth to dine sixteen, and sixteen napkins, and some hock.

Miss King, the Aunt, a silver cruet stand and a pillar lamp for the drawing-room.

Arabella, a papier maché card basket.

Matilda and Emma, an inlaid work box.

Mr. Robert Fowler, a pair of china candlesticks.

The three Ladies Crichton, a flower vase, a papier maché inkstand, and Indian hand skreens.

Miss Clerk an urn stand, the dear little children, two flower vases, Henrietta a gold chain, and sévigné of garnets or carbuncles. Dr. Eckford the watch and polyglott bible, dear little Jack a fan, cost him all his savings—sixteen shillings. The Colonel *fifty pounds*. I, all sorts of old trumpery and one handsome brooch, a mocha, very large, set on purpose for her, and the ruby hoop ring that poor William gave me years and years ago and which she will consider his gift, for he cannot afford her another.

Leslie Whateley, a little prayer-book gild-edged and clasped. Eliza Browne, two embroidered pocket handkerchiefs. Miss Owen, Longfellow's poems. Also I have forgot a black velvet polka, ribbons, flowers, silk handkerchiefs, veils, lace polkas, black and white, etc., and now head and hand are tired—to bed—to bed—to bed.

13. The Colonel is off by the caravan for Dublin, very early this rainy morning. He wants to see Mrs. Haughton, he wants to see Annie and he has to have another talk with Mr. Cathcart about his Will which has to be remade in

consequence of this marriage. Lady Milltown is beginning to forgive me for having a daughter married, well and before hers. Her Lord is very queer. His daughters should marry as quickly as possible any respectable man who could keep them above the *want* they must fall into were their mother to die and he puts every obstacle in the way, never has a creature within his doors hardly, follows up no acquaintance and looks as high as if he were not ruined both in character and circumstances.

14. I was hours making up bundles of patches and rags and old clothes for distribution among the poor who are certainly not so numerous as they used to be though their wretchedness is extreme. They can't mind it, or they would go to the poorhouse.

19. All looks pleasant and I am sad for indeed trouble has fallen on us. John Robinson has given up the Agency. The times are such, his business requires so much attention, the competition in it as in every thing else being so great that he is quite unable to give any part of his head to any affairs but his own. Were it not for the hope of doing something for his boys he would not remain a corn factor but retire to a farm in the country, the sort of life best suited to the tastes both of himself and his wife. He spent a couple of hours teaching me thoroughly to understand his truly exact method of keeping the Agency accounts which is all I had to learn, as I have done the country business for him of late, with the help of Tom Darker; the whole of the rent days' latterly I have been beside him so that I know how he deals with the tenantry and I am not afraid of being able to manage them assisted by Tom Darker.

But here's the hitch. Tom has given up the stewardship—failing health, increasing irritability of temper, low spirits etc., are his reasons for giving timely notice that this will be his last year of service. The real reason is that unfortunate farm which it is a thousand pities that it ever was given him. Though he got it only for a year, he never would believe that it would be resumed. He is very unreasonable—very Irish—but being indispensable to us we must only soothe his selfishness as best we may.

He wants to keep this farm as 'amusement with a *little profit*' for the present, and a provision for his old age, and he does not like relinquishing his Steward's salary of Fifty pounds, though he says he cannot do the work for which he receives it, but his nephew Sam, a clever boy, certainly, but still a boy, only seventeen, could attend here when it did not suit his own health or other affairs to come himself. It is a very nice plan for the Darker side very little thought of the Colonel's pocket in it, so if we agree to it we'll *cut* the money part!

Christmas Day. It is years since the thought even of a merry Christmas crossed a mind of late, almost sad at this so-called cheerful time. This year I feel the season's worth. We are both alive and our children are all with us—so they have hitherto been but we did not realise it for they had not ever left us. Now Annie had gone, taken her new name and her new station and her new duties and ours is to be no more her *home*. But she is with us; *she and he* and they are loving children to us, he as much our son as she our daughter, and so I think that it will ever be for they love each other, they love and respect us and we shall never jar upon their feelings by any airs of authority.

I have laid it down as a rule never to advise them—never that is to offer them advice. Should they want it, they will ask it the more readily that it is not obtruded upon them. The French family politeness is too little followed among us, it may appear ceremonious but it really is well bred and prudent and our ruder frankness leads frequently to scandals never heard of in the domestick affairs of our neighbours.

All are off to church this beautiful Christmas morning, the Colonel the gayest of the party. Ever since his visit to St. Fenton's he has been in tip top spirits, quite like his own younger days, and he is so well, so alive, so awake, it really makes the heart glad to see him. On the 19th, Friday last we expected the Bride and Bridegroom back and that they would drop Jack in passing. They called certainly, much elated at having been again rung through Blesinton and a right merry peal they got, but they would not leave Jack,; they only ate a good luncheon and went on in the pretty carriage which I am glad to see is now shut up for the rest of the winter; the car took them saturday to the post and set them down on their return at school where we were entertaining all our little pupils with tea and bread and butter and the Piper; such dancing: thumping rather, and such slices of bread and butter some of them equal in size to the heads of the devourers; the tea was made in a pot and two kettles and looked black enough. The neatness of the children was remarkable, all quite clean, hair very smooth, no tawdry finery but good decent clothing; how very different from what we can remember those poor ragged creatures.

Their healthy looks struck James so much; he would have remarked otherwise before the Messrs. Chambers' breakfast. God be thanked for the talent he has given me, and the energy to apply it, and those good men who have rendered all this available. Our party at school gave so much pleasure and it was so comfortable to us, done so quietly, not paraded on the wedding day. We really are to get the boys' school up again. I promised to reopen it if they would promise me twenty-five boys and I understand they have already twenty-seven; so I begin and with a Protestant Master. Our whole feeling hereabout's is turning very protestant; no one goes with the Pope and Cardinal Wiseman at all. I really believe all the Roman Catholic gentry will delight in their being defeated and every day the peasantry are caring less about their priest—the Pope they never cared for.

I have had a nice long rest and must now begin to work; thirty-five pounds already from the second set of *Mrs. Wright* and the *Indian Journal* so far. I believe it is not quite all printed yet but I don't know for my book parcel is laying at Webb's, a forgetful somebody forgetting to call for it. I have lent twenty-three pounds ten shillings to the farm to buy some additional stock; we have an abundant stock now but I am to get it back again when I want it in February for my pretty Janey who is to go to some of the gaieties of Dublin. The remainder will more than pay the school. Indeed I think now our stable is so small and our house expenses-lessened we may begin to feel in easy circumstances. If the dear good Colonel will let his *unproductive* improvement lay by till better times we should be very comfortable; they took a mint of money which for all but the *look*, might have as well been in the fire.

27. I spoke to John Hornidge about Tom Darker. He thinks him utterly unreasonable, can hardly indeed credit that he should be so absorbingly selfish as not to see he was quite too encroaching. The threat of resigning the Stewardship he treats as *temper*. He will think better of it. It would never do to yield, it would only make him more the master than he is now which is perfectly unnecessary.

29. I am at last at work at my *Clan*, reading up for it. Gregory I find very useful, dry enough but the facts are there and they are what I wanted. John Graham Dalyell on the superstitions is not useless. A Highland memory is, however, too tenacious to require any promtings on this subject. The Book of Books is that curiously clever Macculloch's *Highlands and Islands* in letters to his friend Sir Walter Scott—full of knowledge, old world lore, information on every point and so amusing either in spite of, or in consequence of its discursiveness that I can never lay it down once I take it up. Colonel Smith is busy with my old *Painters Progress* in the dead and buried *Inspector*. I wish we could rub them up, add to them and republish them, for the work they were published in expired before the series of papers was even half got through and they represent so truthfully the Highlands of my youth, it is really a pity such interesting sketches should be lost sight of, and be incomplete. Jane wants me to write to Mr. Ritchie about them.

31. Good-bye, old year. We are once more all together, though not exactly side by side, dear little Jack being at Russelstown. A gloomy rainy Christmas it is, and windy some nights to that degree one almost fears the house may fall. James and his *two* ladies were up before day, breakfasted at a little after seven and then that active man walked off upon his own ten toes to catch the Bus in Blesinton. May be he won't stir up those two idle monkeys! Early risers all the Kings are; always in exercise

he is. Annie will be enough out of doors at any rate; no fear of her getting ill for want of the open air. And they have no fires in their bedroom in the morning, just one to go warm to bed by and air their linen during the night. All very right; young people require none of these enervating luxuries, time enough for all such indulgence when years bring ailments along with them. It is very pleasant to see the Colonel so roused by this marriage. Really he is quite an altered person, so gay, singing! old hunting songs and mess ditties! No sleepiness, no fretfulness. Almost as young as he was ten years ago. Annie looks so happy too—and Janey—and Jack—and James, all do so well together. Poor old over-anxious Mama had best determine to be happy too.

Index

CANONGATE CLASSICS

Books listed in alphabetical order by author.

The Gowk Storm Nancy Brysson Morrison
ISBN 0 86241 222 6   £3.95
An Autobiography Edwin Muir
ISBN 0 86241 423 7   £5.99
The Wilderness Journeys (The Story of My Boyhood and Youth,
A Thousand Mile Walk to the Gulf, My First Summer in the
Sierra, Travels in Alaska, Stickeen) John Muir
ISBN 0 86241 586 1   £8.99
Imagined Selves: (Imagined Corners, Mrs Ritchie, Mrs Grundy in
Scotland, Women: An Inquiry, Women in Scotland) Willa Muir
ISBN 0 86241 605 1   £8.99
Homeward Journey John MacNair Reid
ISBN 0 86241 178 5   £3.95
A Twelvemonth and a Day Christopher Rush
ISBN 0 86241 439 3   £4.99
End of an Old Song J. D. Scott
0 86241 311 7   £4.95
Grampian Quartet: (The Quarry Wood, The Weatherhouse, A Pass
in the Grampians, The Living Mountain) Nan Shepherd
ISBN 0 86241 589 6   £8.99
Consider the Lilies Iain Crichton Smith
ISBN 0 86241 415 6   £4.99
Diaries of a Dying Man William Soutar
ISBN 0 86241 347 8   £4.99
Listen to the Voice: Selected Stories Iain Crichton Smith
ISBN 0 86241 434 2   £5.99
Shorter Scottish Fiction Robert Louis Stevenson
ISBN 0 86241 555 1   £4.99
Tales of Adventure (Black Arrow, Treasure Island, 'The Sire de
Malétroit's Door' and other stories) Robert Louis Stevenson
ISBN 0 86241 687 6   £7.99
Tales of the South Seas (Island Landfalls, The Ebb-tide,
The Wrecker) Robert Louis Stevenson
ISBN 0 86241 643 4   £7.99
The Scottish Novels: (Kidnapped, Catriona, The Master of
Ballantrae, Weir of Hermiston) Robert Louis Stevenson
ISBN 0 86241 533 0   £5.99
The People of the Sea David Thomson
ISBN 0 86241 550 0   £4.99
City of Dreadful Night James Thomson
ISBN 0 86241 449 0   £4.99
Three Scottish Poets: MacCaig, Morgan, Lochead
ISBN 0 86241 400 8   £4.99
Black Lamb and Grey Falcon Rebecca West
ISBN 0 86241 428 8   £10.99

Most Canongate Classics are available at good bookshops. You can
also order direct from Canongate Books Ltd – by post: 14 High Street,
Edinburgh EH1 1TE, or by telephone: 0131 557 5111. There is no charge
for postage and packing to customers in the United Kingdom.